PEARSON CUSTOM LIBRARY

Human Anatomy Laboratory Manual
Department of Biological Sciences
University of Rhode Island
Fall 2015

PEARSON

ISBN 10: 1-269-83546-7
ISBN 13: 978-1-269-83546-6

Laboratory Safety: General Guidelines

1. Notify your instructor immediately if you are pregnant, color blind, allergic to any insects or chemicals, taking immunosuppressive drugs, or have any other medical condition (such as diabetes, immunologic defect) that may require special precautionary measures in the laboratory.

2. Upon entering the laboratory, place all books, coats, purses, backpacks, etc. in designated areas, not on the bench tops.

3. Locate and, when appropriate, learn to use exits, fire extinguisher, fire blanket, chemical shower, eyewash, first aid kit, broken glass container, and cleanup materials for spills.

4. In case of fire, evacuate the room and assemble outside the building.

5. Do not eat, drink, smoke, or apply cosmetics in the laboratory.

6. Confine long hair, loose clothing, and dangling jewelry.

7. Wear shoes at all times in the laboratory.

8. Cover any cuts or scrapes with a sterile, waterproof bandage before attending lab.

9. Wear eye protection when working with chemicals.

10. Never pipet by mouth. Use mechanical pipeting devices.

11. Wash skin immediately and thoroughly if contaminated by chemicals or microorganisms.

12. Do not perform unauthorized experiments.

13. Do not use equipment without instruction.

14. Report all spills and accidents to your instructor immediately.

15. Never leave heat sources unattended.

16. When using hot plates, note that there is no visible sign that they are hot (such as a red glow). Always assume that hot plates are hot.

17. Use an appropriate apparatus when handling hot glassware.

18. Keep chemicals away from direct heat or sunlight.

19. Keep containers of alcohol, acetone, and other flammable liquids away from flames.

20. Do not allow any liquid to come into contact with electrical cords. Handle electrical connectors with dry hands. Do not attempt to disconnect electrical equipment that crackles, snaps, or smokes.

21. Upon completion of laboratory exercises, place all materials in the disposal areas designated by your instructor.

22. Do not pick up broken glassware with your hands. Use a broom and dustpan and discard the glass in designated glass waste containers; never discard with paper waste.

23. Wear disposable gloves when working with blood, other body fluids, or mucous membranes. Change gloves after possible contamination and wash hands immediately after gloves are removed.

24. The disposal symbol indicates that items that may have come in contact with body fluids should be placed in your lab's designated container. It also refers to liquid wastes that should not be poured down the drain into the sewage system.

25. Leave the laboratory clean and organized for the next student.

26. Wash your hands with liquid or powdered soap prior to leaving the laboratory.

27. The biohazard symbol indicates procedures that may pose health concerns.

The caution symbol points out instruments, substances, and procedures that require special attention to safety. These symbols appear throughout this manual.

Measurement Conversions

Metric to American Standard	American Standard to Metric
Length	
1 mm = 0.039 inches	1 inch = 2.54 cm
1 cm = 0.394 inches	1 foot = 0.305 m
1 m = 3.28 feet	1 yard = 0.914 m
1 m = 1.09 yards	1 mile = 1.61 km
Volume	
1 mL = 0.0338 fluid ounces	1 fluid ounce = 29.6 mL
1 L = 4.23 cups	1 cup = 237 mL
1 L = 2.11 pints	1 pint = 0.474 L
1 L = 1.06 quarts	1 quart = 0.947 L
1 L = 0.264 gallons	1 gallon = 3.79 L
Mass	
1 mg = 0.0000353 ounces	1 ounce = 28.3 g
1 g = 0.0353 ounces	1 pound = 0.454 kg
1 kg = 2.21 pounds	

Temperature

To convert temperature:

$$^{\circ}C = \frac{5}{9}(F - 32) \qquad ^{\circ}F = \frac{9}{5} + 32$$

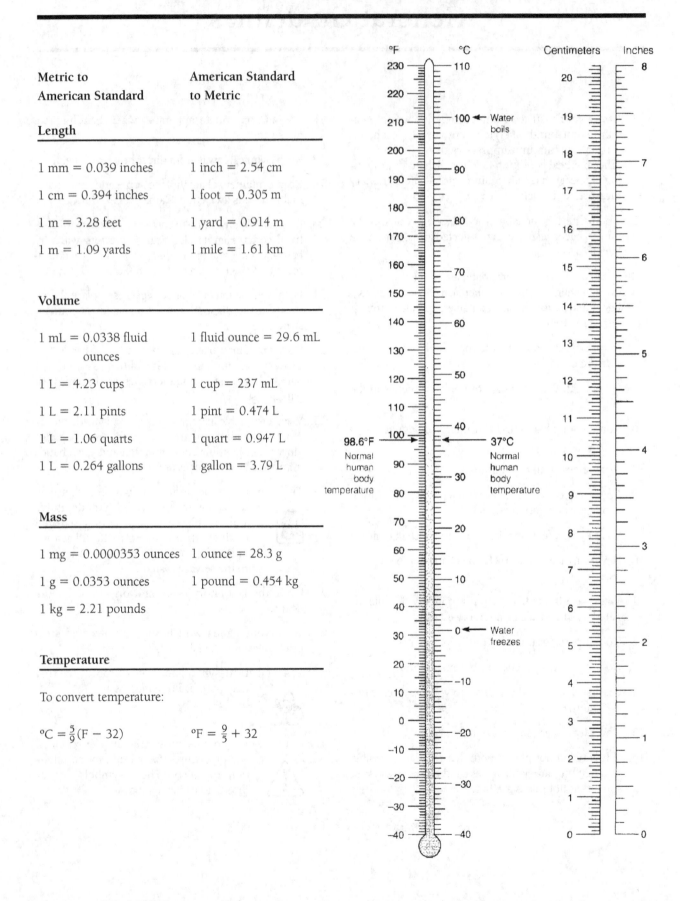

Table of Contents

Anatomical Terms and Regions

There are many terms used in anatomy which describe a region or structure of the body in a number of systems. Knowing these root words is useful in getting oriented in anatomy. It is also important to be able to describe where structures are in relationship to one another. This list of words will help you speak in a technical way about the things you will be studying in this class. As you go through the exercises of lab 1 "Organ System's Overview," make sure you keep these key terms in mind. You will be expected to know them, and you will be quizzed on them before lab 2 begins.

✓	Anatomical Landmarks
	Cephalon – head
	Cranium – skull
	Facies – face
	Frons – forehead
	Oculus or Orbital – eye
	Auris or Otic – ear
	Bucca – cheek
	Nasus – nose
	Oris or Oral – mouth
	Mentis – chin
	Cervicis – neck
	Trunk – body less head, neck and limbs
	Acromial – shoulder
	Dorsum – back
	Thoracis – chest
	Mamma – breast
	Abdomen – abdomen
	Umbilicus – naval
	Pelvis – pelvis
	Upper Extremity – upper limb
	Axilla – armpit
	Brachium – arm
	Antecubitis – front of elbow
	Olecranon – back of elbow
	Antebrachium – forearm
	Carpus – wrist
	Palma – palm
	Pollex – thumb
	Digits or Phalanx – fingers
	Manus – hand
	Inguen – groin
	Pubis – pubis
	Lumbus – loin

✓	Abdominopelvic Regions - Quadrants
	Right & Left Upper Quadrant
	Right & Left Lower Quadrant

✓	Abdominopelvic Regions – Anatomical
	Right & Left Hypochondriac Region
	Epigastric Region
	Right & Left Lumbar Region
	Umbilical Region
	Right & Left Iliac Region
	Hypogastric Region

✓	Directional Terms
	Anterior - front, before
	Posterior - back, behind
	Dorsal - back side, superior
	Ventral - belly side, inferior
	Cranial or Cephalic - towards the head
	Caudal - towards the tail or coccyx
	Superior – above
	Inferior – below
	Medial - towards the midline
	Lateral - away from the midline
	Proximal - toward an attached base
	Distal - away from an attached base

✓	Planes and Sections
	Sagittal or Parasagittal Plane
	Midsagittal Plane
	Frontal or Coronal Plane
	Transverse Plane

✓	Anatomical Landmarks (cont.)
	Gluteus – buttock
	Lower Extremity – lower limb
	Femur – thigh
	Patella – kneecap
	Crus – leg
	Sura – calf
	Tarsus – ankle
	Pes – foot
	Calcaneus – heel of foot
	Planta – sole of foot
	Digits or Phalanx - toes
	Hallus – great toe

✓	Body Cavities
	Dorsal Body Cavity
	Cranial Cavity
	Spinal Cavity
	Ventral Body Cavity
	Thoracic Cavity
	Right & Left Pleural
	Mediastinum
	Pericardial
	Abdominopelvic Cavity
	Abdominal
	Pelvic Cavity

Introduction to the Human Body

Learning Outcomes

On completion of this exercise, you should be able to:

1. Define *anatomy* and *physiology* and discuss the specializations of each.

2. Describe each level of organization in the body.

3. Describe anatomical position and its importance in anatomical studies.

4. Use directional terminology to describe the relationships of the surface anatomy of the body.

5. Describe and identify the major planes and sections of the body.

6. Locate all abdominopelvic quadrants and regions on laboratory models.

7. Locate the major organs of each organ system and briefly describe each organ's function.

8. Identify the location of the cranial, spinal, and ventral body cavities.

9. Describe the two main divisions of the ventral cavity.

10. Describe and identify the serous membranes of the body.

Lab Activities

1 Organization of the Body

2 Anatomical Position and Directional Terminology

3 Regional Terminology

4 Planes and Sections

5 Body Cavities

Clinical Application

Problems with Serous Membranes

Knowledge about what lies beneath the skin and how the body works has been slowly amassed over a span of nearly 3000 years. It may be obvious to us now that any logical practice of medicine depends on an accurate knowledge of human anatomy, yet people have not always realized this. Through most of human history, corpses were viewed with superstitious awe and dread. Observations of anatomy

Need More Practice and Review?

Build your knowledge—and confidence!—in the Study Area of MasteringA&P® at www.masteringaandp.com with Pre-lab Quizzes, Post-lab Quizzes, Practice Anatomy Lab™ (PAL™) 3.0 virtual anatomy practice tool, PhysioEx™ 9.0 laboratory simulations, and A&P Flix™ with Quizzes.

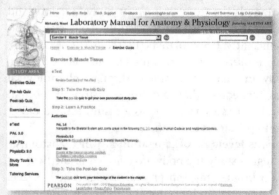

From Exercise 2 of *Laboratory Manual for Anatomy & Physiology featuring Martini Art*, Fifth Edition. Michael G. Wood.

by dissection were illegal, and medicine therefore remained an elusive practice that often harmed rather than helped the unfortunate patient. Despite these superstitions and prohibitions, however, there have always been scientists who wanted to know the human body as it really is rather than how it was imagined to be.

The founder of anatomy was the Flemish anatomist and physician Andreas Vesalius (1514–1564). Vesalius set about to describe human structure accurately. In 1543, he published his monumental work, *De Humani Corporis Faberica (On the Structure of the Human Body)*, the first meaningful text on human anatomy. In this work he corrected more than 200 errors of earlier anatomists and produced drawings that are still useful today. The work done by Vesalius laid the foundation for all future knowledge of the human body. Merely imagining the body's internal structure at last became unacceptable in medical literature.

Many brilliant anatomists and physiologists since the time of Vesalius have contributed significantly to the understanding of human form and function. Advances in medicine and in the understanding of the human body continue at an accelerated pace. For accuracy and consistency, this manual follows the terminology of the publication *Terminologica Anatomica* as endorsed by the International Federation of Associations of Anatomists.

Lab Activity 1   Organization of the Body

Anatomy is the study of body structures. Early anatomists described the body's **gross anatomy,** which includes the large parts such as muscles and bones. As knowledge of the body advanced and scientific tools permitted more detailed observations, the field of anatomy began to diversify into such areas as **microanatomy,** the study of microscopic structures; **cytology,** the study of cells; and **histology,** the study of **tissues,** which are groups of cells coordinating their effort toward a common function.

Physiology is the study of how the body functions and of the work that cells must do to keep the body stable and operating efficiently. **Homeostasis** (hō-mē-ō-STĀ-sis; *homeo-,* unchanging + *stasis,* standing) is the maintenance of a relatively steady internal environment through physiological work. Stress, inadequate diet, and disease disrupt the normal physiological processes and may, as a result, lead to either serious health problems or death.

The various **levels of organization** at which anatomists and physiologists study the body are reflected in the fields of specialization in anatomy and physiology. Each higher level increases in structural and functional complexity, progressing from chemicals to cells, tissues, organs, and finally the organ systems that function to maintain the organism.

Figure 1 uses the cardiovascular system to illustrate these levels of organization. The simplest is the **molecular level,** sometimes called the *chemical level,* shown at the bottom of the figure. Atoms such as carbon and hydrogen bond together and form molecules. The heart, for instance, contains protein molecules that are involved in contraction of the cardiac muscle. Molecules are organized into cellular structures called *organelles,* which have distinct shapes and functions. The organelles collectively constitute the next level of organization, the **cellular level.** Cells are the fundamental level of biological organization because it is cells, not molecules, that are alive. Different types of cells working together constitute the **tissue level.** Although tissues lack a distinct shape, they are distinguishable by cell type, such as the various cells that comprise the pancreas. Tissues function together at the **organ level;** at this level, each organ has a distinct three-dimensional shape and a range of functions that is broader than the range of functions for individual cells or tissues. The **organ system level** includes all the organs of a system interacting to accomplish a common goal. The heart and blood vessels, for example, constitute the cardiovascular organ system and physiologically work to move blood through the body. All organ systems make up the individual, which is referred to as the **organism level.**

QuickCheck Questions

1.1 What is the lowest living level of organization in the body?

1.2 What is homeostasis?

In the Lab   1

Materials

- ☐ Variety of objects and object sets, each representing a level of organization
- ☐ Torso models
- ☐ Articulated skeleton
- ☐ Charts

Procedures

1. Classify each object or object set as to the level of organization it represents. Write your answers in the spaces provided.

   - Molecular level _____
   - Cellular level _____
   - Tissue level _____
   - Organ level _____
   - Organ system level _____
   - Organism level _____ ▪

Figure 1 Levels of Organization

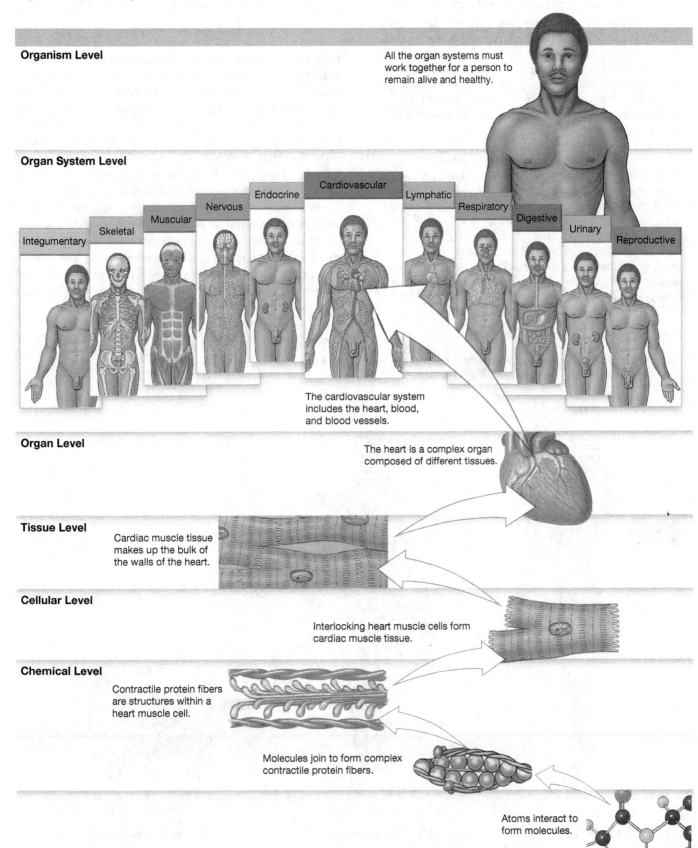

Organism Level

All the organ systems must work together for a person to remain alive and healthy.

Organ System Level

Integumentary | Skeletal | Muscular | Nervous | Endocrine | Cardiovascular | Lymphatic | Respiratory | Digestive | Urinary | Reproductive

The cardiovascular system includes the heart, blood, and blood vessels.

Organ Level

The heart is a complex organ composed of different tissues.

Tissue Level

Cardiac muscle tissue makes up the bulk of the walls of the heart.

Cellular Level

Interlocking heart muscle cells form cardiac muscle tissue.

Chemical Level

Contractile protein fibers are structures within a heart muscle cell.

Molecules join to form complex contractile protein fibers.

Atoms interact to form molecules.

Study Tip Getting Organized for Success

A major challenge in the anatomy and physiology laboratory is organizing and processing a substantial volume of information and working with the language of science. Much of the information is obtained through your reading of the lab manual. It is important that you pay attention to the anatomical terminology. Pronounce each term and note its spelling. Break apart the word into its prefix and suffix. Write the word with a definition or example.

Being prepared for lab enables you to spend more hands-on time with the laboratory material. Before class, read the appropriate exercise(s) in this manual, study the figures, and review the Laboratory Activities in the assigned sections. Relate the laboratory material to the theory concepts covered in the lecture component of the course.

Management of your daily schedule is necessary to dedicate several hours to studying anatomy and physiology. Reading typically takes a considerable time commitment, and more technical material may require several readings for you to clearly understand the concepts. ▪

Lab Activity 2 Anatomical Position and Directional Terminology

The human body can bend and stretch in a variety of directions. Although this flexibility allows us to move and manipulate objects in our environment, it can cause difficulty when describing and comparing structures. For example, what is the correct relationship between the wrist and the elbow? If your upper limb is raised above your head, you might reply that the wrist is above the elbow. With your upper limb at your side, you would respond that the wrist is below the elbow. Each response appears correct, but which is the proper anatomical relationship?

For anatomical study, the body is always referred to as being in the **anatomical position.** In this position, the individual is standing erect with the feet pointed forward, the eyes straight ahead, and the palms of the hands facing forward with the upper limbs at the sides (Figure 2). An individual in the anatomical position is said to be **supine** (soo-PĪN) when lying on the back and **prone** when lying face down.

Figure 2 Directional Terminology Important directional terms used in this text are indicated by arrows; definitions and descriptions are included in Table 1.

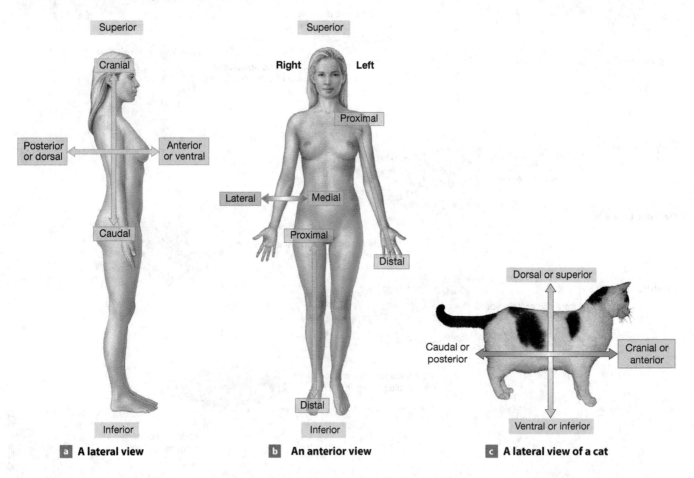

a A lateral view

b An anterior view

c A lateral view of a cat

Imagine attempting to give someone directions if you could not use terms such as *north* and *south* or *left* and *right*. These words have a unique meaning and guide the traveler toward a destination. Describing the body also requires specific terminology. Expressions such as *near, close to,* or *on top of* are too vague for anatomical descriptions. To prevent misunderstandings, precise terms are used to describe the locations and spatial relationships of anatomy. These terms have their roots in the Greek and Latin languages. Table 1 and Figure 2 display the most frequently used directional terms. Notice that most of them can be grouped into opposing pairs, or antonyms.

- **Superior** and **inferior** describe vertical positions. *Superior* means above, *inferior* means below. For example, on a person in the anatomical position, the head is superior to the shoulders and the knee is inferior to the hip.

- **Anterior** and **posterior** refer to front and back. *Anterior* means in front of or forward, and *posterior* means in back of or toward the back. The anterior surface of the body comprises all front surfaces, including the palms of the hand, and the posterior surface includes all the back surfaces. In addition to describing locations, these directional terms describe position *relationships*, which means that one body part can be described using both terms. The heart, for example, is posterior to the breastbone and anterior to the spine.

- In four-legged animals, the anatomical position is with all four limbs on the ground, and therefore the meanings of some directional terms change (Figure 2c). *Superior* now

refers to the back, or **dorsal**, surface, and *inferior* refers to the belly, or **ventral**, surface. **Cranial** and *anterior* mean toward the head in four-legged animals, and **caudal** and *posterior* mean toward the tail in four-legged animals and toward the coccyx in humans.

- **Medial** and **lateral** describe positions relative to the body's *midline*, the vertical middle of the body or any structure in the body. *Medial* has two meanings. It describes one structure as being closer to the body's midline than some other structure; for instance, the ring finger is medial to the middle finger when the hand is held in the anatomical position. *Medial* also describes a structure that is permanently between others, as the nose is medial to the eyes. *Lateral* means either farther from the body's midline or permanently to the side of some other structure; the eyes are lateral to the nose, and, in the anatomical position, the middle finger is lateral to the ring finger.

- **Proximal** refers to parts near another structure. **Distal** describes structures that are distant from other structures. These terms are frequently used to describe the proximity of a structure to its point of attachment on the body. For example, the thigh bone (femur) has a proximal region where it attaches to the hip and a distal region toward the knee.

- **Superficial** and **deep** describe layered structures. *Superficial* refers to parts on or close to the surface. Underneath an upper layer are *deep*, or *bottom*, structures. The skin is superficial to the muscular system, and bones are usually deep to the muscles.

Table 1	Directional Terms (See Figure 2)	
Term	**Region or Reference**	**Example**
Anterior	The front; before	The navel is on the *anterior* surface of the trunk.
Ventral	The belly side (equivalent to anterior when referring to human body)	In humans, the navel is on the *ventral* surface.
Posterior	The back; behind	The shoulder blade is located *posterior* to the rib cage.
Dorsal	The back (equivalent to posterior when referring to human body)	The *dorsal* body cavity encloses the brain and spinal cord.
Cranial or cephalic	The head	The *cranial*, or *cephalic*, border of the pelvis is on the side toward the head rather than toward the thigh.
Superior	Above; at a higher level (in human body, toward the head)	In humans, the cranial border of the pelvis is *superior to* the thigh.
Caudal	The tail (coccyx in humans)	The hips are *caudal* to the waist.
Inferior	Below; at a lower level	The knees are *inferior* to the hips.
Medial	Toward the body's longitudinal axis; toward the midsagittal plane	The *medial* surfaces of the thighs may be in contact; moving medially from the arm across the chest surface brings you to the sternum.
Lateral	Away from the body's longitudinal axis; away from the midsagittal plane	The thigh articulates with the *lateral* surface of the pelvis; moving laterally from the nose brings you to the eyes.
Proximal	Toward an attached base	The thigh is *proximal* to the foot; moving proximally from the wrist brings you to the elbow.
Distal	Away from an attached base	The fingers are *distal* to the wrist; moving distally from the elbow brings you to the wrist.
Superficial	At, near, or relatively close to the body surface	The skin is *superficial* to underlying structures.
Deep	Farther from the body surface	The bone of the thigh is *deep* to the surrounding skeletal muscles.

Some directional terms seem to be interchangeable, but there is usually a precise term for each description. For example, *superior* and *proximal* both describe the upper region of limb bones. When discussing the point of attachment of a bone, *proximal* is the more descriptive term. When describing the location of a bone relative to an inferior bone, the term *superior* is used.

QuickCheck Questions

2.1 Why is having a precisely defined anatomical position important in anatomical studies?

2.2 What is the relationship of the shoulder joint to the elbow joint?

2.3 Which directional term describes the relationship of muscles to the skin?

In the Lab 2

Materials

☐ Yourself or a laboratory partner
☐ Torso models
☐ Anatomical charts
☐ Anatomical models

Procedures

1. Assume the anatomical position. Consider how this orientation differs from your normal stance.

2. Review each directional term presented in Figure 2.

3. Use the laboratory models and charts and your own body (or your partner's) to practice using directional terms while comparing anatomy. The Review & Practice Sheet at the end of this exercise may be used as a guide for comparisons. ■

Lab Activity 3 Regional Terminology

Approaching the body from a regional perspective simplifies the learning of anatomy. Body surface features are used as anatomical landmarks to assist in locating internal structures, and as a result many internal structures are named after an overlying surface structure. For example, the back of the knee is called the popliteal (pop-LIT-ē-al) region, and the major artery in the knee is the popliteal artery. Table 2 and Figure 3 present the major regions of the body.

The head is referred to as the **cephalon** and consists of the **cranium,** or skull, and the **face.** The neck is the **cervical** region. The main part of the body is the **trunk,** which attaches the neck, upper limbs, and lower limbs. The thorax is the chest, or **pectoral,** region. Below the chest is the **abdominal** region, which narrows at the **pelvis.** The back surface of the trunk, the **dorsum,** includes the **loin,** or lower back, and the **gluteal** region of the buttock. The side of the trunk below the ribs is the **flank.**

The shoulder, or **scapular,** region attaches the **upper limb,** which is the arm and forearm, to the trunk and forms the **axilla,** the armpit. The proximal part of the upper limb is the **brachium;** the **antebrachium** is the forearm. Between the brachium and antebrachium is the **antecubitis** region, the elbow. The wrist is called the **carpus,** and the inside surface of the hand is the **palm.**

The pelvis attaches the **lower limb** to the trunk at the **inguinal** area, or **groin.** The proximal part of the lower limb is the **thigh,** the back of the knee is the **popliteal** region, and the leg is the calf, or **sura. Tarsus** refers to the ankle, and the sole of the foot is the **plantar** surface.

Reference to the position of internal abdominal organs is simplified by partitioning the trunk into four equal **quadrants,** the right and left upper quadrants and the right and left lower quadrants (Figure 4). Observe in Figure 4a the vertical and horizontal planes used to delineate the quadrants. Quadrants are used to describe the positions of organs.

Table 2	Regions of the Human Body (See Figure 3)
Structure	**Region**
Cephalon (head)	Cephalic region
Cervicis (neck)	Cervical region
Thoracis (thorax, or chest)	Thoracic region
Axilla (armpit)	Axillary region
Brachium (arm)	Brachial region
Antecubitis (elbow)	Antecubital region
Antebrachium (forearm)	Antebrachial region
Carpus (wrist)	Carpal region
Manus (hand)	Manual region
Abdomen (belly)	Abdominal region
Lumbus (loin)	Lumbar region
Gluteus (buttock)	Gluteal region
Pelvis (hip)	Pelvic region
Pubis (anterior pelvis)	Pubic region
Inguen (groin)	Inguinal region
Femur (thigh)	Femoral region
Popliteus (back of knee)	Popliteal region
Crus (anterior leg)	Crural region
Sura (calf)	Sural region
Tarsus (ankle)	Tarsal region
Pes (foot)	Pedal region
Planta (sole)	Plantar region

Figure 3 Regional Terminology Anatomical terms are shown in boldface type, common names in plain type, and anatomical adjectives in parentheses.

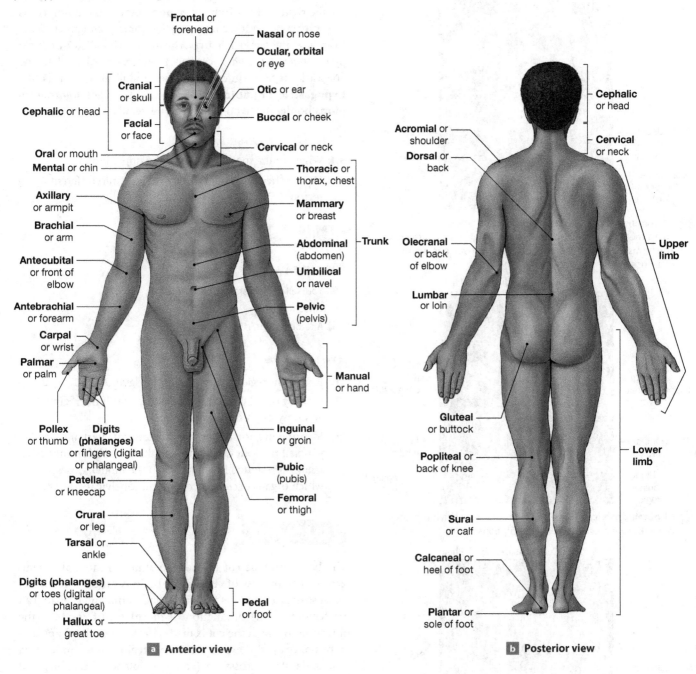

a Anterior view

b Posterior view

The stomach, for example, is mostly located in the left upper quadrant.

For more detailed descriptions, the abdominal surface is divided into nine **abdominopelvic regions,** shown in Figure 4b. Four planes are used to define the regions: two vertical and two transverse planes arranged in the familiar tic-tac-toe pattern. The vertical planes, called the right and left **lateral planes,** are positioned slightly medial to the

nipples, each plane on the side of the nipple that is closer to the body center. The lateral planes divide the trunk into three nearly equal vertical regions. A pair of transverse planes crosses the vertical planes to isolate the nine regions. The **transpyloric plane** is superior to the umbilicus (navel) at the level of the pylorus, the lower region of the stomach. The **transtubercular plane** is inferior to the umbilicus and crosses the abdomen at the level of the superior hips.

Figure 4 Abdominopelvic Quadrants and Regions

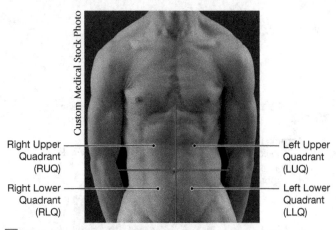

Custom Medical Stock Photo

Right Upper Quadrant (RUQ)

Left Upper Quadrant (LUQ)

Right Lower Quadrant (RLQ)

Left Lower Quadrant (LLQ)

a Abdominopelvic quadrants. The four abdominopelvic quadrants are formed by two perpendicular lines that intersect at the navel. The terms for these quadrants, or their abbreviations, are most often used in clinical discussions.

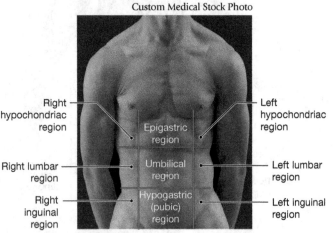

Custom Medical Stock Photo

Right hypochondriac region

Left hypochondriac region

Epigastric region

Right lumbar region

Umbilical region

Left lumbar region

Right inguinal region

Hypogastric (pubic) region

Left inguinal region

b Abdominopelvic regions. The nine abdominopelvic regions provide more precise regional descriptions.

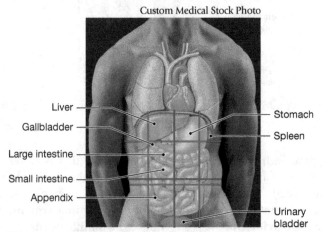

Custom Medical Stock Photo

Liver

Gallbladder

Large intestine

Small intestine

Appendix

Stomach

Spleen

Urinary bladder

c Anatomical relationships. The relationship between the abdominopelvic quadrants and regions and the locations of the internal organs are shown here.

The nine abdominopelvic regions are as follows: The **umbilical region** surrounds the umbilicus. Lateral to this region are the right and left **lumbar regions.** Above the umbilicus is the **epigastric region** containing the stomach and much of the liver. The right and left **hypochondriac** (hī-pō-KON-drē-ak; *hypo,* under + *chondro,* cartilage) **regions** are lateral to the epigastric region. Inferior to the umbilical region is the **hypogastric, or pubic, region.** The right and left **inguinal regions** border the hypogastric region laterally.

QuickCheck Questions

3.1 What are the major regions of the upper limb?

3.2 How is the abdominal surface divided into different regions?

In the Lab 3

Materials

☐ Yourself or a laboratory partner

☐ Torso models

☐ Anatomical charts

Procedures

1. Review the regional terminology in Figure 3 and Table 2.

2. Identify on a laboratory model or yourself the regional anatomy as presented in Figure 3.

3. Identify on a torso model or anatomical chart and on yourself the four quadrants and the nine abdominopelvic regions presented in Figure 4. On the model, observe which organs occupy each abdominopelvic region. ■

Lab Activity 4 Planes and Sections

The body must be cut in order to study its internal organization. The process of cutting the body is called **sectioning.** Most structures, such as the trunk, knee, arm, and eyeball, can be sectioned. The orientation of the **plane of section** (the direction in which the cut is made) determines the shape and appearance of the exposed internal region. Imagine cutting one soda straw crosswise (crosswise plane of section) and another straw lengthwise (lengthwise plane of section). The former produces a circle, and the latter produces a concave U-shaped tube.

Three major types of sections are used in the study of anatomy: two vertical and one transverse (Figure 5). **Transverse** sections are perpendicular to the vertical orientation of the body. (The crosswise cut you made on the imaginary straw yielded a transverse section.) Transverse sections are often called **cross sections** because they go across the body axis.

Figure 5 Planes of Section The three primary planes of section. The photographs of sectional images were derived from the Visible Human data set.

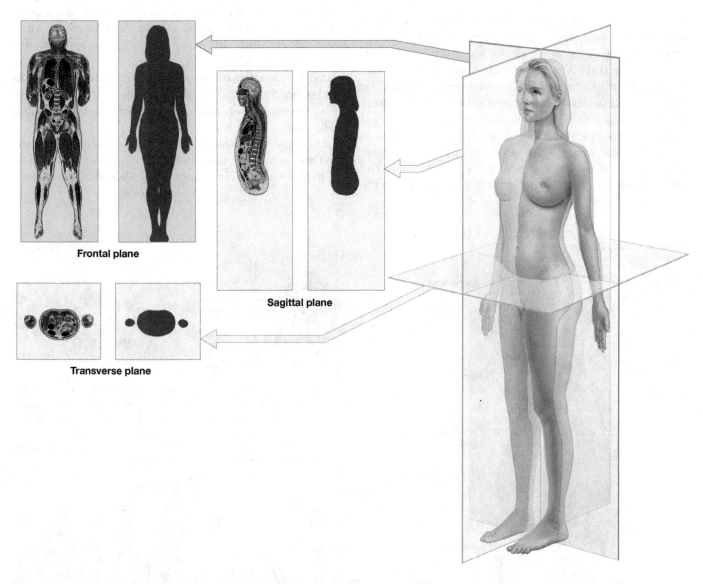

Frontal plane

Transverse plane

Sagittal plane

A transverse section divides superior and inferior structures. **Vertical** sections are parallel to the vertical axis of the body and include sagittal and frontal sections. A **sagittal** vertical section divides a body or organ into right and left portions. A **midsagittal** vertical section equally divides structures, and a **parasagittal** vertical section produces nearly equal divisions. A **frontal,** or **coronal,** vertical section separates anterior and posterior structures.

QuickCheck Questions

4.1 Which type of section separates the kneecap from the lower limb?

4.2 Amputation of the forearm is performed by which type of section?

In the Lab 4

Materials

☐ Anatomical models with various sections
☐ Knife and objects for sectioning

Procedures

1. Review each plane of section shown in Figure 5.

2. Identify the sections on models and other materials presented by your instructor.

3. Cut several common objects, such as an apple and a hot dog, along their sagittal and transverse planes. Compare the exposed arrangement of the interior. ■

Lab Activity 5 Body Cavities

Body cavities are internal spaces that house internal organs, such as the brain in the cranium and the digestive organs in the abdomen. The walls of a body cavity support and protect the soft organs contained in the cavity. In the trunk, large cavities are subdivided into smaller cavities that contain individual organs. The smaller cavities are enclosed by thin sacs, such as those around the heart, lungs, and intestines. Most of the space in a cavity is occupied by the enclosed organ and by a thin film of liquid.

The **cranial cavity** is the space within the oval *cranium* of the skull that encases and protects the delicate brain. The **spinal cavity** is a long, slender canal that passes through the vertebral column. The cranial and spinal cavities are continuous with each other and join at the base of the skull, where the spinal cord meets the brain. The brain and spinal cord are contained within the **meninges,** a protective three-layered membrane. Some anatomists group the cranial and spinal cavities into a larger *dorsal body cavity;* however, this term is not recognized by the international reference *Terminologica Anatomica* and is therefore not used in this manual.

The **ventral body cavity,** also called the **coelom** (SĒ-luhm; *koila,* cavity), is the entire space of the body trunk anterior to the vertebral column and posterior to the sternum (breastbone) and the abdominal muscle wall (**Figure 6**). This large cavity is divided into two major cavities, the **thoracic** (*thorax,* chest)

Figure 6 Body Cavities

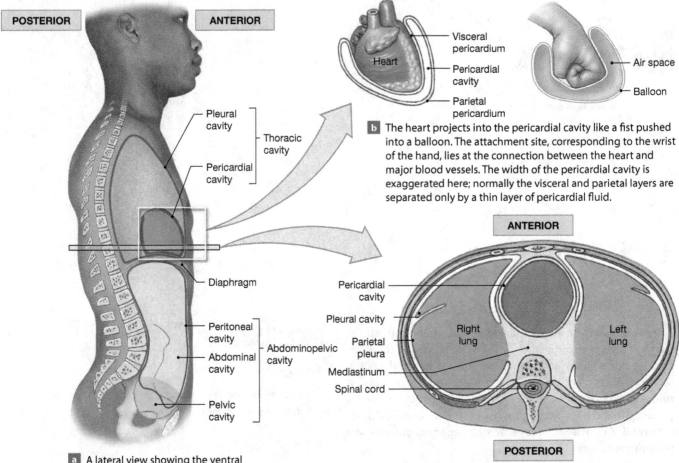

b The heart projects into the pericardial cavity like a fist pushed into a balloon. The attachment site, corresponding to the wrist of the hand, lies at the connection between the heart and major blood vessels. The width of the pericardial cavity is exaggerated here; normally the visceral and parietal layers are separated only by a thin layer of pericardial fluid.

a A lateral view showing the ventral body cavity, which is divided by the muscular diaphragm into a superior thoracic (chest) cavity and an inferior abdominopelvic cavity. Three of the four adult body cavities are shown and outlined in red; only one of the two pleural cavities can be shown in a sagittal section.

c A transverse section through the thoracic cavity, showing the central location of the pericardial cavity. Notice how the mediastinum divides the thoracic cavity into two pleural cavities. Note that this transverse or cross-sectional view is oriented as though the observer were standing at the subject's feet and looking toward the subject's head. This is the standard presentation for clinical images, and unless otherwise noted, sectional views in this text use this same orientation.

cavity and the **abdominopelvic cavity.** These cavities, in turn, are further divided into the specific cavities that surround individual organs. The heart, lungs, stomach, and intestines are covered with a double-layered **serous** (SĒR-us; *seri-*, watery) **membrane.** Each serous membrane isolates one organ and reduces friction and abrasion on the organ surface.

The walls of the thoracic cavity are muscle and bone. The main subdivisions of this cavity are the **mediastinum** (mē-dē-as-TĪ-num *or* mē-dē-AS-ti-num; *media-*, middle) and two **pleural cavities.** The mediastinum is the mass of organs and tissues separating the pleural cavities. Each pleural cavity contains one lung. Inside the mediastinum is a smaller cavity, the **pericardial** (*peri-*, around + *kardia*, heart) **cavity,** and the heart is most often described as being contained inside this cavity rather than simply inside the mediastinum.

The abdominopelvic cavity is separated from the thoracic cavity by a dome-shaped muscle, the diaphragm. The abdominopelvic cavity is the space between the diaphragm and the floor of the pelvis. This cavity is subdivided into the abdominal cavity and the pelvic cavity. The **abdominal cavity** contains most of the digestive organs, such as the liver, gallbladder, stomach, pancreas, kidneys, and small and large intestines. The **pelvic cavity** is the small cavity enclosed by the pelvic girdle of the hips. This cavity contains the internal reproductive organs, parts of the large intestine, the rectum, and the urinary bladder.

The heart, lungs, stomach, and intestines are encased in double-layered serous membranes that have a minuscule fluid-filled cavity between the two layers. Directly attached to the exposed surface of an internal organ is the **visceral** (VIS-er-al; *viscera*, internal organ) **layer** of the serous membrane. The **parietal** (pah-RĪ-e-tal; *pariet-*, wall) **layer** is superficial to the visceral layer and lines the wall of the body cavity. The **serous fluid** between these layers is a lubricant that reduces friction and abrasion between the layers as the enclosed organ moves.

Figure 6b highlights the anatomy of the serous membrane of the heart, the **pericardium.** This membrane consists of an outer **parietal pericardium** and an inner **visceral pericardium.** The parietal pericardium is a fibrous sac attached to the diaphragm and supportive tissues of the thoracic cavity. The visceral pericardium is attached to the surface of the heart. The space between these two serous layers is the pericardial cavity.

The serous membrane of the lungs is called the **pleura** (PLOO-rah). The **parietal pleura** lines the thoracic wall, and the **visceral pleura** is attached to the surface of the lung. Because each lung is contained inside a separate pleural cavity, a puncture wound on one side of the chest usually collapses only the corresponding lung.

Most of the digestive organs are encased in the **peritoneum** (per-i-ton-Ē-um), the serous membrane of the abdomen. The **parietal peritoneum** has numerous folds that wrap around and attach the abdominal organs to the posterior abdominal wall. The **visceral peritoneum** lines the organ surfaces. The **peritoneal cavity** is the space between the parietal and visceral peritoneal layers. The peritoneum has many blood vessels, lymphatic vessels, and nerves that support the digestive organs. The kidneys are **retroperitoneal** (*retro-*, behind) and are located outside the peritoneum.

Clinical Application **Problems with Serous Membranes**

Serous membranes may become inflamed and infected as a result of bacterial invasion or damage to the underlying organ. Liquids often build up in the cavity of the serous membrane, causing additional complications. **Peritonitis** is an infection of the peritoneum that occurs when the digestive tract is damaged—often by ulceration, rupture, or a puncture wound—in a way that permits intestinal bacteria to contaminate the peritoneum. **Pleuritis, or pleurisy,** is an inflammation of the pleura often caused by tuberculosis, pneumonia, or thoracic abscess. Breathing is made painful as the inflamed membranes move when a person inhales and exhales. **Pericarditis** is an inflammation of the pericardium resulting from infection, injury, heart attack, or other causes. In advanced stages, a buildup of liquid causes the heart to compress, a condition resulting in decreased cardiac function. ▪

QuickCheck Questions

5.1 What structures form the walls of the cranial and spinal cavities?

5.2 Name the various subdivisions of the ventral body cavity.

5.3 Describe the two layers of a serous membrane.

5.4 Name the three serous membranes of the body.

In the Lab 5

Materials

☐ Torso models

☐ Articulated skeleton

☐ Anatomical charts

Procedures

1. Review each cavity and serous membrane illustrated in Figure 6.

2. Locate each body cavity on the torso models, anatomical charts, and articulated skeleton.

3. Identify the organ(s) in the various cavities of the ventral body cavity on the torso models.

4. Identify the pericardium, pleura, and peritoneum on the torso models and charts.

Sketch to Learn

Drawing is an excellent study technique to review material. Let's sketch the thoracic cavity and its major organs. "Hey, I'm not an artist," you may say. Just follow the simple examples here and throughout the manual, and you just might learn to draw nearly anything. Most sketching we will do in this manual requires little more than the skill to draw simple shapes with lines, uncomplicated curves, and circles.

First, a few hints are in order:

- Use a pencil while sketching. I personally need more eraser than lead!

- Take your time and plan your sketch. Look at the example and be sure you understand what you need to draw.

- Consider the size of the sketch and its components so your drawing is easy to label and study.

- Organize your labels into anatomical groups as shown in the example.

- Most rewarding of all, relax and enjoy the creative process. Further develop your drawing by using color pencils and adding shade and texture.

Sample Sketch

Step 1
- Draw thorax with the heart and lungs.

Step 2
- Add another layer around organs to show serous membranes.

Step 3
- Label your sketch.

Your Sketch

Name _____

Date _____

Section _____

Introduction
to the Human Body

A. Definitions

Define each directional term.

1. anterior

2. lateral

3. proximal

4. ventral

5. posterior

6. medial

7. distal

8. superficial

9. superior

10. dorsal

11. inferior

12. deep

B. Fill in the Blanks

Use the correct term(s) to complete each sentence.

1. The heart is surrounded by a small cavity called the _____, which is inside a larger cavity, the _____.

2. The _____ cavity surrounds the digestive organs in the abdominal cavity.

3. The kidneys are _____ because they are located superficial to the _____.

4. The inner membrane layer surrounding a lung is the _____.

5. The brain is contained in a cavity called the _____.

6. A lubricating substance in body cavities is called _____.

7. The large medial area of the chest is called the _____.

8. The muscle that divides the ventral body cavity horizontally is the _____.

9. The outer layer of a serous membrane is the _____ layer.

10. In the anatomical position, the palms of the hands are _____.

11. The index finger is _____ to the ring finger.

12. The trunk is _____ to the pubis.

13. Where it attaches to the elbow, the brachium is _____ to the elbow.

14. The buttock is _____ to the pubis.

15. The shoulders are _____ to the hips.

C. Short-Answer Questions

1. Describe the six main levels of organization in the body.

2. List the nine abdominopelvic regions and the location of each.

3. Compare the study of anatomy with that of physiology.

4. Define the term *homeostasis*.

5. In which quadrant is the liver located?

6. Name the abdominopelvic region that contains the urinary bladder.

7. Describe a parasagittal plane of section.

8. What do the brachium, antecubitis, and antebrachium constitute?

9. Where is the dorsal surface of a four-legged animal?

D. Labeling

1. Label the regions of the body in Figure 7.

Figure 7 Regional Terminology

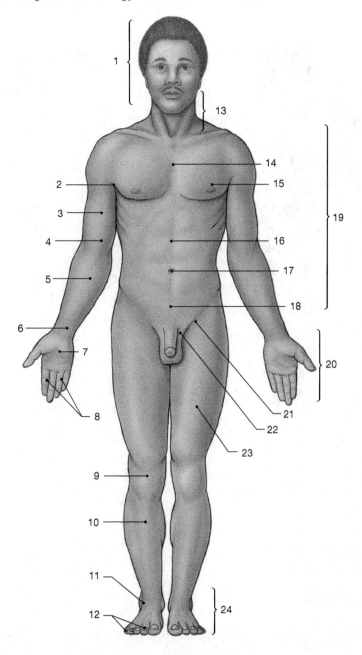

1. _____
2. _____
3. _____
4. _____
5. _____
6. _____
7. _____
8. _____
9. _____
10. _____
11. _____
12. _____
13. _____
14. _____
15. _____
16. _____
17. _____
18. _____
19. _____
20. _____
21. _____
22. _____
23. _____
24. _____

2. Label the directional terms in Figure 8.

Figure 8 **Directional References**

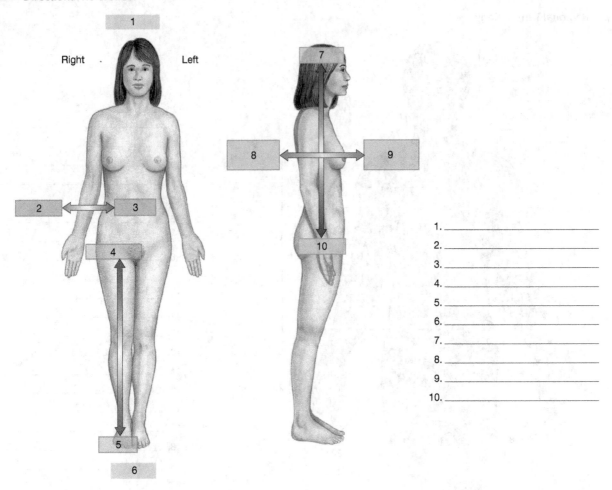

Right   Left

1. _____
2. _____
3. _____
4. _____
5. _____
6. _____
7. _____
8. _____
9. _____
10. _____

3. Label the structures in Figure 9.

Figure 9 **Body Cavity**

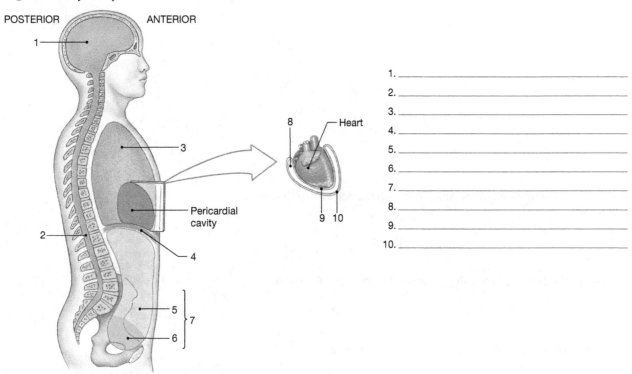

1. _____
2. _____
3. _____
4. _____
5. _____
6. _____
7. _____
8. _____
9. _____
10. _____

E. Drawing

1. *Draw It!* Draw two pictures of a bagel sectioned by a plane. In one drawing, make the sectioning plane parallel to the circular surface of the bagel; in the other drawing, make the sectioning plane perpendicular to that surface.

2. *Draw It!* Sketch the body trunk and the planes that designate the nine abdomino-pelvic regions.

F. Analysis and Application

1. Explain why it is important to use anatomical terminology when describing body parts.

2. Compare the body axis of a four-legged animal to the axis of a human.

3. Describe the cavities that protect the brain and spinal cord.

4. What is the benefit for organs in the ventral body to be surrounded by double-layered membranes instead of single-layered membranes?

G. Clinical Challenge

1. Nicole has a respiratory infection that has caused her right pleura to dry out. Describe the symptoms that could be related to this condition.

2. Doug has a skateboard accident and scrapes his knees, left hip, and left elbow. Using the appropriate regional terminology, describe his injuries as if you were writing them in his medical chart.

Integumentary System
Wish List

Locate and identify selected integumentary structures as you work through the Integumentary system activities

✓	Structure	Description
	Epidermis	epi=above dermis=skin
	stratum corneum	Outermost layer
	stratum lucidum	"Clear" layer below the stratum corneum
	stratum granulosum	Thin granular layer above stratum spinosum
	stratum spinosum	Spinous (prickly) layer above stratum basale
	stratum germinativum/basale	bottom of epidermis (base)

	Dermis	
	papillary layer	"Bumpy" layer. Supplies blood and sensory neurons
	dermal papillae	papillae= small cone. Swirls produce fingerprints
	reticular layer	"little net" of collagen fibers. Accessory organs originate here

	Hypodermis (subcutaneous)	hypo=below
	subcutaneous (cutaneous) plexus	Dermal blood supply

	Accessory Structures	
✓	sebaceous gland	oil glands. Associated with hair folicles
✓	arrector pili muscle	"goose bumps" muscle
✓	sweat gland	exocrine glands that secreate sweat
✓	sweat pore	
	Meissner's corpuscle (tactile receptor)	Touch receptor
	Pacinian corpuscle (lamellated receptor)	Pressure receptor
✓	hair shaft	
✓	adipose cells	Adipose=fat

22

Integumentary System

Learning Outcomes

On completion of this exercise, you should be able to:

1. Identify the two layers of the skin.

2. Identify the layers of the epidermis.

3. Distinguish between the papillary and reticular layers of the dermis.

4. Identify the accessory structures of the skin.

5. Identify a hair follicle, the parts of a hair, and an arrector pili muscle.

6. Distinguish between sebaceous and sweat glands.

7. Describe three sensory organs of the integument.

Lab Activities

1 Epidermis and Dermis

2 Accessory Structures of the Skin

Clinical Applications

Skin Cancer

Acne

Burns

The **integumentary (in-TEG-ū-MEN-ta-ree) system** is the most visible organ system of the human body. The integument (in-TEG-ū-ment), or skin, is classified as an organ system because it is composed of many different types of tissues and organs. Organs of the skin include oil-, wax-, and sweat-producing glands; sensory organs for touch; muscles attached to hair follicles; and blood and lymphatic vessels.

The integument seals the body in a protective barrier that is flexible yet resistant to abrasion and evaporative water loss. People interact with the external environment with the skin. Caressing a baby's head, feeling the texture of granite, and testing the temperature of bath water all involve sensory organs of the integumentary system. Sweat glands in the skin cool the body to regulate body temperature. When exposed to sunlight, the integument manufactures vitamin D_3, a vitamin essential in calcium and phosphorus balance.

Need More Practice and Review?

Build your knowledge—and confidence!—in the Study Area of MasteringA&P® at www.masteringaandp.com with Pre-lab Quizzes, Post-lab Quizzes, Practice Anatomy Lab™ (PAL™) 3.0 virtual anatomy practice tool, PhysioEx™ 9.0 laboratory simulations, and A&P Flix™ with Quizzes.

PAL | practice anatomy lab | For this lab exercise, follow these navigation paths:

• PAL>Anatomical Models>Integumentary System

• PAL>Histology>Integumentary System

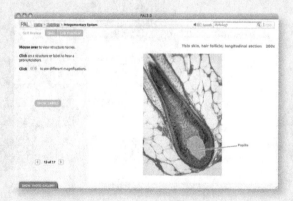

MasteringA&P®

Lab Activity 1 Epidermis and Dermis

There are two principal tissue layers in the integument: a superficial layer of epithelium called the *epidermis* and a deeper layer of connective tissue, the *dermis* (Figure 1). The **epidermis** consists of a stratified squamous epithelium organized into many distinct layers, or *strata*, of cells, as shown in Figure 2. Thick-skinned areas, such as the palms of the hands and soles of the feet, have five layers; thin-skinned areas have only four. Cells called **keratinocytes** are produced deep in the epidermis and pushed superficially toward the surface of the skin. It takes from 15 to 30 days for a cell to migrate from the basal region to the surface of the epidermis. During this migration, the keratinocytes synthesize and accumulate the protein keratin, the internal organization of the cell is disrupted, and the cells die. These dry, scalelike keratinized cells on the surface of the stratified squamous epidermis are resistant to dehydration and friction. Because of these characteristics the integument is also called the **cutaneous membrane.**

Moving superficially from the basal lamina, the five layers of the epidermis are as follows:

- The **stratum basale** (STRA-tum bah-SA-le), or the **stratum germinativum** (STRA-tum jer-mi-na-TĒ-vum), is a layer just one cell thick that joins the basal lamina of the epidermis to the upper surface of the dermis. The cells in this stratum are stem cells and so are in a constant state of mitosis, replacing cells that have rubbed off the epidermal surface. Other cells in this layer, called **melanocytes,** produce the pigment **melanin** (MEL-ă-nin), which protects deeper cells from the harmful effects of ultraviolet (UV) radiation from the sun. Prolonged exposure to UV light causes an increase in melanin synthesis, resulting in a darkening, or tanning, of the integument.

- Superficial to the stratum germinativum is the **stratum spinosum,** which consists of five to seven layers of cells, interconnected by strong protein molecules between cell membranes, forming cell attachments called **desmosomes.** When a slide of epidermal tissue is being prepared, cells in

Figure 1 Components of the Integumentary System This diagrammatic view of skin illustrates the relationships among the epidermis, dermis, and accessory structures of the integumentary system (with the exception of nails, shown in Figure 7).

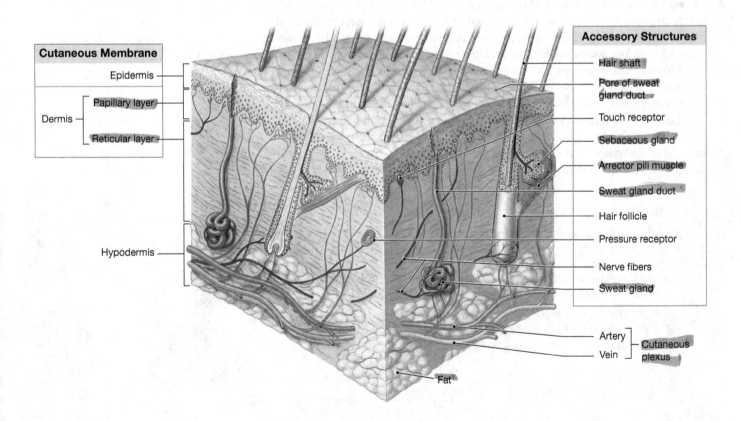

Cutaneous Membrane
- Epidermis
- Dermis
  - Papillary layer
  - Reticular layer
- Hypodermis

Accessory Structures
- Hair shaft
- Pore of sweat gland duct
- Touch receptor
- Sebaceous gland
- Arrector pili muscle
- Sweat gland duct
- Hair follicle
- Pressure receptor
- Nerve fibers
- Sweat gland
- Artery
- Vein
- Cutaneous plexus

Fat

Figure 2 Organization of the Epidermis

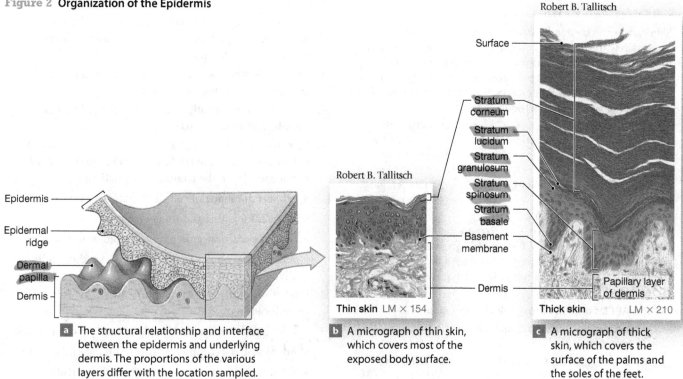

Robert B. Tallitsch

Surface

Stratum corneum

Stratum lucidum

Stratum granulosum

Stratum spinosum

Stratum basale

Basement membrane

Dermis

Papillary layer of dermis

Robert B. Tallitsch

Epidermis

Epidermal ridge

Dermal papilla

Dermis

Thin skin LM × 154

Thick skin LM × 210

a The structural relationship and interface between the epidermis and underlying dermis. The proportions of the various layers differ with the location sampled.

b A micrograph of thin skin, which covers most of the exposed body surface.

c A micrograph of thick skin, which covers the surface of the palms and the soles of the feet.

this layer often shrink, but the desmosome bridges between cells remain intact. This results in cells with a spiny outline; hence the name "spinosum."

- Superficial to the stratum spinosum is a layer of darker cells that make up the **stratum granulosum.** As cells from the stratum germinativum are pushed superficially, they synthesize the protein **keratohyalin** (ker-a-tō-HĪ-a-lin), which increases durability and reduces water loss from the integument surface. Keratohyalin granules stain dark and give this layer its color.

- In thick skin, a thin, transparent layer of cells called the **stratum lucidum** lies superficial to the stratum granulosum. Only the thick skin of the palms and the soles of the feet have the stratum lucidum; the rest of the skin is considered thin and lacks this layer.

- The **stratum corneum** (KOR-nē-um; *cornu,* horn) is the most superficial layer of the epidermis and contains many layers of flattened, dead cells. As cells from the stratum granulosum migrate superficially, keratohyalin granules are converted to the fibrous protein keratin. Cells in the stratum corneum also accumulate the yellow-orange pigment **carotene,** which is common in light-skinned individuals.

Deep to the epidermis is the second of the two layers of the integument, the **dermis,** a thick layer of irregularly arranged connective tissue that supports and nourishes the epidermis

and secures the integument to the underlying structures (Figure 1). The dermis is divided into two layers: *papillary* and *reticular.* Although there is no distinct boundary between these layers, the superficial portion of the dermis is designated the **papillary layer.** It consists of areolar tissue containing numerous collagen and elastic fibers. Folds in the tissue are called **dermal papillae** (pa-PIL-la; *papilla,* a small cone) and project into the epidermis as the swirls of fingerprints. Within the dermal papillae are small sensory receptors for light touch, movement, and vibration, termed **tactile corpuscles** (also called *Meissner's corpuscles*).

Deep to the papillary layer is the **reticular layer** of the dermis. This layer is distinguished by a meshwork of thick bands of collagen fibers in dense irregular connective tissue. Hair follicles and glands from the epidermis penetrate deep into the reticular layer. Sensory receptors in this layer, called **lamallated corpuscles** (*Pacinian corpuscles*), detect deep pressure.

Attaching the dermis to underlying structures is the **hypodermis,** or **subcutaneous layer,** which is composed primarily of adipose tissue and areolar tissue. *Cutaneous membrane* is yet another name for the skin, thus the name *subcutaneous* for this layer. The hypodermis is not part of the integumentary system.

QuickCheck Questions

1.1 Describe the two layers of the skin.

1.2 Why does the epidermis constantly replace its cells?

Clinical Application Skin Cancer

Skin cancer can be deadly. Protect yourself and your loved ones' skin with sunscreen and use common sense when out in the sun. Sunburns greatly increase the chances of getting cancer. During summer, some people can start to burn in just 20 minutes! Know the warning signs for skin cancer and self-examine your skin on a regular basis.

Basal cell carcinoma (Figure 3) is a tumor starting in stem cells in the stratum germinativum. Approximately 65% of the tumors occur in areas of skin exposed to excessive UV light (too much sun). Basal cell carcinoma is the most common form of skin cancer. It rarely spreads and there is a very high survivor rate. Squamous cell carcinoma only occurs in areas with high UV exposure.

Malignant melanoma is an extremely dangerous malignant tumor of melanocytes. Cancer cells grow rapidly and metastasize through the lymphatic system which drains into the bloodstream. This type has only a 14% survival rate if widespread in the lymph.

The ABCDs of Skin Cancer—Warning Signs

A = *asymmetry*, the skin tumor has an uneven shape and may bleed.

B = *border*, the edge is irregular instead of round and smooth.

C = *color*, many colors in a spot may indicate skin cancer.

D = *diameter*, 5 mm or larger is dangerous. ▪

Figure 3 Skin Cancers

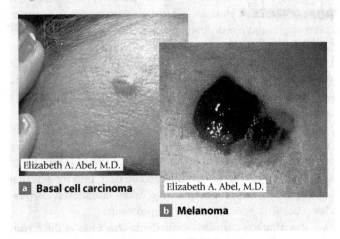

Elizabeth A. Abel, M.D.

a **Basal cell carcinoma**

Elizabeth A. Abel, M.D.

b **Melanoma**

In the Lab 1

Materials

☐ Skin model

☐ Compound microscope

☐ Prepared slide of the scalp (cross section)

Procedures

1. Examine a skin model and identify the epidermis, dermis, and hypodermis. Identify the specific layers of the epidermis and dermis.

2. Place the scalp slide on the microscope and focus on the specimen at low magnification.

3. Scan the slide vertically and identify the epidermis, dermis, and hypodermis.

4. Increase the magnification to medium and examine the epidermis. Locate the epidermal layers, beginning with the deepest layer, the stratum germinativum.

   ▪ What is the shape of cells in the stratum spinosum?

   ▪ What color is the stratum granulosum?

   ▪ Does the scalp specimen have a stratum lucidum?

   ▪ What is the top layer of cells called? Are these cells alive?

5. Study the dermis at low, medium, and high magnifications.

   ▪ Distinguish between the papillary and reticular layers.

   ▪ Are Meissner's corpuscles visible at the papillary folds?

   ▪ What type of connective tissue is in the reticular layer? ▪

Lab Activity 2 Accessory Structures of the Skin

During embryonic development, the epidermis produces accessory integumentary structures called **epidermal derivatives,** which include oil and sweat glands, hair, and nails. These structures are exposed on the surface of the skin and project deep into the dermis.

▪ **Sebaceous** (se-BĀ-shus) **glands** are associated with hair follicles and secrete the oily substance **sebum,** which coats the hair shafts and the epidermal surface to reduce brittleness and prevents excessive drying of the integument (Figure 4). **Sebaceous follicles** secrete sebum onto the surface of the skin to lubricate the skin and provide limited antibacterial action. These follicles are not associated with hair and are distributed on the face, most of the trunk, and the male reproductive organs.

▪ **Sweat glands,** or **sudoriferous** (sū-dor-IF-er-us) **glands,** are scattered throughout the dermis of most of the integument. They are exocrine glands that secrete their liquid either into sweat ducts leading to the skin surface or into sweat ducts leading to hair follicles (Figure 5).

Figure 4 The Structure of Sebaceous Glands and Sebaceous Follicles Sebaceous glands empty their oil (sebum) into hair follicles; sebaceous follicles secrete sebum onto the surface of the skin.

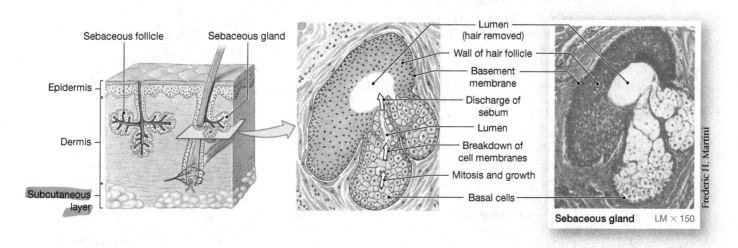

Sebaceous gland LM × 150

Figure 5 Sweat Glands

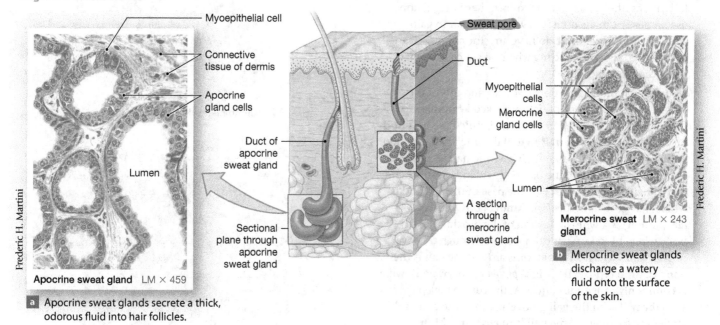

Apocrine sweat gland LM × 459

a Apocrine sweat glands secrete a thick, odorous fluid into hair follicles.

Merocrine sweat LM × 243 gland

b Merocrine sweat glands discharge a watery fluid onto the surface of the skin.

The liquid we call **sweat** can be a thick or a thin substance. To cool the body, **merocrine** (MER-ō-krin) **sweat glands** secrete onto the body surface a thin sweat containing electrolytes, proteins, urea, and other compounds. The sweat absorbs body heat and evaporates from the skin, cooling the body. It also contributes to body odor because of the presence of urea and other wastes. Merocrine glands, also called *eccrine* (EK-rin) *glands,* are not associated with hair follicles and are distributed throughout most of the skin. **Apocrine sweat glands** are found in the groin, nipples, and axillae. These glands secrete a thick sweat into ducts associated with hair follicles. Bacteria on the hair metabolize the sweat and produce the characteristic body odor of, for example, axillary sweat.

- **Hair** covers most of the skin, with only the lips, nipples, portions of the external genitalia, soles, palms, fingers, and toes being without hair. Three major types of hair are found in humans. **Terminal hairs** are the thick, heavy hairs on the scalp, eyebrows, and eyelashes. **Vellus hairs** are lightly pigmented and distributed over much of the skin as fine "peach fuzz." **Intermediate hairs** are the hairs on the arms and legs. Hair generally serves a protective function. It cushions the scalp and prevents foreign objects from entering the eyes, ears, and nose. Hair also serves as a sensory receptor. Wrapped around the base of each hair is a **root hair plexus,** a sensory neuron sensitive to movement of the hair.

Each hair has a **hair root** embedded deep in a hair follicle (Figure 6). At the root tip is a **hair papilla** containing nerves, blood vessels, and the hair **matrix,** which is the living, proliferative part of the hair. Cells in the matrix undergo mitotic divisions that cause the hair to elongate (it "grows"). Above the matrix, keratinization of the hair cells causes them to harden and die. The resulting **hair shaft** contains an outer **cortex** and an inner **medulla.**

A smooth muscle called the **arrector pili** (a-REK-tor PI-lē) **muscle** is attached to each hair follicle. When fur-covered animals are cold, this muscle contracts to raise the hair and trap a layer of warm air next to the skin. In humans, the muscle has no known thermoregulatory use because humans do not have enough hair to gain an insulation benefit. We do have arrector pili muscles, though, and their contracting when we are cold is what produces "gooseflesh."

- **Nails,** which protect the dorsal surface and tips of the fingers and toes, consist of tightly packed keratinized cells (Figure 7). The visible part of the nail, called the **nail body,** protects the underlying **nail bed** of the integument. Blood vessels underneath the nail body give the nail its pinkish color. The **free edge** of the nail body extends past the end of the digit. The **nail root** is at the base of the nail and is where new growth occurs. The **lunula** (LOO-nū-la; *luna,* moon) is a whitish portion of the proximal nail body where blood vessels do not show through the layer of keratinized cells. The epidermis around the nail is the **eponychium** (ep-ō-NIK-ē-um; *epi,* over + *onyx,* nail), what is commonly called the cuticle. At the cuticle the epidermis seals the nail with the nail groove and the raised nail fold. Under the free edge of the nail is the **hyponychium** (hī-pō-NIK-ē-um), a thicker region of the epidermis.

Clinical Application Acne

Many teenagers have dealt with skin blemishes called *acne.* During puberty, hormone levels increase, and sebaceous glands are activated to produce more sebum. If a gland's duct becomes blocked, sebum accumulates and causes inflammation, resulting in a pimple. A pimple with a white head indicates that a duct is blocked and full of sebum. A black head forms when an open sebaceous duct contains solid material infected with bacteria. ■

Figure 6 Structure of a Hair

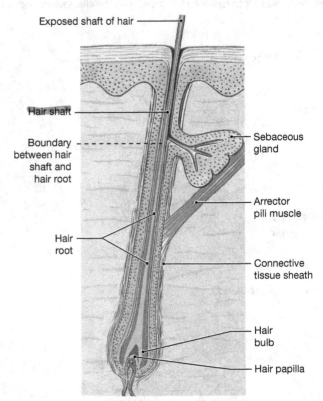

- Exposed shaft of hair
- Hair shaft
- Boundary between hair shaft and hair root
- Hair root
- Sebaceous gland
- Arrector pili muscle
- Connective tissue sheath
- Hair bulb
- Hair papilla

a Diagrammatic view of hair follicle

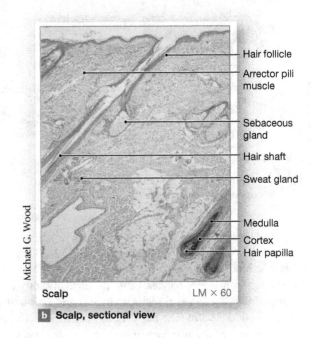

- Hair follicle
- Arrector pili muscle
- Sebaceous gland
- Hair shaft
- Sweat gland
- Medulla
- Cortex
- Hair papilla

Michael G. Wood

Scalp   LM × 60

b Scalp, sectional view

Figure 7 Structure of a Nail The prominent features of a typical fingernail.

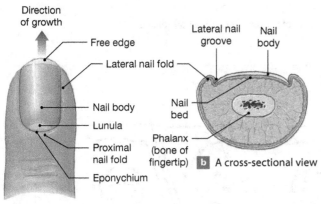

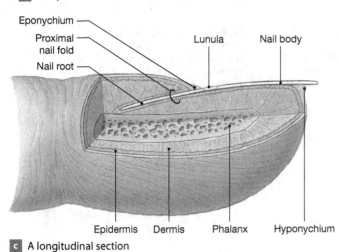

a A superficial view

b A cross-sectional view

c A longitudinal section

QuickCheck Questions

2.1 List the accessory structures of the skin.

2.2 What are the two major types of glands in the skin?

Clinical Application Burns

Burns are classified by the damage they cause to the layers of the integument. First-degree burns injure cells of the epidermis, no deeper than the stratum germinativum. Sunburns and other topical burns are first-degree burns. Second-degree burns destroy the entire epidermis and portions of the dermis but do not injure hair follicles and glands in the dermis. This destruction of portions of the dermis causes blistering, and the wound is extremely painful. Third-degree burns penetrate completely through the integument, severely damaging epidermis, dermis, and subcutaneous structures. This type of wound cannot heal because the restorative layers of the epidermis are lost. To prevent infection in cases of third-degree burns and to reestablish the barrier formed by the skin, a skin graft is used to cover the wound. Nerves are usually damaged by third-degree burns, with the result that these more serious burns may not be as painful as first- and second-degree burns. ■

In the Lab 2

Materials

☐ Compound microscope
☐ Prepared slide of the scalp (cross section)

Procedures

1. On the scalp slide, locate a hair follicle.
   - What is the shape of the hair follicle? In which layer of the skin is it found?
   - Identify the hair shaft, cortex, and medulla.
   - Identify a sebaceous gland. Where does it empty its secretions?
2. Scan the dermis of the slide for a sudoriferous gland.
   - Look for small oval sections of a duct and follow them from the gland to the surface of the skin.

For additional practice, complete the *Sketch to Learn* activity. ■

Sketch to Learn

To reinforce the study of the integument, sketch the major components of the skin. Include a hair follicle and sebaceous and sweat glands in your drawing.

Sample Sketch

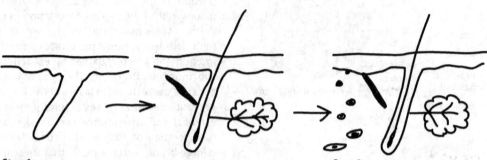

Step 1
- Draw a horizontal line for the surface of the skin.
- Add a wavy line with a long, thin pocket for a hair follicle.

Step 2
- Add a hair to the follicle.
- Attach an arrector pili muscle and a sebaceous gland to the follicle.

Step 3
- Draw a few ovals for sweat glands and smaller ovals leading to the surface for the duct.
- Label your sketch.

Your Sketch

Name Nicole Villa

Date 1/31/18

Section 15

Integumentary System

A. Descriptions

Describe each skin structure.

1. sebaceous follicle – secrete sebum onto surface of skin to lubricate skin / provided some bacterial protection (26)

2. apocrine sweat gland - groin/nipple, axillae – secrete thick sweat

3. keratin – protein accumulated by keratinocytes (24

4. arrector pili – attached to each hair follicle, produces goosebumps (28)

5. stratum corneum – most superficial layer, flattened/dead cells (25)

6. stratum germinativum – 1 layer thick and joins basal lamina to dermis in a constant state of meiosis (24)

7. reticular layer – deep to papillary layer, collagen fibers and dense irregular connective tissue (25)

8. subcutaneous layer – adipose and areolar tissue (25)

9. stratum lucidum – superficial to stratum granulosum, only in thick skin (25)

10. eccrine sweat gland – not associated w/ hair follicles and distributed over most of the skin (25)

B. Short-Answer Questions

1. Describe the layers of epidermis in an area where the skin is thick.

   Stratum corneum, stratum lucidem, stratum granulosum, stratum spinosum, stratum basale (sup → deep) (24-25)

2. How does the skin tan when exposed to sunlight?

   melanocytes produce melanin which protects deeper cells from UV light (24)

3. List the types of sweat glands associated with the skin.

   merocrine sweat glands, eccrine glands, apocrine sweat glands (27)

4. What is the function of arrector pili muscles in animals other than humans?

   raises hair and traps a layer of warmth next to the skin (28)

31

C. Labeling

Label the structures of the skin in Figure 8.

Figure 8 **Components of the Integumentary System** (24)

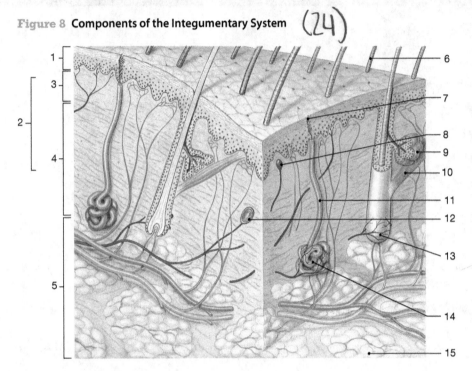
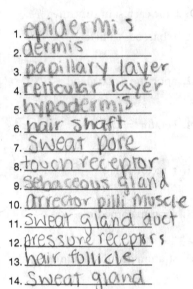

1. epidermis
2. dermis
3. papillary layer
4. reticular layer
5. hypodermis
6. hair shaft
7. sweat pore
8. touch receptor
9. sebaceous gland
10. arrector pilli muscle
11. sweat gland duct
12. pressure receptors
13. hair follicle
14. sweat gland
15. fat

D. Analysis and Application

1. What important function does the keratinized epidermis serve?

resistant to dehydration and friction (24)

2. What is the main cause of acne, and in which part of the skin does it occur?

sebum (sebaceous glands), base of hair follicles

3. How are cells replaced in the epidermis?

keratinocytes (24)

4. What is the difference between sebaceous glands and sebaceous follicles?

glands are associated · w hair follicles (26)

E. Clinical Challenge

A nurse notices a spot on a patient's skin. How can one distinguish between a mass of skin cancer and a mole or freckle on the skin?

assymetry
border (irregular/regular)
color
diameter   (26)

Organization of the Skeletal System and Axial Skeleton Wish List

As you work through this lab, make sure you can identify the five shapes of bones and the different bone markings described in the chapter "Organization of the Skeletal System. Your understanding of bones and bone markings will be critical for your ability to successfully learn muscle origins and insertions later in the semester. After completing the activities that will help you become familiar with the skeletal system in general, work through the activities in the "Axial Skeleton" chapter. The list below is extensive and it will probably take you more than one lab period to learn. Use your lab time wisely, and work with a partner to quiz each other on the structures on the list.

✓	Structure	Description
	SKULL	
	Cranial Bones (8 Bones)	
	Occipital Bone	**posterior head, base of the skull** ✓
	External occipital protuberance	the bump on the posterior side. ✓
	Occipital condyles	articulate with the atlas ✓
	Foramen magnum	large hole for the spinal cord to pass through ✓
	Frontal Bone	**forehead** ✓
	Supraorbital margin	ridge of bone above each eye ✓
	Parietal Bones	**form part of the sidewall and roof of the cranium**
	Coronal suture	junction between frontal bone and 2 parietal bones ✓
	Sagittal suture	junction between 2 parietal bones ✓
	Squamous suture	junction between temporal bone and parietal bones ✓
	Lambdoidal suture	junction between 2 parietal bones and the occipital bone ✓
	Temporal Bones	**form part of the sidewall of cranium, the temple** ✓
	External auditory meatus	ear canal ✓
	Styloid process	elongated, pin-like process on inferior side ✓
	Mastoid process	large bony mass inferior and posterior to ear ✓
	Mandibular fossa	articulates with the mandibular condyles on mandible ✓
	Zygomatic process	projection of temporal bone ✓

Sphenoid	irregular bone on floor of cranium, looks like a "bat"
Optic foramen	hole for the optic nerve to pass through towards each eye
Sella turcica	saddle like structure on superior surface (pituitary gland sits here)
Greater and Lesser wings	large and small wing like structures which help form the floor of the cranium
Pterygoid process	projections from the inferior surface of the bone towards the oral and nasal cavities
Superior orbital fissure	large slits which can be seen in the eye sockets, it is between the greater and lesser wings
Inferior orbital fissure	smaller slits, also seen in the eye sockets, just inferior to the superior orbital fissures.

Ethmoid	irregular bone anterior to sphenoid and between eyes
Crista galli	bony projection on superior surface
Cribriform plate	horizontal plate on the superior surface that is perforated with many small holes for the olfactory nerve
Middle nasal concha	not a named bone, but part of the ethmoid bone. Above inferior nasal concha
Superior nasal concha	not a named bone, but part of the ethmoid bone. Above middle nasal concha
Perpendicular plate	Inferior plate that divides the nasal cavity
Orbital plate	smooth plates which form the medial walls of the eye sockets

✓ Facial Bones (14 Bones)	
Mandible	lower jaw
Ramus	vertical projection on each side
Mandibular condyle	rounded projections on the superior surface of the ramii
Coronoid process	flat process on the superior surface of the ramii
Body	chin area
Mandibular angle	where body and ramii meet

Maxilla	upper jaw

Zygomatic bones	cheek bones
Temporal process	

	Nasal bones	**form bride of nose**

	Lacrimal bones	**located on medial wall of eye socket**
	Lacrimal fossa	deep groove on anterior/medial surface (tear duct or lacrimal duct)

	Palatine bones	**form roof of mouth and walls of nasal cavity**

	Vomer	**in nasal cavity, form lower portion of the nasal septum**

	Inferior nasal concha	found on lateral walls of nasal cavity and project medially just inferior to ethmoid bone

	Middle nasal concha	**not a named bone, but part of the ethmoid bone. Above inferior nasal concha**

	Superior nasal concha	**not a named bone, but part of the ethmoid bone. Above middle nasal concha**

✓	**Other Skull Bones**	
	Middle ear ossicles	**found in each ear**
	Malleus	hammer
	Incus	anvil
	Stapes	stirrup
	Hyoid	horse-shoe bone

	VERTEBRAL COLUMN	* Indicates structures that help distinguish between the groups of vertebrae
	Cervical vertebrae	**7 bones numbered C1-C7**
	Atlas	C1, articulates occipital bone. No body & spinous process
	Superior articular surfaces	
	Inferior articular surface	
	*Facet for odontoid process	
	Transverse process	lateral projections
	*Transverse foramina	hole in transverse process
	Vertebral foramen	hole posterior to body
	Pedicle	connects body to transverse process
	Lamina	connect transverse process to spinous process

Axis	C2, inferior to atlas
Superior articular surfaces	
Inferior articular surface	
Body	
*Odontoid process (Dens)	knob like process on superior surface
Spinous process	most are bifid
Transverse process	lateral projections
*Transverse foramina	hole in transverse process
Vertebral foramen	hole posterior to body
Pedicle	connects body to transverse process
Lamina	connect transverse process to spinous process

C3-C7	
Superior articular surfaces	most are bifid
Inferior articular surface	
Body	
Spinous process	Long and angled
Transverse process	lateral projections
*Transverse foramina	hole in transverse process
Vertebral foramen	hole posterior to body
Pedicle	connects body to transverse process
Lamina	connect transverse process to spinous process
Intervertebral foramina	small openings formed on the lateral side of the vertebral column, formed between 2 vertebra that are stacked on top of each other. Also permits spinal nerve to pass.

Thoracic vertebrae	12 bones named T1-T12
T1-T12	
Superior articular surfaces	
Inferior articular surface	
Body	
*Spinous process	long and angled
Transverse process	lateral projections
Pedicle	connects body to transverse process
Lamina	connect transverse process to spinous process
*Facets for ribs (T1-8 has 2, T9-12 has 1 per side)	lateral side of body
*articular facets for ribs	on the transverse processes

	Intervertebral foramina	small openings formed on the lateral side of the vertebral column, formed between 2 vertebra that are stacked on top of each other. Permits spinal nerve to pass

	Lumbar vertebrae	**5 bones, named L1-L5**
	L1-L5	
	Superior articular surfaces	
	inferior articular surface	
	*Body	Larger body
	*Spinous process	Short and thick
	Transverse process	lateral projections
	Vertebral foramen	hole posterior to body
	Pedicle	connects body to transverse process
	Lamina	connect transverse process to spinous process
	Intervertebral foramina	small openings formed on the lateral side of the vertebral column, formed between 2 vertebra that are stacked on top of each other. Allows spinal nerve to pass

	Sacrum	**5 fused vertebrae in one bone, name S1-S5**
	S1-S5	
	Body	
	Ala	Wings, formed by fused transverse processes
	Superior articular process (facet)	
	Sacral canal	
	Sacral hiatus	
	Medial sacral crest	formed by fused spinous processes
	Sacral foramina	similar to intervertebral foramina

	Coccyx	**Often called the tailbone**

	RIBS	
	General	**paired**
	True ribs	ribs 1-7 with individual costal cartilage
	False ribs	ribs 8-12 that do not have individual cartilages but *may* share common costal cartilage
	Floating ribs	ribs 11-12 that do not attach to the sternum in any way

Ribs	all have similar features and attach on thoracic vertebrae
Head (superior and inferior articular facets)	posterior portion that articulates with thoracic vertebrae
Neck	just lateral to head
Tubercle	articulates with transverse process of thoracic vertebrae
Body/Shaft	curved main part of rib
Costal extremity	sternal extremity that attaches to costal cartilage and sternum

STERNUM	anterior in thorax and made of 3 parts
Manubrium	superior portion
Jugular notch	superior depression
Clavicular notch	superior/lateral depressions where clavicles articulate
Facets for ribs	lateral border for ribs 1 and 2
Sternal angle	transverse ridge on the anterior surface

Body	lower 2/3 of bone, below sternal angle
Facets for ribs	lateral border for ribs 2-10
Xiphoid process	inferior process

✓ FETAL SKULL	
Frontal bone	forehead
Parietal bone	form part of the sidewall and roof of the cranium
Occipital bone	posterior head, base of the skull
Temporal bone	form part of the sidewall of cranium, the temple
Nasal bone	nose
Maxillary bone	upper jaw
Mandible	lower jaw
Fontanel	connective tissue between the sutures

Organization of the Skeletal System

Learning Outcomes

On completion of this exercise, you should be able to:

1. List the components of the axial skeleton and those of the appendicular skeleton.

2. Describe the gross anatomy of a long bone.

3. Describe the histological organization of compact bone and of spongy bone.

4. List the five shapes of bones and give an example of each type.

5. Describe the bone markings visible on the skeleton.

Lab Activities

1 Bone Structure

2 Histological Organization of Bone

3 The Skeleton

4 Bone Classification and Bone Markings

Clinical Application

Osteoporosis

The skeletal system serves many functions. Bones support the body's soft tissues and protect vital internal organs. Calcium, lipids, and other materials are stored in the bones, and blood cells are manufactured in the bones' red marrow. Bones serve as levers that allow the muscular system to produce movement or maintain posture. In this exercise, you will study the gross structure of bone and the individual bones of the skeletal system.

Two types of bone tissue are found in the skeleton: compact and spongy. **Compact bone,** which is also called **dense bone,** seals the outer surface of bones and is found wherever stress arrives from one direction on the bone. **Spongy bone,** or **cancellous tissue,** is found inside the compact-bone envelope.

Need More Practice and Review?

Build your knowledge—and confidence!—in the Study Area of MasteringA&P® at www.masteringaandp.com with Pre-lab Quizzes, Post-lab Quizzes, Practice Anatomy Lab™ (PAL™) 3.0 virtual anatomy practice tool, PhysioEx™ 9.0 laboratory simulations, and A&P Flix™ with Quizzes.

PAL For this lab exercise, follow these navigation paths:
- PAL>Anatomical Models>Axial Skeleton
- PAL>Anatomical Models>Appendicular Skeleton
- PAL>Histology>Connective Tissue

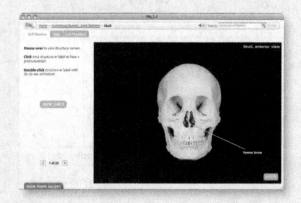

MasteringA&P®

Lab Activity 1 Bone Structure

Bones are encapsulated in a tough, fibrous membrane called the **periosteum** (per-ē-OS-tē-um). This membrane appears shiny and glossy and is sometimes visible on a chicken bone or on the bone in a steak. Histologically, the periosteum is composed of two layers: an outer fibrous layer, where muscle tendons and bone ligaments attach, and an inner cellular layer which produces cells called **osteoblasts** (OS-tē-ō-blasts) for bone growth and repair. **Osteocytes** are mature bone cells that maintain the mineral and protein components of bone matrix.

Long bones, such as the femur of the thigh, have a shaft, called the **diaphysis** (dī-AF-i-sis), with an **epiphysis** (ē-PIF-i-sis) on each end (Figure 1). The proximal epiphysis is on the superior end of the diaphysis, and the distal epiphysis is on the inferior end. Wherever an epiphysis articulates with another bone, a layer of hyaline cartilage, the **articular cartilage,** covers the epiphysis.

The wall of the diaphysis is made primarily of compact bone. The interior of the diaphysis is hollow, forming a space called the **medullary cavity** (or **marrow cavity**). This cavity is lined with spongy bone and is a storage site for **marrow,** a loose connective tissue. The marrow in long bones contains a high concentration of lipids and is called yellow marrow. A membrane called the **endosteum** (en-DOS-tē-um) lines the medullary cavity. **Osteoclasts** in the endosteum secrete carbonic acid, which dissolves bone matrix to tear down bone either so that it can be replaced with new, stronger bone in a

Figure 1 Bone Structure

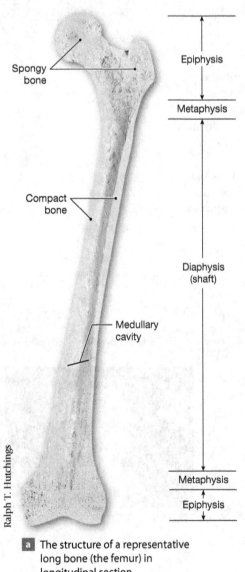

Spongy bone

Compact bone

Medullary cavity

Epiphysis

Metaphysis

Diaphysis (shaft)

Metaphysis

Epiphysis

Ralph T. Hutchings

a The structure of a representative long bone (the femur) in longitudinal section

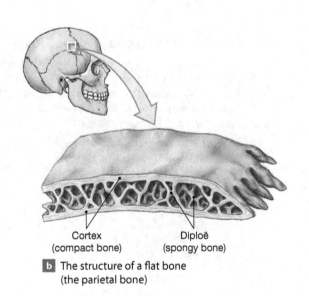

Cortex (compact bone)

Diploë (spongy bone)

b The structure of a flat bone (the parietal bone)

process called **remodeling** or so that minerals stored in the bone can be released into the blood.

Between the diaphysis and either epiphysis is the **metaphysis** (me-TAF-i-sis). In a juvenile's bone, the metaphysis is called the **epiphyseal plate** and consists of a plate of hyaline cartilage that allows the bone to grow longer. By early adulthood, the rate of mitosis in the cartilage plate slows, and ossification fuses the epiphysis to the diaphysis. Bone growth stops when all the cartilage in the metaphysis has been replaced by bone. This bony remnant of the growth plate is now called the **epiphyseal line.**

Flat bones, such as the frontal and parietal bones of the skull, are thin bones with no marrow cavity. Flat bones have a layer of spongy bone sandwiched between layers of compact bone (Figure 1b). The compact bone layers are called the *external* and *internal tables* and are thick in order to provide strength for the bone. The spongy bone between the tables is called the **diploë** (DIP-lō-ē) and is filled with **red marrow,** a type of loose connective tissue made up of stem cells that produces red blood cells, platelets, and most of the white blood cells in the body.

QuickCheck Questions

1.1 What is the location of the two membranes found in long bones?

1.2 Where is spongy bone found?

In the Lab 1

Materials

- ☐ Preserved long bone or fresh long bone from butcher shop
- ☐ Blunt probe
- ☐ Disposable examination gloves
- ☐ Safety glasses

Procedures

1. Put on the safety glasses and examination gloves before you handle the bone.
2. Examine the long bone and locate the periosteum. Does it appear shiny? Are any tendons or ligaments attached to it? _____
3. If the bone has been sectioned, observe the internal bone tissue of the diaphysis. Is the bone tissue similar in all regions of the sectioned bone? _____
4. Locate an epiphysis and its articular cartilage. What is the function of the cartilage? _____
5. Locate the metaphysis and determine if the bone has an epiphyseal plate or an epiphyseal line. ◼

Lab Activity 2 Histological Organization of Bone

Compact bone has supportive columns called either **osteons** or *Haversian systems* (Figure 2). Each osteon consists of many rings of calcified matrix called **concentric lamellae** (lah-MEL-lē; *lamella*, a thin plate). Between the lamellae, in small spaces in the matrix called **lacunae,** are mature bone cells called osteocytes. Bone requires a substantial supply of nutrients and oxygen. Nerves, blood vessels, and lymphatic vessels all pierce the periosteum and enter the bone in a **perforating canal** oriented perpendicular to the osteons. This canal interconnects with **central canals** positioned in the center of osteons. Radiating outward from a central canal

Clinical Application Osteoporosis

As we age, our bones change. They become weaker and thinner, and they produce less collagen and are therefore less flexible. Calcium levels in the bone matrix decline, resulting in brittle bones. Osteopenia is the natural, age-related loss of bone mass that begins as early as 30 to 40 years of age in some individuals. The loss is a result of a decrease in osteoblast activity while osteoblasts continue to remain active. Bone degeneration beyond normal loss is called **osteoporosis** (os-tē-ō-po-RŌ-sis) and affects the epiphysis, vertebrae, and jaws, and leads to weak limbs, decrease in height, and loss of teeth. Bone fractures are common as spongy bone becomes more porous and unable to withstand stress. Osteoporosis is more common in women, with 29% of women 45 years or older having osteoporosis, but only 18% of males 45 years or older having this condition.

Osteoporosis is associated with an age-related decline in circulating sex hormones in the blood. Sex hormones stimulate osteoblasts to deposit calcium into new bone matrix. In menopausal women, decreasing levels of estrogen slow osteoblast activity, and one result is bone loss. As men age, hormone levels decline more gradually than in women, and as a result most men are able to maintain a healthy bone mass.

Exercising more and consuming adequate amounts of calcium can reduce the rate of bone degeneration and occurrence of osteoporosis in both men and women. However, increasing calcium intake is not enough to prevent osteoporosis. New bone matrix must be produced in order to maintain bone density. Hormone replacement therapy is sometimes prescribed to promote new bone growth in postmenopausal women. Unfortunately, many studies link hormone replacement therapy with blood clots in the lungs, uterine cancer, and other clinical complications. ◼

Figure 2 Bone Histology

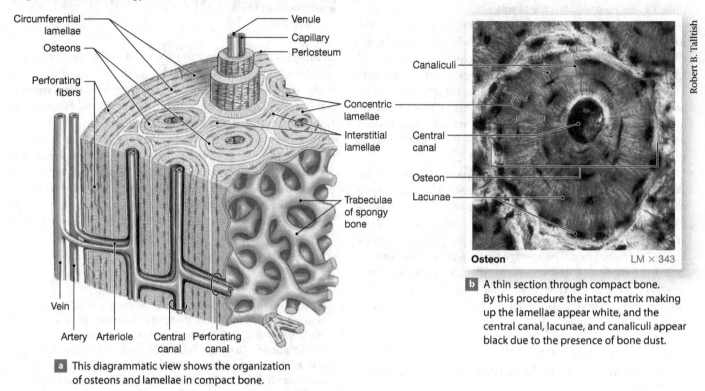

Canaliculi
Concentric lamellae
Central canal
Osteon
Lacunae

Osteon LM × 343

Robert B. Tallitsh

b A thin section through compact bone. By this procedure the intact matrix making up the lamellae appear white, and the central canal, lacunae, and canaliculi appear black due to the presence of bone dust.

Circumferential lamellae
Osteons
Perforating fibers
Venule
Capillary
Periosteum
Concentric lamellae
Interstitial lamellae
Trabeculae of spongy bone
Vein
Artery   Arteriole   Central canal   Perforating canal

a This diagrammatic view shows the organization of osteons and lamellae in compact bone.

are small diffusion channels called **canaliculi** (kan-a-LIK-ū-lē) that facilitate nutrient, gas, and waste exchange with the blood.

To maintain its strength and weight-bearing ability, bone tissue is continuously being remodeled in a process that leaves distinct structural features in compact bone. Old osteons are partially removed, and the concentric rings of lamellae are fragmented, resulting in **interstitial lamellae** (lah-MEL-lē) between intact osteons. Typically, the distal end of a bone is extensively remodeled throughout life, whereas areas of the diaphysis may never be remodeled. Other lamellae occur underneath the periosteum and wrap around the entire bone. These **circumferential lamellae** are added as a bone grows in diameter.

Unlike compact bone, spongy bone is not organized into osteons; instead, it forms a lattice, or meshwork, of bony struts called **trabeculae** (tra-BEK-ū-lē). Each trabecula is composed of layers of lamellae that are intersected with canaliculi. Filling the spaces between the trabeculae is red marrow, the tissue that produces most blood cells. Spongy bone is always sealed with a thin outer layer of compact bone.

QuickCheck Questions

2.1 What are the three types of lamellae found in bone and their characteristics?

2.2 How is blood supplied to an osteon?

In the Lab   2

Materials

☐ Bone model
☐ Compound microscope
☐ Prepared slide of bone tissue (transverse section)

Procedures

1. Review the histology of bone in Figure 2.
2. Examine a bone model and locate each structure shown in Figure 2.
3. Obtain a prepared microscope slide of bone tissue. Most bone slides are a transverse section through bone that is ground very thin. This preparation process removes the bone cells but leaves the bone matrix intact for detailed studies.
4. At low magnification, observe the overall organization of the bone tissue. How many osteons can you locate?
   _____
5. Select an osteon and observe it at a higher magnification. Identify the central canal, canaliculi, and lacunae. What is the function of the canaliculi? _____
6. Locate an area of interstitial lamellae. How do these lamellae differ from the concentric lamellae? _____

For additional practice, complete the *Sketch to Learn* activity. ∎

 *Sketch to Learn*

Let's draw an osteon as observed at medium magnification with the microscope.

Sample Sketch

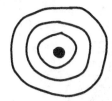

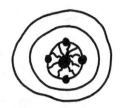

Step 1
- Draw a large oval with several smaller ovals inside.
- Add a dark circle in the middle for the central canal.

Step 2
- Add wavy lines to each concentric lamella. The innermost one is shown as an example.
- Add small dark ovals for osteocytes.
- Label your sketch.

Your Sketch

Lab Activity 3 The Skeleton

The adult skeletal system, shown in Figure 3, consists of 206 bones. Each bone is an organ and includes bone tissue, cartilage, and other connective tissues. The skeleton is organized into the axial and appendicular divisions. The **axial division,** which comprises 80 bones, includes the **skull, vertebral column, sternum, ribs,** and **hyoid bone.** The **appendicular division** (126 bones) consists of the **pectoral girdle, upper limbs, pelvic girdle,** and **lower limbs.** Each girdle attaches its respective limbs to the axial skeleton and allows limb mobility at the points of attachment.

Each side of the pectoral girdle includes a **scapula** (shoulder blade) and a **clavicle** (collar bone). Each upper limb consists of arm, forearm, wrist, and hand. The **humerus** is the arm bone, and the **ulna** and **radius** together form the forearm. The eight wrist bones, called **carpal bones,** articulate with the elongated **metacarpal bones** of the palm. The individual bones of the fingers are the **phalanges.**

The pelvic girdle is fashioned from two coxal bones, each of which is an aggregate of three bones: the superior **ilium** in the hip area, the **ischium** inferior to the ilium, and the **pubis** in the anterior pelvis. Each lower limb comprises thigh, knee-cap, leg, ankle, and foot. The **femur** is the thighbone and is the largest bone in the body. The two bones of the leg are a medial **tibia,** which bears most of the body weight, and a thin, lateral **fibula.** The **patella** occurs at the articulation between femur and tibia. The seven ankle bones are collectively called the **tarsal bones. Metatarsal bones** form the arch of the foot, and **phalanges** form the toes.

QuickCheck Questions

3.1 What are the two major divisions of the skeleton?

3.2 A rib belongs to which division of the skeletal system?

In the Lab 3

Material

☐ Articulated skeleton

Procedures

1. Using Figure 3 as a guide, locate the bones of the axial division of the skeleton. List the major components of the axial division.

2. Using Figure 3 as a guide, locate the major components of the appendicular division of the skeleton.

3. What bones are found in the shoulder and upper limb?

4. What three bones fuse to form the coxal bone?

5. List the bones of the lower limb. ■

Lab Activity 4 Bone Classification and Bone Markings

Bones may be grouped and classified according to shape (Figure 4). Already discussed in this exercise are **long bones,** which are greater in length than in width, and **flat bones,** which are thin and platelike. Bones of the arm, forearm, thigh, and leg are long bones. Bones of the wrist and ankle are

Figure 3 The Skeleton

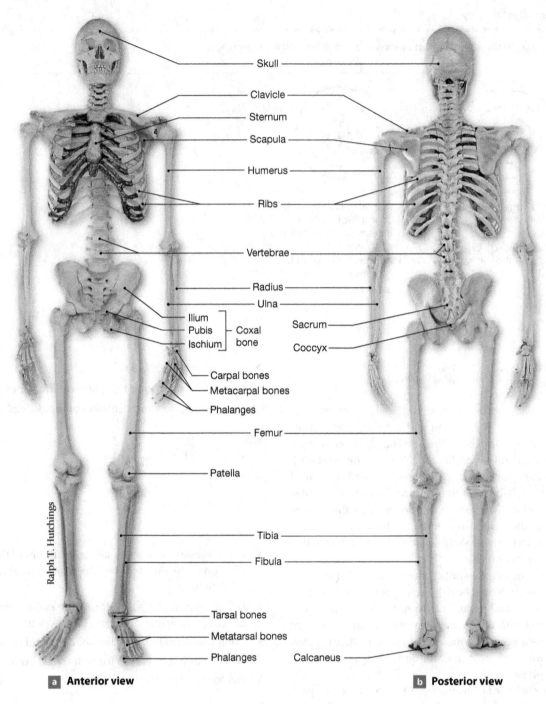

Skull

Clavicle

Sternum

Scapula

Humerus

Ribs

Vertebrae

Radius

Ulna

Ilium
Pubis ⎤ Coxal
Ischium ⎦ bone

Sacrum

Coccyx

Carpal bones

Metacarpal bones

Phalanges

Femur

Patella

Tibia

Fibula

Tarsal bones

Metatarsal bones

Phalanges

Calcaneus

Ralph T. Hutchings

a Anterior view

b Posterior view

short bones, almost as wide as they are long. The vertebrae of the spine are **irregular bones** that are not in any of the just-named categories. **Sesamoid bones** form inside tendons. The largest sesamoid bone is the patella, and it develops inside tendons anterior to the knee. **Sutural bones,** or **Wormian bones,** occur where the interlocking joints of the skull, called **sutures,** branch and isolate a small piece of bone. The number of sutural

bones varies from one person to another and is not included when counting the number of bones in the skeletal system.

Each bone has certain anatomical features on its surface, called either **bone markings** or surface markings. A particular bone marking may be unique to a single bone or may occur throughout the skeleton. Table 1 illustrates examples of bone markings and organizes the markings

Figure 4 Shapes of Bones

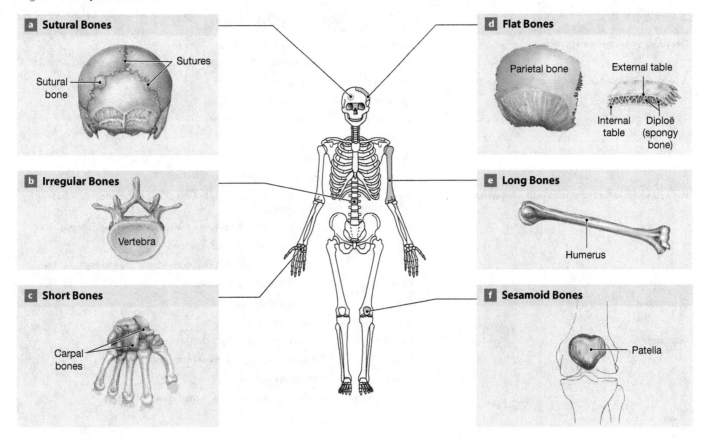

a Sutural Bones
Sutures
Sutural bone

b Irregular Bones
Vertebra

c Short Bones
Carpal bones

d Flat Bones
Parietal bone
External table
Internal table
Diploë (spongy bone)

e Long Bones
Humerus

f Sesamoid Bones
Patella

into five groups. The first group includes general anatomical structures, and the second group lists bony structures for tendon and ligament attachment. The third group contains structures that occur at sites of articulation with other bones. The last two groups include depressions and openings.

QuickCheck Questions

4.1 Give examples of two types of short bones.

4.2 Give an example of an irregular bone.

4.3 What is a foramen?

4.4 What is the neck of a bone?

In the Lab 4

Material

☐ Articulated skeleton

Procedures

1. Examine the articulated skeleton and determine how many of each type of bone is present.
- Long bones:
- Short bones:
- Flat bones:
- Irregular bones:
- Sesamoid bones:
- Sutural bones:

2. Using Table 1 for reference, locate on the skeleton:
- A *foramen* in the skull. Describe this structure. _____
- A *fossa* on the distal end of the humerus. How is the fossa different from a foramen? _____
- A *head* on the femur. Which other bones have a head? _____
- A *condyle* on two different bones. Describe this structure. _____
- A *tuberosity* on the proximal end of the humerus. What is the texture of this structure? _____

3. Locate one instance of each of the other marking types on the skeleton: process, ramus, trochanter, tubercle, crest, line, spine, neck, trochlea, facet, sulcus, canal, fissure, sinus. ■

Table 1	An Introduction to Skeletal Terminology		
General Description		**Anatomical Term**	**Definition**
Elevations and projections (general)		Process	Any projection or bump
		Ramus	An extension of a bone making an angle with the rest of the structure
Processes formed where tendons or ligaments attach		Trochanter	A large, rough projection
		Tuberosity	A smaller, rough projection
		Tubercle	A small, rounded projection
		Crest	A prominent ridge
		Line	A low ridge
		Spine	A pointed process
Processes formed for articulation with adjacent bones		Head	The expanded articular end of an epiphysis, separated from the shaft by the neck
		Neck	A narrow connection between the epiphysis and the diaphysis
		Condyle	A smooth, rounded articular process
		Trochlea	A smooth, grooved articular process shaped like a pulley
		Facet	A small, flat articular surface
Depressions		Fossa	A shallow depression
		Sulcus	A narrow groove
Openings		Foramen	A rounded passageway for blood vessels or nerves
		Canal	A passageway through the substance of a bone
		Fissure	An elongated cleft
		Sinus or antrum	A chamber within a bone, normally filled with air

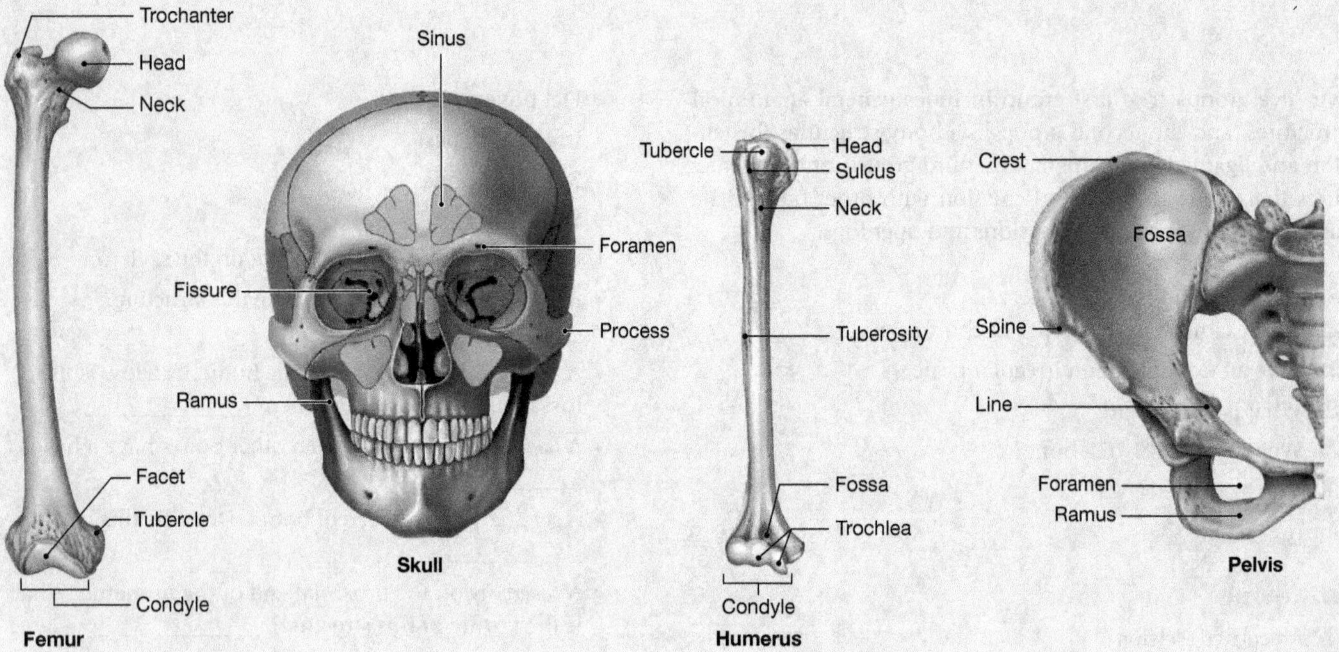

Femur

Skull

Humerus

Pelvis

Name _____

Date _____

Section _____

Organization
of the Skeletal System

A. Definitions

Define each structure.

1. metaphysis

2. trabecula

3. articular cartilage

4. diaphysis

5. epiphyseal plate

6. periosteum

7. epiphysis

8. endosteum

9. medullary cavity

10. epiphyseal line

B. Matching

Match each bone with the correct division and part of the skeleton. Each question may
have more than one answer, and each choice can be used more than once.

_____	**1.** scapula	**A.** axial division
_____	**2.** coxal bone	**B.** appendicular division
_____	**3.** patella	**C.** pectoral girdle
_____	**4.** hyoid	**D.** upper limb
_____	**5.** radius	**E.** pelvic girdle
_____	**6.** metacarpal	**F.** lower limb
_____	**7.** vertebra	
_____	**8.** clavicle	
_____	**9.** rib	
_____	**10.** femur	
_____	**11.** sternum	
_____	**12.** carpal	

C. Short-Answer Questions

1. List the components of the axial skeleton.

2. List the components of the appendicular skeleton.

3. Describe the five types of surface markings on bones.

4. List the different shapes of bones.

D. Labeling

1. Label Figure 5.

Figure 5 Histology of Bone

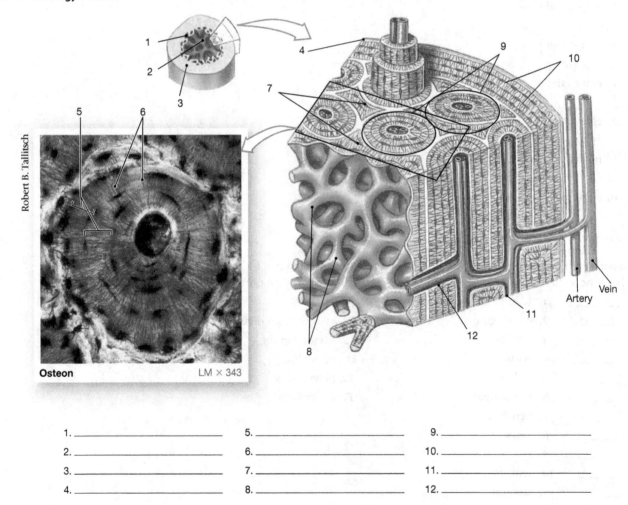

Robert B. Tallitsch

Osteon   LM × 343

1. _____   5. _____   9. _____
2. _____   6. _____   10. _____
3. _____   7. _____   11. _____
4. _____   8. _____   12. _____

2. Label Figure 6.

Figure 6 **Anterior View of the Skeleton**

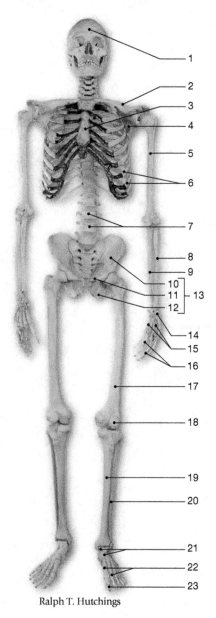

Ralph T. Hutchings

1. _____
2. _____
3. _____
4. _____
5. _____
6. _____
7. _____
8. _____
9. _____
10. _____
11. _____
12. _____
13. _____
14. _____
15. _____
16. _____
17. _____
18. _____
19. _____
20. _____
21. _____
22. _____
23. _____

E. Analysis and Application

1. Where does spongy bone occur in the skeleton?

2. How are the upper limbs attached to the axial skeleton?

3. Where does growth in length occur in a long bone?

F. Clinical Challenge

The result of an elderly woman's bone density test indicates that her bones are losing mass. What preventative measure can she take to slow her bone loss?

Axial Skeleton

Learning Outcomes

On completion of this exercise, you should be able to:

1. Identify the components of the axial skeleton.

2. Identify the cranial and facial bones of the skull.

3. Identify the surface features of the cranial and facial bones.

4. Describe the skull of a fetus.

5. Describe the five regions of the vertebral column and distinguish among the vertebrae of each region.

6. Identify the features of a typical vertebra.

7. Discuss the articulation of the ribs with the thoracic vertebrae.

8. Identify the components of the sternum.

The axial skeleton provides both a central framework for attachment of the appendicular skeleton and protection for the body's internal organs. The 80 bones of the axial skeleton include the skull, a thoracic cage made up of ribs and the sternum, and a flexible vertebral column with 24 vertebrae, 1 sacrum, and 1 coccyx (Figure 1). The 22 bones of the skull are organized into **facial bones** and 8 **cranial bones** that form the **cranium** (Figure 2). The six bones of the middle ear (three per ear) and the hyoid bone are referred to as the *associated bones* of skull.

Need More Practice and Review?

Build your knowledge—and confidence!—in the Study Area of MasteringA&P® at www.masteringaandp.com with Pre-lab Quizzes, Post-lab Quizzes, Practice Anatomy Lab™ (PAL™) 3.0 virtual anatomy practice tool, PhysioEx™ 9.0 laboratory simulations, and A&P Flix™ with Quizzes.

PAL | practice anatomy lab   For this lab exercise, follow these navigation paths:
- PAL>Human Cadaver>Axial Skeleton
- PAL>Anatomical Models>Axial Skeleton

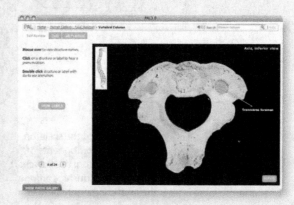

MasteringA&P®

From Exercise 14 of *Laboratory Manual for Anatomy & Physiology featuring Martini Art*, Fifth Edition. Michael G. Wood.
Copyright © 2013 by Pearson Education, Inc. All rights reserved.

Figure 1 The Axial Skeleton An anterior view of the entire skeleton, with the axial components highlighted. The numbers in the boxes indicate the number of bones in the adult skeleton.

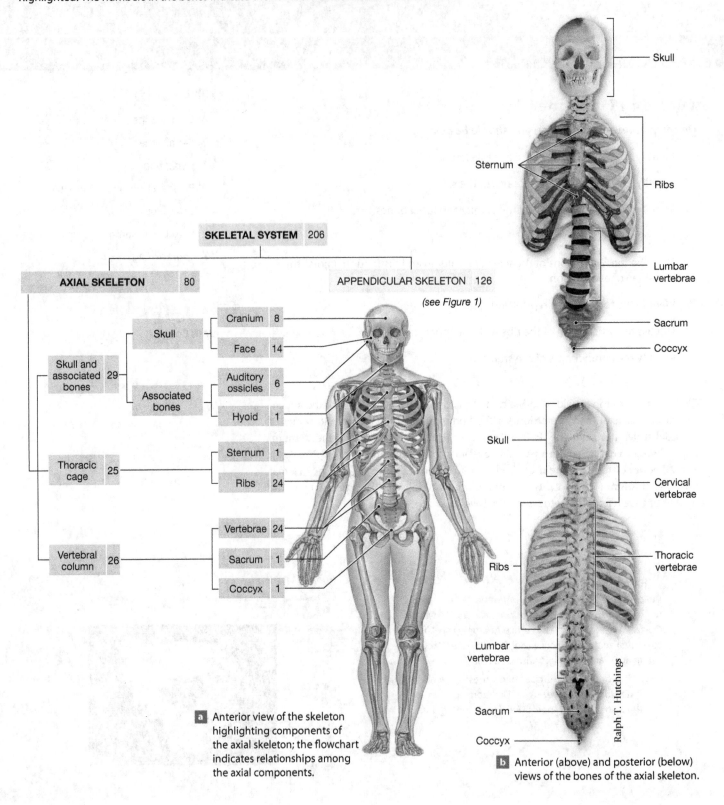

a Anterior view of the skeleton highlighting components of the axial skeleton; the flowchart indicates relationships among the axial components.

b Anterior (above) and posterior (below) views of the bones of the axial skeleton.

Ralph T. Hutchings

Figure 2 **Cranial and Facial Subdivisions of the Skull** The seven associated bones are not illustrated.

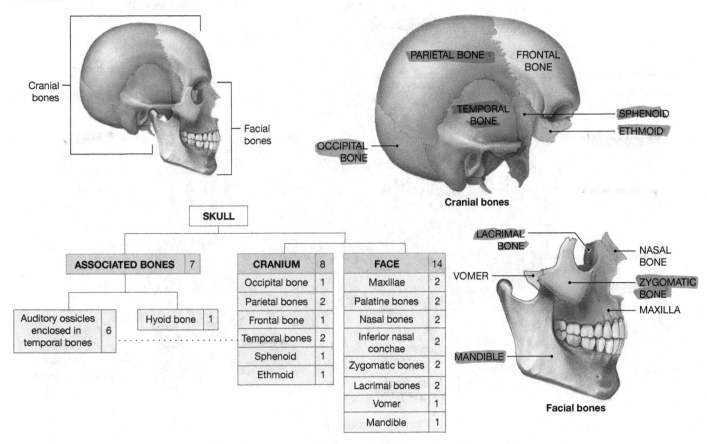

Cranial bones

Facial bones

PARIETAL BONE

FRONTAL BONE

TEMPORAL BONE

SPHENOID

ETHMOID

OCCIPITAL BONE

Cranial bones

LACRIMAL BONE

NASAL BONE

VOMER

ZYGOMATIC BONE

MAXILLA

MANDIBLE

Facial bones

SKULL

ASSOCIATED BONES	7

Auditory ossicles enclosed in temporal bones	6

Hyoid bone	1

CRANIUM	8
Occipital bone	1
Parietal bones	2
Frontal bone	1
Temporal bones	2
Sphenoid	1
Ethmoid	1

FACE	14
Maxillae	2
Palatine bones	2
Nasal bones	2
Inferior nasal conchae	2
Zygomatic bones	2
Lacrimal bones	2
Vomer	1
Mandible	1

Lab Activity 1 Cranial Bones

The skull serves a wide variety of critical functions; it cradles the delicate brain and houses major sensory organs for vision, hearing, balance, taste, and smell. The skull is perforated with many holes called **foramina** where nerves and blood vessels pass to and from the brain and other structures of the head. Facial and cranial bones make sockets, called **orbits,** for the eyes. The joints of the skull are designed for strength instead of movement and only two joints can move: the jaw and the joint between the skull and the vertebral column.

The cranium, shown in **Figure 3**, has eight bones: one frontal bone, two parietal bones, two temporal bones, one occipital bone, one sphenoid, and one ethmoid (Figure 3a). The **frontal bone** of the cranium extends from the forehead posterior to the **coronal suture** and articulates (joins) with the two **parietal bones** on the lateral sides of the skull. The parietal bones are joined at their superior crest by the **sagittal suture** (Figure 3b). The two **temporal bones** are inferior to the parietal bones and are easy to identify by the canals where sound enters the ears. The temporal bone articulates with the parietal bone at the **squamous suture.** The posterior wall of the cranium is the **occipital bone,** which meets the parietals at the **lambdoid** (LAM-doyd) **suture,** also called the *occipitoparietal suture* (Figure 3c).

The **sphenoid** is the bat-shaped bone visible on the cranial floor, anterior to the temporal bone (Figure 3d). The sphenoid forms parts of the floor and lateral walls of the cranium and the posterolateral wall of the orbit. At the

Study Tip An Organized Approach to the Skull

The skull is perhaps the most challenging part of the skeleton to learn. The anatomy is small and very detailed and each bone has several surfaces. When faced with such a volume of material, take some time to survey the topic and formulate a study plan. With the skull, the study plan is: "Start big then go for details." First, start with the big picture—identify each cranial bone —then progress on to the detailed study of the individual cranial bones. ■

Figure 3 Views of the Skull

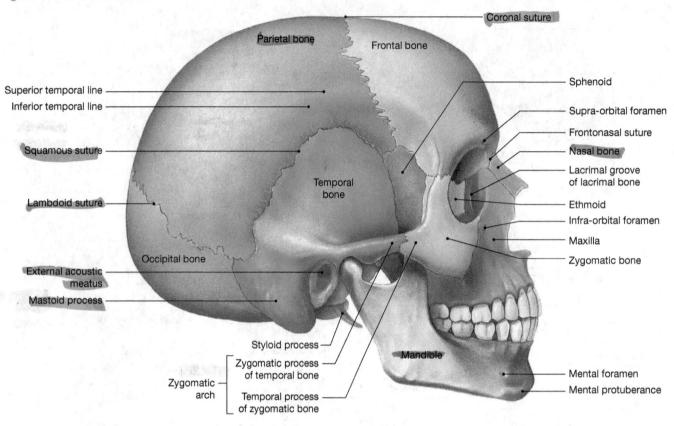

Coronal suture

Parietal bone

Frontal bone

Superior temporal line

Inferior temporal line

Squamous suture

Lambdoid suture

Temporal bone

Sphenoid

Supra-orbital foramen

Frontonasal suture

Nasal bone

Lacrimal groove of lacrimal bone

Ethmoid

Infra-orbital foramen

Maxilla

Zygomatic bone

Occipital bone

External acoustic meatus

Mastoid process

Styloid process

Zygomatic process of temporal bone

Zygomatic arch

Temporal process of zygomatic bone

Mandible

Mental foramen

Mental protuberance

Ralph T. Hutchings

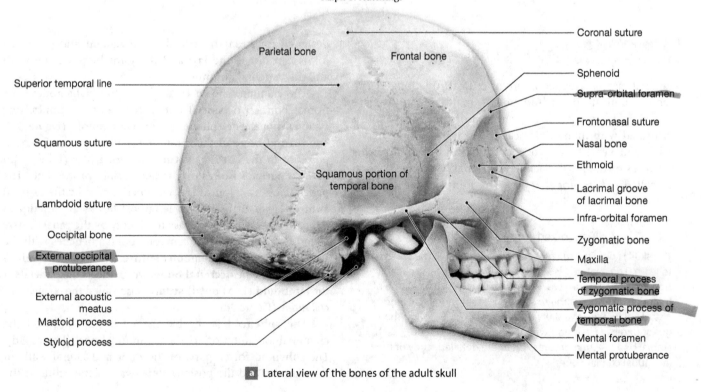

Coronal suture

Parietal bone

Frontal bone

Superior temporal line

Squamous suture

Squamous portion of temporal bone

Sphenoid

Supra-orbital foramen

Frontonasal suture

Nasal bone

Ethmoid

Lacrimal groove of lacrimal bone

Infra-orbital foramen

Zygomatic bone

Maxilla

Temporal process of zygomatic bone

Zygomatic process of temporal bone

Mental foramen

Mental protuberance

Lambdoid suture

Occipital bone

External occipital protuberance

External acoustic meatus

Mastoid process

Styloid process

a Lateral view of the bones of the adult skull

Figure 3   Views of the Skull *(continued)*

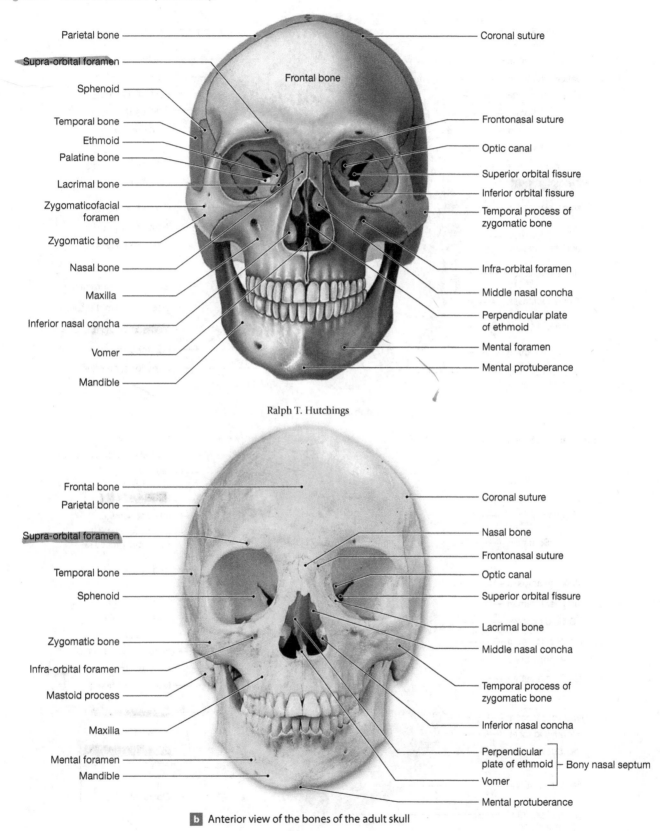

Parietal bone

Supra-orbital foramen

Sphenoid

Temporal bone

Ethmoid

Palatine bone

Lacrimal bone

Zygomaticofacial foramen

Zygomatic bone

Nasal bone

Maxilla

Inferior nasal concha

Vomer

Mandible

Frontal bone

Coronal suture

Frontonasal suture

Optic canal

Superior orbital fissure

Inferior orbital fissure

Temporal process of zygomatic bone

Infra-orbital foramen

Middle nasal concha

Perpendicular plate of ethmoid

Mental foramen

Mental protuberance

Ralph T. Hutchings

Frontal bone

Parietal bone

Supra-orbital foramen

Temporal bone

Sphenoid

Zygomatic bone

Infra-orbital foramen

Mastoid process

Maxilla

Mental foramen

Mandible

Coronal suture

Nasal bone

Frontonasal suture

Optic canal

Superior orbital fissure

Lacrimal bone

Middle nasal concha

Temporal process of zygomatic bone

Inferior nasal concha

Perpendicular plate of ethmoid

Vomer

Bony nasal septum

Mental protuberance

b Anterior view of the bones of the adult skull

Figure 3 **Views of the Skull** *(continued)*

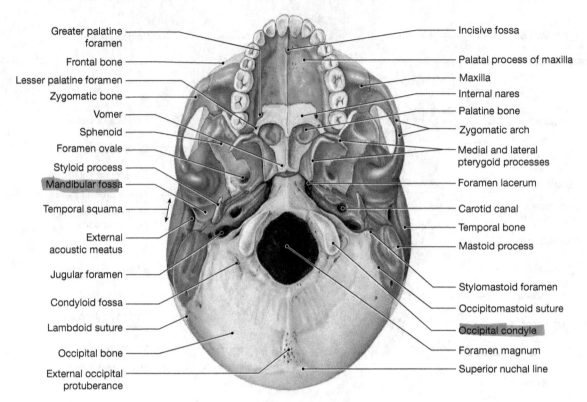

Greater palatine foramen
Frontal bone
Lesser palatine foramen
Zygomatic bone
Vomer
Sphenoid
Foramen ovale
Styloid process
Mandibular fossa
Temporal squama
External acoustic meatus
Jugular foramen
Condyloid fossa
Lambdoid suture
Occipital bone
External occipital protuberance

Incisive fossa
Palatal process of maxilla
Maxilla
Internal nares
Palatine bone
Zygomatic arch
Medial and lateral pterygoid processes
Foramen lacerum
Carotid canal
Temporal bone
Mastoid process
Stylomastoid foramen
Occipitomastoid suture
Occipital condyle
Foramen magnum
Superior nuchal line

Ralph T. Hutchings

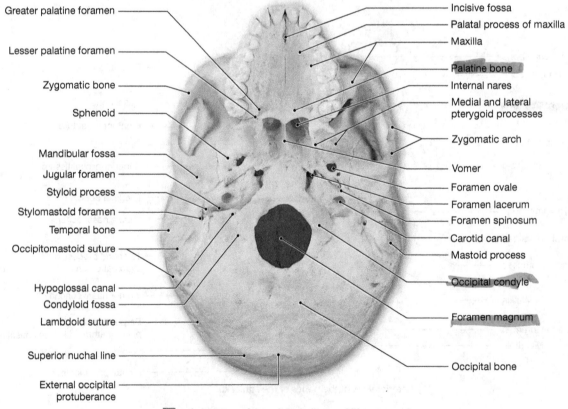

Greater palatine foramen
Lesser palatine foramen
Zygomatic bone
Sphenoid
Mandibular fossa
Jugular foramen
Styloid process
Stylomastoid foramen
Temporal bone
Occipitomastoid suture
Hypoglossal canal
Condyloid fossa
Lambdoid suture
Superior nuchal line
External occipital protuberance

Incisive fossa
Palatal process of maxilla
Maxilla
Palatine bone
Internal nares
Medial and lateral pterygoid processes
Zygomatic arch
Vomer
Foramen ovale
Foramen lacerum
Foramen spinosum
Carotid canal
Mastoid process
Occipital condyle
Foramen magnum
Occipital bone

c Inferior view of the adult skull, mandible removed

Figure 3 **Views of the Skull** *(continued)*

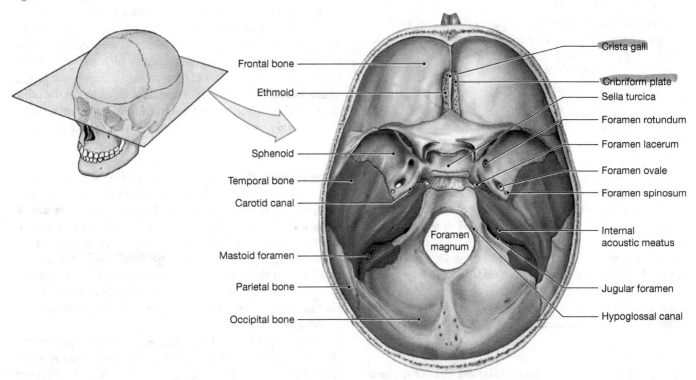

Frontal bone

Ethmoid

Sphenoid

Temporal bone

Carotid canal

Foramen magnum

Mastoid foramen

Parietal bone

Occipital bone

Crista galli

Cribriform plate

Sella turcica

Foramen rotundum

Foramen lacerum

Foramen ovale

Foramen spinosum

Internal acoustic meatus

Jugular foramen

Hypoglossal canal

Ralph T. Hutchings

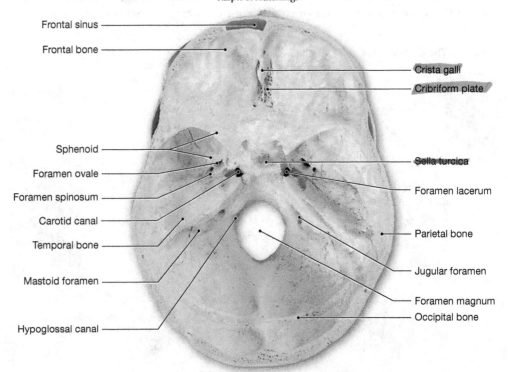

Frontal sinus

Frontal bone

Sphenoid

Foramen ovale

Foramen spinosum

Carotid canal

Temporal bone

Mastoid foramen

Hypoglossal canal

Crista galli

Cribriform plate

Sella turcica

Foramen lacerum

Parietal bone

Jugular foramen

Foramen magnum

Occipital bone

d Horizontal section through the skull showing the floor of the cranial cavity

Study Tip Locating the Ethmoid
Pinching the eye orbit is an easy way to locate the ethmoid. Insert your thumb halfway into one eye orbit of the study skull and your forefinger halfway into the other eye orbit. Gently pinch the bone deep between the orbits, which is the ethmoid. ■

superior margin the squamous and coronal sutures are connected by the **sphenoparietal suture.** The single **ethmoid** is a small, rectangular bone posterior to the bridge of the nose and anterior to the sphenoid (Figure 3d). The ethmoid contributes to the posteromedial wall of both orbits.

The floor of the cranium has three depressions called *fossae* (Figure 3d). The **anterior cranial fossa** is mainly the depression that forms the base of the frontal bone. Small portions of the ethmoid and sphenoid also contribute to the floor of this area. The **middle cranial fossa** is a depressed area extending over the sphenoid and the temporal and occipital bones. The **posterior cranial fossa** is found in the occipital bone.

Frontal Bone

The frontal bone forms the roof, walls, and floor of the anterior cranium (Figure 4). The **frontal squama** is the flattened expanse commonly called the forehead. In the midsagittal plane of the squama is the **frontal (metopic) suture,** where

the two frontal bones fuse in early childhood (typically by the time a child is eight years old). As natural remodeling of bone occurs, this suture typically disappears by age 30. The frontal bone forms the upper portion of the eye orbit. Superior to the orbit is the **supra-orbital foramen,** which on some skulls occurs not as a complete hole but as a small notch, the **supra-orbital notch.** In the anterior and medial regions of the orbit, the frontal bone forms the **lacrimal fossa,** an indentation for the lacrimal gland, which moistens and lubricates the eye.

Occipital Bone

The occipital bone, shown in Figure 5, forms the posterior floor and wall of the skull (Figure 5a). The most conspicuous structure of the occipital bone is the **foramen magnum,** the large hole where the spinal cord enters the skull and joins the brain. Along the lateral margins of the foramen magnum are flattened **occipital condyles** that articulate with the first vertebra of the spine. Passing superior to each occipital condyle is the **hypoglossal canal,** a passageway for the hypoglossal nerve, which controls muscles of the tongue and throat.

The occipital bone has many external surface marks that show where muscles and ligaments attach. The **external occipital crest** is a ridge that extends posteriorly from the foramen magnum to a small bump, the **external occipital protuberance.** Wrapping around the occipital bone lateral from the crest and protuberance are the **superior** and **inferior nuchal**

Figure 4 The Frontal Bone

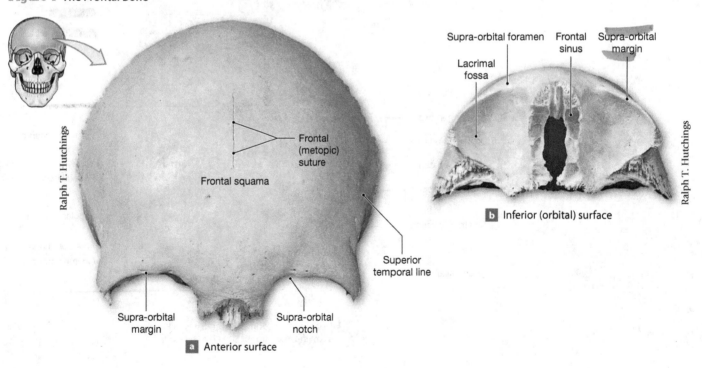

Frontal (metopic) suture

Frontal squama

Superior temporal line

Supra-orbital margin

Supra-orbital notch

a Anterior surface

Supra-orbital foramen

Frontal sinus

Supra-orbital margin

Lacrimal fossa

b Inferior (orbital) surface

Ralph T. Hutchings

Ralph T. Hutchings

Figure 5 The Occipital and Parietal Bones

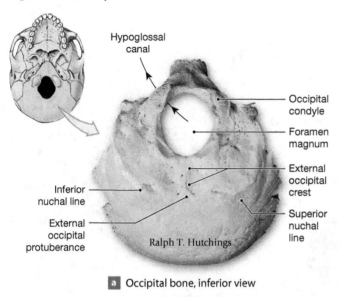

Hypoglossal canal

Occipital condyle

Foramen magnum

External occipital crest

Superior nuchal line

Inferior nuchal line

External occipital protuberance

Ralph T. Hutchings

a Occipital bone, inferior view

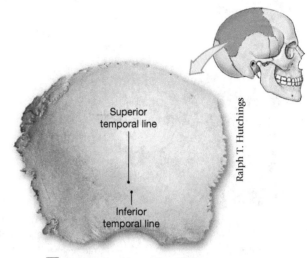

Superior temporal line

Inferior temporal line

Ralph T. Hutchings

b Right parietal bone, lateral view

(NOO-kul) **lines,** surface marks indicating where muscles of the neck attach to the skull.

Parietal Bones

The two parietal bones form the posterior crest of the skull and are joined by the sagittal suture (Figure 5b). The bones are smooth and have few surface features. The low ridges of the **superior** and **inferior temporal lines** (Figure 5b) are superior to the squamous suture, where a muscle for chewing attaches. No major foramina pass through the parietal bones.

Temporal Bones

The two temporal bones constitute the inferior lateral walls of the skull and part of the floor of the middle cranial fossa (Figure 6). One of the most distinct features of a temporal bone is its articulation with the zygomatic bone of the face by the **zygomatic arch** (Figure 3a). The arch is a span of processes from two bones: the **zygomatic process** of the temporal bone and the temporal process of the zygomatic bone. Posterior to the zygomatic process is the region of the temporal bone called the **articular tubercle.** Immediately posterior to the articular tubercle is the **mandibular fossa,** a shallow depression where the mandible bone articulates with the temporal bone.

The broad, flattened superior surface of each temporal bone is the **squamous part.** The hole inferior to the squamous part is the **external acoustic meatus,** which conducts sound waves toward the eardrum. Directly posterior to the external acoustic meatus is the conical **mastoid process,**

where a muscle tendon that moves the head attaches. Within the mastoid process are many small, interconnected sinuses called **mastoid air cells.** The long, needlelike **styloid** (STI-loyd; *stylos,* pillar) **process** is located anteromedial to the mastoid process. Between the styloid and the mastoid processes is a small foramen, the **stylomastoid foramen,** where the facial nerve exits the cranium.

On the cranial floor, the large bony ridge of the temporal bone is the **petrous** (pet-rus; *petra,* a rock) **part,** which houses the organs for hearing and equilibrium and the tiny bones of the ear. The **internal acoustic meatus** is on the posteromedial surface of the petrous part. The union between the temporal and occipital bones creates an elongated **jugular foramen** that serves as a passageway for cranial nerves and the jugular vein, which drains blood from the brain. On the anterior side of the petrous part is the **carotid canal,** where the internal carotid artery enters the skull to deliver oxygenated blood to the brain.

The Sphenoid

The sphenoid is the base of the cranium and each cranial bone articulates with it. The sphenoid is visible from all views of the skull but the easiest aspect of this bone to work with is its superior surface exposed on the floor of the skull. On the anterior side, the sphenoid contributes to the lateral wall of the eye orbit; on the lateral side, it spans the floor of the cranium and braces the walls. The superior surface of the sphenoid is made up of two **lesser wings** and two **greater wings** on either side of the medial line, which give

Figure 6 The Temporal Bones The right temporal bone.

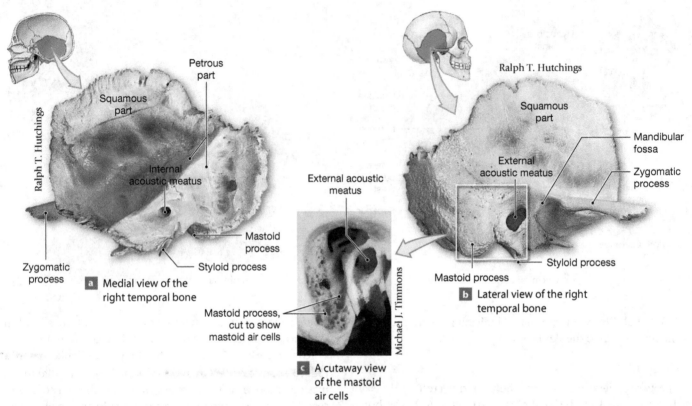

a Medial view of the right temporal bone

b Lateral view of the right temporal bone

c A cutaway view of the mastoid air cells

Ralph T. Hutchings

Michael J. Timmons

Petrous part

Squamous part

Internal acoustic meatus

Mastoid process

Styloid process

Zygomatic process

External acoustic meatus

Mastoid process, cut to show mastoid air cells

Squamous part

Mandibular fossa

Zygomatic process

Styloid process

Mastoid process

External acoustic meatus

the bone the appearance of a bat (**Figure 7**). Each greater wing has an **orbital surface** contributing to the wall of the eye orbit. In the center of the sphenoid is the U-shaped **sella turcica** (TUR-si-kuh), commonly called the Turk's saddle. The depression in the sella turcica is the **hypophyseal** (hī-pō-FIZ-ē-ul) fossa, which contains the pituitary gland of the brain. The anterior part of the sella turcica is the **tuberculum sellae;** the posterior wall is the **posterior clinoid** (KLĪ-noyd; *kline,* a bed) **process.** The two **anterior clinoid processes** are the hornlike projections on either side of the tuberculum sellae. Extending vertically from the inferior surface of the sphenoid are the **pterygoid** (TER-i-goyd; *pterygion,* wing) **processes.** Each process divides into a **lateral plate** and a **medial plate,** where muscles of the mouth attach. At the base of each pterygoid process is a small **pterygoid canal** that serves as a passageway for nerves to the soft palate of the mouth.

Four pairs of foramina are aligned on either side of the sella turcica and serve as passageways for blood vessels and nerves. The oval **foramen ovale** (ō-VAH-lē; oval) and, posterior to it, the small **foramen spinosum** are passageways for parts of the trigeminal nerve of the head. The **foramen rotundum,** anterior to the foramen ovale, is the passageway for a major nerve of the face. Directly medial to the foramen ovale, where the sphenoid joins the temporal bone, is the **foramen lacerum** (LA-se-rum; *lacerare,* to tear), where the auditory (eustachian) tube enters the skull. The sphenoid contribution of the foramen lacerum is visible in Figure 7 as the notch lateral to the posterior clinoid process. Frequently, the carotid canal merges with the nearby foramen lacerum to form a single passageway.

Superior to the foramen rotundum is a cleft in the sphenoid, the **superior orbital fissure,** where nerves to the ocular muscles pass. The **inferior orbital fissure** is the crevice at the inferior margin of the sphenoid. At the base of the anterior clinoid process is the **optic canal,** where the optic nerve enters the skull to carry visual signals to the brain. Medial to the optic canals is an **optic groove** that lies transverse on the tuberculum sellae.

> **Study Tip Using Foramina as Landmarks**
>
> Notice the positions of the foramina as they line up along the sphenoid. This pattern is very similar on all human skulls. Use the foramen ovale as a landmark, because it is easy to identify by its oval shape. Anterior to the foramen ovale is the foramen rotundum; posterior is the foramen spinosum. Medial to the foramen ovale is the foramen lacerum with the nearby carotid canal. ∎

Figure 7 The Sphenoid

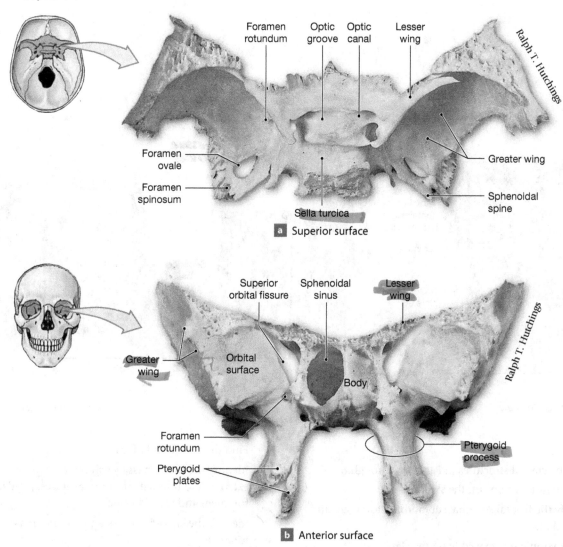

Foramen rotundum · Optic groove · Optic canal · Lesser wing · Foramen ovale · Foramen spinosum · Greater wing · Sphenoidal spine · Sella turcica

Ralph T. Hutchings

a Superior surface

Superior orbital fissure · Sphenoidal sinus · Lesser wing · Greater wing · Orbital surface · Body · Foramen rotundum · Pterygoid plates · Pterygoid process

Ralph T. Hutchings

b Anterior surface

The Ethmoid

The ethmoid (**Figure 8**) is a rectangular bone that is anterior to the sphenoid. It forms the medial orbital walls, the roof of the nose and part of the nasal septum, and the anteromedial cranial floor. On the superior surface is a vertical crest of bone called the **crista galli** (*crista*, crest + gal-lē, *gallus*, chicken; cock's comb), where membranes that protect and support the brain attach. At the base of the crista galli is a screenlike **cribriform** (*cribrum*, sieve) **plate** punctured by many small **olfactory foramina** that are passageways for branches of the olfactory nerve. The inferior ethmoid has a thin sheet of vertical bone, the **perpendicular plate,** which contributes to the septum of the nasal cavity. On each side of the perpendicular plate are the **lateral masses** that contain the **ethmoidal labyrinth,** which are full of connected **ethmoidal air cells,** also called the *ethmoidal sinuses*, which open into the nasal cavity. Extending inferiorly into the nasal cavity from the lateral masses are the **superior** and **middle nasal conchae.**

QuickCheck Questions

1.1 Where is the sella turcica located?

1.2 Describe the location of the ethmoid in the orbit of the eye.

1.3 Where are the squamous and petrous parts of the temporal bone located?

In the Lab 1

Materials

☐ Skull sectioned horizontally

☐ Disarticulated ethmoid

Figure 8 The Ethmoid

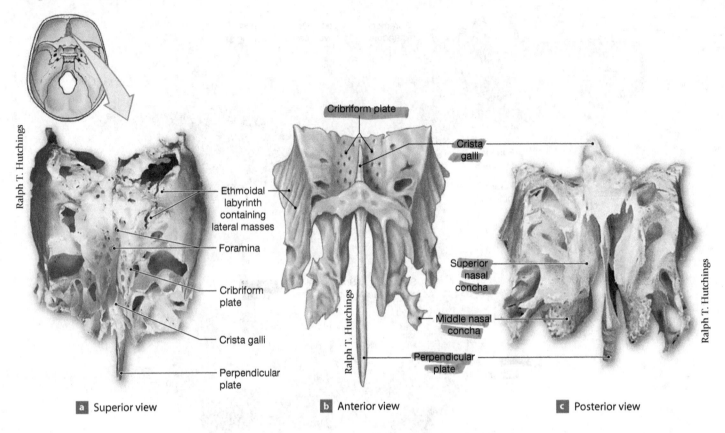

Ralph T. Hutchings

Cribriform plate

Crista galli

Ethmoidal
labyrinth
containing
lateral masses

Foramina

Cribriform
plate

Crista galli

Perpendicular
plate

Superior
nasal
concha

Middle nasal
concha

Perpendicular
plate

Ralph T. Hutchings

Ralph T. Hutchings

a Superior view   **b** Anterior view   **c** Posterior view

Procedures

1. Review the cranial structures in Figures 3 through 8.
2. Locate the frontal bone on the skull.
   - Identify the frontal squama, supraorbital foramen, and lacrimal fossa.
   - Is the metopic suture visible on the skull?
3. Locate the parietal bones on the skull. Examine the lateral surface of a parietal bone and locate the superior and inferior temporal lines.
4. Identify the occipital bone on the skull.
   - Locate the foramen magnum, the occipital condyles, and the hypoglossal canal.
   - Locate the external occipital crest, external occipital protuberance, and superior and inferior nuchal lines.
5. Examine the temporal bones on the skull.
   - Locate the squamous and petrous parts, mastoid processes, and zygomatic processes. Can you feel the mastoid process on your own skull?
   - Find the mandibular fossa.
   - Identify the major passageways of the temporal bone: external and internal auditory meatuses, jugular foramen, and carotid canal.
   - Identify the styloid process and the stylomastoid foramen.
6. Examine the sphenoid and determine its borders with other bones.
   - Identify the lesser wings, greater wings, and sella turcica.
   - Observe the structure of the sella turcica, which includes the anterior, middle, and posterior clinoid processes.
   - Identify each foramen of the sphenoid: ovale, spinosum, rotundum, and lacerum.
   - Locate the optic canal and the superior and inferior orbital fissure.
   - On the inferior sphenoid, identify the pterygoid processes and the pterygoid plates.

7. Identify the ethmoid on the skull. Closely examine its location within the orbit.

- ■ Observe on the floor of the skull the crista galli, cribriform plate, and olfactory foramina.

- ■ Examine the perpendicular plate in the nasal cavity. Examine a disarticulated ethmoid and identify the lateral masses and the superior and middle nasal conchae. ■

Lab Activity 2 Facial Bones

The face is constructed of 14 bones: two nasal, two maxillary, two lacrimal, two zygomatic, two palatine, two inferior nasal conchae, the vomer, and the mandible (see Figure 3b). The small **nasal** bones form the bridge of the nose. Lateral to the nasals are the **maxillary** bones, or maxillae; these bones form the floor of the eye orbits and extend inferiorly to form the upper jaw. Below the eye orbits are the **zygomatic** bones, commonly called the cheekbones. At the bridge of the nose, lateral to each maxillary bone, are the small **lacrimal** bones of the medial eye orbitals. Through each lacrimal bone passes a small canal that allows tears to drain into the nasal cavity. The **inferior nasal conchae** (KONG-kē) are the lower shelves of bone in the nasal cavity. The other conchae in the nasal cavity are part of the ethmoid. The bone of the lower jaw is the **mandible.**

On the inferior surface of the skull, the **palatine** bones form the posterior roof of the mouth next to the last molar tooth (see Figure 3c). A thin bone called the **vomer** divides the nasal cavity.

Maxillary Bones

The paired maxillary bones, or *maxillae*, are the foundation of the face (**Figure 9**). Inferior to the orbit is the **infra-orbital foramen.** The **alveolar** (al-VĒ-ō-lar) **process** consists of the U-shaped ridge where the upper teeth are embedded in the maxilla. From the inferior aspect, the **palatal process** of the maxilla is visible. This bony shelf forms the anterior hard palate of the mouth. At the anterior margin of the palatal process is the **incisive fossa.**

Zygomatic Bones

The zygomatic bones contribute to the inferior and lateral walls of the orbits (Figure 9). These bones also contribute to the floor and lateral walls of the orbit. Lateral and slightly inferior to the orbit is the small **zygomaticofacial foramen.** The posterior margin of the zygomatic bone narrows inferiorly to the **temporal process,** which joins the temporal bone's zygomatic process to complete the zygomatic arch.

Nasal Bones

The nasal bones form the bridge of the nose, and the maxilla separates them from the bones of the eye orbit (Figure 9). The superior margin of nasal bone articulates with the frontal

Figure 9 The Smaller Bones of the Face

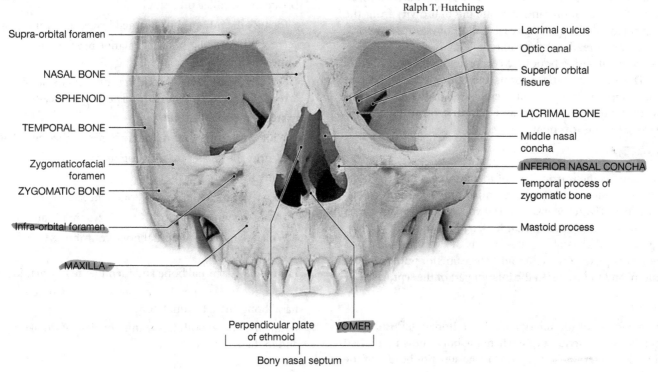

Ralph T. Hutchings

Supra-orbital foramen
NASAL BONE
SPHENOID
TEMPORAL BONE
Zygomaticofacial foramen
ZYGOMATIC BONE
Infra-orbital foramen
MAXILLA

Lacrimal sulcus
Optic canal
Superior orbital fissure
LACRIMAL BONE
Middle nasal concha
INFERIOR NASAL CONCHA
Temporal process of zygomatic bone
Mastoid process

Perpendicular plate of ethmoid   VOMER
Bony nasal septum

bone at the **frontonasal suture;** the posterior surface joins the ethmoid deep in the skull.

Lacrimal Bones

The lacrimal bones are the anterior portions of the medial orbital wall (Figure 9). Each lacrimal bone is named after the lacrimal glands that produce tears to lubricate and protect the eyeball. Tears flow medially across the eye and drain into the **lacrimal fossa,** which directs the lacrimal secretions toward the nasal cavity.

Inferior Nasal Conchae

The inferior nasal conchae are shelves that extend medially from the lower lateral portion of the nasal wall (Figure 9). They cause inspired air to swirl in the nasal cavity so that the moist mucous membrane lining can warm, cleanse, and moisten the air. Similar shelves of bone occur on the lateral walls of the ethmoid bone.

Palatine Bones

The palatine bones are posterior to the palatine processes of the maxilla. The palatine bones and maxillary bones fashion the roof of the mouth and separate the oral cavity from the nasal cavity (Figure 10). This separation of cavities allows us to chew and breathe at the same time. Only the inferior surfaces of the palatine bones are completely visible (see Figure 3c). The superior surface forms the floor of the nasal cavity and supports the base of the vomer. On the lateral margins of the bone are the **greater palatine foramen** and the **lesser palatine foramen** (Figure 3c).

The Vomer

The vomer is the inferior part of the **nasal septum,** the bony wall that partitions the nasal chamber into right and left nasal cavities (Figures 9 and 10). The vomer is also visible from the inferior aspect of the skull looking into the nasal cavities (Figure 3c). The nasal septum consists of two bones: the perpendicular plate of the ethmoid at the superior portion of the septum, and the vomer in the inferior part of the septum.

The Mandible

The mandible of the inferior jaw has a horizontal **body** that extends to a posterior **angle** where the bone turns to a raised projection, the **ramus** (Figure 11). The superior border of the

ramus terminates at the **mandibular notch** that has two processes extend upward: the anterior **coronoid** (kuh-RŌ-noyd) **process** and a posterior **condylar process,** also called the **mandibular condyle.** The smooth **articular surface** of the condylar **head** articulates in the mandibular fossa on the temporal bone at the **temporomandibular joint (TMJ).** The **alveolar process** of the mandible is the crest of bone where the lower teeth articulate with the mandible bone. Lateral to the chin, or **mental protuberance** (*mental,* chin), is the **mental foramen.** The medial mandibular surface features the **submandibular fossa,** a depression where the submandibular salivary gland rests against the bone. At the posterior end of the fossa is the **mandibular foramen,** a passageway for the sensory nerve from the lower teeth and gums.

QuickCheck Questions

2.1 Which facial bones contribute to the orbit of the eye?

2.2 Which facial bones form the roof of the mouth?

2.3 How does the mandible bone articulate with the cranium?

In the Lab   2

Material

☐ Skull

Procedures

1. Review the skeletal features of the face in Figures 3, 9, and 10.

2. Locate the maxillae on a skull.
   - Identify the infraorbital foramen below the orbit.
   - Locate the alveolar process, palatine process, and incisive fossa.
   - Feel your hard palate by placing your tongue on the roof of your mouth just behind your upper teeth.

3. Examine the palatine bones.
   - With which part of the maxillary bones do they articulate?
   - Identify the greater palatine foramen.

4. Identify the zygomatic bones.
   - Locate the zygomaticofacial foramen.
   - Locate the temporal process of the zygomatic arch.
   - Which part of the temporal bone contributes to the zygomatic arch?

5. Examine the lacrimal bone and identify the lacrimal fossa.

6. Locate the nasal bones. Which bone occurs between a nasal bone and a lacrimal bone?

7. Locate the vomer both in the inferior view of the skull and in the nasal cavity.

Figure 10 **Sectional Anatomy of the Skull** Medial view of a sagittal section through the skull.

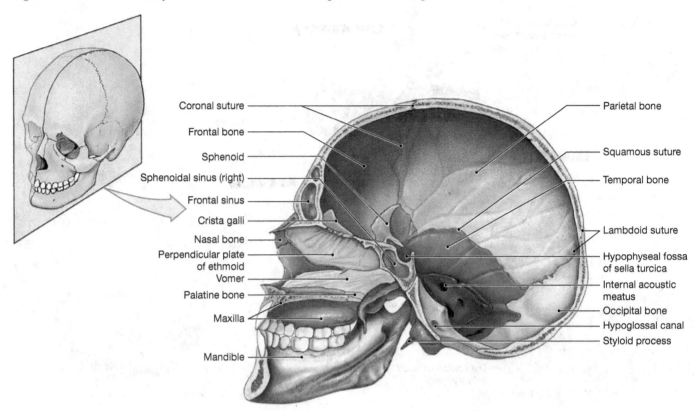

Coronal suture
Frontal bone
Sphenoid
Sphenoidal sinus (right)
Frontal sinus
Crista galli
Nasal bone
Perpendicular plate of ethmoid
Vomer
Palatine bone
Maxilla
Mandible

Parietal bone
Squamous suture
Temporal bone
Lambdoid suture
Hypophyseal fossa of sella turcica
Internal acoustic meatus
Occipital bone
Hypoglossal canal
Styloid process

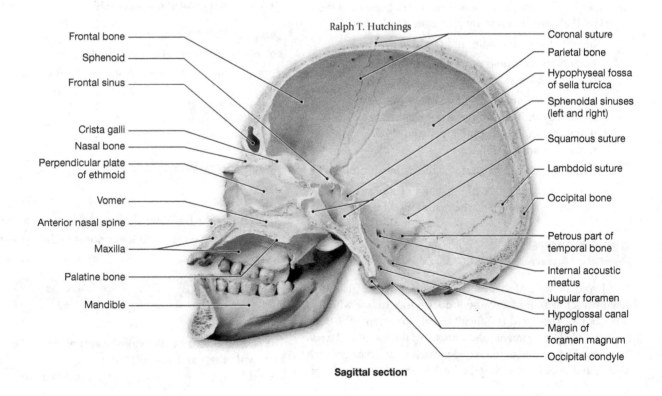

Ralph T. Hutchings

Frontal bone
Sphenoid
Frontal sinus
Crista galli
Nasal bone
Perpendicular plate of ethmoid
Vomer
Anterior nasal spine
Maxilla
Palatine bone
Mandible

Coronal suture
Parietal bone
Hypophyseal fossa of sella turcica
Sphenoidal sinuses (left and right)
Squamous suture
Lambdoid suture
Occipital bone
Petrous part of temporal bone
Internal acoustic meatus
Jugular foramen
Hypoglossal canal
Margin of foramen magnum
Occipital condyle

Sagittal section

65

Figure 11 The Mandible and Hyoid Bone

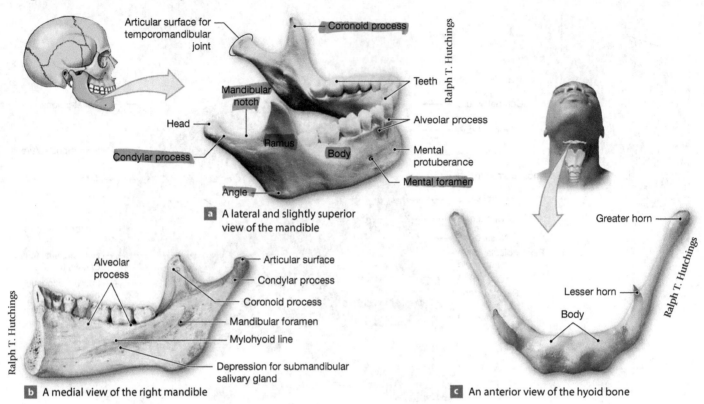

a A lateral and slightly superior view of the mandible

b A medial view of the right mandible

c An anterior view of the hyoid bone

8. Identify the inferior nasal conchae in the nasal cavity.

9. Examine the mandible. Disarticulate this bone from the skull if allowed to do so by your instructor.

- Identify the body, angle, and ramus.
- Identify the coronoid process, mandibular notch, and condylar process.
- Note how the articular surface of the mandible articulates with the temporal bone at the temporomandibular joint. Open and close your mouth to feel this articulation.
- Locate the alveolar process and the mental protuberance.
- On the medial surface of the mandible, locate the mandibular groove and the mandibular foramen. ■

Lab Activity 3 Hyoid Bone

The hyoid bone, a U-shaped bone inferior to the mandible (Figure 11c), is unique because it does not articulate with any other bones. The hyoid is difficult to palpate because the bone is surrounded by ligaments and muscles of the throat and neck. Two hornlike processes for muscle attachment occur on each side of the hyoid bone, an anterior **lesser horn** and a larger

posterior **greater horn.** These bony projections are also called the **lesser** and **greater cornua** (KOR-nū-uh; *cornu-*, horn).

QuickCheck Questions

3.1 Where is the hyoid bone located?

3.2 Does the hyoid bone articulate with other bones?

In the Lab 3

Material

☐ Articulated skeleton

Procedures

1. Examine the hyoid bone on an articulated skeleton.
2. Identify the greater and lesser horns of the hyoid bone. ■

Lab Activity 4 Paranasal Sinuses of the Skull

The skull contains cavities called **paranasal sinuses** that connect with the nasal cavity (Figure 12). The sinuses lighten the skull and, like the nasal cavity, are lined with a mucous

Figure 12 Paranasal Sinuses

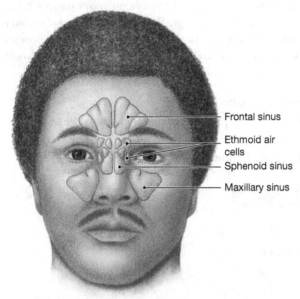

- Frontal sinus
- Ethmoid air cells
- Sphenoid sinus
- Maxillary sinus

a This anterior view shows the general location of the four paranasal sinuses.

Frederic H. Martini

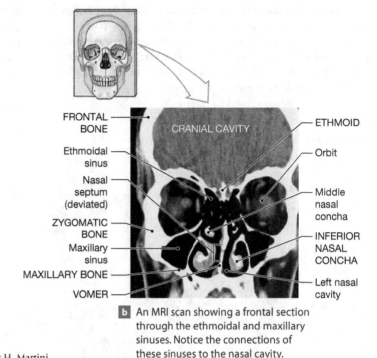

- FRONTAL BONE
- Ethmoidal sinus
- Nasal septum (deviated)
- ZYGOMATIC BONE
- Maxillary sinus
- MAXILLARY BONE
- VOMER
- CRANIAL CAVITY
- ETHMOID
- Orbit
- Middle nasal concha
- INFERIOR NASAL CONCHA
- Left nasal cavity

b An MRI scan showing a frontal section through the ethmoidal and maxillary sinuses. Notice the connections of these sinuses to the nasal cavity.

Clinical Application Sinus Congestion

In some individuals, allergies or changes in the weather can make the sinus membranes swell and secrete more mucus. The resulting congestion blocks connections with the nasal cavity, and the increased sinus pressure is felt as a headache. The sinuses also serve as resonating chambers for the voice, much like the body of a guitar amplifies its music, and when the sinuses and nasal cavity are congested, the voice sounds muffled. ▪

membrane that cleans, warms, and moistens inhaled air. The **frontal sinus** extends laterally over the orbit of the eyes. The **sphenoidal sinus** is located in the sphenoid directly inferior to the sella turcica. The **ethmoid labyrinth** houses **ethmoidal air cells** that collectively constitute the **ethmoidal sinus.** Each maxilla contains a large **maxillary sinus** positioned lateral to the nasal cavity.

QuickCheck Questions

4.1 What are the names of the various paranasal sinuses?

4.2 What are the functions of the paranasal sinuses?

In the Lab 4

Material

☐ Skull (midsagittal section)

Procedures

1. Compare the frontal sinus on several sectioned skulls. Is the sinus the same size on each skull?
2. Locate the sphenoidal sinus on a sectioned skull. Under which sphenoidal structure is this sinus located?
3. Examine the maxillary sinus on a sectioned skull. How does the size of this sinus compare with the sizes of the other three sinuses?
4. Identify the ethmoidal air cells. What sinus do these cells collectively form? ▪

Lab Activity 5 Fetal Skull

As the fetal skull develops, the cranium must remain flexible to accommodate the growth of the brain. This flexibility is possible because the cranial bones remain incompletely fused until after birth (Figure 13). Between wide developing sutures are expanses of fibrous connective tissue called **fontanels** (fon-tuh-NELZ). It is these so-called *soft spots* that allow the skull to expand as brain size increases and enable the skull to flex in order to squeeze through the birth canal during delivery. By the age of four to five years, the brain is nearly adult size, the fibrous connective tissue of the fontanels ossifies, and the cranial sutures interlock to securely support the articulating bones.

Four major fontanels are present at birth: the large **anterior fontanel** is between the frontal and parietal bones where

Figure 13 **The Skull of an Infant** The skull of an infant contains more individual bones than that of an adult. Many of the bones eventually fuse; thus, the adult skull has fewer bones. The flat bones of the skull are separated by areas of fibrous connective tissue, allowing for cranial expansion and the distortion of the skull during birth. The large fibrous areas are called fontanels. By about age four or five, these areas will disappear.

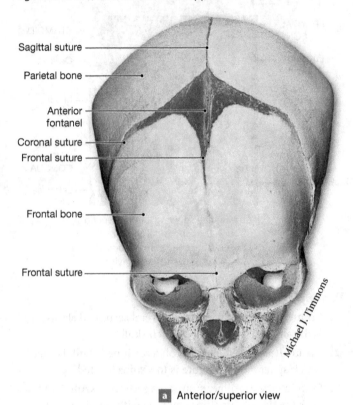

Sagittal suture

Parietal bone

Anterior fontanel

Coronal suture

Frontal suture

Frontal bone

Frontal suture

Michael J. Timmons

a Anterior/superior view

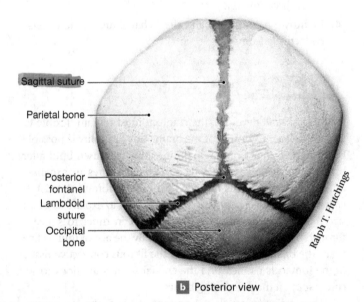

Sagittal suture

Parietal bone

Posterior fontanel

Lambdoid suture

Occipital bone

Ralph T. Hutchings

b Posterior view

the frontal, coronal, and sagittal sutures intersect; the **posterior fontanel** is at the juncture of the occipital and parietal bones where the lambdoid and sagittal sutures join; the **sphenoidal fontanel** is at the union of the coronal and squamous sutures; and the **mastoid fontanel** is posterolateral where the squamous and lambdoid sutures meet.

QuickCheck Questions

5.1 What does the presence of fontanels allow the fetal skull to do?

5.2 How long are fontanels present in the skull?

In the Lab 5

Materials

☐ Fetal skull

☐ Adult skull

Procedures

1. Identify each fontanel on a fetal skull, using Figure 13 as a guide.

2. Compare the fetal and adult skulls. Which has more bones? ▨

Lab Activity 6 Vertebral Column

The **vertebral column,** or **spine,** is a flexible chain of 26 bones; 24 vertebrae (singular: *vertebra*), the sacrum, and the coccyx. The column articulates at the superior end with the skull, the inferior portion with the pelvic girdle, and the ribs laterally. The bones of the vertebral column are grouped into five regions based on location and anatomical features (**Figure 14**). Starting at the superior end of the spine, the first seven vertebrae are the **cervical** vertebrae of the neck. Twelve **thoracic** vertebrae articulate with the ribs. The lower back has five **lumbar** vertebrae, and a single **sacrum** joining the hips is comprised of five fused **sacral vertebrae.** The **coccyx** (KOK-siks), commonly called the *tailbone,* is the inferior portion of the spine and consists of (usually) four fused **coccygeal vertebrae.**

The vertebral column is curved to balance the body weight while standing. Toward the end of gestation, the fetal spine develops **accommodation curves** in the thoracic and sacral regions, curves that provide space for internal organs in these regions. Because accommodation curves occur first they are also called **primary curves.** At birth, the accommodation curves are still forming, and the vertebral column is relatively straight. During early childhood, as the individual learns to hold the head up, crawl, and then walk, **compensation (secondary) curves** form in the cervical and lumbar regions

Figure 14 **The Vertebral Column** The major divisions of the vertebral column, showing the four spinal curvatures.

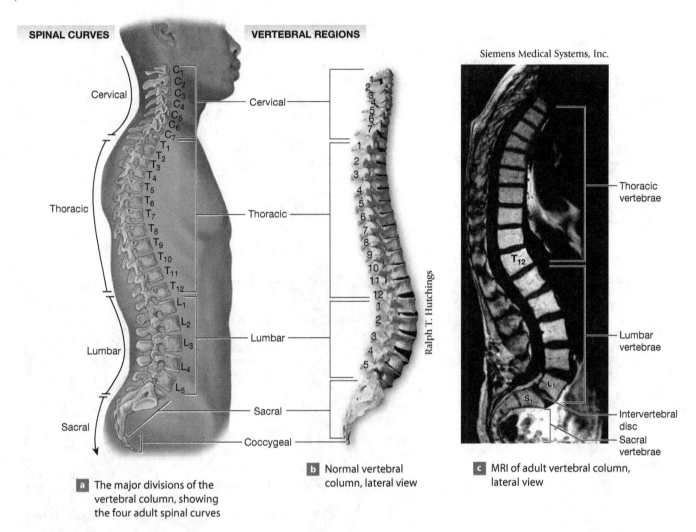

a The major divisions of the vertebral column, showing the four adult spinal curves

b Normal vertebral column, lateral view

c MRI of adult vertebral column, lateral view

to move the body weight closer to the body's axis for better balance. Once the child is approximately 10 years old, the spinal curves are established and the fully developed column has alternating secondary and primary curves.

In the cervical, thoracic, and lumbar regions are **intervertebral discs,** cushions of fibrocartilage between the articulating vertebrae. Each disc consists of an outer layer of strong fibrocartilage, the **annulus fibrosus,** surrounding a deeper mass, the **nucleus pulposus.** Water and elastic fibers in the gelatinous mass of the nucleus pulposus absorb stresses that arise between vertebrae whenever a person is either standing or moving.

Vertebral Anatomy

The anatomical features of a typical vertebra include a large, anterior, disc-shaped **vertebral body** (the *centrum*) and a posterior elongated **spinous process** (**Figure 15**). Lateral on

each side of the spinous process is a **transverse process.** The **lamina** (LA-mi-na) is a flat plate of bone between the transverse and spinous processes that forms the curved **vertebral arch.** The **pedicle** (PE-di-kul) is a strut of bone extending posteriorly from the vertebral body to a transverse process. The pedicle and lamina on each side form the wall of the large posterior **vertebral foramen,** which contributes to the spinal cavity where the spinal cord is housed. Inferior to the pedicle is an inverted U-shaped region called the **inferior vertebral notch.** Two articulating vertebrae contribute to fashion an **intervertebral foramen,** with the **inferior vertebral notch** of the superior vertebra joining the pedicle of the inferior vertebra. Spinal nerves pass through the intervertebral foramen to access the spinal cord.

The vertebral column moves much like a gooseneck lamp: Each joint moves only slightly, but the combination

Figure 15 Vertebral Anatomy The anatomy of a typical vertebra and the arrangement of articulations between vertebrae.

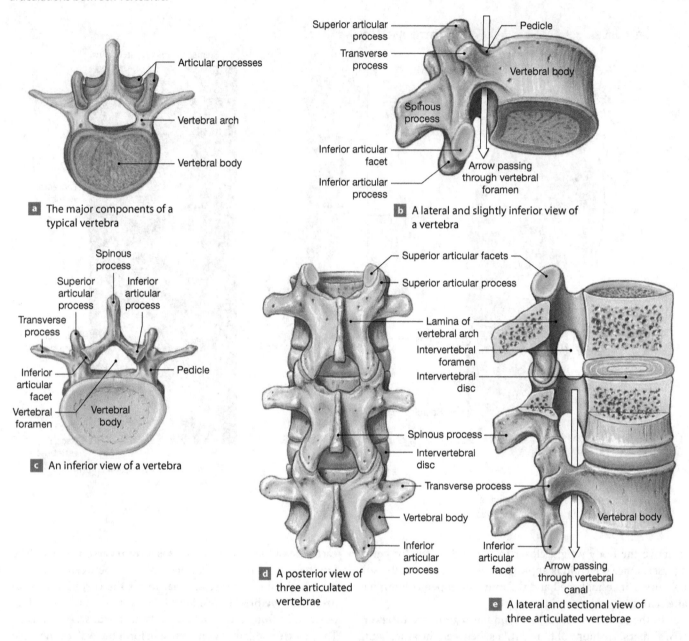

a The major components of a typical vertebra

- Articular processes
- Vertebral arch
- Vertebral body

b A lateral and slightly inferior view of a vertebra

- Superior articular process
- Transverse process
- Pedicle
- Vertebral body
- Spinous process
- Inferior articular facet
- Inferior articular process
- Arrow passing through vertebral foramen

c An inferior view of a vertebra

- Spinous process
- Superior articular process
- Inferior articular process
- Transverse process
- Inferior articular facet
- Pedicle
- Vertebral foramen
- Vertebral body

d A posterior view of three articulated vertebrae

- Superior articular facets
- Superior articular process
- Lamina of vertebral arch
- Intervertebral foramen
- Intervertebral disc
- Spinous process
- Intervertebral disc
- Transverse process
- Vertebral body
- Inferior articular process
- Inferior articular facet
- Vertebral body
- Arrow passing through vertebral canal

e A lateral and sectional view of three articulated vertebrae

of all the individual movements permits the column a wide range of motion. Joints between adjacent vertebrae occur at smooth articular surfaces called *facets* that project from *articular processes*. The **superior articular process** is on the superior surface of the pedicle of each vertebra and has a **superior articular facet** at the posterior tip. The **inferior articular process** is a downward projection of the inferior lamina wall and has an **inferior articular facet** on the anterior tip. At a vertebral joint, the inferior articular facet of the superior vertebra

glides across the superior articular facet of the inferior vertebra. The greatest movement of these joints is in the cervical region for head movement.

Cervical Vertebrae

The seven cervical vertebrae in the neck are recognizable by the presence of a **transverse foramen** on each transverse process (**Figure 16**). The vertebral artery travels up the neck through these foramina to enter the skull. The first two cervical vertebrae

Figure 16 The Cervical Vertebrae

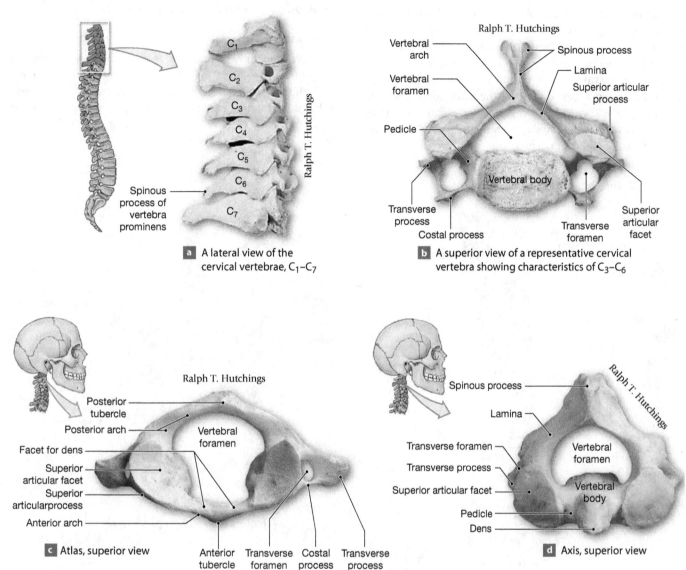

a A lateral view of the cervical vertebrae, C₁–C₇

b A superior view of a representative cervical vertebra showing characteristics of C₃–C₆

c Atlas, superior view

d Axis, superior view

are modified for special articulations with the skull. The tip of the spinous process is **bifid** (branched) in vertebrae C₂ through C₆. The last cervical vertebra, C₇, is called the **vertebra prominens** because of the broad tubercle at the end of the spinous process. The tubercle can be palpated at the base of the neck.

The first cervical vertebra, C₁, is called the **atlas** (Figure 16c), named after the Greek mythological character who carried the world on his shoulders. The atlas is the only vertebra that articulates with the skull. The superior articular facets of the atlas are greatly enlarged, and the occipital condyles of the occipital bone fit into the facets like spoons nested together. When you nod your head, the atlas remains stationary while the occipital condyles glide in the facets.

The atlas is unusual in that it lacks a vertebral body and a spinous process and has a very large vertebral foramen formed by the **anterior** and **posterior arches.** A small, rough **posterior tubercle** occurs where the spinous process normally resides. A long spinous process would interfere with occipitoatlas articulation.

The **axis** is the second cervical vertebra, C₂. It is specialized to articulate with the atlas. A peglike **dens** (DENZ; *dens,* tooth), or *odontoid process,* arises superiorly from the body of the axis (Figure 16d). It fits against the anterior wall of the vertebral foramen and provides the atlas with a pivot point for when the head is turned laterally and medially. A **transverse ligament** secures the atlas around the dens.

Thoracic Vertebrae

The 12 thoracic vertebrae, which articulate with the 12 pairs of ribs, are larger than the cervical vertebrae and increase in size as they approach the lumbar region. Most ribs attach to their thoracic vertebra at two sites on the vertebra: on a **transverse costal facet** at the tip of the transverse process and on a **costal facet** located on the posterior of the vertebral body (**Figure 17**). Two costal facets usually are present on the same vertebral body, a **superior costal facet** and an **inferior costal facet.** The costal facets are unique to the thoracic vertebrae, and there is variation in where these facets occur on the various thoracic vertebrae.

Lumbar Vertebrae

The five lumbar vertebrae are large and heavy in order to support the weight of the head, neck, and trunk. Compared with thoracic vertebrae, lumbar vertebrae have a wider body, a blunt and horizontal spinous process, and shorter transverse processes (**Figure 18**). The lumbar vertebral foramen is smaller than that in thoracic vertebrae. To prevent the back

Figure 17 The Thoracic Vertebrae

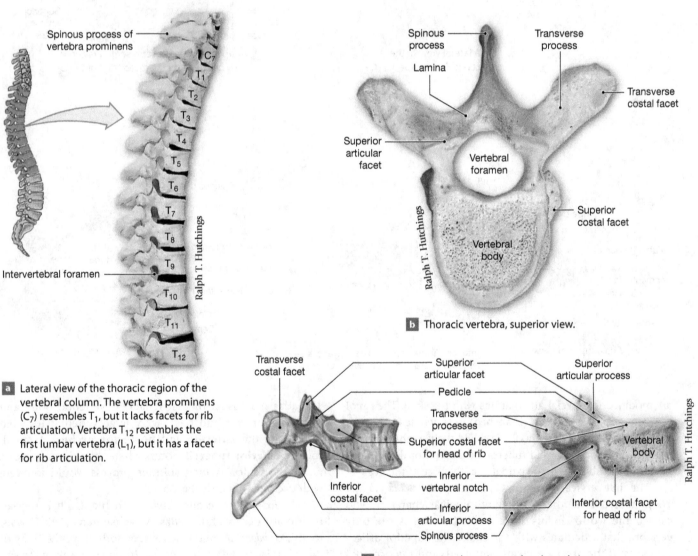

a Lateral view of the thoracic region of the vertebral column. The vertebra prominens (C$_7$) resembles T$_1$, but it lacks facets for rib articulation. Vertebra T$_{12}$ resembles the first lumbar vertebra (L$_1$), but it has a facet for rib articulation.

b Thoracic vertebra, superior view.

c A representative thoracic vertebra, lateral view.

Figure 18 The Lumbar Vertebrae

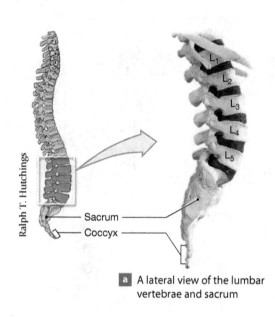

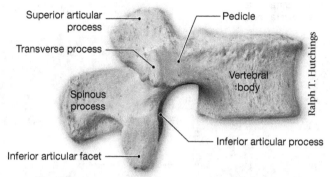

Superior articular process

Transverse process

Spinous process

Inferior articular facet

Pedicle

Vertebral body

Inferior articular process

Ralph T. Hutchings

b A lateral view of a typical lumbar vertebra

Ralph T. Hutchings

L₁
L₂
L₃
L₄
L₅

Sacrum
Coccyx

a A lateral view of the lumbar vertebrae and sacrum

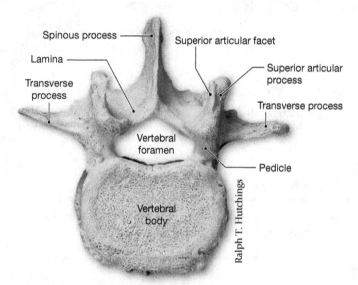

Spinous process

Lamina

Transverse process

Superior articular facet

Superior articular process

Transverse process

Vertebral foramen

Pedicle

Vertebral body

Ralph T. Hutchings

c A superior view of the same vertebra shown in part b

from twisting when objects are being lifted or carried, the lumbar superior articular process is turned medially and the lumbar inferior articular processes are oriented laterally to interlock the lumbar vertebrae. No facets or transverse foramina occur on the lumbar vertebrae.

Sacral and Coccygeal Vertebrae

As noted earlier, the sacrum is a single bony element composed of five fused sacral vertebrae (Figure 19). It articulates with the ilium of the pelvic girdle to form the posterior wall of the pelvis. Fusion of the sacral bones before birth consolidates the vertebral canal into the **sacral canal.** On the fifth sacral vertebra, the sacral canal opens as the **sacral hiatus** (hi-Ā-tus). Along the lateral margin of the fused vertebral bodies are **sacral foramina.** The spinous processes fuse to form an elevation called the **median sacral crest.** A **lateral sacral crest** extends from the lateral margin of the sacrum. The sacrum articulates with each pelvic bone at the large **auricular surface** on the

lateral border. Dorsal to this surface is the **sacral tuberosity,** where ligaments attach to support the **sacroiliac joint.**

The coccyx (Figure 19) articulates with the fifth fused sacral vertebra at the **coccygeal cornu.** There may be anywhere from three to five coccygeal bones, but most people have four.

QuickCheck Questions

6.1 What are the five major regions of the vertebral column and the number of vertebrae in each region?

6.2 What are three features found on all vertebrae?

In the Lab 6

Materials

☐ Articulated skeleton

☐ Articulated vertebral column

☐ Disarticulated vertebral column

Figure 19 The Sacrum and Coccyx

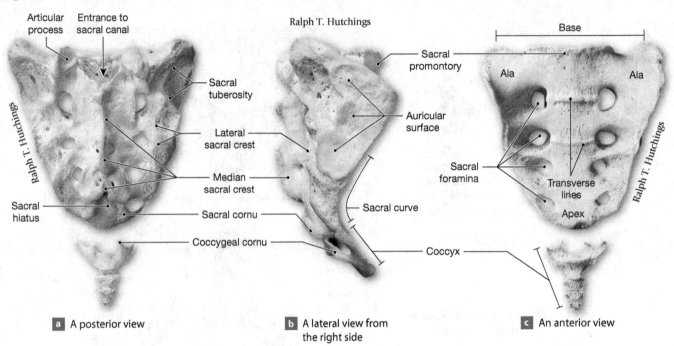

Articular process

Entrance to sacral canal

Ralph T. Hutchings

Sacral tuberosity

Lateral sacral crest

Median sacral crest

Sacral hiatus

Sacral cornu

Coccygeal cornu

Ralph T. Hutchings

Sacral promontory

Auricular surface

Sacral curve

Coccyx

Base

Ala

Ala

Sacral foramina

Transverse lines

Apex

Coccyx

Ralph T. Hutchings

| a | A posterior view |

| b | A lateral view from the right side |

| c | An anterior view |

 Sketch to Learn

Let's draw a lateral view of a thoracic vertebra and label the facets where articulations occur. Refer to a thoracic vertebra or Figure 17c while sketching.

Sample Sketch

Step 1
- Draw a 3-sided cube for the vertebral body.
- Add a notch for the intervertebral foramen.

Step 2
- Complete the vertebra by drawing the long spinous process.

Step 3
- Add small ovals for the various facets of thoracic vertebrae.
- Label your sketch.

Your Sketch

Procedures

1. Review the vertebral anatomy presented in Figures 14 to 19.
2. Identify the four regions of the vertebral column on an articulated skeleton.
3. Describe the type of curves found in each region.
4. Describe the anatomy of a typical vertebra. Locate each feature on a disarticulated vertebra.
   - Distinguish the anatomical differences among cervical, thoracic, and lumbar vertebrae.
   - Identify the unique features of the atlas and the axis. How do these two vertebrae articulate with the skull and with each other?
   - Discuss how a lumbar vertebra differs from a thoracic vertebra.
5. Describe the anatomy of the sacrum and the coccyx. ■

Lab Activity 7 Thoracic Cage

The 12 pairs of ribs articulate with the thoracic vertebrae posteriorly and the sternum anteriorly to enclose the thoracic organs in a protective cage. In breathing, muscles move the ribs to increase or decrease the size of the thoracic cavity and cause air to move into or out of the lungs.

Sternum

The **sternum** is the flat bone located anterior to the thoracic region of the vertebral column. It is composed of three bony elements: a superior **manubrium** (ma-NOO-brē-um), a middle **sternal body,** and an inferior **xiphoid** (ZĪ-foyd) **process** (Figure 20). The manubrium is triangular and articulates with the first pair of ribs and the clavicle. Muscles that move the head and neck attach to the manubrium. The sternal body is elongated and receives the costal cartilage of ribs 2 through 7. The xiphoid process is shaped like an arrowhead and projects inferiorly off the sternal body. This process is cartilaginous until late adulthood, when it completely ossifies.

Ribs

Ribs, also called **costae,** are classified according to how they articulate with the sternum (Figure 20). The first seven pairs are called either **true ribs** or **vertebrosternal ribs** because their cartilage, the **costal cartilage,** attaches directly to the sternum. Rib pairs 8 through 12 are called **false ribs** or **vertebrochondral ribs** because their costal cartilage does not connect directly with the sternum but instead fuse with the costal cartilage of rib 7. Rib pairs 11 and 12 are called **floating ribs** or **vertebral ribs** because they do not articulate with the sternum.

Each rib has a **head,** or **capitulum** (ka-PIT-ū-lum), and on the head are two **articular facets** for articulating with the costal facets of the rib's thoracic vertebra. The **tubercle** of the rib articulates with the transverse costal facet of the rib's vertebra. Between the head and tubercle is a slender **neck.**

Differences in the way ribs articulate with the thoracic vertebrae are reflected in variations in the vertebral costal facets. Vertebrae T_1 through T_8 all have paired costal facets, one superior and one inferior as noted in our previous thoracic discussion. The first rib articulates with a transverse costal facet of T_1. The second rib articulates with the inferior costal facet of T_1 and the superior costal facet of T_2. Ribs 3 through 9 continue this pattern of articulating with two adjacent costal facets. Vertebrae T_9 through T_{12} have a single costal facet on the vertebral body, and the ribs articulate entirely on the one costal facet. After each rib articulates on the single costal facet, the rib bends laterally and articulates on the transverse costal facet. Rib pairs 11 and 12 do not articulate on costal facets.

QuickCheck Questions

7.1 Which part of the sternum articulates with the clavicle?

7.2 Which ribs are true ribs, which are false ribs, and which are floating ribs?

In the Lab 7

Materials

- ☐ Articulated skeleton
- ☐ Articulated vertebral column with ribs
- ☐ Disarticulated vertebral column and ribs

Procedures

1. Review the anatomy in Figure 20.
2. Identify the manubrium, body, and xiphoid process of the sternum.
3. Discuss the anatomy of a typical rib.
   - How many pairs of ribs do human males have? How many pairs do human females have?
   - Describe the anatomical features involved in the articulation of a rib on a thoracic vertebra.
   - Identify the differences of articular facets along the thoracic region and relate this to how each rib articulates with the vertebrae. ■

Figure 20 The Thoracic Cage The thoracic cage is the articulated ribs and sternum.

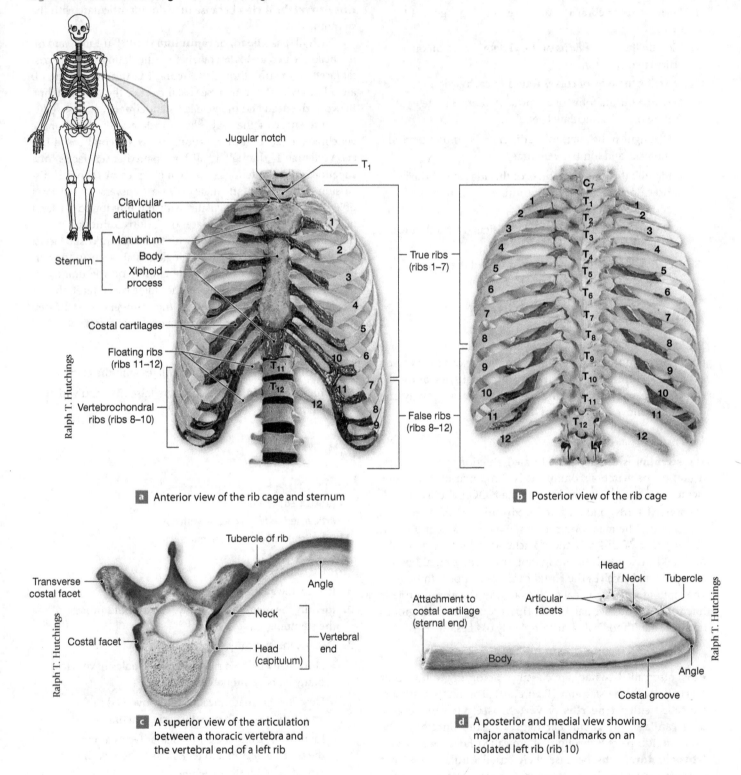

Jugular notch

T₁

Clavicular articulation

Manubrium

Body

Xiphoid process

Sternum

Costal cartilages

Floating ribs (ribs 11–12)

Vertebrochondral ribs (ribs 8–10)

T₁₁

T₁₂

True ribs (ribs 1–7)

False ribs (ribs 8–12)

Ralph T. Hutchings

a Anterior view of the rib cage and sternum

C₇

T₁ T₂ T₃ T₄ T₅ T₆ T₇ T₈ T₉ T₁₀ T₁₁ T₁₂

L₁

b Posterior view of the rib cage

Tubercle of rib

Angle

Transverse costal facet

Neck

Costal facet

Head (capitulum)

Vertebral end

Ralph T. Hutchings

c A superior view of the articulation between a thoracic vertebra and the vertebral end of a left rib

Head

Neck

Tubercle

Articular facets

Attachment to costal cartilage (sternal end)

Body

Angle

Costal groove

Ralph T. Hutchings

d A posterior and medial view showing major anatomical landmarks on an isolated left rib (rib 10)

Name Nicole Villa

Date 1/31/18

Section 15

Axial Skeleton

A. Identification

Identify the bone that each structure occurs on.

1. sella turcica

center of sphnoid

2. crista galli

ethmoid

3. external acoustic meatus

temperal bone

4. foramen magnum

occipital bone

5. zygomatic process

temperol bone

6. condylar process

mandible

7. mandibular fossa

mandible

8. styloid process

temporol

9. coronoid process

mandible

10. jugular foramen

temporal

11. superior nuchal line

occipital

12. superior temporal line

parietal

B. Description

Describe each structure of the vertebral column and thoracic cage.

1. spinous process — posterior and elongated (70)

2. transverse foramen — on each transverse process (70)

3. manubrium – superior bony element of the sternum (75)

4. capitulum – (head) of rib (75)

5. pedicle – strut of bone extending posteriorly from vertebral body → transverse process (65)

6. xiphoid process –

7. dens

8. vertebral foramen

9. vertebrochondral rib

10. costal facet

C. Labeling

1. Label Figure 21, an anterior view of the skull.

Figure 21 **Anterior View of the Skull** (55)

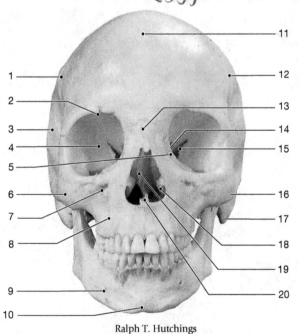

Ralph T. Hutchings

1. parietal bone
2. supra-orbital foramen
3. temporal bone
4. sphenoid
5. lacrimal bone
6. zygomatic bone
7. infra orbital foramen
8. maxilla
9. mandible
10. mental protuberance
11. frontal bone
12. coronal structure
13. nasal bone
14. optic canal
15. superior orbital fissure
16. temporal process of zygomatic
17. mastoid process
18. inferior nasal concha
19. perp plate of ethmoid
20. vomer

2. Label Figure 22, a lateral view of the skull.

Figure 22 **Lateral View of the Skull** (54)

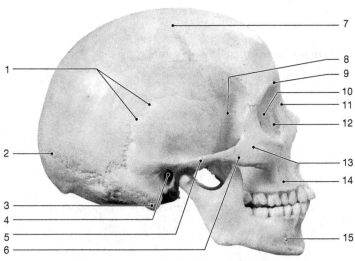

Ralph T. Hutchings

1. squamous suture
2. lamboid suture
3. mastoid process
4. external acoustic meatus
5. zygomatic proc. of temporal
6. temporal proc. of zygomatic
7. coronal suture
8. sphenoid
9. supra orbital foramen
10. ethmoid
11. nasal bone
12. lacrimal groove of lacrimal
13. zygomatic bone
14. maxilla
15. mental foramen

3. Label Figure 23, a typical cervical vertebra.

Figure 23 **Typical Cervical Vertebra, Superior View** (71)

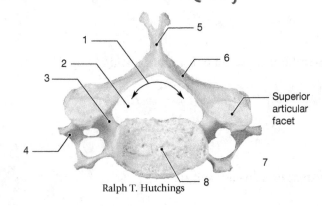

Superior articular facet

Ralph T. Hutchings

1. vertebral arch
2. vertebral foramen
3. pedicle
4. transverse process
5. spinous process
6. lamina
7. _____
8. vertebral body

D. Short-Answer Questions

1. List the three primary components of the axial skeleton.

2. How many bones are found in the cranium and the face?

3. Describe the three cranial fossae and the bones that form the floor of each.

4. List the six primary sutures of the skull and the bones that articulate at each suture.

5. Describe the five regions of the vertebral column.

E. **Analysis and Application**

1. Name two passageways in the floor of the skull for major blood vessels that serve the brain.

2. Describe the skeletal features at the point where the vertebral column articulates with the skull.

3. Compare the articulation on the thoracic vertebrae of rib pairs 7 and 10.

F. **Clinical Challenge**

A patient is scheduled for surgery to correct a deviated nasal septum. Which bones and other facial features may be involved in this procedure?

Appendicular Skeleton Wish List

By the end of today's lab, you should be able to identify all the structures listed below. As you go through the ID list, make sure that you pay special attention to bone markings that will help your understanding of origins and insertions of muscles (our next major topic). Also pay special attention to left and right handedness of bones since you might have to provide this information during the practical. If you finish the list before your lab time is over, make sure you review items from the axial wish list.

✓	Item	Description
	UPPER EXTREMITY	
	Pectoral Girdle	
	Scapula	two bones often called the shoulder blades
	Superior border	superior edge
	Medial border	medial edge, next to vertebral column
	Lateral border	lateral edge, next to the axilla
	Superior angle	between superior and medial borders
	Lateral angle	inferior glenoid fossa
	Inferior angle	between medial and lateral borders
	Acromion process	lateral point of the shoulder, articulates with clavicle
	Coracoid process	Inferior and anterior to acromion process
	Glenoid fossa or cavity	shoulder "socket"
	Spine of the scapula	posterior structure
	Supraspinous fossa -	posterior, superior to spine
	Infraspinous fossa	posterior, inferior to spine
	Subscapular fossa	anterior, concave towards rib cage
	Clavicle	**two bones that connect to sternum on either side**
	Sternal end	medial end, articulates with sternum
	Acromial end	lateral end, articulates with acromion process
	Conoid tubercle	inferior, on acromial end
✓	**Upper extremity**	
	Humerus	**previously known as brachial bone**
	Head	smooth rounded proximal portion
	Anatomical neck	narrowing distal to head

	Greater tubercle	proximal
	Lesser tubercle	proximal
	Intertubercular groove (bicipital)	between 2 tubercles
	Shaft	
	Deltoid tuberosity	Lateral shaft
	Olecranon fossa	posterior, inferior fossa for olecranon process
	Capitulum	distal, lateral smooth, rounded knuckle
	Trochlea	distal, medial, pointed knuckle
	Medial and lateral epicondyle	bony mass proximal to the capitulum and trochlea

	Ulna	medial forearm bone
	Olecranon process	proximal, posterior, point of elbow, fits in olecranon fossa
	Radial notch	articulates with head of radius
	Shaft	
	Head	distal end
	Styloid process	distal, projection from head

	Radius	**lateral forearm bone**
	Head	proximal end, looks like spool
	Neck	distal to head
	Radial tuberosity	proximal end
	Shaft	
	Ulnar notch	distal end, articulates with ulna
	Styloid process	distal end, projection on lateral side

	Carpals	**two rows of 4. Some Lovers Try Positions That They Can't Handle! Names Lateral to Medial, proximal row then distal row**
	Scaphoid	looks like a boat or spoon
	Lunate	moon shaped
	Triquetral	triangular shaped, superman sign
	Pisiform	pea shaped
	Trapezium	small table or stool shaped

	Trapezoid	four sides but not really square
	Capitate	dome, Darth Vader
	Hamate	has a hook
	Metacarpals	**five bones, numbered from the lateral (thumb) side**
	Phalanges (Phalanx for one)	**each finger has 3 except the thumb that only has 2**
	Proximal	
	Middle	thumb does not have middle
	Distal	

	LOWER EXTREMITY	
✓	**Pelvic Girdle**	
	Sacrum	**posterior portion of girdle. See structures from axial skeleton**
	Os Coxa (innominate bone)	hip bones that form anterior and lateral portions of girdle. 3 fused bones (ischium, ilium, pubis)
	Acetabulum	cup shaped cavity on lateral aspect of girdle, holds head of femur
	Obturator foramen	largest foramen, between ischium and pubis

	Ilium	**superior portion of hip bone**
	Iliac crest	superior border
	Anterior Superior Iliac Spine (ASIS)	anterior, superior
	Anterior Inferior Iliac Spine (AIIS)	anterior, inferior
	Posterior Superior Iliac Spine (PSIS)	posterior, superior
	Posterior Inferior Iliac Spine (PIIS)	posterior, inferior
	Greater sciatic notch	inferior to PIIS
	Iliac fossa	anterior, concave surface distal to crest
	Auricular surface	ear shaped surface on medial border, articulates with sacrum
	Iliac tuberosity	medial aspect of crest
	Iliopectineal line	inner rim that separates true pelvis from false pelvis

	Ischium	posterior, inferior portion
	Ischial spine	inferior to greater sciatic notch
	Lesser sciatic notch	inferior to ischial spine
	Ischial tuberosity	inferior
	Ischial ramus	projects from tuberosity towards the pubis
	Pubis	**anterior, inferior portion**
	Symphaseal surface	medial articulating surface between 2 pubis bones
	Symphysis pubis	cartilage between symphaseal surfaces
	Superior ramus	projects towards acetabulum
	Inferior ramus	projects from pubis to ischium
	Pubic Crest	area superior to symphaseal surfaces
✓	**Lower Extremity**	
	Femur	**longest bones in the body**
	Head	medial ball like structure that fits into the acetabulum
	Neck	lateral to head
	Greater trochanter	superior, lateral
	Trochanteric fossa	depression on medial surface of greater trochanter
	Lesser trochanter	posterior, inferior to head
	Gluteal tuberosity	posterior, lateral surface of shaft
	Shaft	
	Linea Aspera	two lipped line on posterior shaft
	Popliteal surface	concave, triangular shaped surface at distal, posterior end of femur (where linea aspera splits)
	Medial and Lateral condyles	distal rounded knuckles
	Intercondylar fossa	notch found between condyles on posterior side
	Medial and Lateral Epicondyles	bony tissue superior to condyles
	Adductor tubercle	projection on medial epicondyle for adductor muscles (groin)
	Patellar surface	smooth anterior surface that articulates with patella

Patella		knee caps, triangular in shape
	Base	superior surface
	Apex	pointy, inferior surface
Tibia		**weight bearing bone on the medial side of the lower extremity**
	Medial and Lateral Condyles	2 large, almost flat condyles on the superior surface and that articulate with the condyles of the femur. They look like large facets
	Intercondylar eminence	enlarged ridge on the superior surface, between the condyles
	Anterior intercondylar fossa	small depression between condyles anterior to the eminence and serves as a point of attachment for ligaments
	Posterior intercondylar fossa	small depression between condyles posterior to the eminence and serves as a point of attachment for ligaments
	Tibial tuberosity	anterior and superior projection
	Shaft	
	Fibular notch	lateral and distal and articulates with fibula
	Articular facet	surface inferior to the lateral condyle that articulates with fibula
	Inferior articulating facet	depression on inferior surface of tibia that articulates with talus
	Medial malleolus	projection on the medial and distal side
Fibula		**long slender bones on the lateral side of the lower leg**
	Head	rounded proximal end
	Tibial facet	medial side of head, articulates with the articular facet of the tibia
	Shaft	
	Articulating facet for talus	smooth surface, inferior and medial and articulates with talus (more anterior)
	Lateral malleolus	projection on the lateral and distal side
Tarsals		
Talus		**has large rounded top**
	Trochlea	rounded superior surface that tibia articulates with

	Calcaneus	largest tarsal, heel bone
	Calcaneal tuberosity	posterior and inferior projection that we stand on
	Sustentaculum tali	medial projection on the superior surface that supports the talus
	Navicular	**anterior to talus, on medial side**
	Cuboid	**anterior to calcaneus, on lateral side**
	Cuneiforms (3)	**anterior to navicular, medial to cuboid**
	Medial (I)	
	Intermediate (II)	
	Lateral (III)	
	Metatarsals	five bones, numbered from the medial (Big Toes) side
	Phalanges (Phalanx for one)	**each toe has 3 except the big toe that only has 2**
	Proximal	
	Middle	big toe does not have middle
	Distal	

Appendicular Skeleton

Learning Outcomes

On completion of this exercise, you should be able to:

1. Identify the bones and surface features of the pectoral girdle and upper limbs.

2. Articulate the clavicle with the scapula.

3. Articulate the scapula, humerus, radius, and ulna.

4. Identify the bones and surface features of the pelvic girdle and lower limbs.

5. Articulate the coxal bones with the sacrum to form the pelvis.

6. Articulate the coxa, femur, tibia, and fibula.

The appendicular skeleton provides the bony structure of the limbs, permitting us to move and to interact with our surroundings. It is attached to the vertebral column and sternum of the axial skeleton. The appendicular skeleton consists of two pectoral girdles and the attached upper limbs and a pelvic girdle and the attached lower limbs (Figure 1). The pectoral girdle is loosely attached to the axial skeleton, and as a result the shoulder joints have a great range of movement. The pelvic girdle is securely attached to the sacrum of the spine to support the weight of the body.

Make a Prediction

How much does the pelvic girdle move in comparison to the pectoral girdle? Support your prediction with anatomical observations of both girdles.

Need More Practice and Review?

Build your knowledge—and confidence!—in the Study Area of MasteringA&P® at www.masteringaandp.com with Pre-lab Quizzes, Post-lab Quizzes, Practice Anatomy Lab™ (PAL™) 3.0 virtual anatomy practice tool, PhysioEx™ 9.0 laboratory simulations, and A&P Flix™ with Quizzes.

PAL ｜practice anatomy lab For this lab exercise, follow these navigation paths:
  • PAL>Human Cadaver>Appendicular Skeleton
  • PAL>Anatomical Models>Appendicular Skeleton

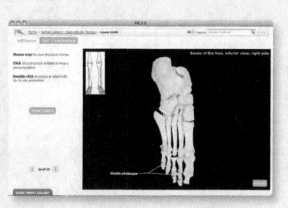

From Exercise 15 of *Laboratory Manual for Anatomy & Physiology featuring Martini Art*, Fifth Edition. Michael G. Wood.
Copyright © 2013 by Pearson Education, Inc. All rights reserved.

Figure 1 **The Appendicular Skeleton** An anterior view of the skeleton detailing the appendicular components. The numbers in the boxes indicate the number of bones in each type or within each category.

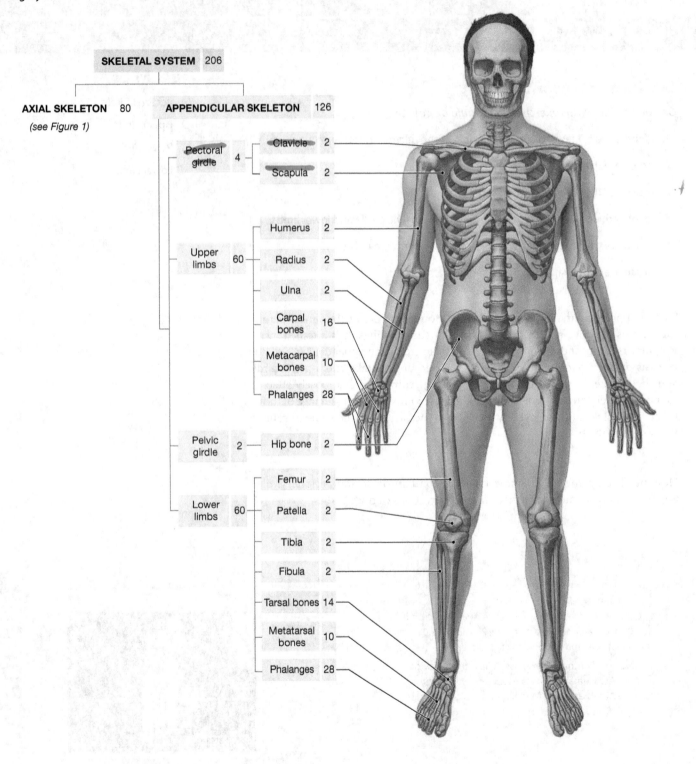

As you study the appendicular skeleton, keep in mind that each bone is one member of a left/right pair. Carefully observe the orientation of major surface features on the bones and use these features as landmarks for determining whether a given bone is from the left side of the body or from the right side.

Lab Activity 1 Pectoral Girdle

The **pectoral girdle** consist of four bones: two *clavicles*, commonly called collarbones, and two *scapulae*, the shoulder blades. These four bones are arranged in an incomplete ring that constitutes the bony architecture of the superior trunk. Each scapula rests against the posterior surface of the rib cage and against a clavicle, and provides an anchor for tendons of arm and shoulder muscles. The clavicles are like struts, providing support by connecting the scapulae to the sternum.

Clavicle

The S-shaped **clavicle** (KLAV-i-kul) is the only bony connection between the pectoral girdle and the axial skeleton. The **sternal end** articulates medially with the sternum, and laterally the flat **acromial** (a-KRO-mě-al) **end** joins the scapula (**Figure 2**). Inferiorly, toward the acromial end, where the clavicle bends, is the **conoid tubercle,** an attachment site for the coracoclavicular ligament. Near the inferior sternal end is the rough **costal tuberosity.**

The sternal end of the clavicle articulates lateral to the jugular notch on the manubrium of the sternum. The point where these two bones articulate is called the **sternoclavicular joint.** From this joint, the clavicle curves posterior and articulates with the scapula at the **acromioclavicular joint.**

Scapula

The **scapula** (SKAP-ū-la) is composed of a triangular **body** defined by long edges called the **superior, medial,** and **lateral borders** (**Figure 3**). The corners where the borders meet are the **superior, lateral,** and **inferior angles.** An indentation in the superior border is the **suprascapular notch.** The **subscapular fossa** is the smooth, triangular surface where the anterior surface of the scapula faces the ribs.

A prominent ridge, the **spine,** extends across the scapula body on the posterior surface and divides the convex surface into the **supraspinous fossa** superior to the spine and the **infraspinous fossa** inferiorly. At the lateral tip of the spine is the **acromion** (a-KRŌ-mē-on), which is superior to the **glenoid cavity** (also called the *glenoid fossa*) where the humerus articulates. Superior and inferior to the glenoid cavity are the **supraglenoid** and **infraglenoid tubercles** where the biceps brachii and triceps brachii muscles of the arm attach. Superior to the glenoid cavity is the beak-shaped **coracoid** (KOR-uh-koyd) **process.** The **scapular neck** is the ring of bone around the base of the coracoid process and the glenoid cavity.

QuickCheck Questions

1.1 Which bones form the pectoral girdle?

1.2 Where does the clavicle articulate with the axial skeleton?

Figure 2 The Clavicle

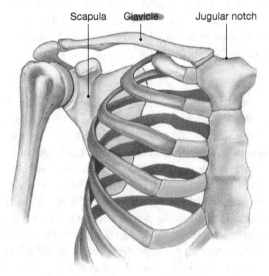

a The position of the clavicle within the pectoral girdle, anterior view.

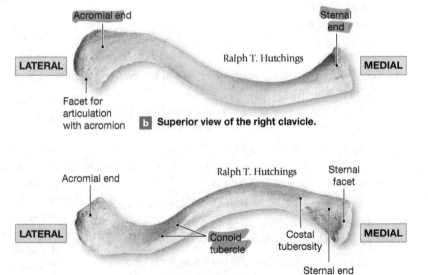

b Superior view of the right clavicle.

c Inferior view of the right clavicle. Stabilizing ligaments attach to the conoid tubercle and the costal tuberosity.

Figure 3 **The Scapula**

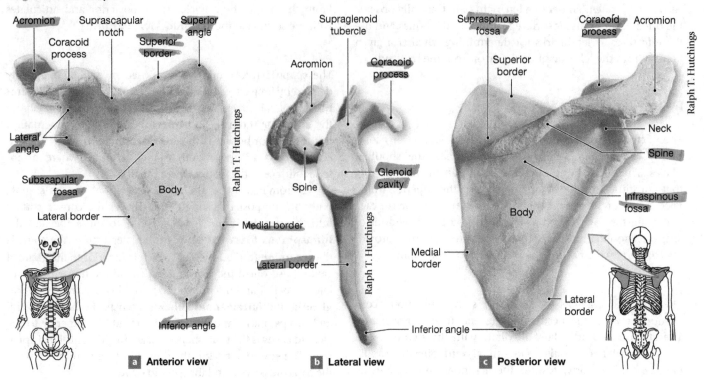

a Anterior view

b Lateral view

c Posterior view

Materials

☐ Articulated skeleton

☐ Disarticulated skeleton

Procedures

1. Locate a clavicle on the study skeleton and review the anatomy shown in Figure 2.

   ▪ Identify the sternal and acromial ends of the clavicle. Can you feel these ends on your own clavicles?

   ▪ Identify the conoid tubercle of the clavicle.

2. Locate a scapula on the study skeleton. Review the surface features of the scapula in Figure 3.

   ▪ Identify the borders, angles, and fossae of the scapula.

   ▪ Identify the spine, the acromion, the coracoid process, and the glenoid cavity.

   ▪ Can you feel the spine and acromion on your own scapula?

3. Place a clavicle from the disarticulated skeleton on your shoulder and determine how it would articulate with your scapula. ▪

Lab Activity 2   Upper Limb

Each **upper limb,** also called an *upper extremity*, includes the bones of the arm, forearm, and hand—a total of 30 bones, with all but three of them in the wrist and hand. Note that the correct anatomical usage of the term *arm* is in reference to the **brachium,** the part of the upper limb between the shoulder and elbow.

Humerus

The bone of the **arm** (brachium) is the **humerus,** shown in Figure 4. The proximal **head** articulates with the glenoid cavity of the scapula. Lateral to the head is the **greater tubercle,** and medial to the head is the **lesser tubercle;** both are sites for muscle tendon attachment. The **intertubercular groove** separates the tubercles. Between the head and the tubercles is the **anatomical neck;** inferior to the tubercles is the **surgical neck.** Inferior to the greater tubercle is the rough **deltoid tuberosity,** where the deltoid muscle of the shoulder attaches. Along the diaphysis, at the inferior termination of the deltoid tuberosity, is the **radial groove,** a depression that serves as the passageway for the radial nerve.

The distal end of the humerus has a specialized **condyle** to accommodate two joints: the hingelike elbow joint and a pivot joint of the forearm, the latter used when doing

Figure 4 The Humerus

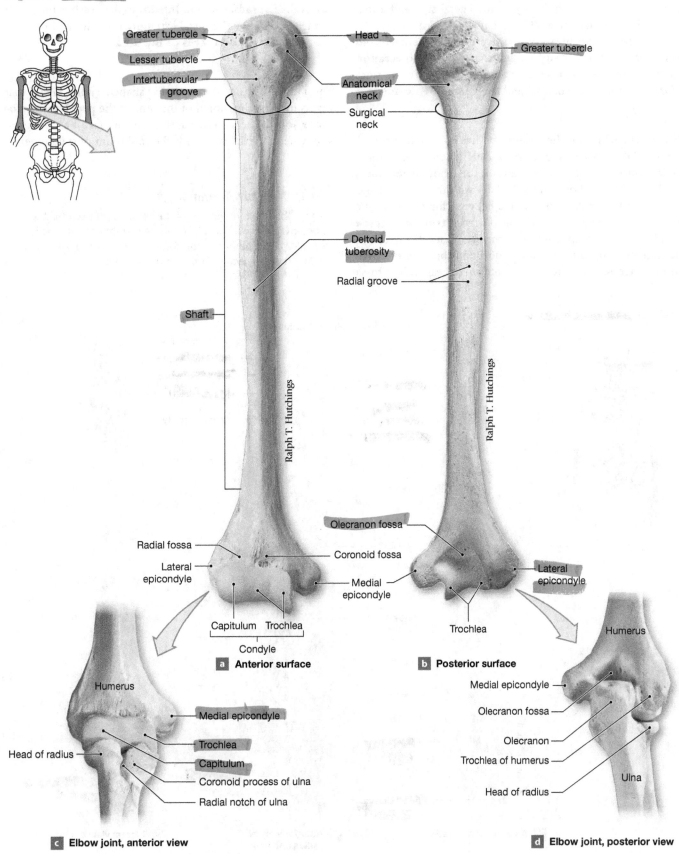

Greater tubercle

Lesser tubercle

Intertubercular groove

Head

Greater tubercle

Anatomical neck

Surgical neck

Deltoid tuberosity

Radial groove

Shaft

Ralph T. Hutchings

Ralph T. Hutchings

Olecranon fossa

Radial fossa

Coronoid fossa

Lateral epicondyle

Medial epicondyle

Lateral epicondyle

Capitulum   Trochlea

Condyle

Trochlea

Humerus

a **Anterior surface**

b **Posterior surface**

Humerus

Medial epicondyle

Medial epicondyle

Trochlea

Olecranon fossa

Head of radius

Capitulum

Olecranon

Coronoid process of ulna

Trochlea of humerus

Radial notch of ulna

Head of radius

Ulna

c **Elbow joint, anterior view**

d **Elbow joint, posterior view**

such movements as turning a doorknob. The condyle has a round **capitulum** (*capit,* head) on the lateral side and a medial cylindrical **trochlea** (TROK-lē-uh) (*trochlea,* a pulley). Superior to the trochlea are two depressions, the **coronoid fossa** on the anterior surface and the triangular **olecranon** (ō-LEK-ruh-non) **fossa** on the posterior surface. To the sides of the condyle are the **medial** and larger **lateral epicondyles.**

Ulna

The **antebrachium** is the *forearm* and has two parallel bones, the medial **ulna** and the lateral **radius** (Figure 5), both of which articulate with the humerus at the elbow. The ulna is the larger forearm bone and articulates with the humerus and radius. A fibrocartilage disc occurs between the ulna and the wrist. The ulna has a conspicuous U-shaped **trochlear notch** that is like a C clamp, with two processes that articulate with the humerus: the superior **olecranon** and the inferior **coronoid process.** Each process fits into its corresponding fossa

on the humerus. On the lateral surface of the coronoid process is the flat **radial notch.** Inferior to the notch is the rough **ulnar tuberosity.** The distal extremity is the **ulnar head** and the pointed **styloid process of the ulna.**

Radius

The radius (Figure 5) has a disc-shaped **radial head** that pivots in the radial notch of the ulna at the **proximal radio-ulnar joint.** The superior surface of the head has a depression where it articulates with the capitulum of the humerus.

> **Study Tip Elbow Terminology**
>
> Notice that the terminology of the elbow is consistent in the humerus and ulna. The trochlear notch of the ulna fits into the trochlea of the humerus. The coronoid process and olecranon fit into their respective fossae on the humerus. ■

Figure 5 The Radius and Ulna

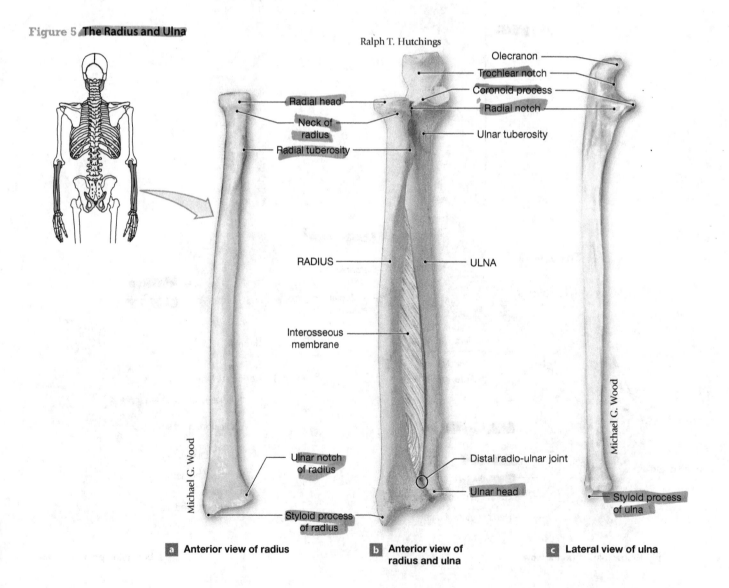

Ralph T. Hutchings

Michael G. Wood

Michael G. Wood

- Radial head
- Neck of radius
- Radial tuberosity
- Olecranon
- Trochlear notch
- Coronoid process
- Radial notch
- Ulnar tuberosity
- RADIUS
- ULNA
- Interosseous membrane
- Ulnar notch of radius
- Distal radio-ulnar joint
- Ulnar head
- Styloid process of radius
- Styloid process of ulna

a Anterior view of radius

b Anterior view of radius and ulna

c Lateral view of ulna

Supporting the head is the **neck,** and inferior to the neck is the **radial tuberosity.** On the distal portion, the **styloid process of the radius** is larger and not as pointed as the styloid process of the ulna. The **ulnar notch** on the medial surface articulates with the ulna at the **distal radioulnar joint.** The **interosseous membrane** extends between the ulna and radius to support the bones.

Bones of the Hand

The **carpus** is the *wrist* and consists of eight **carpal** (KAR-pul) **bones** arranged in two rows of four, the **proximal** and **distal carpal bones.** An easy method of identifying the carpal bones is to use the anterior wrist and start with the carpal bone next to the styloid process of the radius (**Figure 6**). From this reference point moving medially, the proximal carpal bones are the **scaphoid bone, lunate bone, triquetrum,** and small **pisiform** (PIS-i-form) **bone.** Returning on the lateral side, the four distal carpal bones are the **trapezium, trapezoid bone, capitate bone,** and **hamate bone.** The hamate bone has a process called the **hook of the hamate.**

The five long bones of the palm are **metacarpal bones.** Each metacarpal bone is numbered with a roman numeral, with the lateral metacarpal bone that articulates with the thumb being digit I.

The 14 bones of the fingers are called **phalanges.** Digits II, III, IV, and V each have a **proximal, middle,** and **distal phalanx.** The thumb, or **pollex,** has only proximal and distal phalanges.

QuickCheck Questions

2.1 List the three bones that constitute the arm and forearm.

2.2 What are the three major groups of bones in the hand?

In the Lab 2

Materials

☐ Articulated skeleton

☐ Disarticulated skeleton

Procedures

1. Review the anatomy of the humerus in Figure 4.

2. Locate a humerus of your study skeleton and review its surface features.

   ▪ Identify the head, surgical and anatomical necks, tubercles, and intertubercular groove.

   ▪ Identify the deltoid tuberosity and radial groove.

Figure 6 **Bones of the Hand**

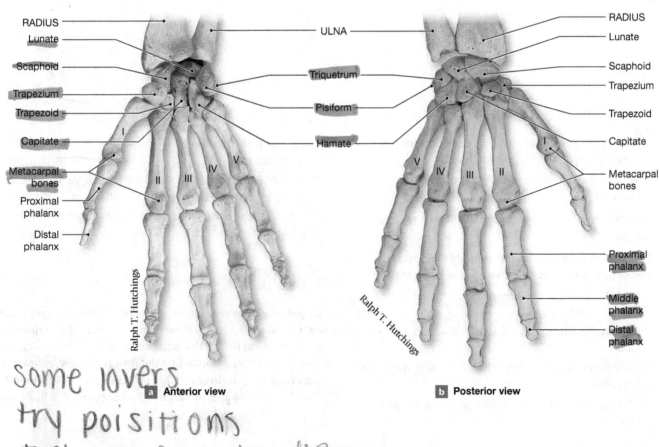

RADIUS
Lunate
Scaphoid
Trapezium
Trapezoid
Capitate
Metacarpal bones
Proximal phalanx
Distal phalanx

ULNA
Triquetrum
Pisiform
Hamate

RADIUS
Lunate
Scaphoid
Trapezium
Trapezoid
Capitate
Metacarpal bones
Proximal phalanx
Middle phalanx
Distal phalanx

Ralph T. Hutchings

a Anterior view

b Posterior view

some lovers try poisitions that they can't handle

Sketch to Learn

Make a quick sketch of the distal end of the humerus to help you remember all those bony features.

Sample Sketch

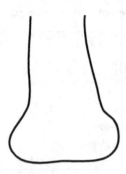 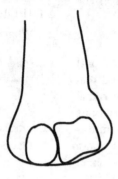 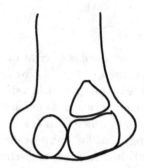

Step 1
- Draw a bell shape (the sides represent the epicondyles).

Step 2
- Add a circle for the capitulum.
- Sketch in a rectangle with top and bottom lines curving inward. This represents the trochlea.

Step 3
- Add a triangle fossa above the trochlea.
- Label your sketch.

Your Sketch

- Identify the epicondyles and the condyle. Can you feel the epicondyles on your own humerus?
- Identify the capitulum, trochlea, and fossae of the distal humerus.

For additional practice, complete the *Sketch to Learn* activity.

3. Locate an ulna and radius of your study skeleton and review their surface features using Figure 5 as reference.
   - Study the processes that fit into the corresponding fossae of the humerus.
   - Identify the articulating anatomy between the ulna and radius.
4. Review Figure 6 and locate the bones of the hand on the study skeleton.
   - Distinguish between the carpals, metacarpals, and phalanges.

- Identify the four proximal carpals and the four distal carpals.
- Identify the metacarpals and the phalanges. Do all the fingers have the same number of phalanges?

5. Articulate the bones of the upper limb with those of the pectoral girdle. ■

Lab Activity 3 Pelvic Girdle

The **pelvic girdle** is made up of the two hipbones, called the **coxal bones,** which articulate with the vertebral column and attach the lower limbs. The coxal bone, also called the *os coxae* (plural *ossa coxae*) is formed by the fusion of three bones: the **ilium** (IL-ē-um), **ischium** (IS-kē-um), and **pubis** (PŪ-bis). By 20 to 25 years of age, these three bones ossify and fuse into a single os coxae, but the three bones are still referred to and used to name related structures. The **pelvis** is the bony ring of the two coxal bones of the appendicular skeleton and the sacrum and coccyx of the axial skeleton.

Coxal Bone

A conspicuous feature of the coxal bone is the deep socket, the **acetabulum** (a-se-TAB-ū -lum), where the head of the femur articulates (**Figure 7**). The smooth inner wall of the acetabulum is the C-shaped **lunate surface.** The center of the acetabulum is the **acetabular fossa.** The anterior and inferior rims of the acetabulum are not continuous; instead, there is an open gap between them, the **acetabular notch.**

The superior ridge of the ilium is the **iliac crest.** It is shaped like a shovel blade, with the **anterior** and **posterior superior iliac spines** at each end. The large indentation below the posterior superior iliac spine is the **greater sciatic (sī-A-tik) notch.** A conspicuous feature on the posterior iliac crest is the rough **auricular surface,** where the **sacroiliac joint** attaches the pelvic girdle to the sacrum of the axial skeleton. On the flat expanse of the ilium are ridges, the **anterior, posterior,** and **inferior gluteal lines,** which are attachment sites for muscles that move the femur.

The ischium is the bone we sit on. The greater sciatic notch terminates at a bony point, the **ischial spine.** Inferior to this spine is the **lesser sciatic notch.** The **ischial tuberosity** is in

Figure 7 The Pelvic Girdle

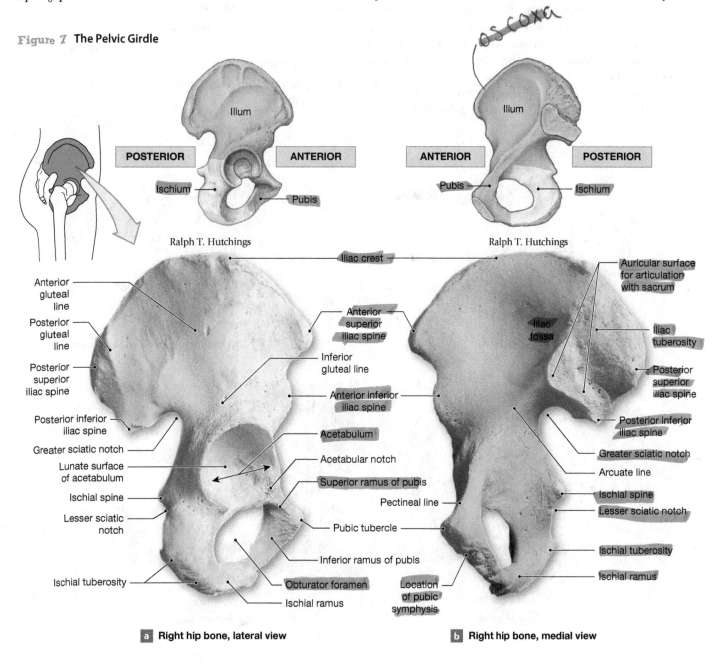

Ralph T. Hutchings

Ralph T. Hutchings

a Right hip bone, lateral view

b Right hip bone, medial view

the most inferior portion of the ischium and is a site for muscle attachment. The **ischial ramus** extends from the tuberosity and fuses with the pubis bone.

The pubis forms the anterior portion of the coxal bone. The most anterior region of the pubis is the pointed **pubic tubercle.** The **superior ramus** of the pubis is above the tubercle and extends to the ilium. On the medial surface, the superior ramus narrows to a rim called the **pectineal line** of the pubis. The **inferior ramus** joins the ischial ramus, creating the **obturator** (OB-tŭ-rā-tor) **foramen.**

The pelvis has three articulations; two **sarcoiliac joints** between the coxal bones and sacrum, and the **pubic symphysis,** a strong joint of fibrocartilage holding the pubis bones together (**Figure 8**). On the medial surface of each os coxae, the **iliac fossa** forms the wall of the upper pelvis, called the **false pelvis.** The **arcuate line** on this same surface marks where the pelvis narrows into the lower pelvis, called the **true pelvis.**

The pelvis of the male differs anatomically from that of the female (Figure 8c, d). The female pelvis has a wider pelvic outlet, which is the space between the two ischii. The circle formed by the top of the pelvis, called the **brim,** defines the **pelvic inlet.** This opening is wider and rounder in females. Additionally, the **pubic angle** at the pubis symphysis is wider in the female and more U-shaped. This angle is V-shaped in the male. The wider female pelvis provides a larger passageway for childbirth.

Make a Prediction

How much does the pelvic girdle move in comparison to the pectoral girdle? Support your prediction with anatomical observations of both girdles.

QuickCheck Questions

3.1 Which bones make up the pelvic girdle?

3.2 With what structure of the pelvic girdle does the lower limb articulate?

3.3 Explain the difference between the terms *pelvic girdle* and *pelvis.*

Figure 8 The Pelvis

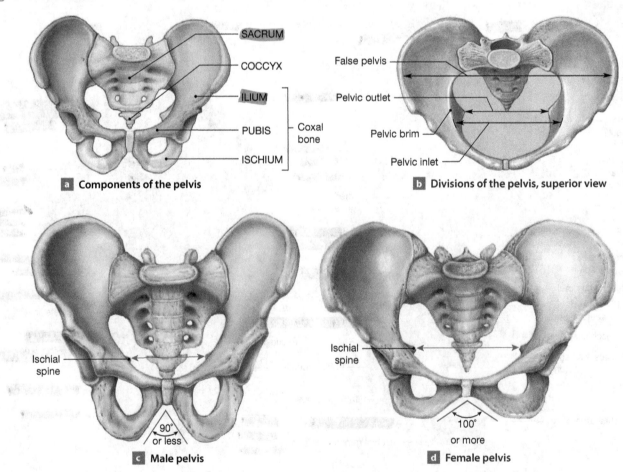

a **Components of the pelvis**

b **Divisions of the pelvis, superior view**

c **Male pelvis**

d **Female pelvis**

In the Lab 3

Materials

☐ Articulated skeleton
☐ Disarticulated skeleton

Procedures

1. Locate a coxal bone on your study skeleton and review the anatomy in Figures 7 and 8.

2. Identify the ilium, ischium, and pubis bones.

   ▪ Are sutures visible where these bones fused?

   ▪ Locate the acetabulum and obturator foramen.

   ▪ Identify other features of the ilium.

3. Trace along the iliac crest and down the posterior surface.

   ▪ Identify the greater and lesser sciatic notches and the ischial spine.

   ▪ What is the large rough area on the inferior ischium called?

   ▪ Identify other features of the ischium and pubis.

4. Locate the auricular surface of the sacroiliac joint and the pubic symphysis.

5. Articulate the two coxal bones and the sacrum to form the pelvis.

6. Examine the pelvis on several articulated skeletons in the laboratory. How can you distinguish a male pelvis from a female pelvis? ▪

Lab Activity 4 Lower Limb

Each **lower limb,** also called the *lower extremity*, includes the bones of the thigh, knee, leg, and foot—a total of 30 bones. Recall that the term *leg* refers not to the entire lower limb but only to the region between the knee and ankle. Superior to the leg is the *thigh*.

The Femur

The **femur** is the largest bone of the skeleton (Figure 9). It supports the body's weight and bears the stress from the leg. The smooth, round **head** fits into the acetabulum of the coxal bone and permits the femur a wide range of movement. The depression on the head is the **fovea capitis,** where the *ligamentum capitis femoris* stabilizes the hip joint during movement. A narrow **neck** joins the head to the proximal shaft. Lateral to the head is a large stump, the **greater trochanter** (trō-KAN-ter); on the inferiomedial surface is the **lesser trochanter.** These large processes are attachment sites for tendons of powerful hip and thigh muscles. On the anterior surface of the femur, between the trochanters, is the **intertrochanteric line,** where the *iliofemoral ligament* inserts to encase the hip joint. Posteriorly, the **intertrochanteric crest** lies between the trochanters.

On the lateral side of the intertrochanteric crest, the **gluteal tuberosity** continues inferiorly and joins with the medial **pectineal line** of the femur as the **linea aspera,** a rough line for thigh muscle attachment. Toward the distal end of the femur, the linea aspera divides into the **medial** and **lateral supracondylar ridges** encompassing a flat triangle called the **popliteal surface.** The medial supracondylar ridge terminates at the **adductor tubercle.**

The largest condyles of the skeleton are the **lateral** and **medial condyles** of the femur, which articulate with the tibial head. The condyles are separated posteriorly by the **intercondylar fossa.** A smooth **patellar surface** spans the condyles and serves as a gliding platform for the patella. To the sides of the condyles are **lateral** and **medial epicondyles.**

The Patella

The **patella** is the kneecap and protects the knee joint during movement. It is a sesamoid bone encased in the distal tendons of the anterior thigh muscles. The superior border of the patella is the flat **base;** the **apex** is at the inferior tip (Figure 10). Along the base is the attachment site of the quadriceps muscle tendons that straighten (*extend*) the leg. The patellar ligament joins around the apex of the bone. Tendons attach to the rough anterior surface, and the smooth posterior facets glide over the condyles of the femur. The **medial facet** is narrower than the **lateral facet.**

The Tibia

The **tibia** (TI-bē-uh) is the large medial bone of the leg (Figure 11). The proximal portion of the tibia flares to develop the **lateral** and **medial condyles,** which articulate with the corresponding femoral condyles. Separating the tibial condyles is a ridge of bone, the **intercondylar eminence.** This eminence has two projections, the **medial** and **lateral tubercles,** that fit into the intercondylar fossa of the femur. On the anterior surface of the tibia, inferior to the condyles, is the large **tibial tuberosity,** where the patellar

Study Tip Patella Pointers

It is easy to distinguish a right patella from a left one. Lay the bone on its facets, and point the apex away from you. Notice that the bone leans to one side. Because the lateral facet is larger, the bone will tilt and lean on that facet. Therefore, if the patella leans to the left, it is a left patella. ▪

Figure 9 The Femur

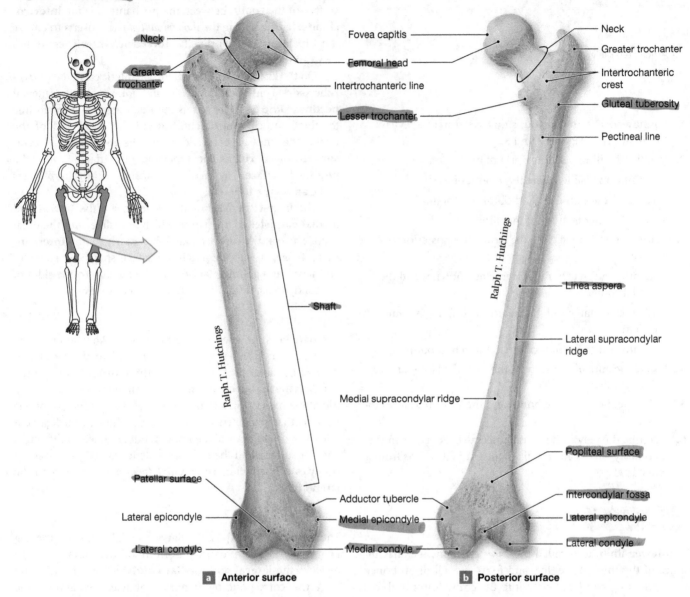

Neck

Greater trochanter

Fovea capitis

Femoral head

Intertrochanteric line

Lesser trochanter

Neck

Greater trochanter

Intertrochanteric crest

Gluteal tuberosity

Pectineal line

Ralph T. Hutchings

Ralph T. Hutchings

Shaft

Linea aspera

Lateral supracondylar ridge

Medial supracondylar ridge

Popliteal surface

Patellar surface

Lateral epicondyle

Lateral condyle

Adductor tubercle

Medial epicondyle

Medial condyle

Intercondylar fossa

Lateral epicondyle

Lateral condyle

a Anterior surface

b Posterior surface

Figure 10 The Patella The right patella.

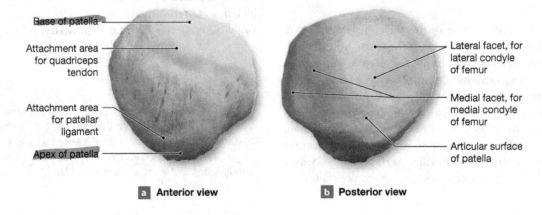

Base of patella

Attachment area for quadriceps tendon

Attachment area for patellar ligament

Apex of patella

Lateral facet, for lateral condyle of femur

Medial facet, for medial condyle of femur

Articular surface of patella

a Anterior view

b Posterior view

Figure 11 The Tibia and Fibula Bones of the right leg.

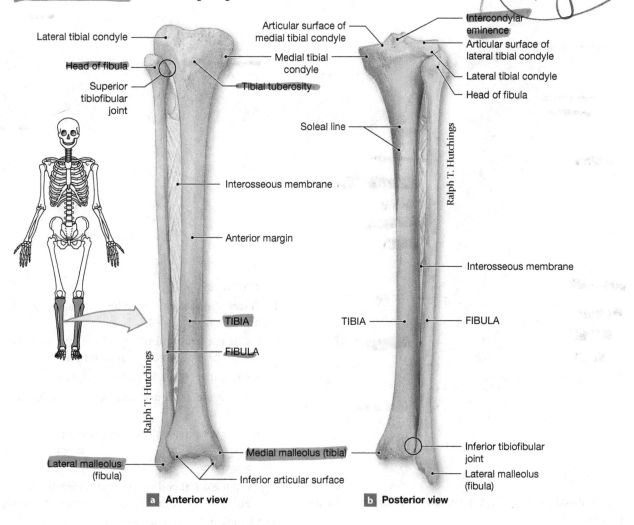

a **Anterior view**

b **Posterior view**

ligament attaches. Along most of the length of the anterior shaft is the **anterior margin,** a ridge commonly called the *shin*. The distal tibia is constructed to articulate with the ankle. A large wedge, the **medial malleolus** (ma-LĒ-rō-lus) **of the tibia,** stabilizes the ankle joint. The inferior **articular surface** is smooth so that it can slide over the talus of the ankle. Posteriorly, the proximal tibial shaft has a rough line, the **popliteal line,** where leg muscles attach.

The Fibula

The **fibula** (FIB-ū-la) is the slender bone lateral to the tibia (Figure 11). The proximal and distal regions of the fibula appear very similar at first, but closer examination reveals the proximal head to be more rounded (less pointed) than the distal **lateral malleolus of the fibula.** The head of the fibula articulates below the lateral condyle of the tibia at the **superior tibiofibular joint.** The distal articulation creates the **inferior tibiofibular joint.**

Study Tip Hands and Feet

Because their names are so similar, it is easy to confuse the carpal and metacarpal bones of the wrist and hand with the tarsal and metatarsal bones of the ankle and foot. Just remember, when you listen to music you *clap* your *carpal bones* and *tap* your *tarsal bones*! ■

Bones of the Foot

The ankle is formed by seven **tarsal bones** (Figure 12). One of them, the **talus** (TĀ-lus), sits on top of the heel bone, the **calcaneus** (kal-KĀ-nē-us), and articulates with the tibia and the lateral malleolus of the fibula. Anterior to the talus is the tarsal bone called the **navicular bone,** which articulates with the **medial, intermediate,** and **lateral cuneiform** (kū-NĒ-i-form) **bones.** Lateral to the lateral cuneiform bone

Figure 12 Bones of the Foot

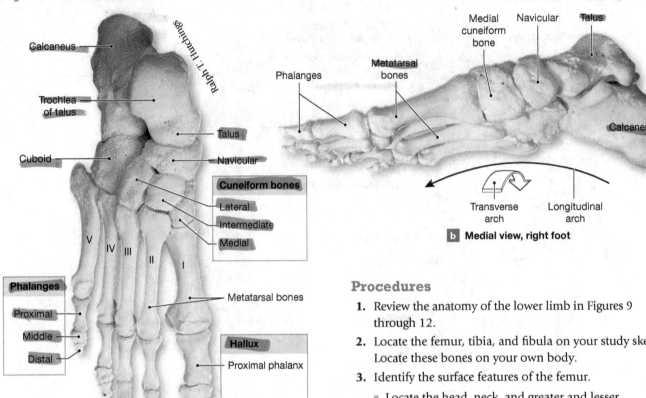

Calcaneus

Trochlea of talus

Cuboid

Talus

Navicular

Cuneiform bones
Lateral
Intermediate
Medial

V IV III II I

Phalanges
Proximal
Middle
Distal

Metatarsal bones

Hallux
Proximal phalanx
Distal phalanx

a Superior view, right foot

Medial cuneiform bone Navicular Talus

Phalanges

Metatarsal bones

Calcaneus

Transverse arch Longitudinal arch

b Medial view, right foot

Ralph T. Hutchings

is the **cuboid bone,** which articulates posteriorly with the calcaneus.

The arch of the foot is formed by five **metatarsal bones.** Each metatarsal bone is named with a roman numeral, with the medial metatarsal that articulates with the big toe being designated as toe I.

The 14 bones of the toes are called **phalanges.** Like the fingers of the hand, toes II through V have a **proximal, middle,** and **distal phalanx.** The big toe, or **hallux,** has only a proximal and a distal phalanx.

QuickCheck Questions

4.1 What are the bones of the thigh, knee, and leg?

4.2 What are the three major groups of bones in the foot?

`In the Lab  4`

Materials

☐ Articulated skeleton
☐ Disarticulated skeleton

Procedures

1. Review the anatomy of the lower limb in Figures 9 through 12.
2. Locate the femur, tibia, and fibula on your study skeleton. Locate these bones on your own body.
3. Identify the surface features of the femur.
   - Locate the head, neck, and greater and lesser trochanters.
   - Trace your hand along the posterior of the diaphysis and feel the linea aspera. What attaches to this rough structure?
   - On the distal end of the femur, identify the epicondyles, condyles, and intercondylar fossa.
4. Identify the surface features of the patella.
   - Examine the two facets of the patella.
   - How can the facets be used to determine whether the patella is from a right leg or a left one?
5. Review the anatomy of the tibia and fibula.
   - What is the ridge on the tibial head called?
   - On the tibia, locate the condyles and the tibial tuberosity.
   - On the distal tibia, locate the medial malleolus.
   - Locate the lateral malleolus of the fibula. How does its shape differ from the fibular head?
6. Identify the bones of the foot.
   - Identify the tarsals, metatarsals, and phalanges.
   - Which tarsal bone directly receives body weight?
   - Which bones form the arch of the foot?
   - Do the toes all have the same number of phalanges?
7. Articulate the bones of the lower limb with the pelvis. ■

Name Nicole Villa

Date

Section

Appendicular Skeleton

PPE next week

A. Matching

Match each surface feature in the left column with its correct bone from the right column. Each choice from the right column may be used more than once.

_____	1. acromion	A. clavicle
_____	2. intercondylar fossa	B. patella
_____	3. trochlea	C. fibula
_____	4. glenoid cavity	D. humerus
_____	5. ulnar notch	E. femur
_____	6. deltoid tuberosity	F. scapula
_____	7. greater trochanter	G. tibia
_____	8. sternal end	H. radius
_____	9. lateral malleolus	
_____	10. linea aspera	
_____	11. capitulum	
_____	12. medial malleolus	
_____	13. intercondylar eminence	
_____	14. base	

B. Short-Answer Questions

1. List the bones of the pectoral girdle and the upper limb.

2. List the bones of the pelvic girdle and the lower limb.

3. Compare the pelvis of males and females.

4. Which bony process acts like a doorstop to prevent excessive movement of the elbow?

5. On what two structures does the radial head pivot during movements such as turning a doorknob?

6. How are the carpal bones arranged in the wrist?

7. Where is the deltoid tuberosity located?

8. Which appendicular bones have a styloid process?

9. Which bone of the ankle articulates with the tibia?

10. What are the major features of the proximal portion of the femur?

11. Do the toes all have the same number of phalanges?

12. Which bones form the arch of the foot?

13. What is the ridge on the tibial head called?

14. Where is the glenoid cavity located?

C. Labeling

1. Label the surface features of the scapula in Figure 13.

Figure 13 Posterior Surface of Right Scapula

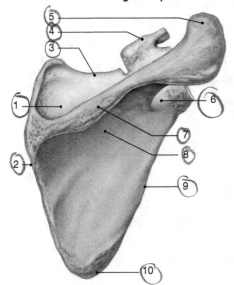

1. supraspinous process
2. medial border
3. superior border
4. corocoid process
5. acromonion
6. lateral angle
7. spine
8. intraspinous fossa
9. lateral border
10. inferior angle

2. Label the surface features of the coxal bone in Figure 14.

Figure 14 Right Coxal Bone

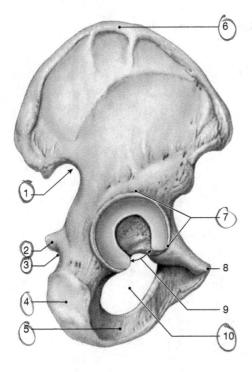

1. greater sciatic notch
2. ischial spine
3. lesser sciatic notch
4. ischial tuberosity
5. ischial ramus
6. illiac crest
7. acetebelum
8. _____
9. _____
10. obturator foramen

3. Label the surface features of the foot in Figure 15.

Figure 15 Right Foot

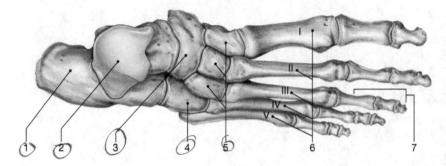

1. calcaneous
2. talus
3. navicular
4. cuboid
5. cuneiforms
6. metatarsals
7. phalanges

D. Analysis and Application

1. Describe the condyle of the humerus where the ulna and radius articulate.

2. Compare the bones of the hand with the bones of the foot.

3. Name a tuberosity for shoulder muscle attachment and a tuberosity for thigh muscle attachment.

E. Clinical Challenge

The clavicle can break when catching a fall with outstretched hands. Describe how the impact on the hands could cause damage to the clavicle.

Articulations Wish List

In previous wish lists, we provided a description of each structure next to its name to help you ID and remember such structure. As you go through this list and the activities associated with the chapter on Articulations, add identifying characteristics using correct anatomical terminology to help you remember the location of these items.

✓	Item	Description
	Skull + Thoracic Joints	
	sagittal suture	from frontal → occipital
	coronal suture	Separates frontal / parietal
	lamboidal suture	Separates parietal / occipital
	temporomandibular joint	round part of mandible meets temporal
	atlanto-occipital joint	occipital atlas
	atlanto-axial joint	atlas to axis
	intervertebral joint sternoclavicular joint	inbetween vertebrae	clavicle meets sternum
	sternocostal joint	sternum → ribs
	vertebrocostal joint	ribs → vertebrae

✓	Item	Description
✓	**Shoulder Joint (glenohumeral)**	
	coracoacromial ligament	coracoid process to acromion
	acromioclavicular ligament	acromion to clavicle
	coracoclavicular ligament	coracoid process to clavicle
	coracohumeral ligament	coracoid process to humerus
	glenohumeral ligament	glenoid cavity to humerus

✓	Item	Description
✓	**Elbow Joint (humeroulnar + humeroradial)**	
	articular capsule	capsule around joint
	annular ligament	circular, radius → ulna
	ulnar collateral ligament	humerus → ulna (triangle)

✓	Item	Description
✓	**Wrist and Hand Joints**	
	radioulnar joint (proximal, distal)	radius to ulna
	radiocarpal articulation	radius to carpals
	intercarpal joint	carpal to carpal
	carpometacarpal joint	carpal to metacarpal
	metacarpalphalangeal joint	metacarpal to phalange

	interphalangeal joint (proximal, distal)	

✓	**Pelvic Joints**	
	sacroiliac joint	sacrum to iliac
	pubic symphysis	superior rami
	sacrococcygeal joint	
	ischiofemoral ligament	
	iliofemoral ligament	
	pubofemoral ligament	
	acetabulofemoral joint (hip joint)	

✓	**Knee Joint**	
	tibiofibular joint (proximal, distal)	tibia to fibula
	tibial collateral ligament	tibia to femur
	fibular collateral ligament	fibula to femur
	medial meniscus	cartilage medial
	lateral meniscus	cartilage lateral
	patellar ligament	patella to tibia
	anterior cruciate ligament	front
	posterior cruciate ligament	back

	Ankle and Foot Joints	
	talocrural joint	ankle
	intertarsal joint	in between tarsals
	tarsometatarsal joint	tarsals → metatarsals
	metatarsalphalangeal joint	metatarsals → phalanges
	interphalangeal joint (proximal, distal)	phalange → phalange

Articulations

Learning Outcomes

On completion of this exercise, you should be able to:

1. List the three types of functional joints and give an example of each.

2. List the four types of structural joints and give an example of each.

3. Describe the three types of diarthroses and the movement each produces.

4. Describe the anatomy of a typical synovial joint.

5. Describe and demonstrate the various movements of synovial joints.

Arthrology is the study of the structure and function of **joints;** a joint is defined as any location where two or more bones articulate. (In anatomic terminology, a synonym for *joint* is **articulation.**) If you were asked to identify joints in your body, you would most likely name those that allow a large range of movement, such as your knee or hip joint. In large-range joints like these, a cavity between the two bones of the joint permits free movement. In some joints, however, the bones are held closely together, a condition that allows no movement; an example of this type of nonmoving joint is found in the bones of the cranium.

Some individuals have more movement in a particular joint than most other people and are called "double jointed." Of course, they do not have two joints; the additional movement is a result of either the anatomy of the articulating bones or the position of tendons and ligaments around the joint.

Lab Activities

1 Joint Classification

2 Structure of Synovial Joints

3 Types of Diarthroses

4 Skeletal Movement at Diarthrotic Joints

5 Selected Synovial Joints: Elbow and Knee Joints

Clinical Application

Arthritis

Need More Practice and Review?

Build your knowledge—and confidence!—in the Study Area of MasteringA&P® at www.masteringaandp.com with Pre-lab Quizzes, Post-lab Quizzes, Practice Anatomy Lab™ (PAL™) 3.0 virtual anatomy practice tool, PhysioEx™ 9.0 laboratory simulations, and A&P Flix™ with Quizzes.

PAL | practice anatomy lab™ For this lab exercise, follow these navigation paths:
- PAL>Human Cadaver>Joints
- PAL>Anatomical Models>Joints

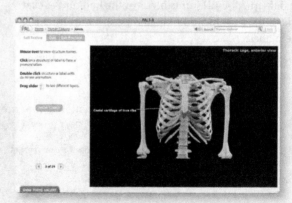

MasteringA&P®

From Exercise 16 of *Laboratory Manual for Anatomy & Physiology featuring Martini Art,* Fifth Edition. Michael G. Wood.

Lab Activity 1   Joint Classification

Two classification schemes are commonly used for articulations. The functional scheme groups joints by the amount of movement permitted, and the structural scheme groups joints by the type of connective tissue between the articulating bones. The three kinds of functional joints permit no, some, or free movement of the articulating bones. Four types of structural joints occur: bony fusion, fibrous, cartilaginous, and synovial.

Functional Classification

The functional classification scheme divides joints into three groups: immovable joints, the *synarthroses*; semimovable joints, the *amphiarthroses*; and freely movable joints, the *diarthroses*. Table 1 summarizes these three groups.

1. **Synarthroses** (sin-ar-THRŌ-sēz; *syn-*, together + *arthros*, joint) are immovable joints in which the bones are either closely fitted together or surrounded by a strong ligament. Sutures of the skull are synarthroses.

2. **Amphiarthroses** (am-fē-ar-THRŌ-sēz) are joints held together by strong connective tissue; they are capable of only minimal movement. Examples of an amphiarthrosis include the joint between the tibia and fibula and the joints between vertebral bodies.

3. **Diarthroses** (dī-ar-THRŌ-sēz) are joints in which the bones are separated by a small membrane-lined cavity. The cavity allows a wide range of motion which makes diarthroses freely movable **synovial** (sin-NŌ-vē-ul) joints. Movements are classified according to the number of planes through which the bones move.

   - **Monaxial** (mon-AX-ē-ul) joints, like the elbow, move in one plane.
   - **Biaxial** (bī-AX-ē-ul) joints allow movement in two planes; move your wrist up and down and side to side to demonstrate biaxial movement.
   - **Triaxial** (trī-AX-ē-ul) joints occur in the ball-and-socket joints of the shoulder and hip and permit movement in three planes.
   - **Nonaxial** joints, also called **multiaxial,** are glide joints where the articulating bones can move slightly in a

variety of directions. The anatomy of a diarthrotic joint is examined in more detail later in this exercise.

Structural Classification

The structural classification scheme for joints is important when discussing joint anatomy rather than movement. As Table 2 summarizes, four types of structural joints occur in the skeleton.

1. **Bony fusion** occurs where bones have fused together, and this type of joint permits no movement. These joints are also called **synostoses** (sin-os-TŌ-sēz; *-osteo*, bone) and occur in the frontal bone, coxal bones, and mandible bone. A good example of a synostosis is the frontal bone. Humans are born with two frontal bones that, by the age of eight, fuse into a single frontal bone. The old articulation site is then occupied by bony tissue to form a bony fusion joint. The joint between the diaphysis and either epiphysis of a mature long bone is also a synostosis.

2. **Fibrous joints** are synarthroses that have fibrous connective tissue between the articulating bones, and as a result little to no movement occurs in these strong joints. There are three main types of fibrous joints: suture, the gomphosis, and syndesmosis.

   - **Sutures** (*sutura*, a sewing together) occur in the skull wherever the bones interlock. This strong synarthrosis has no movement.
   - A **gomphosis** (gom-FŌ-sis; *gompho*, a peg or nail) is characterized by the insertion of a conical process into a socket in the alveolar bone of the jaw. The gomphosis is the joint between the tooth and the socket of alveolar bone of the jaw. The fibrous periodontal ligament lined the joint and holds the tooth firmly in place and permits no movement.
   - **Syndesmoses** (sin-dez-MŌ-sēz; *syn-*, together + *desmo-*, band) occur between the parallel bones of the forearm and leg. A ligament of fibrous connective tissue forms a strong band that wraps around the bones. The syndesmosis thus formed prevents excessive movement in the joint.

Table 1	A Functional Classification of Articulation	
Functional Category	**Description**	**Examples**
Synarthrosis	Strong joint with no movement. Bones are held together with fibrous connective tissue or cartilage.	Sutures of the skull, fusion of frontal bones
Amphiarthrosis	Strong joint with limited movement.	Between the tibia and fibula, between right and left halves of pelvis; between adjacent vertebral bodies
Diarthrosis	Complex joint with free movement that is bounded by joint capsule containing synovial fluid.	Elbow, ankle, wrist, shoulder, hip

Table 2   A Structural Classification of Articulations

Structure	Type	Functional Category	Example
Bony fusion	Synostosis (illustrated)	Synarthrosis	Metopic suture (fusion) — Frontal bone
Fibrous joint	Suture (illustrated) Gomphosis Syndesmosis	Synarthrosis Synarthrosis Amphiarthrosis	Lambdoid suture — Skull
Cartilaginous joint	Synchondrosis Symphysis (illustrated)	Synarthrosis Amphiarthrosis	Pubic symphysis — Pelvis
Synovial joint	Monaxial Biaxial Triaxial (illustrated)	Diarthroses	Synovial joint

3. **Cartilaginous joints,** as their name implies, have cartilage between the bones. The type of cartilage—hyaline or fibrocartilage—determines the type of cartilaginous joint.

   ▪ **Symphyses** are amphiarthroses characterized by the presence of fibrocartilage between the articulating bones. The intervertebral disks, for instance, construct a symphysis between any two articulating vertebrae. Another symphysis in the body occurs where the coxal bones unite at the pubis. This strong joint, called the pubic symphysis, limits flexion of the pelvis. During childbirth, a hormone softens the fibrocartilage to widen the pelvic bowl.

   ▪ **Synchondroses** (sin-kon-DRŌ-sēz; *syn-*, together + *condros,* cartilage) are synarthroses that have cartilage between the bones making up the joints. Two examples of this type of synarthrosis are the epiphyseal plate in a child's long bones and the cartilage between the ribs and sternum.

4. **Synovial joints** have a joint cavity lined by a **synovial membrane.** All the free-moving joints—in other words, the diarthroses—are synovial joints. The four types are the monaxial, biaxial, triaxial, and multiaxial joints, described earlier.

Clinical Application Arthritis

Arthritis, a disease that destroys synovial joints by damaging the articular cartilage, comes in two forms. **Rheumatoid arthritis** is an autoimmune disease that occurs when the body's immune system attacks the cartilage and synovial membrane of the joint. As the disease progresses, the joint cavity is eliminated and the articulating bones fuse, which results in painful disfiguration of the joint and loss of joint function. **Osteoarthritis** is a degenerative joint disease that often occurs due to age and wearing of the joint tissues. The articular cartilage is damaged, and bone spurs may project into the joint cavity. Osteoarthritis tends to occur in the knee and hip joints, whereas rheumatoid arthritis is more common in the smaller joints of the hand. ▪

QuickCheck Questions

1.1 What is the difference between the functional classification scheme for joints and the structural classification scheme?

1.2 What are the three types of functional joints and how much movement does each allow?

1.3 What are the four types of structural joints and the type of connective tissue found in each?

Material

☐ Articulated skeleton

Procedures

1. Locate on an articulated skeleton or on your body a joint from each functional group and one from each structural group.

2. Identify on your body and give an example of each of the following joints.

   ▪ Synarthrosis _____

   ▪ Amphiarthrosis _____

   ▪ Diarthrosis _____

   ▪ Syndesmosis _____

   ▪ Synchondrosis _____

   ▪ Synostosis _____

   ▪ Symphysis _____

   ▪ Suture _____

3. Identify two monaxial joints, two biaxial joints, and two triaxial joints on your body.

   ▪ Monaxial joints _____

   ▪ Biaxial joints _____

   ▪ Triaxial joints _____ ▪

Lab Activity 2 Structure of Synovial Joints

The wide range of motion of synovial joints is attributed to the small **joint cavity** between articulating bones (**Figure 1**). When you consider how a door can swing open even though there is only a small space between the metal pieces of the hinges, you can appreciate how a joint cavity permits free movement of a joint. The epiphyses are capped with **articular cartilage,** a slippery gelatinous surface of hyaline cartilage that protects the epiphyses and prevents the bones from making contact across the joint cavity. A membrane called the **synovial membrane** lines the cavity and produces **synovial fluid.** Injury to a joint may cause inflammation of the membrane and lead to excessive fluid production.

A **bursa** (BUR-sa; *bursa,* a pouch) is similar to a synovial membrane except that, instead of lining a joint cavity, the bursa provides padding between bones and other structures. The periosteum of each bone is continuous with the strong **articular capsule** that encases the joint.

As mentioned previously, all diarthrotic joints are capable of free movement. This large range of motion is due to the anatomical organization of the joint: Between the bones of every diarthrotic joint is a cavity lined with a synovial membrane.

Figure 1 Structure of a Synovial Joint

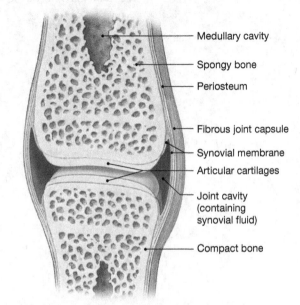

Medullary cavity
Spongy bone
Periosteum
Fibrous joint capsule
Synovial membrane
Articular cartilages
Joint cavity (containing synovial fluid)
Compact bone

a Synovial joint, sagittal section

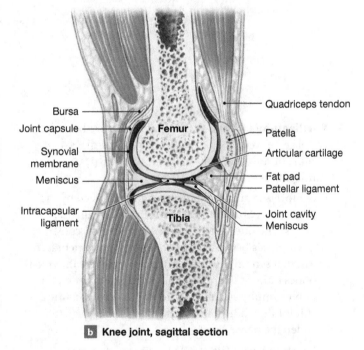

Bursa
Joint capsule
Synovial membrane
Meniscus
Intracapsular ligament
Femur
Tibia
Quadriceps tendon
Patella
Articular cartilage
Fat pad
Patellar ligament
Joint cavity
Meniscus

b Knee joint, sagittal section

QuickCheck Questions

2.1 Where is the synovial membrane located in a joint?

2.2 Where is cartilage found in a synovial joint?

In the Lab 2

Material

☐ Fresh beef joint

Procedures

1. Review the anatomy of the synovial joint in Figure 1.
2. On the fresh beef joint, locate and describe the joint cavity.
3. Identify the articular cartilage and articular capsule. ▪

Lab Activity 3 Types of Diarthroses

Six types of diarthroses (synovial joints) occur in the skeleton. Each type permits a certain amount of movement owing to the joining surfaces of the articulating bones. Figure 2 details each type of joint and includes a mechanical representation of each joint to show planes of motion.

- **Gliding joints** (also called *plane joints*) are common where flat articular surfaces, such as in the wrist, slide by neighboring bones. The movement is typically nonaxial. In addition to the wrist, glide joints also occur between bones of the sternum and between the tarsals. When you place your open hand, palm facing down, on your desktop and press down hard, you can observe the gliding of your wrist bones.
- **Hinge joints** are monaxial, operating like a door hinge, and are located in the elbows, fingers, toes, and knees. Bending your legs at the knees and your arms at the elbows is possible because of your hinge joints.
- **Pivot joints** are monaxial joints that permit one bone to rotate around another. Shake your head "no" to operate the pivot joint between your first two cervical vertebrae. The first cervical vertebra (the atlas) pivots around the second cervical vertebra (the axis).
- **Ellipsoid joints** (also called *condyloid joints*) are characterized by a convex surface of one bone that articulates in a concave depression of another bone. This concave-to-convex spooning of articulating surfaces permits biaxial movement. The articulation between the bones of the forearm and wrist is an ellipsoidal joint.
- The **saddle joint** is a biaxial joint found only at the junction between the thumb metacarpus and the trapezium bone of the wrist. Place a finger on your lateral wrist and feel the saddle joint move as you touch your little finger with your thumb. This joint permits you to oppose your thumb to grasp and manipulate objects in your hand.
- **Ball-and-socket joints** occur where a spherical head of one bone fits into a cup-shaped fossa of another bone, as in the joint between the humerus and the scapula. This triaxial joint permits dynamic movement in many planes.

QuickCheck Questions

3.1 What are the six types of diarthroses?

3.2 What type of diarthrosis is a knuckle joint?

In the Lab 3

Material

☐ Articulated skeleton

Procedures

1. Locate each type of synovial joint on an articulated skeleton or on your body. On the skeleton, notice how the structure of the joining bones determines the amount of joint movement.
2. Give an example of each type of synovial joint.
   - Gliding _____
   - Hinge _____
   - Pivot _____
   - Ellipsoidal _____
   - Saddle _____
   - Ball-and-socket _____ ▪

Lab Activity 4 Skeletal Movement at Diarthrotic Joints

The diversity of bone shapes and joint types permits the skeleton to move in a variety of ways. Figure 3 illustrates angular movements, which occur either front to back in the anterior/posterior plane or side to side in the lateral plane. Figure 4 illustrates rotational movements. For clarity, these figures include a small dot at the joint where a demonstrated movement is described. Table 3 summarizes articulations of the axial skeleton and Table 4 summarizes articulations of the appendicular divisions.

- **Flexion** is movement that decreases the angle between the articulating bones, and **extension** is movement that increases the angle between the bones (Figure 3a). Hang your arm down at your side in anatomical position. Now flex your arm by moving the elbow joint. Your hand should be up by your shoulder. Notice how close the antebrachium is to the brachium and how the angle between them has decreased. Is your flexed arm still in anatomical position? Now extend your arm to return it to anatomical position. How has the angle changed? **Hyperextension** moves the body beyond anatomical position.
- **Abduction** is movement away from the midline of the body (Figures 3b, c). **Adduction** is movement toward the midline. Notice how you move your arm at the shoulder for these two motions. Practice this movement first with your shoulder joint and then with your wrist joint.

Figure 2 Movements at Synovial Joints The types of movement permitted are illustrated on the left anatomically and on the right by a mechanical model.

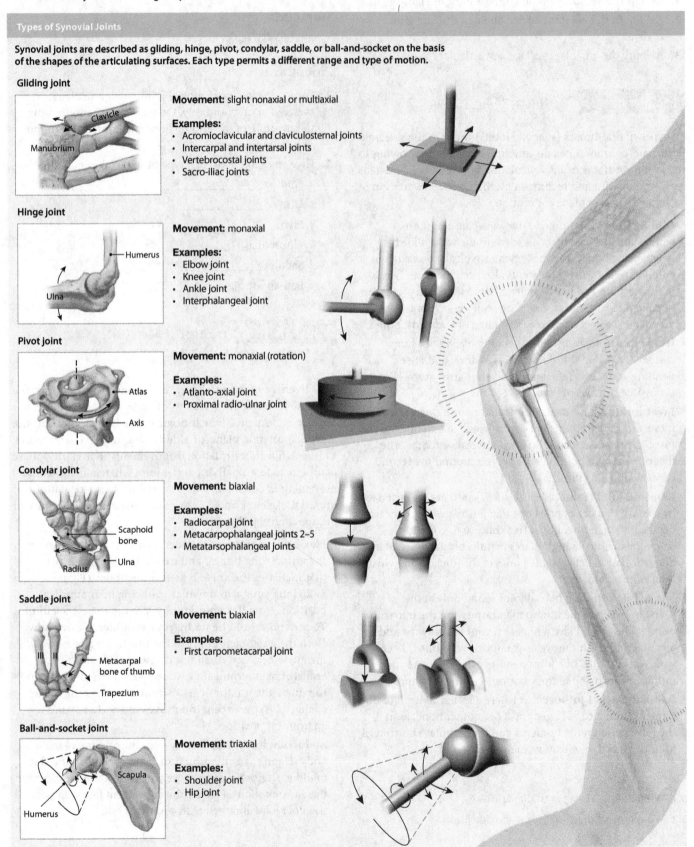

Types of Synovial Joints

Synovial joints are described as gliding, hinge, pivot, condylar, saddle, or ball-and-socket on the basis of the shapes of the articulating surfaces. Each type permits a different range and type of motion.

Gliding joint

Clavicle
Manubrium

Movement: slight nonaxial or multiaxial

Examples:
- Acromioclavicular and claviculosternal joints
- Intercarpal and intertarsal joints
- Vertebrocostal joints
- Sacro-iliac joints

Hinge joint

Humerus
Ulna

Movement: monaxial

Examples:
- Elbow joint
- Knee joint
- Ankle joint
- Interphalangeal joint

Pivot joint

Atlas
Axis

Movement: monaxial (rotation)

Examples:
- Atlanto-axial joint
- Proximal radio-ulnar joint

Condylar joint

Scaphoid bone
Ulna
Radius

Movement: biaxial

Examples:
- Radiocarpal joint
- Metacarpophalangeal joints 2–5
- Metatarsophalangeal joints

Saddle joint

III II
Metacarpal bone of thumb
Trapezium

Movement: biaxial

Examples:
- First carpometacarpal joint

Ball-and-socket joint

Scapula
Humerus

Movement: triaxial

Examples:
- Shoulder joint
- Hip joint

Figure 3 Angular Movements Examples of angular movements that change the angle between the two bones making up a joint. The red dots indicate the locations of the joints involved in the illustrated movement.

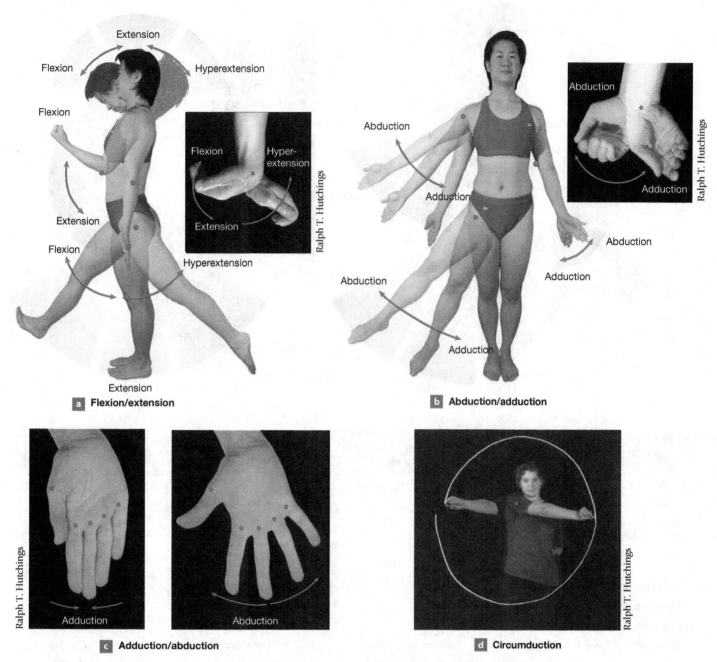

a Flexion/extension

b Abduction/adduction

c Adduction/abduction

d Circumduction

Ralph T. Hutchings

- **Circumduction** is circular movement at a ball-and-socket joint (Figure 3d). During this movement, motion of the proximal region of the upper limb is relatively stationary while the distal portion traces a wide circle in the air.

- **Rotation** is a turning movement of bones at a joint (Figure 4a). **Left rotation** or **right rotation** occur when the head is turned, as in shaking to indicate "no."

Lateral rotation and **medial rotation** of the limbs occur at ball-and-socket joints and at the radioulnar joint. These movements turn the rounded head of one bone in the socket of another bone.

- **Supination** (soo-pi-NĀ-shun) is movement that moves the palm into the anatomical position (Figure 4b). **Pronation** (pro-NĀ-shun) is movement that moves the

Figure 4 Rotational Movements Examples of motion in which a body part rotates.

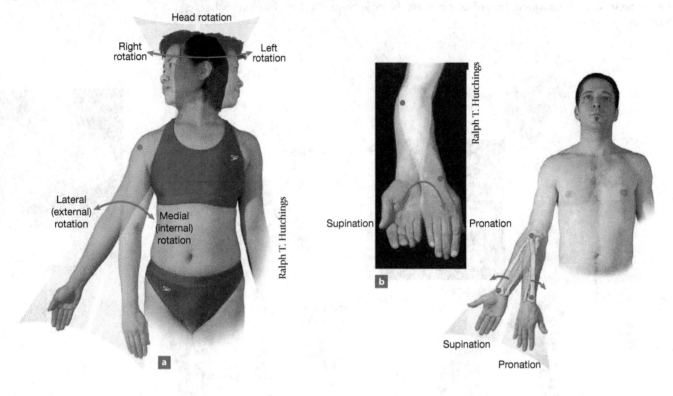

Table 3   Articulations of the Axial Skeleton

Element	Joint	Type of Articulation	Movements
SKULL			
Cranial and facial bones of skull	Various	Synarthroses (suture or synostosis)	None
Maxillary bone/teeth and mandible/teeth	Alveolar	Synarthrosis (gomphosis)	None
Temporal bone/mandible	Temporomandibular	Combined gliding joint and hinge diarthrosis	Elevation, depression, and lateral gliding
VERTEBRAL COLUMN			
Occipital bone/atlas	Atlanto-occipital	Ellipsoidal diarthrosis	Flexion/extension
Atlas/axis	Atlanto-axial	Pivot diarthrosis	Rotation
Other vertebral elements	Intervertebral (*between vertebral bodies*)	Amphiarthrosis (symphysis)	Slight movement
	Intervertebral (*between articular processes*)	Gliding diarthrosis	Slight rotation and flexion/extension
L_5/sacrum	Between L_5 body and sacral body	Amphiarthrosis (symphysis)	Slight movement
	Between inferior articular processes of L_5 and articular processes of sacrum	Gliding diarthrosis	Slight flexion/extension
Sacrum/coxal bone	Sacroiliac	Gliding diarthrosis	Slight movement
Sacrum/coccyx	Sacrococcygeal	Gliding diarthrosis (*may become fused*)	Slight movement
Coccygeal bones		Synarthrosis (synostosis)	No movement

(continued)

Table 3	Articulations of the Axial Skeleton *(continued)*		
Element	**Joint**	**Type of Articulation**	**Movements**
THORACIC CAGE			
Bodies of T$_1$–T$_{12}$ and heads of ribs	Costovertebral	Gliding diarthrosis	Slight movement
Transverse processes of T$_1$–T$_{10}$	Costovertebral	Gliding diarthrosis	Slight movement
Ribs and costal cartilages		Synarthrosis (synchondrosis)	No movement
Sternum and first costal cartilage	Sternocostal (1st)	Synarthrosis (synchondrosis)	No movement
Sternum and costal cartilages 2–7	Sternocostal (2nd–7th)	Gliding diarthrosis*	Slight movement

*Commonly converts to synchondrosis in elderly individuals.

Table 4	Articulations of the Appendicular Skeleton		
Element	**Joint**	**Type of Articulation**	**Movements**
ARTICULATIONS OF THE PECTORAL GIRDLE AND UPPER LIMB			
Sternum/clavicle	Sternoclavicular	Gliding diarthrosis*	Protraction/retraction, elevation/depression, slight rotation
Scapula/clavicle	Acromioclavicular	Gliding diarthrosis	Slight movement
Scapula/humerus	Shoulder, or glenohumeral	Ball-and-socket diarthrosis	Flexion/extension, adduction/abduction, circumduction, rotation
Humerus/ulna and humerus/radius	Elbow (humeroulnar and humeroradial)	Hinge diarthrosis	Flexion/extension
Radius/ulna	Proximal radioulnar	Pivot diarthrosis	Rotation
	Distal radioulnar	Pivot diarthrosis	Pronation/supination
Radius/carpal bones	Radiocarpal	Ellipsoidal diarthrosis	Flexion/extension, adduction/abduction, circumduction
Carpal bone to carpal bone	Intercarpal	Gliding diarthrosis	Slight movement
Carpal bone to metacarpal bone (I)	Carpometacarpal of thumb	Saddle diarthrosis	Flexion/extension, adduction/abduction, circumduction, opposition
Carpal bone to metacarpal bone (II–V)	Carpometacarpal	Gliding diarthrosis	Slight flexion/extension, adduction/abduction
Metacarpal bone to phalanx	Metacarpophalangeal	Ellipsoidal diarthrosis	Flexion/extension, adduction/abduction, circumduction
Phalanx/phalanx	Interphalangeal	Hinge diarthrosis	Flexion/extension
ARTICULATIONS OF THE PELVIC GIRDLE AND LOWER LIMB			
Sacrum/ilium os coxae	Sacroiliac	Gliding diarthrosis	Slight movement
Coxal bone	Pubic symphysis	Amphiarthrosis (symphysis)	None†
Coxal bone/femur	Hip	Ball-and-socket diarthrosis	Flexion/extension, adduction/abduction, circumduction, rotation
Femur/tibia	Knee	Complex, functions as hinge	Flexion/extension, limited rotation
Tibia/fibula	Tibiofibular (proximal)	Gliding diarthrosis	Slight movement
	Tibiofibular (distal)	Gliding diarthrosis and amphiarthrotic syndesmosis	Slight movement
Tibia and fibula with talus	Ankle, or talocrural	Hinge diarthrosis	Flexion/extension (dorsiflexion/plantar flexion)
Tarsal bone to tarsal bone	Intertarsal	Gliding diarthrosis	Slight movement
Tarsal bone to metatarsal bone	Tarsometatarsal	Gliding diarthrosis	Slight movement
Metatarsal bone to phalanx	Metatarsophalangeal	Ellipsoidal diarthrosis	Flexion/extension, adduction/abduction
Phalanx/phalanx	Interphalangeal	Hinge diarthrosis	Flexion/extension

*A "double gliding joint," with two joint cavities separated by an articular cartilage.
†During pregnancy, hormones weaken the symphysis and permit movement important to childbirth.

palm to face posteriorly. During these two motions, the humerus serves as a foundation for the radius to pivot around the ulna.

The following specialized motions are illustrated in Figure 5.

- **Eversion** (ē-VER-zhun) is lateral movement of the ankle to move the foot so that the toes point away from the body's midline. Moving the sole medially so that the toes point toward the midline is **inversion;** the foot moves "in." Eversion and inversion are commonly mistaken for pronation and supination of the ankle.

- Two other terms describing ankle movement are dorsiflexion and plantar flexion. **Dorsiflexion** is the joint movement that permits you to walk on your heels, which means the soles of your feet are raised up off the floor and the angle between the ankle and the bones of the leg is decreased. **Plantar flexion** (*plantar,* sole) moves the foot so that you can walk on your tiptoes; here the angle between the ankle and the tibia/fibula is increased.

- **Opposition** is touching the thumb pad with the pad of the little finger.

- **Retraction,** which means to take back, moves structures posteriorly out of the anatomical position, as when the mandible is moved posteriorly to demonstrate an overbite.

Protraction moves a structure anteriorly, as when you jut your mandible forward.

- **Depression** lowers bones. This motion occurs, for instance, when you lower your mandible bone to take a bite of food. Closing your mouth is **elevation** of the mandible bone.

Study Tip Movements of the Upper Limb

To see the difference between medial and lateral rotation, start with your right upper limb in the anatomical position and then flex your right elbow until the forearm is parallel to the floor. Keeping your forearm parallel to the floor, move your right hand until it hits your torso; the movement of your humerus at the shoulder when you do this is medial rotation. Still keeping your right forearm parallel to the floor, now swing your right hand away from your torso. In this motion, the humerus is rotating laterally.

To see the difference between supination and pronation, return your right upper limb to the anatomical position and again flex the elbow to bring your right forearm parallel to the floor. Now twist your hand as if turning a doorknob and observe the movement of the forearm and hand. Twisting your hand until the palm faces the floor is pronation; twisting your hand back until the palm faces the ceiling is supination. ▪

Figure 5 Special Movements Special movements occur at specific joints.

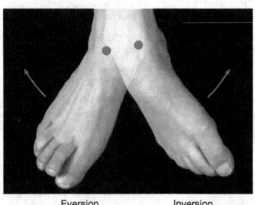

Eversion   Inversion

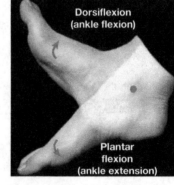

Dorsiflexion (ankle flexion)

Plantar flexion (ankle extension)

Opposition

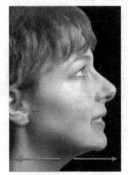

Retraction   Protraction

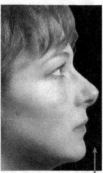

Depression

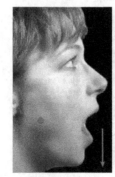

Elevation

Lateral flexion

Sketch to Learn

Let's sketch the knee joint from a superior view and detail the seven ligaments that surround this joint.

Sample Sketch

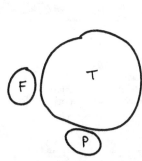 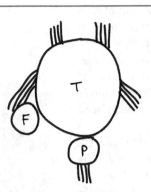 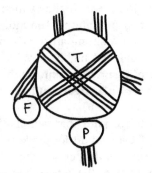

Step 1
- Draw a large oval for the tibial head and two smaller ovals for the fibula and patella.
- Place a letter in each oval to identify the bones.

Step 2
- Use a series of lines to represent each popliteal ligament.
- Add the two collateral ligaments.
- Add the patellar ligament.

Step 3
- Include the anterior and posterior cruciate ligaments.
- Label your sketch.

Your Sketch

- **Lateral flexion** is the bending of the vertebral column from side to side. Most of the movement occurs in the cervical and lumbar regions.

QuickCheck Questions

4.1 How does flexion differ from extension?

4.2 How does hyperextension differ from extension?

4.3 What are pronation and supination?

4.4 How does dorsiflexion differ from plantar flexion?

In the Lab 4

Material

☐ Articulated skeleton

Procedures

1. Use an articulated skeleton or your body to demonstrate each of the movements in Figures 3, 4, and 5.

2. Label the movements illustrated in Figures 3 and 4.

3. Give an example of each of the following movements.
   - Abduction _____
   - Extension _____
   - Hyperextension _____
   - Pronation _____
   - Supination _____
   - Depression _____
   - Retraction _____
   - Lateral rotation _____

For additional practice, complete the *Sketch to Learn* activity. ■

Lab Activity 5 Selected Synovial Joints: Elbow and Knee Joints

The elbow is a hinge joint involving humeroradial and humeroulnar articulations. (Within the elbow complex is also the radioulnar joint, which allows the radius to pivot during supination and pronation.) The morphology of the articulating bones and a strong articular capsule and ligaments result in a strong and highly movable elbow. **Radial** and **ulnar collateral ligaments** reinforce the lateral aspects of the joint, and the **annular ligament** holds the radial head in position to pivot (Figure 6).

The knee is a hinge joint that permits flexion and extension of the leg. Most support for the knee is provided by seven bands of ligaments that encase the joint (Figure 7). Cushions of fibrocartilage, the **lateral meniscus** (men-IS-kus; *meniskos*, a crescent) and the **medial meniscus,** pad the area between the condyles of the femur and tibia. Areas where tendons move against the bones in the knee are protected with bursae.

The seven ligaments of the knee occur in three pairs and a single patellar ligament. **Tibial** and **fibular collateral ligaments** provide medial and lateral support when a person is standing. Two **popliteal ligaments** extend from the head of the femur to the fibula and tibia to support the posterior of the knee. The **anterior** and **posterior cruciate ligaments** are inside the articular capsule. The cruciate (*cruciate,* crosslike) ligaments originate on the tibial head and cross each other as they pass through the intercondylar fossa of the femur. The **patellar ligament** attaches the inferior aspect of the patella to the tibial tuberosity, adding anterior support to the knee. The large quadriceps tendon is attached to the superior margin of the patella. Cords of ligaments called the **patellar retinaculae** contribute to anterior support of the knee.

QuickCheck Questions

5.1 What structure reinforces the radial head?

5.2 How many ligaments are in the knee?

5.3 What structures cushion the knee?

In the Lab 5

Materials

☐ Articulated skeleton
☐ Elbow model
☐ Knee model

Figure 6 **The Right Elbow** The right elbow joint.

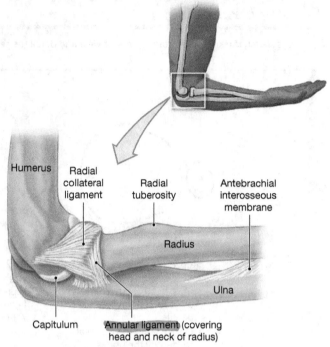

Humerus — Radial collateral ligament — Radial tuberosity — Antebrachial interosseous membrane

Radius

Ulna

Capitulum — Annular ligament (covering head and neck of radius)

a Lateral view

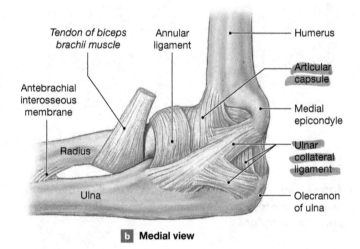

Tendon of biceps brachii muscle — Annular ligament — Humerus

Antebrachial interosseous membrane

Articular capsule

Medial epicondyle

Radius

Ulnar collateral ligament

Ulna

Olecranon of ulna

b Medial view

Procedures

1. Examine the elbow of the articulated skeleton and review the skeletal anatomy of the joint.

2. Locate the annular and collateral ligaments on the elbow model.

3. Review the skeletal components of the knee joint on the articulated skeleton.

4. On the knee model, examine the relationship of the ligaments and determine how each supports the knee. Note how the menisci cushion between the bones. ■

Figure 7 **The Knee Joint** The right knee joint.

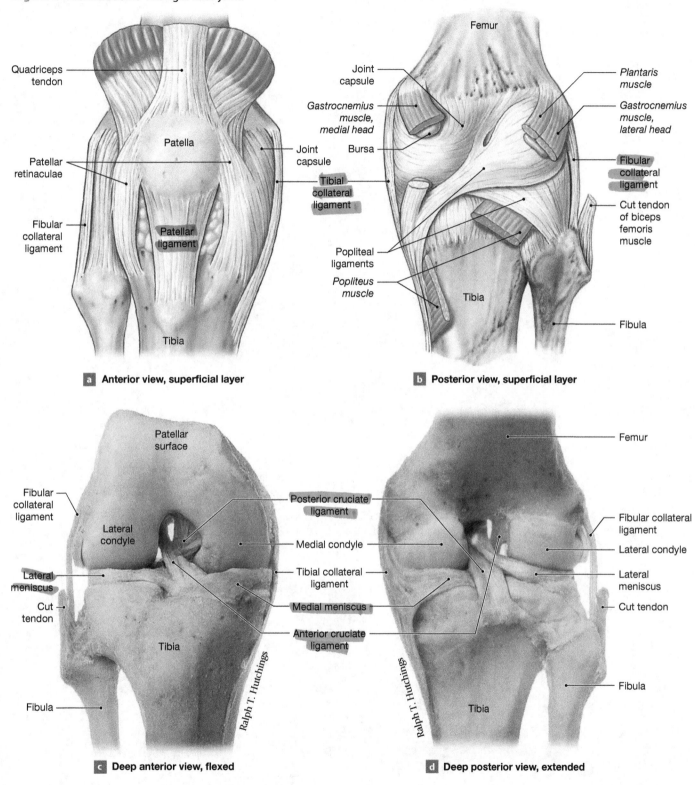

Quadriceps tendon

Patella

Patellar retinaculae

Fibular collateral ligament

Patellar ligament

Tibia

a **Anterior view, superficial layer**

Femur

Joint capsule

Gastrocnemius muscle, medial head

Joint capsule

Bursa

Tibial collateral ligament

Popliteal ligaments

Popliteus muscle

Tibia

Plantaris muscle

Gastrocnemius muscle, lateral head

Fibular collateral ligament

Cut tendon of biceps femoris muscle

Fibula

b **Posterior view, superficial layer**

Patellar surface

Fibular collateral ligament

Lateral condyle

Lateral meniscus

Cut tendon

Tibia

Fibula

Posterior cruciate ligament

Medial condyle

Tibial collateral ligament

Medial meniscus

Anterior cruciate ligament

Ralph T. Hutchings

c **Deep anterior view, flexed**

Femur

Posterior cruciate ligament

Fibular collateral ligament

Lateral condyle

Lateral meniscus

Cut tendon

Fibula

Tibia

Ralph T. Hutchings

d **Deep posterior view, extended**

Name _____

Date _____

Section _____

Articulations

A. Matching

Match each joint in the left column with its correct description from the right.

_____	**1.** pivot	**A.**	forearm-to-wrist joint
_____	**2.** symphysis	**B.**	joint between parietal bones
_____	**3.** ball and socket	**C.**	rib-to-sternum joint
_____	**4.** gomphosis	**D.**	joint between vertebral bodies
_____	**5.** hinge	**E.**	femur-to-coxal bone joint
_____	**6.** suture	**F.**	phalangeal joint
_____	**7.** synostosis	**G.**	distal tibia-to-fibula joint
_____	**8.** syndesmosis	**H.**	atlas-to-axis joint
_____	**9.** condyloid	**I.**	fused frontal bones
_____	**10.** synchondrosis	**J.**	joint holding tooth in a socket

B. Matching

Match each movement in the left column with its correct description from the right column.

_____	**1.** retraction	**A.**	movement away from midline
_____	**2.** dorsiflexion	**B.**	movement to turn foot outward
_____	**3.** eversion	**C.**	palm moved to face posteriorly
_____	**4.** inversion	**D.**	palm moved to face anteriorly
_____	**5.** pronation	**E.**	movement to posterior plane
_____	**6.** plantar flexion	**F.**	movement to stand on tiptoes
_____	**7.** protraction	**G.**	movement in anterior plane
_____	**8.** supination	**H.**	movement to turn foot inward
_____	**9.** adduction	**I.**	movement to stand on heels
_____	**10.** abduction	**J.**	movement toward midline

C. Labeling

1. Label the anatomy of a synovial joint in Figure 8.

2. Label the five numbered joint movements in Figure 9.

Figure 8 Synovial Joint

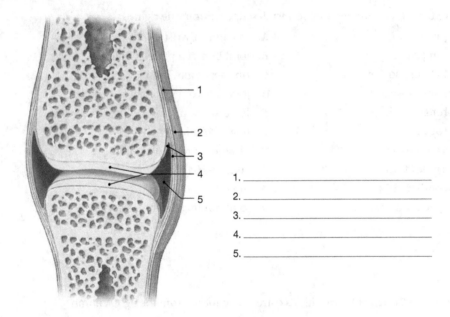

1. _____
2. _____
3. _____
4. _____
5. _____

Figure 9 Angular Movements

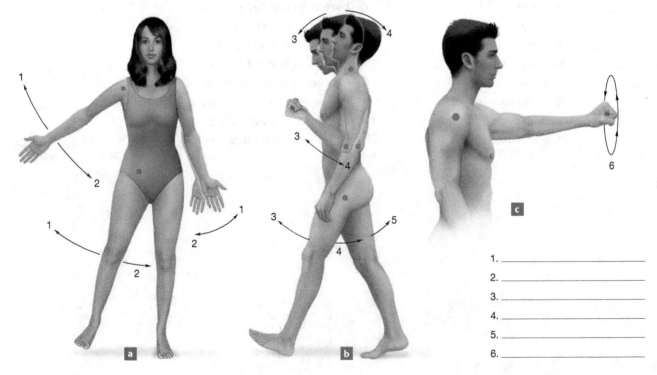

1. _____
2. _____
3. _____
4. _____
5. _____
6. _____

3. Label the four numbered joint movements in Figure 10.

Figure 10 **Rotational Movements**

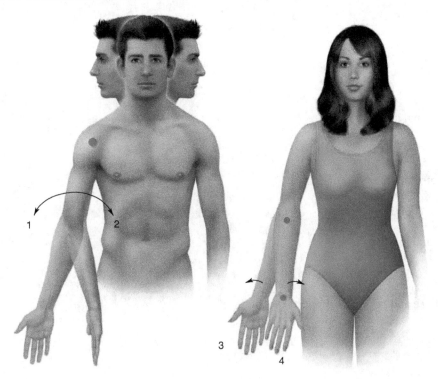

1. _____
2. _____
3. _____
4. _____

D. Description

Describe the joints and movements involved in:

1. walking

2. throwing a ball

3. turning a doorknob

4. crossing your legs while sitting

5. shaking your head "no"

6. chewing food

E. Short-Answer Questions

    1. Describe the three types of functional joints.

    2. What factors limit the range of movement of a joint?

    3. Describe the four types of structural joints.

    4. List the seven ligaments of the knee and how each supports the joint.

F. Analysis and Application

    1. Describe how the articulating bones of the elbow prevent hyperextension of this joint.

    2. Which joint is unique to the hand, and how does this joint move the hand?

    3. Which structural feature enables diarthrotic joints to have free movement?

G. Clinical Challenge

    1. Why do bones fuse in joints damaged by rheumatoid arthritis?

    2. Why is the lateral meniscus often associated with a knee injury?

Organization of Skeletal Muscles

Learning Outcomes

On completion of this exercise, you should be able to:

1. Describe the basic functions of skeletal muscles.

2. Describe the organization of a skeletal muscle.

3. Describe the microanatomy of a muscle fiber.

4. Discuss and provide examples of a lever system.

5. Understand the rules that determine the names of some muscles.

Lab Activities

1 Skeletal Muscle Organization

2 The Neuromuscular Junction

3 Naming Muscles

Clinical Application

Muscular Dystrophies (MD)

E very time you move some part of your body, either consciously or unconsciously, you use muscles. There are three kinds of muscle tissue: skeletal, smooth, and cardiac. Skeletal muscles are primarily responsible for **locomotion,** or movement of the body. Locomotions such as rolling your eyes, writing your name, and speaking are the result of highly coordinated muscle contractions. Other functions of skeletal muscle include maintenance of posture and body temperature and support of soft tissues, as with the muscles of the abdomen.

In addition to the ability to contract, muscle tissue has several other unique characteristics. Like nerve tissue, muscle tissue is **excitable** and, in response to a stimulus, produces electrical impulses called **action potentials.** Muscle tissue can stretch and is therefore **extensible.** When the ends of a stretched muscle are released, it recoils to its original size, like a rubber band. This property is called **elasticity.**

Need More Practice and Review?

Build your knowledge—and confidence!—in the Study Area of MasteringA&P® at www.masteringaandp.com with Pre-lab Quizzes, Post-lab Quizzes, Practice Anatomy Lab™ (PAL™) 3.0 virtual anatomy practice tool, PhysioEx™ 9.0 laboratory simulations, and A&P Flix™ with Quizzes.

PAL For this lab exercise, follow these navigation paths:
- PAL>Anatomical Models>Muscular System
- PAL>Histology>Muscular System

A&PFlix For this lab exercise, go to these topics:
- Events at the Neuromuscular Junction
- Excitation-Contraction Coupling

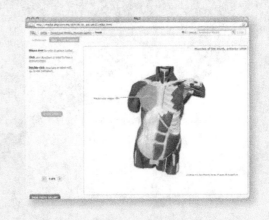

From Exercise 17 of *Laboratory Manual for Anatomy & Physiology featuring Martini Art,* Fifth Edition. Michael G. Wood.

Lab Activity 1 Skeletal Muscle Organization

Connective Tissue Coverings

Connective tissues support and organize skeletal muscles and attach them to bones. Three layers of connective tissue partition a muscle. Superficially, a collagenous connective tissue layer called the **epimysium** (ep-i-MĪ Z-ē-um; *epi*, on + *mys*, muscle) covers the muscle and separates it from neighboring structures (Figure 1). The epimysium folds into the muscle as the **perimysium** (per-i-MĪ Z-ē-um; *peri-*, around), and divides the muscle fibers into groups called **fascicles** (FAS-i-kl). Connective tissue fibers of the perimysium extend deep into the fascicles, as the **endomysium** (en-dō-MĪ Z-ē-um; *endo-*, inside), and surround each muscle fiber (cell). The parallel, threadlike fascicles can be easily seen when a muscle is teased apart with a probe.

Figure 1 **The Organization of Skeletal Muscles** A skeletal muscle consists of fascicles (bundles of muscle fibers) enclosed by the epimysium. The bundles are separated by the connective tissue fibers of the perimysium, and within each bundle the muscle fibers are surrounded by the endomysium. Each muscle fiber has many superficial nuclei, as well as mitochondria and other organelles (see Figure 2).

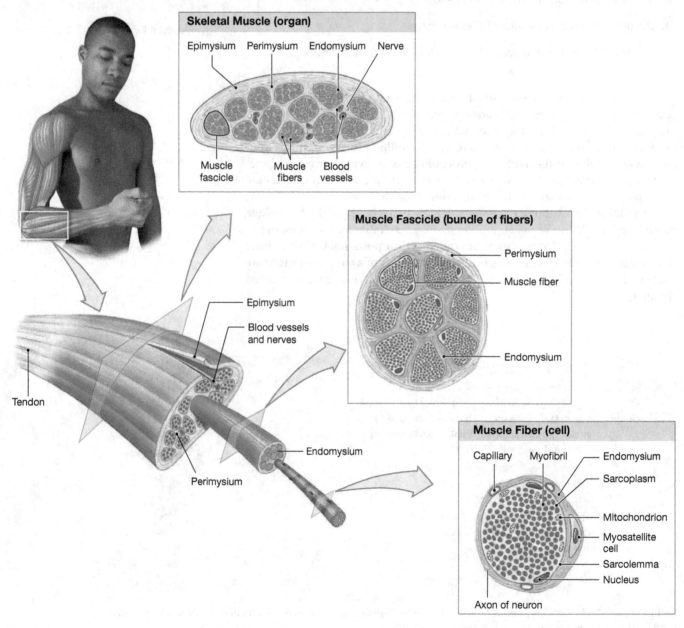

The connective tissues of the muscle interweave and combine as the **tendon** at each end of the muscle. The fibers of the tendon and the bone's periosteum interlace to firmly attach the tendon to the bone. When the muscle fibers contract and generate tension, they transmit this force through the connective tissue layers to the tendon, which pulls on the associated bone and produces movement. As the muscle contracts, its two ends move closer together and the central part of the muscle, called the **belly,** increases in diameter.

Structure of a Skeletal Muscle Fiber

Each muscle fiber is a composite of many cells that fused into a single cell during embryonic development. The cell membrane of a muscle fiber is called the **sarcolemma** (sar-cō-LEM-uh; *sarkos*, flesh + *lemma*, husk) and the cytoplasm is called **sarcoplasm** (Figure 2). Many **transverse tubules,** also called *T tubules*, connect the sarcolemma to the interior of the muscle fiber. The function of these tubules is to pass contraction stimuli to deeper regions of the muscle fiber.

Inside the muscle fiber are proteins arranged in thousands of rods, called **myofibrils,** that extend the length of the fiber. Each myofibril is surrounded by the **sarcoplasmic reticulum,** a modified endoplasmic reticulum where calcium ions are stored. Branches of the sarcoplasmic reticulum fuse to form large calcium ion storage chambers called **terminal cisternae** (sis-TUR-nē), which lie adjacent to the transverse tubules. A **triad** is a "sandwich" consisting of a transverse tubule plus the terminal cisterna on either side of the tubule. In order for a muscle to contract, calcium ions must be released from the cisternae; the transverse tubules stimulate this ion release. When a muscle relaxes, protein carriers in the sarcoplasmic reticulum transport calcium ions back into the cisternae.

Each myofibril consists of several kinds of proteins arranged in about 3000 **thin filaments** and 1500 **thick filaments** (Figure 3). During contraction, thick and thin protein molecules interact to produce tension and shorten the muscle. The thin filaments are mostly composed of the protein **actin,** and the thick filaments are made of the protein **myosin.**

Figure 2 The Structure of a Skeletal Muscle Fiber The internal organization of a muscle fiber.

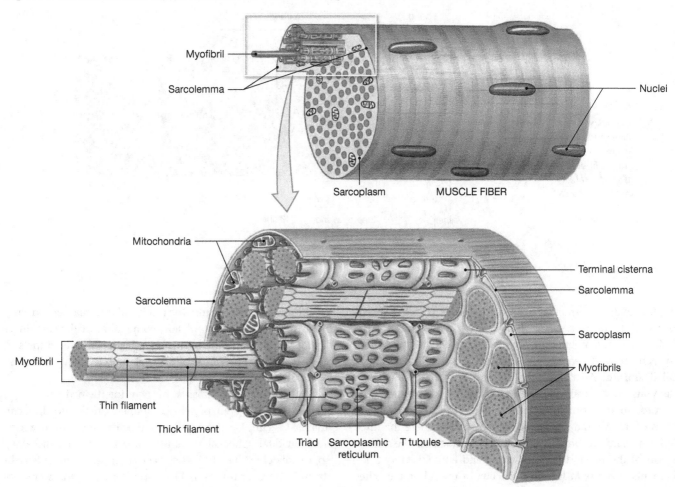

Figure 3 **Sarcomere Structure**

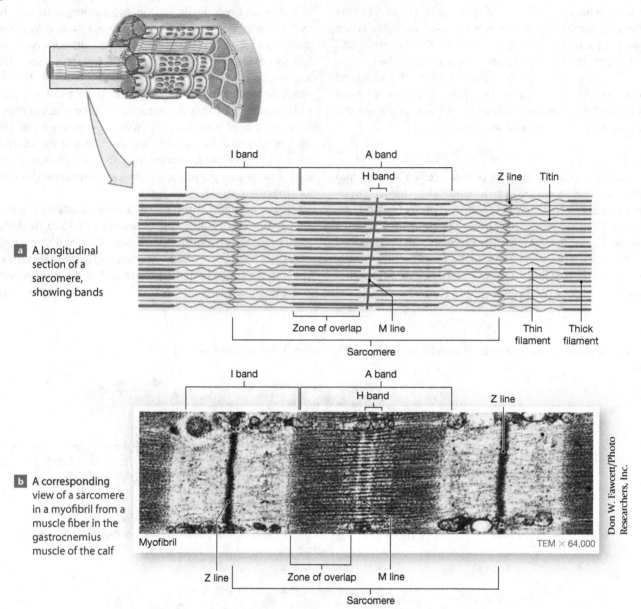

a A longitudinal section of a sarcomere, showing bands

I band · A band · H band · Z line · Titin · Zone of overlap · M line · Sarcomere · Thin filament · Thick filament

b A corresponding view of a sarcomere in a myofibril from a muscle fiber in the gastrocnemius muscle of the calf

I band · A band · H band · Z line · Myofibril · TEM × 64,000 · Z line · Zone of overlap · M line · Sarcomere

Don W. Fawcett/Photo Researchers, Inc.

The filaments are arranged in repeating patterns called **sarco-meres** (SAR-kō-mĕrz; *sarkos*, flesh + *meros*, part) along a myofibril. The thin filaments connect to one another at the **Z lines** on each end of the sarcomere. Each Z line is made of a protein called **actinin.** Areas near the Z line that contain only thin filaments are **I bands.** Between I bands in a sarcomere is the **A band,** an area containing both thin and thick filaments. The edges of the A band are the **zone of overlap** where the thick and thin filaments bind during muscle contraction. The middle region of the A band is the **H zone** and contains only thick filaments. A dense **M line** in the center of the A band attaches the thick filaments. Because the thick and thin filaments do not overlap one another completely, some areas of the sarcomere appear lighter than others. This organization results in the striated (striped) appearance of skeletal muscle tissue visible in Figure 3b.

A thin filament consists of two intertwined strands of actin (**Figure 4**). Four protein components make up the actin strands: G actin, F actin, nebulin, and active sites. The **G actins** are individual spherical molecules, like pearls on a necklace. Approximately 300 to 400 G actins twist together into an **F-actin strand.** The G actins are held in position along the strand by

Figure 4 Thick and Thin Filaments

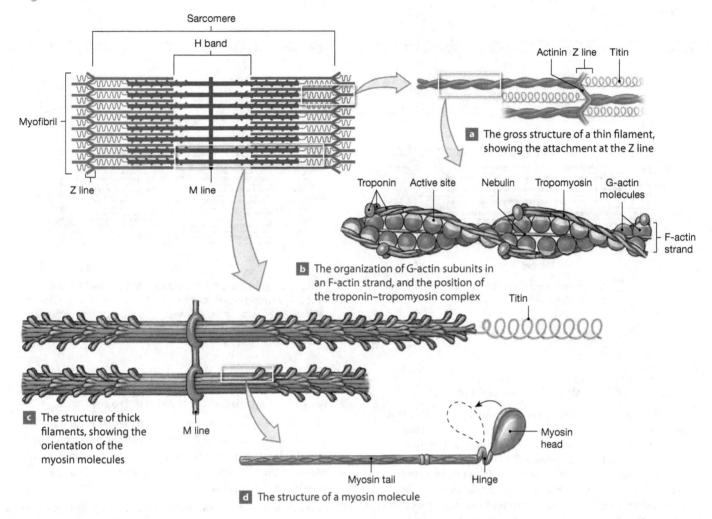

a The gross structure of a thin filament, showing the attachment at the Z line

b The organization of G-actin subunits in an F-actin strand, and the position of the troponin–tropomyosin complex

c The structure of thick filaments, showing the orientation of the myosin molecules

d The structure of a myosin molecule

the protein **nebulin,** much like the string of a necklace holds the beads in place. On each G-actin molecule is an **active site** where myosin molecules in the thick filaments bind during contraction. Associated with the actin strands are two other proteins, **tropomyosin** (trō-pō-MĪ-ō-sin; *trope,* turning) and **troponin** (TRŌ-pō-nin). Tropomyosin follows the twisted actin strands and blocks active sites to regulate muscle contraction. Troponin holds tropomyosin in position and has binding sites for calcium ions. When calcium ions are released into the sarcoplasm, they bind to and cause troponin to change shape. This change in shape moves tropomyosin away from the binding sites, exposing the sites to myosin heads so that the interactions necessary for contraction can take place.

A thick filament is made of approximately 300 subunits of myosin. Each subunit consists of two strands: two intertwined **tail** regions and two globular **heads.** Bundles of myosin subunits, with the tails parallel to one another and the heads projecting outward, constitute a thick filament. A protein called **titin** attaches

the thick filament to the Z line on the end of the sarcomere. Each myosin head contains a **binding site** for actin and a region that functions as an **ATPase enzyme.** This portion of the head splits an ATP molecule and absorbs the released energy to bind to a thin filament and then pivot and slide the thin filament inward.

When a muscle fiber contracts, the thin filaments are pulled deep into the sarcomere (**Figure 5**). As the thin filaments slide inward, the I band and H zone become smaller. Each myofibril consists of approximately 10,000 sarcomeres that are joined end to end. During contraction, the sarcomeres compress and the myofibril shortens and pulls on the sarcolemma, causing the muscle fiber to shorten as well.

QuickCheck Questions

1.1 Describe the connective tissue organization of a muscle.

1.2 What is the relationship between myofibrils and sarcomeres?

1.3 Where are calcium ions stored in a muscle fiber?

Figure 5 **Changes in the Appearance of a Sarcomere During the Contraction of a Skeletal Muscle Fiber**

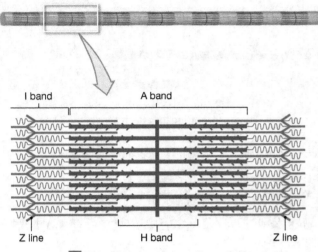

I band   A band

Z line   H band   Z line

a This relaxed sarcomere shows the location of the A band, Z lines, and I band.

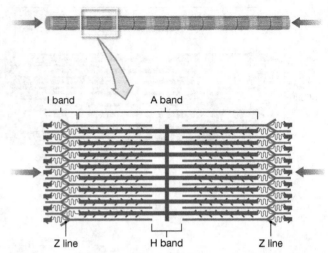

I band   A band

Z line   H band   Z line

b During a contraction, the A band stays the same width, but the Z lines move closer together and the I band gets smaller. When the ends of a myofibril are free to move, the sarcomeres shorten simultaneously and the ends of the myofibril are pulled toward its center.

Clinical Application Muscular Dystrophies (MD)

Muscular dystrophies (DIS-trŏ-fēz) are inherited diseases that cause changes in muscle proteins that result in progressive weakening and deterioration of skeletal muscles. The most common type of MD, Duchenne's (DMD), starts in childhood and is often fatal with cardiac and respiratory failure by the age of 20. DMD occurs with a mutation of the gene for muscle protein **dystrophin** that is part of the anchoring complex that attaches thin filaments to the sarcolemma. In the absence of normal dystrophin molecules, calcium channels in the sarcoplasmic reticulum remain open. Elevated calcium levels gradually deteriorate muscle proteins important in contraction. The dystrophin gene is located on the X chromosome. Mothers can carry the mutated MD form and have a 50 percent chance of passing it on to each of their male offspring. Steroids are used to slow degeneration and inflammation of muscles; however, treatment for the disease is still in the research phase. ■

In the Lab 1

Materials

☐ Muscle model
☐ Muscle fiber model
☐ Round steak or similar cut of meat
☐ Preserved muscle tissue
☐ Dissecting microscope

Procedures

1. Review the organization of muscles in Figures 1 to 5.
2. Identify the connective tissue coverings of muscles on the laboratory models. If your instructor has prepared a muscle demonstration from a cut of meat, examine the meat for the various connective tissues. Are fascicles visible on the specimen?
3. Examine the muscle fiber model and identify each feature. Describe the location of the sarcoplasmic reticulum, myofibrils, sarcomeres, and filaments.
4. Examine a specimen of preserved muscle tissue by placing the tissue in saline solution and then teasing the muscle apart using tweezers and a probe. Notice how the fascicles appear as strands of muscle tissue. Examine the fascicles under a dissecting microscope. How are they arranged in the muscle?

For additional practice, complete the *Sketch to Learn* Activity. ■

Lab Activity 2   The Neuromuscular Junction

Each skeletal muscle fiber is controlled by a nerve cell called a **motor neuron.** To excite the muscle fiber, the motor neuron releases a chemical message called **acetylcholine** (as-ē-til-KŌ-lēn), abbreviated ACh. The motor neuron and the

Sketch to Learn

Let's draw a relaxed sarcomere and label each region.

Sample Sketch

Step 1
- Draw 2 stacks of 3 horizontal lines. Be sure to keep the lines the same length.

Step 2
- Connect the outer edges of lines together for the 2 stacks.
- Add thick lines between the thin ones.

Step 3
- Add small bristle-like heads on thick filaments.
- Label your drawing.

Your Sketch

muscle fiber meet at a **neuromuscular junction** (Figure 6), also called a **myoneural junction.** The end of the neuron, called the *axon*, expands to form a bulbous **synaptic terminal,** also called a **synaptic knob.** In the synaptic terminal are **synaptic vesicles** that contain ACh. A small gap, the **synaptic cleft,** separates the synaptic terminal from a folded area of the sarcolemma called the **motor end plate.** At the motor end plate, the sarcolemma releases into the synaptic cleft the enzyme **acetylcholinesterase (AChE),** which prevents overstimulation of the muscle fiber by deactivating ACh.

An Overview of Muscle Contraction

When a nerve impulse, called an **action potential,** travels down a neuron and reaches the synaptic terminal, the synaptic vesicles release ACh into the synaptic cleft. The ACh diffuses across the cleft and binds to ACh receptors embedded in the sarcolemma at the motor end plate of the muscle fiber. This binding of the chemical stimulus causes the sarcolemma to generate an action potential. The potential spreads across the sarcolemma and down transverse tubules, causing calcium ions to be released from the sarcoplasmic reticulum into the sarcoplasm of the muscle fiber. The calcium ions bind to troponin, which in turn moves tropomyosin and exposes the active sites on the G actins. The myosin heads attach to the active sites and ratchet the thin filaments inward, much like a tug-of-war team pulling on a rope. As thin filaments slide into the H zone, the sarcomere shortens. The additive effect of the shortening of many sarcomeres along the myofibril results in a decrease in the length of the myofibril and contraction of the muscle.

In a relaxed muscle fiber, the calcium ion concentration in the sarcoplasm is minimal. When the muscle fiber is stimulated, calcium channels in the sarcoplasmic reticulum open and calcium ions rapidly flow down the concentration gradient into the sarcoplasm. Because each myofibril is surrounded by sarcoplasmic reticulum, calcium ions are quickly and efficiently released among the thick and thin filaments of the myofibril. For the muscle to relax, calcium-ion pumps in the sarcoplasmic reticulum actively transport calcium ions out of the sarcoplasm and into the cisternae.

QuickCheck Questions

2.1 What molecules are in the synaptic vesicles?

2.2 Where is the motor end plate?

Figure 6 **Skeletal Muscle Innervation**

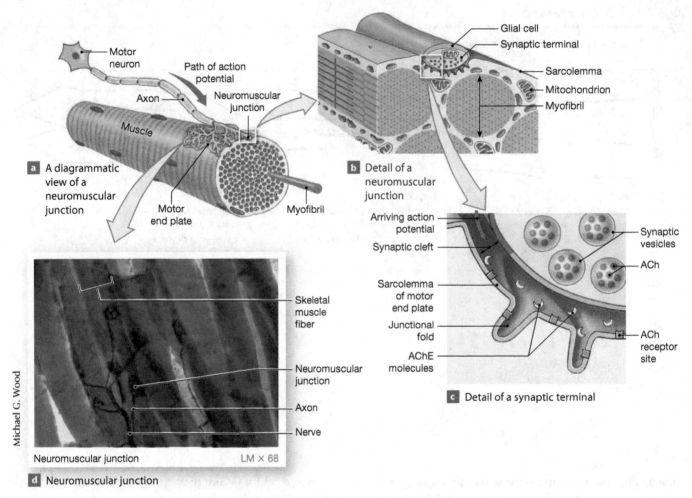

a A diagrammatic view of a neuromuscular junction

Motor neuron

Path of action potential

Axon

Muscle

Neuromuscular junction

Motor end plate

Myofibril

b Detail of a neuromuscular junction

Glial cell
Synaptic terminal
Sarcolemma
Mitochondrion
Myofibril

Arriving action potential
Synaptic cleft
Sarcolemma of motor end plate
Junctional fold
AChE molecules

Synaptic vesicles
ACh
ACh receptor site

c Detail of a synaptic terminal

Skeletal muscle fiber

Neuromuscular junction

Axon

Nerve

Neuromuscular junction   LM × 68

Michael G. Wood

d Neuromuscular junction

In the Lab 2

Materials

☐ Compound microscope
☐ Neuromuscular junction slide

Procedures

1. Review the structure of the neuromuscular junction in Figure 6.

2. Examine the slide of the neuromuscular junction at low and medium powers. Identify the long, dark, threadlike structures and the oval disks. Describe the appearance of the muscle fibers.

3. **Draw It!** In the space provided, sketch several muscle fibers and their neuromuscular junctions. ■

Muscle fibers

Lab Activity 3 Naming Muscles

Numerous methods are used to name skeletal muscles (Table 1). One method names muscles according to either the bones they attach to or the region of the body in which they are found. For example, the temporalis muscle is found on the temporal bone, and the rectus abdominis muscle forms the anterior muscular wall of the abdomen. Another easily identifiable muscle is the sternocleidomastoid, which is attached to the sternum (*sterno-*), the

Table 1 Muscle Terminology

Terms Indicating Specific Regions of the Body	Terms Indicating Position, Direction, or Fascicle Organization	Terms Indicating Structural Characteristics of the Muscle	Terms Indicating Actions
Abdominis (abdomen)	Anterior (front)	**NATURE OF ORIGIN**	**GENERAL**
Anconeus (elbow)	Externus (superficial)	Biceps (two heads)	Abductor
Auricularis (auricle of ear)	Extrinsic (outside)	Triceps (three heads)	Adductor
Brachialis (brachium)	Inferioris (inferior)	Quadriceps (four heads)	Depressor
Capitis (head)	Internus (deep internal)		Extensor
Carpi (wrist)	Intrinsic (inside)	**SHAPE**	Flexor
Cervicis (neck)	Lateralis (lateral)	Deltoid (triangle)	Levator
Cleido-/-clavius (clavicle)	Medialis/medius (medial middle)	Orbicularis (circle)	Pronator
Coccygeus (coccyx)	Oblique	Pectinate (comblike)	Rotator
Costalis (ribs)	Posterior (back)	Piriformis (pear-shaped)	Supinator
Cutaneous (skin)	Profundus (deep)	Platy- (flat)	Tensor
Femoris (femur)	Rectus (straight parallel)	Pyramidal (pyramid)	
Genio- (chin)	Superficialis (superficial)	Rhomboid	**SPECIFIC**
Glosso-/-glossal (tongue)	Superions (superior)	Serratus (serrated)	Buccinator (trumpeter)
Hallucis (great toe)	Transversus (transverse)	Splenius (bandage)	Risorius (laughter)
Ilio- (ilium)		Teres (long and round)	Sartorius (like a tailor)
Inguinal (groin)		Trapezius (trapezoid)	
Lumborum (lumbar region)			
Nasalis (nose)		**OTHER STRIKING FEATURES**	
Nuchal (back of neck)		Alba (white)	
Oculo- (eye)		Brevis (short)	
Oris (mouth)		Gracilis (slender)	
Palpebrae (eyelid)		Lata (wide)	
Pollicis (thumb)		Latissimus (widest)	
Popliteus (posterior to knee)		Longissimus (longest)	
Psoas (loin)		Longus (long)	
Radialis (radius)		Magnus (large)	
Scapularis (scapula)		Major (larger)	
Temporalis (temples)		Maximus (largest)	
Thoracis (thoracic region)		Minimus (smallest)	
Tibialis (tibia)		Minor (smaller)	
Ulnaris (ulna)		Tendinosus (tendinous)	
Uro- (urinary)		Vastus (great)	

clavicle (*cleido-*), and the mastoid process of the temporal bone. The size of a muscle or the direction of fibers in a muscle is often reflected in its name. Many muscles have multiple origins. Look for the prefixes *bi-* for two, *tri-* for three, and *quad-* for four origins. Anatomists also conceive names based on muscle shape. The deltoid has a broad origin and inserts on a very narrow region of the humerus. This gives this muscle a triangular, or *deltoid*, shape; hence the name.

Many muscles are named based on how they move the body. The name *flexor carpi ulnaris* appears complex, but it is really quite easy to understand if you examine it step by step. *Flexor* means the muscle flexes something. *Carpi* refers to carpals, the bones of the wrist, and *ulnaris* suggests that the muscle flexes the carpi on the medial side of the wrist, where the ulna is located. Therefore, the flexor carpi ulnaris is a muscle that flexes and adducts the wrist.

Make a Prediction

What does the muscle name *biceps femoris* mean?

QuickCheck Questions

3.1 Give two examples of how muscles are named.

3.2 What does the name *sternocleidomastoid* mean?

In the Lab 3

Material

☐ Torso model

Procedures

1. Review the muscle terminology in Table 1.
2. Using the names of the following muscles, locate each muscle on the torso model.
   - Rectus abdominis
   - Gluteus maximus
   - Deltoid ■

Name _____

Date _____

Section _____

Organization
of Skeletal Muscles

A. Definitions

Write a definition for each term.

1. sarcomere

2. epimysium

3. perimysium

4. endomysium

5. myofibril

6. striations

7. sarcolemma

8. transverse tubule

9. sarcoplasmic reticulum

10. actin

11. myosin

12. fascicle

B. Matching

Match each term in the left column with its correct description from the right column.

_____	1. glossal	A. mouth
_____	2. cleido	B. clavicle
_____	3. scapularis	C. moves away
_____	4. abductor	D. great
_____	5. oris	E. tongue
_____	6. brevis	F. moves toward
_____	7. adductor	G. eye
_____	8. oculi	H. scapula
_____	9. vastus	I. tenses
_____	10. rectus	J. head
_____	11. tensor	K. short
_____	12. capitis	L. straight

C. Drawing

1. *Draw It!* Draw the organization of a skeletal muscle and show the various types of connective tissue, fascicles, and muscle fiber.

2. *Draw It!* Draw a sarcomere and label each band and zone.

D. **Short-Answer Questions**

1. Describe the structure of a fascicle, including the connective tissue covering around and within the fascicle.

2. How does a motor neuron stimulate a muscle fiber to contract?

3. Describe the structure of a sarcomere.

E. **Labeling**

Label the structure of the muscle fiber in Figure 7.

Figure 7 Structure of a Muscle Fiber

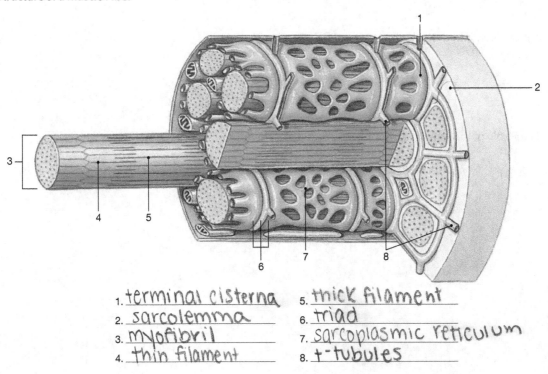

1. _terminal cisterna_   5. _thick filament_
2. _sarcolemma_   6. _triad_
3. _myofibril_   7. _sarcoplasmic reticulum_
4. _thin filament_   8. _t-tubules_

F. **Analysis and Application**

   1. What gives skeletal muscle fibers their striations?

   2. Describe the role of each thin-filament protein and each thick-filament protein in muscle contraction.

   3. Many insecticides contain a compound that is an acetylcholinesterase inhibitor. How would exposure to this poison affect skeletal muscles in a human?

G. **Clinical Challenge**

   1. How can children inherit Duchenne's muscular dystrophy (DMD)?

   2. What is the role of the protein dystrophin in normal muscle function and in DMD?

Muscles of the Head and the Neck Wish List

During the unit on muscles, you will be required to learn the same muscles for lecture and lab. As you review the activities of the 4 muscle chapters, make sure you work on memorizing origins, insertions and actions on your wish lists.

✓	Cranial, Face and Eye	Description/Action	Origin Bone/marking	Insertion Bone/marking
	Occipitofrontalis frontal belly	Raises eyebrows, wrinkles forehead	Epicranial aponeurosis	Skin of eyebrow and bridge of nose
	Orbicularis Oculi	Closes eye	Medial margin of orbit	Skin around eyelids
	Levator Labii Superioris	Elevates upper lip	Inferior margin of orbit	Orbicularis oris
	Depressor Labii Inferioris	Depresses lower lip	Mandible	Skin of lower lip
	Orbicularis Oris	Compresses, purses lips	Maxilla and Mandible	Lips
	Inferior rectus	Eyes looks down	Sphenoid	Inferior surface
	Medial rectus	Eye looks medially	Sphenoid	Medial surface
	Superior rectus	Eye looks up	Sphenoid	Superior surface
	Lateral rectus	Eye looks laterally	Sphenoid	Lateral surface
	Inferior oblique	Eye rolls, looks up and laterally	Maxilla	Inferior/Lateral surface
	Superior oblique	Eye rolls, looks down and laterally	Sphenoid	Superior/Lateral surface
✓	**Muscles of Mastication**	**Description/Action**	**Origin Bone**	**Insertion Bone/marking**
	Temporalis	Elevates/closes jaw	Temporal bone	Coronoid process of mandible
	Masseter	Elevates mandible	Zygomatic arch	Angle/ramus of mandible
	Trapezius	Superior portion-rotate scapula upward, middle portion-adduct scapula, inferior portion-depress scapula. Together-stabilize scapula.	Occipital bone/spinous processes of C7-T12 (mostly thoracic vertebrae)	Clavicle/acromion/spine of scapula

Muscles of the Head and Neck

Learning Outcomes

On completion of this exercise, you should be able to:

1. Identify the origin, insertion, and action of the muscles used for facial expression and mastication.

2. Identify the origin, insertion, and action of the muscles that move the eye.

3. Identify the origin, insertion, and action of the muscles that move the tongue, head, and anterior neck.

Muscles are organized into the axial and appendicular divisions to reflect their attachment to either the axial or appendicular skeleton. Axial muscles include the muscles of the head and neck, and muscles of the vertebral column, abdomen, and pelvis. Appendicular muscles are muscles of the pectoral girdle and upper limb and the pelvic girdle and lower limb.

The movement and attachments of a muscle are often reflected in its name. Each muscle causes a movement, called the **action,** that depends on many factors, especially the shape of the attached bones. For a muscle to produce a smooth, coordinated action, one end of it must serve as an attachment site while the other end moves the intended bone. The relatively stationary part of the muscle is called the **origin.** The opposite end of the muscle, the part that moves the bone, is called the **insertion.** As the muscle contracts, the insertion moves toward the origin to generate a pulling force and cause the muscle's action. Muscles can generate only a pulling force; they can never push. Usually, when one muscle, called

Need More Practice and Review?

Build your knowledge—and confidence!—in the Study Area of MasteringA&P® at www.masteringaandp.com with Pre-lab Quizzes, Post-lab Quizzes, Practice Anatomy Lab™ (PAL™) 3.0 virtual anatomy practice tool, PhysioEx™ 9.0 laboratory simulations, and A&P Flix™ with Quizzes.

PAL For this lab exercise, follow these navigation paths:
- PAL>Human Cadaver>Muscular System>Head and Neck
- PAL>Anatomical Models>Muscular System>Head and Neck

    For this lab exercise, go to these topics:
- Origins, Insertions, Actions, and Innervations
- Group Muscle Actions and Joints

A&PFlix

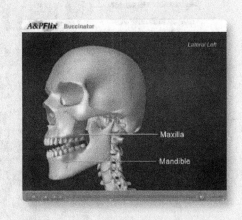

From Exercise 18 of *Laboratory Manual for Anatomy & Physiology featuring Martini Art*, Fifth Edition. Michael G. Wood.

an **agonist,** pulls in one direction, an **antagonistic** muscle pulls in the opposite direction to produce resistance and promote smooth movement. **Synergists** are muscles that work together and are often classified together in a **muscle group,** such as the oblique group of the abdomen.

The muscles of the head and neck produce a wide range of motions for making facial expressions, processing food, producing speech, and positioning the head. The names of

these muscles usually indicate either the bone to which a muscle is attached or the structure a muscle surrounds. In this exercise you will identify the major muscles used for facial expression and mastication, the muscles that move the eyes, and those that position the head and neck. As you study each group, attempt to find the general location of each muscle on your body. Contract the muscle and observe its action as your body moves.

Study Tip Muscle Modeling

Your fingers and hands can be used to simulate the origin, insertion, and action of muscles. For example, place the base of your right index finger on your right zygomatic bone and the tip of the index finger at the right corner of your mouth. The finger now represents the zygomatic major muscle, which elevates the edge of the mouth. The base of the finger represents the muscle's origin at the zygomatic bone, and the tip represents the insertion. When you flex your finger and elevate your mouth, you are mimicking the major action of this muscle. Smile! ∎

Lab Activity 1 Muscles of Facial Expression

The muscles of facial expression are those associated with the mouth, eyes, nose, ears, scalp, and neck. These muscles are unique in that one or both attachments are to the dermis of the skin rather than to a bone. Refer to Figure 1 and Table 1 for details on the origin, insertion, and actions of these muscles.

Make a Prediction

The face has two sphincter muscles. Where are they and what action does each perform?

Figure 1 Muscles of Facial Expression Anterior view.

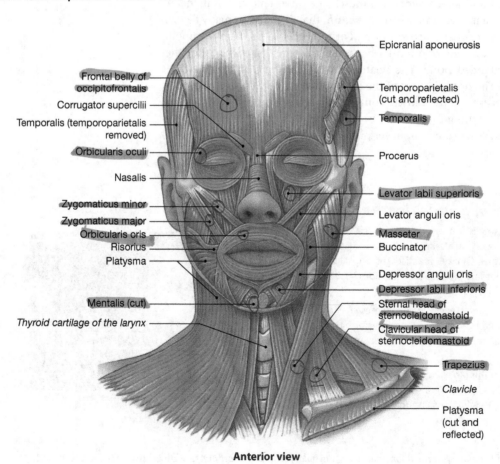

Frontal belly of occipitofrontalis
Corrugator supercilii
Temporalis (temporoparietalis removed)
Orbicularis oculi
Nasalis
Zygomaticus minor
Zygomaticus major
Orbicularis oris
Risorius
Platysma
Mentalis (cut)
Thyroid cartilage of the larynx

Epicranial aponeurosis
Temporoparietalis (cut and reflected)
Temporalis
Procerus
Levator labii superioris
Levator anguli oris
Masseter
Buccinator
Depressor anguli oris
Depressor labii inferioris
Sternal head of sternocleidomastoid
Clavicular head of sternocleidomastoid
Trapezius
Clavicle
Platysma (cut and reflected)

Anterior view

Scalp

The **occipitofrontalis muscle** is the major muscle of the scalp, which is called the *epicranium*. It consists of two muscle bellies, the **frontal belly** and the **occipital belly,** which are separated by a flat sheet of connective tissue attached to the scalp called the **epicranial aponeurosis** (ep-i-KRĀ-nē-ul ap-ō-nū-RŌ-sis; *epi-,* on + *kranion,* skull). The frontal belly of the occipitofrontalis muscle is the broad anterior muscle on the forehead that covers the frontal bone. It originates at the epicranial aponeurosis and inserts on the superior margin of the eye orbit, near the eyebrow and on the bridge of the nose. The actions of the frontal belly include wrinkling the forehead, raising the eyebrows, and pulling the scalp forward. The occipital belly of the occipitofrontalis muscle covers the posterior of the skull. It originates on the superior nuchal line and inserts on the epicranial aponeurosis. This muscle tenses and retracts the scalp, an action difficult for most people to isolate and perform.

Ear

The **temporoparietalis** muscle occurs on the lateral sides of the epicranium. The muscle is cut and reflected (pulled up) in Figure 1 to illustrate deeper muscles of the epicranium. The action of the temporoparietalis is to tense the scalp and move the auricle (flap) of the ear. The origin and insertion for this muscle are on the epicranial aponeurosis.

Eye

Muscles of the face that surround the eyes wrinkle the brow and move the eyelids. Muscles that move the eyeball are covered in an upcoming activity in this exercise.

The sphincter muscle of the eye is the **orbicularis oculi** (or-bik-ū-LA-ris OK-ū-lī). It arises from the medial wall of the eye orbit, and its fibers form a band of muscle that passes around the circumference of the eye, which serves as the insertion. The muscle acts to close the eye, as during an exaggerated blink. The **corrugator supercilii** muscle is a small muscle that originates on the orbital rim of the frontal bone and inserts on the eyebrow. It acts to pull the skin inferiorly and wrinkles the forehead into a frown. The **levator palpebrae superioris** muscle inserts on and elevates the upper eyelid. (This muscle is not visible in Figure 1. See Figure 2.)

Nose

The human nose has limited movement, and the related muscles serve mainly to change the shape of the nostrils. The **procerus muscle** has a vertical orientation over the nasal bones; the **nasalis muscle** horizontally spans the inferior nasal bridge.

Mouth

The **buccinator** (BUK-si-nā-tor) **muscle** is the horizontal muscle spanning between the jaws. It compresses the cheeks when you are eating or sucking on a straw. The **orbicularis oris muscle** is a sphincter muscle that inserts on the skin surrounding the mouth. This muscle shapes the lips for a variety of functions, including speech, food manipulation, and facial expressions, and purses the lips together for a kiss. The **levator labii superioris muscle** is lateral to the nose and inserts on the superolateral edge of the orbicularis oris muscle. As its name implies, the levator labii superioris muscle elevates the upper lip. Muscles that act on the lower lip are inferior to the mouth. The **depressor anguli oris muscle** inserts on the skin at the angle of the mouth to depress the corners of the mouth. The **depressor labii inferioris muscle** is medial to the anguli muscle and inserts along the edge of the lower lip to depress the lower lip. On the medial chin is the **mentalis muscle,** which elevates and protrudes the lower lip.

The **risorius muscle** is a narrow muscle that inserts on the angle of the mouth. When it contracts, the risorius muscle pulls and produces a grimace-like tensing of the mouth. Although the term *risorius* refers to a smile, the muscle is probably more associated with the expression of pain than pleasure. In the disease tetanus, the risorius is involved in the painful contractions that pull the corners of the mouth back into "lockjaw."

The **zygomaticus major** and **zygomaticus minor muscles** originate on the zygomatic bone and insert on the skin and corners of the mouth. These muscles retract and elevate the corners of the mouth when you smile.

Neck

The **platysma** (pla-TIZ-muh; *platy,* flat) is a thin, broad muscle covering the sides of the neck. It originates on the fascia covering the pectoralis and deltoid muscles and extends upward to insert on the inferior edge of the mandible. Some of the fibers of the platysma also extend into the fascia and muscles of the lower face. The platysma depresses the mandible and the soft structures of the lower face, resulting in an expression of horror and disgust.

QuickCheck Questions

1.1 What are the two facial muscles that are circular?

1.2 What are the muscles associated with the epicranial aponeurosis?

In the Lab   1

Materials

☐ Head model

☐ Muscle chart

Table 1 — *ORIGINS AND INSERTIONS* Muscles of Facial Expression (See Figure 1)

Region/Muscle	Origin	Insertion	Action	Innervation
MOUTH				
Buccinator	Alveolar processes of maxilla and mandible	Blends into fibers of orbicularis oris	Compresses cheeks	Facial nerve (N VII)*
Depressor labii inferioris	Mandible between the anterior midline and the mental foramen	Skin of lower lip	Depresses lower lip	As above
Levator labii superioris	Inferior margin of orbit, superior to the infraorbital foramen	Orbicularis oris	Elevates upper lip	As above
Levator anguli oris	Maxilla below the infraorbital foramen	Corner of mouth	Elevates mouth corner	As above
Mentalis	Incisive fossa of mandible	Skin of chin	Elevates and protrudes lower lip	As above
Orbicularis oris	Maxilla and mandible	Lips	Compresses, purses lips	As above
Risorius	Fascia surrounding parotid salivary gland	Angle of mouth	Draws corner of mouth to the side	As above
Depressor anguli oris	Anterolateral surface of mandibular body	Skin at angle of mouth	Depresses corner of mouth	As above
Zygomaticus major	Zygomatic bone near zygomaticomaxillary suture	Angle of mouth	Retracts and elevates corner of mouth	As above
Zygomaticus minor	Zygomatic bone posterior to zygomaticotemporal suture	Upper lip	Retracts and elevates upper lip	As above
EYE				
Corrugator supercilii	Orbital rim of frontal bone near nasal suture	Eyebrow	Pulls skin inferiorly and anteriorly; wrinkles brow	As above
Levator palpebrae superioris (*Figure 2*)	Tendinous band around optic foramen	Upper eyelid	Elevates upper eyelid	Oculomotor nerve (N III)**
Orbicularis oculi	Medial margin of orbit	Skin around eyelids	Closes eye	Facial nerve (N VII)
NOSE				
Procerus	Nasal bones and lateral nasal cartilages	Aponeurosis at bridge of nose and skin of forehead	Moves nose, changes position and shape of nostrils	As above
Nasalis	Maxilla and alar cartilage of nose	Bridge of nose	Compresses bridge, depresses tip of nose; elevates corners of nostrils	As above
EAR				
Temporoparietalis	Fascia around external ear	Epicranial aponeurosis	Tenses scalp, moves auricle of ear	As above
SCALP (EPICRANIUM)				
Occipitofrontalis frontal belly	Epicranial aponeurosis	Skin of eyebrow and bridge of nose	Raises eyebrows, wrinkles forehead	As above
Occipital belly	Epicranial aponeurosis	Epicranial aponeurosis	Tenses and retracts scalp	As above
NECK				
Platysma	Superior thorax between cartilage of 2nd rib and acromion of scapula	Mandible and skin of cheek	Tenses skin of neck; depresses mandible	As above

*An uppercase N and Roman numerals refer to a cranial nerve.
**This muscle originates in association with the extrinsic eye muscles, so its innervation is unusual.

Procedures

1. Review the muscles of the head in Figure 1.
2. Examine the head model and/or the muscle chart, and locate each muscle described in the preceding paragraphs.
3. Find the general location of the muscles of facial expression on your face. Practice the action of each muscle and observe how your facial expression changes. ■

Lab Activity 2 Muscles of the Eye

The **extrinsic muscles** of the eye, also called **extraocular eye muscles** or **oculomotor muscles,** are the muscles that move the eyeballs. (In general, any muscle located outside the structure it controls is called an **extrinsic muscle,** and any muscle inside the structure it controls is referred to as an **intrinsic muscle.**) The extraocular muscles insert on the *sclera*, which is the white, fibrous covering of the eye. **Intrinsic eye muscles** are involved in focusing the eye for vision.

Six extraocular eye muscles control eye movements (**Figure 2** and **Table 2**). The **superior rectus, inferior rectus, medial rectus,** and **lateral rectus** muscles are straight muscles that move the eyeball in the superior, inferior, medial, and lateral directions, respectively. They originate around the optic foramen in the eye orbit and insert on the sclera. The **superior** and **inferior oblique** muscles attach diagonally on the eyeball. The superior oblique muscle has a tendon passing through a trochlea (pulley) located on the upper orbit. This muscle rolls the eye downward, and the inferior oblique muscle rolls the eye upward.

QuickCheck Questions

2.1 What are the four rectus muscles of the eye?

2.2 Which eye muscle passes through a pulleylike structure?

Figure 2 Extrinsic Eye Muscles

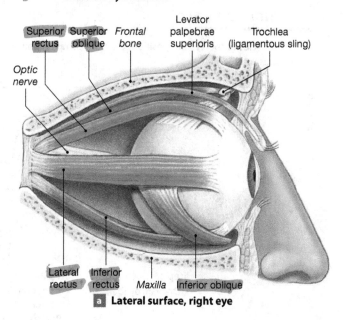

a **Lateral surface, right eye**

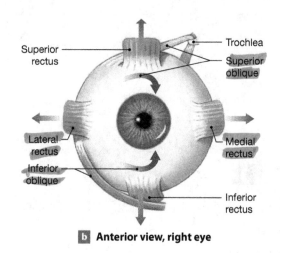

b **Anterior view, right eye**

Table 2	ORIGINS AND INSERTIONS Extrinsic Eye Muscles (See Figure 2)			
Muscle	**Origin**	**Insertion**	**Action**	**Innervation**
Inferior rectus	Sphenoid around optic canal	Inferior, medial surface of eyeball	Eye looks down	Oculomotor nerve (N III)
Medial rectus	As above	Medial surface of eyeball	Eye looks medially	As above
Superior rectus	As above	Superior surface of eyeball	Eye looks up	As above
Lateral rectus	As above	Lateral surface of eyeball	Eye looks laterally	Abducens nerve (N VI)
Inferior oblique	Maxilla at anterior portion of orbit	Inferior, lateral surface of eyeball	Eye rolls, looks up and laterally	Oculomotor nerve (N III)
Superior oblique	Sphenoid around optic canal	Superior, lateral surface of eyeball	Eye rolls, looks down and laterally	Trochlear nerve (N IV)

Sketch to Learn

The muscles of the eye are positioned on the compass points. Let's draw an eyeball with the extraocular muscles included.

Sample Sketch

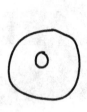

Step 1
- Draw an eyeball.

Step 2
- Add some lines "at the compass points" to represent the rectus muscles.

Step 3
- Draw the superior oblique and inferior oblique muscles.
- Label your drawing.

Your Sketch

In the Lab   2

Materials

☐ Eye model

☐ Eye muscle chart

Procedures

1. Review the muscles of the eye in Figure 2.
2. Examine the eye model and/or the eye muscle chart, and locate each extrinsic eye muscle.
3. Practice the action of each eye muscle by moving your eyeballs.

For additional practice, complete the *Sketch to Learn* activity. ■

Lab Activity   3   Muscles of Mastication

The muscles involved in mastication depress and elevate the mandible to open and close the jaws and grind the teeth against the food (**Figure 3** and **Table 3**). The **masseter** (MAS-se-tur) muscle is a short, thick muscle originating on the zygomatic arch and inserting on the angle and the ramus of the mandible. The **temporalis** (tem-pō-RA-lis) muscle covers almost the entire temporal fossa. This muscle has its origin on the temporal lines of the cranium and inserts on the coronoid process of the mandible.

Deep to the masseter and other cheek muscles are the **lateral** and **medial pterygoid** (TER-i-goyd; *pterygoin*, wing) muscles, which assist in mastication by elevating and depressing the mandible and moving the mandible from side to side, an action called *lateral excursion*.

Study Tip   The Mighty Masseter

Put your fingertips at the angle of your jaw and clench your teeth. You should feel the masseter bunch up as it forces the teeth together. ■

Figure 3 **Muscles of Mastication**

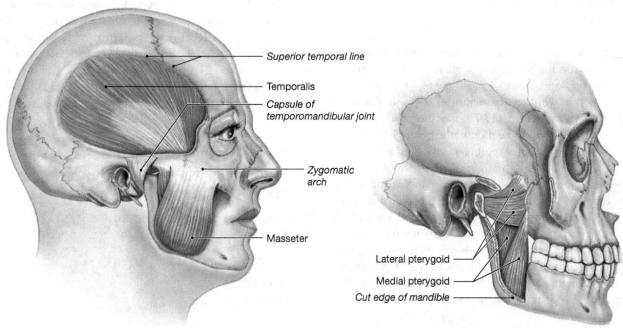

a **Lateral view.** The temporalis muscle passes medial to the zygomatic arch to insert on the coronoid process of the manible. The masseter inserts on the angle and lateral surface of the mandible.

b **Lateral view, pterygoid muscles exposed.** The location and orientation of the pterygoid muscles can be seen after the overlying muscles, along with a portion of the mandible, are removed.

Table 3	*ORIGINS AND INSERTIONS* **Muscles of Mastication (See Figure 3)**			
Muscle	**Origin**	**Insertion**	**Action**	**Innervation**
Masseter	Zygomatic arch	Lateral surface of mandibular ramus	Elevates mandible and closes the jaws	Trigeminal nerve (N V), mandibular branch
Temporalis	Along temporal lines of skull	Coronoid process of mandible	Elevates mandible	As above
Pterygoids (medial and lateral)	Lateral pterygoid plate	Medial surface of mandibular ramus	*Medial:* Elevates the mandible and closes the jaws, or performs lateral excursion	As above
			Lateral: Opens jaws, protrudes mandible, or performs lateral excursion	As above

QuickCheck Questions

3.1 To which bones do the muscles for mastication attach?

3.2 Which muscle protracts the mandible?

In the Lab 3

Materials

☐ Head model

☐ Muscle chart

Procedures

1. Review the mastication muscles in Table 3 and Figures 1 and 3.

2. Examine the head model and/or the muscle chart, and locate each mastication muscle described in this activity.

3. Find the general location of the muscles of mastication on your face. Practice the action of each muscle and observe how your mandible moves. ■

Lab Activity 4 Muscles of the Tongue and Pharynx

Extrinsic muscles of the tongue constitute the floor of the oral cavity and assist in the complex movements of the tongue for speech, chewing, and initiating swallowing (**Figure 4** and **Table 4**). The root word for these muscles is *glossus*, Greek for "tongue." Each prefix in the name indicates the muscle's origin.

In the anterior floor of the mouth, the **genioglossus** muscle originates on the medial mandibular surface around the chin and inserts on the body of the tongue and the hyoid bone. It depresses and protracts the tongue, as in initiating the licking of an ice cream cone. The **hyoglossus** muscle originates on the hyoid bone, inserts on the side of the tongue, and acts to both depress and retract the tongue. The **palatoglossus** muscle arises from the soft palate, inserts on the side of the tongue, elevates the tongue, and depresses the soft palate. The **styloglossus** muscle has its origin superior to the tongue on the styloid process. This muscle retracts the tongue and elevates its sides.

Muscles of the pharynx are involved in swallowing (Figure 4b and **Table 5**). The **superior, middle,** and **inferior constrictor** muscles constrict the pharynx to push food into the esophagus. The **levator veli palatini** and **tensor veli palatini** muscles elevate the soft palate during swallowing. The larynx is elevated by the **palatopharyngeus** (pal-āt-ō-far-IN-jē-us), **salpingopharyngeus** (sal-pin-gō-far-IN-jē-us), and **stylopharyngeus** muscles, and by some of the neck muscles.

QuickCheck Questions

4.1 What does the word *glossus* mean?

4.2 Where do the styloglossus and the hyoglossus muscles originate?

In the Lab 4

Materials

☐ Head model
☐ Muscle chart

Figure 4 Muscles of the Tongue and Pharynx

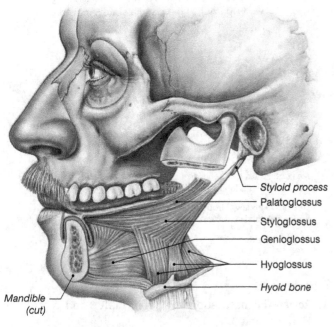

a The left mandibular ramus has been removed to show the extrinsic muscles on the left side of the tongue.

- Styloid process
- Palatoglossus
- Styloglossus
- Genioglossus
- Hyoglossus
- Hyoid bone
- *Mandible (cut)*

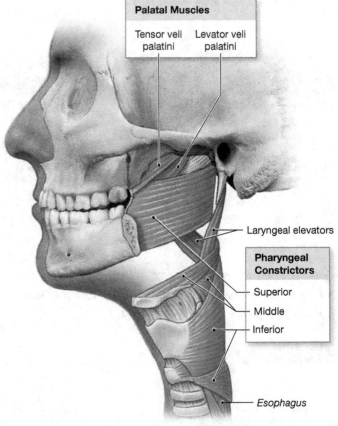

Palatal Muscles

Tensor veli palatini Levator veli palatini

- Laryngeal elevators

Pharyngeal Constrictors
- Superior
- Middle
- Inferior

- *Esophagus*

b Pharyngeal muscles for swallowing are shown in lateral view.

Table 4   *ORIGINS AND INSERTIONS* Muscles of the Tongue (See Figure 4a)

Muscle	Origin	Insertion	Action	Innervation
Genioglossus	Medial surface of mandible around chin	Body of tongue, hyoid bone	Depresses and protracts tongue	Hypoglossal nerve (N XII)
Hyoglossus	Body and greater horn of hyoid bone	Side of tongue	Depresses and retracts tongue	As above
Palatoglossus	Anterior surface of soft palate	As above	Elevates tongue, depresses soft palate	Internal branch of accessory nerve (N XI)
Styloglossus	Styloid process of temporal bone	Along the side to tip and base of tongue	Retracts tongue, elevates side	Hypoglossal nerve (N XII)

Table 5   *ORIGINS AND INSERTIONS* Muscles of the Pharynx (See Figure 4b)

Muscle	Origin	Insertion	Action	Innervation
PHARYNGEAL CONSTRICTORS				
Superior constrictor	Pterygoid process of sphenoid, medial surfaces of mandible	Median raphe attached to occipital bone	Constricts pharynx to propel bolus into esophagus	Branches of pharyngeal plexus (N X)
Middle constrictor	Horns of hyoid bone	Median raphe	As above	As above
Inferior constrictor	Cricoid and thyroid cartilages of larynx	As above	As above	As above
LARYNGEAL ELEVATORS*				
	Ranges from soft palate, to cartilage around inferior portion of auditory tube, to styloid process of temporal bone	Thyroid cartilage	Elevate larynx	Branches of pharyngeal plexus (N IX and N X)
PALATAL MUSCLES				
Levator veli palatini	Petrous part of temporal bone; tissues around the auditory tube	Soft palate	Elevates soft palate	Branches of pharyngeal plexus (N X)
Tensor veli palatini	Sphenoidal spine; tissues around the auditory tube	As above	As above	Trigeminal nerve (N V)

*Refers to the palatopharyngeus, salpingopharyngeus, and stylopharyngeus, assisted by the thyrohyoid, geniohyoid, stylohyoid, and hyoglossus muscles, discussed in Tables 4 and 6.

Procedures

1. Review the extrinsic muscles of the tongue in Figure 4 and Table 4.
2. Examine the head model and/or the muscle chart and identify each muscle of the tongue.
3. Practice the action of each tongue muscle. The ability to curl your tongue with the styloglossus is genetically controlled by a single gene. Individuals with the dominant gene are "rollers" and can curl the tongue. Those with the recessive form of the gene are "nonrollers." Is it possible for nonrollers to learn how to roll the tongue? Are you, your parents, or your children rollers or nonrollers?
4. Review the muscles of the pharynx in Figure 4b and Table 5.
5. Locate each pharyngeal muscle on the head model and/or muscle chart.
6. Place your finger on your larynx (Adam's apple) and swallow. Which muscles caused the larynx to move? ▪

Lab Activity 5   Muscles of the Anterior Neck

Muscles of the anterior neck, which stabilize and move the neck, act on the mandible and the hyoid bone (Figure 5 and Table 6). The principal muscle of the anterior neck is the **sternocleidomastoid** (ster-nō-klī-dō-MAS-toyd) muscle. This long, slender muscle occurs on both sides of the neck and is named after its points of attachment on the sternum, clavicle, and mastoid process of the temporal bone. When

Figure 5 Muscles of the Anterior Neck Muscles of the anterior neck adjust the position of the larynx, mandible, and floor of the mouth and establish a foundation for tongue and pharyngeal muscles.

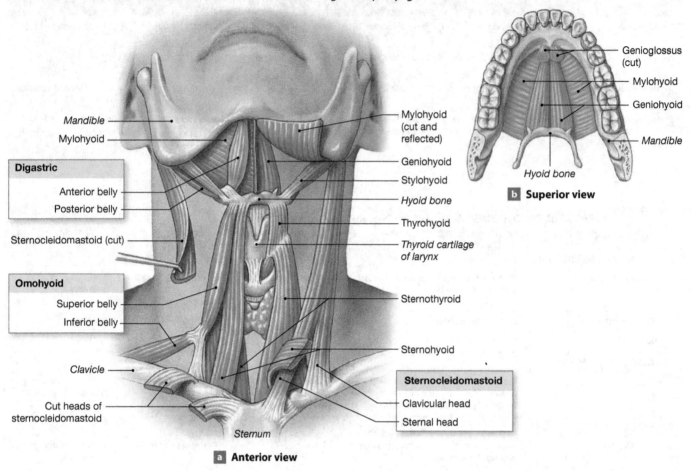

a Anterior view

b Superior view

the sternocleidomastoid muscles on the two sides of the neck contract, they act together to flex the neck; when only one sternocleidomastoid muscle contracts, it bends the head toward the shoulder and turns the face to the opposite side.

The *suprahyoid muscles* are a group of neck muscles that originate superior to, and act on, the hyoid bone. The suprahyoid muscle known as the **digastric muscle** has two parts: The **anterior belly** originates on the inferior surface of the mandible near the chin, and the **posterior belly** arises on the mastoid process of the temporal bone. The bellies insert on the hyoid bone and form a muscular swing that elevates the hyoid bone or depresses the mandible. The **mylohyoid** muscle is a wide muscle posterior to the anterior belly of the digastric muscle. The mylohyoid muscle elevates the hyoid bone or depresses the mandible. Deep and medial to the mylohyoid muscle is the **geniohyoid** muscle, which depresses the mandible, elevates the larynx, and can also retract the hyoid

bone. The **stylohyoid** muscle originates on the styloid process of the temporal bone, inserts on the hyoid bone, and elevates the hyoid bone and the larynx.

The *infrahyoid muscles* are a group of neck muscles that arise inferior to the hyoid bone, and their actions depress that bone and the larynx. The infrahyoid called the **omohyoid** (ō-mō-HĪ-ōyd) muscle has two bellies that meet at a central tendon attached to the clavicle and the first rib. Medial to the omohyoid muscle is the straplike **sternohyoid** muscle, which originates on the sternal end of the clavicle. Deep to the sternohyoid is the **sternothyroid** muscle, which arises on the manubrium of the sternum and inserts on the thyroid cartilage of the larynx. The omohyoid, sternohyoid, and sternothyroid muscles depress the hyoid bone and larynx. The **thyrohyoid** muscle originates on the thyroid cartilage of the larynx and inserts on the hyoid bone. It depresses this bone and elevates the larynx.

Table 6	ORIGINS AND INSERTIONS Anterior Muscles of the Neck (See Figure 5)			
Muscle	**Origin**	**Insertion**	**Action**	**Innervation**
Digastric	Two bellies *anterior* from inferior surface of mandible at chin; *posterior* from mastoid region of temporal bone	Hyoid bone	Depresses mandible or elevates larynx	*Anterior belly:* Trigeminal nerve (N V), mandibular branch *Posterior belly:* Facial nerve (N VII)
Geniohyoid	Medial surface of mandible at chin	Hyoid bone	As above and pulls hyoid bone anteriorly	Cervical nerve C_1 via hypoglossal nerve (N XII)
Mylohyoid	Mylohyoid line of mandible	Median connective tissue band (raphe) that runs to hyoid bone	Elevates floor of mouth and hyoid bone or depresses mandible	Trigeminal nerve (N V), mandibular branch
Omohyoid (superior and inferior bellies united at central tendon anchored to clavicle and first rib)	Superior border of scapula near scapular notch	Hyoid bone	Depresses hyoid bone and larynx	Cervical spinal nerves C_2–C_3
Sternohyoid	Clavicle and manubrium	Hyoid bone	As above	Cervical spinal nerves C_1–C_3
Sternothyroid	Dorsal surface of manubrium and first costal cartilage	Thyroid cartilage of larynx	As above	As above
Stylohyoid	Styloid process of temporal bone	Hyoid bone	Elevates larynx	Facial nerve (N VII)
Thyrohyoid	Thyroid cartilage of larynx	Hyoid bone	Elevates thyroid, depresses hyoid bone	Cervical spinal nerves C_1–C_2 via hypoglossal nerve (N XII)
Sternocleidomastoid	Two bellies: *clavicular head* attaches to sternal end of clavicle; *sternal head* attaches to manubrium	Mastoid region of skull and lateral portion of superior nuchal line	Together, they flex the neck; alone, one side bends head toward shoulder and turns face to opposite side	Accessory nerve (N XI) and cervical spinal nerves (C_2–C_3) of cervical plexus

QuickCheck Questions

5.1 Where does the sternocleidomastoid muscle attach?

5.2 What is the suffix in the names of muscles that insert on the hyoid bone?

5.3 Where is the digastric muscle located?

In the Lab 5

Materials

☐ Head–torso model

☐ Muscle chart

Procedures

1. Review the anterior neck muscles in Figure 5 and Table 6.

2. Locate each muscle on the head–torso model and/or the muscle chart.

3. Produce the actions of your suprahyoid and infrahyoid muscles and observe how your larynx moves.

4. Locate the sternocleidomastoid on the head–torso model and/or on the muscle chart.

5. Contract your sternocleidomastoid on one side and observe your head movement. Next, contract both sides and note how your head flexes.

6. Rotate your head until your chin almost touches your right shoulder and locate your left sternocleidomastoid just above the manubrium of the sternum. ■

Name _____

Date _____

Muscles of the Head and Neck

Section _____

A. Matching

Match each term in the left column with its correct description from the right column.

_____	**1.** orbicularis oculi	**A.** retracts scalp
_____	**2.** buccinator	**B.** elevates upper lip
_____	**3.** stylohyoid	**C.** thin muscle on sides of neck, depresses jaw
_____	**4.** masseter	
_____	**5.** frontal belly of occipitofrontalis	**D.** attached to styloid process and hyoid bone
_____	**6.** platysma	**E.** tenses angle of mouth laterally
_____	**7.** corrugator supercilii	**F.** elevates corner of mouth
_____	**8.** zygomaticus major	**G.** elevates jaw
_____	**9.** occipital belly of occipitofrontalis	**H.** two-bellied neck muscle
_____	**10.** levator labii superioris	**I.** wrinkles forehead
_____	**11.** digastric	**J.** tenses cheeks
_____	**12.** risorius	**K.** protracts scalp
		L. closes eye

B. Descriptions

Describe the location of each of the following muscles.

1. masseter

2. sternocleidomastoid

3. sternohyoid

4. orbicularis oris

5. zygomaticus minor

6. platysma

7. risorius

8. temporoparietalis

9. superior constrictor

10. digastric

C. Labeling

1. Label the eye muscles in Figure 6.

Figure 6 **Muscles of the Right Eye** Anterior view.

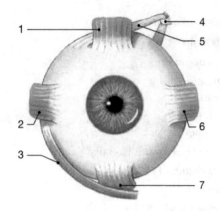

1. Superior rectus
2. lateral rectus
3. inferior oblique
4. trochlea
5. Superior oblique
6. medial rectus
7. inferior rectus

2. Label the muscles of the head in Figure 7.

Figure 7 **Muscles of the Head and Neck** Lateral view.

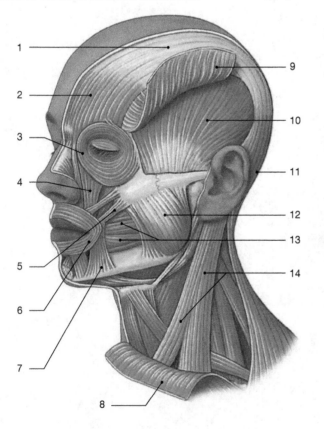

1.
2. frontalis
3. orbicularis oculi
4. levator labii superioris
5. zygomaticus major
6. orbicularis oris
7. depressor lavii inferioris
8.
9.
10. temporalis
11.
12. masseter
13.
14. trapezius

3. Label the muscles of the anterior neck in Figure 8.

Figure 8 **Muscles of the Anterior Neck** Anterior view.

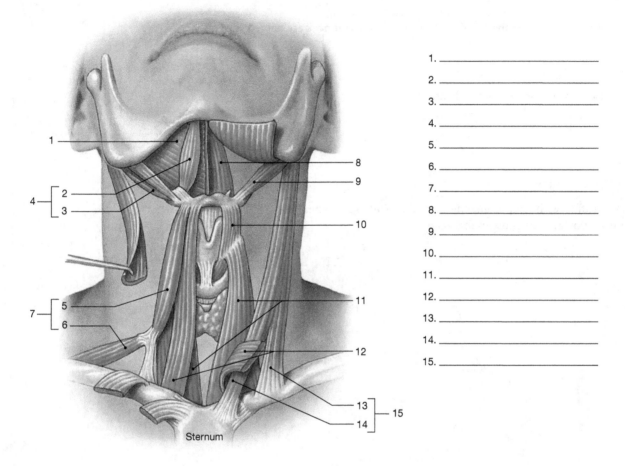

Sternum

1. _____
2. _____
3. _____
4. _____
5. _____
6. _____
7. _____
8. _____
9. _____
10. _____
11. _____
12. _____
13. _____
14. _____
15. _____

D. Analysis and Application

1. Describe the position and action of the muscles of mastication. Which muscles oppose the action of these muscles?

2. What anatomical descriptions are in the name *epicranial aponeurosis*?

3. Describe the movement produced by each extraocular eye muscle.

4. Explain how the muscles of the tongue and anterior neck are named.

5. Describe the actions of the digastric muscle.

E. Clinical Challenge

Mary suffers with temporomandibular joint (TMJ) syndrome. Describe the bones at this articulation and the muscles that act on them.

42
4

Muscles of the Vertebral Column, Abdomen, and Pelvis

Wish List

During the unit on muscles, you will be required to learn the same muscles for lecture and lab. As you review the activities of the 4 muscle chapters, make sure you work on memorizing origins, insertions and actions on your wish lists.

✓	Muscles of Respiration	Description/Action	Origin Bone/marking	Insertion Bone/marking
	Diaphragm	When contracted, it flattens and increases vertical dimension of thoracic cavity for inhalation. When relaxed, it moves superiorly and decrease vertical dimension of cavity for exhalation.	Xiphoid process of sternum/costal cartilage ribs/Lumbar vertebrae and discs.	Central Tendon (towards the center of diaphragm)
	External Intercostals	When contracted, they elevate ribs and increase anteroposterior dimension of thoracic cavity for inhalation. When relaxed, they depress ribs and decrease dimension of cavity for exhalation.	Inferior border of rib ABOVE	Superior border of rib BELOW
	Internal Intercostals	When contracted, draws adjacent ribs together to decrease dimensions of cavity during FORCED exhalation.	Superior border of rib BELOW	Inferior border of rib ABOVE

✓	Abdominal Muscles	Description/Action	Origin Bone/marking	Insertion Bone/marking
	Rectus Abdominis	Flexes vertebral column	Pubic crest/pubic Symphysis of Pubis/Os Coxa	Ribs 5-7/Xiphoid process of sternum
	External Oblique	Acting together (bilaterally)- compress abdomen/flex vertebral column. Acting separately (unilaterally)-lateral flexion of vertebral column.	Ribs 5-12	Iliac crest of Ilium/Os Coxa and linea alba (midline)

		Acting together (bilaterally)- compress abdomen/flex vertebral column. Acting separately (unilaterally)-lateral flexion of vertebral column.		
	Internal Oblique		Iliac crest of Ilium/Os Coxa	Ribs 7-10 and linea alba
	Transverse Abdominis	Compresses abdomen	Iliac crest of Ilium/Os Coxa and ribs 5-10	Xiphoid process of sternum, linea alba (midline) and pubis/Os Coxa

✓	Back Muscles	Description/Action	Origin Bone/marking	Insertion Bone/marking
	Erector Spinae	When contracting together (bilaterally)-they extend the vertebral column and maintain posture. When contracting separately (unilaterally)-they rotate and laterally flex the vertebral column.	Large muscle group extending from sacrum to the base of the skull. They attach to the vertebra and ribs along the way.	Large muscle group extending from sacrum to the base of the skull. The attach to the vertebra and ribs along the way

Muscles of the Vertebral Column, Abdomen, and Pelvis

Learning Outcomes

On completion of this exercise, you should be able to:

1. Locate the muscles of the vertebral column, abdomen, and pelvis on laboratory models and charts.

2. Identify on the models the origin, insertion, and action of the muscles of the vertebral, abdominal, and pelvic regions.

3. Demonstrate or describe the action of the major muscles of the vertebral column, abdomen, and pelvis.

Lab Activities

1. Muscles of the Vertebral Column

2. Oblique and Rectus Muscles

3. Muscles of the Pelvic Region

The body torso has both axial and appendicular muscles. Axial muscles of the torso are the muscles that act on the vertebral column, abdomen, and pelvis. The muscles that flex, extend, and support the spine are on the posterior surface of the vertebral column. Oblique and rectus muscles occur in the neck and the abdomen. The primary functions of the abdominal muscles are to support the abdomen, viscera, and lower back, and to move the legs. Muscles of the pelvic region form the floor and walls of the pelvis and support local organs of the reproductive and digestive systems. The appendicular muscles of the torso are the large chest and back muscles that act on the shoulder and arm.

Lab Activity 1 Muscles of the Vertebral Column

The muscles of the back are organized into three layers: *superficial*, *intermediate*, and *deep* (Figure 1 and Table 1,). Except for two superficial muscles that act on the appendicular skeleton, the trapezius and latissimus dorsi muscles, all the back muscles move the vertebral column. The superficial vertebral muscles move the head and neck. The

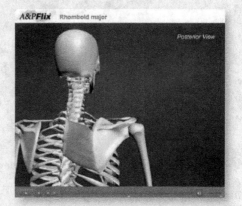

Need More Practice and Review?

Build your knowledge—and confidence!—in the Study Area of MasteringA&P® at www.masteringaandp.com with Pre-lab Quizzes, Post-lab Quizzes, Practice Anatomy Lab™ (PAL™) 3.0 virtual anatomy practice tool, PhysioEx™ 9.0 laboratory simulations, and A&P Flix™ with Quizzes.

PAL | practice anatomy lab   For this lab exercise, follow these navigation paths:
• PAL>Human Cadaver>Muscular System>Trunk
• PAL>Anatomical Models>Muscular System>Trunk

For this lab exercise, go to these topics:
A&PFlix ...s, Insertions, Actions, and Innervations
• Group Muscle Actions and Joints

Figure 1 Muscles of the Vertebral Column These muscles adjust the position of the vertebral column, head, neck, and ribs.

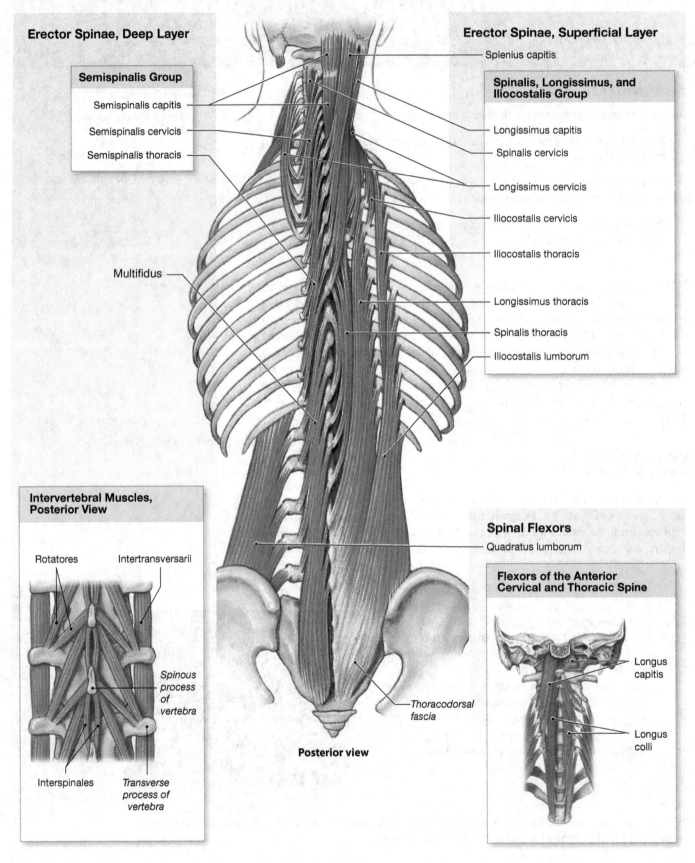

Erector Spinae, Deep Layer

Semispinalis Group

Semispinalis capitis

Semispinalis cervicis

Semispinalis thoracis

Multifidus

Erector Spinae, Superficial Layer

Splenius capitis

Spinalis, Longissimus, and Iliocostalis Group

Longissimus capitis

Spinalis cervicis

Longissimus cervicis

Iliocostalis cervicis

Iliocostalis thoracis

Longissimus thoracis

Spinalis thoracis

Iliocostalis lumborum

Intervertebral Muscles, Posterior View

Rotatores

Intertransversarii

Spinous process of vertebra

Interspinales

Transverse process of vertebra

Spinal Flexors

Quadratus lumborum

Thoracodorsal fascia

Posterior view

Flexors of the Anterior Cervical and Thoracic Spine

Longus capitis

Longus colli

intermediate muscles are in long bands that stabilize and extend the vertebral column. The deep layer consists of small muscles that connect adjacent vertebrae to each other.

Most of the vertebral muscles are *extensor muscles* that extend the vertebral column and in doing so resist the downward pull of gravity. The extensors are located on the back, posterior to the spine. *Flexor muscles* are muscles that cause flexion; the vertebral flexors are positioned lateral to the vertebral column. There are few flexor muscles for the vertebral column because most of the body's mass is positioned anterior to the vertebral column, and consequently the force of gravity naturally pulls the column to flex.

Many vertebral muscles are named after their insertion to assist with grouping and identification. Muscles that insert on the skull include *capitis* in their name. Muscles that insert on the neck are called *cervicis*, those that insert on the thoracic vertebrae are *thoracis*, and those that insert on the lumbar are *lumborum*.

Superficial Layer

The superficial vertebral muscles are the **splenius capitis muscle** (Figure 1) and the **splenius cervicis muscle.** When the two left splenius muscles and the two right ones contract in concert, the neck is extended. When the splenius capitis and splenius cervicis muscles on only one side of the neck contract, the neck is rotated laterally and flexed.

Intermediate Layer

The **erector spinae group** of muscles forms the intermediate layer of the back musculature. This group is made up of three subgroups: *spinalis*, *longissimus*, and *iliocostalis*. The **spinalis cervicis** muscles extend the neck, and the **spinalis thoracis** muscles extend the vertebral column.

The **longissimus capitis** and **longissimus cervicis** muscles act on the neck (Figure 1). When either both longissimus capitis muscles or both longissimus cervicis muscles contract, the head is extended. When only one longissimus capitis or one longissimus cervicis contracts, the neck is flexed and rotated laterally. The **longissimus thoracis** muscles extend the vertebral column, and when only one of these muscles contracts, the column is flexed laterally.

The **iliocostalis cervicis, iliocostalis thoracis,** and **iliocostalis lumborum** muscles all extend the neck and vertebral column and stabilize the thoracic vertebrae.

Deep Layer

The back muscles that make up the deep layer are collectively called the *transversospinalis muscles*; they interconnect and support the vertebrae. The various types in this layer are the semispinalis group and the multifidus, rotatores, interspinales, and intertransversarii muscles.

The **semispinalis capitis** muscles extend the neck when both of them contract; if only one semispinalis capitis contracts, it extends and laterally flexes the neck and turns the head to the opposite side. The **semispinalis cervicis** muscles extend the vertebral column when both contract and rotate the column to the opposite side when only one of them contracts. The **semispinalis thoracis** muscles work in the same way.

The **multifidus muscles** are a deep band of muscles that span the length of the vertebral column. Each portion of the band originates either on the sacrum or on a transverse process of a vertebra and inserts on the spinous process of a vertebra that is three or four vertebrae superior to the origin.

Between transverse processes are the **rotatores cervicis, rotatores thoracis,** and **rotatores lumborum** muscles, each named after the vertebra of origin (Figure 1). The multifidus and rotatores muscles act with the semispinalis thoracis to extend and flex the vertebral column. Spanning adjacent spinous processes are **interspinales muscles,** which extend the vertebral column. Contiguous transverse processes have **intertransversarii muscles,** which laterally flex the column.

Spinal Flexors

The spinal flexor muscles are located along the lateral and anterior surfaces of the vertebrae. The **longus capitis** (Figure 1) muscles are visible as bands along the anterior margin of the vertebral column that insert on the occipital bone and flex the neck; when only one longus capitis contracts, it rotates the head to the side of contraction. The **longus colli** muscles insert on the cervical vertebrae, flex and rotate the neck, and limit extension. The **quadratus lumborum** muscles originate on the iliac crest and the iliolumbar ligament, and insert on the inferior border of the 12th pair of ribs and the transverse processes of the lumbar vertebrae. These muscles flex the vertebral column; when only one quadratus lumborum contracts, the column is flexed laterally toward the side of contraction.

QuickCheck Questions

1.1 Name the three muscles of the longissimus group and describe the action of each.

1.2 Which muscle inserts on the 12th pair of ribs?

In the Lab 1

Materials

☐ Torso model
☐ Muscle chart

Procedures

1. Review the muscles of the vertebral column in Figure 1 and Table 1.

2. Examine the back of the torso model and identify the superficial vertebral muscles. Note the insertion of each muscle.

3. Distinguish the various erector spinae muscles in the intermediate layer of vertebral muscles. Note the insertion of each muscle group.

Group and Muscle(s)		Origin	Insertion	Action	Innervation
SUPERFICIAL LAYER					
Splenius (splenius capitis, splenius cervicis)		Spinous processes and ligaments connecting inferior cervical and superior thoracic vertebrae	Mastoid process, occipital bone of skull, and superior cervical vertebrae	Together, the two sides extend neck; alone, each rotates and laterally flexes neck to that side	Cervical spinal nerves
INTERMEDIATE LAYER					
Erector spinae					
Spinalis group	Spinalis cervicis	Inferior portion of ligamentum nuchae and spinous process of C_7	Spinous process of axis	Extends neck	As above
	Spinalis thoracis	Spinous processes of inferior thoracic and superior lumbar vertebrae	Spinous processes of superior thoracic vertebrae	Extends vertebral column	Thoracic and lumbar spinal nerves
Longissimus group	Longissimus capitis	Transverse processes of inferior cervical and superior thoracic vertebrae	Mastoid process of temporal bone	Together, the two sides extend head; alone, each rotates and laterally flexes neck to that side	Cervical and thoracic spinal nerves
	Longissimus cervicis	Transverse processes of superior thoracic vertebrae	Transverse processes of middle and superior cervical vertebrae	As above	As above
	Longissimus thoracis	Broad aponeurosis and transverse processes of inferior thoracic and superior lumbar vertebrae; joins iliocostalis	Transverse processes of superior vertebrae and inferior surfaces of ribs	Extends vertebral column; alone, each produces lateral flexion to that side	Thoracic and lumbar spinal nerves
Iliocostalis group	Iliocostalis cervicis	Superior borders of vertebrosternal ribs near the angles	Transverse processes of middle and inferior cervical vertebrae	Extends or laterally flexes neck, elevates ribs	Cervical and superior thoracic spinal nerves
	Iliocostalis thoracis	Superior borders of inferior seven ribs medial to the angles	Upper ribs and transverse process of last cervical vertebra	Stabilizes thoracic vertebrae in extension	Thoracic spinal nerves
	Iliocostalis lumborum	Iliac crest, sacral crests, and spinous processes	Inferior surfaces of inferior seven ribs near their angles	Extends vertebral column, depresses ribs	Inferior thoracic and lumbar spinal nerves
DEEP LAYER (TRANSVERSOSPINALIS)					
Semispinalis group	Semispinalis capitis	Articular processes of inferior cervical and transverse processes of superior thoracic vertebrae	Occipital bone, between nuchal lines	Together, the two sides extend head; alone, each extends and laterally flexes neck	Cervical spinal nerves
	Semispinalis cervicis	Transverse processes of T_1–T_5 or T_6	Spinous processes of C_2–C_5	Extends vertebral column and rotates toward opposite side	As above
	Semispinalis thoracis	Transverse processes of T_6–T_{10}	Spinous processes of C_5–T_4	As above	Thoracic spinal nerves
	Multifidus	Sacrum and transverse processes of each vertebra	Spinous processes of the third or fourth more superior vertebra	As above	Cervical, thoracic, and lumbar spinal nerves
	Rotatores	Transverse processes of each vertebra	Spinous processes of adjacent, more superior vertebra	As above	As above
	Interspinales	Spinous processes of each vertebra	Spinous processes of more superior vertebra	Extends vertebral column	As above
	Intertransversarii	Transverse processes of each vertebra	Transverse processes of more superior vertebra	Laterally flexes the vertebral column	As above
SPINAL FLEXORS					
Longus capitis		Transverse processes of cervical vertebrae	Base of the occipital bone	Together, the two sides flex the neck; alone, each rotates head to that side	Cervical spinal nerves
Longus colli		Anterior surfaces of cervical and superior thoracic vertebrae	Transverse processes of superior cervical vertebrae	Flexes or rotates neck; limits hyperextension	As above
Quadratus lumborum		Iliac crest and iliolumbar ligament	Last rib and transverse processes of lumbar vertebrae	Together, they depress ribs; alone, each side laterally flexes vertebral column	Thoracic and lumbar spinal nerves

4. Identify the transversospinalis muscles associated with the individual vertebrae on the torso model and/or muscle chart.

5. Locate the flexor muscles of the vertebral column on the torso model and/or muscle chart.

6. Extend and flex your vertebral column and consider the muscles producing each action. ■

Lab Activity 2   Oblique and Rectus Muscles

Muscles between the vertebral column and the anterior midline are grouped into either the *oblique* (slanted) or *rectus* muscle groups. As the names imply, the oblique muscles are slanted relative to the body's vertical central axis and the rectus muscles are oriented either parallel or perpendicular to this axis. Both muscle groups are found in the cervical, thoracic, and abdominal regions (Figure 2 and Table 2). All these muscles support the vertebral column, provide resistance against the erector spinae muscles, move the ribs during respiration, and constitute the abdominal wall. Another major action of these muscles is to increase intra-abdominal pressure during urination, defecation, and childbirth.

Make a Prediction

In the abdomen, what muscle is superficial to the internal oblique muscle?

Oblique Muscles

The oblique muscles of the neck, collectively called the *scalene group*, are the **anterior, middle,** and **posterior scalene muscles** (see Figure 1). Each originates on the transverse process of a cervical vertebra and inserts on a first or second rib. When the ribs are held in position, the scalene muscles flex the neck. When the neck is stationary, they elevate the ribs during inspiration.

Oblique muscles of the thoracic region include the intercostal and transversus thoracis muscles (Figure 2). The intercostal muscles are located between the ribs and, along with the diaphragm, change the size of the chest for breathing. The superficial **external intercostal muscles** and the deep **internal intercostal muscles** span the gaps between the ribs. These muscles are difficult to palpate because they are deep to other chest muscles. The **transversus thoracis muscle** lines the posterior surfaces of the sternum and the cartilages of the ribs. The muscle is covered by the serous membrane of the lungs (pleura). It depresses the ribs.

The serratus posterior muscles insert on the ribs and assist the intercostal muscles in moving the rib cage. The **superior serratus posterior muscle** elevates the ribs, and the **inferior serratus posterior muscle** (Figure 2b) pulls the rib inferiorly and opposes the diaphragm.

The abdomen has layers of oblique and rectus muscles organized in crossing layers, much like the laminar structure of a sheet of plywood (Figure 3; also Figure 2). On the lateral abdominal wall is the thin, membranous **external oblique muscle.** This muscle originates on the external and inferior borders of ribs 5 through 12 and inserts on the external oblique aponeurosis that extends to the iliac crest and to a midsagittal fibrous line called the **linea alba.** The **internal oblique muscle** lies deep and at a right angle to the external oblique muscle. The internal oblique muscle arises from the thoracolumbar fascia and iliac crest and inserts on the inferior surfaces of the lower ribs and costal cartilages, the linea alba, and the pubis. Both the external and internal oblique muscles compress and flex the abdomen, depress the ribs, and rotate the vertebral column.

The **transversus abdominis muscle,** located deep to the internal oblique muscle, originates on the lower ribs, the iliac crest, and the thoracolumbar fascia and inserts on the linea alba and the pubis. It contracts with the other abdominal muscles to compress the abdomen.

Rectus Muscles

Rectus muscles are found in the cervical, thoracic, and abdominal regions of the body. Those of the cervical region are the suprahyoid and infrahyoid muscles.

The **diaphragm** is a sheet of muscle that forms the thoracic floor and separates the thoracic cavity from the abdominopelvic cavity (Figure 2). The diaphragm originates at many points along its edges, and the muscle fibers meet at a central tendon. Contracting the diaphragm to expand the thoracic cavity is the muscular process by which air is inhaled into the lungs.

The **rectus abdominis muscle** is the vertical muscle along the midline of the abdomen between the pubic symphysis and the xiphoid process of the sternum. This muscle is divided by the linea alba. A well-developed rectus abdominis muscle has a washboard appearance because transverse bands of collagen called **tendinous inscriptions** separate the muscle into many segments. Bodybuilders often call the rectus abdominis the "six pack" because of the bulging segments of the muscle. During exercise, the rectus abdominis flexes and compresses the vertebral column and depresses the ribs for forced exhalation that occurs during increased activity.

Study Tip   Fiber Orientation

Find the external oblique and internal oblique muscles on a muscle model, and notice the difference in the way the muscle fibers are oriented. The fibers of the external oblique muscle flare laterally as they are traced from bottom to top, whereas those of the internal oblique muscle are directed medially. Just remember: From bottom up the externals flare out and internals go in. This tip is also useful in examining the external and internal intercostal muscles between the ribs. By the way, the intercostal muscles of beef and pork are the barbecue "ribs" that you might enjoy. ■

Figure 2 **Oblique and Rectus Muscles and the Diaphragm** Oblique muscles compress underlying structures between the vertebral column and the ventral midline; rectus muscles are flexors of the vertebral column.

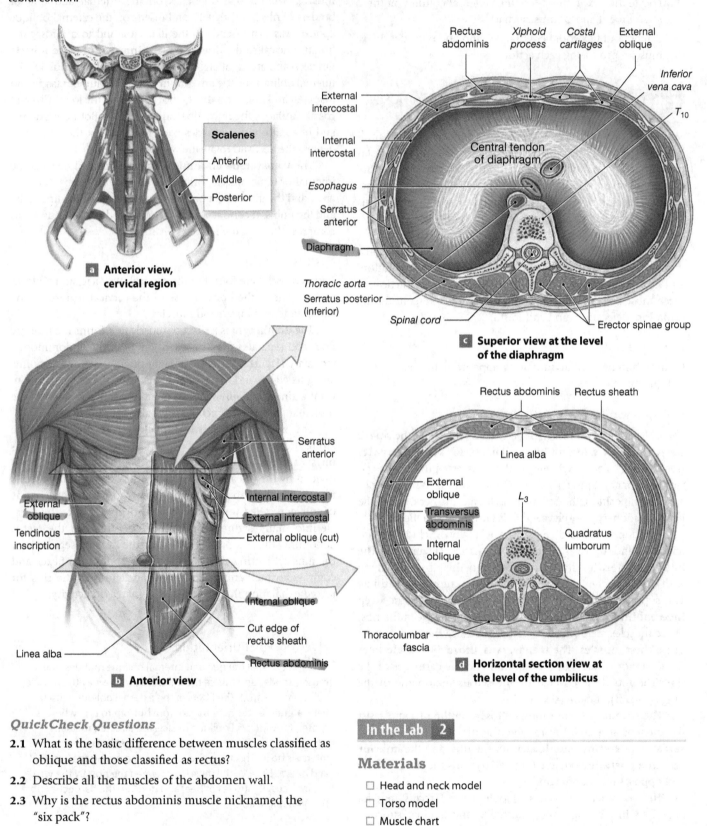

Scalenes
- Anterior
- Middle
- Posterior

a **Anterior view, cervical region**

Rectus abdominis — *Xiphoid process* — *Costal cartilages* — External oblique

Inferior vena cava

External intercostal

Internal intercostal

Central tendon of diaphragm

T_{10}

Esophagus

Serratus anterior

Diaphragm

Thoracic aorta

Serratus posterior (inferior)

Spinal cord

Erector spinae group

c **Superior view at the level of the diaphragm**

Serratus anterior

Internal intercostal

External intercostal

External oblique (cut)

External oblique

Tendinous inscription

Internal oblique

Cut edge of rectus sheath

Linea alba

Rectus abdominis

b **Anterior view**

Rectus abdominis   Rectus sheath

Linea alba

External oblique

L_3

Transversus abdominis

Internal oblique

Quadratus lumborum

Thoracolumbar fascia

d **Horizontal section view at the level of the umbilicus**

QuickCheck Questions

2.1 What is the basic difference between muscles classified as oblique and those classified as rectus?

2.2 Describe all the muscles of the abdomen wall.

2.3 Why is the rectus abdominis muscle nicknamed the "six pack"?

In the Lab 2

Materials

☐ Head and neck model
☐ Torso model
☐ Muscle chart

Table 2	ORIGINS AND INSERTIONS Oblique and Rectus Muscles (See Figure 2)			
Group and Muscle(s)	Origin	Insertion	Action	Innervation*
OBLIQUE GROUP				
Cervical region				
Scalenes (anterior, middle, and posterior)	Transverse and costal processes of cervical vertebrae	Superior surfaces of first two ribs	Elevate ribs or flex neck	Cervical spinal nerves
Thoracic region				
External intercostals	Inferior border of each rib	Superior border of more inferior rib	Elevate ribs	Intercostal nerves (branches of thoracic spinal nerves)
Internal intercostals	Superior border of each rib	Inferior border of the preceding rib	Depress ribs	As above
Transversus thoracis	Posterior surface of sternum	Cartilages of ribs	As above	As above
Serratus posterior superior (Figure 2b)	Spinous processes of C_7–T_3 and ligamentum nuchae	Superior borders of ribs 2–5 near angles	Elevates ribs, enlarges thoracic cavity	Thoracic nerves (T_1–T_4)
Serratus posterior inferior	Aponeurosis from spinous processes of T_{10}–L_3	Inferior borders of ribs 8–12	Pulls ribs inferiorly; also pulls outward, opposing diaphragm	Thoracic nerves (T_9–T_{12})
Abdominal region				
External oblique	External and inferior borders of ribs 5–12	Linea alba and iliac crest	Compresses abdomen, depresses ribs, flexes or bends spine	Intercostal, iliohypogastric, and ilioinguinal nerves
Internal oblique	Thoracolumbar fascia and iliac crest	Inferior ribs, xiphoid process, and linea alba	As above	As above
Transversus abdominis	Cartilages of ribs 6–12, iliac crest, and thoracolumbar fascia	Linea alba and pubis	Compresses abdomen	As above
RECTUS GROUP				
Cervical region	See muscles in Table 1			
Thoracic region				
Diaphragm	Xiphoid process, cartilages of ribs 4–10, and anterior surfaces of lumbar vertebrae	Central tendinous sheet	Contraction expands thoracic cavity, compresses abdominopelvic cavity	Phrenic nerves (C_3–C_5)
Abdominal region				
Rectus abdominis	Superior surface of pubis around symphysis	Inferior surfaces of costal cartilages (ribs 5–7) and xiphoid process	Depresses ribs, flexes vertebral column, compresses abdomen	Intercostal nerves (T_7–T_{12})

*Where appropriate, spinal nerves involved are given in parentheses.

Procedures

1. Review the oblique and rectus muscles in Figures 1 to Figure 3 and in Table 2.
2. Examine the head and neck model and distinguish each muscle of the scalene group.
3. Locate the intercostal muscles on the torso model and note differences in the orientation of the fibers of each muscle.
4. Identify each abdominal muscle on the torso model and/or on the muscle chart.
5. Locate the general position of each oblique muscle and the rectus muscles on the torso model.

For additional practice, complete the *Sketch to Learn* activity. ■

Lab Activity 3 Muscles of the Pelvic Region

The pelvic floor and wall form a bowl that supports the organs of the reproductive and digestive systems. The floor mainly consists of the **coccygeus muscle** and the **levator ani muscle,** peritoneal muscles, and muscles associated with the reproductive organs (Figure 4 and Table 3). The coccygeus muscle originates on the ischial spine, passes posteriorly, and inserts on the lateral and inferior borders of the sacrum. The levator ani muscle, anterior to the coccygeus muscle, originates on the inside edge of the pubis and the ischial spine and inserts on the coccyx.

Figure 3 Dissectional View of Muscles of the Trunk

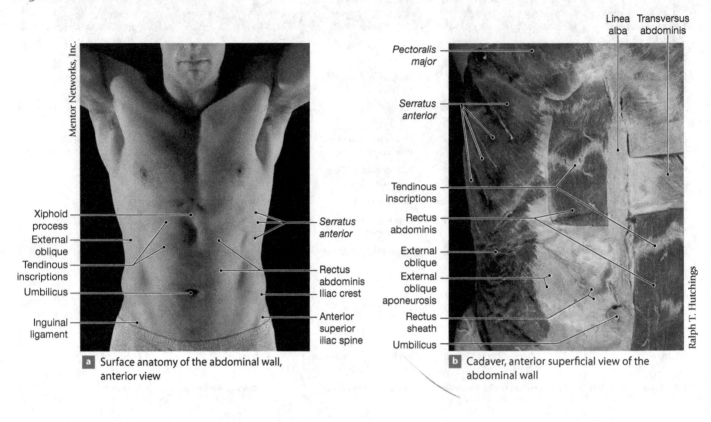

Pectoralis major

Serratus anterior

Linea alba

Transversus abdominis

Tendinous inscriptions

Rectus abdominis

External oblique

External oblique aponeurosis

Rectus sheath

Umbilicus

Xiphoid process

External oblique

Tendinous inscriptions

Umbilicus

Inguinal ligament

Serratus anterior

Rectus abdominis

Iliac crest

Anterior superior iliac spine

Mentor Networks, Inc.

Ralph T. Hutchings

a Surface anatomy of the abdominal wall, anterior view

b Cadaver, anterior superficial view of the abdominal wall

Sketch to Learn!

Let's do a simple sketch of the abdominal muscles and show the overlapping muscles.

Sample Sketch

Step 1
- Draw three vertical lines for the rectus abdominis muscle.
- Add horizontal lines on each side for the transverse abdominis.

Step 2
- Add the internal oblique muscles slanted toward the rectus abdominis.

Step 3
- Sketch the external obliques as lines slanted away from the midline.
- Label your drawing.

Your Sketch

Figure 4 Muscles of the Pelvic Floor The muscles of the pelvic floor form the urogenital triangle and the anal triangle to support organs of the pelvic cavity, flex the sacrum and coccyx, and control material movement through the urethra and anus.

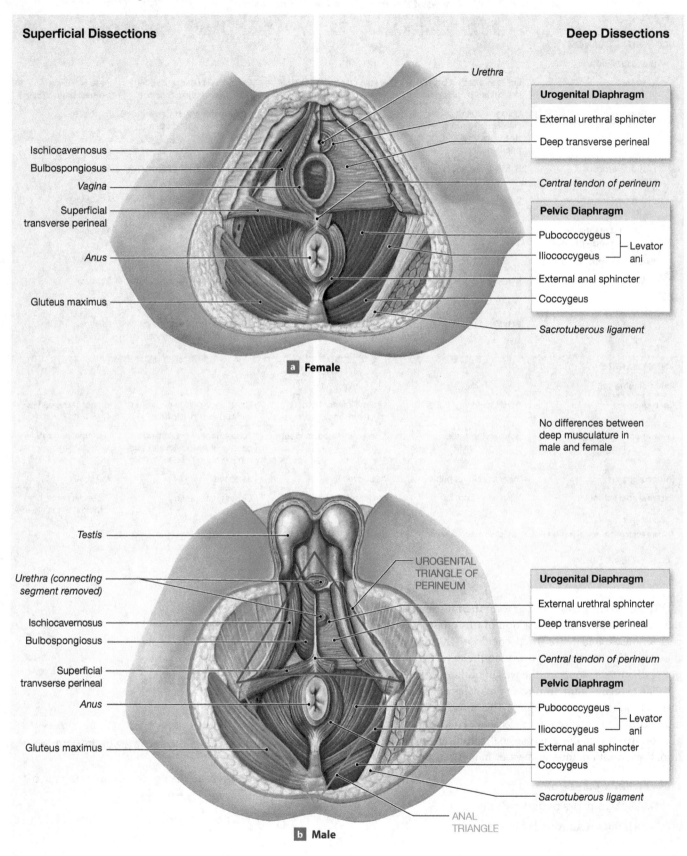

Superficial Dissections

Deep Dissections

Urethra

Urogenital Diaphragm

External urethral sphincter

Deep transverse perineal

Ischiocavernosus

Bulbospongiosus

Vagina

Central tendon of perineum

Superficial transverse perineal

Pelvic Diaphragm

Pubococcygeus ⎤
Iliococcygeus ⎦ Levator ani

Anus

External anal sphincter

Coccygeus

Gluteus maximus

Sacrotuberous ligament

a Female

No differences between deep musculature in male and female

Testis

Urethra (connecting segment removed)

UROGENITAL TRIANGLE OF PERINEUM

Urogenital Diaphragm

External urethral sphincter

Deep transverse perineal

Ischiocavernosus

Bulbospongiosus

Central tendon of perineum

Superficial transverse perineal

Pelvic Diaphragm

Anus

Pubococcygeus ⎤
Iliococcygeus ⎦ Levator ani

External anal sphincter

Coccygeus

Gluteus maximus

Sacrotuberous ligament

ANAL TRIANGLE

b Male

Table 3 ORIGINS AND INSERTIONS Muscles of the Pelvic Floor (See Figure 4)

Group and Muscle(s)	Origin	Insertion	Action	Innervation*
UROGENITAL TRIANGLE				
Superficial muscles — **Bulbospongiosus:**				
Males	Collagen sheath at base of penis; fibers cross over urethra	Median raphe and central tendon of perineum	Compresses base and stiffens penis; ejects urine or semen	Pudendal nerve, perineal branch (S_2–S_4)
Females	Collagen sheath at base of clitoris; fibers run on either side of urethral and vaginal opening	Central tendon of perineum	Compresses and stiffens clitoris; narrows vaginal opening	As above
Ischiocavernosus	Ischial ramus and tuberosity	Pubic symphysis anterior to base of penis or clitoris	Compresses and stiffens penis or clitoris	As above
Superficial transverse perineal	Ischial ramus	Central tendon of perineum	Stabilizes central tendon of perineum	As above
Deep muscles — **Urogenital diaphragm Deep transverse perineal**	Ischial ramus	Median raphe of urogenital diaphragm	As above	As above
External urethral sphincter:				
Males	Ischial and pubic rami	To median raphe at base of penis; inner fibers encircle urethra	Closes urethra; compresses prostate and bulbourethral glands	As above
Females	Ischial and pubic rami	To median raphe; inner fibers encircle urethra	Closes urethra; compresses vagina and greater vestibular glands	As above
ANAL TRIANGLE				
Pelvic diaphragm:				
Coccygeus	Ischial spine	Lateral, inferior borders of sacrum and coccyx	Flexes coccygeal joints; tenses and supports pelvic floor	Inferior sacral nerves (S_4–S_5)
Levator ani Iliococcygeus	Ischial spine, pubis	Coccyx and median raphe	Tenses floor of pelvis; flexes coccygeal joints; elevates and retracts anus	Pudendal nerve (S_2–S_4)
Pubococcygeus	Inner margins of pubis	As above	As above	As above
External anal sphincter	Via tendon from coccyx	Encircles anal opening	Closes anal opening	Pudendal nerve, hemorrhoidal branch (S_2–S_4)

*Where appropriate, spinal nerves involved are given in parentheses.

These two muscles together form the muscle group called the **pelvic diaphragm.** The action of this group is to flex the coccyx muscle and tense the pelvic floor. During pregnancy, the expanding uterus bears down on the pelvic floor, and the pelvic diaphragm supports the weight of the fetus.

The **external anal sphincter** originates on the coccyx and inserts around the anal opening. This muscle closes the anus and is consciously relaxed for defecation. Following depression and protrusion of the external anal sphincter during defecation, the levator ani muscle elevates and retracts the anus.

QuickCheck Questions

3.1 Name the muscles of the pelvic floor.

3.2 Which muscle surrounds the anus?

In the Lab 3

Materials

☐ Torso model
☐ Muscle chart

Procedures

1. Review the muscles of the pelvic region in Figure 4 and Table 3.
2. Locate each muscle of the pelvic region on the torso model and/or muscle chart. ■

Name _____

Date _____

Section _____

Muscles of the Vertebral Column, Abdomen, and Pelvis

A. Matching

Match each term in the left column with its correct description from the right column.

_____	**1.** rectus abdominis	**A.** neck muscles that extend head
_____	**2.** quadratus lumborum	**B.** superficial lateral muscle of abdomen
_____	**3.** levator ani	**C.** middle lateral muscle layer of abdomen
_____	**4.** transverse abdominis	**D.** major muscle of inhalation
_____	**5.** external oblique	**E.** abdominal muscle with horizontal fibers
_____	**6.** external intercostal	**F.** muscle at trunk midline that compresses abdomen
_____	**7.** linea alba	
_____	**8.** longissimus cervicis	**G.** circular muscle in pelvic floor
_____	**9.** diaphragm	**H.** found between ribs; elevates rib cage
_____	**10.** internal intercostal	**I.** fibrous line located along midline of trunk
_____	**11.** external anal sphincter	**J.** elevates anal sphincter
_____	**12.** internal oblique	**K.** posterior vertebral muscle that flexes spine
		L. found between ribs; depresses rib cage

B. Descriptions

Describe the location of each of the following muscles.

1. splenius cervicis

2. longissimus thoracis

3. multifidus

4. anterior scalene

5. internal intercostal

6. transverse abdominis

7. coccygeus

8. diaphragm

C. Labeling

Label the muscles that act on the vertebral column in Figure 5.

Figure 5 **Muscles of the Vertebral Column** Posterior view.

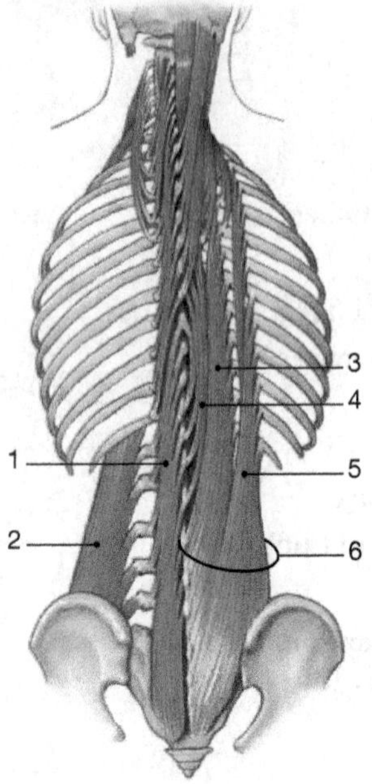

1. _____
2. _____
3. _____
4. _____
5. _____
6. _____

D. Analysis and Application

1. The anterior abdominal wall lacks bone. This being true, on what structure do the abdominal muscles insert?

2. Describe the longissimus muscle group of the vertebral column.

E. Clinical Challenge

1. A patient is admitted to the surgery ward for an appendectomy. Describe the layers of muscles the surgeon must cut in order to reach the appendix.

2. Frank uses improper body position to lift a heavy box and strains the muscles in his lumbar region. Which muscles are most likely to be involved in this injury?

Muscles of the Pectoral Girdle and Upper Limb

Wish List

During the unit on muscles, you will be required to learn the same muscles for lecture and lab. As you review the activities of the 4 muscle chapters, make sure you work on memorizing origins, insertions and actions on your wish lists.

✓	Thorax Muscles	Description/Action	Origin Bone	Insertion Bone/marking
	Pectoralis Major	As a whole- flexes/adducts/internally rotates shoulder.	Clavicle/sternum/costal cartilage of ribs	Greater tubercle/intertubercular groove of humerus
	Latissimus Dorsi	Extend/adducts/internally rotates shoulder.	Spinous processes T7-L5/sacrum/iliac crest	Intertubercular groove of humerus

✓	Shoulder Muscles	Description/Action	Origin Bone/marking	Insertion Bone/marking
	Deltoid	Lateral fibers-abduct humerus, anterior fibers-flex and internally rotate humerus, posterior fibers-extend and externally rotate humerus.	Acromial end of clavicle (anterior)/acromion process of scapula (lateral)/spine of scapula (posterior).	Deltoid tuberosity of Humerus
	Supraspinatus (RC)	Assists Deltoid in abduction of shoulder	Supraspinous fossa of scapula	Greater tubercle of humerus
	Infraspinatus (RC)	Externally rotates shoulder	Infraspinous fossa of scapula	Greater tubercle of humerus
	Teres Minor (RC)	Externally rotates /extends shoulder	Lateral border of scapula	Greater tubercle of humerus
	Subscapularis (RC)	Internally rotates shoulder	Subscapular fossa of scapula	Lesser tubercle of humerus
	Teres Major	Extends shoulder and assists in adduction/internal rotation	Inferior angle of scapula	Intertubercular groove of humerus

✓	Upper Arm Muscles	Description/Action	Origin Bone/marking	Insertion Bone/marking
	Biceps Brachii Long Head	Flexes elbow/flexes shoulder/supinates forearm	Tubercle above glenoid fossa of scapula (supraglenoid tubercle)	Radial tuberosity of radius
	Biceps Brachii Short Head	Flexes elbow/flexes shoulder/supinates forearm	Coracoid process of scapula	Radial tuberosity of radius
	Brachialis	Flexes elbow	Distal/anterior shaft of humerus	Ulnar tuberosity/coronoid process of ulna

Triceps Brachii-Long Head	Extend elbow and shoulder	Tubercle inferior to glenoid fossa (infraglenoid tubercle) of scapula	Olecranon process of ulna
Triceps Brachii-Lateral Head	Extend elbow and shoulder	Posterior/lateral surface humerus	Olecranon process of ulna
Triceps Brachii-Medial Head	Extend elbow and shoulder	posterior surface of humerus	Olecranon process of ulna

✓ Superficial, Anterior Forearm Muscles	Description/Action	Origin Bone/marking	Insertion Bone/marking
Brachioradialis	Flexes arm at elbow. Brings arm to mid-prone position	Lateral supracondylar ridge of humerus	Base of styloid procees of radius
Pronator Teres	Pronates forearm	Medial epicondyle of humerus/coronoid process of ulna	Middle/lateral shaft of radius
Flexor Carpi Radialis	Flexes and abducts wrist in the radial direction	Medial epicondyle of humerus	Metacarpals (II, III)
Flexor Carpi Ulnaris	Flexes and abducts wrist in the ulnar direction	Medial epicondyle of humerus	Pisiform, hamate and metacarpal V
Flexor Digitorum Superficialis	Flexes middle phalanges (interphalangeal, metacarpophalangeal joints) and flexes wrist.	Medial epicondyle of humerus/coronoid process of ulna/ lateral and anterior surface of radius	Middle phalanx of each finger

✓ Superficial, Posterior, Forearm	Description/Action	Origin Bone/marking	Insertion Bone/marking
Extensor Digitorum	Extends distand and middle phalanges (interphalangeal, metacarpophalangeal joints) and extends wrist).	Lateral epicondyle of humerus	Distal and middle phalanges of each finger

✓ Deep, Anterior, Forearm Muscles	Description/Action	Origin Bone/marking	Insertion Bone/marking
Pronator Quadratus	Pronates forearm	Distal shaft of ulna	Distal shaft of radius

✓	Deep, Posterior, Forearm Muscles	Description/Action	Origin Bone/marking	Insertion Bone/marking
	Supinator	Supinates forearm	Lateral epicondyle of humerus and ridge near radial notch of ulna (supinator crest)	Proximal/lateral shaft of radius

Muscles of the Pectoral Girdle and Upper Limb

Learning Outcomes

On completion of this exercise, you should be able to:

1. Locate the muscles of the pectoral and upper limb on lab models and charts.

2. Identify on the models the origin, insertion, and action of the muscles of the shoulder and upper limb.

3. Demonstrate or describe the action of the major muscles of the scapula and upper limb.

The appendicular musculature supports and moves the pectoral girdle and upper limb and the pelvic girdle and lower limb. Many of the muscles of the pectoral and pelvic girdles are on the body trunk but move appendicular bones (Figure 1). For example, the largest muscle that moves the arm, the latissimus dorsi, is located on the lumbus.

Muscles of the pectoral girdle and upper limb are covered in this exercise.

Lab Activity 1 Muscles That Move the Pectoral Girdle

The muscles of the pectoral girdle support and position the scapula and clavicle and help maintain the articulation between the humerus and scapula (Figure 2). The shoulder joint is the most movable and least stable joint of the body, and many of the surrounding muscles help keep the humerus articulated in the scapula. Origin, insertion, action, and innervation for these muscles are detailed in Table 1.

Lab Activities

1 Muscles That Move the Pectoral Girdle

2 Muscles That Move the Arm

3 Muscles That Move the Forearm

4 Muscles That Move the Wrist and Hand

Clinical Applications

Rotator Cuff Injuries

Carpal Tunnel Syndrome

Need More Practice and Review?

Build your knowledge—and confidence!—in the Study Area of MasteringA&P® at www.masteringaandp.com with Pre-lab Quizzes, Post-lab Quizzes, Practice Anatomy Lab™ (PAL™) 3.0 virtual anatomy practice tool, PhysioEx™ 9.0 laboratory simulations, and A&P Flix™ with Quizzes.

PAL   For this lab exercise, follow these navigation paths:
- PAL>Human Cadaver>Muscular System>Upper Limb
- PAL>Anatomical Models>Muscular System>Upper Limb

   For this lab exercise, go to these topics:
- Origins, Insertions, Actions, and Innervations
- A&PFlix Group Muscle Actions and Joints

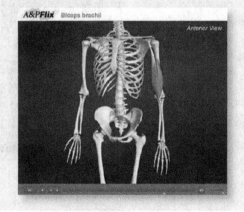

Figure 1 Superficial and Deep Muscles of the Neck, Shoulder, and Back A posterior view of many
of the major muscles of the neck, trunk, and proximal portions of the upper limbs.

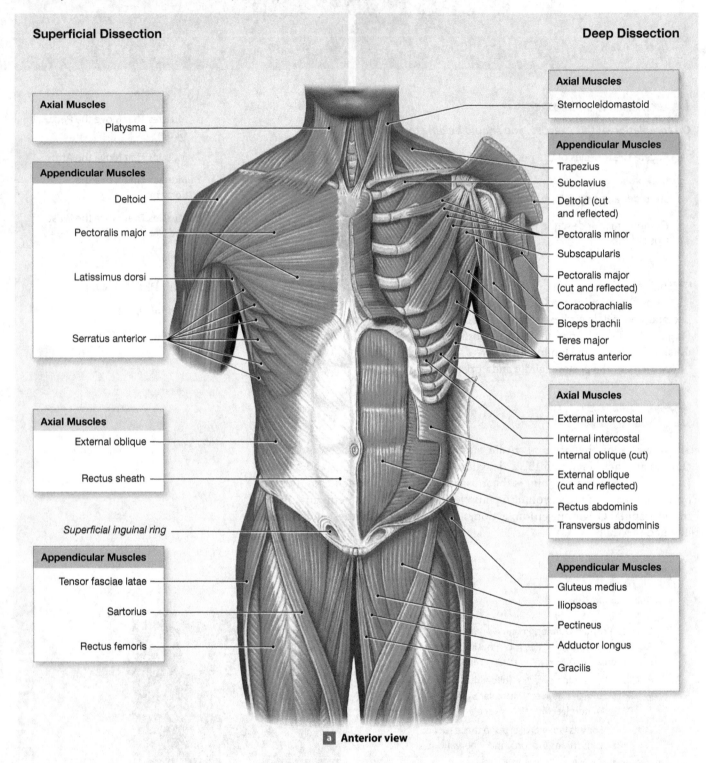

Superficial Dissection

Deep Dissection

Axial Muscles

Platysma

Appendicular Muscles

Deltoid

Pectoralis major

Latissimus dorsi

Serratus anterior

Axial Muscles

External oblique

Rectus sheath

Superficial inguinal ring

Appendicular Muscles

Tensor fasciae latae

Sartorius

Rectus femoris

Axial Muscles

Sternocleidomastoid

Appendicular Muscles

Trapezius

Subclavius

Deltoid (cut
and reflected)

Pectoralis minor

Subscapularis

Pectoralis major
(cut and reflected)

Coracobrachialis

Biceps brachii

Teres major

Serratus anterior

Axial Muscles

External intercostal

Internal intercostal

Internal oblique (cut)

External oblique
(cut and reflected)

Rectus abdominis

Transversus abdominis

Appendicular Muscles

Gluteus medius

Iliopsoas

Pectineus

Adductor longus

Gracilis

a Anterior view

Figure 1 **Superficial and Deep Muscles of the Neck, Shoulder, and Back** *(continued)*

Superficial Dissection

Deep Dissection

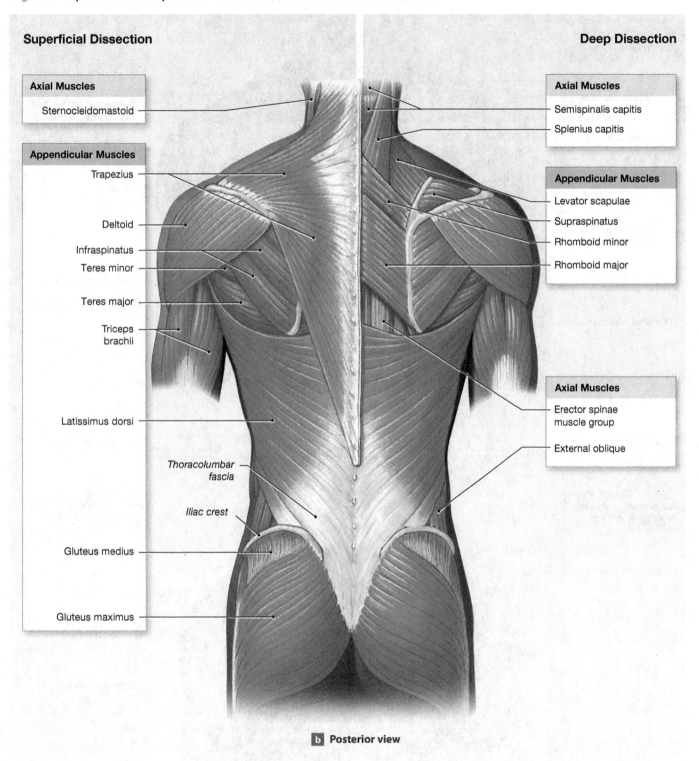

Axial Muscles

Sternocleidomastoid

Appendicular Muscles

Trapezius

Deltoid

Infraspinatus

Teres minor

Teres major

Triceps brachii

Latissimus dorsi

Thoracolumbar fascia

Iliac crest

Gluteus medius

Gluteus maximus

Axial Muscles

Semispinalis capitis

Splenius capitis

Appendicular Muscles

Levator scapulae

Supraspinatus

Rhomboid minor

Rhomboid major

Axial Muscles

Erector spinae muscle group

External oblique

b **Posterior view**

Figure 2 Superficial and Deep Muscles of the Trunk and Proximal Portion of the Limbs Anterior view of the axial muscles of the trunk and the appendicular muscles associated with the pectoral and pelvic girdles and the proximal portion of the upper and lower limbs.

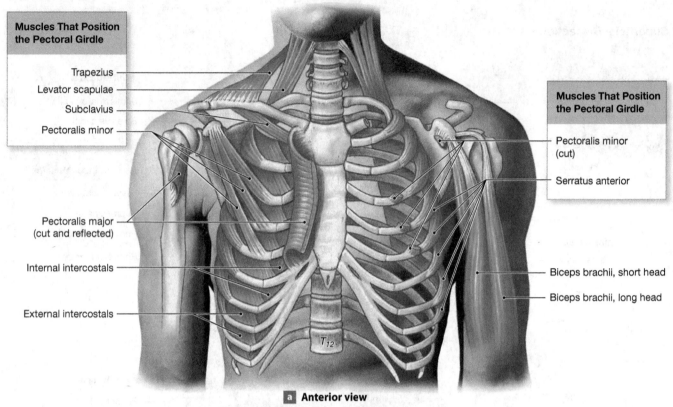

Muscles That Position the Pectoral Girdle

Trapezius
Levator scapulae
Subclavius
Pectoralis minor

Pectoralis major (cut and reflected)

Internal intercostals

External intercostals

T_{12}

Muscles That Position the Pectoral Girdle

Pectoralis minor (cut)

Serratus anterior

Biceps brachii, short head

Biceps brachii, long head

a Anterior view

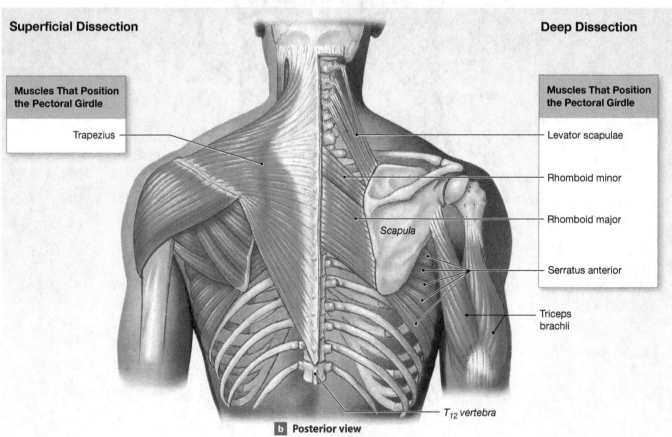

Superficial Dissection

Deep Dissection

Muscles That Position the Pectoral Girdle

Trapezius

Muscles That Position the Pectoral Girdle

Levator scapulae

Rhomboid minor

Rhomboid major

Scapula

Serratus anterior

Triceps brachii

T_{12} vertebra

b Posterior view

Table 1	ORIGINS AND INSERTIONS Muscles That Position the Pectoral Girdle (See Figures 1 and 2)			
Muscle	Origin	Insertion	Action	Innervation*
Levator scapulae	Transverse processes of first four cervical vertebrae	Vertebral border of scapula near superior angle	Elevates scapula	Cervical nerves C_3–C_4 and dorsal scapular nerve (C_5)
Pectoralis minor	Anterior and superior surfaces of ribs 3–5	Coracoid process of scapula	Depresses and protracts shoulder; rotates scapula so glenoid cavity moves inferiorly (downward rotation); elevates ribs if scapula is stationary	Medial pectoral nerve (C_8, T_1)
Rhomboid major	Spinous processes of superior thoracic vertebrae	Vertebral border of scapula from spine to inferior angle	Adducts scapula and performs downward rotation	Dorsal scapular nerve (C_5)
Rhomboid minor	Spinous processes of vertebrae C_7–T_1	Vertebral border of scapula near spine	As above	As above
Serratus anterior	Anterior and superior margins of ribs 1–8 or 1–9	Anterior surface of vertebral border of scapula	Protracts shoulder, rotates scapula so glenoid cavity moves superiorly (upward rotation)	Long thoracic nerve (C_5–C_7)
Subclavius	First rib	Clavicle (inferior border)	Depresses and protracts shoulder	Nerve to subclavius (C_5–C_6)
Trapezius	Occipital bone, ligamentum nuchae, and spinous processes of thoracic vertebrae	Clavicle and scapula (acromion and scapular spine)	Depends on active region and state of other muscles; may (1) elevate, retract, depress, or rotate scapula upward, (2) elevate clavicle, or (3) extend neck	Accessory nerve (N XI) and cervical spinal nerves (C_3–C_4)

*Where appropriate, spinal nerves involved are given in parentheses.

On the anterior of the trunk, the **subclavius** (sub-KLĀ-vē-us) muscle is inferior to the clavicle (Figure 2a). It arises from the first rib, inserts on the underside of the clavicle, and depresses and protracts the clavicle. The **serratus** (ser-Ā-tus; *serratus*, a saw) **anterior** muscle appears as fan-shaped wedges on the side of the chest. This arrangement gives the muscle a sawtooth appearance similar to that of a bread knife with its *serrated* cutting edge. The muscle protracts the shoulder and rotates the scapula upward.

The **pectoralis** (pek-tō-RĀ-lis; *pectus*; chest) **minor** muscle is a deep muscle of the anterior trunk. Its origin is the anterior surfaces and superior margins of ribs 3 through 5, and it inserts on the coracoid process of the scapula. The function of this muscle is to pull the top of the scapula forward and depressv the shoulders. It also elevates the ribs during forced inspiration, as during strenuous exercise.

The large, diamond-shaped muscle of the upper back is the **trapezius** (tra-PĒ-zē-us) muscle. It spans the gap between the scapulae and extends from the lower thoracic vertebrae to the back of the head (Figure 2b). The superior portion of the trapezius originates at three places: on the occipital bone; on the **ligamentum nuchae** (li-guh-MEN-tum NŪ-kē; *nucha*, nape), which is a ligament extending from the cervical vertebrae to the occipital bone; and on the spinous processes of thoracic vertebrae. It inserts on the clavicle and on the acromion and scapular spine of the scapula. Because the trapezius has origins superior and inferior to its insertion, it may elevate, depress, retract, or rotate the scapula and/or the

clavicle upward. The trapezius also can extend the neck. Deep to the trapezius are the **rhomboid** (rom-boyd) **major** and **rhomboid minor** muscles, which extend between the upper thoracic vertebrae and the scapula. The rhomboid muscles adduct the scapula and rotate it downward. The **levator scapulae** (lē-VĀ-tor SKAP-ū-lē; *levator*, lifter) muscle originates on cervical vertebrae 1 through 4 and inserts on the superior border of the scapula. As its name implies, it elevates the scapula.

QuickCheck Questions

1.1 Describe the actions of the trapezius muscle.

1.2 Describe the action of the rhomboid muscles.

In the Lab 1

Materials

- ☐ Torso model
- ☐ Articulated skeleton
- ☐ Muscle chart

Procedures

1. Review the anterior and posterior muscles of the chest in Table 1 and Figures 1 and 2.

2. Identify each muscle on the torso model and the muscle chart.

3. Examine an articulated skeleton and note the origin, insertion, and action of the major muscles that act on the shoulder.

4. Locate the position of these muscles on your body and practice each muscle's action. ■

Lab Activity 2 Muscles That Move the Arm

Muscles that move the arm originate either on the scapula or on the vertebral column, span the ball-and-socket joint of the shoulder, and insert on the humerus to abduct, adduct, flex, or extend the arm (**Figure 3**). Refer to Table 2 for details on origin, insertion, action, and innervation for these muscles.

The **coracobrachialis** (kor-uh-kō-brā-kē-AL-is) muscle is a small muscle that originates on the coracoid process of the scapula and adducts and flexes the shoulder (Figure 3a). The largest muscle of the chest is the **pectoralis major** muscle, which covers most of the upper rib cage on the two sides of the chest, and is one of the main muscles that move the arm. It originates on the clavicle, on the body of the sternum, and on costal cartilages for ribs 2 through 6, and inserts on the humerus at the greater tubercule and lateral surface of the intertubercular groove. This muscle flexes, adducts, and medially rotates the arm. In females, the breasts cover the inferior part of the pectoralis major muscle. Lateral to the pectoralis major muscle is the **deltoid** (DEL-toyd; *delta*, triangular) muscle, the triangular muscle of the shoulder. It originates on the anterior edge of the clavicle, on the inferior margins of the scapular spine, and on the acromion process of the scapula. The deltoid inserts on the deltoid tuberosity and is the major abductor of the humerus.

The **subscapularis** (sub-skap-ū-LAR-is) muscle is deep to the scapula next to the posterior surface of the rib cage (Figure 2). It originates on the subscapular fossa, inserts on the lesser tubercle of the humerus, and medially rotates the shoulder.

The **latissimus dorsi** (la-TIS-i-mus DOR-sē; *lati*, broad) muscle is the large muscle wrapping around the lower back (Figure 3b). This muscle has a broad origin from the sacral and lumbar vertebrae up to the sixth thoracic vertebra and sweeps up and inserts on the humerus. The latissimus dorsi muscle extends, adducts, and medially rotates the arm.

Two muscles occur superior and inferior to the spine of the posterior scapular surface. The **supraspinatus** (sū-pra-spī-NĀ-tus; *supra*, above + *spin*, spine) muscle originates on the supraspinous fossa, the depression located superior to the scapular spine (Figure 3b). It abducts the shoulder. The **infraspinatus** (inf-ra-spī-NĀ-tus; *infra*, below) muscle arises from the infraspinous fossa of the scapula and inserts on the greater tubercle of the humerus to laterally rotate the humerus at the shoulder.

Clinical Application Rotator Cuff Injuries

Four shoulder muscles—the supraspinatus, infraspinatus, teres minor, and subscapularis muscles—all act to position the head of the humerus firmly in the glenoid fossa to prevent dislocation of the shoulder. Collectively these muscles are called the **rotator cuff**. Remember the acronym **SITS** (supraspinatus, infraspinatus, teres minor, subscapularis) for the rotator cuff muscles. Although part of the rotator cuff, the supraspinatus is not itself a rotator; rather, it is an abductor. You may be familiar with rotator cuff injuries if you are a baseball fan. The windup and throw of a pitcher involve circumduction of the humerus. This motion places tremendous stress on the shoulder joint and on the rotator cuff—stress that can cause premature degeneration of the joint. To protect the shoulder joint and muscles, bursal sacs are interspersed between the tendons of the rotator cuff muscles and the neighboring bony structures. Repeated friction on the bursae may result in an inflammation called *bursitis*. ■

The **teres** (TER-ēs; *teres*, round) **major** muscle is a thick muscle that arises on the inferior angle of the posterior surface of the scapula. The muscle converges up and laterally into a flat tendon that ends on the anterior side of the humerus. On the lateral border of the scapula is the small and flat **teres minor** muscle. The teres major muscle extends, adducts, and medially rotates the humerus; the teres minor muscle laterally rotates the humerus at the shoulder.

QuickCheck Questions

2.1 Which muscles adduct the arm?

2.2 Which muscle flexes the arm?

In the Lab 2

Materials

☐ Torso model   ☐ Articulated skeleton
☐ Upper limb model   ☐ Muscle chart

Procedures

1. Review the muscles that move the arm in Table 2 and Figures 1 through 3.

2. Locate each muscle that moves the arm on the torso model, upper limb model, and muscle chart.

3. Examine the articulated skeleton and note the origin, insertion, and action of the major muscles that act on the arm.

4. Locate the general position of each arm muscle on your body. Contract each muscle and observe how your arm moves. ■

Figure 3 Muscles That Move the Arm Muscles that move the arm are located on the trunk and insert on the proximal portions of the humerus.

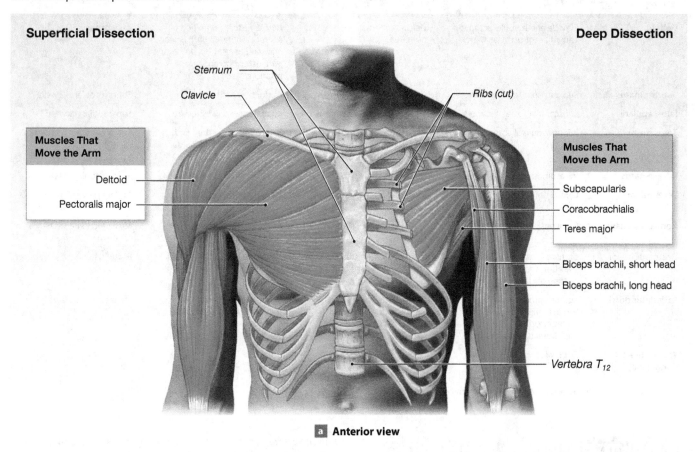

Superficial Dissection

Muscles That Move the Arm

Deltoid

Pectoralis major

Sternum

Clavicle

Deep Dissection

Ribs (cut)

Muscles That Move the Arm

Subscapularis

Coracobrachialis

Teres major

Biceps brachii, short head

Biceps brachii, long head

Vertebra T₁₂

a Anterior view

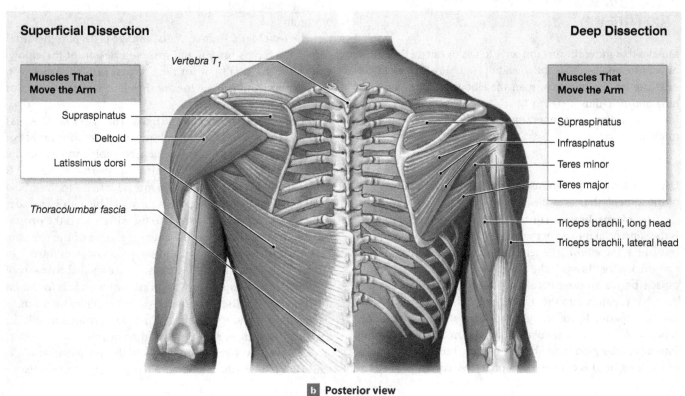

Superficial Dissection

Vertebra T₁

Muscles That Move the Arm

Supraspinatus

Deltoid

Latissimus dorsi

Thoracolumbar fascia

Deep Dissection

Muscles That Move the Arm

Supraspinatus

Infraspinatus

Teres minor

Teres major

Triceps brachii, long head

Triceps brachii, lateral head

b Posterior view

Table 2	ORIGINS AND INSERTIONS Muscles That Move the Arm (See Figures 1, 2, and 3)			
Muscle	**Origin**	**Insertion**	**Action**	**Innervation***
Deltoid	Clavicle and scapula (acromion and adjacent scapular spine)	Deltoid tuberosity of humerus	*Whole muscle:* abduction at shoulder; *anterior part:* flexion and medial rotation, *posterior part:* extension and lateral rotation	Axillary nerve (C_5–C_6)
Supraspinatus	Supraspinous fossa of scapula	Greater tubercle of humerus	Abduction at the shoulder	Suprascapular nerve (C_5)
Subscapularis	Subscapular fossa of scapula	Lesser tubercle of humerus	Medial rotation at shoulder	Subscapular nerves (C_5–C_6)
Teres major	Inferior angle of scapula	Passes medially to reach the medial lip of intertubercular groove of humerus	Extension, adduction, and medial rotation at shoulder	Lower subscapular nerve (C_5–C_6)
Infraspinatus	Infraspinous fossa of scapula	Greater tubercle of humerus	Lateral rotation at shoulder	Suprascapular nerve (C_5–C_6)
Teres minor	Lateral border of scapula	Passes laterally to reach the greater tubercle of humerus	Lateral rotation at shoulder	Axillary nerve (C_5)
Coracobrachialis	Coracoid process	Medial margin of shaft of humerus	Adduction and flexion at shoulder	Musculocutaneous nerve (C_5–C_7)
Pectoralis major	Cartilages of ribs 2–6, body of sternum, and inferior, medial portion of clavicle	Crest of greater tubercle and lateral lip of intertubercular groove of humerus	Flexion, adduction, and medial rotation at shoulder	Pectoral nerves (C_5–T_1)
Latissimus dorsi	Spinous processes of inferior thoracic and all lumbar vertebrae, ribs 8–12, and thoracolumbar fascia	Floor of intertubercular groove of the humerus	Extension, adduction, and medial rotation at shoulder	Thoracodorsal nerve (C_6–C_8)
Triceps brachii (long head)	*See Table 3*			

*Where appropriate, spinal nerves involved are given in parentheses.

Lab Activity 3 Muscles That Move the Forearm

Muscles that move the forearm serve to flex or extend the elbow, or pronate and supinate the forearm (**Figure 4**). These muscles originate on the humerus, span the elbow, and insert on the ulna and/or radius. Refer to Table 3 for details on the origin, insertion, action, and innervation for muscles that move the forearm.

Make a Prediction

Use your knowledge of muscle actions and predict the action of the muscles that span the anterior of the elbow.

The **biceps brachii** (BĪ-ceps BRĀ-kē-ī) muscle (Figure 4) is the superficial muscle of the anterior brachium that flexes the forearm at the elbow. The term *biceps* refers to the presence of two origins, or "heads." The **short head** of the biceps brachii muscle begins on the coracoid process of the scapula as a tendon that expands into the muscle belly. The **long head** arises on the superior lip of the glenoid fossa at the supraglenoid tubercle. A tendon passes over the top of the humerus into the intertubercular groove and blends into the muscle. The tendon of the long head is enclosed in a protective covering called the

intertubercular synovial sheath. The two heads of the biceps brachii muscle fuse and constitute most of the mass of the anterior brachium.

The **brachialis** (brā-kē-AL-is) muscle is deep to the distal end of the biceps brachii and assists in flexion of the elbow. You can feel a small part of the brachialis muscle when you flex your arm and palpate the area just lateral to the tendon of the biceps brachii muscle.

The superficial **brachioradialis** (brā-kē-ō-rā-dē-AL-is) muscle is easily felt on the lateral side of the anterior surface of the forearm (Figure 4). It spans the elbow joint and assists the biceps brachii in flexion of this joint. The **pronator teres** (PR Ō-nā-tōr TE-rēs) muscle is a thin muscle inferior to the elbow and medial to the brachioradialis muscle, which it dives under to insert on the radius. Proximal to the wrist joint is the **pronator quadratus** muscle on the anterior surface of the forearm. This muscle acts as a synergist to the pronator teres muscle in pronating the forearm and can also cause medial rotation of the forearm. The **supinator** (SŪ-pi-nā-tor) muscle is found on the lateral side of the forearm deep to the brachioradialis muscle. It contracts and rotates the radius into a position parallel to the ulna, resulting in supination of the forearm.

The **triceps brachii** muscle on the posterior arm extends the elbow and is therefore the principal antagonist to

Figure 4 **Muscles That Move the Forearm and Hand—Anterior View** Muscles of the right upper limb.

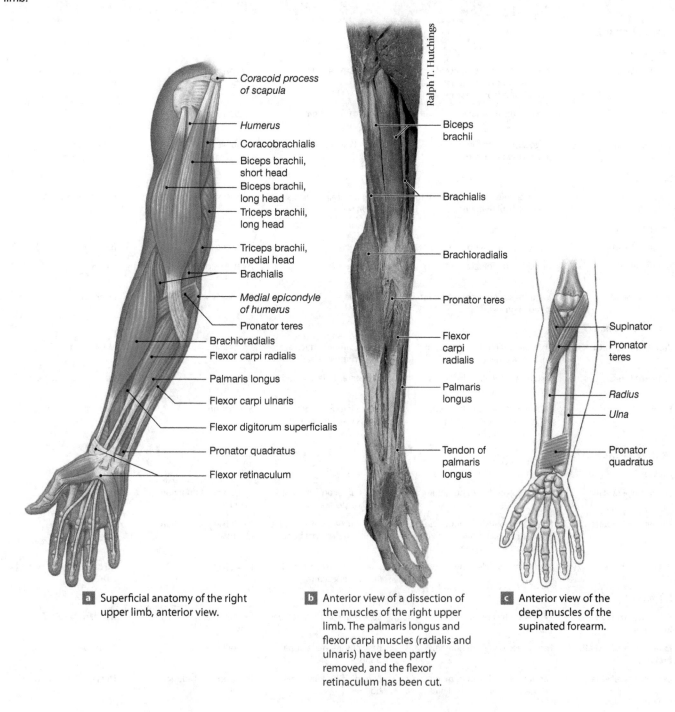

Ralph T. Hutchings

a Superficial anatomy of the right upper limb, anterior view.

b Anterior view of a dissection of the muscles of the right upper limb. The palmaris longus and flexor carpi muscles (radialis and ulnaris) have been partly removed, and the flexor retinaculum has been cut.

c Anterior view of the deep muscles of the supinated forearm.

the biceps brachii and brachialis muscles (**Figure 5**). The muscle arises from three heads, called the **long, lateral,** and **medial heads,** which merge into a common tendon that begins near the middle of the muscle and inserts on the olecranon process of the ulna. At the posterior lateral humerus is the small **anconeus** (ang-KŌ-nē-ūs; *ankon,* elbow) muscle, which assists the triceps brachii muscle in extending the elbow.

QuickCheck Questions

3.1 Which muscles are antagonistic to the triceps brachii?

3.2 Which muscles are involved when you turn a doorknob?

Table 3 *ORIGINS AND INSERTIONS* Muscles That Move the Forearm and Hand (See Figures 4 to 6)

Muscle	Origin	Insertion	Action	Innervation
ACTION AT THE ELBOW				
Flexors				
Biceps brachii	*Short head* from the coracoid process; *long head* from the supraglenoid tubercle (both on the scapula)	Tuberosity of radius	Flexion at elbow and shoulder; supination	Musculocutaneous nerve $(C_5–C_6)$
Brachialis	Anterior, distal surface of humerus	Tuberosity of ulna	Flexion at elbow	As above and radial nerve $(C_7–C_8)$
Brachioradialis	Ridge superior to the lateral epicondyle of humerus	Lateral aspect of styloid process of radius	As above	Radial nerve $(C_5–C_6)$
Extensors				
Anconeus	Posterior, inferior surface of lateral epicondyle of humerus	Lateral margin of olecranon on ulna	Extension at elbow	Radial nerve $(C_7–C_8)$
Triceps brachii				
lateral head	Superior lateral margin of humerus	Olecranon of ulna	As above	Radial nerve $(C_6–C_8)$
long head	Infraglenoid tubercle of scapula	As above	As above, plus extension and adduction at the shoulder	As above
medial head	Posterior surface of humerus inferior to radial groove	As above	Extension at elbow	As above
Pronators/Supinators				
Pronator quadratus	Anterior and medial surfaces of distal portion of ulna	Anterolateral surface of distal portion of radius	Pronation	Median nerve $(C_8–T_1)$
Pronator teres	Medial epicondyle of humerus and coronoid process of ulna	Midlateral surface of radius	As above	Median nerve $(C_6–C_7)$
Supinator	Lateral epicondyle of humerus, annular ligament, and ridge near radial notch of ulna	Anterolateral surface of radius distal to the radial tuberosity	Supination	Deep radial nerve $(C_6–C_8)$
ACTION AT THE HAND				
Flexors				
Flexor carpi radialis	Medial epicondyle of humerus	Bases of second and third metacarpal bones	Flexion and abduction at wrist	Median nerve $(C_6–C_7)$
Flexor carpi ulnaris	Medial epicondyle of humerus; adjacent medial surface of olecranon and anteromedial portion of ulna	Pisiform, hamate, and base of fifth metacarpal bone	Flexion and adduction at wrist	Ulnar nerve $(C_8–T_1)$
Palmaris longus	Medial epicondyle of humerus	Palmar aponeurosis and flexor retinaculum	Flexion at wrist	Median nerve $(C_6–C_7)$
Extensors				
Extensor carpi radialis longus	Lateral supracondylar ridge of humerus	Base of second metacarpal bone	Extension and abduction at wrist	Radial nerve $(C_6–C_7)$
Extensor carpi radialis brevis	Lateral epicondyle of humerus	Base of third metacarpal bone	As above	As above
Extensor carpi ulnaris	Lateral epicondyle of humerus; adjacent dorsal surface of ulna	Base of fifth metacarpal bone	Extension and adduction at wrist	Deep radial nerve $(C_6–C_8)$

In the Lab   3

Materials

- ☐ Torso model
- ☐ Upper limb model
- ☐ Articulated skeleton
- ☐ Muscle chart

Procedures

1. Review the muscles of the forearm in Figures 4 and 5 and in Table 3.

2. Identify each muscle on the torso and upper limb models and on the muscle chart.

Figure 5 **Muscles That Move the Forearm, Wrist, and Hand—Posterior View** Muscles of the right limb, posterior view.

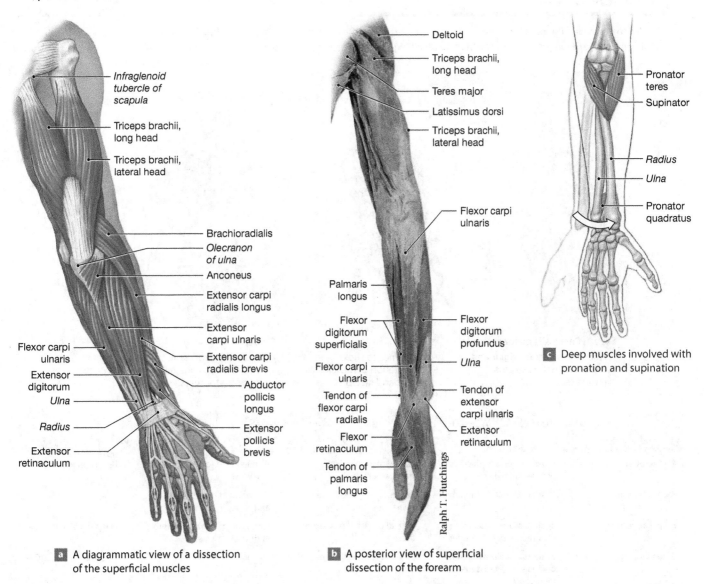

Infraglenoid tubercle of scapula

Triceps brachii, long head

Triceps brachii, lateral head

Brachioradialis
Olecranon of ulna
Anconeus
Extensor carpi radialis longus
Extensor carpi ulnaris
Extensor carpi radialis brevis
Abductor pollicis longus
Extensor pollicis brevis

Flexor carpi ulnaris
Extensor digitorum
Ulna
Radius
Extensor retinaculum

a A diagrammatic view of a dissection of the superficial muscles

Deltoid
Triceps brachii, long head
Teres major
Latissimus dorsi
Triceps brachii, lateral head

Flexor carpi ulnaris

Palmaris longus
Flexor digitorum superficialis
Flexor carpi ulnaris
Tendon of flexor carpi radialis
Flexor retinaculum
Tendon of palmaris longus

Flexor digitorum profundus
Ulna
Tendon of extensor carpi ulnaris
Extensor retinaculum

Ralph T. Hutchings

b A posterior view of superficial dissection of the forearm

Pronator teres
Supinator

Radius
Ulna

Pronator quadratus

c Deep muscles involved with pronation and supination

3. Examine the articulated skeleton and note the origin, insertion, and action of the muscles that act on the forearm.

4. On your body, locate the general position of each muscle involved with movement of the forearm. Flex and extend your elbow joint and watch the action of the muscles on your arm. ■

Lab Activity 4 Muscles That Move the Wrist and Hand

The muscles of the wrist and hand can be organized into two groups based on location: extrinsic muscles in the forearm and intrinsic muscles in the hand. The extrinsic muscles flex and extend the wrist and fingers, and the intrinsic muscles control fine finger and thumb movements. Refer to Table 3 as well as Table 4 and Table 5 for descriptions of the origins, insertions, actions, and innervation for muscles of the wrist and hand.

The flexor muscles that move the wrist and hand are on the anterior forearm and the extensor muscles are on the posterior forearm. The brachioradialis muscle is between the flexor and extensor muscles of the forearm and is a good anatomical landmark. At the wrist, the long tendons of the flexor muscles are supported and stabilized by a wide sheath called the **flexor retinaculum** (ret-i-NAK-ū-lum; *retinaculum*, a halter or band). Many of the extensor muscles on the posterior forearm originate from a common tendon on the lateral epicondyle of the humerus.

Sketch to Learn

Use the provided figure of the skeleton as a template and add the pronator teres, supinator, brachioradialis, and palmaris longus muscles. The brachioradialis will cover the supinator muscle.

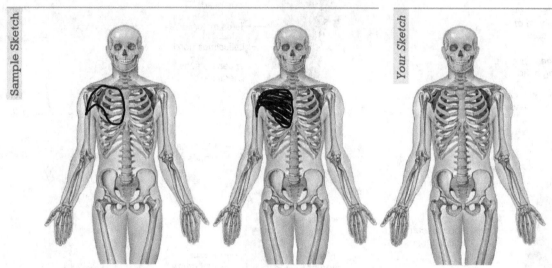

Sample Sketch

Your Sketch

Step 1: Pectoralis major example
- Trace the muscle's origins and insertion on the skeleton template.

Step 2
- Add lines to show orientation of muscle fibers and fascicles.

Step 3
- Repeat the process for the deltoid, biceps brachii, brachialis, and pronator teres.

Table 4	*ORIGINS AND INSERTIONS* Muscles That Move the Hand and Fingers (See Figure 6)			
Muscle	**Origin**	**Insertion**	**Action**	**Innervation***
Abductor pollicis longus	Proximal dorsal surfaces or ulna and radius	Lateral margin of first metacarpal bone	Abduction at joints of thumb and wrist	Deep radial nerve (C_6–C_7)
Extensor digitorum	Lateral epicondyle of humerus	Posterior surfaces of the phalanges, fingers 2–5	Extension at finger joints and wrist	Deep radial nerve (C_6–C_8)
Extensor pollicis brevis	Shaft of radius distal to origin of adductor pollicis longus	Base of proximal phalanx of thumb	Extension at joints of thumb; abduction at wrist	Deep radial nerve (C_6–C_7)
Extensor pollicis longus	Posterior and lateral surfaces of ulna and interosseous membrane	Base of distal phalanx of thumb	As above	Deep radial nerve (C_6–C_8)
Extensor indicis	Posterior surface of ulna and interosseous membrane	Posterior surface of phalanges of index finger (2), with tendon of extensor digitorum	Extension and adduction at joints of index finger	As above
Extensor digiti minimi	Via extensor tendon to lateral epicondyle of humerus and from intermuscular septa	Posterior surface of proximal phalanx of little finger (5)	Extension at joints of little finger	As above
Flexor digitorum superficialis	Medial epicondyle of humerus; adjacent anterior surfaces of ulna and radius	Midlateral surfaces of middle phalanges of fingers 2–5	Flexion at proximal interphalangeal, metacarpophalangeal, and wrist joints	Median nerve (C_7–T_1)
Flexor digitorum profundus	Medial and posterior surfaces of ulna, medial surface of coronoid process, and interosseus membrane	Bases of distal phalanges of fingers 2–5	Flexion at distal interphalangeal joints and, to a lesser degree, proximal interphalangeal joints and wrist	Palmar interosseous nerve, from median nerve, and ulnar nerve (C_8–T_1)
Flexor pollicis longus	Anterior shaft of radius, interosseous membrane	Base of distal phalanx of thumb	Flexion at joints of thumb	Median nerve (C_8–T_1)

*Where appropriate, spinal nerves involved are given in parentheses.

Table 5	ORIGINS AND INSERTIONS	Intrinsic Muscles of the Hand (See Figures 6 and 7)		
Muscle	**Origin**	**Insertion**	**Action**	**Innervation***
Adductor pollicis	Metacarpal and carpal bones	Proximal phalanx of thumb	Adduction of thumb	Ulnar nerve; deep branch (C_8–T_1)
Opponens pollicis	Trapezium and flexor retinaculum	First metacarpal bone	Opposition of thumb	Median nerve (C_6–C_7)
Palmaris brevis	Palmar aponeurosis	Skin of medial border of hand	Moves skin on medial border toward midline of palm	Ulnar nerve, superficial branch (C_8)
Abductor digiti minimi	Pisiform	Proximal phalanx of little finger	Abduction of little finger and flexion at its metacarpophalangeal joint	Ulnar nerve, deep branch (C_8–T_1)
Abductor pollicis brevis	Transverse carpal ligament, scaphoid and trapezium	Radial side of base of proximal phalanx of thumb	Abduction of thumb	Median nerve (C_6–C_7)
Flexor pollicis brevis	Flexor retinaculum, trapezium, capitate, and ulnar side of first metacarpal bone	Radial and ulnar sides of proximal phalanx of thumb	Flexion and adduction of thumb	Branches of median and ulnar nerves
Flexor digiti minimi brevis	Hamate	Proximal phalanx of little finger	Flexion at joints of little finger	Ulnar nerve deep branch (C_8–T_1)
Opponens digiti minimi	As above	Fifth metacarpal bone	Opposition of fifth metacarpal bone	As above
Lumbrical (4)	Tendons of flexor digitorum profundus	Tendons of extensor digitorum to digits 2–5	Flexion at metacarpophalangeal joints 2–5; extension at proximal and distal interphalangeal joints, digits 2–5	No. 1 and no. 2 by median nerve; no. 3 and no. 4 by ulnar nerve; deep branch
Dorsal interosseus (4)	Each originates from opposing faces of two metacarpal bones (I and II, II and III, and IV, IV, and V)	Bases of proximal phalanges of fingers 2–4	Adduction at metacarpophalangeal joints of fingers 2 and 4; flexion at metacarpophalangeal joints; extension at interphalangeal joints	Ulner nerve, deep branch (C_8–T_1)
Palmar interosseus** (3–4)	Sides of metacarpal bones II, IV, and V	Bases of proximal phalanges of fingers 2, 4, and 5	Adduction at metacarpophalangeal joints of fingers 2, 4, and 5; flexion at metacarpophalangeal joints; extension at interphalangeal joints	As above

*Where appropriate, spinal nerves involved are given in parentheses.

**The deep, medial portion of the flexor pollicis brevis originating on the first metacarpal bone is sometimes called the *first palmar interosseus muscle;* it inserts on the ulnar side of the phalanx and is innervated by the ulnar nerve.

Study Tip Use a Reference Muscle to Remember the Forearm

Here's a quick method to learn the muscles of the forearm. Follow the tendon of the palmaris longus muscle from the middle of flexor retinaculum to the belly of the muscle. Next, identify the flexor carpi radialis longus and the flexor carpi ulnaris muscles on each side of the palmaris longus by remembering the radius bone is medial and the ulna is lateral. On the posterior forearm, trace the tendon on the middle finger toward the belly of the extensor digitorum muscle. Now identify the other extensor muscles on each side. ∎

Tendons of these muscles are secured across the posterior aspect of the wrist by the **extensor retinaculum** (Figure 6).

Medial to the brachioradialis is the **flexor carpi radialis** muscle, the flexor muscle closest to the radius. The fibers of this muscle blend into a long tendon that inserts on the second and third metacarpals. The **palmaris longus** muscle is medial to the flexor carpi radialis muscle and is easy to locate by its tendon that inserts on the flexor retinaculum. Medial to the palmaris longus muscle is the **flexor carpi ulnaris** muscle. This muscle rests on the ulnar side of the forearm and inserts on the pisiform and hamate bones of the carpus and on the base of metacarpal IV. The **flexor digitorum superficialis** muscle is located deep to the superficial flexors of the hand. It has four tendons that insert on the midlateral surface of the middle phalanges of fingers 2 through 5. Deeper flexors are also shown in Figure 6.

Posterior to the brachioradialis muscle, the long **extensor carpi radialis longus** muscle is the only extensor that does not originate on a tendon attached to the humerus lateral epicondyle. Instead, it arises from the humerus just proximal to the lateral epicondyle, although a few fibers do extend

Figure 6 **Muscles That Move the Wrist, Hand, and Fingers** Middle and deep muscle layers of the right forearm.

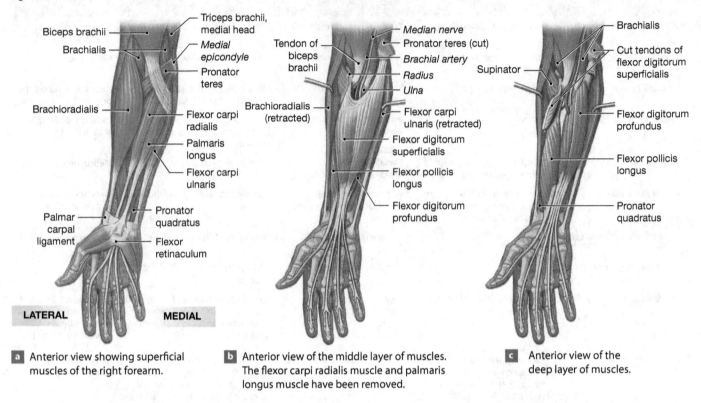

Biceps brachii
Brachialis
Triceps brachii, medial head
Medial epicondyle
Pronator teres
Brachioradialis
Flexor carpi radialis
Palmaris longus
Flexor carpi ulnaris
Palmar carpal ligament
Pronator quadratus
Flexor retinaculum

LATERAL **MEDIAL**

Tendon of biceps brachii
Brachioradialis (retracted)
Median nerve
Pronator teres (cut)
Brachial artery
Radius
Ulna
Flexor carpi ulnaris (retracted)
Flexor digitorum superficialis
Flexor pollicis longus
Flexor digitorum profundus

Brachialis
Cut tendons of flexor digitorum superficialis
Supinator
Flexor digitorum profundus
Flexor pollicis longus
Pronator quadratus

a Anterior view showing superficial muscles of the right forearm.

b Anterior view of the middle layer of muscles. The flexor carpi radialis muscle and palmaris longus muscle have been removed.

c Anterior view of the deep layer of muscles.

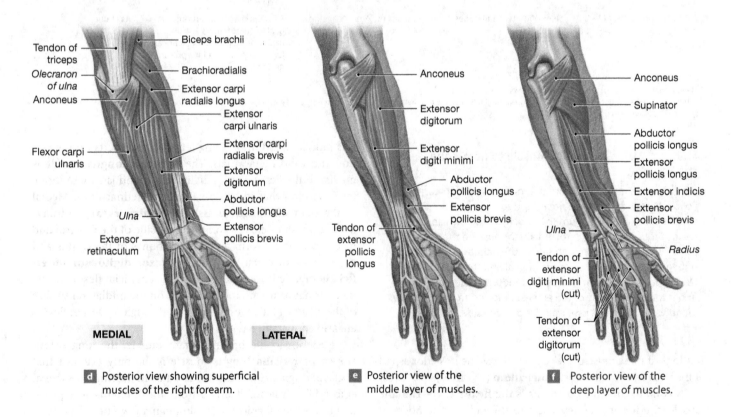

Tendon of triceps
Olecranon of ulna
Anconeus
Flexor carpi ulnaris
Ulna
Extensor retinaculum
Biceps brachii
Brachioradialis
Extensor carpi radialis longus
Extensor carpi ulnaris
Extensor carpi radialis brevis
Extensor digitorum
Abductor pollicis longus
Extensor pollicis brevis

MEDIAL

Anconeus
Extensor digitorum
Extensor digiti minimi
Abductor pollicis longus
Extensor pollicis brevis
Tendon of extensor pollicis longus

LATERAL

Anconeus
Supinator
Abductor pollicis longus
Extensor pollicis longus
Extensor indicis
Extensor pollicis brevis
Ulna
Radius
Tendon of extensor digiti minimi (cut)
Tendon of extensor digitorum (cut)

d Posterior view showing superficial muscles of the right forearm.

e Posterior view of the middle layer of muscles.

f Posterior view of the deep layer of muscles.

188

Clinical Application Carpal Tunnel Syndrome

The tendons of the flexor digitorum superficialis muscle pass through a narrow valley, the *carpal tunnel*, bounded by carpal bones. A protective synovial sheath lubricates the tendons in the tunnel, but repeated flexing of the hand and fingers, such as with prolonged typing or piano playing, causes the sheath to swell and compress the median nerve. Pain and numbness occur in the palm during flexion, a condition called *carpal tunnel syndrome.* ▪

from the common tendon. Inferior to the longus muscle is the **extensor carpi radialis brevis** muscle. The carpi muscles extend and abduct the wrist. The **extensor digitorum** muscle is medial to the extensor carpi radialis muscles and is easy to identify by the three or four tendons that insert on the posterior surface of the phalanges of fingers 2 through 5. Lateral to the digitorum muscle is the **extensor carpi ulnaris** muscle. Deeper extensor muscles are shown in Figure 6.

Muscles of the Hand

The masses of tissue at the base of the thumb and along the medial margin of the hand are called **eminences.** See Tables 4 and 5 for details on the origins, insertions, and actions of these muscles. The **thenar** (THĒ-nar; *thenar,* palm) eminence of the thumb consists of several muscles (**Figure 7**). The most medial of the thenar muscles is the **flexor pollicis brevis** (POL-i-sis; *pollex,* thumb, BREV-is; *brevis,* short) muscle, which flexes and adducts the thumb. Lateral to this flexor is the **abductor pollicis brevis** muscle, which abducts the thumb. The most lateral thenar muscle is the **opponens pollicis** muscle, which opposes the thumb toward the little finger.

The **adductor pollicis** muscle is often not considered part of the thenar eminence, as it is found just medial to the flexor pollicis brevis muscle and deep in the web of tissue between the thumb and palm. This muscle adducts the thumb and opposes the action of the abductor pollicis brevis muscle.

The **hypothenar eminence** is fleshy mass on the medial side of the palm at the base of the little finger and consists of three muscles (Figure 7). The most lateral is the **opponens digiti minimi** muscle, which opposes the little finger toward the thumb. Medial to this muscle is the **flexor digiti minimi brevis** muscle, which flexes the little finger. The most medial muscle of the hypothenar eminence is the **abductor digiti minimi** muscle, which abducts the little finger.

You should note that no muscles originate on the fingers. Instead, the phalanges of the fingers serve as insertion points for muscles whose origins are more proximal.

QuickCheck Questions

4.1 What is the general action of the muscles on the posterior forearm?

4.2 What are the muscles of the thenar eminence?

In the Lab 4

Materials

- ☐ Torso model
- ☐ Upper limb model
- ☐ Articulated skeleton
- ☐ Muscle chart

Procedures

1. Review the muscles of the wrist and hand in Figures 4 through 7 and in Tables 3 through 5.
2. Examine the articulated skeleton and note the origin, insertion, and action of the muscles that act on the wrist and hand.
3. On your body, locate the tendons of the extensor digitorum on the posterior of the hand. Also identify on your forearm the general position of each muscle involved with movement of the wrist and hand. Contract each muscle and observe the action of your wrist. ▪

Figure 7 Muscles of the Wrist and Hand Anatomy of the right wrist and hand.

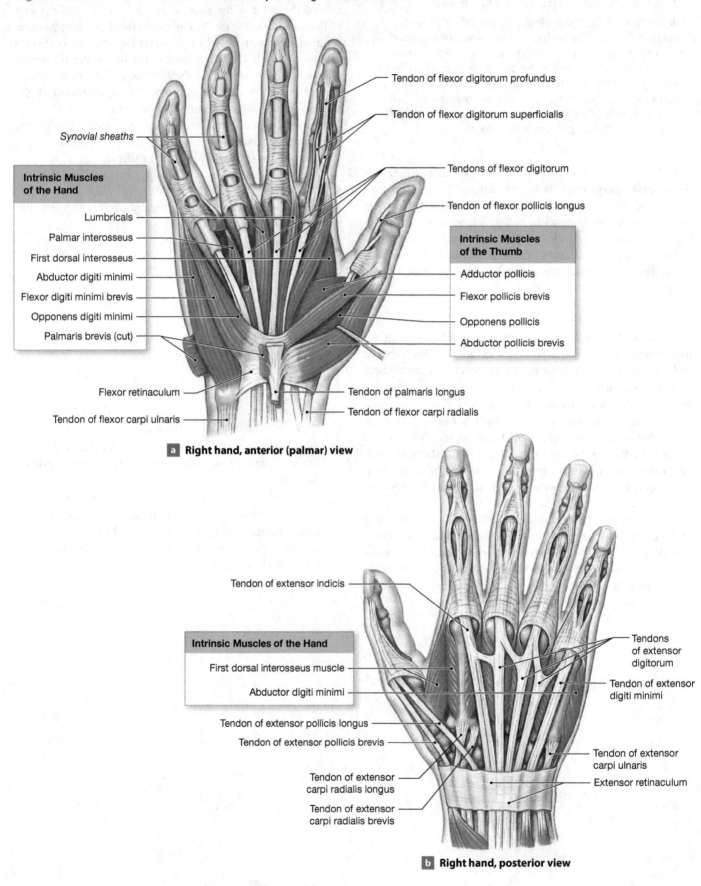

Tendon of flexor digitorum profundus

Tendon of flexor digitorum superficialis

Synovial sheaths

Tendons of flexor digitorum

Tendon of flexor pollicis longus

**Intrinsic Muscles
of the Hand**

Lumbricals

Palmar interosseus

First dorsal interosseus

Abductor digiti minimi

Flexor digiti minimi brevis

Opponens digiti minimi

Palmaris brevis (cut)

**Intrinsic Muscles
of the Thumb**

Adductor pollicis

Flexor pollicis brevis

Opponens pollicis

Abductor pollicis brevis

Flexor retinaculum

Tendon of palmaris longus

Tendon of flexor carpi radialis

Tendon of flexor carpi ulnaris

a Right hand, anterior (palmar) view

Tendon of extensor indicis

Intrinsic Muscles of the Hand

First dorsal interosseus muscle

Abductor digiti minimi

Tendons
of extensor
digitorum

Tendon of extensor
digiti minimi

Tendon of extensor pollicis longus

Tendon of extensor pollicis brevis

Tendon of extensor
carpi ulnaris

Extensor retinaculum

Tendon of extensor
carpi radialis longus

Tendon of extensor
carpi radialis brevis

b Right hand, posterior view

190

Name _____

Date _____

Section _____

Muscles of the Pectoral Girdle and Upper Limb

A. Matching

Match each term in the left column with its correct description from the right column.

_____	**1.** opponens digiti minimi	**A.** tenses palmar fascia and flexes wrist
_____	**2.** palmaris longus	**B.** major pronator of arm
_____	**3.** pronator teres	**C.** flexes and adducts wrist
_____	**4.** flexor carpi ulnaris	**D.** opposes thumb
_____	**5.** extensor carpi ulnaris	**E.** major supinator of forearm
_____	**6.** extensor digitorum	**F.** extends and adducts wrist
_____	**7.** extensor carpi radialis	**G.** band of connective tissue on flexor tendons
_____	**8.** supinator	**H.** brings little finger toward thumb
_____	**9.** flexor retinaculum	**I.** extends fingers
_____	**10.** opponens pollicis	**J.** extends and abducts wrist

B. Descriptions

Describe the location of each of the following muscles.

1. triceps brachii

2. infraspinatus

3. teres minor

4. biceps brachii

5. supraspinatus

6. brachialis

7. coracobrachialis

8. teres major

9. deltoid

10. subscapularis

C. Labeling

1. Label the muscles that move the pectoral girdle in Figure 8.

Figure 8 **Muscles That Move the Pectoral Girdle** Anterior view.

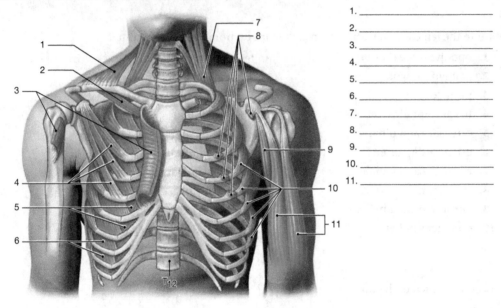

1. _____
2. _____
3. _____
4. _____
5. _____
6. _____
7. _____
8. _____
9. _____
10. _____
11. _____

2. Label the muscles that move the arm in Figure 9.

Figure 9 **Muscles That Move the Arm** Posterior view.

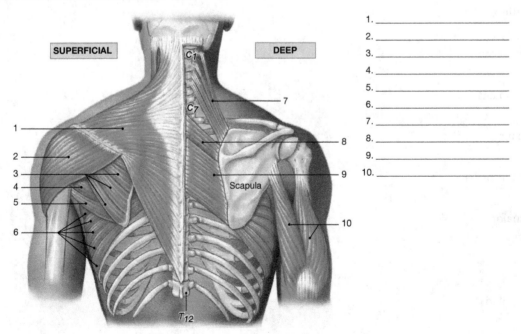

1. _____
2. _____
3. _____
4. _____
5. _____
6. _____
7. _____
8. _____
9. _____
10. _____

3. Label the muscles that move the forearm and hand in Figure 10.

Figure 10 **Muscles That Move the Forearm and Hand** Anterior view.

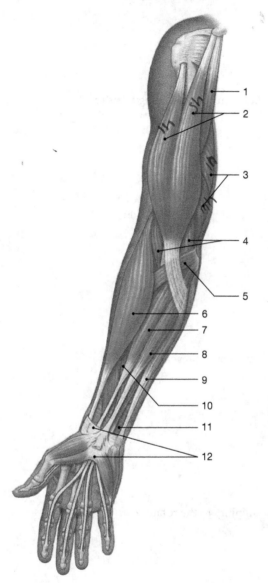

1. coracobrachialis
2. biceps brachii
3. triceps
4. brachialis
5. pronator teres
6. brachioradialis
7. flexor carpi radialis
8. palmaris longus
9. flexor carpi ulnaris
10. flexor digitorum superficialis
11. pronator quadratus
12. flexor retinaculum

D. **Short-Answer Questions**

   1. Describe the muscles involved in turning the hand, as when twisting a doorknob back and forth.

   2. Name the muscles responsible for flexing the arm. Which muscles are antagonists to these flexors?

   3. Name a muscle for each movement of the wrist: flex, extend, abduct, and adduct.

E. **Analysis and Application**

   A brace placed on your wrist to treat carpal tunnel syndrome would prevent what wrist action? What would you accomplish by limiting this action?

F. **Clinical Challenge**

   How would a dislocated shoulder also potentially result in injury to the rotator cuff?

Muscles of the Pelvic Girdle and Lower Limb

Wish List

During the unit on muscles, you will be required to learn the same muscles for lecture and lab. As you review the activities of the 4 muscle chapters, make sure you work on memorizing origins, insertions and actions on your wish lists.

✓	Muscle of Pelvic Region	Description/Action	Origin Bone/marking	Insertion Bone/marking
	Iliopsoas group	Psoas major, minor and Iliacus		
	Psoas Major	Psoas and iliacus acting together-flex hip/externally	Transverse processes and bodies of lumbar vertebrae	With iliacus to lesser trochanter of femur
	Iliacus	Psoas and iliacus acting together-flex hip/externally rotate hip/flex vertebral column	Transverse processes and bodies of Iliac fossa of Ilium/Os Coxa and sacrum	With psoas major to lesser trochanter of femur
	Gluteus Maximus	Extends hip/externally rotates hip	Iliac crest of ilium/Os Coxa/sacrum/coccyx	IT band/gluteal tuberosity of femur
	Tensor Fascia Latae	Flexes/abducts hip	Iliac crest of ilium/Os coxa	Tibia via IT band

✓	Medial Thigh Muscles	Description/Action	Origin Bone/marking	Insertion Bone/marking
	Gracilis	Adducts hip/internally rotates and flexes knee	Body and inferior ramus of pubis/Os coxa	Medial shaft of tibia
	Adductor Magnus	Adducts hip/anterior portion-flexes hip/posterior portion extends hip	Inferior ramus of pubis and ischium/ischial tuberosity	Linear aspera of femur
	Adductor Longus	Adduction/flexion/external rotation of hip (open chain)	Pubic crest/pubic symphysis of Pubis/Os coxa	Linea aspera of femur

✓	Anterior Thigh Muscles	Description/Action	Origin Bone/marking	Insertion Bone/marking
	Sartorius	Weakly flexes knee and weakly flexes/externally rotates hip	Anterior Superior Iliac Spine of Ilium/Os Coxa	Medial shaft of tibia

	Muscle	Description/Action	Origin Bone/marking	Insertion Bone/marking
	Rectus Femoris	All four quads extend the knee. The rectus femoris also flexes the hip.	Anterior Inferior Iliac Spine of Ilium/Os Coxa	Patella and tibial tuberosity of tibia via patellar tendon/ligament
	Vastus Lateralis	All four quads extend the knee. The rectus femoris also flexes the hip.	Greater trochanter and linea aspera of femur	Patella and tibial tuberosity of tibia via patellar tendon/ligament
	Vastus Medialis	All four quads extend the knee. The rectus femoris also flexes the hip.	Linea aspera of femur	Patella and tibial tuberosity of tibia via patellar tendon/ligament
	Vastus Intermedius*	All four quads extend the knee. The rectus femoris also flexes the hip.	Anterior/lateral surface of femur	Patella and tibial tuberosity of tibia via patellar tendon/ligament

✓	Anterior Crural Muscles	Description/Action	Origin Bone/marking	Insertion Bone/marking
	Tibialis Anterior	Dorsiflexes/inverts ankle	Lateral condyle/body of tibia and interosseous membrane	Metatarsal I and medial cuneiform
	Extensor Digitorum Longus	Dorsiflexes ankle/extend middle and distal phalanges of toes (interphalangeal, metatarsophalangeal joints)	Lateral condyle of tibia/body of fibula/interosseous membrane	Middle and distal phalanges of toes

✓	Posterior Thigh Muscles	Description/Action	Origin Bone/marking	Insertion Bone/marking
	Biceps Femoris- Long Head	Flexes knee/extends hip	Ischial tuberosity of Ischium/Os Coxa	Head of fibula/lateral condyle of tibia
	Biceps Femoris- Short Head**	Flexes knee/extends hip	Linea aspera of femur	Head of fibula/lateral condyle of tibia
	Semitendinosus	Flexes knee/extends hip	Ischial tuberosity of Ischium/Os Coxa	Proximal/medial shaft of tibia
	Semimembranosus	Flexes knee/extends hip	Ischial tuberosity of Ischium/Os Coxa	Medial condyle of tibia

✓	Lateral Crural Muscles	Description/Action	Origin Bone/marking	Insertion Bone/marking
	Peroneus (Fibularis) Longus	plantarflexes/everts ankle	head/body fibula	Metatarsal I/medial cuneiform
	Peroneus (Fibularis) Brevis	plantarflexes/everts ankle	Body of fibula	Base of metatarsal V

✓	Superficial, Posterior, Crural Muscle	Description/Action	Origin Bone/marking	Insertion Bone/marking
	Gastrocnemius	Plantarflexes ankle/flexes knee	Lateral and medial condyle of femur	Calcaneus via Achilles tendon
	Soleus	Plantar flexes ankle	Head of fibula/medial border of tibia	Calcaneus via Achilles tendon

✓	Deep, Posterior, Crural Muscles	Description/Action	Origin Bone/marking	Insertion Bone/marking
	Popliteus	Flexes knee/internally rotates tibia to unlock extended knee	Lateral condyle of femur	Proximal tibia
	Tibialis Posterior	Plantarflexes ankle/inverts foot	Tibia/fibula/interosseous membrane	Metatarsals (II-V) and navicular/cuneiforms/cuboid
	Flexor Digitorum Longus	Plantarflexes ankle/flexes distal and middle phalanges (interphalangeal, metatarsophalangeal joints)	Posterior tibia	Distal phalanges of toes

*Deep to vastus medialis. See "Muscles of the anterior thigh" section in Anatomy Coloring Book chapter on muscles.
** Deep to Biceps femoris-long head. See "Muscles of the posterior thigh" section in Anatomy Coloring Book chapter on muscles.

Muscles of the Pelvic Girdle and Lower Limb

Learning Outcomes

On completion of this exercise, you should be able to:

1. Locate the muscles of the pelvic girdle and lower limb on lab models and charts.

2. Identify on the models the origin, insertion, and action of the muscles of the pelvic girdle and lower limb.

3. Demonstrate or describe the action of the major muscles of the pelvic girdle and lower limb.

The muscles of the pelvis help support the mass of the body and stabilize the pelvic girdle. Leg muscles move the thigh, knee, and foot. Flexors of the knee are on the posterior thigh, and knee extensors are anterior. Muscles that abduct the thigh are on the lateral side of the thigh, and the adductors are on the medial thigh.

Lab Activity 1   Muscles That Move the Thigh

Unlike the articulations between the axial skeleton and the pectoral girdle, which give this region great mobility, the articulations between the axial skeleton and the pelvic girdle limit movement of the hips. Muscles that move the thigh insert on the femur and cause movement at the ball-and-socket joint. These muscles are organized into four groups: gluteal, lateral rotator, adductor, and iliopsoas. Refer to Figure 1 and Table 1 for details on these muscles.

Need More Practice and Review?

Build your knowledge—and confidence!—in the Study Area of MasteringA&P® at www.masteringaandp.com with Pre-lab Quizzes, Post-lab Quizzes, Practice Anatomy Lab™ (PAL™) 3.0 virtual anatomy practice tool, PhysioEx™ 9.0 laboratory simulations, and A&P Flix™ with Quizzes.

PAL | practice anatomy lab   For this lab exercise, follow these navigation paths:
- PAL>Human Cadaver>Muscular System>Lower Limb
- PAL>Anatomical Models>Muscular System>Lower Limb

A&PFlix   For this lab exercise, go to these topics:
- Origins, Insertions, Actions, and Innervations
- Group Muscle Actions and Joints

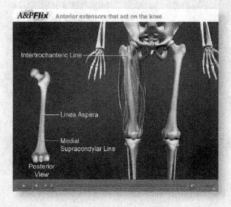

Figure 1 Anterior Muscles That Move the Thigh The gluteal and lateral rotator muscle groups of the right hip.

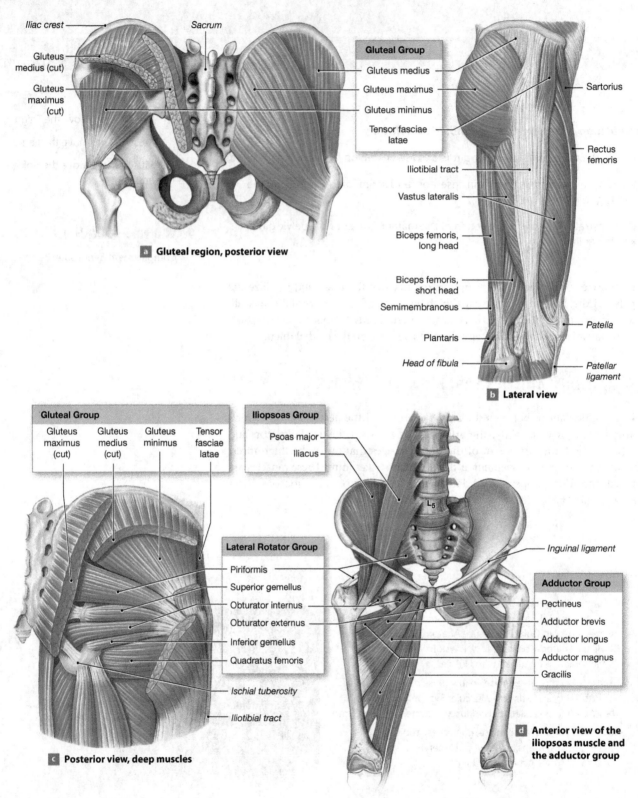

Iliac crest

Sacrum

Gluteus medius (cut)

Gluteus maximus (cut)

Gluteal Group

Gluteus medius

Gluteus maximus

Gluteus minimus

Tensor fasciae latae

Iliotibial tract

Vastus lateralis

Biceps femoris, long head

Biceps femoris, short head

Semimembranosus

Plantaris

Head of fibula

Sartorius

Rectus femoris

Patella

Patellar ligament

a Gluteal region, posterior view

b Lateral view

Gluteal Group

| Gluteus maximus (cut) | Gluteus medius (cut) | Gluteus minimus | Tensor fasciae latae |

Iliopsoas Group

Psoas major

Iliacus

L₅

Lateral Rotator Group

Piriformis

Superior gemellus

Obturator internus

Obturator externus

Inferior gemellus

Quadratus femoris

Ischial tuberosity

Iliotibial tract

Inguinal ligament

Adductor Group

Pectineus

Adductor brevis

Adductor longus

Adductor magnus

Gracilis

c Posterior view, deep muscles

d Anterior view of the iliopsoas muscle and the adductor group

Gluteal Group

The posterior muscles originating on the ilium of the pelvis are the three gluteal muscles that constitute the buttocks. The most superficial and prominent is the **gluteus maximus** muscle (Figure 1). It is a large, fleshy muscle and is easily located as the major muscle of the buttocks. Its muscle fibers pass inferiorolaterally and insert on a thick band of tendon called the **iliotibial** (il-ē-ō-TIB-ē-ul) **tract** that attaches to the lateral condyle of the tibia.

The **gluteus medius** muscle originates on the iliac crest and on the lateral surface of the ilium, and gathers laterally into a thick tendon that inserts posteriorly on the greater trochanter of the femur. The **gluteus minimus** muscle begins on the lateral surface of the ilium, tucked under the origin of the gluteus medius muscle. The fibers of the gluteus minimus muscle also pass laterally to insert on the anterior surface of the greater trochanter. Both the gluteus medius muscle and the gluteus minimus muscle abduct and medially rotate the thigh.

The **tensor fasciae latae** (TEN-sor FAH-shē-āy LAH-tāy) muscle is a small muscle on the proximal part of the lateral thigh. It originates on the iliac crest and on the outer surface of the anterior superior iliac spine. It is a gluteal muscle because it shares its insertion on the iliotibial tract with the gluteus maximus. As the name implies, the tensor fasciae latae muscle tenses the fascia of the thigh and helps stabilize the pelvis on the femur. The muscle also abducts and medially rotates the thigh.

Lateral Rotator Group

The lateral rotator group consists of the obturator internus and externus muscles and the piriformis, gamellus, and quadratus femoris muscles (Figure 1b–d). All of these muscles rotate the thigh laterally, and the piriformis muscle also abducts the thigh. Both the **obturator internus** muscle and the **obturator externus** muscle originate along the medial and lateral edges of the obturator foramen of the os coxae and insert on the trochanteric fossa, a shallow depression on the medial side of the greater trochanter of the femur.

The **piriformis** (pir-i-FOR-mis) muscle arises from the anterior and lateral surfaces of the sacrum and inserts on the greater trochanter of the femur. Inferior to the piriformis is the **quadratus femoris** muscle. Its origin is on the lateral surface of the ischial tuberosity and inserts on the femur between the greater and lesser trochanters.

The **superior gemellus** muscle and **inferior gemellus** muscle are deep to the gluteal muscles. These small rotators originate on the ischial spine and ischial tuberosity and insert on the greater trochanter with the tendon of the obturator internus. Both muscles rotate the thigh laterally.

Iliopsoas Group

The iliopsoas (il-ē-ō-SŌ-us) group consists of two muscles, the psoas major and the iliacus (Figure 1d). The **psoas** (SŌ-us) **major** muscle originates on the body and transverse processes of vertebrae T_{12} through L_5. The muscle sweeps inferiorly, passing between the femur and the ischial ramus, and inserts on the lesser trochanter of the femur. The **iliacus** (il-Ē-ah-kus) muscle originates on the iliac fossa on the medial portion of the ilium and joins the tendon of the psoas major muscle. The psoas major and iliacus muscles work together to flex the thigh, bringing its anterior surface toward the abdomen.

Adductor Group

Muscles that adduct the thigh are organized into the adductor group and the pectineus and gracilis muscles. The **pectineus** (pek-TIN-ē-us) muscle is another superficial adductor muscle of the medial thigh (Figure 1d). It is located next to the iliacus muscle. It originates along the superior ramus of the pubic bone and inserts on the pectineal line of the femur.

The **gracilis** (GRAS-i-lis) muscle is the most superficial of the thigh adductors and is located at the midline of the medial thigh (Figure 2). It arises from the superior ramus of the pubic bone, near the symphysis, extends inferiorly along the medial surface of the thigh, and inserts just medial to the insertion of the sartorius near the tibial tuberosity. Because it passes over both the hip and knee joints, it acts to adduct and medially rotate the thigh and flex the knee.

Three additional adductor muscles originate on the inferior pubis and insert on the posterior femur and are powerful adductors of the thigh (Figure 2). They also allow the thigh to flex and rotate medially. The **adductor magnus** muscle is the largest of the adductor muscles. It arises on the inferior ramus of the pubis and the ischial tuberosity and inserts along the length of the linea aspera of the femur. It is easily observed on a leg model if the superficial muscles are removed. Superficial to the adductor magnus is the **adductor longus** muscle. Not visible on the surface is the **adductor brevis** muscle, which is positioned superior and posterior to the adductor longus muscle (see Figure 1d).

> **Study Tip Learning by Anatomical Association**
>
> An easy method for remembering the superficial muscles of the medial thigh is to reference them to other regional muscles. Locate the gracilis muscle in the midline of the thigh. Anterior to the gracilis is the adductor longus, which is next to the long sartorius muscle (described in the next activity). Posterior to the gracilis is the adductor magnus, which is by the gluteus maximus. ∎

Table 1   *ORIGINS AND INSERTIONS*   Muscles That Move the Thigh (See Figures 1 and 2)

Group and Muscle(s)	Origin	Insertion	Action	Innervation*
GLUTEAL GROUP				
Gluteus maximus	Iliac crest, posterior gluteal line, and lateral surface of ilium; sacrum, coccyx, and thoracolumbar fascia	Iliotibial tract and gluteal tuberosity of femur	Extension and lateral rotation at hip	Inferior gluteal nerve (L_5–S_2)
Gluteus medius	Anterior iliac crest of ilium, lateral surface between posterior and anterior gluteal lines	Greater trochanter of femur	Abduction and medial rotation at hip	Superior gluteal nerve (L_4–S_1)
Gluteus minimus	Lateral surface of ilium between inferior and anterior gluteal lines	As above	As above	As above
Tensor fasciae latae	Iliac crest and lateral surface of anterior superior iliac spine	Iliotibial tract	Flexion and medial rotation at hip; tenses fascia lata, which laterally supports the knee	As above
LATERAL ROTATOR GROUP				
Obturators (externus and internus)	Lateral and medial margins of obturator foramen	Trochanteric fossa of femur (externus); medial surface of greater trochanter (internus)	Lateral rotation at hip	Obturator nerve (externus: L_3–L_4) and special nerve from sacral plexus (internus: L_5–S_2)
Piriformis	Anterolateral surface of sacrum	Greater trochanter of femur	Lateral rotation and abduction at hip	Branches of sacral nerves (S_1–S_2)
Gemelli (superior and inferior)	Ischial spine and tuberosity	Medial surface of greater trochanter with tendon of obturator internus	Lateral rotation at hip	Nerves to obturator internus and quadratus femoris
Quadratus femoris	Lateral border of ischial tuberosity	Intertrochanteric crest of femur	As above	Special nerve from sacral plexus (L_4–S_1)
ADDUCTOR GROUP				
Adductor brevis	Inferior ramus of pubis	Linea aspera of femur	Adduction, flexion, and medial rotation at hip	Obturator nerve (L_3–L_4)
Adductor longus	Inferior ramus of pubis anterior to adductor brevis	As above	As above	As above
Adductor magnus	Inferior ramus of pubis posterior to adductor brevis and ischial tuberosity	Linea aspera and adductor tubercle of femur	Adduction at hip; superior part produces flexion and medial rotation; inferior part produces extension and lateral rotation	Obturator and sciatic nerves
Pectineus	Superior ramus of pubis	Pectineal line inferior to lesser trochanter of femur	Flexion medial rotation and adduction at hip	Femoral nerve (L_2–L_4)
Gracilis	Inferior ramus of pubis	Medial surface of tibia inferior to medial condyle	Flexion at knee; adduction and medial rotation at hip	Obturator nerve (L_3–L_4)
ILIOPSOAS GROUP				
Iliacus	Iliac fossa of ilium	Femur distal to lesser trochanter; tendon fused with that of psoas major	Flexion at hip	Femoral nerve (L_2–L_3)
Psoas major	Anterior surfaces and transverse processes of vertebrae (T_{12}–L_5)	Lesser trochanter in company with iliacus	Flexion at hip or lumbar intervertebral joints	Branches of the lumbar plexus (L_2–L_3)

*Where appropriate, spinal nerves involved are given in parentheses.

Figure 2 Medial Muscles That Move the Leg Medial view of the muscles of the right thigh.

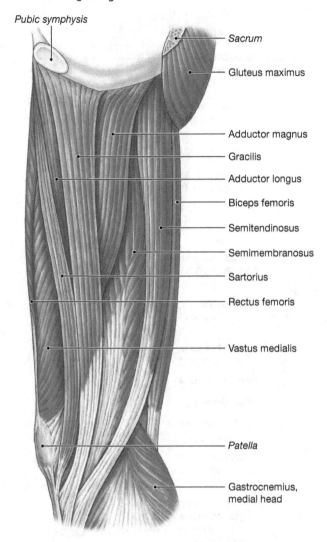

Pubic symphysis

Sacrum

Gluteus maximus

Adductor magnus

Gracilis

Adductor longus

Biceps femoris

Semitendinosus

Semimembranosus

Sartorius

Rectus femoris

Vastus medialis

Patella

Gastrocnemius, medial head

QuickCheck Questions

1.1 Where are the abductors of the thigh located?

1.2 What is the iliotibial tract?

1.3 Name two muscles that rotate the thigh.

In the Lab 1

Materials

☐ Torso model ☐ Articulated skeleton

☐ Lower limb model ☐ Muscle chart

Procedures

1. Review the pelvic and gluteal muscles in Figures 1 and 2 and in Table 1.

2. Identify each muscle on the torso and lower limb models and on the muscle chart.

3. On the lower limb model, observe how the gluteal muscles and the tensor fasciae latae muscle insert on the lateral portion of the femur.

4. Locate as many of your own thigh muscles as possible. Practice the actions of the muscles and observe how your lower limb moves.

5. Examine the articulated skeleton and note the origin, insertion, and action of the major muscles that act on the thigh. ∎

Lab Activity 2 Muscles That Move the Leg

Muscles that flex and extend the leg at the knee joint are on the posterior and anterior sides of the femur. Refer to Table 2 for details on these muscles. Some of these muscles originate on the pelvis and cross both the hip and the knee joints and can therefore also move the thigh.

The major muscles of the posterior thigh are collectively called the **hamstrings.** They all have a common origin on the ischial tuberosity and flex the knee. The **biceps femoris** muscle is the lateral muscle of the posterior thigh (Figure 3). It has two heads and two origins, one on the ischial tuberosity and a second on the linea aspera of the femur. The two heads merge to form the belly of the muscle and insert on the lateral condyle of the tibia and the head of the fibula. Because this muscle spans both the hip and knee joints, it can extend the thigh and flex the knee. Medial to the biceps femoris muscle is the **semitendinosus** (sem-ē-ten-di-NŌ-sus) muscle. It is a long muscle that passes the posterior knee to insert on the proximomedial surface of the tibia near the insertion of the gracilis. The **semimembranosus** (sem-ē-mem-bra-NŌ-sus) muscle is medial to the semitendinosus muscle and inserts on the medial tibia. These muscles cross both the hip joint and the knee joint and extend the thigh and flex the knee. The hamstrings are therefore antagonists to the quadriceps muscles. When the thigh is flexed and drawn up toward the pelvis, the hamstrings extend the thigh.

The extensors of the leg are collectively called either the **quadriceps** muscles or the **quadriceps femoris.** They make up the bulk of the anterior mass of the thigh and are consequently easy to locate. The largest muscle in the group, the **rectus femoris** muscle (Figure 4), is located along the midline of the anterior surface of the thigh. Covering almost the entire medial surface of the femur is the **vastus medialis** muscle. The **vastus lateralis** muscle is located on the lateral side of the rectus femoris muscle, and the **vastus intermedius** muscle is directly deep to the rectus femoris muscle. The quadriceps muscles converge on a patellar tendon and insert on the

Figure 3 Posterior Muscles That Move the Leg

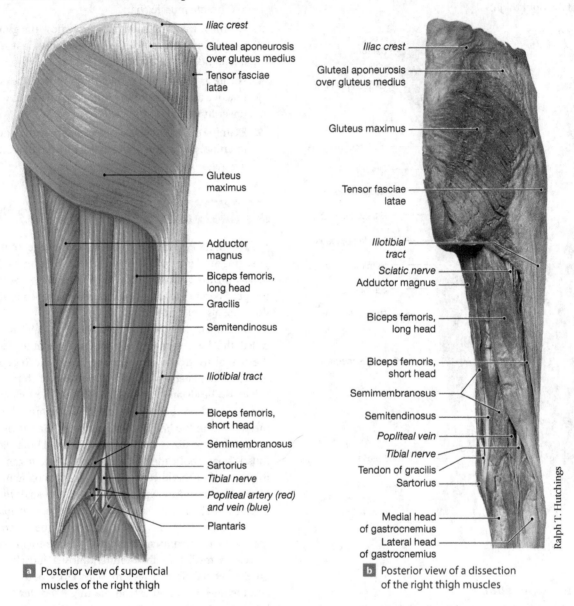

- Iliac crest
- Gluteal aponeurosis over gluteus medius
- Tensor fasciae latae
- Gluteus maximus
- Adductor magnus
- Biceps femoris, long head
- Gracilis
- Semitendinosus
- Iliotibial tract
- Biceps femoris, short head
- Semimembranosus
- Sartorius
- Tibial nerve
- Popliteal artery (red) and vein (blue)
- Plantaris

- Iliac crest
- Gluteal aponeurosis over gluteus medius
- Gluteus maximus
- Tensor fasciae latae
- Iliotibial tract
- Sciatic nerve
- Adductor magnus
- Biceps femoris, long head
- Biceps femoris, short head
- Semimembranosus
- Semitendinosus
- Popliteal vein
- Tibial nerve
- Tendon of gracilis
- Sartorius
- Medial head of gastrocnemius
- Lateral head of gastrocnemius

Ralph T. Hutchings

a Posterior view of superficial muscles of the right thigh

b Posterior view of a dissection of the right thigh muscles

tibial tuberosity. Because the rectus femoris muscle crosses two joints, the hip and knee, it allows the hip to flex and the leg to extend.

The **sartorius** (sar-TOR-ē-us; *sartor*, a tailor) muscle is a thin, ribbonlike muscle originating on the anterior superior iliac spine and passing inferiorly, cutting obliquely across the thigh (Figure 3b). It is the longest muscle in the body. It crosses the knee joint to insert on the medial surface of the tibia near the tibial tuberosity. This muscle is a flexor of the knee and thigh and a lateral rotator of the thigh. Figures 3b and 4b show the anterior and posterior thigh muscles in superficial

dissection for comparison with the muscles illustrated in Figures 3a and 4a.

A small muscle on the posterior of the knee assists in flexing the knee. The **popliteus** (pop-LI-tē-us) muscle crosses from its origin on the lateral condyle of the femur to insert on the posterior surface of the tibial shaft.

QuickCheck Questions

2.1 Name all the quadriceps muscles.

2.2 Name all the hamstrings.

Figure 4 Anterior Muscles That Move the Leg

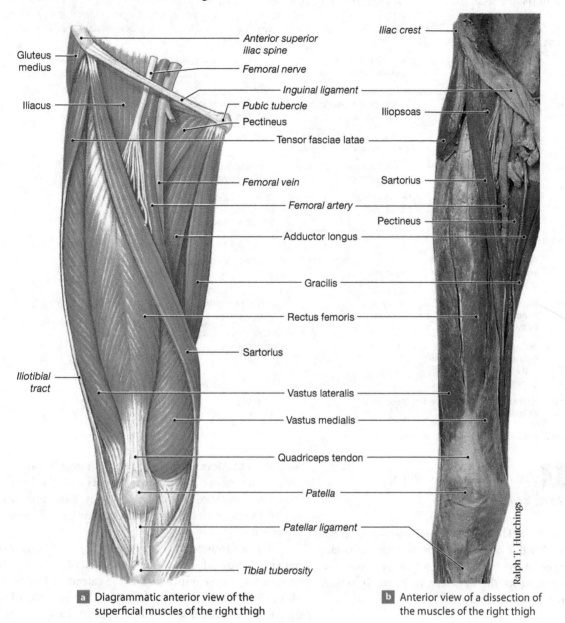

Anterior superior iliac spine
Gluteus medius
Femoral nerve
Iliacus
Inguinal ligament
Pubic tubercle
Pectineus
Tensor fasciae latae
Femoral vein
Femoral artery
Adductor longus
Gracilis
Rectus femoris
Sartorius
Iliotibial tract
Vastus lateralis
Vastus medialis
Quadriceps tendon
Patella
Patellar ligament
Tibial tuberosity

Iliac crest
Iliopsoas
Sartorius
Pectineus

Ralph T. Hutchings

a Diagrammatic anterior view of the superficial muscles of the right thigh

b Anterior view of a dissection of the muscles of the right thigh

Materials

☐ Torso model
☐ Lower limb model
☐ Articulated skeleton
☐ Muscle chart

Procedures

1. Review the muscles that move the leg in Figures 2 through 4. On the torso and lower limb models and the muscle chart, identify the muscles that move the leg, categorizing each muscle as being a flexor, extensor, adductor, or abductor.

2. Flex your knee and feel the tendons of the semimembranosus and semitendinosus muscles, located just above the posterior knee on the medial side. Similarly, on the lateral side of the knee, just above the fibular head, the tendon of the biceps femoris muscle can be palpated.

3. Examine the articulated skeleton and note the origin, insertion, and action of the major muscles that act on the thigh, knee, and leg. ■

Table 2	ORIGINS AND INSERTIONS Muscles That Move the Leg (See Figures 3 and 4)			
Muscle	Origin	Insertion	Action	Innervation*
FLEXORS OF THE KNEE				
Biceps femoris	Ischial tuberosity and linea aspera of femur	Head of fibula, lateral condyle of tibia	Flexion at knee; extension and lateral rotation at hip	Sciatic nerve; tibial portion (S_1–S_3; to long head) and common fibular branch (L_5–S_2; to short head)
Semimembranosus	Ischial tuberosity	Posterior surface of medial condyle of tibia	Flexion at knee; extension and medial rotation at hip	Sciatic nerve (tibial portion; L_5–S_2)
Semitendinosus	As above	Proximal, medial surface of tibia near insertion of gracilis	As above	As above
Sartorius	Anterior superior iliac spine	Medial surface of tibia near tibial tuberosity	Flexion at knee; flexion and lateral rotation at hip	Femoral nerve (L_2–L_3)
Popliteus	Lateral condyle of femur	Posterior surface of proximal tibial shaft	Medial rotation of tibia (or lateral rotation of femur); flexion at knee	Tibial nerve (L_4–S_1)
EXTENSORS OF THE KNEE				
Rectus femoris	Anterior inferior iliac spine and superior acetabular rim of ilium	Tibial tuberosity via patellar ligament	Extension at knee; flexion at hip	Femoral nerve (L_2–L_4)
Vastus intermedius	Anterolateral surface of femur and linea aspera (distal half)	As above	Extension at knee	As above
Vastus lateralis	Anterior and inferior to greater trochanter of femur and along linea aspera (proximal half)	As above	As above	As above
Vastus medialis	Entire length of linea aspera of femur	As above	As above	As above

*Where appropriate, spinal nerves involved are given in parentheses.

Lab Activity 3 Muscles That Move the Ankle and Foot

Muscles that move the ankle arise on the leg and insert on the tarsal bones. Muscles that move the foot and toes originate either on the leg or in the foot. Details for origin, insertion, action, and innervation for the muscles that move the ankle, foot, and toes are in Tables 3 and 4.

Make a Prediction

Consider the action of flexing the toes and then predict the location of the contracting flexor muscle.

The **tibialis** (tib-ē-A-lis) **anterior** muscle is located on the anterior side of the leg (Figure 5). This muscle is easy to locate as the lateral muscle mass of the shin on the anterior edge of the tibia bone. Its tendon passes over the dorsal surface of the foot, and the muscle dorsiflexes and inverts the foot. Two extensor muscles arise on the anterior leg and insert on the various phalanges of the foot. The **extensor hallucis** (HAL-i-sis; *hallux*, great toe) **longus** muscle (not shown in any illustration here) is lateral and deep to the tibialis anterior muscle. Lateral to the extensor hallucis longus muscle is the **extensor digitorum longus** muscle with four tendons that

spread on the dorsal surface of toes 2 through 5. On the lateral side of the leg are the **fibularis longus** and **fibularis brevis** muscles, also called the *peroneus* muscles. These muscles insert on the foot to evert the foot by laterally turning the sole to face outward.

The calf muscles of the posterior leg are the **gastrocnemius** (gas-trok-NĒ-mē-us) and the **soleus** (SŌ-lē-us) muscles (Figure 5d). These muscles share the **calcaneal** (Achilles) **tendon,** which inserts on the calcaneus of the foot. The **plantaris** (plan-TAR-is; *planta*, sole of foot) muscle is a short muscle of the lateral popliteal region, deep to the gastrocnemius muscle. The plantaris muscle has a long tendon that inserts on the posterior of the calcaneus. The gastrocnemius, soleus, and plantaris muscles plantarflex the ankle; the soleus is also a postural muscle for support while standing.

Deep to the soleus muscle is the **tibialis posterior** muscle (Figure 5e), which adducts and inverts the foot and plantar flexes the ankle. Its tendon passes medially to the calcaneus and inserts on the plantar surface of the navicular and cuneiform bones and metatarsals II, III, and IV. The **flexor hallucis longus** muscle begins lateral to the origin of the tibialis posterior muscle on the fibular shaft. Its tendon runs parallel to that of the tibialis posterior muscle, passes medial to the calcaneus, and inserts on the plantar surface of the distal phalanx of the

Figure 5 Muscles That Move the Ankle, Foot, and Toes Relationships among the muscles of the right leg and foot.

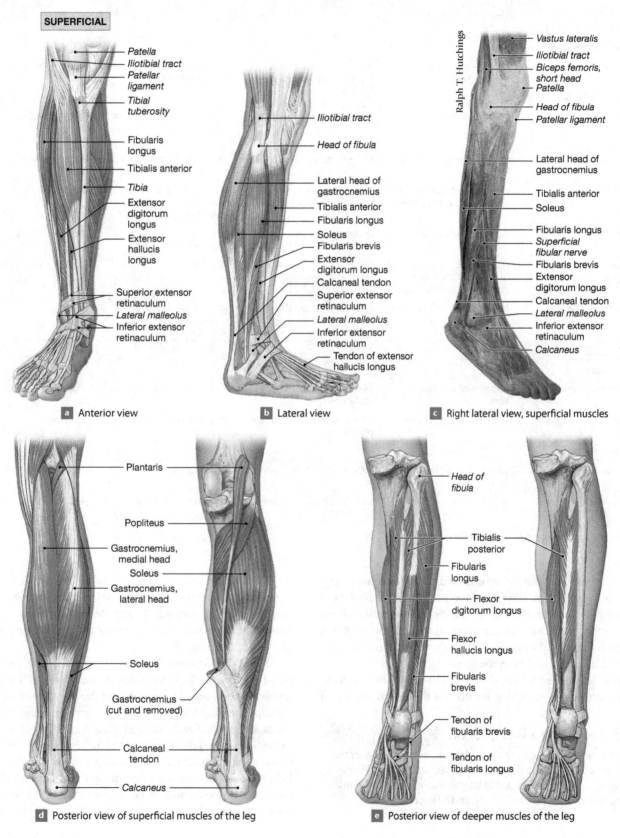

SUPERFICIAL

Patella
Iliotibial tract
Patellar ligament
Tibial tuberosity
Fibularis longus
Tibialis anterior
Tibia
Extensor digitorum longus
Extensor hallucis longus
Superior extensor retinaculum
Lateral malleolus
Inferior extensor retinaculum

a Anterior view

Iliotibial tract
Head of fibula
Lateral head of gastrocnemius
Tibialis anterior
Fibularis longus
Soleus
Fibularis brevis
Extensor digitorum longus
Calcaneal tendon
Superior extensor retinaculum
Lateral malleolus
Inferior extensor retinaculum
Tendon of extensor hallucis longus

b Lateral view

Ralph T. Hutchings

Vastus lateralis
Iliotibial tract
Biceps femoris, short head
Patella
Head of fibula
Patellar ligament
Lateral head of gastrocnemius
Tibialis anterior
Soleus
Fibularis longus
Superficial fibular nerve
Fibularis brevis
Extensor digitorum longus
Calcaneal tendon
Lateral malleolus
Inferior extensor retinaculum
Calcaneus

c Right lateral view, superficial muscles

Plantaris
Popliteus
Gastrocnemius, medial head
Soleus
Gastrocnemius, lateral head
Soleus
Gastrocnemius (cut and removed)
Calcaneal tendon
Calcaneus

d Posterior view of superficial muscles of the leg

Head of fibula
Tibialis posterior
Fibularis longus
Flexor digitorum longus
Flexor hallucis longus
Fibularis brevis
Tendon of fibularis brevis
Tendon of fibularis longus

e Posterior view of deeper muscles of the leg

Table 3 *ORIGINS AND INSERTIONS* Extrinsic Muscles That Move the Foot and Toes (See Figure 5)

Muscle	Origin	Insertion	Action	Innervation*
ACTION AT THE ANKLE				
Flexors (Dorsiflexors)				
Tibialis anterior	Lateral condyle and proximal shaft of tibia	Base of first metatarsal bone and medial cuneiform bone	Flexion (dorsiflexion) at ankle; inversion of foot	Deep fibular nerve (L_4–S_1)
Extensors (Plantarflexors)				
Gastrocnemius	Femoral condyles	Calcaneus via calcaneal tendon	Extension (plantar flexion) at ankle; inversion of foot; flexion at knee	Tibial nerve (S_1–S_2)
Fibularis brevis	Midlateral margin of fibula	Base of fifth metatarsal bone	Eversion of foot and extension (plantar flexion) at ankle	Superficial fibular nerve (L_4–S_1)
Fibularis longus	Lateral condyle of tibia, head and proximal shaft of fibula	Base of fifth metatarsal bone and medial cuneiform bone	Eversion of foot and extension (plantar flexion) at ankle; supports longitudinal arch	As above
Plantaris	Lateral supracondylar ridge	Posterior portion of calcaneus	Extension (plantar flexion) at ankle; flexion at knee	Tibial nerve (L_4–S_1)
Soleus	Head and proximal shaft of fibula and adjacent posteromedial shaft of tibia	Calcaneus via calcaneal tendon (with gastrocnemius)	Extension (plantar flexion) at ankle	Sciatic nerve, tibial branch (S_1–S_2)
Tibialis posterior	Interosseous membrane and adjacent shafts of tibia and fibula	Tarsal and metatarsal bones	Adduction and inversion of foot; extension (plantar flexion) at ankle	As above
ACTION AT THE TOES				
Digital Flexors				
Flexor digitorum longus	Posteromedial surface of tibia	Inferior surfaces of distal phalanges, toes 2–5	Flexion at joints of toes 2–5	Sciatic nerve, tibial branch (L_5–S_1)
Flexor hallucis longus	Posterior surface of fibula	Inferior surface, distal phalanx of great toe	Flexion at joints of great toe	As above
Digital Extensors				
Extensor digitorum longus	Lateral condyle of tibia, anterior surface of fibula	Superior surfaces of phalanges, toes 2–5	Extension at joints of toes 2–5	Deep fibular nerve (L_4–S_1)
Extensor hallucis longus	Anterior surface of fibula	Superior surface, distal phalanx of great toe	Extension at joints of great toe	As above

*Where appropriate, spinal nerves involved are given in parentheses.

hallux, or great toe. The **flexor digitorum longus** muscle originates on the posterior tibia and inserts on the distal phalanges of toes 2 through 5. The flexor hallucis longus muscle flexes the joints of the great toe; the flexor digitorum longus flexes the joints of toes 2 through 5. Both of these flexor muscles also dorsiflex the ankle and evert the foot.

Muscles of the foot are shown in Figure 6. The **extensor digitorum brevis** muscle is located on the dorsal surface of

the foot and passes obliquely across the foot with four tendons that insert into the dorsal surface of the proximal phalanges of toes 1 through 4. The **flexor digitorum brevis** muscle on the plantar surface inserts tendons on the phalanges of toes 2 through 5.

The **abductor hallucis** muscle is found on the inner margin of the foot on the plantar side of the calcaneus. The **flexor hallucis brevis** muscle originates on the plantar surface of the cuneiform and cuboid bones of the foot and splits into two heads, one medial and one lateral. Each head sends a tendon to the base of the first phalanx of the hallux, to either the lateral or the medial side. The **abductor digiti minimi** muscle of the little toe is located on the outer margin of the foot and originates on the plantar and lateral surfaces of the calcaneus. It inserts on the lateral side of the proximal phalanx of the little toe.

Study Tip **The Tibia's Guide to the Leg**

An excellent approach to learning the superficial muscles of the leg is to locate the tibia bone and then sequence the following muscles in order from medial to lateral: tibialis anterior, extensor digitorum longus, fibularis longus, and gastrocnemius. ■

Figure 6 Muscles of the Foot

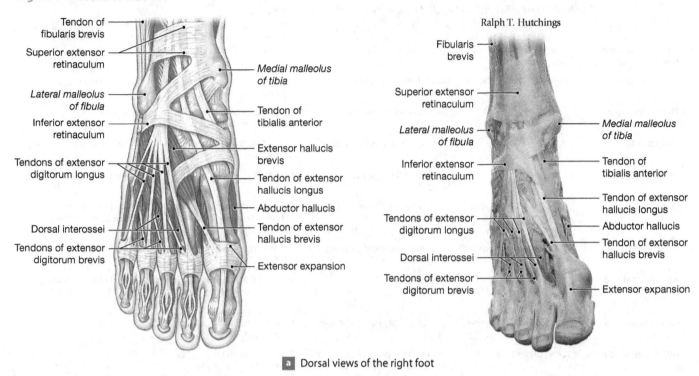

Tendon of fibularis brevis
Superior extensor retinaculum
Lateral malleolus of fibula
Inferior extensor retinaculum
Tendons of extensor digitorum longus
Dorsal interossei
Tendons of extensor digitorum brevis

Medial malleolus of tibia
Tendon of tibialis anterior
Extensor hallucis brevis
Tendon of extensor hallucis longus
Abductor hallucis
Tendon of extensor hallucis brevis
Extensor expansion

Ralph T. Hutchings

Fibularis brevis
Superior extensor retinaculum
Lateral malleolus of fibula
Inferior extensor retinaculum
Tendons of extensor digitorum longus
Dorsal interossei
Tendons of extensor digitorum brevis

Medial malleolus of tibia
Tendon of tibialis anterior
Tendon of extensor hallucis longus
Abductor hallucis
Tendon of extensor hallucis brevis
Extensor expansion

a Dorsal views of the right foot

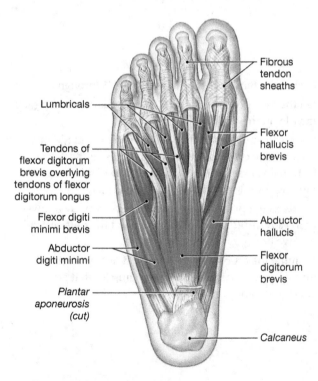

Lumbricals
Tendons of flexor digitorum brevis overlying tendons of flexor digitorum longus
Flexor digiti minimi brevis
Abductor digiti minimi
Plantar aponeurosis (cut)

Fibrous tendon sheaths
Flexor hallucis brevis
Abductor hallucis
Flexor digitorum brevis
Calcaneus

b Plantar (inferior) view, superficial layer of the right foot

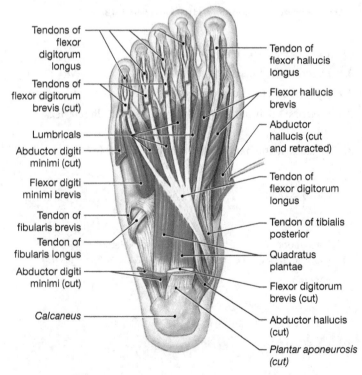

Tendons of flexor digitorum longus
Tendons of flexor digitorum brevis (cut)
Lumbricals
Abductor digiti minimi (cut)
Flexor digiti minimi brevis
Tendon of fibularis brevis
Tendon of fibularis longus
Abductor digiti minimi (cut)
Calcaneus

Tendon of flexor hallucis longus
Flexor hallucis brevis
Abductor hallucis (cut and retracted)
Tendon of flexor digitorum longus
Tendon of tibialis posterior
Quadratus plantae
Flexor digitorum brevis (cut)
Abductor hallucis (cut)
Plantar aponeurosis (cut)

c Plantar (inferior) view, deep layer of the right foot

Table 4   *ORIGINS AND INSERTIONS*   Intrinsic Muscles of the Foot (See Figure 6)

Muscle	Origin	Insertion	Action	Innervation*
Extensor digitorum brevis	Calcaneus (superior and lateral surfaces)	Dorsal surfaces of toes 1–4	Extension at metatarsophalangeal joints of toes 1–4	Deep fibular nerve (L_5–S_1)
Abductor hallucis	Calcaneus (tuberosity on inferior surface)	Medial side of proximal phalanx of great toe	Abduction at metatarsophalangeal joint of great toe	Medial plantar nerve (L_4–L_5)
Flexor digitorum brevis	As above	Sides of middle phalanges, toes 2–5	Flexion at proximal interphalangeal joints of toes 2–5	As above
Abductor digiti minimi	As above	Lateral side of proximal phalanx, toe 5	Abduction at metatarsophalangeal joint of toe 5	Lateral plantar nerve (L_4–L_5)
Quadratus plantae	Calcaneus (medial, inferior surfaces)	Tendon of flexor digitorum longus	Flexion at joints of toes 2–5	As above
Lumbrical (4)	Tendons of flexor digitorum longus	Insertions of extensor digitorum longus	Flexion at metatarsophalangeal joints; extension at proximal interphalangeal joints of toes 2–5	Medial plantar nerve (1), lateral plantar nerve (2–4)
Flexor hallucis brevis	Cuboid and lateral cuneiform bones	Proximal phalanx of great toe	Flexion at metatarsophalangeal joints of great toe	Medial plantar nerve (L_4–L_5)
Adductor hallucis	Bases of metatarsal bones II–IV and plantar ligaments	As above	Adduction at metatarsophalangeal joint of great toe	Lateral plantar nerve (S_1–S_2)
Flexor digiti minimi brevis	Base of metatarsal bone V	Lateral side of proximal phalanx of toe 5	Flexion at metatarsophalangeal joint of toe 5	As above
Dorsal interosseus (4)	Sides of metatarsal bones	Medial and lateral sides of toe 2; lateral sides of toes 3 and 4	Abduction at metatarsophalangeal joints of toes 3 and 4	As above
Plantar interosseus (3)	Bases and medial sides of metatarsal bones	Medial sides of toes 3–5	Adduction at metatarsophalangeal joints of toes 3–5	As above

*Where appropriate, spinal nerves involved are given in parentheses.

QuickCheck Questions

3.1 Describe the muscles of the calf.

3.2 Which muscles move the great toe?

3.3 Describe the insertions of the muscles that plantar flex the foot.

3.4 What does the name *flexor hallucis brevis* mean?

In the Lab 3

Materials

- ☐ Torso model
- ☐ Lower limb model
- ☐ Foot model
- ☐ Articulated skeleton
- ☐ Muscle chart

Procedures

1. Review the muscles of the leg in Figures 5 through 6.
2. On the lower limb model and muscle chart, identify each muscle on the leg.
3. Review the muscles of the foot in Figure 6 and identify each muscle on the foot model and muscle chart. If sectional views of the lower limb are available, study the muscles found in each muscle compartment.
4. Locate as many leg and foot muscles on your own lower limb as possible. Practice the actions of the muscles and observe how your leg and foot move.
5. Examine the articulated skeleton and note the origin, insertion, and action of the major muscles that act on the ankle, foot, and toes. ■

Compartment Syndrome

Muscles on the upper and lower limbs are surrounded by the deep fascia and isolated in saclike muscle **compartments.** These compartments separate the various muscles into anterior, posterior, lateral, and deep groups that have similar muscle actions. Within a muscle compartment are arteries, veins, nerves, and other structures.

Lower limb compartments and the muscles, blood vessels, and nerves in each compartment are illustrated in **Figure 7**.

Examine the figure and observe how superficial and deep muscles of the limb are in different compartments.

Treating a limb injury includes watching for blood trapped in a muscle compartment. Bleeding increases pressure in the compartment and causes compression of local nerves and blood vessels. If the compression persists beyond four to six hours, permanent damage to nerve and muscle tissue may occur, a condition called *compartment syndrome*. To prevent compartment syndrome, drains are inserted into wounds to remove blood and other liquids both from the muscle and from the compartment. ∎

Figure 7 Muscle Compartments of the Lower Limb

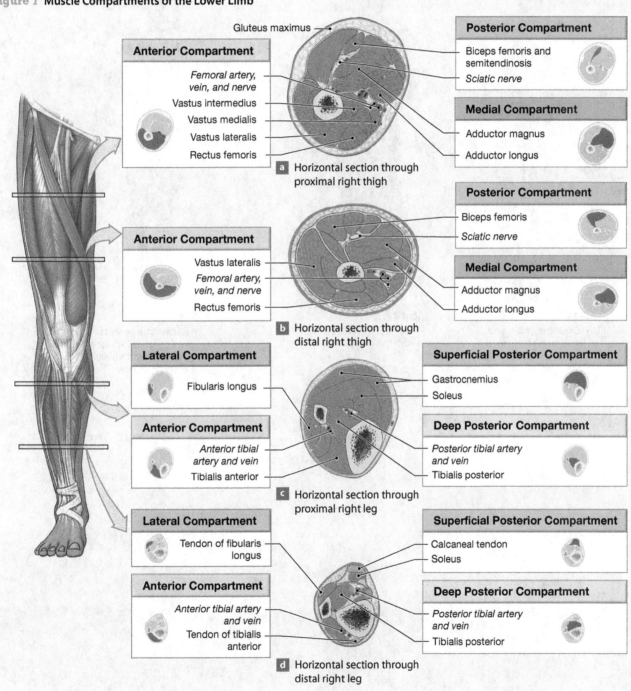

Gluteus maximus

Anterior Compartment
- *Femoral artery, vein, and nerve*
- Vastus intermedius
- Vastus medialis
- Vastus lateralis
- Rectus femoris

Posterior Compartment
- Biceps femoris and semitendinosis
- *Sciatic nerve*

Medial Compartment
- Adductor magnus
- Adductor longus

a Horizontal section through proximal right thigh

Anterior Compartment
- Vastus lateralis
- *Femoral artery, vein, and nerve*
- Rectus femoris

Posterior Compartment
- Biceps femoris
- *Sciatic nerve*

Medial Compartment
- Adductor magnus
- Adductor longus

b Horizontal section through distal right thigh

Lateral Compartment
- Fibularis longus

Anterior Compartment
- *Anterior tibial artery and vein*
- Tibialis anterior

Superficial Posterior Compartment
- Gastrocnemius
- Soleus

Deep Posterior Compartment
- *Posterior tibial artery and vein*
- Tibialis posterior

c Horizontal section through proximal right leg

Lateral Compartment
- Tendon of fibularis longus

Anterior Compartment
- *Anterior tibial artery and vein*
- Tendon of tibialis anterior

Superficial Posterior Compartment
- Calcaneal tendon
- Soleus

Deep Posterior Compartment
- *Posterior tibial artery and vein*
- Tibialis posterior

d Horizontal section through distal right leg

Sketch to Learn

Use the provided figure of the skeleton and add the vastus lateralis, vastus medialis, and tibialis anterior muscles. The rectus femoris muscle is shown as an example.

Sample Sketch

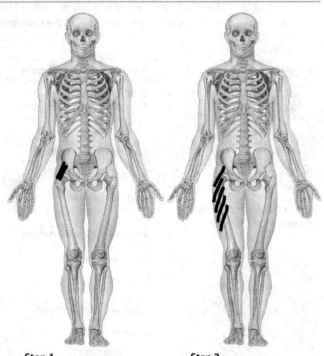

Your Sketch

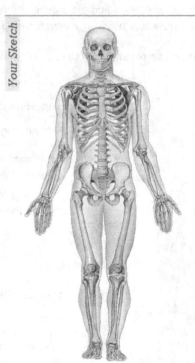

Step 1
- Draw the origin and insertion of the rectus femoris muscle.

Step 2
- Connect the two ends with the muscle's belly.

Step 3
- Repeat the process for the vastus lateralis, vastus medialis, and tibialis anterior muscles.

Name _____

Date _____

Section _____

Muscles of the Pelvic Girdle and Lower Limb

A. Descriptions

Describe the location of each of the following muscles.

1. sartorius

2. semitendinosus

3. psoas major

4. adductor magnus

5. gracilis

6. tensor fasciae latae

7. fibularis longus

8. vastus intermedius

B. Labeling

1. Label each muscle in Figure 8.

Figure 8 **An Overview of the Major Anterior Skeletal Muscles**

1. trapezius
2. deltoid
3. pectoralis major
4. biceps brachii
5. triceps
6. brachioradialis
7. pronator teres
8. palmaris longus
9. flexor carpi radialis
10. flexor carpi ulnaris
11. tensor fascie latae
12. rectus femoris
13. vastus lateralis
14. iliotibial tract
15. tibialis anterior
16. extensor digitorum longus
17. frontalis
18. temporalis
19. sternocleidomastoid
20. _____
21. external intercostals
22. external oblique
23. rectus abdominus
24. sartorius
25. fibularis longus

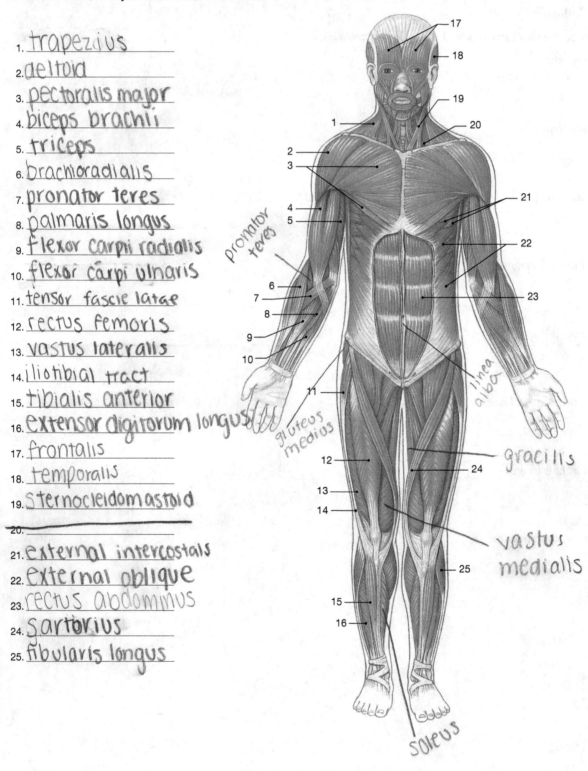

2. Label each muscle in Figure 9.

Figure 9 **An Overview of the Major Posterior Skeletal Muscles**

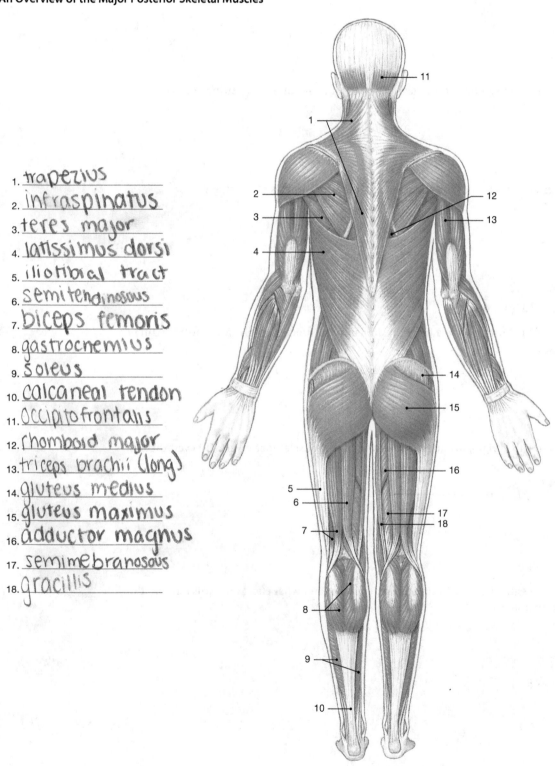

1. trapezius
2. infraspinatus
3. teres major
4. latissimus dorsi
5. iliotibial tract
6. semitendinosous
7. biceps femoris
8. gastrocnemius
9. soleus
10. calcaneal tendon
11. occipitofrontalis
12. rhomboid major
13. triceps brachii (long)
14. gluteus medius
15. gluteus maximus
16. adductor magnus
17. semimebranosous
18. gracillis

C. Short-Answer Questions

1. Describe how the hamstring muscle group moves the leg.

2. Which muscle group is the antagonist to the muscles of the hamstring group?

3. Describe the action of the abductor and adductor muscles of the thigh.

D. Analysis and Application

1. Which leg muscles serve a function similar to the function of the arm's rotator cuff muscles?

2. Describe the origin, insertion, and action of the muscles that invert and evert the foot.

E. Clinical Challenge

How can pressure increase around injured muscles, and what effect does this have on the regional anatomy?

SKELETAL MUSCLE

A typical **skeletal muscle** (e.g., biceps brachii) is a discrete entity, characterized by a muscle mass (**belly**) with fibrous **tendons** at each end. The muscle consists of **muscle cells** and three degrees of layers of protective connective tissue **coverings**. The muscle and its coverings are packaged in deep fascia along with other muscles and neurovascular bundles.

Each skeletal muscle is arranged into **fascicles**. The outer covering of the muscle is the fibrous **epimysium**. Each fascicle of the muscle is wrapped in a thinner fibrous tissue, **perimysium**, along with nerves, small arteries, and small veins (neurovascular bundles). These nerve fibers and small vessels branch off to reach individual muscle cells. Each muscle fiber is surrounded by a thin sheath of fibrous tissue (**endomysium**), which secures the important neurovascular structures for that muscle fiber. Each of these fibrous coverings contributes to ensuring the uniform distribution of muscle tension during contraction, and to maintaining the natural elasticity of muscle, permitting it to recoil to its resting length following stretching. The merging of these fibrous layers at the ends of the muscle fibers forms the *tendons* that integrate with and secure the muscle to its attachment site(s), such as the periosteum or another tendon.

MUSCLE LEVER SYSTEM

Skeletal muscles work like simple machines, such as levers, to increase the efficiency of their contractile work about a joint. Mechanically, the degree of muscular effort required to overcome resistance to movement at a **joint (fulcrum)** depends on: (1) the force of that **resistance (weight)**; (2) the relative distances from the anatomical fulcrum to the anatomical sites of *muscular effort;* and (3) the anatomical sites of *resistance* (joints). The position of the joint relative to the site of muscle pull and the site of imposed load determines the class of the lever system in use.

In a **1st class lever**, the joint lies between the muscle and the load. This is the most efficient class of lever.

In a **2nd class lever**, the load lies between the joint and the pulling muscle. This lever system operates in lifting a wheelbarrow (the wheel is the fulcrum) as well as lifting a 75 kg (165 lb) body onto the metatarsal heads at the metatarsophalangeal joints.

In a **3rd class lever**, the muscle lies between the joint and the load and gives little mechanical advantage.

MUSCULAR SYSTEM
INTRODUCTION TO SKELETAL MUSCLE

CN: The list of names of colorable structures for this page is arranged from large to small. *However, the coloring sequence is from small to large.* (1) Begin by coloring the muscle fiber, C, and its name, a moderately dark color. (2) Color the endomysial covering, C¹, of the muscle fibers a much lighter color than, C. (3) Color the endomysium in the cross sections of fascicles, avoiding the septa of perimysium, and then color over the cross sections again with the darker color of the muscle fibers. (4) Color the perimysium and its septa, B¹, a light color. (5) Color the epimysium of the muscle belly, A¹, a light color. (6) Color the muscle belly, A, and tendon, D, at the top of the page. (7) Color the lower illustrations of muscle lever systems in the body.

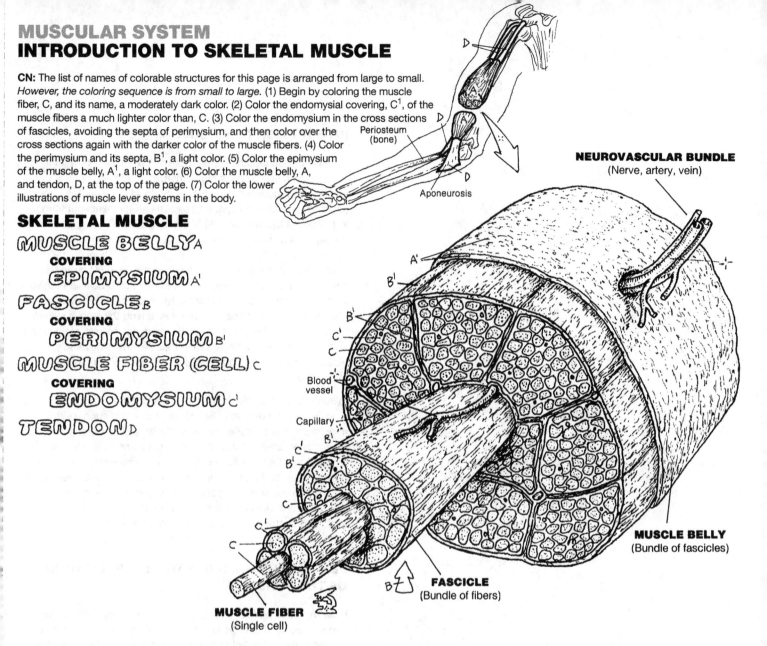

Periosteum (bone)

Aponeurosis

NEUROVASCULAR BUNDLE
(Nerve, artery, vein)

SKELETAL MUSCLE

MUSCLE BELLY A
   COVERING
     EPIMYSIUM A'
FASCICLE B
   COVERING
     PERIMYSIUM B'
MUSCLE FIBER (CELL) C
   COVERING
     ENDOMYSIUM C'
TENDON D

Blood vessel

Capillary

MUSCLE BELLY
(Bundle of fascicles)

FASCICLE
(Bundle of fibers)

MUSCLE FIBER
(Single cell)

MUSCLE LEVER SYSTEM

FULCRUM E (JOINT) E'
EFFORT A² (MUSCLE) A
RESISTANCE F (WEIGHT) F'

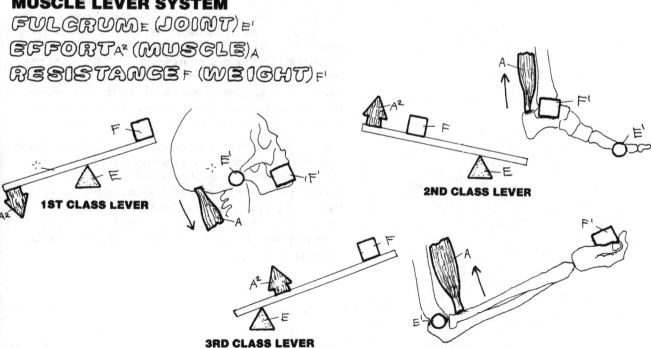

1ST CLASS LEVER

2ND CLASS LEVER

3RD CLASS LEVER

INTEGRATION OF MUSCLE ACTION

Here we investigate the simple case of flexing the elbow joint. The fixed (nonmoving) bone is the humerus; the moving bone is the radius. The muscle attachments at the fixed bone are the *origins* (O) of the muscles (biceps, triceps). The attachments at the moving bone are the *insertions* (I) of those muscles. Here, biceps is the **agonist (prime mover)** and triceps is the **antagonist** for the action of elbow flexion. Starting at a neutral position (center), contraction of the biceps brachii brings the hand closer to the shoulder. At the same time, the muscle triceps brachii stretches with some resistance (contraction) to accommodate the desired movement. With both sets of muscles at rest, the limb is said to be "neutral." In this situation, both biceps and triceps are relaxed with a mild degree of background muscle tone. Conversely, in elbow extension, the agonist shortens while the antagonist is **stretched**.

In summary, the prime mover is the primary muscle effecting a desired joint movement. Secondary movers in such a joint movement may be called **synergists**. Synergists often act as neutralizers, assisting intended movements or resisting unintended movements. Muscles opposing a prime mover's action are antagonists. **Fixators** serve to "fix" more proximal muscles to stabilize the background conditions for a specific joint movement, as trapezius is doing in the action at lower left and right. Agonists, synergists, antagonists, and fixators often work together to move a limb into a desired position (integration of muscle action).

ELBOW FLEXION, SUPINATION, & PRONATION OF THE FOREARM

Here we focus on four muscles that act on the right elbow joint and the proximal and distal radioulnar joints of a right-handed person in the act of holding up the right hand gripping a screwdriver and driving a screw clockwise into the frame of a door. In the first case (lower left illustration), the forearm is repeatedly supinated (and repeatedly pronated to return the forearm to a new starting point for each act of supination) as the screw is driven into the wood. Here biceps is the prime mover and supinator is a synergist in this action of supination. This is so because the rotation of the radius during supination puts tension on the insertion of biceps brachii, inducing its contraction in the face of the desired action (supination). Biceps is stronger than supinator. Test this on yourself: as you supinate the forearm, feel biceps contract.

In the second case (lower right illustration) the forearm is pronated repeatedly which backs the screw out of the wood. Pronation of the forearm is the weaker of the two rotational actions. Contraction of biceps is limited when supination of the forearm is resisted by pronator teres and pronator quadratus. Try it. If pronation is the weaker action, isn't it possible one can't get the screw out? Nah...bring in the cordless impact driver, and click it in reverse.

MUSCULAR SYSTEM
INTEGRATION OF MUSCLE ACTION

CN: (1) Color the names at upper right, and relate them to the small arrows A and C, the large outline letters O and I, and the flexor and extensor muscles of the elbow joint. Note the directions of the arrows. Color left to right. The relaxed muscles of a neutral elbow have a degree of tension (tone) even though they are relaxed. (2) Color the muscle actor names A[1] to E relating to supination and pronation of the forearm and apply those colors to the muscles in the two lower illustrations.

MUSCLE ACTION
CONTRACTED A
RELAXED B
STRETCHED C

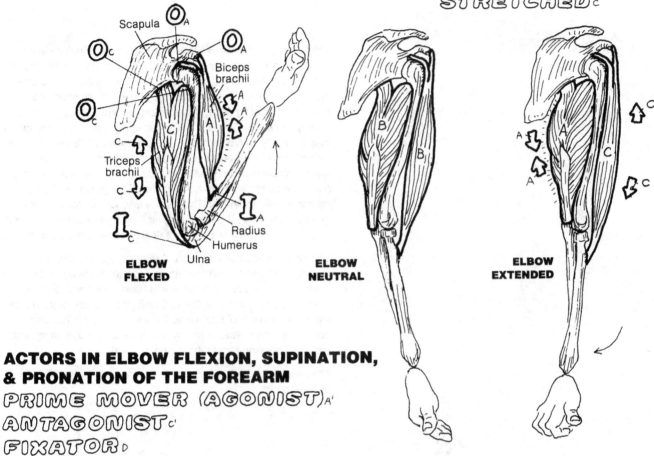

Scapula

Biceps brachii

Triceps brachii

Radius

Humerus

Ulna

ELBOW FLEXED

ELBOW NEUTRAL

ELBOW EXTENDED

ACTORS IN ELBOW FLEXION, SUPINATION, & PRONATION OF THE FOREARM
PRIME MOVER (AGONIST) A'
ANTAGONIST C'
FIXATOR D
SYNERGIST E

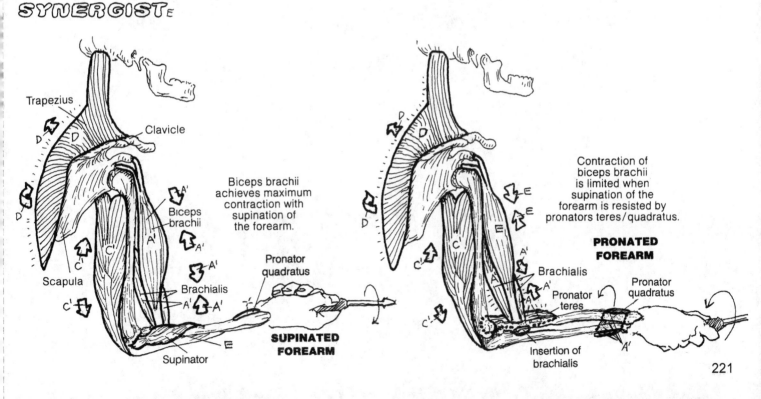

Trapezius

Clavicle

Biceps brachii

Biceps brachii achieves maximum contraction with supination of the forearm.

Pronator quadratus

Scapula

Brachialis

Supinator

SUPINATED FOREARM

Contraction of biceps brachii is limited when supination of the forearm is resisted by pronators teres/quadratus.

PRONATED FOREARM

Brachialis

Pronator teres

Pronator quadratus

Insertion of brachialis

221

The **muscles of facial expression** are generally thin, flat bands arising from a facial bone or cartilage and inserting into the dermis of the skin or the fibrous tissue enveloping the sphincter muscles of the orbit or mouth. These muscles are generally arranged into the following regional groups: (1) the epicranial group (*occipitofrontalis,* moving the scalp); (2) the orbital group (*orbicularis oculi,* **corrugator supercilii**); (3) the nasal group (*nasalis,* **procerus**); (4) the oral group (*orbicularis oris,* **zygomaticus major** and **minor,** the **levators** and the **depressors** of the lips and angles of the mouth, **risorius,** *buccinator,* and part of **platysma**); and (5) the group moving the ears (**auricular muscles**). The general function of each of these muscles is to move the skin wherever they insert. As you color each muscle, try contracting it on yourself while looking into a mirror.

The **orbicularis oculi** and **orbicularis oris** are sphincter muscles, tending to close the skin over the eyelids and tighten the lips, respectively. Contractions of the cheek muscle **buccinator** makes possible rapid changes in the volume of the oral cavity, as in playing a trumpet or squirting water. The **nasalis** muscle has both compressor and dilator parts, which influence the size of the anterior nasal openings (as in the flaring of nostrils).

The muscles of facial expression are innervated by the 7th cranial or facial nerve.

MUSCLES OF FACIAL EXPRESSION

CN: Use your lightest colors for O and Q. Use cheerful colors for names and muscles on the cheerful side and sad colors for the names and muscles on the non-smiling side. (1) Begin with the smiling side (muscles A-H). (2) Color the names and muscles on the sad side. (3) Color the names and muscles in the profile view below. Note that some of frontalis, I, have been cut away to reveal corrugator supercilii, J.

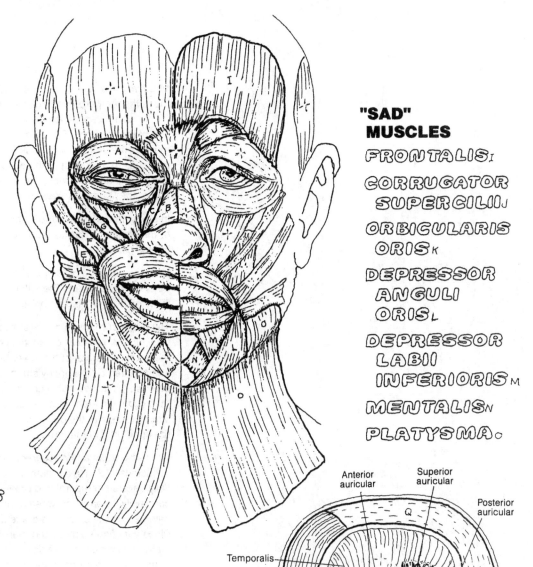

"CHEERFUL" MUSCLES

ORBICULARIS OCULI A
NASALIS B
LEVATOR LABII SUPERIORIS ALAEQUE NASI C
LEVATOR LABII SUPERIORIS D
LEVATOR ANGULI ORIS E
ZYGOMATICUS MAJOR F
ZYGOMATICUS MINOR G
RISORIUS H

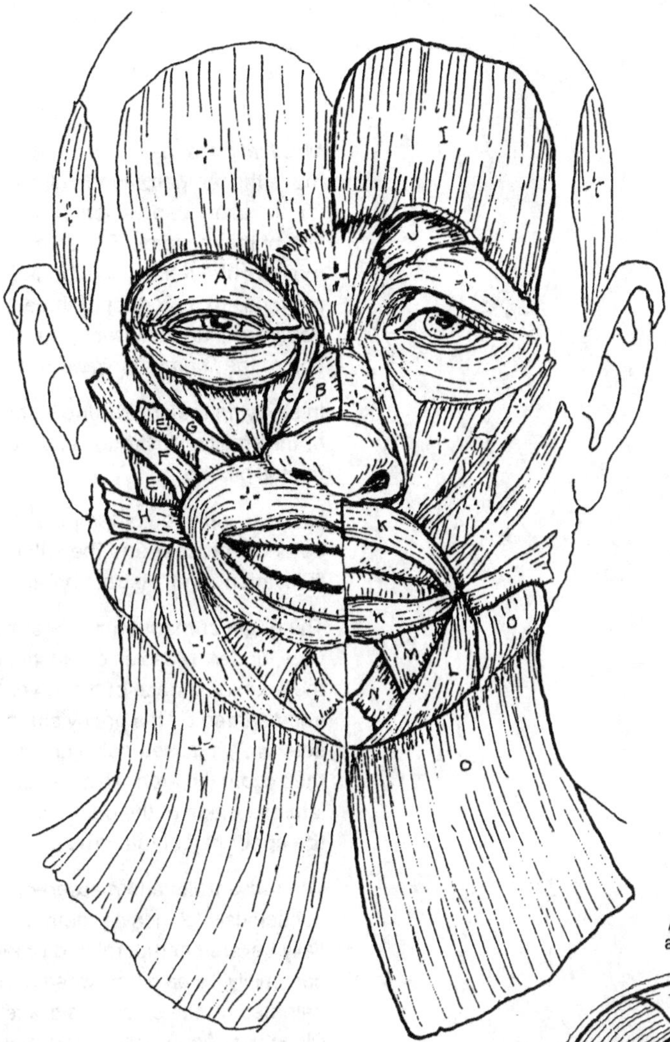

"SAD" MUSCLES

FRONTALIS I
CORRUGATOR SUPERCILII J
ORBICULARIS ORIS K
DEPRESSOR ANGULI ORIS L
DEPRESSOR LABII INFERIORIS M
MENTALIS N
PLATYSMA O

ADDITIONAL MUSCLES

BUCCINATOR P
GALEA APONEUROTICA Q
OCCIPITALIS R
AURICULAR MUSCLES S
PROCERUS T

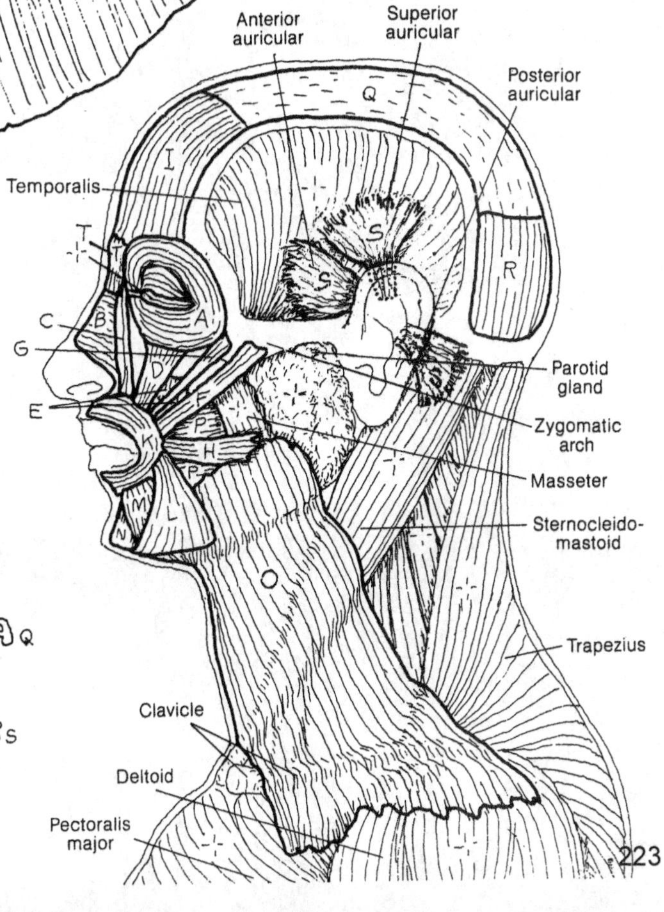
Anterior auricular
Superior auricular
Posterior auricular
Temporalis
Parotid gland
Zygomatic arch
Masseter
Sternocleido-mastoid
Trapezius
Clavicle
Deltoid
Pectoralis major

Mastication is the act of chewing. The **muscles of mastication** move the temporomandibular joint and are largely responsible for elevation, depression, protrusion, retraction, and lateral motion of the mandible. These muscles function bilaterally to effect movements of the single bone (mandible) at two joints. Chewing motions are a product of the action of the elevator muscles (*temporalis* and *masseter*) on one side combined with the contraction of the *lateral pterygoid* muscle on the opposite side.

In studying the origins and insertions of these muscles, make use of the smaller illustrations as well as the larger views above to get the full picture.

Note the insertion of temporalis on the anterior border of the coronoid process and the anterior ramus of the **mandible** in the "Elevation" and "Retraction" illustrations.

The origin of **masseter** is best seen in the upper left "superficial" view, under "Muscles of Mastication"; this muscle arises from the anterior surface of the lower border of the zygomatic arch (represented by the grainy site of origin labeled "Origin of masseter m."). Masseter also arises from the deep (medial) surface of the zygomatic arch. This muscle essentially inserts on the entire lateral surface of the coronoid process of the mandible as well as the upper half of the ramus.

The **temporalis** and *masseter* **muscles** are often contracted unconsciously (clenching teeth) during stress, giving rise to potentially severe bitemporal and preauricular headaches. The muscles can easily be palpated when contracted. The masseter is easily palpated on the external surface of the ramus of the mandible. Place your fingers there and then contract the muscle (clench your teeth). The temporalis, in contrast, inserts on the internal surface of the coronoid process and is best be palpated at the side of the head. Its dense fascia prevents the bulging you experienced with the masseter.

The **medial** and **lateral pterygoids** are in the infratemporal fossa and cannot be palpated.

The muscles of mastication are all innervated by branches of the fifth cranial nerve (trigeminal) mandibular division.

MUSCLES OF MASTICATION

CN: Use a yellowish "bone" color for the mandible, E. (1) Begin with the upper left illustration and proceed to the two dissected views exposing the deeper muscles of mastication. On the smaller skull, two colors A + E are needed to indicate the insertion of temporalis on the deep side of the mandible. Three colors A + B + E are needed to color the part of the external surface where the broad insertion of the masseter also covers part of the representation of the temporalis on the underside. (2) Color the directional arrows and the muscles that move the mandible.

MUSCLES
TEMPORALIS A
MASSETER B
MEDIAL PTERYGOID C
LATERAL PTERYGOID D

BONE
MANDIBLE E

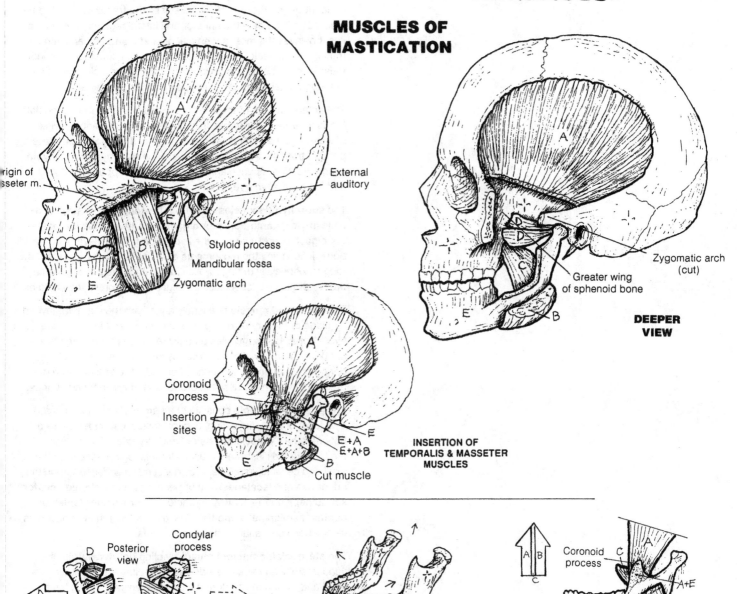

MUSCLES OF MASTICATION

Origin of masseter m.
External auditory
Styloid process
Mandibular fossa
Zygomatic arch
E
B
A

A
Zygomatic arch (cut)
Greater wing of sphenoid bone
D
D
C
B
E
DEEPER VIEW

Coronoid process
Insertion sites
A
E+A
E+A+B
E
B
Cut muscle
INSERTION OF TEMPORALIS & MASSETER MUSCLES

ACTION OF MUSCLES ON MANDIBLE

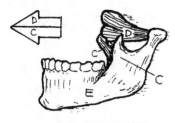

Posterior view
Condylar process
D
C
E
LATERAL

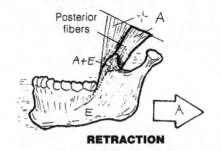

A B
C
Coronoid process
A
C
D
A+E
B
E
ELEVATION

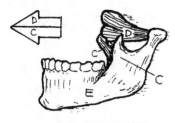

D
C
C
E
PROTRUSION

Posterior fibers
A
A+E
E
A
RETRACTION

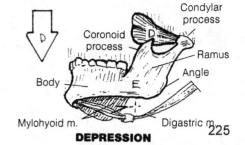

Condylar process
Coronoid process
D
Ramus
Angle
Body
E
Mylohyoid m.
Digastric m.
DEPRESSION

The neck is a complex tubular region of muscles, viscera, vessels, and nerves surrounding the cervical vertebrae. The muscles of the neck are arranged in superficial and deep groups. Here we will concentrate on the superficial muscles. The trapezius is not to be colored as it is not in the anterior and lateral regions of the neck; it is, however, the most superficial posterior and posterolateral muscle of the neck. The platysma is the most superficial anterior muscle of the neck. The *sternocleidomastoid muscle* divides the anterior and lateral muscle groups into triangular areas.

The anterior region of the neck is divided in the midline; each half forms an **anterior triangle**. The borders of the anterior triangle of superficial neck muscles are illustrated. The **hyoid bone**, suspended from the styloid processes of the skull by the **stylohyoid** ligaments, divides each anterior triangle into upper *suprahyoid* and lower *infrahyoid* regions.

The **suprahyoid muscles** arise from the tongue (glossus), mandible (**mylo-, genio-,** anterior **digastric**), and skull (stylo-, posterior digastric) and insert on the hyoid bone. They elevate the hyoid bone, influencing the movements of the floor of the mouth and the tongue, especially during swallowing. With a fixed hyoid, the suprahyoid muscles, especially the digastrics, depress the mandible.

The **infrahyoid muscles** generally arise from the sternum, thyroid cartilage of the larynx, or the scapula (*omo-*) and insert on the hyoid bone. These muscles partially resist elevation of the hyoid bone during swallowing. The **thyrohyoid** elevates the larynx during production of high-pitched sounds; the **sternohyoid** depresses the larynx to assist in production of low-pitched sounds.

The **posterior triangle** consists of an array of muscles covered by a layer of deep (investing) cervical fascia just under the skin between the sternocleidomastoid and trapezius. The borders of the triangle are illustrated. Muscles of this region arise from the skull and cervical vertebrae; they descend to and insert upon the upper two ribs (**scalenes**), the upper scapula (**omohyoid, levator scapulae**), and the cervical/thoracic vertebral spines (**splenius capitis, semispinalis capitis**). These muscles' function becomes clear when you visualize their attachments.

The **sternocleidomastoid muscle**, acting unilaterally, tilts the head laterally on the same side while simultaneously rotating the head and pulling the back of the head downward, lifting the chin, and rotating the front of the head to the opposite side. Both muscle bellies acting together move the head forward (anteriorly) while extending the upper cervical vertebrae, lifting the chin upward.

ANTERIOR & LATERAL MUSCLES

CN: Except for the hyoid bone, E, use your lightest colors throughout the plate. (1) Begin with the diagrams of the triangles of the neck, A and C, and the sternocleidomastoid, B. Color over all the muscles within the triangles. (2) Then work top and bottom illustrations simultaneously, coloring each muscle in as many views as you can find it. Note the relationship between muscle name and attachment.

ANTERIOR TRIANGLE OF THE NECK

SUPRAHYOID MUSCLES

STYLOHYOID ᴅ¹

DIGASTRIC ᴅ²

MYLOHYOID ᴅ³

HYOGLOSSUS ᴅ⁴

GENIOHYOID ᴅ⁵

HYOID BONE ᴇ

INFRAHYOID MUSCLES

STERNOHYOID ꜰ¹

OMOHYOID ꜰ²

THYROHYOID ꜰ³

STERNOTHYROID ꜰ⁴

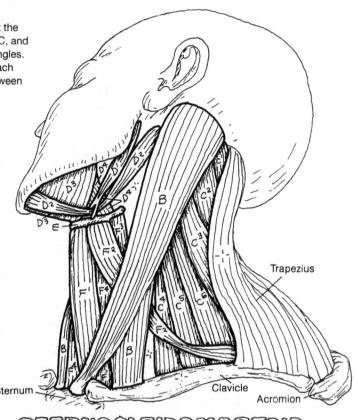

STERNOCLEIDOMASTOID ʙ

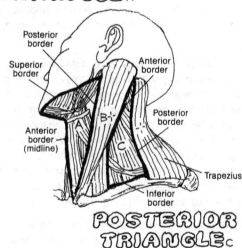

ANTERIOR TRIANGLE ᴀ

POSTERIOR TRIANGLE ᴄ

POSTERIOR TRIANGLE OF THE NECK

SEMISPINALIS CAPITIS ᴄ¹

SPLENIUS CAPITIS ᴄ²

LEVATOR SCAPULAE ᴄ³

SCALENUS ANTERIOR ᴄ⁴

SCALENUS MEDIUS ᴄ⁵

SCALENUS POSTERIOR ᴄ⁶

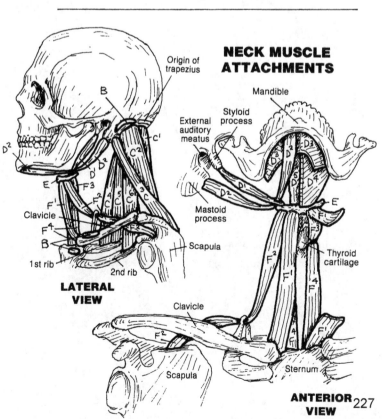

NECK MUSCLE ATTACHMENTS

LATERAL VIEW

ANTERIOR VIEW

The **deep muscles of the back and posterior neck** extend, rotate, or laterally flex one or more of the 24 paired facet joints and the 22 intervertebral disc joints of the vertebral column. The long muscles move several motion segments with one contraction, while the short muscles can move one or two motion segments at a time (see **intrinsic movers**).

The **splenius** muscles extend and rotate the neck and head in concert with the opposite sternocleidomastoid muscle. The *splenius capitis* covers the deeper muscles of the upper spine.

The **erector spinae group** comprises the principal extensors of the vertebral motion segments. Oriented vertically along the longitudinal axis of the back, they are thick, quadrilateral muscles in the lumbar region, splitting into smaller, thinner separate bundles attaching to the ribs (**iliocostalis**), and upper vertebrae and head (**longissimus, spinalis**). The erector spinae muscles arise from the lower thoracic and lumbar spines, the sacrum, ilium, and intervening ligaments.

The **transversospinalis group** extends the motion segments of the back, and rotates the thoracic and cervical vertebral joints. These muscles generally run from the transverse processes of one vertebra to the spine of the vertebra above, spanning three or more vertebrae. The **semispinales** are the largest muscles of this group, reaching from mid-thorax to the posterior skull; the **multifidi** consist of deep fasciculi spanning 1–3 motion segments from sacrum to C2; the **rotatores** are well defined only in the thoracic region (the lumbar vertebrae, for the most part, do not rotate).

These small, deep-lying **(deepest) muscles** cross the joints of only one motion segment. They are collectively important for making small adjustments among the cervical and lumbar vertebrae. Electromyographic evidence has shown that these short muscles remain in sustained contraction for long periods of time during movement and standing/sitting postures. They are most prominent in the cervical and lumbar regions. The small muscles set deep in the posterior, suboccipital region (deep to semispinalis and erector spinae) rotate and extend the joints between the skull and C1 and C2 vertebrae.

Intrinsic movers are the small muscles that cross the joints of one motion segment, and include the deepest muscles noted above. These function in stabilization and facilitate getting proprioceptive information to the spinal cord and brain.

DEEP MUSCLES OF THE BACK & POSTERIOR NECK

CN: Use very light colors on the vertical, B–B³, and oblique, C–C³, muscle groups. Note that the splenius, A, and semispinalis, C, each have more than one part (e.g., cervicis, capitis); each is identified in the illustration. (1) Color the muscles of the main figure one group at a time. The function of these muscles is related to their orientation (vertical, oblique). (2) Color the suboccipital muscle group, F, in the upper boxed inset along with the sites of origin of the overlying muscles. (3) Color the intrinsic movers and their names below.

COVERING MUSCLE

SPLENIUS ᴀ

VERTICAL MUSCLES

ERECTOR SPINAE ʙ
SPINALIS ʙ'
LONGISSIMUS ʙ²
ILIOCOSTALIS ʙ³

OBLIQUE MUSCLES

TRANSVERSOSPINALIS GROUP

SEMISPINALIS ᴄ
MULTIFIDUS ᴄ'
ROTATORES ᴄ²

DEEPEST MUSCLES

INTERTRANSVERSARII ᴅ
INTERSPINALIS ᴇ
SUBOCCIPITAL MUSCLES ꜰ

INTRINSIC MOVERS

EXTENSOR ᴇ
ROTATOR ᴄ³
LATERAL FLEXOR ᴅ

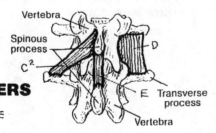

Vertebra

Spinous process

C²

E Transverse process

Vertebra

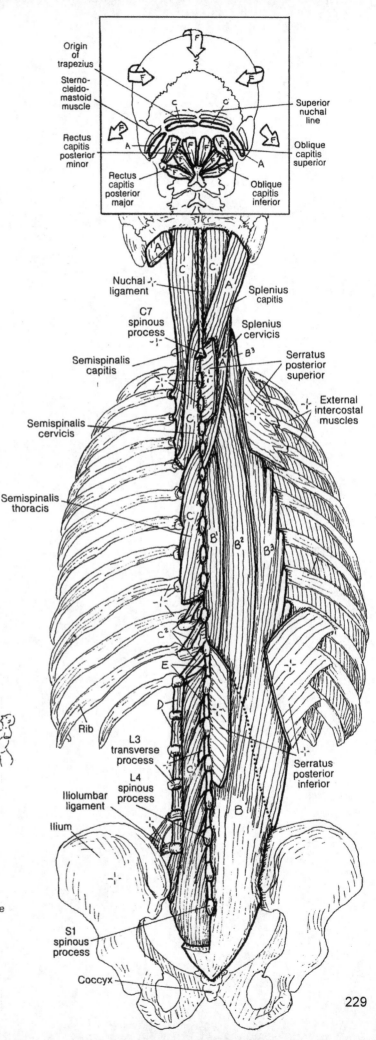

Origin of trapezius

Sterno-cleido-mastoid muscle

Rectus capitis posterior minor

Rectus capitis posterior major

Oblique capitis inferior

Superior nuchal line

Oblique capitis superior

Nuchal ligament

Splenius capitis

C7 spinous process

Splenius cervicis

Semispinalis capitis

Serratus posterior superior

Semispinalis cervicis

External intercostal muscles

Semispinalis thoracis

Rib

L3 transverse process

L4 spinous process

Iliolumbar ligament

Ilium

Serratus posterior inferior

S1 spinous process

Coccyx

229

The thoracic diaphragm is a broad, thin muscle spanning the thoracoabdominal cavity, arising posteriorly from the lumbar vertebrae as muscular crura and aponeurotic arches (lumbar part), from the internal surfaces of the lower six ribs and costal cartilages (costal part), and from the internal surface of the xiphoid process (sternal part); these muscular fibers converge toward the center forming a great musculotendinous oval dome of which the top is the tendinous insertion known as the *central tendon.* At the level of T12, the descending thoracic aorta courses posterior to the diaphragm through the aortic hiatus (foramen) to become the abdominal **aorta**. The azygos vein and the thoracic duct have been known to pass through this hiatus as well. The esophageal hiatus can be found at the level of T10 among the fibers of the right crus as it joins the central tendon. It transmits the right and left vagal nerves as well as the **esophagus**. The **inferior vena** passes through a tendinous hiatus/foramen in the central tendon.

The diaphragm is innervated by the phrenic nerve (C3–C5). How is it that the thoracic diaphragm is supplied by branches of the cervical plexus (of the neck)? Hint: look to embryology.

The **intercostal muscles,** primarily the **external** and **internal intercostals**, alter the dimensions of the thoracic cavity by collectively moving the ribs, resulting in 25% of the total respiratory effort. The **innermost intercostals** are an inconstant layer and here include the transversus thoracis and subcostal muscles.

Below the level of the **12th rib**, the *quadratus lumborum* and the **psoas** (so-az) **major** and **minor** muscles of the posterior abdominal wall span the posterior lumbar gap from the diaphragm to the iliac crests bilaterally. The psoas major and minor are muscles of the lower limb. The major arises from the transverse processes of T12 and the lumbar vertebrae as well as the bodies of the lumbar vertebrae; it passes under the inguinal ligament to join with the fibers of the **iliacus**, converging to a single insertion (**iliopsoas**) on the lesser trochanter of the femur. The iliacus primarily arises from the iliac fossa. The iliopsoas, a strong flexor of the hip joint, is a powerful flexor of the lumbar vertebrae; a weak psoas may contribute to low back pain. The **quadratus lumborum** arises from the posterior iliac crest and inserts on the lower part of the 12th rib and the transverse processes of the upper four lumbar vertebrae. It is an extensor of the lumbar vertebrae bilaterally and a lateral flexor unilaterally.

MUSCLES OF THE BONY THORAX & POSTERIOR ABDOMINAL WALL

CN: Use blue for E, red for G. Color all names as you color the related structures. (1) On the left, color the diaphragm on the posterior abdominal wall to the 12th rib. (2) Color the back of the diaphragm, its lighter central tendon of insertion, and the paired 12th ribs (posterior view). To its left, color the side view of the curved diaphragm between xiphoid and the 12th rib; color its passengers E, F, and G. (3) Color the intercostal muscles at upper right.

MUSCLES OF THORACIC WALL

THORACIC DIAPHRAGM A
EXTERNAL INTERCOSTAL B
INTERNAL INTERCOSTAL C
INNERMOST INTERCOSTAL D

INFERIOR VENA CAVA E
ESOPHAGUS F
AORTA G

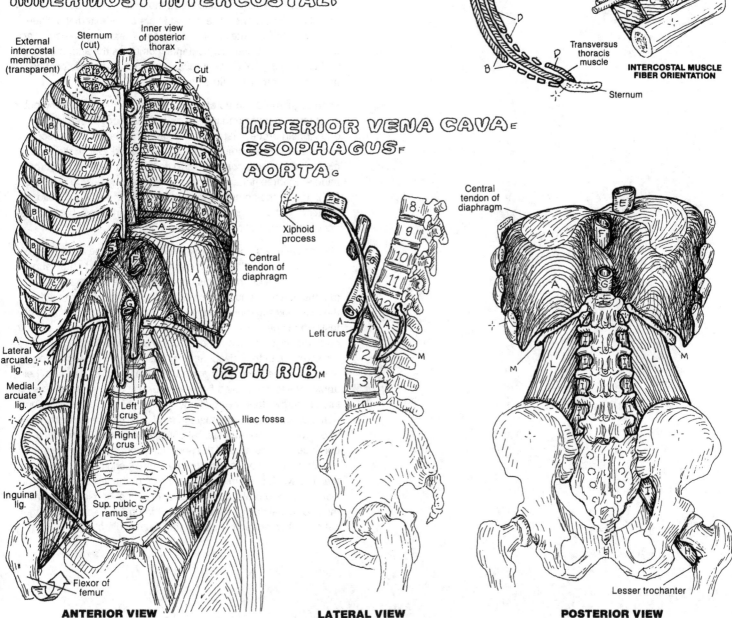

INTERCOSTAL MUSCLES

CROSS SECTION AT LEVEL T5 (Ribs removed)

Subcostal muscle

Intercostal membrane (transparent)

5th thoracic vertebra

Cut rib

Intercostal vessels and nerve

Transversus thoracis muscle

Sternum

INTERCOSTAL MUSCLE FIBER ORIENTATION

External intercostal membrane (transparent)

Sternum (cut)

Inner view of posterior thorax

Cut rib

Xiphoid process

Central tendon of diaphragm

Central tendon of diaphragm

12TH RIB M

Left crus

Lateral arcuate lig.

Medial arcuate lig.

Left crus

Right crus

Iliac fossa

Inguinal lig.

Sup. pubic ramus

Flexor of femur

Lesser trochanter

ANTERIOR VIEW

LATERAL VIEW

POSTERIOR VIEW

POSTERIOR ABDOMINAL WALL MUSCLES

ILIOPSOAS H
PSOAS MAJOR I MINOR J
ILIACUS K
QUADRATUS LUMBORUM L

231

The **anterior abdominal wall** consists of three layers of flat muscles: the **transversus abdominis**, the **internal oblique**, and the **external oblique**. The tendons (aponeuroses) of these muscles interlace in the midline, forming an incomplete sheath around a vertically oriented pair of segmented muscles (*rectus abdominis*). The left and right aponeuroses interlace in the midline (linea alba) The flat muscles arise bilaterally from the lateral aspect of the torso (*inguinal ligament*, iliac crest, thoracolumbar fascia, lower costal cartilages, ribs). The lowest fibers of the external oblique roll inward to form the *inguinal ligament*. These three muscles act to support the abdominal contents; compress the abdominal contents during expiration, regurgitation, urination, and defecation; and may indirectly facilitate flexion of the spine.

Each segmented **rectus abdominis muscle** arises from the pubic crest and tubercles and inserts on the lower costal cartilages and xiphoid process (sternum). Clearly, the sheath of the rectus becomes more superficial from below upward. Below the arcuate line, no muscle contributes to its posterior layer (E^{2*}); in the middle, all three flat aponeuroses contribute equally to the sheath (E^{1*}); above, the anterior sheath is formed from external oblique; posteriorly, the rectus contacts the costal cartilages. They are flexors of the vertebral column.

The **inguinal region** is the lower medial part of the abdominal wall, characterized by a canal with inner (deep) and outer (superficial) openings or rings. This canal carries the **spermatic cord** (ductus deferens and its vessels, testicular vessels, lymphatics) in the male and the round ligament of the uterus in the female. The testes and spermatic cords "descend" (by differential growth) into outpocketings of the anterior abdominal wall, collectively called the *scrotum*. In their descent, they push in front of them layers of fibers from the three flat muscles of the abdominal wall and their aponeuroses, much as a finger might push against four layers of latex to form a four-layered finger glove. These are the coverings of the cord: internal, cremasteric, and external spermatic fasciae. The lower fibers of the internal oblique are unique in that they continue in loops around the spermatic cord as the **cremaster muscle**; the two are connected by cremasteric fascia. The canal area is a weak point in the construction of the anterior abdominal wall, subject to protrusions of fat or intestine (hernias) from within the abdominal cavity, either directly through the wall (direct inguinal hernia) or indirectly through the canal (indirect inguinal hernia).

MUSCLES OF THE ANTERIOR ABDOMINAL WALL & INGUINAL REGION

CN: Use a dark color for J, a bright one for B, and a light one for I. (1) Color the three layers of the anterior abdominal wall above. (2) Color gray the sheath of the rectus abdominis, E, as well as the layers of the abdominal wall in the lower left illustration. (3) Beginning with J and K, and followed by H, color the coverings of the spermatic cord. Use different values of the same color for the epididymis and testis, K.

ANTERIOR ABDOMINAL WALL

TRANSVERSUS ABDOMINIS_A
RECTUS ABDOMINIS_B
INTERNAL OBLIQUE_C
EXTERNAL OBLIQUE_D

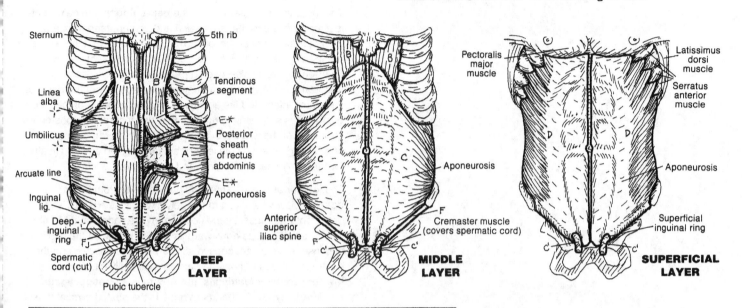

INGUINAL REGION

INGUINAL LIGAMENT_F
CREMASTER MUSCLE_C'
PYRAMIDALIS MUSCLE_G
PERITONEUM_H
TRANSVERSALIS FASCIA_I
SPERMATIC CORD_J
TESTIS/EPIDIDYMIS_K

233

The muscles of the pelvis form the **pelvic floor** in the pelvic outlet *(coccygeus* and the *levator ani)* and contribute to the pelvic "wall" *(obturator internus, piriformis)*. The **pelvic wall** includes part of the bony pelvis, and the **sacrotuberous** and **sacrospinous ligaments**. The fascia-covered pelvic floor muscles constitute the pelvic diaphragm, separating pelvic viscera from the perineal structures inferiorly. Like all muscular diaphragms (thoracic, urogenital), it is a dynamic structure. It is also incomplete; posteriorly, the fusion of the two coccygeus muscles is interrupted by the coccyx and anteriorly the levator ani provides an opening (hiatus) for the anal canal, the vagina, and the urethra.

The **levator ani** arises anteriorly on each side from the pubic bone, the ischial spine, and the pelvic wall, where a thickening of the obturator fascia *(tendinous arch)* gives attachment to the levator ani. It droops downward as it passes toward the midline, and inserts on the anococcygeal ligament, the coccyx, and the contralateral levator ani. The muscle essentially has four parts: **levator prostatae/vaginalis**, **puborectalis**, **pubococcygeus**, and **iliococcygeus**). The **coccygeus** is the posterior-most muscle of the pelvic floor; it is on the same plane as and immediately posterior to the iliococcygeus. The pelvic diaphragm counters abdominal pressure, and, with the thoracic diaphragm, assists in micturition, defecation, and childbirth. It is an important support mechanism for the uterus in resisting vaginal, bladder, and rectal prolapse.

The **obturator internus** is a lateral rotator of the hip joint. It arises, in part, from the margins of the obturator foramen on the pelvic side. It passes downward and posterolaterally past the obturator foramen to and through the lesser sciatic foramen, inserting on the medial surface of the greater trochanter of the femur.

The **piriformis** is a lateral rotator of the hip joint, arises from the sacral component of the pelvic wall, above and posterior to the obturator internus, and exits the pelvis through the greater sciatic foramen.

CN: Use light colors so as not to obscure detail and the identifying letters. (1) Color the pelvic diaphragm (pelvic floor) at upper left and the muscles that constitute it, as well as their names. (2) Color the muscles at upper right that make up the pelvic floor and walls, and their names at lower left. (3) Color the muscles in the middle tier. (4) Color the muscles in the three views below.

VIEW FROM ABOVE
(Male pelvis)

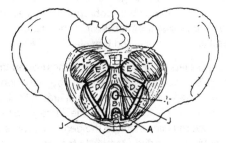

PELVIC DIAPHRAGM / FLOOR

LEVATOR ANI+
  LEVATOR PROSTATAE/VAGINAE A
  PUBORECTALIS B
  PUBOCOCCYGEUS C
  ILIOCOCCYGEUS D
COCCYGEUS E

PELVIC FLOOR & WALL
(Coronal section, anterior view)

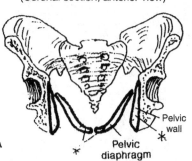

Pelvic wall
Pelvic diaphragm

VIEW FROM ABOVE
(Male pelvis)

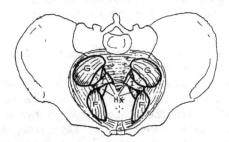

PELVIC WALL

OBTURATOR INTERNUS F
PIRIFORMIS G
SACROTUBEROUS LIGAMENT H*
SACROSPINOUS LIGAMENT I*
TENDINOUS ARCH J

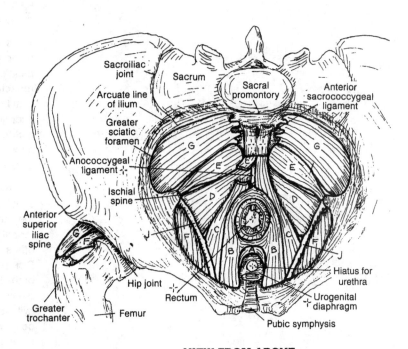

Sacroiliac joint
Sacrum
Sacral promontory
Arcuate line of ilium
Anterior sacrococcygeal ligament
Greater sciatic foramen
Anococcygeal ligament +
Ischial spine
Anterior superior iliac spine
Hiatus for urethra
Rectum
Urogenital diaphragm
Hip joint
Greater trochanter
Femur
Pubic symphysis

VIEW FROM ABOVE
(Male pelvis)

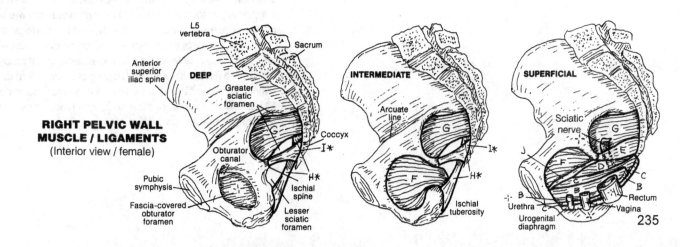

L5 vertebra
Sacrum
Anterior superior iliac spine
DEEP
Greater sciatic foramen
Coccyx
Obturator canal
RIGHT PELVIC WALL MUSCLE / LIGAMENTS
(Interior view / female)
Pubic symphysis
Ischial spine
Fascia-covered obturator foramen
Lesser sciatic foramen

INTERMEDIATE
Arcuate line
Ischial tuberosity

SUPERFICIAL
Sciatic nerve
Urethra
Urogenital diaphragm
Rectum
Vagina

235

The **perineum** is the region below the pelvic diaphragm within the outlet of the pelvis. The *perineal "floor"* is skin and fascia. Its superior border is the *pelvic diaphragm* and the *bilateral ischio-pubic rami* (see coronal section of the urogenital triangle). The perineum is bordered by the **symphysis pubis, ischiopubic rami, ischial tuberosities, sacrotuberous ligaments**, and **coccyx**. It is divided into urogenital and anal regions called triangles.

A triangular muscular diaphragm characterizes the **urogenital region (triangle).** It is attached bilaterally to the bony ischiopubic rami. The deep transverse perineal and external urethral sphincter muscles (not shown in detail), and their fasciae, largely make up this diaphragm. These muscles stabilize the perineal body, support the membranous urethra and prostate in the male and the urethra and vagina in the female.

The inferior fascial layer of this diaphragm (perineal membrane, I) is significantly thicker than the superior fascia; it gives attachment to the vagina and erectile bodies of the penis. Now correlate the coronal section through the urogenital triangle with the illustrations of the muscles of the female and male perinei at the bottom of the page.

The **superficial transverse perineal muscles** are attached to the posterior edge of the urogenital diaphragm, and support/fix the perineal body in both sexes. In the male, the **bulbospongiosus muscle** arises from the median raphe of the penis and the perineal body and inserts on the perineal membrane and the corpus spongiosum (erectile body). It assists in erection of the penis. The **ischiocavernosus muscles** largely arise from the ischiopubic rami and insert on the crura and corpora of the erectile corpora cavernosa.

The **perineal body** is composed of fibromuscular tissue and is situated between the anus and the vagina/bulb of the penis. It is the site of insertion of a number of muscles, including the levator ani, the external sphincter ani, and all the perineal muscles. It offers stability to the pelvic viscera, especially during childbirth. Disruption or tearing of the perineal body can lead to prolapse of the bladder or uterus through the vagina or ureth. The attachments of the superficial perineal muscles in the female are similar (with respect to the clitoris) but much reduced in size. The bulbospongiousus muscle arises from the perineal body, and splits to wrap around the bulb of the vestibule and the vagina; it also sends muscle fibers around the body of the clitoris (corpus clitoridis). The ischiocavernosus muscles arise from the ischiopubic rami and wrap around the crura of the corpus clitoridis.

The **anal triangle** contains the anal canal and orifice and supporting entourage: the **external sphincter ani muscle**, the **anococcygeal ligament** posteriorly, and the perineal body anteriorly. The cavity of this region—the *ischiorectal fossa*—is divided into two fossae separated by the anal canal and its muscle. These fossae are filled with adipose tissue (not shown) that can give way to an expanding anal canal during a voluminous defecation. The anterior recesses of the ischiorectal fossa pass deep to the **urogenital diaphragm.**

MUSCLES OF THE PERINEUM

1) Color the names and the boundaries of the perineum above.
(2) Color the two upper triangular outlines, and the names and coronal section through the male urogenital region. (3) Color the names/components of the male/female urogenital regions in the perinei below. (4) Color the two lower triangular outlines and the related names. Color the anal triangles and their component structures in the perinei below.

PERINEUM * (Boundaries)
SYMPHYSIS PUBIS A
COCCYX B
ISCHIAL TUBEROSITY C
SACROTUBEROUS LIGAMENT D
ISCHIOPUBIC RAMUS E

UROGENITAL TRIANGLE *¹
ISCHIOCAVERNOSUS M. F
BULBOSPONGIOSUS M. G
SUPERIOR TRANSVERSE PERINEAL M. H
UROGENITAL DIAPHRAGM I

ANAL TRIANGLE *²
LEVATOR ANI M. J
EXTERNAL SPHINCTER ANI M. K
ANOCOCCYGEAL LIGAMENT L

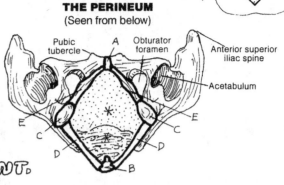

BOUNDARIES OF THE PERINEUM
(Seen from below)

Pubic tubercle — A — Obturator foramen — Anterior superior iliac spine — Acetabulum — E — C — E — C — D — D — B

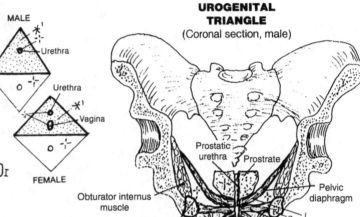

UROGENITAL TRIANGLE
(Coronal section, male)

MALE — *¹ — Urethra
Urethra — *¹ — Vagina
FEMALE

Prostatic urethra — Prostrate — Pelvic diaphragm — Obturator internus muscle — Anterior recess of ischiorectal fossa — Crus of penis — Penile bulb

MALE — *² — Anus
*² — Anus
FEMALE

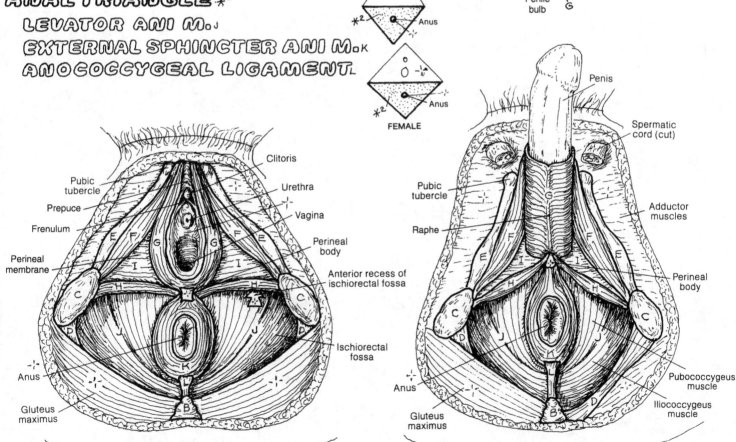

FEMALE PERINEUM

Clitoris — Urethra — Vagina — Perineal body — Anterior recess of ischiorectal fossa — Ischiorectal fossa
Pubic tubercle — Prepuce — Frenulum — Perineal membrane — Anus — Gluteus maximus

MALE PERINEUM

Penis — Spermatic cord (cut) — Adductor muscles — Perineal body — Pubococcygeus muscle — Iliococcygeus muscle
Pubic tubercle — Raphe — Anus — Gluteus maximus

237

The scapulae slide on the posterior thorax, roughly from T2 to T8. It has no direct bony attachment with the axial skeleton. Enveloped by muscle, it glides over the fascia-covered thoracic wall during upper limb movement (scapulothoracic motion). Bursae have been reported between the thorax and the scapula; so has bursitis. The scapula is dynamically moored to the axial skeleton by the six **muscles of scapular stabilization**. These muscles make possible considerable scapular mobility and, therefore, upper limb mobility. Note the roles of these six muscles in scapular movement and note how the shoulder and arm are affected. The **pectoralis minor** assists the **serratus anterior** in protraction of the scapula, such as in pushing against a wall; it also helps in depression of the shoulder and downward rotation of the scapula. Consider the power resident in the serratus anterior and *trapezius* in pushing or swinging a bat. Note the especially broad sites of attachment of the **trapezius** muscle. This muscle commonly manifests significant tension with hard work—mental or physical. A brief massage of the upper and mid back (trapezius) often brings quick relief.

MUSCLES OF SCAPULAR STABILIZATION

CN: (1) Color the muscles in the three main views, the nuchal ligament, and their names. (2) Color the insertion sites at upper right. (3) In the five illustrations below, note that three different parts of the trapezius, A, make possible different scapular movements. Color gray the scapulae and the direction-of-movement arrows.

MUSCLES

*TRAPEZIUS*ᴀ
*RHOMBOID MAJOR*ʙ *MINOR*ʙ'
*LEVATOR SCAPULAE*ᴄ
*SERRATUS ANTERIOR*ᴅ
*PECTORALIS MINOR*ᴇ

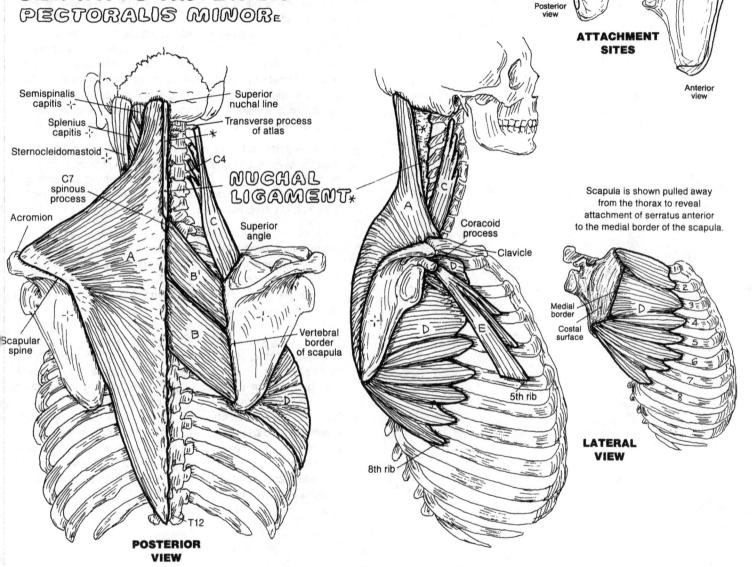

ATTACHMENT SITES

POSTERIOR VIEW

LATERAL VIEW

MOVEMENTS OF THE SCAPULA

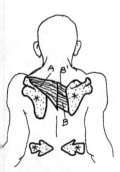

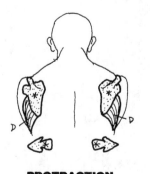

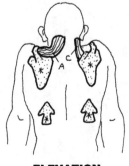

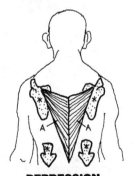

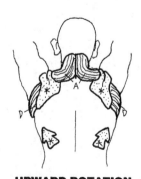

RETRACTION
Military posture
("squaring the shoulders")

PROTRACTION
Pushing forward with
outstretched arms and hands.

ELEVATION
Shrugging the shoulders
or protecting the head.

DEPRESSION
Straight arms on parallel
bars, holding weight.

UPWARD ROTATION
Lifting or reaching
over head.

The socket at the glenohumeral joint (glenoid fossa) is too shallow to offer any bony security for the head of the humerus. As ligaments would severely limit joint movement, muscle tension must be employed to pull the humeral head in to the shallow scapular socket during shoulder movements. Four muscles fulfill this function: the **supraspinatus**, **infraspinatus**, **teres minor**, and **subscapularis** ("SITS") muscles. These muscles form a musculotendinous cuff around the head of the humerus, enforcing joint security. Especially effective during robust shoulder movements, they generally permit the major movers of the joint to work without risking joint dislocation in normal, reasonable applications. Long-term abuse and overuse are quite another matter.

The **SITS muscles** have come to be known as the *rotator cuff muscles,* even though one of them, the supraspinatus, is an **abductor** of the shoulder joint and not a rotator. Indeed, among some health care providers, the supraspinatus is known as the *rotator cuff* in the context of a "rotator cuff tear."

The shoulder joint and the supraspinatus muscle/tendon are subject to early degeneration from overuse. The problem is generally one of impingement (chronic physical contact and friction) and degeneration among the acromion (1), the coracoacromial ligament (2), the distal clavicle and related acromioclavicular (AC) joint (3), the tendon of the supraspinatus as it passes under the acromion (4), and the subacromial bursa (5), which takes the heat of friction...to a point. Those with a down-turned acromion or a previously dislocated, offset acromioclavicular joint are especially vulnerable to impingement (supraspinatus tendinitis and subsequent tearing, subacromial bursitis, acromioclavicular joint degeneration, limitation of shoulder motion, and pain). All overhead activities (such as those of professional drapery hangers, ceiling plasterers, baseball pitchers, etc.) and acromial loading (hose-carrying firemen, those carrying heavy purses/bags by straps over the shoulder, mail delivery persons, etc.) if pursued over a sustained period, can induce changes (bony spurring, bursal destruction) with painful signs and symptoms.

MUSCLES OF MUSCULOTENDINOUS CUFF

CN: (1) Color the four muscles, their names, the open arrows, and the terms describing their actions. (2) Color the muscular attachment sites and the functional diagrams/arrows of these muscles at mid- and lower right. (3) Color the shoulder problem sites at the bottom of the page.

MUSCLES

SUPRASPINATUS_A
INFRASPINATUS_B
TERES MINOR_C
SUBSCAPULARIS_D

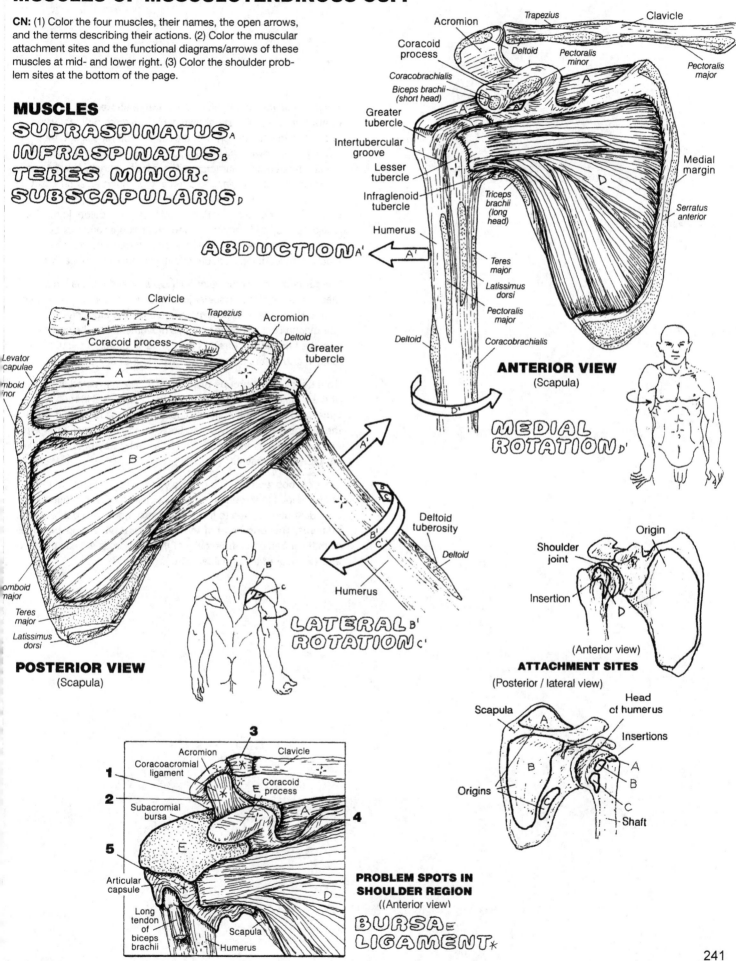

ABDUCTION A'

ANTERIOR VIEW
(Scapula)

MEDIAL ROTATION D'

POSTERIOR VIEW
(Scapula)

LATERAL ROTATION B' C'

ATTACHMENT SITES
(Posterior / lateral view)

PROBLEM SPOTS IN SHOULDER REGION
((Anterior view)

BURSA E
LIGAMENT *

241

The *principal movers* of the freely movable **shoulder (glenohumeral) joint** are shown here from three different views. They work in conjunction with the rotator cuff muscles to move the humerus powerfully in lifting, pushing, pulling, and twisting loads. The **deltoid**, characterized by a multipennate form of construction, a broad origin, and a remarkably short lever arm, is a powerful mover of the humerus in flexion, extension, and abduction. The anterior fibers of deltoid adduct the shoulder joint. The clavicular (upper) fibers of the **pectoralis major** are effective in flexing the shoulder joint; the sternal/abdominal (lower) fibers *extend* the *flexed* joint. Both are effective medial rotators as well.

The **teres major,** a muscle of the posterior shoulder, is a major medial rotator of the shoulder joint because its tendon of insertion is on the *anterior* aspect of the humerus; it therefore has an excellent mechanical advantage for this movement. For the same reason, the **latissimus dorsi** is also a medial rotator of the shoulder joint, in addition to being a major extensor of the joint.

Both heads of the **biceps brachii** are active in resisted flexion of the shoulder joint when the forearm is fixed and immobile. Otherwise, its chief function is supination of the forearm. Note that the biceps brachii has two insertions: one to the radial tuberosity and one to the deep fascia of the forearm by way of an aponeurosis (lacertus fibrosus).

The **coracobrachialis** is a relatively insignificant mover of the shoulder joint in flexion. It does function in shoulder adduction to a modest degree, due to its insertion into the medial border of the humerus. The **long head of the triceps brachii**, arising as it does from the infraglenoid tuberosity of the scapula, is a weak adductor and extensor of the shoulder joint.

MOVERS OF THE SHOULDER JOINT
MUSCLES

DELTOID_A PECTORALIS MAJOR_B
LATISSIMUS DORSI_C TERES MAJOR_D
CORACOBRACHIALIS_E BICEPS BRACHII_F
TRICEPS BRACHII (LONG HEAD)_G

CN: (1) Begin with both posterior views; note that the biceps and triceps are not shown on the lateral view.
(2) When coloring the muscles below, note the actions of different parts of the deltoid, A, and pectoralis major, B.

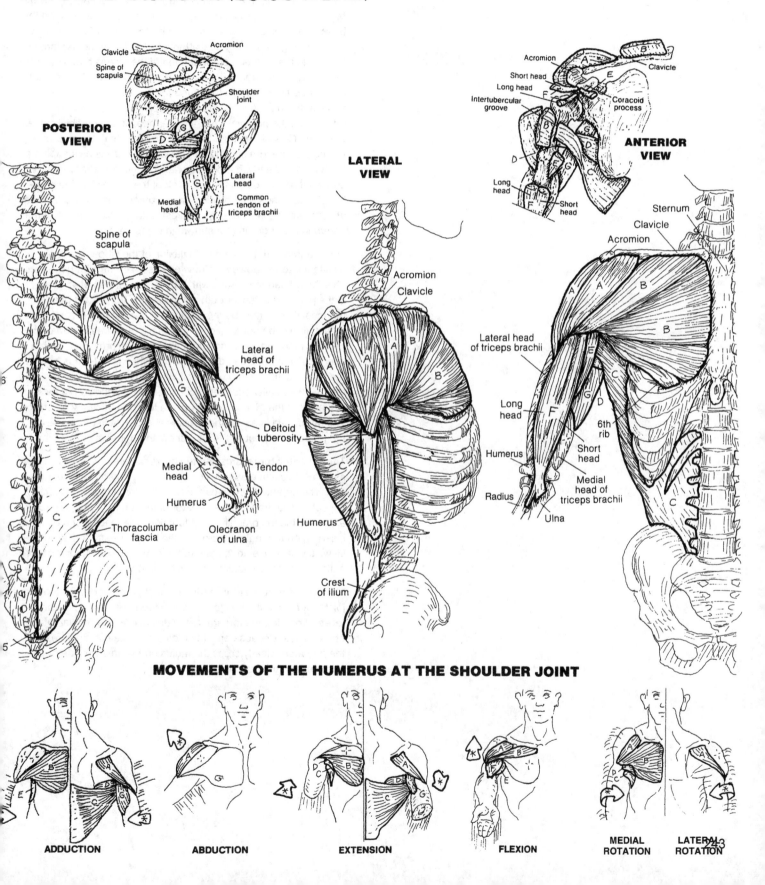

MOVEMENTS OF THE HUMERUS AT THE SHOULDER JOINT

ADDUCTION   ABDUCTION   EXTENSION   FLEXION   MEDIAL ROTATION   LATERAL ROTATION

The **brachialis muscle** is the principal flexor of the **elbow joint**, because its attachment sites provide the best mechanical advantage in responding to loads on the joint—certainly better than the **biceps brachii**, as you can see. Yet it's the bulge of a contracted biceps that gets all the visual attention! The key to understanding this lies in the insertion of the tendon of the biceps brachii on the tuberosity of the radius. Try flexing the elbow joint with the palm and curled fingers down (pronated forearm). Lift a load with the hand in that position. The biceps muscle has a poor mechanical advantage; the brachialis has a better one, so the brachialis does the work. Now slowly supinate the forearm with that same load, feeling the strength coming into the biceps muscle as it supinates the forearm. Clearly, the biceps brachii is the prime mover in forearm supination, adding to the power of the brachialis. The combined load brings on a bulging biceps brachii. Note the additional attachment of the biceps aponeurosis into the deep fascia of the common flexor group (not shown) in the forearm.

The **brachioradialis** is active in flexion of the elbow and rapid resistance to the powerful elbow extensors of the **triceps brachii**. This three-headed muscle, with its massive tendon of insertion, is the principal extensor of the elbow joint. Of the three heads, the medial head may be the primary antagonist to the brachialis. In fact, it may be not a medial head at all, but a *deep* head of the muscle. Many an olecranon fracture has been prevented by the interface of the thick tendon of the three heads of triceps between the proximal ulna and a potentially injurious force striking the olecranon. The smaller *anconeus*, considered an extension of the medial head of the triceps, assists in the function of elbow extension. The **anconeus** is a very thin muscle almost lost in the fascia on the posterior aspect of the olecranon and upper posterior ulna.

The **pronator teres**, crossing the proximal forearm on its *anterior* aspect, assists in elbow flexion as well as pronation of the forearm. The **supinator** crosses the proximal forearm on its *posterior* aspect; it is an important supinator of the forearm though secondary to the biceps brachii in that function. The tendon of the biceps inserting on the radial tuberosity (see lowest illustration, anterior view) is what gives advantage to the power of supination over pronation when the radioulnar joint is supinated.

The **pronator quadratus** is the principal pronator of the elbow joint, superior in its mechanical advantage over the **pronator teres**. Pronating the forearm (palm down) involves medial rotation of the radius. Because only the radius can rotate in the forearm, the pronators clearly cross the radius on the anterior side of the forearm, and their origin is ulnar.

MOVERS OF ELBOW & RADIOULNAR JOINTS

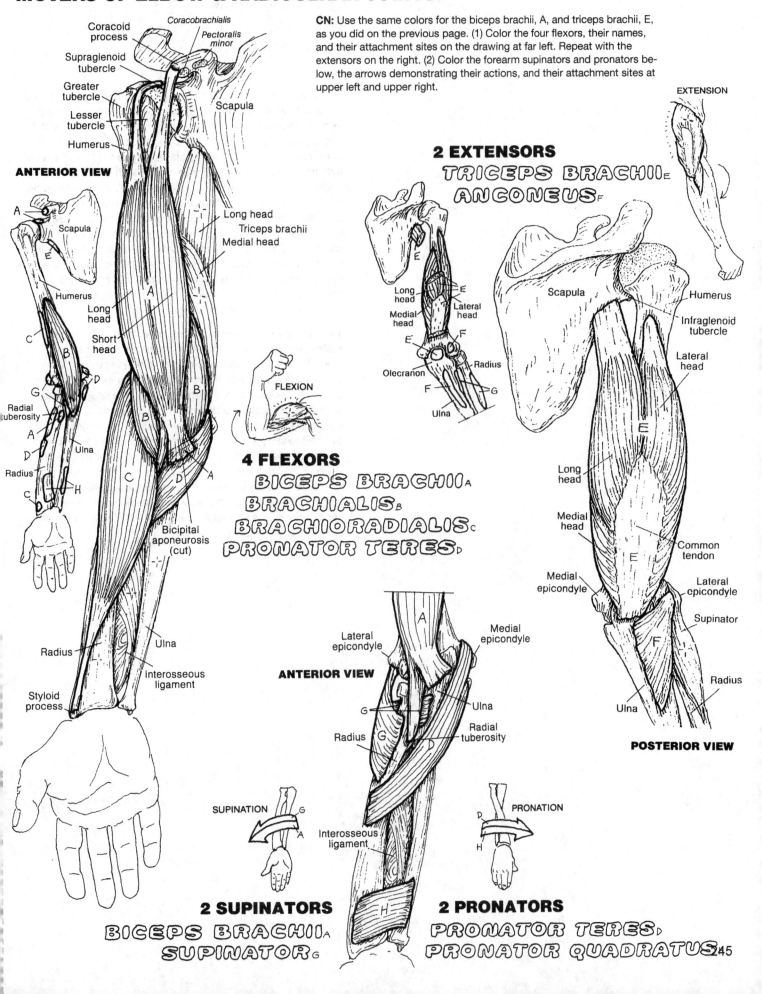

CN: Use the same colors for the biceps brachii, A, and triceps brachii, E, as you did on the previous page. (1) Color the four flexors, their names, and their attachment sites on the drawing at far left. Repeat with the extensors on the right. (2) Color the forearm supinators and pronators below, the arrows demonstrating their actions, and their attachment sites at upper left and upper right.

Coracobrachialis
Coracoid process
Pectoralis minor
Supraglenoid tubercle
Greater tubercle
Lesser tubercle
Humerus
Scapula

EXTENSION

ANTERIOR VIEW

Long head
Triceps brachii
Medial head

2 EXTENSORS
TRICEPS BRACHII E
ANCONEUS F

A
Scapula
E
Humerus
Long head
Short head
C
B
D
G
Radial tuberosity
A
D
Ulna
Radius
C
H

Long head
Medial head
E
Lateral head
E
F
Olecranon
Radius
F
G
Ulna

Scapula
Humerus
Infraglenoid tubercle
Lateral head

A
B
B
C
D
A

FLEXION

4 FLEXORS
BICEPS BRACHII A
BRACHIALIS B
BRACHIORADIALIS C
PRONATOR TERES D

Long head
Medial head
E
Medial epicondyle
E
Common tendon
Lateral epicondyle
Supinator
F
Radius
Ulna

Bicipital aponeurosis (cut)

Radius
Ulna
Interosseous ligament
Styloid process

Lateral epicondyle
A
Medial epicondyle

ANTERIOR VIEW

G
Radius
G
Ulna
D
Radial tuberosity
Interosseous ligament

POSTERIOR VIEW

SUPINATION
G
A

PRONATION
D
H

2 SUPINATORS
BICEPS BRACHII A
SUPINATOR G

2 PRONATORS
PRONATOR TERES D
PRONATOR QUADRATUS 245

The **flexors** of the wrist (carpus) and fingers (digits) take up most of the anterior compartment of the forearm, arising as a group from the medial epicondyle, the upper radius and ulna, and the intervening interosseous membrane. The deep layer of muscles in the anterior forearm (**flexor pollicis longus** or FPL in the radial half, **flexor digitorum profundus** or FDP in the ulnar half) lies in contact with the radius and ulna. The superficial layer of muscles (wrist flexors: the **carpi muscles** and **palmaris longus**) is seen just under the skin and thin superficial fascia. The intermediate layer (**flexor digitorum superficialis**, FDS) lies between the superficial and deep groups. In the anterior (palmar) fingers, note how the tendons of the FDS, which insert on the sides of the middle phalanges, split at the level of the proximal phalanges, permitting the deeper (posterior) tendons of the FDP to pass on through to the bases of the distal phalanges.

The **extensors** of the wrist and fingers arise from the lateral epicondyle and upper parts of the bones and interosseous membrane of the forearm, forming an extensor compartment on the posterior side of the forearm. The wrist extensors insert on the distal carpal bones or metacarpals. The finger extensors form an expansion of tendon over the middle and distal phalanges to which the small intrinsic muscles of the hand insert. The wrist extensors are critical to hand function: With your left wrist *extended,* use the fingers of that same hand to grasp the index finger of the other hand as tightly as you can. Now, maximally *flex* the left wrist, and *keep it flexed* while once again grasping the index finger of the other hand with the fingers in your left hand. What sports or hobbies can you think of that depend on an extended wrist joint to play or work?

MOVERS OF WRIST & HAND JOINTS (Extrinsics)

CN: A more detailed view of the tendons of these muscles (with the same designations) can be seen among the intrinsic muscles of the hand on the next plate. (1) Begin with the flexors; note that the deeper muscles have been omitted from the superficial view. Color gray the entire flexor mass in the smaller illustration. (2) Continue with the extensors, coloring gray the entire extensor mass in the smaller illustration.

ANTERIOR VIEW

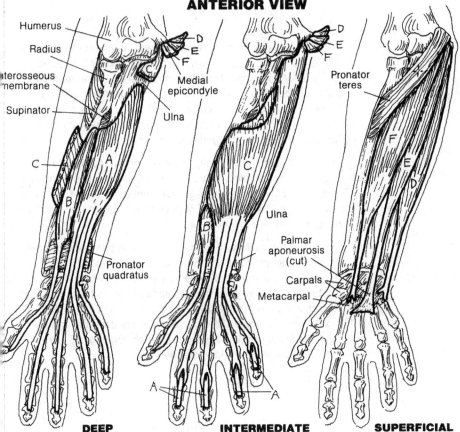

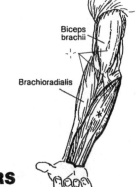

FLEXORS

DEEP LAYER

F. DIGITORUM PROFUNDUS A

F. POLLICIS LONGUS B

INTERMEDIATE LAYER

F. DIGITORUM SUPERFICIALIS C

SUPERFICIAL LAYER

F. CARPI ULNARIS D

PALMARIS LONGUS E

F. CARPI RADIALIS F

EXTENSORS

DEEP LAYER

E. INDICIS G

E. POLLICIS LONGUS H

E. POLLICIS BREVIS I

SUPERFICIAL LAYER

E. CARPI ULNARIS J

E. DIGITI MINIMI K

E. DIGITORUM L

E. CARPI RADIALIS LONGUS M

E. CARPI RADIALIS BREVIS N

ABDUCTOR POLLICIS LONGUS O

POSTERIOR VIEW

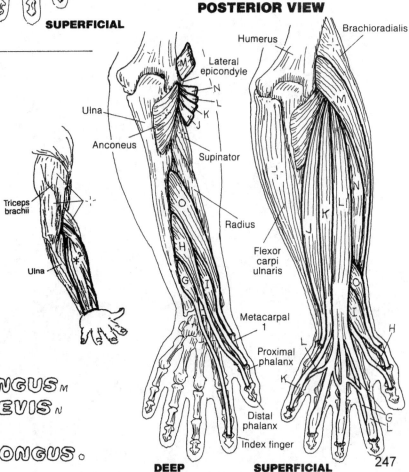

247

Note the palpable bulge of muscle (**thenar eminence**) just proximal to the thumb on your own hand. Integrated with the action of the other thumb movers, these three muscles (the **opponens pollicis**, **abductor pollicis brevis**, and **flexor pollicis brevis**) make possible complex movements of the thumb. The thenar muscles arise/insert in the same general area as one another; however, their different orientation allows different functions.

The hypothenar muscles (**hypothenar eminence**) move the fifth digit; they are complementary to the thenar muscles in attachment and function. Note the two **opponens muscles** in the thumb and the fifth digit. The function of opposition is basic to some of the complex grasping functions of the hand.

The **adductor pollicis,** in concert with the first **dorsal interosseus muscle**, provides great strength in grasping an object between thumb and index finger...try it. The **interossei** and **lumbrical muscles** insert into expanded finger extensor tendons (extensor expansion; see posterior view), forming a complex mechanism for flexing the metacarpophalangeal joints and extending the interphalangeal joints. By their phalangeal insertions, the interossei abduct/adduct certain digits.

MOVERS OF HAND JOINTS (Intrinsics)

CN: The extrinsic wrist and finger joint movers were covered on the previous page; their tendons are shown in dark line and labeled here for reference but not for coloring. (1) Color the muscles of the two anterior views, as well as the flexor retinaculum (gray). (2) Color the posterior view. (3) In the illustration of finger abduction (at the bottom of the page), note that the little finger is not moved by the dorsal interosseus, U.

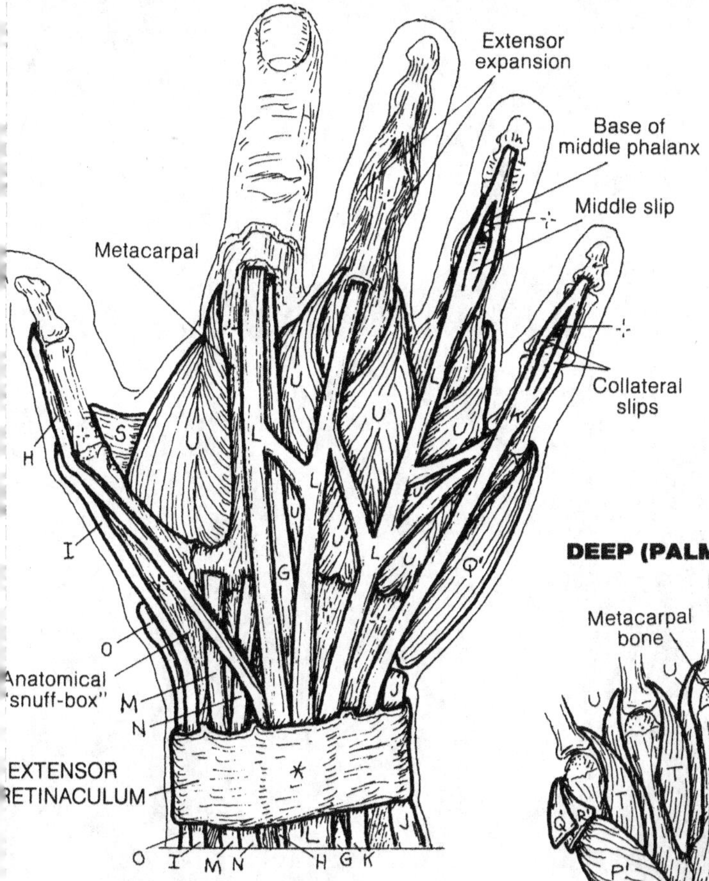

Extensor expansion
Base of middle phalanx
Middle slip
Metacarpal
Collateral slips
Anatomical "snuff-box"
EXTENSOR RETINACULUM

POSTERIOR (DORSAL) VIEW

DEEP (PALMAR) VIEW

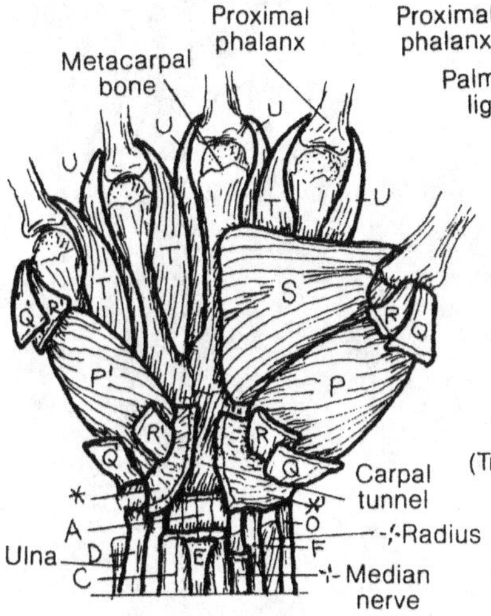

Proximal phalanx
Metacarpal bone
Carpal tunnel
Radius
Ulna
Median nerve

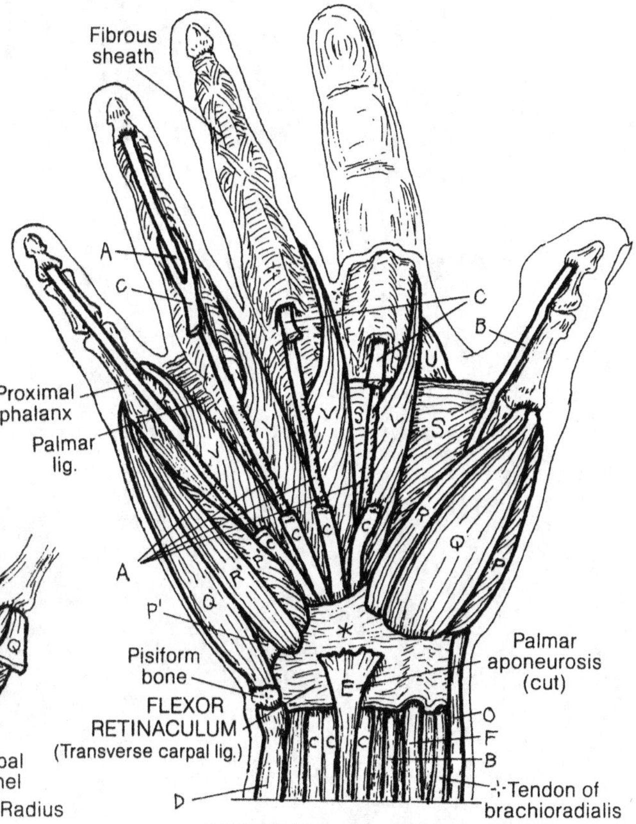

Fibrous sheath
Proximal phalanx
Palmar lig.
Pisiform bone
FLEXOR RETINACULUM (Transverse carpal lig.)
Palmar aponeurosis (cut)
Tendon of brachioradialis

ANTERIOR (PALMAR) VIEW

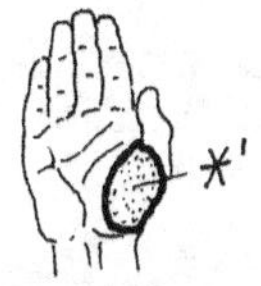

THENAR EMINENCE *'
OPPONENS POLLICIS P
ABDUCTOR POLLICIS BREVIS Q
FLEXOR POLLICIS BREVIS R

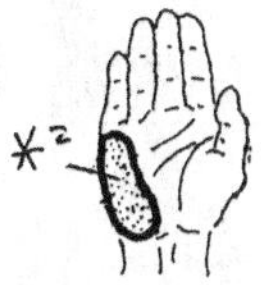

HYPOTHENAR EMINENCE *²
OPPONENS DIGITI MINIMI P'
ABDUCTOR DIGITI MINIMI Q'
FLEXOR DIGITI MINIMI BREVIS R'

DEEP MUSCLES

ADDUCTOR POLLICIS S
PALMAR INTEROSSEUS T
DORSAL INTEROSSEUS U
LUMBRICAL V

ACTIONS OF INTRINSIC MUSCLES

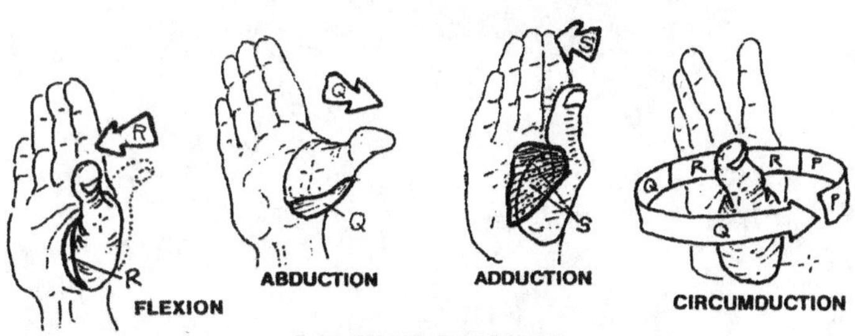

FLEXION
ABDUCTION
ADDUCTION
CIRCUMDUCTION

ON THE THUMB

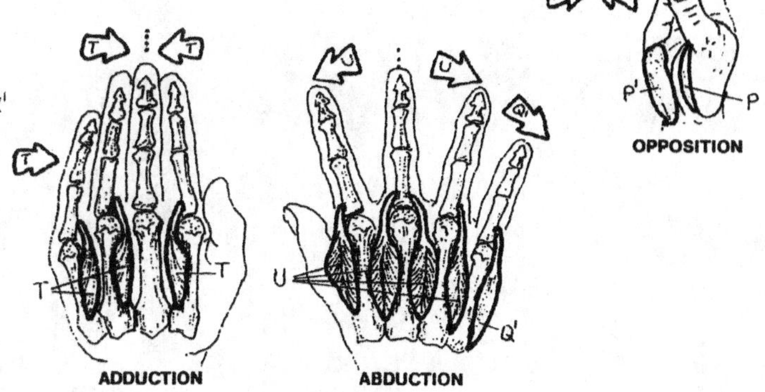

ADDUCTION
ABDUCTION
OPPOSITION

ON THE FINGERS

MUSCULAR SYSTEM / UPPER LIMB
REVIEW OF MUSCLES

CN: Start with the three muscles labeled "A." On the lines provided, write the names of the superficial muscles shown with the color used for each labeled muscle. Some of these muscles have more than one function assigned to them by these categories.
(See the end of this section for answers.)

MUSCLES ACTING PRIMARILY ON THE SCAPULA

A _____
A¹ _____
A² _____

MUSCLES MOVING THE SHOULDER JOINT

B _____
B¹ _____
B² _____
B³ _____
B⁴ _____
B⁵ _____
B⁶ _____

MUSCLES MOVING ELBOW & RADIOULNAR JOINTS

C _____
C¹ _____
C² _____
C³ _____
C⁴ _____
C⁵ _____

MUSCLES MOVING WRIST & HAND JOINTS

D _____
D¹ _____
D² _____
D³ _____
D⁴ _____
D⁵ _____
D⁶ _____
D⁷ _____

FOREARM MUSCLES MOVING THE THUMB

E _____
E¹ _____
E² _____

THENAR MUSCLES MOVING THE THUMB

F _____
F¹ _____
F² _____

HYPOTHENAR MUSCLES MOVING THE 5TH DIGIT

G _____
G¹ _____
G² _____

OTHER MUSCLES ACTING ON THE THUMB & FINGERS

H _____
H¹ _____
H² _____

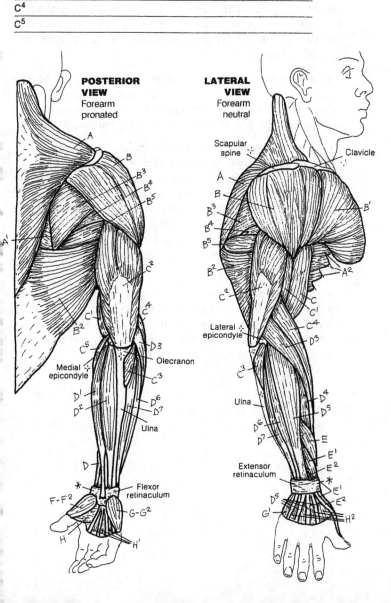

POSTERIOR VIEW
Forearm pronated

LATERAL VIEW
Forearm neutral

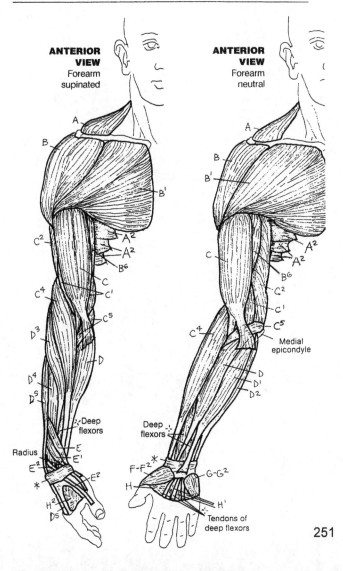

ANTERIOR VIEW
Forearm supinated

ANTERIOR VIEW
Forearm neutral

251

The **gluteal muscles** (A, B, and C) are arranged in three layers, with the gluteus maximus being superficial-most, and the gluteus minimus buried deep to the gluteus medius. **Gluteus maximus** arises from the tendinous fibers of the erector spinae muscles (seen here as an impression under the skin), along the posterior gluteal line of the postero-superior aspect of the ilium, from the sacrotuberous ligament, and the lateral edge of the sacrum and coccyx. This huge muscle covers most of the other two gluteal muscles, and covers all of the six lateral rotators of the hip joint as it courses inferiorly and laterally to insert along the upper *ilio-tibial tract* and the gluteal tuberosity of the femur. It lies just below the skin and superficial fascia that in some people abounds with adipose tissue. It is the most powerful hip extensor of the lot, and adducts and laterally rotates the hip joint. It is a tensor of the fasciae latae.

The large sciatic nerve (roughly the size of your thumb) arises from the sacral plexus on the deep surface of the **piriformis muscle**, one of the lateral rotators of the hip joint. The nerve emerges from the greater sciatic foramen, under piriformis, and comes to lie deep to the gluteus maximus muscle in the lower medial quadrant of the buttock. The thickness of the gluteus maximus varies. Intramuscular injections are delivered to the upper and outer quadrant of the buttock.

The **gluteus medius** is a prime mover in abduction of the hip joint and an important stabilizer (leveler) of the pelvis when the opposite lower limb is lifted off the ground. The gluteus minimus is also a major contributor to the abduction effort of the hip joint.

The deepest layer of gluteal muscles includes the **gluteus minimus** and the **deep lateral rotators** of the hip joint. They cover up/fill the greater and lesser sciatic notches. These muscles generally insert at the posterior aspect of the greater trochanter of the femur. The gluteal muscles (less gluteus maximus) correspond to some degree with the rotator cuff of the shoulder joint: lateral rotators posteriorly, abductor (gluteus medius) superiorly, and medial rotators (gluteus medius and minimus, tensor fasciae latae) anteriorly.

The **iliotibial tract**, a thickening of the deep fascia (fascia lata) of the thigh, runs from ilium to tibia and helps stabilize the knee joint laterally. The **tensor fasciae latae** muscle, a frequently visible and palpable flexor and medial rotator of the hip joint, inserts into this fibrous band, tensing it.

MUSCULAR SYSTEM / LOWER LIMB
MUSCLES OF THE GLUTEAL REGION

CN: In the posterior and lateral views of superficial dissections, the upper fibers of the iliotibial tract have been cut and pulled away, exposing gluteus medius. (1) Color the names and structures of the three gluteal muscles in all views. (2) Color the six deep lateral rotators and their names. Color the directional arrows.

3 GLUTEAL MUSCLES

GLUTEUS MAXIMUS_A
GLUTEUS MEDIUS_B
GLUTEUS MINIMUS_C

TENSOR FASCIAE LATAE_D

6 DEEP, LATERAL ROTATORS

PIRIFORMIS_E
OBTURATOR INTERNUS_F
OBTURATOR EXTERNUS_G
QUADRATUS FEMORIS_H
GEMELLUS SUPERIOR_I
GEMELLUS INFERIOR_J

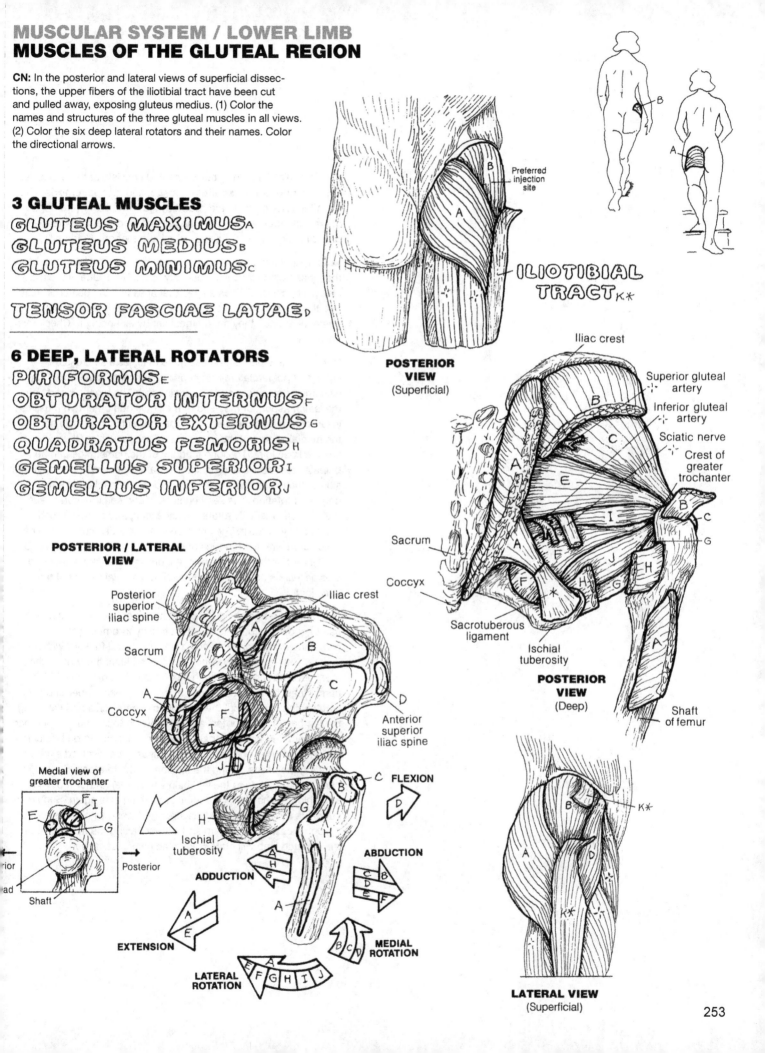

ILIOTIBIAL TRACT_K*

Preferred injection site

POSTERIOR VIEW
(Superficial)

Iliac crest
Superior gluteal artery
Inferior gluteal artery
Sciatic nerve
Crest of greater trochanter
Sacrum
Coccyx
Sacrotuberous ligament
Ischial tuberosity

POSTERIOR VIEW
(Deep)

Shaft of femur

POSTERIOR / LATERAL VIEW

Posterior superior iliac spine
Iliac crest
Sacrum
Coccyx
Anterior superior iliac spine
Ischial tuberosity

Medial view of greater trochanter
Shaft
Posterior

FLEXION
ABDUCTION
ADDUCTION
MEDIAL ROTATION
EXTENSION
LATERAL ROTATION

LATERAL VIEW
(Superficial)

253

The musculature of the **posterior thigh** consists of three muscles: **semimembranosus**, **semitendinosus**, and **biceps femoris**. They are often referred to as the "**hamstrings**," the "ham" referring to the muscle/fat in the back of the porcine hindlimb, and the extraordinarily long (and vulnerable) related tendons ("strings").

Note the origins of these muscles. All three have at least one head that arise from the ischial tuberosity of the ilium. One of the muscles (biceps femoris) has a head that arises on the posterior thigh. See the illustration. Since these muscles cross the hip joint on the posterior aspect, they act on that joint by extending it. Check this on yourself.

Note that the tendons of these three muscles also cross the knee joint posterolaterally (biceps femoris) and posteromedially (semimembranosus and semitendinosus). The biceps inserts on the *lateral* aspect of the head of the fibula; the other two muscles insert on the posterior aspect of the medial tibial condyle and the medial aspect of the upper tibia. These muscles, therefore, flex the knee joint. The long tendons of the hamstrings can be palpated just above and behind the partially flexed knee on either side of the joint's midline. The knee joint is capable of a small degree of rotation. The semitendinosus and semimembranosus muscles can medially rotate the knee joint, and biceps femoris can laterally rotate it. The insertion of semitendinosus is intimately associated with the tendons of insertion of sartorius and gracilis (SGT). Part of this collection of tendons, shaped like a goose foot (*pes anserinus*), can be seen here on the medial aspect of the knee joint.

Discomfort on stretching tight hamstrings can result from overuse to underuse (chronic couch potato syndrome). Test your own hamstrings from a standing posture. Bend forward without locking your knees; stop when you feel tension. It is written that most young people can touch their toes in this maneuver. Tight hamstrings, by their ischial origin, pull the posterior pelvis down, lengthening (stretching) the erector spinae muscles and flattening the lumbar lordosis, potentially contributing to limitation of lumbar movement and low back pain. Low back discomfort on stretching the hamstrings is common, and can usually be resolved simply by bending the knees, taking the tension off the tendons. Sharp low back pain radiating to the leg (below the knee) and/or foot while stretching the hamstrings can be something else again. Such pain suggests the sciatic nerve was stretched along with the tendons; in such a case, standing up and plantar flexing the ankle joint of the affected limb will often relieve the painful sensation.

MUSCLES OF THE POSTERIOR THIGH

CN: Use light colors. (1) Color each hamstring muscle in the deep view before going on to the superficial. Color the two smaller muscle diagrams with respect to flexion and extension of the hip and knee joints. (2) Color gray the two diagrams of stippled muscles at upper right.

"HAMSTRINGS"

SEMIMEMBRANOSUS.ₐ

SEMITENDINOSUS.ᵦ

BICEPS FEMORIS.c

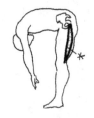

Tight hamstrings limit flexion of hip when knee joint is extended

Lordotic curve

Pelvis

Tight hamstrings (at right) tilt pelvis backward, flattening lordotic curve of lower back.

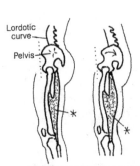

Gluteus maximus

Powerful extensors of the hip joints.

POSTERIOR VIEW

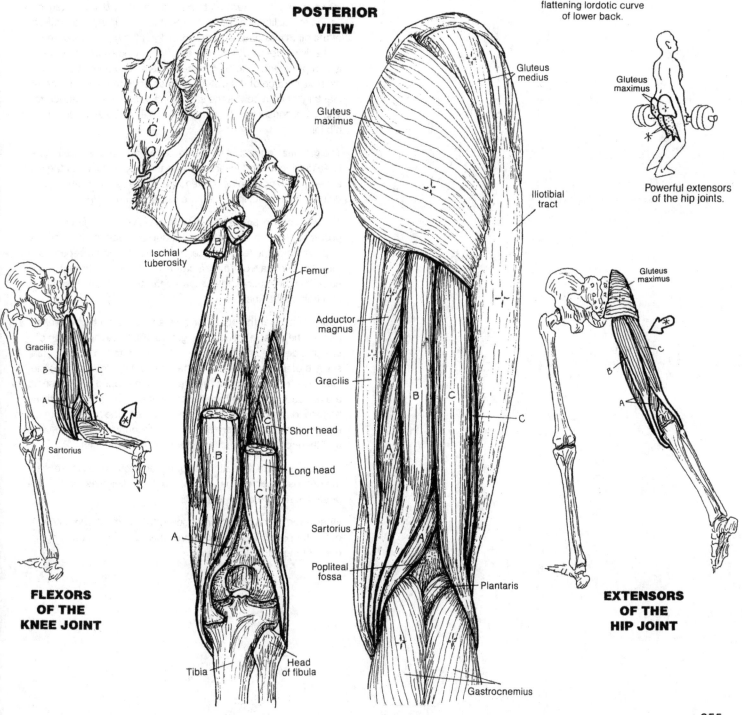

Gluteus medius

Gluteus maximus

Ischial tuberosity

Femur

Iliotibial tract

Adductor magnus

Gracilis

Short head

Long head

A

B

C

Sartorius

Popliteal fossa

Plantaris

Tibia

Head of fibula

Gastrocnemius

Gracilis

B — C

A

Sartorius

FLEXORS OF THE KNEE JOINT

DEEP

SUPERFICIAL

Gluteus maximus

EXTENSORS OF THE HIP JOINT

255

The **medial thigh muscles** consist of the hip joint *adductors* (**pectineus, adductor brevis, adductor longus,** *adductor magnus,* and *gracilis*) and the *obturator externus,* a lateral rotator of that joint. These can all be seen in the illustration, and their relationship to one another at their origin is a relationship you should spend some time with. They are a powerful set of muscles.

The **obturator externus** is part of the medial thigh group because of its location within the adductor group and because it is innervated by the obturator nerve which supplies the adductors. The insertion site of "externus" has a mechanically disadvantaged location to qualify as a hip adductor; it is more likely a lateral rotator of the hip. Unfortunately, electromyographic study of this muscle in the living does not seem to be currently possible. However, it is compartmentalized by fasciae in the medial thigh, covers the external surface of the obturator foramen in the deep upper medial thigh, and receives the same innervation as the adductors. Thus, it is considered by many authorities to be an adductor of the hip joint.

The **gracilis**, longest of the adductor group, crosses the medial knee (flexing it), and inserts only on the medial tibia (not the linea aspera); its tendon joins the tendons of the sartorius and semitendinosus to form its insertion, the *pes anserinus.*

The **adductor magnus** is the most massive of the group (see posterior view). In its lower half, adductor magnus fibers give way to passage of the femoral artery and vein through a separation of muscle fibers called the *adductor hiatus.* Passing through this canal within the muscle, the vessels enter the popliteal fossa above and behind the knee.

Look carefully at the posterior view and focus on the medial aspect of the muscle adjacent to gracilis (E). Note the column of straight, descending fibers that reach down to the distal medial surface of the femur where it attaches to the adductor tubercle (see far left illustration just above the medial condyle). These fibers are not adductors; they are flexors of the knee joint, essentially a hamstring muscle! The more lateral fibers of the adductor magnus attach to the linea aspera and the supracondylar line of the femur and therefore function as an adductor of the hip joint.

This fact is worth repeating: all of the adductor muscles, except the gracilis, insert on the vertical rough line (linea aspera) on the posterior surface of the femur.

Innervation of the adductor muscles, for the most part, is by the obturator nerve. The sciatic nerve innervates the "hamstring fibers" of the adductor magnus.

MUSCLES OF THE MEDIAL THIGH

CN: (1) Color one muscle at a time through the five main views before going to the next one. (2) The dotted lines at far left represent the sites of insertion (linea aspera) for muscles A, B, C, and D on the *posterior* aspect of the femur.

MUSCLES

*PECTINEUS*ᴀ
*ADDUCTOR BREVIS*ʙ
*ADDUCTOR LONGUS*ᴄ
*ADDUCTOR MAGNUS*ᴅ
*GRACILIS*ᴇ
*OBTURATOR EXTERNUS*ꜰ

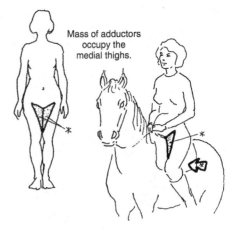

Mass of adductors occupy the medial thighs.

ANTERIOR VIEW

ATTACHMENT SITES

Coxal bone
Superior pubic ramus
Inter-anteric ossa posterior face)
A
F
F
C
B
E
D
Inferior pubic ramus
Obturator foramen
D
A
B
C
Femur
D
Adductor tubercle (on posterior surface)
D
Knee joint
Patella
E
Insertion of sartorius semitendinosus
E
Fibula
Tibia

DEEP

A
F
C
B
E
A
D
B
C
D
Adductor hiatus for femoral artery and vein
E

POSTERIOR VIEW

F
D
E
Linea aspera
Adductor hiatus

INTERMEDIATE

Iliac crest
Sacrum
Anterior superior iliac spine
Greater trochanter
F
A
Lesser trochanter
B
C
D
E

SUPERFICAL

Psoas major
Psoas minor
Iliacus
Iliopsoas
Inguinal ligament
Tensor fasciae latae
Sartorius
A
Vastus lateralis
C
Rectus femoris
Vastus medialis
B
E
Iliotibial tract
Pes anserinus
E

What we have here in the **anterior muscles of the thigh** is a very powerful and fascinating group of muscles. They are all innervated by branches of the lumbar plexus (L1–4), most often in the form of the femoral nerve (L2, 3, 4) and its branches.

The **sartorius**, called the "tailor's muscle" for its role in enabling a crossed-legs sitting posture, one used for centuries to sit and be able to create a posture that takes up little room and so readily facilitates hand work, as in sewing, drawing, etc. The muscle arises from the anterior superior iliac spine, and crosses obliquely medially as it descends to insert on the superior medial surface of the tibia. It is a flexor and lateral rotator of the hip joint and a flexor of the knee joint, as you can infer from its illustrated attachments. It is innervated by the femoral nerve.

The **quadriceps femoris** muscle arises from four heads. The **rectus femoris** arises from the anterior inferior iliac spine. The **vastus medialis** and **lateralis** each arise from the linea aspera on the posterior aspect of the femur; the **vastus intermedius** arises from the anterior and lateral femoral shaft. The four tendons converge at the patella as the tendon of quadriceps femoris.

The **patella** is the largest sesamoid bone in the body. It developed as a cartilaginous body in the tendon of quadriceps femoris as it passed over the anterior inferior surface of the femur and anterior superior surface of the tibia. Absent the patella, the tendon of quadriceps femoris would be subjected to serious abrasive forces when the tendon is brought into contact with the femur over which it is passing during flexion and extension of the knee joint. The patella thus incorporates the tendon of quadriceps in its bony structure. At the inferior aspect (apex) of the patella, the tendinous fibers of quadriceps continue to the tibial tuberosity as the **patellar ligament**.

The rectus femoris, a strong hip joint flexor, is the only member of the quadriceps to cross the hip joint. The four heads of the quadriceps femoris are the only knee extensors. The significance of the role of quadriceps becomes clear to those having experienced a knee injury; the muscles tend to atrophy and weaken rapidly with disuse, and "quad" exercises are essential to maintain structural stability of the joint. The muscle also suffers from insufficient stretching, except by athletes who depend on it. A "tight quad" can be a real pain, not to mention subtracting from a fully functioning and powerful knee extensor

The **iliopsoas** is the most powerful flexor of the hip, having a broad origin from the iliac fossa, iliac crest and the sacrum and sacroiliac ligaments (in the form of iliacus), as well as the narrow triangular psoas major and the much more slender psoas minor. These muscles all attach at the lesser trochanter at the proximal end of the femoral shaft.

MUSCLES OF THE ANTERIOR THIGH

CN: The patellar ligament, G*, is colored gray but the patella is left uncolored.
(1) Begin with the deep view of the thigh and then complete the superficial view.
(2) On the far left, color the visualized portions of the quadriceps that are antagonists to the hamstring group. (3) Complete the action diagrams along the right margin.

MUSCLES

SARTORIUS_A

QUADRICEPS FEMORIS ÷

  RECTUS FEMORIS_B

  VASTUS LATERALIS_C

  VASTUS INTERMEDIUS_D

  VASTUS MEDIALIS_E

ILIOPSOAS_F

PATELLAR
LIGAMENT_{G*}

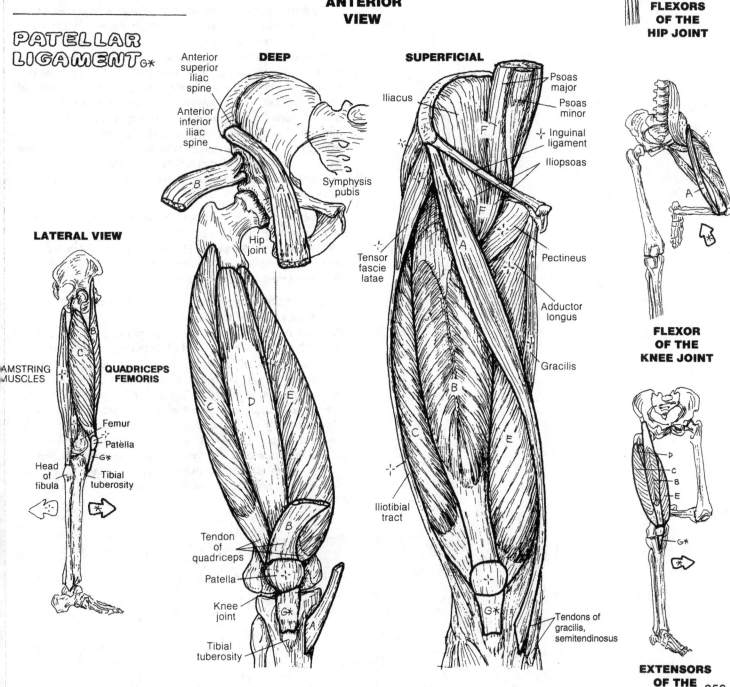

ANTERIOR VIEW

DEEP

Anterior superior iliac spine
Anterior inferior iliac spine
Symphysis pubis
Hip joint

SUPERFICIAL

Iliacus
Psoas major
Psoas minor
Inguinal ligament
Iliopsoas
Tensor fascie latae
Pectineus
Adductor longus
Gracilis
Iliotibial tract
Tendons of gracilis, semitendinosus

LATERAL VIEW

HAMSTRING MUSCLES
QUADRICEPS FEMORIS
Femur
Patella
G*
Head of fibula
Tibial tuberosity

Tendon of quadriceps
Patella
Knee joint
Tibial tuberosity

FLEXORS OF THE HIP JOINT

Tensor fasciae latae
Pectineus
Gracilis

FLEXOR OF THE KNEE JOINT

EXTENSORS OF THE KNEE JOINT

259

The **muscles of the leg** are arranged into anterolateral, lateral, and posterior compartments. These muscles attached to the anterolateral surface of the tibia, the anterior aspect of the fibula, and the intervening interosseous membrane/ligament. The anteromedial surface of the tibia is bare of muscle attachments (as you can feel on yourself). The muscles of the posterior compartment arise from the fibula, tibia, and the interosseous membrane. Insertions of these muscles are discussed below.

Three muscles arise in the anterolateral compartment: the **tibialis anterior** largely originates on the tibia, and its fellows the **extensor hallucis longus** and **extensor digitorum longus** arise from the interosseous membrane and the fibula. All of the anterior leg muscles are dorsiflexors (extensors) of the ankle; the extensors hallucis and digitorum longus are toe extensors; the tibialis anterior is an invertor of the subtalar joint as well, and the **fibularis tertius** (the fifth tendon of the extensor digitorum) is an evertor of the subtalar joint. Due to rotation of the lower limb during embryonic development, these extensors are anterior to the bones of attachment in the anatomical position (unlike the upper limb wrist extensors, which are posterior). In walking, the three anterolateral muscles of the leg are particularly helpful in lifting the foot up (plantar flexion) during the swing phase and avoiding "stubbing" of the toes.

The **fibular (peroneal) muscles** (*longus* and *brevis*) make up the lateral compartment of the leg. They arise largely from the fibula and interosseous membrane. They are principally evertors of the foot, and are especially active during plantar flexion (walking on the toes or pushing off with the great toe).

Look now at the diagram of foot movements at lower right and the plantar view above of the foot with muscle attachments. Tendons from certain anterior, lateral, and posterior muscle groups come around the side of the foot to attach to the plantar surfaces of certain tarsal and metatarsal bones. When these muscles contract, they pull up the side of the foot to which they are attached. Simply defined, these movements are **inversion** if the great-toe side of the foot is lifted, and **eversion** if the little-toe side of the foot is lifted. Clearly, then, the muscles inverting the foot will pass around the medial aspect of the foot; muscles everting the foot will pass around the lateral aspect of the foot. Remember: the muscles from the lateral leg compartment of the foot (fibularis longus and brevis) are both evertors of the subtalar joint.

MUSCLES OF THE ANTERIOR & LATERAL LEG

CN: The interosseous ligament (site of origin) has been left out of the attachment-sites illustration for simplification. Insertion sites on the plantar surface of the foot are shown at upper right. (1) Color the anterior muscles and related names, starting with the attachment sites (with a sharp pencil!). Note the insertion of tibialis anterior at the plantar surface of the foot in the small upper drawing. (2) Color the muscles in the lateral view and the plantar view. (3) Color the "Movements of the Foot" diagram and related muscles and arrows.

LATERAL LEG

*FIBULARIS LONGUS*ᴇ
*FIBULARIS BREVIS*ꜰ

ANTERIOR LEG

*TIBIALIS ANTERIOR*ᴀ
*EXTENSOR DIGITORUM LONGUS*ʙ
*EXTENSOR HALLUCIS LONGUS*ᴄ
*FIBULARIS TERTIUS*ᴅ

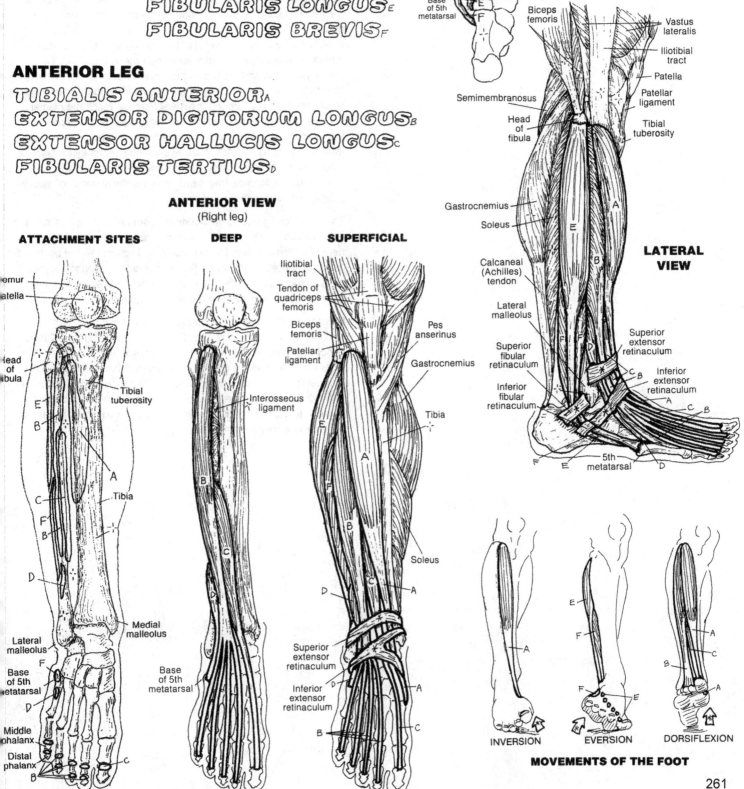

PLANTAR VIEW (Bottom)

1st metatarsal
1st cuneiform
Base of 5th metatarsal

Biceps femoris
Vastus lateralis
Iliotibial tract
Patella
Patellar ligament
Tibial tuberosity

Semimembranosus
Head of fibula
Gastrocnemius
Soleus
Calcaneal (Achilles) tendon
Lateral malleolus
Superior fibular retinaculum
Inferior fibular retinaculum
Superior extensor retinaculum
Inferior extensor retinaculum
5th metatarsal

LATERAL VIEW

ANTERIOR VIEW
(Right leg)

ATTACHMENT SITES

Femur
Patella
Head of fibula
Tibial tuberosity
Tibia
Medial malleolus
Lateral malleolus
Base of 5th metatarsal
Middle phalanx
Distal phalanx

DEEP

Interosseous ligament
Base of 5th metatarsal

SUPERFICIAL

Iliotibial tract
Tendon of quadriceps femoris
Biceps femoris
Patellar ligament
Pes anserinus
Gastrocnemius
Tibia
Soleus
Superior extensor retinaculum
Inferior extensor retinaculum

INVERSION   EVERSION   DORSIFLEXION

MOVEMENTS OF THE FOOT

261

The **muscles of the posterior leg** (calf) are arranged into deep and superficial compartments between which is a fascial septum (barrier): the deep transverse fascia (not shown). The four muscles of the deep compartment arise from the tibia, the fibula, and/or the intervening interosseous membrane (see the "Deep View" and the "Attachment Sites"). The **popliteus** is all by itself in the upper part of the deep compartment, where it flexes the knee joint and rotates the tibia. The **tibialis posterior** occupies the center position in the deep compartment. Its tendon swings to the big-toe side, wraps around the medial aspect of the foot, and inserts on a host of bones on the plantar surface of the foot (cuboid, cuneiforms, navicular, and the base of the metatarsals). It flexes and inverts the foot. The tendons of **flexors hallucis longus** and **digitorum longus** wrap around the medial arch to reach the plantar surface of the great toe and the plantar surface of the bones of the forefoot. The deep fascial compartments of the posterior leg muscles are fairly inelastic. Muscle swelling secondary to vascular insufficiency can result in serious muscle compression with loss of the muscles (compartment syndrome) in the absence of fascial (surgical) decompression.

The superficial group (**gastrocnemius, soleus**) of muscles insert on the calcaneus by way of a common tendon, the tendocalcaneus (Achilles tendon). These muscles collectively lift the posterior calcaneus (heel) up in plantar flexion of the foot, leaving the toes to carry the weight of the body. The gastrocnemius crosses the knee joint and is therefore a flexor of that joint.

Plantaris is a small muscle that arises just above the lateral femoral condyle and continues distally as a variably narrow, thin, pencil-size tendon to insert in the tendocalcaneus just above the latter's insertion on the calcaneus. Players of court games (tennis, racquetball, squash, etc.) may become familiar with the tendon of this muscle when it "snaps" (more like "pops") under excessive tension during dorsiflexion (extension) of the ankle joint. Its loss is of no significant consequence.

MUSCLES OF THE POSTERIOR LEG

MUSCLES

TIBIALIS POSTERIOR·G
FLEXOR DIGITORUM LONGUS·H
FLEXOR HALLUCIS LONGUS·I
POPLITEUS·J
PLANTARIS·K
SOLEUS·L
GASTROCNEMIUS·M

CN: Use light colors different from those used on the previous page. (1) Color one muscle at a time, from deep to superficial, in each of the posterior views. Note that, soleus, L, and gastrocnemius, M, share the same tendon (tendocalcaneus, M). (2) Color the upper and lower medial views, noting the arrangements of tendons on the plantar surface. (3) Color the attachment sites of the posterior leg muscles at far left.

POSTERIOR VIEW (Right leg)

PLANTAR FLEXION

INVERSION

MEDIAL VIEW

Semitendinosus
Semi-membranosus
Gracilis
Sartorius
Vastus lateralis
Biceps femoris
Popliteal fossa

Femur
M
K
J
Semi-membranosus
Head of fibula
J
L
Fibula
Soleal line
G
Tibia
H
I
Interosseous ligament
Medial malleolus
M
K
Lateral malleolus
Calcaneus
Subtalar joint
Tuberosity of the navicular
1st cuneiform
G
Tibialis anterior
Metatarsals
Peroneus longus
Middle phalanx
Distal phalanx
I
H

Tibia
Fibula
H
G

M
J
K
L
G
H
I
K
M
I
G

TENDO-CALCANEUS
Fibularis longus, brevis

Rectus femoris
Vastus medialis
Femur
Pes anserinus
Patellar ligament
Tuberosity of tibia
A
Anterior margin of tibia
Superior extensor retinaculum
Inferior extensor retinaculum
Semi-membranosus
M
L
H
I
Medial malleolus
G

Great toe
C
A
H
G
Flexor retinaculum
Calcaneus

ATTACHMENT SITES   **DEEP VIEW**   **INTERMEDIATE**   **SUPERFICIAL**

263

The dorsal intrinsic **muscles of the foot** (those that arise and insert within the dorsum of the foot) are limited to two small extensors of the toes (the **extensor digitorum brevis** and the **extensor hallucis brevis**), shown at right. Most of the extensor function is derived from extrinsic extensors.

The intrinsic muscles of the plantar region of the foot are shown here in four layers. The **plantar interossei**, wedged between the metatarsal bones, constitute the deepest (**fourth**) **layer**. They adduct toes 3–5, flex the metatarsophalangeal (MP) joints of these toes, and contribute to extension of the interphalangeal (IP) joints of these toes through the mechanism of the extensor expansion. The **dorsal interossei** abduct toes 3–5 and facilitate the other actions of the plantar interossei.

The **third layer** of muscles acts on the great toe (hallux) and fifth digit (digiti minimi).

The **second layer** includes the **quadratus plantae**, which inserts into the lateral border of the common tendon (H) of the flexor digitorum longus (FDL). It assists that muscle in flexion of the toes. The **lumbricals** arise from the individual tendons of the FDL and insert into the medial aspect of the extensor expansion (dorsal aspect). They flex the MP joints and extend the IP joints of toes 2–5 via the extensor expansion.

The superficial **(first) layer** consists of the abductors (**abductor hallucis** and **abductor digiti minimi**) of the first and fifth digits and the **flexor digitorum brevis**. The plantar muscles are covered by the thickened deep fascia of the sole and the plantar aponeurosis, extending from the calcaneus to the fibrous sheath of the flexor tendons.

It seems an injustice to only know these complex, critical muscle layers by virtue of walking on them under all sorts of difficult conditions. When they work, you work. When they don't, you don't...and you may soon make friends with your podiatrist or other appropriate health care provider.

MUSCLES OF THE FOOT (Intrinsics)

CN: Only color the muscles whose names are listed on this page. Letter labels taken from the previous page are for identification purposes only. You may have to use the same color more than once. (1) Attachment sites of extrinsic foot muscles can be found on the two preceding pages. (2) Begin with the fourth (deepest) layer and complete each illustration before going on to the next.

MUSCLES

FOURTH LAYER

3 PLANTAR INTEROSSEI P
4 DORSAL INTEROSSEI Q

THIRD LAYER

FLEXOR HALLUCIS BREVIS R
ADDUCTOR HALLUCIS S
FLEXOR DIGITI MINIMI BREVIS T

SECOND LAYER

QUADRATUS PLANTAE U
4 LUMBRICALS V

FIRST LAYER

ABDUCTOR HALLUCIS W
ABDUCTOR DIGITI MINIMI X
FLEXOR DIGITORUM BREVIS Y

DORSAL SURFACE

EXTENSOR DIGITORUM BREVIS N
EXTENSOR HALLUCIS BREVIS O

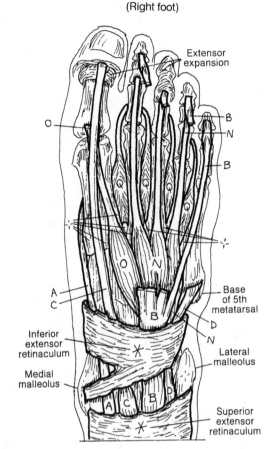

DORSAL SURFACE
(Right foot)

Extensor expansion

Base of 5th metatarsal

Inferior extensor retinaculum

Medial malleolus

Lateral malleolus

Superior extensor retinaculum

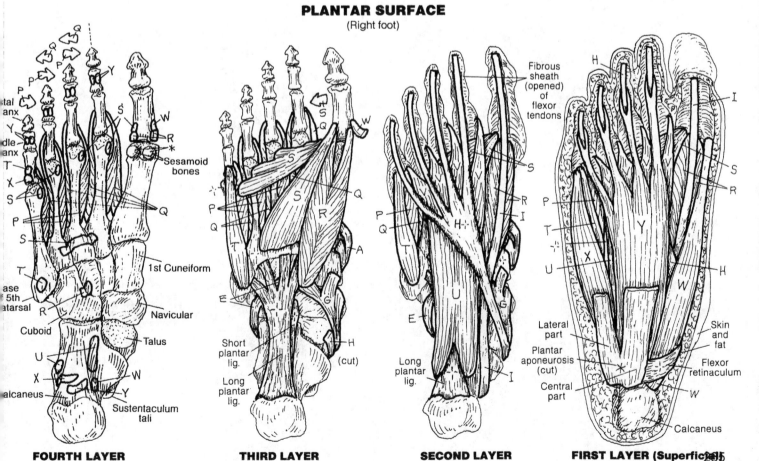

PLANTAR SURFACE
(Right foot)

FOURTH LAYER

Sesamoid bones

1st Cuneiform

Navicular

Cuboid

Talus

Calcaneus

Sustentaculum tali

Base of 5th metatarsal

THIRD LAYER

Short plantar lig.

Long plantar lig.

(cut)

SECOND LAYER

Fibrous sheath (opened) of flexor tendons

Long plantar lig.

FIRST LAYER (Superficial)

Lateral part

Plantar aponeurosis (cut)

Central part

Skin and fat

Flexor retinaculum

Calcaneus

MUSCULAR SYSTEM / LOWER LIMB
REVIEW OF MUSCLES

CN: Start with the three muscles labeled "A." On the lines provided, write the names of the superficial muscles shown with the color used for each labeled muscle. Some of these muscles have more than one function assigned to them by these categories. Be sure to look for the muscle in each of the four drawings before committing its name to writing. The key word in the listings is "primarily." (*See the end of this section for answers.*)

MUSCLES ACTING PRIMARILY ON THE HIP JOINT

A _____
A¹ _____
A² _____
A³ _____
A⁴ _____
A⁵ _____
A⁶ _____
A⁷ _____

MUSCLES ACTING PRIMARILY ON THE KNEE JOINT

B _____
B¹ _____
B² _____
B³ _____
B⁴ _____
B⁵ _____
B⁶ _____
B⁷ _____

MUSCLES ACTING PRIMARILY ON THE ANKLE JOINT

C _____
C¹ _____
C² _____
C³ _____
C⁴ _____
C⁵ _____
C⁶ _____
C⁷ _____
C⁸ _____

MUSCLES ACTING PRIMARILY ON THE SUBTALAR JOINT

D _____
D¹ _____

MUSCLES ACTING ON THE DIGITS OF THE FOOT

E _____
E¹ _____
E² _____

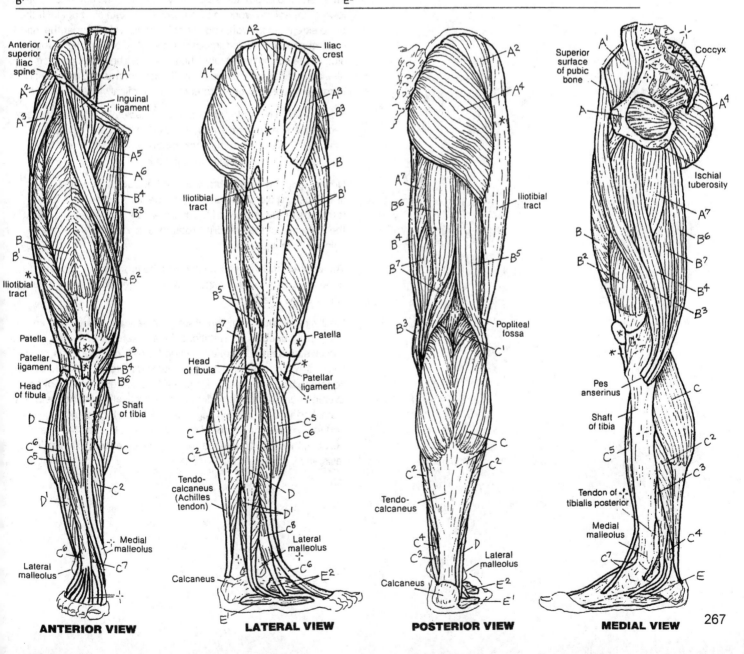

ANTERIOR VIEW   **LATERAL VIEW**   **POSTERIOR VIEW**   **MEDIAL VIEW**

267

Having completed coloring the A and B muscles in the three illustrations, consider the following as you review your handiwork.

The upper body joint **flexors** can be very helpful in taking on loads and getting work done (bending, lifting, pushing, pulling, etc.). Their arrangement makes it handy for picking up stuff and carrying it. Almost anything you do with your upper limbs involves a lot of joint flexion. When you are done, you need your antigravity **extensors** to get you back to an upright posture. Most of these muscles cannot be seen in this illustration, as they are deep muscles supporting the vertebral column. What side of the vertebral column are they on? These muscles are collectively represented in the lower illustration by the "Erector spinae and deeper muscles." You can see that these extensors keep you upright, maintaining an extensor platform (an erect body) to which one can return following upper limb work and from which one can start again. If the deep extensors fail you, you are going to fall down under the influence of gravity. The abdominal muscles (A) work to offer compression to the abdominal cavity when needed. These muscles are also powerful flexors of the trunk. Tightly contracted, they resist intrusive forces and thus protect the abdominal viscera.

Now color the **scapular stabilization** muscles (F). The six of them secure the scapula to the posterior body wall and at the same time make possible a remarkably mobile scapulo-thoracic frame from which the shoulder joints can work.

Now color the **rotator**, **abductor**, and **adductor muscles** (C, D, and E) as you did above. These provide added mobility and performance of the upper and lower limbs during work and sport. At the extremes of their mobility, rotators and abductors are often vulnerable to injury.

The **evertor** and **invertor** muscles of the foot are not shown to good advantage on this page; they are presented in some detail earlier in the chapter.

Finally, recall that extension of weight-bearing joints is often an antigravity function. The relationship of flexors and extensor muscles of the trunk is one of second-by-second tradeoffs. In the lower drawing, note the line of gravity and its relationship to the vertebral, hip, knee, and ankle joints. The center of gravity of an average human being standing with theoretically perfect posture is just anterior to the motion segment of S1–S2. Flexion of the neck and torso move the center of gravity forward, loading the posterior cervical, thoracic, and lumbar paraspinal (extensor) muscles in resistance.

MUSCULAR SYSTEM
FUNCTIONAL OVERVIEW
FUNCTIONAL ACTORS

FLEXOR_A   ROTATOR_E
EXTENSOR_B   SCAPULAR STABILIZER_F
ABDUCTOR_C   EVERTOR_G
ADDUCTOR_D   INVERTOR_H

CN: (1) First check the text and color in conjunction with its organization. Color the muscles labeled A on the left side. Then color the unlabeled A muscles on the opposite side of the same figure. Repeat this sequence with the muscles B through H. (2) Go to the opposite figure (on the right) and color the muscles as you did on the left. (3) Color the A and B muscles in the lower figure.

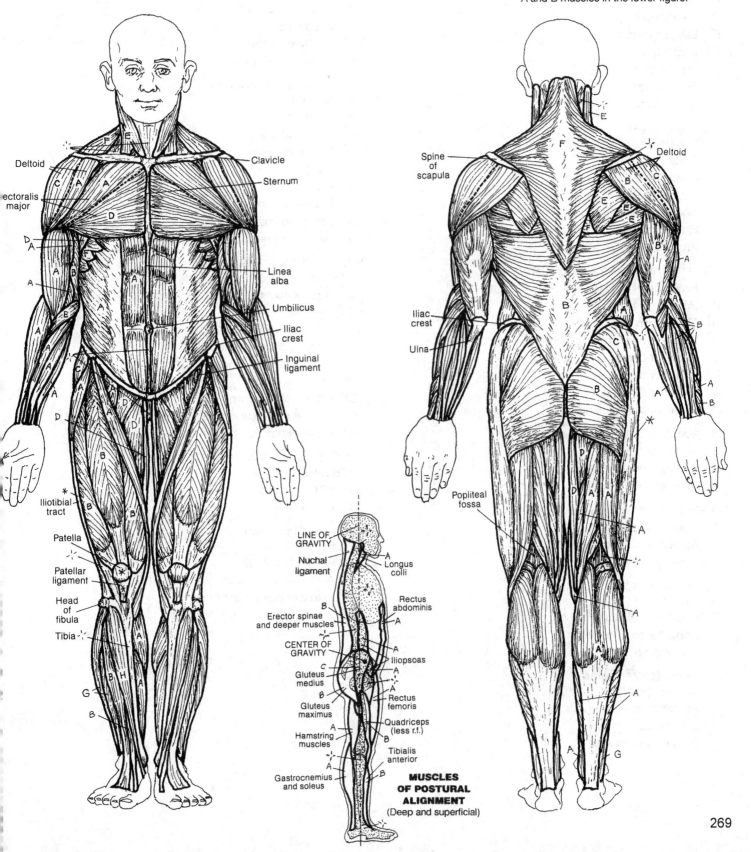

Deltoid
Clavicle
Sternum
Pectoralis major
Linea alba
Umbilicus
Iliac crest
Inguinal ligament
Iliotibial tract
Patella
Patellar ligament
Head of fibula
Tibia

Spine of scapula
Deltoid
Iliac crest
Ulna
Popliteal fossa

LINE OF GRAVITY
Nuchal ligament
Longus colli
Rectus abdominis
Erector spinae and deeper muscles
CENTER OF GRAVITY
Iliopsoas
Gluteus medius
Rectus femoris
Gluteus maximus
Quadriceps (less r.f.)
Hamstring muscles
Tibialis anterior
Gastrocnemius and soleus

MUSCLES OF POSTURAL ALIGNMENT
(Deep and superficial)

269

ANSWERS

Upper Limb: Review of Muscles

MUSCLES ACTING PRIMARILY ON THE SCAPULA

A   Trapezius
A^1 Rhomboids
A^2 Serratus anterior

MUSCLES MOVING THE SHOULDER JOINT

B   Deltoid
B^1 Pectoralis major
B^2 Latissimus dorsi
B^3 Infraspinatus
B^4 Teres minor
B^5 Teres major
B^6 Coracobrachialis

MUSCLES MOVING ELBOW & RADIOULNAR JOINTS

C   Biceps brachii
C^1 Brachialis
C^2 Triceps brachii
C^3 Anconeus
C^4 Brachioradialis
C^5 Pronator teres

MUSCLES MOVING WRIST & HAND JOINTS

D   Flexor carpi radialis
D^1 Palmar longus
D^2 Flexor carpi ulnaris
D^3 Extensor carpi radialis longus
D^4 Extensor carpi radialis brevis
D^5 Extensor digitorum
D^6 Extensor digiti minimi
D^7 Extensor carpi ulnaris

FOREARM MUSCLES MOVING THE THUMB

E   Abductor pollicis
E^1 Extensor pollicis longus
E^2 Extensor pollicis brevis

THENAR MUSCLES MOVING THE THUMB

F   Opponens pollicis
F^1 Abductor pollicis brevis
F^2 Flexor pollicis brevis

HYPOTHENAR MUSCLES MOVING THE 5TH DIGIT

G   Opponens digiti minimi
G^1 Abductor digiti minimi
G^2 Flexor digiti minimi brevis

OTHER MUSCLES ACTING ON THE THUMB & FINGERS

H   Adductor pollicis
H^1 Lumbricals
H^2 Dorsal interosseous

Lower Limb: Review of Muscles

MUSCLES ACTING PRIMARILY ON THE HIP JOINT

A   Obturator internus
A^1 Iliopsoas
A^2 Gluteus medius
A^3 Tensor fasciae latae
A^4 Gluteus maximus
A^5 Pectineus
A^6 Adductor longus
A^7 Adductor magnus

MUSCLES ACTING PRIMARILY ON THE KNEE JOINT

B   Rectus femoris
B^1 Vastus lateralis
B^2 Vastus medialis
B^3 Sartorius
B^4 Gracilis
B^5 Biceps femoris
B^6 Semitendinosus
B^7 Semimembranosus

MUSCLES ACTING PRIMARILY ON THE ANKLE JOINT

C   Gastrocnemius
C^1 Plantaris
C^2 Soleus
C^3 Flexor digitorum longus
C^4 Flexor hallucis longus
C^5 Tibialis anterior
C^6 Extensor digitorum longus
C^7 Extensor hallucis longus
C^8 Fibularis tertius

MUSCLES ACTING PRIMARILY ON THE SUBTALAR JOINT

D   Fibularis longus
D^1 Fibularis brevis

MUSCLES ACTING ON THE DIGITS OF THE FOOT

E   Abductor hallucis
E^1 Abductor digiti minimi
E^2 Extensor digitorum brevis

Nervous System Part 1: Spinal Cord and Spinal Nerves Wish List

As you work through the activities in this chapter, keep in mind that we will NOT be covering the section on reflexes (lab activity 4). Remember to identify the following structures in models or in materials for dissection. Add a description next to the nerve to help you remember key aspects of that structure.

✓	Structure	Description
	Spinal cord	
	anterior horn	
	posterior horn	
	gray commissure	
√	gray matter	
√	white matter	
	dorsal root ganglion	
	ventral root	
	central canal	
	epidural space	
√	dura mater	
√	arachnoid mater	
√	subarachnoid space	
√	pia mater	

✓	Structure	Description
	Plexuses	
√	cervical plexus	
√	brachial plexus	
	phrenic nerve	
	axillary nerve	
	musculocutaneous nerve	
√	lumbar plexus	
√	sacral plexus	

✓	Structure	Description
	Spinal Nerves	
	ulnar nerve	
	median nerve	
	radial nerve	
	femoral nerve	
	sciatic nerve	
	tibial nerve	
	peroneal (common fibular) nerve	
	cauda equina	
	filum terminale	
	sympathetic chain	

The Spinal Cord, Spinal Nerves, and Reflexes

Learning Outcomes

On completion of this exercise, you should be able to:

1. Identify the major surface features of the spinal cord, including the spinal meninges.

2. Identify the sectional anatomy of the spinal cord.

3. Describe the organization and distribution of spinal and peripheral nerves.

4. List the events of a typical reflex arc.

5. Describe how to perform and interpret the stretch reflex, and the biceps and triceps reflexes.

Lab Activities

1 Gross Anatomy of the Spinal Cord

2 Spinal Meninges

3 Spinal and Peripheral Nerves

4 Spinal Reflexes

5 Dissection of the Spinal Cord

Clinical Application

Epidural Injections and Spinal Taps

The **spinal cord** is the long, cylindrical portion of the central nervous system located in the spinal cavity of the vertebral column. It connects the peripheral nervous system (PNS) with the brain. Sensory information from the PNS enters the spinal cord and ascends to the brain. Motor signals from the brain descend the spinal cord and exit the spinal cord to reach the effectors. The spinal cord is more than just a conduit to and from the brain, however. It also processes information and produces **spinal reflexes.** A classic example of a spinal reflex is the stretch reflex that occurs when the tendon over the patella is struck; the spinal cord responds to the tap by stimulating the extensor muscles of the leg in the well-known "knee-jerk" reflex.

Need More Practice and Review?

Build your knowledge—and confidence!—in the Study Area of MasteringA&P® at www.masteringaandp.com with Pre-lab Quizzes, Post-lab Quizzes, Practice Anatomy Lab™ (PAL™) 3.0 virtual anatomy practice tool, PhysioEx™ 9.0 laboratory simulations, and A&P Flix™ with Quizzes.

PAL | practice anatomy lab   For this lab exercise, follow these navigation paths:
- PAL>Human Cadaver>Nervous System
- PAL> Anatomical Models>Nervous System
- PAL>Histology>Nervous Tissue

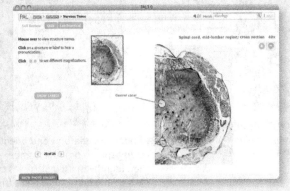

From Exercise 24 of *Laboratory Manual for Anatomy & Physiology featuring Martini Art*, Fifth Edition. Michael G. Wood.

Lab Activity 1 Gross Anatomy of the Spinal Cord

The spinal cord is continuous with the inferior portion of the brain stem (Figure 1). It passes through the foramen magnum, descends approximately 45 cm (18 in.) down the spinal canal of the vertebral column, and terminates between lumbar vertebrae L_1 and L_2. In young children, the spinal cord extends through most of the spine. After the age of four, the spinal cord stops lengthening, but the spine continues to grow. By adulthood, therefore, the spinal cord is shorter than the spine and descends only to the level of the upper lumbar vertebrae.

Figure 1 Gross Anatomy of the Adult Spinal Cord

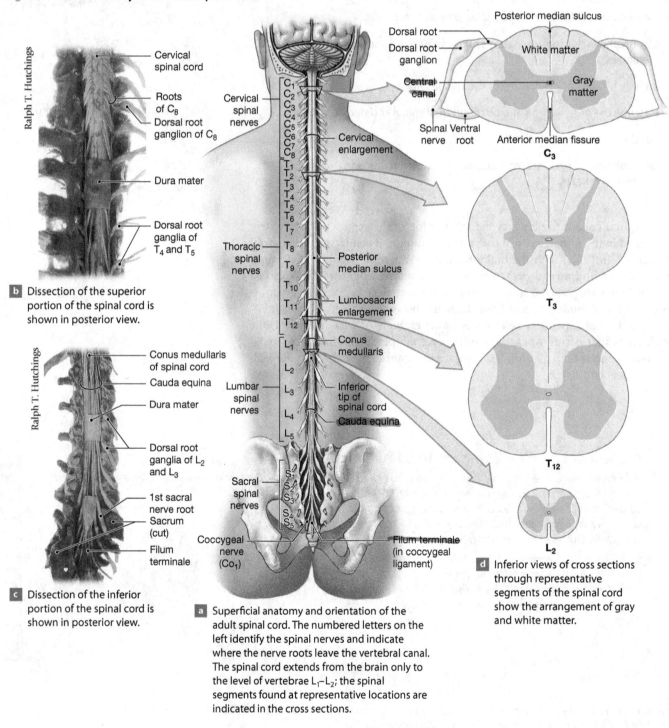

Ralph T. Hutchings

- Cervical spinal cord
- Roots of C_8
- Dorsal root ganglion of C_8
- Dura mater
- Dorsal root ganglia of T_4 and T_5

b Dissection of the superior portion of the spinal cord is shown in posterior view.

Ralph T. Hutchings

- Conus medullaris of spinal cord
- Cauda equina
- Dura mater
- Dorsal root ganglia of L_2 and L_3
- 1st sacral nerve root
- Sacrum (cut)
- Filum terminale

c Dissection of the inferior portion of the spinal cord is shown in posterior view.

Cervical spinal nerves — C_1 C_2 C_3 C_4 C_5 C_6 C_7 C_8

Thoracic spinal nerves — T_1 T_2 T_3 T_4 T_5 T_6 T_7 T_8 T_9 T_{10} T_{11} T_{12}

Lumbar spinal nerves — L_1 L_2 L_3 L_4 L_5

Sacral spinal nerves — S_1 S_2 S_3 S_4 S_5

Coccygeal nerve (Co_1)

- Cervical enlargement
- Posterior median sulcus
- Lumbosacral enlargement
- Conus medullaris
- Inferior tip of spinal cord
- Cauda equina
- Filum terminale (in coccygeal ligament)

a Superficial anatomy and orientation of the adult spinal cord. The numbered letters on the left identify the spinal nerves and indicate where the nerve roots leave the vertebral canal. The spinal cord extends from the brain only to the level of vertebrae L_1–L_2; the spinal segments found at representative locations are indicated in the cross sections.

Posterior median sulcus

- Dorsal root
- Dorsal root ganglion
- Central canal
- Spinal nerve
- Ventral root
- White matter
- Gray matter
- Anterior median fissure

C_3

T_3

T_{12}

L_2

d Inferior views of cross sections through representative segments of the spinal cord show the arrangement of gray and white matter.

The diameter of the spinal cord is not constant along its length. Two enlarged regions occur where the spinal nerves of the limbs join the spinal cord. The **cervical enlargement** in the neck supplies nerves to the upper limbs. The **lumbar enlargement** occurs near the distal end of the cord, where nerves supply the pelvis and lower limbs. Inferior to the lumbar enlargement, the spinal cord narrows and terminates at the **conus medullaris.** Spinal nerves fan out from the conus medullaris in a group called the **cauda equina** (KAW-duh ek-WI-nuh), the "horse's tail." A thin thread of fibrous tissue, the **filum terminale,** extends past the conus medullaris to anchor the spinal cord in the sacrum.

The spinal cord is organized into 31 segments. Each segment is attached to two spinal nerves, one on each side of the segment (Figure 2). Each of the two spinal nerves on a given cord segment is formed by the joining of two lateral extensions of the segment. One of these extensions, called the **dorsal root,** contains sensory neurons entering the spinal cord from sensory receptors. The dorsal root swells at the **dorsal root ganglion,** which is where cell bodies of sensory neurons cluster. The other extension, the **ventral root,** consists of motor neurons exiting the CNS and leading to effectors. The two roots join to form the spinal nerve. Each spinal nerve is therefore a *mixed nerve,* carrying both sensory and motor information. (The first spinal nerve does not have a dorsal root and is therefore a motor nerve.)

Figure 2 illustrates the spinal cord in transverse section to show the internal anatomy, also called the *sectional anatomy.* The cord is divided by the deep and conspicuous **anterior median fissure** and by the shallow **posterior median sulcus.** The periphery of the cord consist of myelinated neurons grouped into three masses called **columns** (*funiculi*). Deep to the white columns is gray matter organized into horns. The **gray horns** contain many glial cells and neuron cell bodies. Each horn contains a specific type of neuron. The **posterior gray horns** carry sensory neurons into the spinal cord, and the **anterior gray horns** carry somatic motor neurons out of the cord and to skeletal muscles. In the sacral region, the anterior gray horns have preganglionic neurons of the parasympathetic nervous system. The **lateral gray horns** occur in spinal segments T_1 through L_2 and consist of visceral motor neurons. Axons may cross to the opposite side of the spinal cord at the crossbars of the horns, called the **anterior** and **posterior gray commissures.** Between the gray commissures is a hole, called the **central canal,** which contains cerebrospinal fluid. The central canal is continuous with the fluid-filled ventricles of the brain. Collectively, all these structures are sometimes referred to as the spinal cord's **gray matter.**

The columns are organized on each side of the cord into the **posterior, lateral,** and **anterior white columns.** The two anterior white columns are connected by the **anterior white commissure.** Within each white column, myelinated axons form distinct bundles of neurons, called either **tracts** (*fasciculi*). (Recall that a bundle of neurons in the PNS is called a *nerve.*)

Make a Prediction

Consider what you know about myelinated neurons. Which anatomical structure's sensory information in the spinal cord ascends to the brain?

QuickCheck Questions

1.1 How is the white and gray matter of the spinal cord organized?

1.2 Which structure is useful in determining which portion of a spinal cord cross section is the anterior region?

1.3 Why is the spinal cord shorter than the vertebral column?

In the Lab 1

Materials

- ☐ Spinal cord model
- ☐ Spinal cord chart
- ☐ Dissection microscope
- ☐ Compound microscope
- ☐ Prepared slide of transverse section of spinal cord

Procedures

1. Review Figures 1 and 2.
2. Locate each surface feature of the spinal cord on the spinal cord model and chart.
3. Review the internal anatomy of the spinal cord on the spinal cord model.
4. Examine the microscopic features of the spinal cord in transverse section by following this sequence:
   - View the slide at low magnification with the dissection microscope. Identify the anterior and posterior regions.
   - Transfer the slide to a compound microscope. Move the slide around to survey the preparation at low magnification, again identifying the posterior and anterior aspects.
   - Examine the central canal and gray horns. Can you distinguish among the posterior, lateral, and anterior gray horns? Locate the gray commissures.
   - Examine the white columns. What is the difference between gray and white matter in the CNS?

For additional practice, complete the *Sketch to Learn* activity. ■

Lab Activity 2 Spinal Meninges

The spinal cord is protected within three layers of **spinal meninges** (me-NIN-jēz). The outer layer, the **dura mater** (DOO-ruh MĀ-ter), is composed of tough, fibrous connective tissue (Figure 3). The fibrous tissue attaches to the bony

Figure 2 **The Sectional Organization of the Spinal Cord**

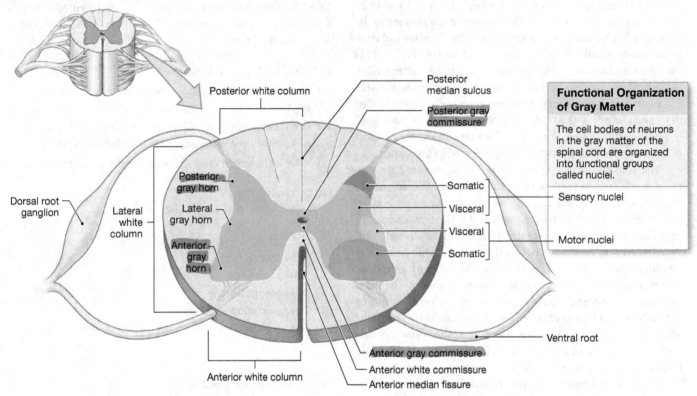

Posterior white column

Posterior median sulcus

Posterior gray commissure

Posterior gray horn

Lateral gray horn

Anterior gray horn

Dorsal root ganglion

Lateral white column

Somatic
Visceral
Visceral
Somatic

Ventral root

Anterior gray commissure

Anterior white commissure

Anterior median fissure

Anterior white column

Functional Organization of Gray Matter

The cell bodies of neurons in the gray matter of the spinal cord are organized into functional groups called nuclei.

Sensory nuclei

Motor nuclei

a The left half of this sectional view shows important anatomical landmarks, including the three columns of white matter. The right half indicates the functional organization of the nuclei in the anterior, lateral, and posterior gray horns.

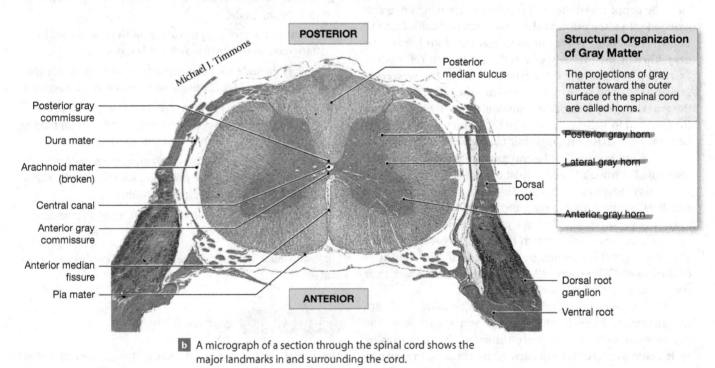

POSTERIOR

Michael J. Timmons

Posterior median sulcus

Posterior gray commissure

Dura mater

Arachnoid mater (broken)

Central canal

Anterior gray commissure

Anterior median fissure

Pia mater

ANTERIOR

Dorsal root

Dorsal root ganglion

Ventral root

Structural Organization of Gray Matter

The projections of gray matter toward the outer surface of the spinal cord are called horns.

Posterior gray horn

Lateral gray horn

Anterior gray horn

b A micrograph of a section through the spinal cord shows the major landmarks in and surrounding the cord.

Figure 3 **The Spinal Cord and Spinal Meninges**

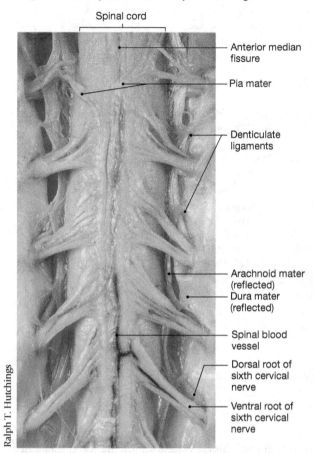

Spinal cord

Anterior median fissure

Pia mater

Denticulate ligaments

Arachnoid mater (reflected)

Dura mater (reflected)

Spinal blood vessel

Dorsal root of sixth cervical nerve

Ventral root of sixth cervical nerve

Ralph T. Hutchings

a Anterior view of the spinal cord and spinal nerve roots in the vertebral canal. The dura mater and arachnoid mater have been reflected.

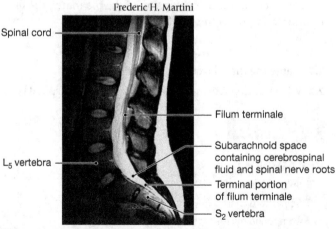

Frederic H. Martini

Spinal cord

Filum terminale

Subarachnoid space containing cerebrospinal fluid and spinal nerve roots

Terminal portion of filum terminale

L₅ vertebra

S₂ vertebra

b MRI of inferior portion of spinal cord is shown in sagittal view.

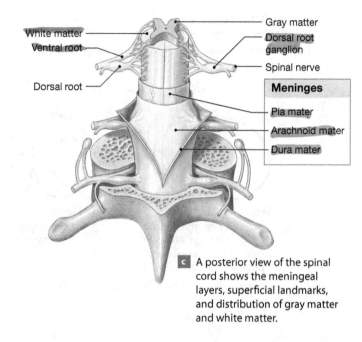

White matter
Ventral root

Dorsal root

Gray matter

Dorsal root ganglion

Spinal nerve

Meninges

Pia mater

Arachnoid mater

Dura mater

c A posterior view of the spinal cord shows the meningeal layers, superficial landmarks, and distribution of gray matter and white matter.

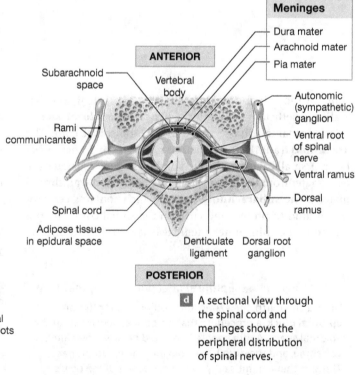

Meninges

Dura mater

Arachnoid mater

Pia mater

ANTERIOR

Subarachnoid space

Vertebral body

Autonomic (sympathetic) ganglion

Ventral root of spinal nerve

Ventral ramus

Dorsal ramus

Rami communicantes

Spinal cord

Adipose tissue in epidural space

Denticulate ligament

Dorsal root ganglion

POSTERIOR

d A sectional view through the spinal cord and meninges shows the peripheral distribution of spinal nerves.

Sketch to Learn

Let's reinforce our understanding of the spinal cord by drawing a section of one. It's easier than it might seem.

Sample Sketch

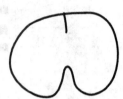

Step 1
- Draw an oval with a fold for the anterior median fissure.
- Include a line on top for the posterior median sulcus.

Step 2
- Add the gray horns and central canal.

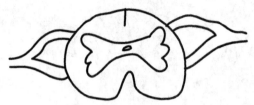

Step 3
- Draw the dorsal and ventral roots by starting at the spinal cord and sketching outward.
- Label your sketch.

Your Sketch

walls of the spinal canal and supports the spinal cord laterally. Superficial to the dura mater is the **epidural space,** which contains adipose tissue to pad the spinal cord. The **arachnoid** (a-RAK-noyd) **mater** is the second meningeal layer. A small cavity called the **subdural space** separates the dura mater from the arachnoid mater. Deep to the arachnoid mater is the **subarachnoid space,** which contains cerebrospinal fluid to protect and cushion the spinal cord. The **pia mater** is the thin, inner meningeal layer that lies directly over the spinal cord. Blood vessels supplying the spinal cord are held in place by the pia mater. The pia mater extends laterally on each side of the spinal cord as the **denticulate ligament,** which joins the dura mater for lateral support to the spinal cord. Another extension of the pia mater, the filum terminale, supports the spinal cord inferiorly.

QuickCheck Questions

2.1 Name the three layers of spinal meninges.

2.2 Where does cerebrospinal fluid circulate in the spinal cord?

Clinical Application Epidural Injections and Spinal Taps

During childbirth, the expectant mother may receive an **epidural block,** a procedure that introduces anesthesia in the epidural space. A thin needle is inserted between two lumbar vertebrae, and the drug is injected into the epidural space. The anesthetic numbs only the spinal nerves of the pelvis and lower limbs and reduces the discomfort the woman feels during the powerful labor contractions of her uterus.

A **spinal tap** is a procedure in which a needle is inserted into the subarachnoid space to withdraw a sample of cerebrospinal fluid. The fluid is then analyzed for the presence of microbes, wastes, and metabolites. To prevent injury to the spinal cord, the needle is inserted into the lower lumbar region inferior to the cord. ∎

In the Lab 2

Materials

- ☐ Spinal cord model
- ☐ Spinal cord chart
- ☐ Compound microscope
- ☐ Prepared slide of transverse section of spinal cord

Procedures

1. Review the spinal meninges in Figure 3.
2. Locate the spinal meninges on the spinal cord model and chart.

3. Use the compound microscope to examine the spinal meninges in transverse section. Move the slide around to survey the preparation. Locate the dura mater, arachnoid mater, and pia mater and the associated spaces between the meninges.

4. Add the spinal meninges to the Sketch to Learn activity you began in Lab Activity 1. ■

Lab Activity 3   Spinal and Peripheral Nerves

Two types of nerves connect PNS sensory receptors and effectors to the CNS: 12 pairs of cranial nerves and 31 pairs of spinal nerves. As their names indicate, cranial nerves connect with the brain and spinal nerves communicate with the spinal cord. As noted at the opening of this exercise, spinal nerves branch into PNS nerves, and it is spinal nerves that make up the axons of PNS sensory and motor neurons.

The two spinal nerves on a given spine segment exit the vertebral canal by passing through an intervertebral foramen between two adjacent vertebrae (shown in Figure 3). Each spinal nerve divides into a series of **peripheral nerves.** The posterior branch is called the **dorsal ramus** and supplies the skin and muscles of the back, and the anterior branch, called the **ventral ramus,** innervates the anterior and lateral skin and muscles. The ventral ramus has additional branches, called the **rami communicantes,** that innervate autonomic ganglions. The rami communicantes consists of two branches: a **white ramus,** which passes ANS preganglionic neurons from the spinal nerve into the ganglion, and a **gray ramus,** which carries ganglionic neurons back into the spinal nerve. Once in the spinal nerve, the ganglionic neurons travel in the ventral or dorsal ramus to their target effector. As their names imply, the white ramus has *myelinated* preganglionic neurons and the gray ramus has *unmyelinated* ganglionic neurons.

The 31 pairs of spinal nerves are named after the vertebral region in which they are associated (Figure 4). There are 8 **cervical nerves** (C_1 through C_8), 12 **thoracic nerves** (T_1 through T_{12}), 5 **lumbar nerves** (L_1 through L_5), 5 **sacral nerves** (S_1 through S_5), and a single **coccygeal nerve** (Co_1). The cervical nerves exit superior to their corresponding vertebrae, except for C_8, which exits inferior to vertebra C_7. The thoracic and lumbar spinal nerves are named after the vertebra immediately above each nerve, which means that thoracic nerve T_1 is inferior to vertebra T_1. Only the spinal nerves that have autonomic neurons carry visceral motor information. Cervical, some lumbar, and coccygeal spinal nerves do not have ANS neurons.

Groups of spinal nerves join in a network called a **plexus.** As muscles form during fetal development, the spinal nerves that supplied the individual muscles interconnect and create a plexus. There are four of these regions: the cervical, brachial, lumbar, and sacral plexuses (Figure 5). Note that thoracic

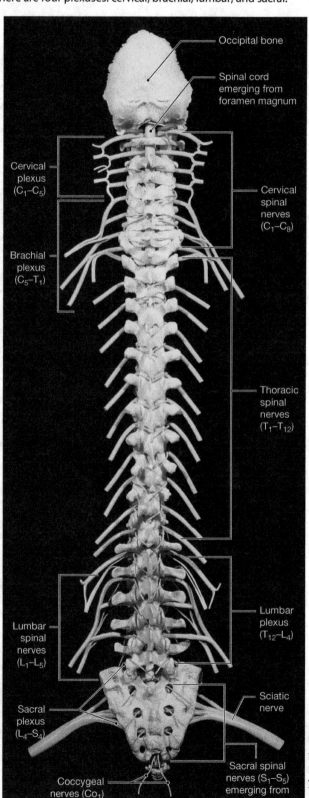

Figure 4 Posterior View of Spinal Nerves Exiting Vertebral Column The yellow wires represent the 31 pairs of spinal nerves. Groups of nerves are interwoven into a network called a plexus. There are four plexuses: cervical, brachial, lumbar, and sacral.

Occipital bone

Spinal cord emerging from foramen magnum

Cervical plexus (C_1–C_5)

Cervical spinal nerves (C_1–C_8)

Brachial plexus (C_5–T_1)

Thoracic spinal nerves (T_1–T_{12})

Lumbar spinal nerves (L_1–L_5)

Lumbar plexus (T_{12}–L_4)

Sacral plexus (L_4–S_4)

Sciatic nerve

Sacral spinal nerves (S_1–S_5) emerging from sacral foramina

Coccygeal nerves (Co_1)

Patrick M. Timmons

279

Figure 5 Peripheral Nerves and Plexuses Spinal nerves branch as peripheral nerves that spread to specific regions of the body. The major peripheral nerves are illustrated in this figure. Groups of peripheral nerves may intertwine into a network called a plexus. There are four major nerve plexuses: cervical, brachial, lumbar, and sacral.

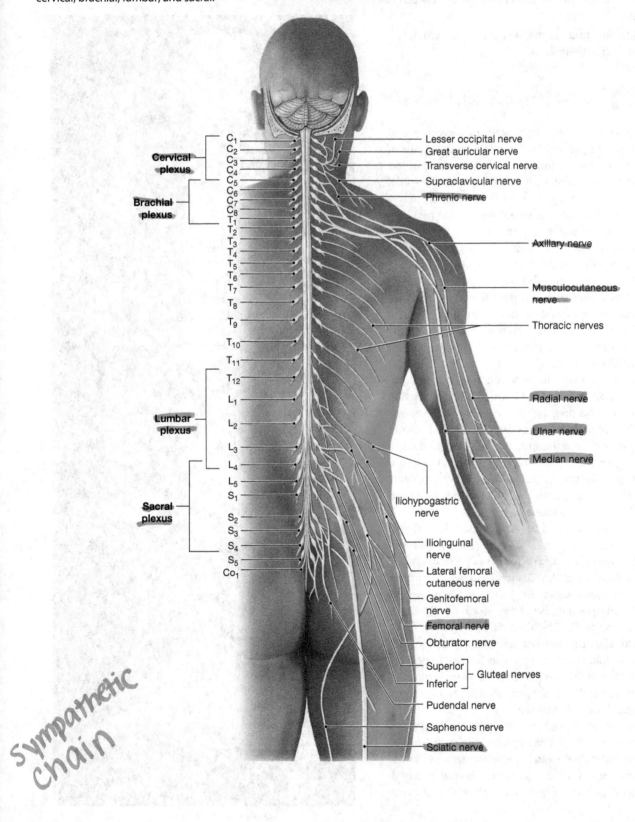

Cervical plexus

Brachial plexus

Lumbar plexus

Sacral plexus

C_1
C_2
C_3
C_4
C_5
C_6
C_7
C_8
T_1
T_2
T_3
T_4
T_5
T_6
T_7
T_8
T_9
T_{10}
T_{11}
T_{12}
L_1
L_2
L_3
L_4
L_5
S_1
S_2
S_3
S_4
S_5
Co_1

Lesser occipital nerve
Great auricular nerve
Transverse cervical nerve
Supraclavicular nerve
Phrenic nerve

Axillary nerve

Musculocutaneous nerve

Thoracic nerves

Radial nerve

Ulnar nerve

Median nerve

Iliohypogastric nerve

Ilioinguinal nerve

Lateral femoral cutaneous nerve

Genitofemoral nerve

Femoral nerve

Obturator nerve

Superior | Gluteal nerves
Inferior |

Pudendal nerve

Saphenous nerve

Sciatic nerve

Sympathetic chain

spinal nerves T_2 through T_{11} are not part of any plexus but instead constitute **intercostal nerves** that enter the spaces between the ribs. The intercostal nerves innervate the intercostal muscles and abdominal muscles and receive sensations from the lateral and anterior trunk.

Cervical Plexus

The eight cervical spinal nerves supply the neck, shoulder, upper limb, and diaphragm. The various branches of the **cervical plexus** contain nerves C_1 through C_4 and parts of C_5. This plexus innervates muscles of the larynx plus the sternocleidomastoid, trapezius, and the skin of the upper chest, shoulder, and ear. Nerves C_3 through C_5, called the phrenic nerves, control the diaphragm, the muscle used for breathing.

Brachial Plexus

The **brachial plexus** includes the parts of spinal nerve C_5 not involved with the cervical plexus plus nerves C_6, C_7, C_8, and T_1. This plexus is more complex than the cervical plexus and branches to innervate the shoulder, the upper limb, and some muscles on the trunk. The major branches of this plexus are the axillary, radial, musculocutaneous, median, and ulnar nerves. The **axillary nerve** (C_5 and C_6) supplies the deltoid and teres minor muscles and the skin of the shoulder. The **radial nerve** (C_5 through T_1) controls the extensor muscles of the upper limb as well as the skin over the posterior and lateral margins of the arm. The **musculocutaneous nerve** (C_5 through C_7) supplies the flexor muscles of the upper limb and the skin of the lateral forearm. The **median nerve** (C_6 through T_1) innervates the flexor muscles of the forearm and digits, the pronator muscles, and the lateral skin of the hand. The **ulnar nerve** (C_8 and T_1) controls the flexor carpi ulnaris muscle of the forearm, other muscles of the hand, and the medial skin of the hand. Notice how overlap occurs in the brachial plexus. For example, spinal nerve C_6 innervates both flexor and extensor muscles.

Lumbar and Sacral Plexuses

The largest nerve network is called the **lumbosacral plexus.** It is a combination of the **lumbar plexus** (T_{12}, L_1 through L_4) and the **sacral plexus** (L_4, L_5, S_1 through S_4). The major nerves of the lumbar plexus innervate the skin and muscles of the abdominal wall, genitalia, and thigh. The **genitofemoral nerve** supplies some of the external genitalia and the anterior and lateral skin of the thigh. The **lateral femoral cutaneous nerve** innervates the skin of the thigh from all aspects except the medial region. The **femoral nerve** controls the muscles of the anterior thigh and the adductor muscles and medial skin of the thigh.

The sacral plexus consists of two major nerves, the sciatic and the pudendal. The **sciatic nerve** descends the posterior

lower limb and sends branches into the posterior thigh muscles and the musculature and skin of the leg. The **pudendal nerve** supplies the muscular floor of the pelvis, the perineum, and parts of the skin of the external genitalia.

QuickCheck Questions

3.1 What are the two groups of nerves in the PNS?

3.2 Which branch of a peripheral nerve innervates the limbs?

3.3 Name the four plexuses in the body.

In the Lab   3

Materials

☐ Spinal cord model

☐ Spinal cord chart

Procedures

1. Review the major spinal nerves and plexuses shown in Figures 4 and 5.

2. Locate each nerve plexus on the spinal cord model and chart.

3. Locate the spinal nerves assigned by your instructor on the spinal cord model. ■

Lab Activity 4   Spinal Reflexes

Reflexes are automatic neural responses to specific stimuli. Most reflexes have a protective function. Touch something hot, and the withdrawal reflex removes your hand to prevent tissue damage. Shine a bright light into someone's eyes, and the pupils constrict to protect the retina from excessive light. Reflexes cause rapid adjustments to maintain homeostasis. The CNS does minimal processing to respond to the stimulus. The sensory and motor components of a reflex are "prewired" and initiate the reflex upon stimulation.

Figure 6 depicts the five steps involved in a typical reflex pathway, called a **reflex arc**. First, a receptor is activated by a stimulus. The receptor in turn activates a sensory neuron that enters the CNS, where the third step, information processing, occurs. The processing is performed at the synapse between the sensory and motor neurons. A conscious thought or recognition of the stimulus is not required to evaluate the sensory input of the reflex. The processing results in activation of a motor neuron that elicits the appropriate action, a response by the effectors. In this basic reflex arc, only two neurons are involved: one sensory and one motor. Complex reflex arcs include **interneurons** between the sensory and motor neurons.

There are many types of reflexes. **Innate** reflexes are the inborn responses of a newborn baby, such as grasping an

Figure 6 Components of a Reflex Arc in the Patellar Reflex A reflex has five main components: a sensory receptor, a sensory neuron, the CNS, a motor neuron, and an effector.

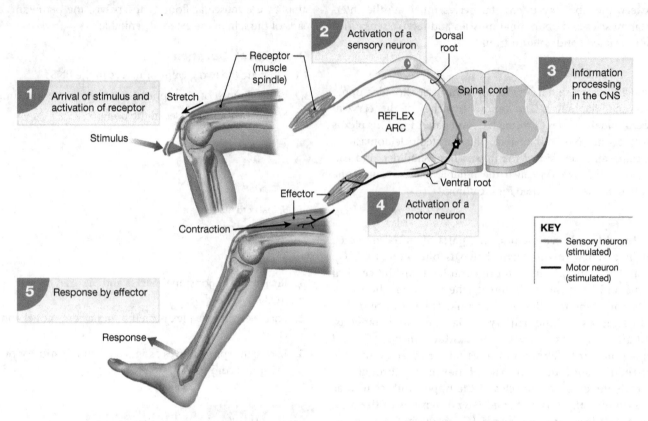

object and suckling the breast for milk. **Cranial** reflexes have pathways in cranial nerves. **Visceral** reflexes pertain to the internal organs. **Spinal** reflexes process information in the spinal cord rather than the brain. **Somatic** reflexes involve skeletal muscles. The number of synapses in a reflex can also be used to classify reflexes. In the arc of a **monosynaptic reflex,** there is only one synapse between the sensory and motor neurons. In the arc of a **polysynaptic reflex,** there are numerous interneurons between sensory and motor neurons. The response of a polysynaptic reflex is more complex and may include both stimulation and inhibition of muscles. Reflexes are used as a diagnostic tool to evaluate the function of specific regions of the brain and spinal cord. An abnormal reflex or the lack of a reflex indicates a loss of neural function resulting from disease or injury.

You are probably familiar with the "knee jerk," a type of **stretch reflex** called the **patellar reflex,** shown in Figure 6. This reflex occurs when the tendon over the patella is hit with a rubber percussion hammer. Tapping on the patellar tendon stretches receptors called **muscle spindles** in the quadriceps muscle group of the anterior thigh. This stimulus evokes a rapid motor reflex to contract the quadriceps and shorten the muscles. **Figure 7** shows other tendons that may be gently struck to study additional somatic reflexes.

QuickCheck Questions

4.1 What are the components of a reflex arc?

4.2 How can reflexes be used diagnostically?

In the Lab 4

Materials

☐ Reflex (percussion) hammer (with rubber head)
☐ Lab partner

Procedures

1. Patellar reflex (Figure 6):
   - Have your partner sit and cross the legs at the knee.
   - On the partner's top leg, gently tap below the patella with the percussion hammer to stimulate the tendon of the rectus femoris muscle.
   - What is the response?
   - How might this reflex help maintain upright posture?

2. Biceps reflex (Figure 7b):
   - This reflex tests the response of the biceps brachii muscle.
   - Have your partner rest an arm on the laboratory benchtop.

Figure 7 Somatic Reflexes Effectors for somatic reflexes are skeletal muscles. Stretch reflexes involve tapping a tendon with a percussion hammer and stimulating the attached muscle.

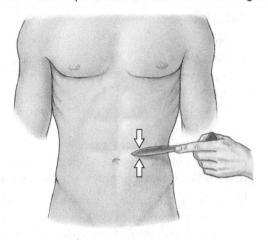

a Abdominal reflex. Gently stroking the sides of the abdomen causes the abdominal reflex, an example of a superficial reflex.

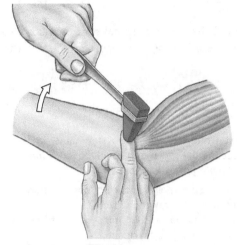

b Biceps reflex. Tapping the tendon initiates a stretch reflex.

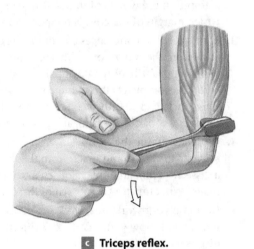

c Triceps reflex.

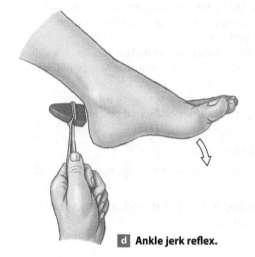

d Ankle jerk reflex.

- Place a finger over the tendon of the biceps brachii and gently tap your finger with the percussion hammer.
- What is the response?

3. Triceps reflex (Figure 7c):

- This reflex tests the response of the triceps brachii muscle.
- Loosely support one of your partner's forearms.
- Gently tap the tendon of the triceps brachii at the posterior elbow.
- What is the response?

4. Ankle calcanean reflex (Figure 7d):

- This reflex tests the response of the gastrocnemius muscle when the calcanean (Achilles) tendon is stretched.
- Have your partner sit in a chair and extend one leg forward so that the foot is off the floor.
- Gently tap the calcanean tendon with the percussion hammer.
- What is the response? ■

Lab Activity 5 Dissection of the Spinal Cord

Dissecting a preserved sheep or cow spinal cord provides you the opportunity to examine the meningeal layers and the internal anatomy.

⚠ Safety Alert: Dissecting the Spinal Cord

You *must* practice the highest level of laboratory safety while handling and dissecting the spinal cord. Keep the following guidelines in mind during the dissection.

1. Be sure to use only a *preserved* spinal cord for dissection because fresh spinal cords can carry disease.
2. Wear gloves and safety glasses to protect yourself from the fixatives used to preserve the specimen.
3. Do not dispose of the fixative from your specimen. You will later store the specimen in the fixative to keep the specimen moist and to prevent it from decaying.
4. Be extremely careful when using a scalpel or other sharp instrument. Always direct cutting and scissor motions away from you to prevent an accident if the instrument slips on moist tissue.
5. Before cutting a given tissue, make sure it is free from underlying and/or adjacent tissues so that they will not be accidentally severed.
6. Never discard tissue in the sink or trash. Your instructor will inform you of the proper disposal procedure. ▲

QuickCheck Questions

5.1 What safety equipment is required for the spinal cord dissection?

5.2 Describe the disposal procedure as discussed by your laboratory instructor.

In the Lab 5

Materials

- ☐ Gloves
- ☐ Safety glasses
- ☐ Segment of preserved sheep or cow spinal cord
- ☐ Dissection pan
- ☐ Dissection pins
- ☐ Scissors
- ☐ Scalpel
- ☐ Forceps
- ☐ Blunt probe

Procedures

Put on gloves and safety glasses before opening the container of preserved spinal cord segments or handling one of the segments.

1. Lay the spinal cord on the dissection pan and cut a thin cross section about 2 cm (0.75 in.) thick. Lay this cross section flat on the dissection pan and observe the internal anatomy. Use Figure 8 as a guide to help locate the various anatomical features of the spinal cord.
2. Identify the gray horns, central canal, and white columns. What type of tissue is found in the gray horns? What type is found in the white columns? How can you determine which margin of the cord is the posterior margin?
3. Locate the spinal meninges by pulling the outer tissues away from the spinal cord with a forceps and blunt probe. Slip your probe between the meninges on the lateral spinal cord. Cut completely through the meninges and gently peel them back to expose the ventral and dorsal roots. How does the dorsal root differ in appearance from the ventral root?
4. Closely examine the meninges. With your probe, separate the arachnoid mater from the dura mater. With a dissection pin, attempt to loosen a free edge of the pia mater. What function does each of these membranes serve?
5. Clean up your work area, wash the dissection pan and tools, and follow your instructor's directions for proper disposal of the specimen. ■

Figure 8 Sheep Spinal Cord Dissection The sheep spinal cord in this transverse section shows its internal organization and the three spinal meninges.

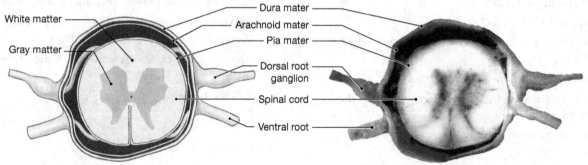

Shawn Miller & Mark Nielsen/Pearson Education

Name _____

Date _____

Section _____

The Spinal Cord, Spinal Nerves, and Reflexes

A. Matching

Match each term in the left column with its correct description from the right column.

_____ 1. lateral gray horn
_____ 2. bundle of axons
_____ 3. rami communicantes
_____ 4. subarachnoid space
_____ 5. ventral root
_____ 6. dorsal ramus
_____ 7. dorsal root ganglion
_____ 8. conus medullaris
_____ 9. endoneurium
_____ 10. dorsal root

A. site of cerebrospinal fluid circulation
B. sensory branch entering spinal cord
C. surrounds axons of peripheral nerve
D. contains visceral motor cell bodies
E. tapered end of spinal cord
F. fascicle
G. posterior branch of a spinal nerve
H. motor branch exiting spinal cord
I. leads to autonomic ganglion
J. contains sensory cell bodies

B. Labeling

1. Label the sectional anatomy of the spinal cord in Figure 9.

Figure 9 Anatomy of the Spinal Cord

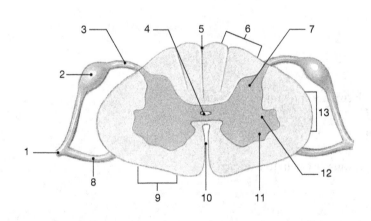

1. _____
2. dorsal root ganglion
3. dorsal root
4. central canal
5. _____
6. _____
7. posterior gray horn
8. ventral root
9. _____
10. _____
11. Anterior gray horn
12. lateral gray horn
13. _____

C. Short-Answer Questions

1. Describe the organization of white and gray matter in the spinal cord.

2. Describe the spinal meninges.

3. Discuss the major nerves of the brachial plexus.

4. List the five basic steps of a reflex.

D. Analysis and Application

1. Starting in the spinal cord, trace a motor pathway to the adductor muscles of the thigh. Include the spinal cord root, spinal nerve, nerve plexus, and specific peripheral nerve involved in the pathway.

2. Compare the types of neurons that synapse in the posterior, lateral, and anterior gray horns of the spinal cord.

E. Clinical Challenge

1. How can an injury to a peripheral nerve cause loss of both sensory and motor functions?

2. How does the stretch reflex cause the quadriceps femoris muscle group to contract?

3. A woman injures her neck in a car accident and now has difficulty breathing. Which spinal nerves may be involved in this case?

Anatomy of the Brain
Wish List

Locate and identify structures of the brain and cranial nerves using models or/and fixed specimens. For cranial nerves, you must know their name and number. Remember that you will be required to be able to identify the structures marked with an * in the sheep brain.

✓	Structure	Description
	Brain	
	Cerebrum	Telencephalon
	cerebral hemisphere	
	*corpus callosum	
	lateral ventricles	
	choroid plexus	
	gyri	
	sulci	
	longitudinal fissure	
	transverse fissure	
	frontal lobe	
	parietal lobe	
	occipital lobe	
	temporal lobe	

✓	Structure	Description
	Epithalamus	
	pineal gland	
	third ventricle	

✓	Structure	Description
	Thalamus	Diencephalon
	<u>Hypothalamus</u>	
	infundibulum	
	pituitary gland	
	*optic chiasma	
	optic tract	
	mammillary body	

✓	Structure	Description
	Midbrain	Mesencephalon
	*corpora quadrigemina	
	*superior colliculi	
	*inferior colliculi	

✓	Structure	Description
	***Cerebellum**	Metencephalon
	*arbor vitae	
	cerebral aqueduct	

	*Pons	Metencephalon
	fourth ventricle	

	*Medulla oblongata	Myelencephalon

✓	Structure	Description	Innervation
	Cranial Nerves		
	Olfactory I		olfactory epithelium
	Optic II		retina of eye
	Occulomotor III		eye muscles
	Trochlear IV		eye muscle
	Trigeminal V		eye and jaw area
	Abducens VI		eye muscle
	Facial VII		face muscles
	Vestibulocochlear (Acoustic) VIII		inner ear
	Glossopharyngeal IX		tongue + pharynx
	Vagus X		visceral organs
	Accessory (Spinal Accessory) XI		pharynx + neck muscles
	Hypoglossal XII		tongue muscles

Anatomy of the Brain

Learning Outcomes

On completion of this exercise, you should be able to:

1. Name the three meninges that cover the brain.

2. Describe the extensions of the dura mater.

3. Identify the six major regions of the brain and a basic function of each.

4. Identify the surface features of each region of the brain.

5. Identify the 12 pairs of cranial nerves.

6. Identify the anatomy of a dissected sheep brain.

Lab Activities

1. Cranial Meninges and Ventricles of the Brain

2. Regions of the Brain

3. Cranial Nerves

4. Sheep Brain Dissection

Clinical Application

Hydrocephalus

The brain, which occupies the cranial cavity, is one of the largest organs in the body. The adult brain weighs approximately 1.4 kg (3 pounds) and has an average volume of 1,200 cc; the brain of a newborn weighs only 350 to 400 g. Adult males tend to have larger bodies and therefore have larger brains than females, but of course, this size difference offers no intellectual advantage to the males.

Approximately 100 billion neurons in the brain interconnect with over 1 trillion synapses as vast biological circuitry that no electronic computer has yet to surpass. Every second, the brain performs a huge number of calculations, interpretations, and visceral-activity adjustments and coordinations to maintain homeostasis.

The brain is organized into six major regions: cerebrum (se-RĒ-brum or SER-e-brum), diencephalon (dī-en-SEF-a-lon), mesencephalon, pons, medulla oblongata, and cerebellum (Figure 1). The medulla oblongata, pons, and mesencephalon (midbrain) are collectively called the **brain stem.** Some anatomists also include the diencephalon as part of the brain stem.

Need More Practice and Review?

Build your knowledge—and confidence!—in the Study Area of MasteringA&P® at www.masteringaandp.com with Pre-lab Quizzes, Post-lab Quizzes, Practice Anatomy Lab™ (PAL™) 3.0 virtual anatomy practice tool, PhysioEx™ 9.0 laboratory simulations, and A&P Flix™ with Quizzes.

PAL practice anatomy lab For this lab exercise, follow these navigation paths:
- PAL>Human Cadaver>Nervous System>Central Nervous System
- PAL>Anatomical Models>Nervous System>Central Nervous System

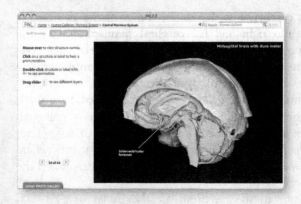

Figure 1 The Human Brain The major regions of the human brain.

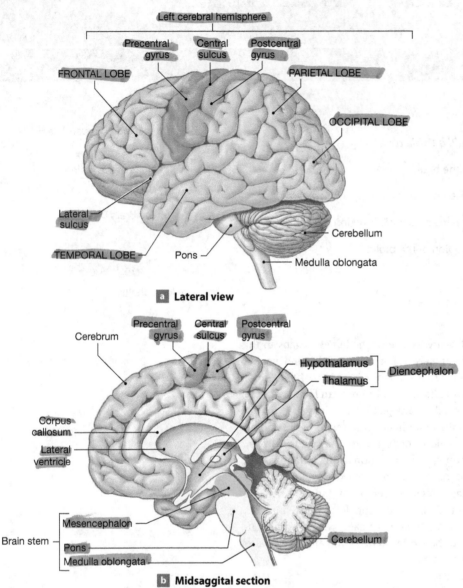

a Lateral view

b Midsaggital section

diencephalon (Figure 1b). Inferior to the diencephalon is the **mesencephalon** (midbrain) of the brain stem. The **pons** is the large, swollen region of the brain stem just inferior to the mesencephalon, and the **medulla oblongata** is the most inferior part of the brain stem, connecting the brain to the spinal cord. The **cerebellum** is the oval mass posterior to the brain stem.

Cranial Meninges and Ventricles of the Brain

Cranial Meninges

The brain is encased in layers of tough, protective **cranial meninges.** Circulating between certain meningeal layers, **cerebrospinal fluid (CSF)** cushions the brain and prevents it from contacting the cranial bones during a head injury, much like a car's airbag prevents a passenger from hitting the dashboard. The cranial meninges are anatomically similar to, and continuous with, the spinal meninges of the spinal cord. Like their spinal counterparts, the cranial meninges consist of three layers: dura mater, arachnoid mater, and pia mater (**Figure 2**).

Make a Prediction

Which body fluid is filtered to produce CSF?

The **cerebrum** is the largest region of the brain. It is divided into right and left **cerebral hemispheres** by the deep groove known as the **longitudinal fissure.** A left cerebral hemisphere is shown in Figure 1a. The hemispheres are covered with a folded **cerebral cortex** (*cortex,* bark or rind) of gray matter, where neurons are not myelinated. Each small fold of the cerebral cortex is called a **gyrus** (JĪ-rus; plural *gyri*), and each shallow groove is called a **sulcus** (SUL-kus; plural *sulci*). Deep in the cerebrum is the brain's white matter, where myelinated neurons that occur in thick bands interconnect the various regions of the brain.

Inferior to the cerebrum are the **thalamus** (THAL-a-mus) and **hypothalamus,** which together make up the

The **dura mater** (DOO-ruh MĀ-ter; *dura,* tough + *mater,* mother), the outer meningeal covering, consists of an **endosteal layer** fused with the periosteum of the cranial bones and a **meningeal layer** that faces the arachnoid mater. The endosteal layer is referred to as the *outer dural layer,* and the meningeal layer is

Study Tip A Sea Horse's Guide to the Brain

When examining the brain in sagittal section, most people notice how the brain stem and diencephalon form the shape of a sea horse. The pons is the horse's belly, the mesencephalon the neck, the diencephalon the head, and the medulla oblongata the tail. Imagine the sea horse is wearing the cerebellum as a backpack and the cerebrum as a very large hat. ■

Figure 2 Brain, Cranium, and Meninges The brain is protected by the cranium and by a three-layered covering called the cranial meninges.

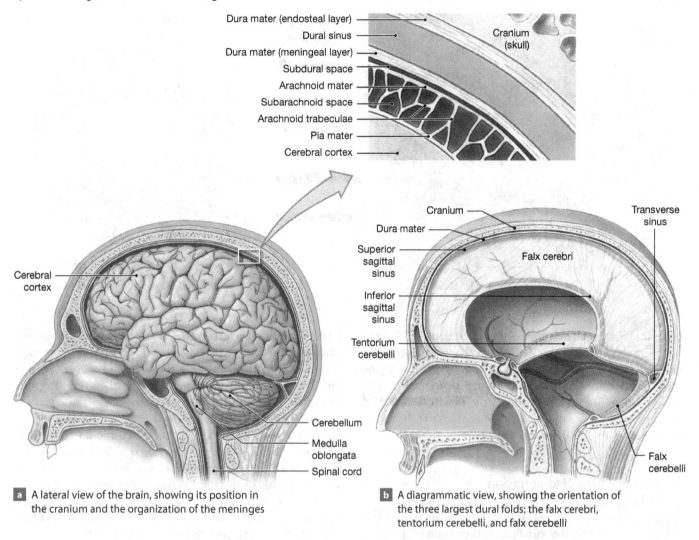

Dura mater (endosteal layer)
Dural sinus
Dura mater (meningeal layer)
Subdural space
Arachnoid mater
Subarachnoid space
Arachnoid trabeculae
Pia mater
Cerebral cortex

Cranium (skull)

Cerebral cortex

Cerebellum
Medulla oblongata
Spinal cord

Cranium
Dura mater
Superior sagittal sinus
Inferior sagittal sinus
Tentorium cerebelli

Transverse sinus
Falx cerebri
Falx cerebelli

a A lateral view of the brain, showing its position in the cranium and the organization of the meninges

b A diagrammatic view, showing the orientation of the three largest dural folds: the falx cerebri, tentorium cerebelli, and falx cerebelli

referred to as the *inner dural layer*. Between the two layers are large blood sinuses, collectively called **dural sinuses,** that drain blood from cranial veins into the jugular veins. The **superior** and **inferior sagittal sinuses** are large veins in the dura mater between the two hemispheres of the cerebrum. The **transverse sinus** is in the dura mater between the cerebrum and the cerebellum. Between the dura mater and the underlying arachnoid mater is the **subdural space.**

Deep to the dura mater is the **arachnoid** (a-RAK-noyd; *arachno,* spider) **mater,** named after the weblike connection this membrane has with the underlying pia mater. The arachnoid mater forms a smooth covering over the brain.

On the surface of the brain is the **pia** (PĒ-uh; *pia,* delicate) **mater,** which contains many blood vessels supplying the brain. Between the arachnoid mater and pia mater is the **subarachnoid space,** where the CSF circulates.

The dura mater has extensions that help stabilize the brain (Figure 2b). A midsagittal fold in the dura mater forms the **falx cerebri** (FALKS SER-e-brī; *falx,* sickle shaped) and separates the right and left hemispheres of the cerebrum. Posteriorly, the dura mater folds again as the **tentorium cerebelli** (ten-TŌ-rē-um ser-e-BEL-ē; *tentorium,* a covering) and separates the cerebellum from the cerebrum. The **falx cerebelli** is a dural fold between the hemispheres of the cerebellum.

Ventricles

Deep in the brain are four chambers called **ventricles** (Figure 3). Two **lateral ventricles,** one in each cerebral hemisphere, extend deep into the cerebrum as horseshoe-shaped chambers. At the midline of the brain, the lateral ventricles are separated by a thin membrane called the **septum pellucidum** (pe-LOO-si-dum; *pellucid,* transparent). A brain sectioned

Figure 3 Ventricles of the Brain The orientation and extent of the ventricles as they would appear if the brain were transparent.

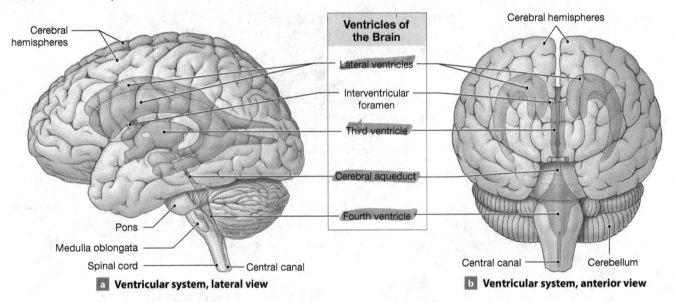

Ventricles of the Brain
Lateral ventricles
Interventricular foramen
Third ventricle
Cerebral aqueduct
Fourth ventricle

Cerebral hemispheres

Pons
Medulla oblongata
Spinal cord
Central canal

a **Ventricular system, lateral view**

Cerebral hemispheres

Central canal
Cerebellum

b **Ventricular system, anterior view**

at the midsagittal plane exposes this membrane. CSF circulates from the lateral ventricles through the **interventricular foramen** (also called the *foramen of Monro*) and enters the **third ventricle,** a small chamber in the diencephalon. CSF in the third ventricle passes through the **cerebral aqueduct** (*aqueduct of the midbrain* or *aqueduct of Sylvius*) and enters the **fourth ventricle** between the brain stem and the cerebellum.

Clinical Application Hydrocephalus

The choroid plexus of an adult brain produces approximately 500 mL of cerebrospinal fluid daily, constantly replacing the 150 mL that circulates in the ventricles and subarachnoid space. Because CSF is constantly being made, a volume equal to that produced must be removed from the central nervous system to prevent a buildup of fluid pressure in the ventricles. In an infant, if CSF production exceeds CSF reabsorption, the increase in cranial pressure expands the unfused skull, creating a condition called *hydrocephalus*. There are two types of hydrocephalus; internal and external. Internal hydrocephalus occurs when CSF accumulates in the ventricles inside the brain. This form of hydrocephalus is almost always fatal because of damaging distortion of the brain tissue. External hydrocephalus is the buildup of CSF in the subdural space, resulting in an enlarged skull and possible brain damage caused by high fluid pressure on the delicate neural tissues. Surgical treatment of external hydrocephalus involves installation of small tubes called shunts to drain the excess CSF and reduce intracranial pressure. ■

In the fourth ventricle, two **lateral apertures** and a single **median aperture** direct CSF laterally to the exterior of the brain and spinal cord and into the subarachnoid space. CSF then circulates around the brain and spinal cord and is reabsorbed at **arachnoid granulations,** which project into the veins of the dural sinuses (**Figure 4**).

Inside each ventricle is a specialized capillary called the **choroid plexus** (KŌ-royd PLEK-sus; *choroid*, vascular coat + *plexus*, network) where cerebrospinal fluid is produced. The choroid plexus of the third ventricle has two folds that pass through the interventricular foramen and expand to line the floor of the lateral ventricles. The choroid plexus of the fourth ventricle lies on the posterior wall of the ventricle.

QuickCheck Questions

1.1 What are the functions of the cranial meninges?

1.2 Between which meningeal layers does CSF circulate?

1.3 Where does CSF circulate, and where is it returned to the blood?

In the Lab   1

Materials

☐ Brain model

☐ Brain chart

☐ Ventricular system model

☐ Preserved and sectioned human brain (if available)

Figure 4 Formation and Circulation of Cerebrospinal Fluid

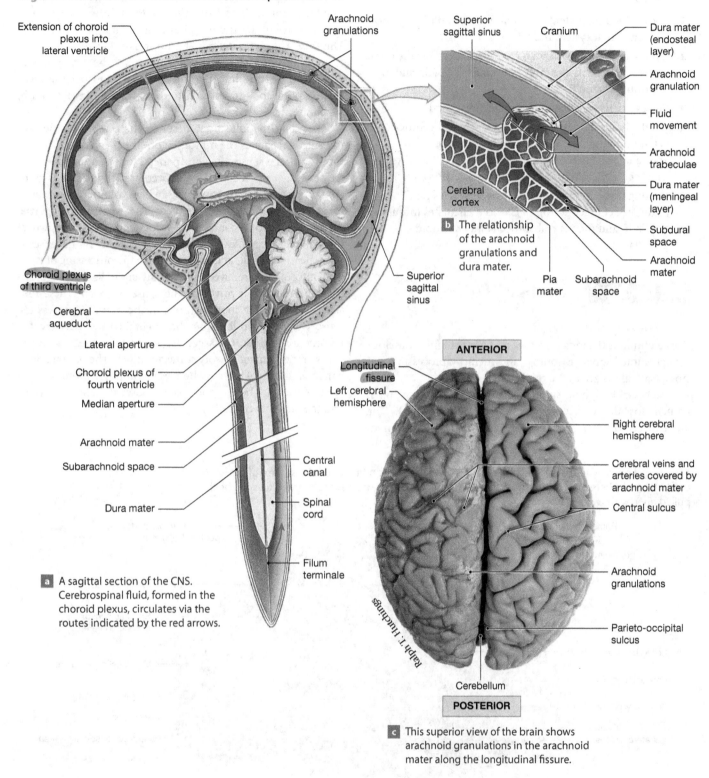

Extension of choroid plexus into lateral ventricle

Arachnoid granulations

Superior sagittal sinus

Cranium

Dura mater (endosteal layer)

Arachnoid granulation

Fluid movement

Arachnoid trabeculae

Dura mater (meningeal layer)

Subdural space

Arachnoid mater

Cerebral cortex

b The relationship of the arachnoid granulations and dura mater.

Pia mater

Subarachnoid space

Choroid plexus of third ventricle

Cerebral aqueduct

Lateral aperture

Choroid plexus of fourth ventricle

Median aperture

Arachnoid mater

Subarachnoid space

Dura mater

Superior sagittal sinus

Central canal

Spinal cord

Filum terminale

a A sagittal section of the CNS. Cerebrospinal fluid, formed in the choroid plexus, circulates via the routes indicated by the red arrows.

ANTERIOR

Longitudinal fissure

Left cerebral hemisphere

Right cerebral hemisphere

Cerebral veins and arteries covered by arachnoid mater

Central sulcus

Arachnoid granulations

Parieto-occipital sulcus

Ralph T. Hutchings

Cerebellum

POSTERIOR

c This superior view of the brain shows arachnoid granulations in the arachnoid mater along the longitudinal fissure.

Procedures

1. Locate the dura mater, arachnoid mater, and pia mater on the ventricular system model.
2. On the brain model or preserved brain, examine the dura mater and identify the falx cerebri, falx cerebelli, and tentorium cerebelli.
3. Review the ventricular system in Figures 3 and 4.
4. On the brain model, observe how the lateral ventricles extend into the cerebrum. If your model is detailed enough, locate the interventricular foramen. Identify the third ventricle, cerebral aqueduct, and fourth ventricle.
5. Starting from one of the two lateral ventricles on the brain model, trace a drop of CSF as it circulates through the brain and then is reabsorbed at an arachnoid granulation. ■

Lab Activity 2   Regions of the Brain

Cerebrum

The cerebrum is the most complex part of the brain. Conscious thought, intellectual reasoning, and memory processing and storage all take place in the cerebrum.

Each cerebral hemisphere consists of five lobes, most named for the overlying cranial bone (Figure 5). The anterior cerebrum is the **frontal lobe,** and the prominent

central sulcus, located approximately midposterior, separates the frontal lobe from the **parietal lobe.** The **occipital lobe** lies under the occipital bone of the posterior skull. The **lateral sulcus** defines the boundary between the large frontal lobe and the **temporal lobe** of the lower lateral cerebrum. Cutting into the lateral sulcus and peeling away the temporal lobe reveals a fifth lobe, the **insula** (IN-sū-luh; *insula,* island).

Regional specializations occur in the cerebrum. The central sulcus separates the motor region of the cerebrum (frontal lobe) from the sensory region (parietal lobe). Immediately anterior to the central sulcus is the **precentral gyrus.** This gyrus contains the primary motor cortex, where voluntary commands to skeletal muscles are generated. The **postcentral gyrus,** on the parietal lobe, contains the primary sensory cortex, where the general sense of touch is perceived. The other four senses—sight, hearing, smell, and taste—involve the processing of complex information received from many more sensory neurons than the number involved in the sense of touch. These four senses thus require more neurons in the brain to process the sensory signals, and therefore the cerebral cortex areas devoted to processing these messages are larger than the postcentral gyrus of the primary sensory cortex for touch. The occipital lobe contains the visual cortex, where visual impulses from the eyes are interpreted. The temporal lobe houses the auditory cortex and the olfactory cortex.

Figure 5 Lobes of a Cerebral Hemisphere Major anatomical landmarks on the surface of the left cerebral hemisphere. Association areas are colored. To expose the insula, the lateral sulcus has been pulled open with two retractors.

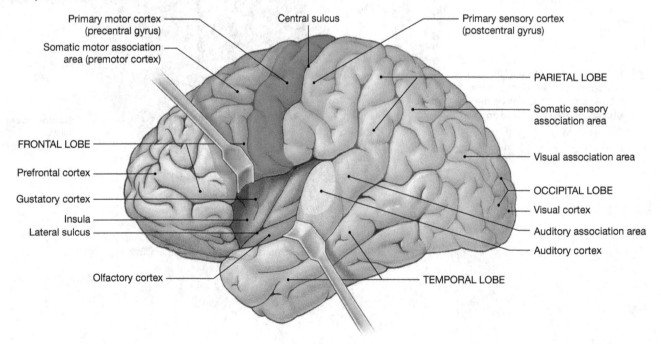

Figure 5 also shows numerous **association areas,** regions that either interpret sensory information from more than one sensory cortex or integrate motor commands into an appropriate response. The **premotor cortex** is the somatic motor association area of the anterior frontal lobe. Auditory and visual association areas occur near the corresponding sensory cortex in the occipital lobe.

Deep structures of the cerebrum are visible when the brain is sectioned, as in Figures 6 and 7. The cerebral hemispheres are connected by a deep, thick tract of white matter called the **corpus callosum** (kōr-pus ka-LŌ-sum; *corpus*, body + *callosum*, hard). This structure, which bridges the two hemispheres at the base of the longitudinal fissure, is easily identified as the curved white structure at the base of the cerebrum. The inferior portion of the corpus callosum is the **fornix** (FOR-niks), a white tract connecting deep structures of the limbic system, the "emotional" brain. The fornix narrows anteriorly and meets the **anterior commissure** (kom-MIS-sur), another tract of white matter connecting the cerebral hemispheres.

In each cerebral hemisphere, paired masses of gray matter called **basal nuclei** are involved in automating voluntary muscle contractions. Each basal nucleus consists of a medial **caudate nucleus** and a lateral **lentiform nucleus** (see Figures 6 and 7). The latter is made up of two parts: a **putamen** (pū-TĀ-men; shell) and a **globus pallidus** (glō-bus PAL-i-dus; *globus*, ball + *pallidus*, pale). At the tip of the caudate nucleus is the **amygdaloid** (ah-MIG-da-loyd; almond) **body.** Between the caudate nucleus and the lentiform nucleus lies the **internal capsule,** a band of white matter that connects the cerebrum to the diencephalon, brain stem, and cerebellum.

Diencephalon: The Thalamus and Hypothalamus

The diencephalon is embedded in the cerebrum and is exposed only at the inferior aspect of the brain. The thalamus region of the diencephalon maintains a crude sense of awareness. All sensory impulses except smell and proprioception (the sense of muscle, bone, and joint position) pass into the thalamus and are relayed to the proper sensory cortex for interpretation. Nonessential sensory data are filtered out by the thalamus and do not reach the sensory cortex. In sagittal section, the **interthalamic adhesion,** also called the *massa intermedia*, is an oval structure in the diencephalon that connects the right and left sides of the thalamus (Figure 7). The **pineal** (PIN-ē-ul) **gland** is the cone-shaped structure superior to the mesencephalon positioned between the cerebrum and the cerebellum.

The hypothalamus is the floor of the diencephalon. On the inferior surface of the brain, a pair of rounded **mamillary** (MAM-i-lar-ē; *mammilla*, little breast) **bodies** are visible inferior to the hypothalamus (Figure 7). These bodies are hypothalamic nuclei that control eating reflexes for licking, chewing, sucking, and swallowing. Anterior to the mamillary bodies is the **infundibulum** (in-fun-DIB-ū-lum; *infundibulum*, funnel), the stalk that attaches the **pituitary gland** to the hypothalamus.

Mesencephalon (Midbrain)

The mesencephalon (Figure 8; also see Figure 7) is posteriorly covered by the cerebrum. Posterior to the cerebral aqueduct is the **corpora quadrigemina** (KOR-pōr-uh qui-dri-JEM-i-nuh), a series of four bulges next to the pineal gland of the diencephalon. The two members of the superior pair of bulges are the **superior colliculi** (ko-LĪK-u-lē; *colliculus*, small hill), which function as a visual reflex center to move the eyeballs and the head, to keep an object centered on the retina of the eye. The two members of the inferior pair of bulges are the **inferior colliculi,** which function as an auditory reflex center to move the head, to locate and follow sounds. The anterior mesencephalon between the pons and the hypothalamus consists of the **cerebral peduncles** (*peduncles*, little feet), a group of white fibers connecting the cerebral cortex with other parts of the brain.

Pons

The pons is located inferior to the mesencephalon (Figures 7 and 8). The pons functions as a relay station to direct sensory information to the thalamus and cerebellum. It also contains certain sensory, somatic motor, and autonomic cranial nerve nuclei.

Medulla Oblongata

The medulla oblongata is the inferior part of the brain stem and is continuous with the spinal cord (Figures 7 and 8). Sensory information in ascending tracts in the spinal cord enter the brain at the medulla oblongata, and motor commands in descending tracts pass through the medulla oblongata and into the spinal cord. The anterior surface of the medulla oblongata has two prominent folds called **pyramids** where some motor tracts cross over, or *decussate*, to the opposite side of the body. The medulla oblongata also functions as an autonomic center for visceral functions. Nuclei in this portion of the brain are vital reflex centers for the regulation of cardiovascular, respiratory, and digestive activities.

Cerebellum

The cerebellum (Figure 9) is inferior to the occipital lobe of the cerebrum and is covered by a layer called the **cerebellar cortex.** Small folds on the cerebellar cortex are called **folia** (FŌ-lē-uh; *folia*, leaves; singular *folium*). The cerebellum is divided into right and left **cerebellar hemispheres,** which are separated by a narrow **vermis** (VER-mis; *vermis*, worm). Each cerebellar hemisphere consists of two lobes: a smaller **anterior lobe,** which is directly inferior to the cerebrum, and a

Figure 6 The Basal Nuclei The basal nuclei are masses of gray matter deep in the cerebrum.

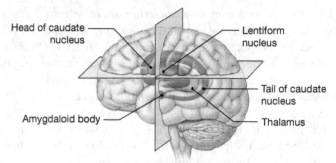

Head of caudate nucleus

Lentiform nucleus

Tail of caudate nucleus

Thalamus

Amygdaloid body

a The relative positions of the basal nuclei in the brain

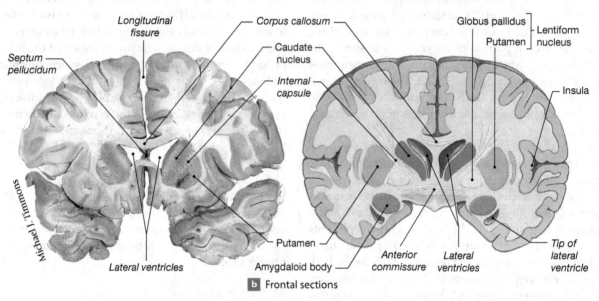

Longitudinal fissure

Corpus callosum

Globus pallidus ⎱ Lentiform
Putamen ⎰ nucleus

Septum pellucidum

Caudate nucleus

Internal capsule

Insula

Michael J. Timmons

Putamen

Lateral ventricles

Amygdaloid body

Anterior commissure

Lateral ventricles

Tip of lateral ventricle

b Frontal sections

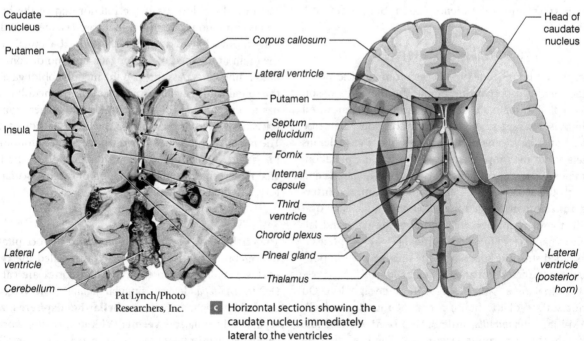

Caudate nucleus

Putamen

Corpus callosum

Head of caudate nucleus

Lateral ventricle

Insula

Putamen

Septum pellucidum

Fornix

Internal capsule

Third ventricle

Choroid plexus

Lateral ventricle

Pineal gland

Cerebellum

Thalamus

Lateral ventricle (posterior horn)

Pat Lynch/Photo Researchers, Inc.

c Horizontal sections showing the caudate nucleus immediately lateral to the ventricles

Figure 7 The Brain in Midsagittal and Frontal Sections Midsagittal and frontal sections show the relationship among internal structures of the brain.

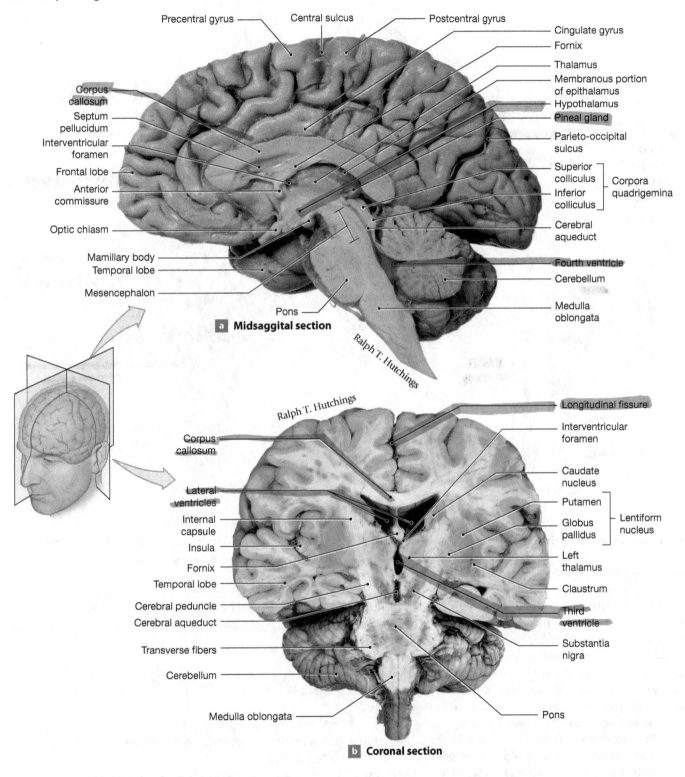

Precentral gyrus

Central sulcus

Postcentral gyrus

Cingulate gyrus

Fornix

Thalamus

Membranous portion of epithalamus

Hypothalamus

Pineal gland

Parieto-occipital sulcus

Superior colliculus

Inferior colliculus

Corpora quadrigemina

Cerebral aqueduct

Fourth ventricle

Cerebellum

Medulla oblongata

Corpus callosum

Septum pellucidum

Interventricular foramen

Frontal lobe

Anterior commissure

Optic chiasm

Mamillary body

Temporal lobe

Mesencephalon

Pons

a Midsaggital section

Ralph T. Hutchings

Ralph T. Hutchings

Corpus callosum

Lateral ventricles

Internal capsule

Insula

Fornix

Temporal lobe

Cerebral peduncle

Cerebral aqueduct

Transverse fibers

Cerebellum

Medulla oblongata

Longitudinal fissure

Interventricular foramen

Caudate nucleus

Putamen

Globus pallidus

Lentiform nucleus

Left thalamus

Claustrum

Third ventricle

Substantia nigra

Pons

b Coronal section

Figure 8 Brain Stem and Diencephalon The medulla, pons, and mesencephalon constitute the brain stem.

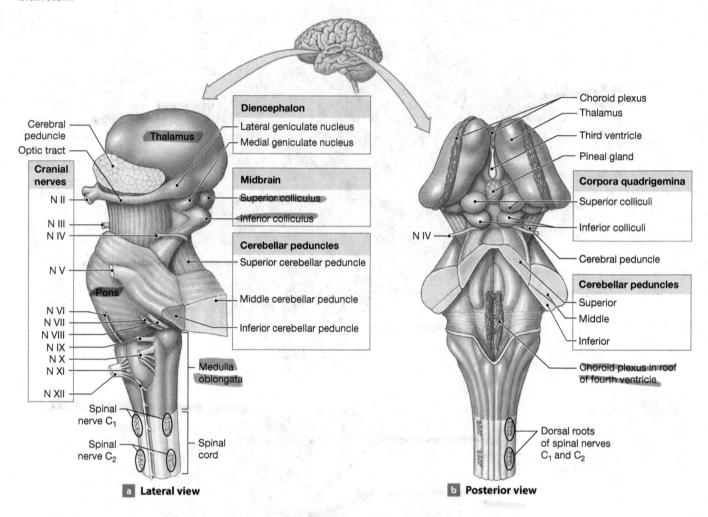

a Lateral view

b Posterior view

posterior lobe. The **primary fissure** separates the anterior and posterior cerebellar lobes. In a sagittal section, a smaller **flocculonodular** (flok-ū-lō-NOD-ū-lar) **lobe** is visible where the anterior wall of the cerebellum faces the pons.

In a sagittal section, the white matter of the cerebellum is apparent. Because this tissue is highly branched, it is called the **arbor vitae** (ar-bor VĪ-tē; *arbor*, tree + *vitae*, life). In the middle of the arbor vitae are the **cerebellar nuclei,** which function in the regulation of involuntary skeletal muscle contraction. The cortex of the cerebellum contains large neurons called **Purkinje** (pur-KIN-jē) cells that branch extensively and synapse with up to 200,000 other neurons.

The cerebellum is primarily involved in the coordination of somatic motor functions, which means principally skeletal muscle contractions. Adjustments to postural muscles occur when impulses from the cranial nerve of the inner ear pass into the flocculonodular lobe, the part of the cerebellum where information concerning equilibrium is processed. Learned muscle patterns, such as those involved in serving a tennis ball or playing the guitar, are stored and processed in the cerebellum.

QuickCheck Questions

2.1 What are the six major regions of the brain?

2.2 How are the cerebral hemispheres connected to each other?

2.3 Where is the mesencephalon?

In the Lab 2

Materials

- ☐ Brain model (midsagittal, frontal, and horizontal sections)
- ☐ Brain chart
- ☐ Preserved and sectioned human brain (if available)
- ☐ Compound microscope
- ☐ Microscope slide of cerebellar cortex

Figure 9 Cerebellum The cerebellum is posterior to the brain stem.

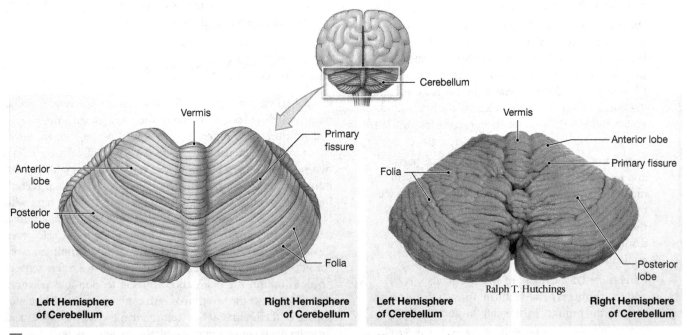

Cerebellum

Vermis

Primary fissure

Anterior lobe

Posterior lobe

Folia

Left Hemisphere of Cerebellum

Right Hemisphere of Cerebellum

Vermis

Anterior lobe

Primary fissure

Folia

Posterior lobe

Ralph T. Hutchings

Left Hemisphere of Cerebellum

Right Hemisphere of Cerebellum

a The posterior, superior surface of the cerebellum, showing major anatomical landmarks and regions

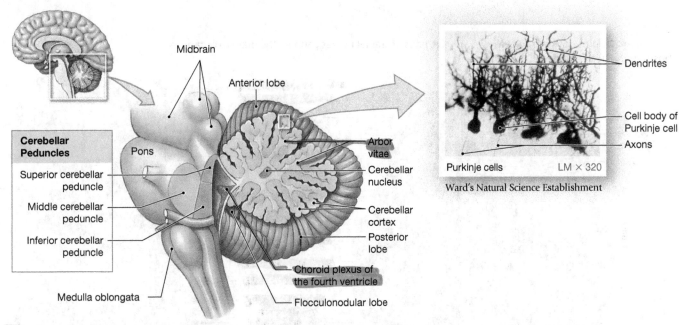

Midbrain

Anterior lobe

Dendrites

Cell body of Purkinje cell

Axons

Purkinje cells   LM × 320

Ward's Natural Science Establishment

Cerebellar Peduncles

Pons

Superior cerebellar peduncle

Middle cerebellar peduncle

Inferior cerebellar peduncle

Medulla oblongata

Arbor vitae

Cerebellar nucleus

Cerebellar cortex

Posterior lobe

Choroid plexus of the fourth ventricle

Flocculonodular lobe

b A sectional view of the cerebellum, showing the arrangement of gray matter and white matter

Procedures

1. Review the brain anatomy in Figures 5 through 9.
2. On the brain model, identify the following:

   ▪ *Cerebrum* Note how the longitudinal fissure separates it into two cerebral hemispheres. Identify the five lobes of each hemisphere, along with the central sulcus, precentral gyri, and postcentral gyri. View the brain model in midsagittal section and identify the corpus callosum, fornix, and anterior commissure. In a frontal section and a horizontal section, locate the internal capsule, lentiform nucleus, and caudate nucleus.

Distinguish between the putamen and the globus pallidus of the lentiform nucleus.

- **Diencephalon** In a midsagittal section of the brain model, identify the thalamus, recognizable as the lateral wall around the diencephalon, and the wedge-shaped hypothalamus, inferior to the thalamus. Observe the third ventricle around the thalamus and the interthalamic adhesion. Identify the infundibulum, which attaches the pituitary gland to the hypothalamus. Locate the mamillary bodies and pineal gland.

- **Brain stem** Identify the medulla oblongata, pons, and mesencephalon. Locate the two pyramids on the medulla's anterior surface and the cerebral peduncles on the lateral sides of the mesencephalon. Identify the corpora quadrigemina of the mesencephalon, distinguishing between the superior and inferior colliculi.

- **Cerebellum** Locate the right and left hemispheres and the vermis separating them. In each hemisphere, identify the primary fissure and the anterior and posterior lobes. In a midsagittal section, locate the arbor vitae and the cerebellar nuclei.

3. Observe the cerebellar cortex slide and identify the Purkinje cells. Note the large size and many branched dendrites and a single thin axon. ■

Lab Activity 3   Cranial Nerves

Cranial nerves emerge from the brain at specific locations and pass through various foramina of the skull to reach the peripheral structures they innervate. Like spinal nerves, cranial nerves occur in pairs, 12 pairs in the case of the cranial nerves. The nerves are identified by name and are numbered with Roman numerals from N I to N XII. The numbers are assigned according to the locations at which the nerves contact the brain, with N I being most anterior and N XII most posterior. Some cranial nerves are entirely sensory nerves, but most are mixed. However, those mixed nerves that conduct primarily motor commands are considered motor nerves even though they have a few sensory fibers to inform the brain about muscle tension and position. Figure 10 shows the position of each cranial nerve on the inferior surface of the brain. Table 1 summarizes the cranial nerves and includes the foramen through which each nerve passes.

Figure 10 Origins of the Cranial Nerves Twelve pairs of cranial nerves connect the brain to organs mostly in the head and neck.

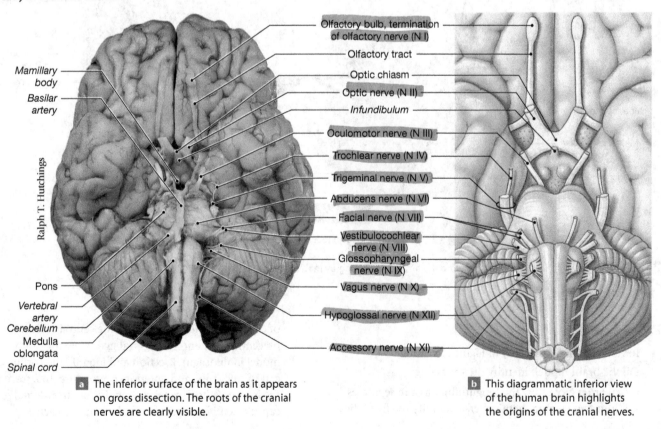

Ralph T. Hutchings

Mamillary body
Basilar artery
Pons
Vertebral artery
Cerebellum
Medulla oblongata
Spinal cord

Olfactory bulb, termination of olfactory nerve (N I)
Olfactory tract
Optic chiasm
Optic nerve (N II)
Infundibulum
Oculomotor nerve (N III)
Trochlear nerve (N IV)
Trigeminal nerve (N V)
Abducens nerve (N VI)
Facial nerve (N VII)
Vestibulocochlear nerve (N VIII)
Glossopharyngeal nerve (N IX)
Vagus nerve (N X)
Hypoglossal nerve (N XII)
Accessory nerve (N XI)

a The inferior surface of the brain as it appears on gross dissection. The roots of the cranial nerves are clearly visible.

b This diagrammatic inferior view of the human brain highlights the origins of the cranial nerves.

Table 1	Cranial Nerve Branches and Functions				
Cranial Nerve (Number)	Sensory Ganglion	Branch	Primary Function	Foramen	Innervation
Olfactory (I)			Special sensory	Olfactory foramina of ethmoid	Olfactory epithelium
Optic (II)			Special sensory	Optic canal	Retina of eye
Oculomotor (III)			Motor	Superior orbital fissure	Inferior, medial, superior rectus, inferior oblique, and levator palpebrae superioris muscles; intrinsic eye muscles
Trochlear (IV)			Motor	Superior orbital fissure	Superior oblique muscle
Trigeminal (V)	Semilunar		Mixed	Superior orbital fissure	Areas associated with the jaws
		Ophthalmic	Sensory	Superior orbital fissure	Orbital structures, nasal cavity, skin of forehead, upper eyelid, eyebrows, and nose (part)
		Maxillary		Foramen rotundum	Lower eyelid; superior lip, gums, and teeth; cheek, nose (part) palate, and pharynx (part)
		Mandibular		Foramen ovale	*Sensory:* inferior gums, teeth, lips, palate (part), and tongue (part) *Motor:* muscles of mastication
Abducens (VI)			Motor	Superior orbital fissure	Lateral rectus muscle
Facial (VII)	Geniculate		Mixed	Internal acoustic canal to facial canal; exits at stylomastoid foramen	*Sensory:* taste receptors on anterior 2/3 of tongue *Motor:* muscles of facial expression, lacrimal gland, submandibular gland, and sublingual salivary glands
Vestibulocochlear (Acoustic) (VIII)		Cochlear Vestibular	Special sensory	Internal acoustic canal	Cochlea (receptors for hearing) Vestibule (receptors for motion and balance)
Glossopharyngeal (IX)	Superior (jugular) and inferior (petrosal)		Mixed	Jugular foramen	*Sensory:* posterior 1/3 of tongue; pharynx and palate (part); receptors for blood pressure, pH, oxygen, and carbon dioxide concentrations *Motor:* pharyngeal muscles and parotid salivary gland
Vagus (X)	Jugular and nodose		Mixed	Jugular foramen	*Sensory:* pharynx; auricle and external acoustic canal; diaphragm; visceral organs in thoracic and abdominopelvic cavities *Motor:* palatal and pharyngeal muscles and visceral organs in thoracic and abdominopelvic cavities
Accessory (XI)		Internal	Motor	Jugular foramen	Skeletal muscles of palate, pharynx, and larynx (with vagus nerve)
		External	Motor	Jugular foramen	Sternocleidomastoid and trapezius muscles
Hypoglossal (XII)			Motor	Hypoglossal canal	Tongue musculature

Make a Prediction

Consider the major sensory organs of the head and predict how many cranial nerves are sensory nerves.

Olfactory Nerve (N I)

The **olfactory nerve** is composed of bundles of sensory fibers for the sense of smell and is located in the roof of the nasal cavity. The nerve passes through the cribriform plate of the ethmoid bone and enters an enlarged **olfactory bulb,** which then extends into the cerebrum as the **olfactory tract.**

Optic Nerve (N II)

The **optic nerve** carries visual information. This nerve originates in the retina, the neural part of the eye that is sensitive to changes in the amount of light entering the eye. The nerve is easy to identify as the X-shaped structure at the **optic chiasm** inferior to the hypothalamus. It is at this point that some of the sensory fibers cross to the nerve on the opposite side of the brain. The optic nerve enters the thalamus, which relays the visual signal to the occipital lobe. Some of the fibers enter the superior colliculus for visual reflexes.

Oculomotor Nerve (N III)

The **oculomotor nerve** innervates four extraocular eye muscles—the superior, medial, and inferior rectus muscles, and the inferior oblique muscle—and the levator palpebrae muscle of the eyelid. Autonomic motor fibers also control the intrinsic muscles of the iris and the ciliary body. The oculomotor nerve is located on the ventral mesencephalon just posterior to the optic nerve.

Trochlear Nerve (N IV)

The **trochlear** (TRŌK-lē-ar) **nerve** supplies motor fibers to the superior oblique muscle of the eye and originates where the mesencephalon joins the pons. The root of the nerve exits the mesencephalon on the lateral surface. Because it is easily cut or twisted off during removal of the dura mater, many dissection specimens do not have this nerve intact. The superior oblique eye muscle passes through a trochlea, or "pulley"; hence the name of the nerve.

Trigeminal Nerve (N V)

The **trigeminal** (tri-JEM-i-nal) **nerve** is the largest of the cranial nerves. It is located on the lateral pons near the medulla oblongata and services much of the face. In life, the nerve has three branches: *ophthalmic, maxillary,* and *mandibular.* The ophthalmic branch innervates sensory structures of the forehead, eye orbit, and nose. The maxillary branch contains sensory fibers for structures in the roof of the mouth, including half of the maxillary teeth. The mandibular branch carries the motor portion of the nerve to the muscles of mastication. Sensory signals from the lower lip, gum, muscles of the tongue, and one-third of the mandibular teeth are also part of the mandibular branch.

Abducens Nerve (N VI)

The **abducens** (ab-DŪ-senz) **nerve** controls the lateral rectus extraocular muscle. When this muscle contracts, the eyeball is abducted; hence the name. The nerve originates on the medulla oblongata and is positioned posterior and medial to the trigeminal nerve.

Facial Nerve (N VII)

The **facial nerve** is located on the medulla oblongata, posterior and lateral to the abducens nerve. It is a mixed nerve, with sensory fibers for the anterior two-thirds of the taste buds and somatic and autonomic motor fibers. The somatic motor neurons innervate the muscles of facial expression, such as the zygomaticus muscle. Visceral motor neurons control the activity of the salivary glands, lacrimal (tear) glands, and nasal mucous glands.

Vestibulocochlear Nerve (N VIII)

The **vestibulocochlear nerve,** also called the *auditory nerve,* is a sensory nerve of the inner ear located on the medulla oblongata near the facial nerve. The vestibulocochlear nerve has two branches. The vestibular branch gathers information regarding the sense of balance from the vestibule and semicircular canals of the inner ear. The cochlear branch conducts auditory sensations from the cochlea, the organ of hearing in the inner ear.

Glossopharyngeal Nerve (N IX)

The **glossopharyngeal** (glos-ō-fah-RIN-jē-al) **nerve** is a mixed nerve of the tongue and throat. It supplies the medulla oblongata with sensory information from the posterior third of the tongue (remember, the facial nerve innervates the anterior two-thirds of the taste buds) and from the palate and pharynx. The glossopharyngeal nerve also conveys barosensory and chemosensory information from the carotid sinus and the carotid body, where blood pressure and dissolved blood gases are monitored, respectively. Motor innervation by the glossopharyngeal nerve controls the pharyngeal muscles involved in swallowing and in the activity of the salivary glands.

Vagus Nerve (N X)

The **vagus** (VĀ-gus) **nerve** is a complex nerve on the medulla oblongata that has mixed sensory and motor functions. Sensory neurons from the pharynx, diaphragm, and most of the internal organs of the thoracic and abdominal cavities ascend along the vagus nerve and synapse with autonomic nuclei in the medulla. The motor portion controls the involuntary muscles of the respiratory, digestive, and cardiovascular systems. The vagus is the only cranial nerve to descend below the neck. It enters the ventral body cavity, but it does not pass to the thorax via the spinal cord; rather, it follows the musculature of the neck. Because this nerve regulates the activities of the organs of the thoracic and abdominal cavities, disorders of the nerve result in systemic disruption of homeostasis. Parasympathetic fibers in the vagus nerve control swallowing, digestion, heart rate, and respiratory patterns. If this control is compromised, sympathetic stimulation goes unchecked, and the organs respond as during exercise or stress. The cardiovascular and respiratory systems increase their activities, and the digestive system shuts down.

Accessory Nerve (N XI)

The **accessory nerve** is a motor nerve controlling the skeletal muscles involved in swallowing and the sternocleidomastoid and trapezius muscles of the neck. It is the only cranial nerve with fibers originating from both the medulla oblongata and the spinal cord. Numerous threadlike branches from these two regions unite in the spinal accessory nerve.

Hypoglossal Nerve (N XII)

The **hypoglossal** (hī-pō-GLOS-al) **nerve** is located on the medulla oblongata medial to the vagus nerve. This motor nerve supplies motor fibers that control tongue movements for speech and swallowing.

QuickCheck Questions

3.1 List three cranial nerves that are sensory nerves.

3.2 Which cranial nerve enters the ventral body cavity?

In the Lab   3

Materials

☐ Brain model
☐ Brain chart
☐ Isopropyl (rubbing) alcohol
☐ Wintergreen oil
☐ Eye chart

☐ Sugar solution
☐ Quinine solution
☐ Tuning fork
☐ Beaker of ice and cold probes
☐ Beaker of warm water and warm probes

Procedures

1. Review the cranial nerves in Figure 10.
2. Locate each cranial nerve on the brain model and chart.
3. Your instructor may ask you to test the function of selected cranial nerves. Table 2 lists the basic tests used to assess the general function of each nerve.

For additional practice, complete the *Sketch to Learn* activity. ■

Sketch to Learn

To help you remember the cranial nerves, let's draw each nerve on the provided picture of the brain. Pay close attention to the location of the base of each nerve and identify that part of the brain where the nerve emerges. Refer to Figure 10 for each nerve's exact location.

Sample Sketch

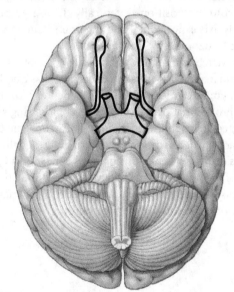

Your Sketch

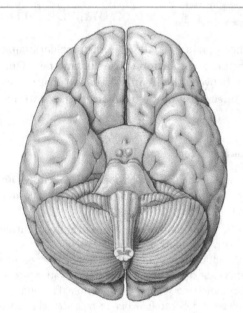

Step 1
• Draw the olfactory nerve lateral to the longitudinal fissure.
• Make a large x-shape for the optic nerve and chiasma.

Step 2
• Use the sample as reference for nerve placement and add the remaining nerves to the brain template.
• Label each nerve.

Table 2	Cranial Nerve Tests
Cranial Nerve	**Nerve Function Test**
I. Olfactory	Hold open container of rubbing alcohol under subject's nose and have subject identify odor. Repeat with open container of wintergreen oil.
II. Optic	Test subject's visual field by moving a finger back and forth in front of subject's eyes. Use eye chart to test visual acuity.
III. Oculomotor	Examine subject's pupils for equal size. Have subject follow an object with eyes.
IV. Trochlear	Tested with oculomotor nerve. Have subject roll eyes downward.
V. Trigeminal	Check motor functions of nerve by having subject move mandible in various directions. Check sensory functions with warm and cold probes on forehead, upper lip, and lower jaw.
VI. Abducens	Tested with oculomotor nerve. Have subject move eyes laterally.
VII. Facial	Use sugar solution to test anterior of tongue for sweet taste reception. Observe facial muscle contractions for even muscle tone on each side of face while subject smiles, frowns, and purses lips.
VIII. Vestibulocochlear	Cochlear branch—Hold vibrating tuning fork in air next to ear, and then touch fork to mastoid process for bone-conduction test. Vestibular branch—Have subject close eyes and maintain balance.
IX. Glossopharyngeal	While subject coughs, check position of uvula on posterior of soft palate. Use quinine solution to test posterior of tongue for bitter taste reception.
X. Vagus	While subject coughs, check position of uvula on posterior of soft palate.
XI. Spinal accessory	Hold subject's shoulder while the subject rotates it to test the strength of sternocleidomastoid muscle. Hold head while subject rotates it to test trapezius strength.
XII. Hypoglossal	Observe subject protract and retract tongue from mouth, and check for even movement on two lateral edges of tongue.

Lab Activity 4   Sheep Brain Dissection

The sheep brain, like all other mammalian brains, is similar in structure and function to the human brain. One major difference between the human brain and that of other animals is the orientation of the brain stem relative to the body axis.

! Safety Alert: Brain Dissection

You *must* practice the highest level of laboratory safety while handling and dissecting the brain. Keep the following guidelines in mind during the dissection.

1. Wear gloves and safety glasses to protect yourself from the fixatives used to preserve the specimen.
2. Do not dispose of the fixative from your specimen. You will later store the specimen in the fixative to keep the specimen moist and prevent it from decaying.
3. Be extremely careful when using a scalpel or other sharp instrument. Always direct cutting and scissor motions away from you to prevent an accident if the instrument slips on moist tissue.
4. Before cutting a given tissue, make sure it is free from underlying and/or adjacent tissues so that they will not be accidentally severed.
5. Never discard tissue in the sink or trash. Your instructor will inform you of the proper disposal procedure.

The human body has a vertical axis, and the brain stem and spinal cord are positioned vertically. In four-legged animals, the body axis is horizontal and the brain stem and spinal cord are also horizontal.

All vertebrate animals—sharks, fish, amphibians, reptiles, birds, and mammals—have a brain stem for basic body functions. These animals can learn through experience, a complex neurological process that requires higher-level processing and memory storage, as occurs in the human cerebrum. Imagine the complex motor activity necessary for locomotion in these animals.

Dissecting a sheep brain enhances your study of models and charts of the human brain. Take your time during the dissection and follow the directions carefully. Refer to this manual and its illustrations often during the procedures.

In the Lab   4

Materials

- ☐ Gloves
- ☐ Safety glasses
- ☐ Preserved sheep brain (preferably with dura mater intact)
- ☐ Dissection pan
- ☐ Scissors
- ☐ Blunt probe
- ☐ Large dissection knife

Procedures

Put on gloves and safety glasses before handling the brain.

I. The Meninges

If your sheep brain does not have the dura mater, skip to part II.

1. On the intact dura mater, locate the falx cerebri and the tentorium cerebelli on the overlying dorsal surface of the dura mater. How does the tissue of the falx cerebri compare with the dura mater covering the hemispheres?

2. If your specimen still has the ethmoid, a mass of bone on the anterior frontal lobe, slip a probe between the bone and the dura mater. Carefully pull the bone off the specimen, using scissors to snip away any attached dura mater. Examine the removed ethmoid and identify the crista galli, which is the crest of bone where the meninges attach.

3. Gently insert a probe between the dura mater and the brain and gently work the probe back and forth to separate the two. With scissors, cut completely around the base of the dura mater, leaving the inferior portion intact over the cranial nerves. Make small cuts with the scissors and be careful not to cut or remove any of the cranial nerves. Do not lift the dura too high or the cranial nerves will detach from the brain.

4. Cut completely through the lateral sides of the tentorium cerebelli and then remove the dura mater in one piece by grasping it with your (gloved) hand and peeling it off the brain.

5. Open the detached dura mater and identify the falx cerebri and tentorium cerebelli. (One difference between the sheep brain and the human brain is that the sheep brain does not have a falx cerebelli.)

II. External Brain Anatomy

1. Examine the cerebrum, identifying the frontal, parietal, occipital, and temporal lobes. The insula is a deep lobe and is not visible externally. Note the longitudinal fissure separating the right and left cerebral hemispheres. Observe the gyri and sulci on the cortical surface. Examine the surface between sulci for the arachnoid mater and pia mater.

2. Identify the cerebellum and compare the size of the folia with the size of the cerebral gyri. Unlike the human brain, the sheep cerebellum is not divided medially into two lateral hemispheres.

3. To examine the dorsal anatomy of the mesencephalon, position the sheep brain as in Figure 11 and use your fingers to gently depress the cerebellum. The mesencephalon will then be visible between the cerebrum and cerebellum. Now identify the four elevated masses of the corpora quadrigemina and distinguish between the superior colliculi and the inferior colliculi. The pineal gland of the diencephalon is superior to the mesencephalon.

Figure 11 Dorsal View of the Sheep Brain The cerebellum is pushed down to show the location of the corpora quadrigemina of the mesencephalon.

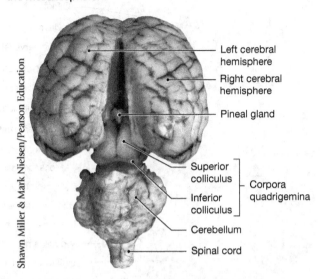

Shawn Miller & Mark Nielsen/Pearson Education

Left cerebral hemisphere
Right cerebral hemisphere
Pineal gland
Superior colliculus
Inferior colliculus
Corpora quadrigemina
Cerebellum
Spinal cord

4. Turn the brain over to view the ventral surface, as in Figure 12. Note how the spinal cord joins the medulla oblongata. Identify the pons and the cerebral peduncles of the mesencephalon. Locate the single mamillary body on the hypothalamus. (Remember that the mamillary body of the human brain is a *paired* mass.) The pituitary gland has most likely been removed from your specimen; however, you can still identify the stub of the infundibulum that attaches the pituitary to the hypothalamus.

5. Using Figure 12 as a guide, identify as many cranial nerves on your sheep brain as possible. Nerves I through III and nerve V are usually intact and easy to identify. Your laboratory instructor may ask you to observe several sheep brains in order to study all the cranial nerves. The three branches of the trigeminal nerve were cut when the brain was removed from the sheep and therefore are not present on any specimen. The glossopharyngeal nerve may have been removed inadvertently when the specimen was being prepared. Even if this nerve is present in your specimen, however, it is difficult to identify on the sheep brain.

III. Internal Brain Anatomy—Sagittal and Frontal Sections

Sagittal Section

1. To study the internal organization of the brain, make a midsagittal section to expose the deep structures. Lay the sheep brain in the dissection pan so that the superior surface faces you, as in Figure 11. Place the blade of a large dissection knife in the anterior region of the longitudinal fissure and section the brain by cutting it

Figure 12 Ventral View of the Sheep Brain Cranial nerves are clearly visible in the ventral view of the sheep brain.

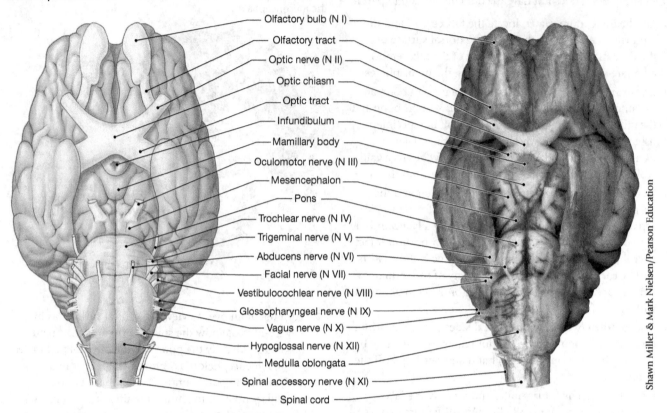

Olfactory bulb (N I)
Olfactory tract
Optic nerve (N II)
Optic chiasm
Optic tract
Infundibulum
Mamillary body
Oculomotor nerve (N III)
Mesencephalon
Pons
Trochlear nerve (N IV)
Trigeminal nerve (N V)
Abducens nerve (N VI)
Facial nerve (N VII)
Vestibulocochlear nerve (N VIII)
Glossopharyngeal nerve (N IX)
Vagus nerve (N X)
Hypoglossal nerve (N XII)
Medulla oblongata
Spinal accessory nerve (N XI)
Spinal cord

Shawn Miller & Mark Nielsen/Pearson Education

in half along the fissure. Use as few cutting strokes as possible to prevent damage to the brain tissue.

2. Using Figure 13 as a guide, identify the internal anatomical features of the sheep brain. Gently slide a blunt probe between the corpus callosum and fornix and into the lateral ventricle to determine how deep the ventricle extends into the cerebrum. Inside the lateral ventricle, locate the choroid plexus, which appears as a granular mass of tissue.

Frontal Section

1. To view deep structures of the cerebrum and diencephalon, put the two halves of the brain together and use a large dissection knife to cut a frontal section through the infundibulum. Make another frontal section

just posterior to the first to slice off a thin slab of brain. Lay the slab in the dissection pan with the anterior side up. (The anterior side is the surface where you made your first cut.)

2. Using Figure 14 as a guide, notice the distribution of gray matter and white matter. Observe how the corpus callosum joins each cerebral hemisphere. Lateral to the lateral ventricles is the gray matter of the basal nuclei.

IV. Cleanup and Disposal of Brain

When finished, store or discard the sheep brain as directed by your laboratory instructor. Proper disposal of all biological waste protects the local environment and is mandated by local, state, and federal regulations. ■

Figure 13 Midsagittal Section of the Sheep Brain Internal anatomy of the sheep brain in sagittal section.

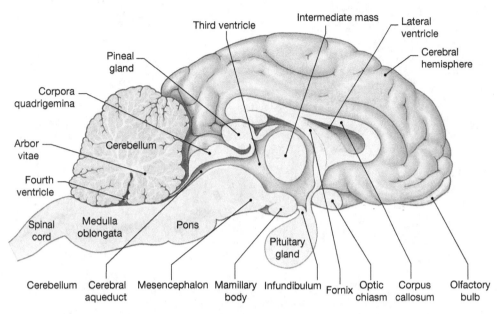

Labels (clockwise from top): Third ventricle · Intermediate mass · Lateral ventricle · Cerebral hemisphere · Pineal gland · Corpora quadrigemina · Arbor vitae · Cerebellum · Fourth ventricle · Spinal cord · Medulla oblongata · Pons · Pituitary gland

Bottom labels: Cerebellum · Cerebral aqueduct · Mesencephalon · Mamillary body · Infundibulum · Fornix · Optic chiasm · Corpus callosum · Olfactory bulb

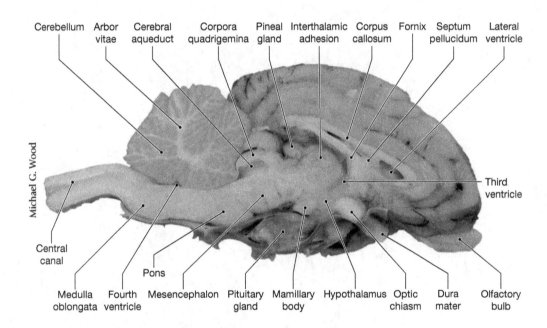

Michael G. Wood

Top labels: Cerebellum · Arbor vitae · Cerebral aqueduct · Corpora quadrigemina · Pineal gland · Interthalamic adhesion · Corpus callosum · Fornix · Septum pellucidum · Lateral ventricle · Third ventricle

Bottom labels: Central canal · Medulla oblongata · Fourth ventricle · Pons · Mesencephalon · Pituitary gland · Mamillary body · Hypothalamus · Optic chiasm · Dura mater · Olfactory bulb

Figure 14 Frontal Section of the Sheep Brain Internal anatomy of the sheep brain in frontal section.

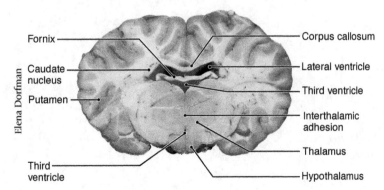

Elena Dorfman

Labels: Fornix · Corpus callosum · Caudate nucleus · Lateral ventricle · Putamen · Third ventricle · Interthalamic adhesion · Thalamus · Third ventricle · Hypothalamus

Name _____

Date _____

Section _____

Anatomy of the Brain

A. Description

Describe each of the following structures.

1. cerebrum

2. mamillary body

3. longitudinal fissure

4. optic chiasm

5. falx cerebri

6. hypothalamus

7. dura mater

8. vermis

9. subarachnoid space

10. septum pellucidum

11. thalamus

12. corpus callosum

13. pineal gland

14. superior colliculus

15. arbor vitae

B. Labeling

1. Label **Figure 15**, which shows the inferior surface of the brain.

Figure 15 **Inferior Surface of the Human Brain**

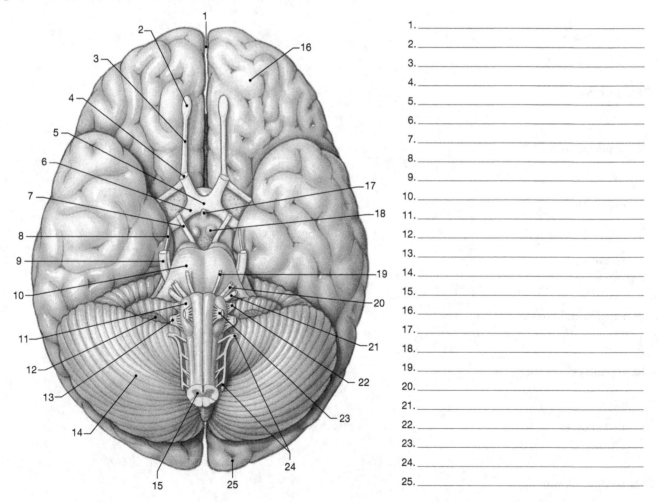

1. _____
2. _____
3. _____
4. _____
5. _____
6. _____
7. _____
8. _____
9. _____
10. _____
11. _____
12. _____
13. _____
14. _____
15. _____
16. _____
17. _____
18. _____
19. _____
20. _____
21. _____
22. _____
23. _____
24. _____
25. _____

2. Label **Figure 16**, a midsagittal close-up view of the human brain.

Figure 16 Detail of Sagittal Section of the Human Brain

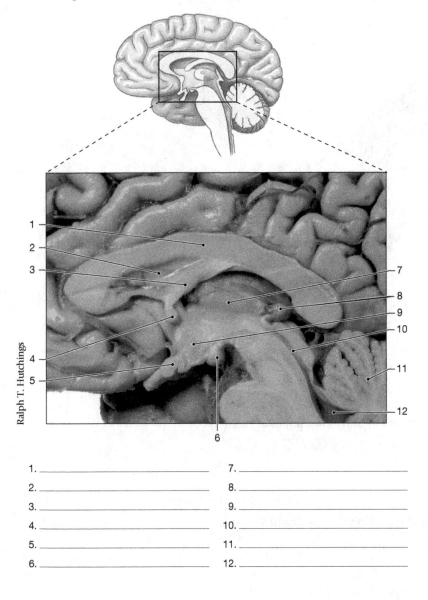

Ralph T. Hutchings

1. _____   7. _____
2. _____   8. _____
3. _____   9. _____
4. _____   10. _____
5. _____   11. _____
6. _____   12. _____

3. Label Figure 17, a cast of the ventricles of the brain.

Figure 17 **Ventricles of the Brain** A cast of the ventricles.

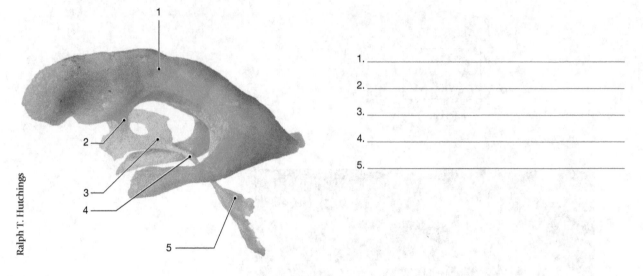

Ralph T. Hutchings

1. _____

2. _____

3. _____

4. _____

5. _____

C. Short-Answer Questions

1. List the six major regions of the brain.

2. Which cranial nerves conduct the sensory and motor impulses of the eye?

3. List the location and specific anatomy of the corpora quadrigemina.

4. Describe the extensions of the dura mater.

5. What is the function of the precentral gyrus?

6. Trace a drop of CSF from a lateral ventricle to reabsorption at an arachnoid granulation.

D. Analysis and Application

1. Imagine watching a bird fly across your line of vision. What part of your brain is active in keeping an image of the moving bird on your retina?

2. You have just eaten a medium-sized pepperoni pizza and are now laying down to digest it. Which cranial nerve stimulates the muscular activity of your digestive tract?

3. A child is preoccupied with a large cherry lollipop. What part of the child's brain is responsible for the licking and eating reflexes?

4. Your favorite movie has made you cry yet again. Which cranial nerve is responsible for your tears?

E. Clinical Challenge

1. A patient is brought into the emergency room with severe whiplash. He is not breathing and has lost cardiac function. What part of the brain has most likely been damaged?

2. A woman is admitted to the hospital with Bell's palsy caused by an inflamed facial nerve. What symptoms will you, as the attending physician, observe, and how would you test her facial nerve?

Nervous System part 3: Autonomic Nervous System
Wish List

✓	<u>Sympathetic Division</u>	
	Sympathetic chain	
	Sympathetic ganglia	
	Collateral ganglia	
	Splanchnic nerves	

Autonomic Nervous System

Learning Outcomes

On completion of this exercise, you should be able to:

1. Compare the location of the preganglionic outflow from the CNS in the sympathetic and parasympathetic divisions.

2. Compare the lengths of and the neurotransmitters released by each fiber in the sympathetic and parasympathetic divisions.

3. Trace the sympathetic pathways into a chain ganglion, into a collateral ganglion, and into the adrenal medulla.

4. Trace the parasympathetic pathways into cranial nerves III, VII, IX, and X, and into the pelvic nerves.

5. Compare the responses to sympathetic and parasympathetic innervation.

Lab Activities

1. The Sympathetic (Thoracolumbar) Division

2. The Parasympathetic (Craniosacral) Division

Clinical Application

Stress and the ANS

The autonomic nervous system (ANS) controls the motor and glandular activity of the visceral effectors. Most internal organs have **dual innervation** in that they are innervated by both sympathetic and parasympathetic nerves of the ANS. Thus, the two divisions of the ANS share the role of regulating autonomic function. Typically, one division stimulates a given effector, and the other division inhibits that same effector. Autonomic motor pathways originate in the brain and enter the cranial and spinal nerves.

An autonomic pathway consists of two groups of neurons, both of which have names that reflect the fact that they synapse with one another in bulblike PNS structures called **ganglia** (GANG-lē-uh). An autonomic neuron between the CNS and a sympathetic or parasympathetic ganglion is called a **preganglionic neuron;** an autonomic neuron between the ganglion and the target muscle or gland is a

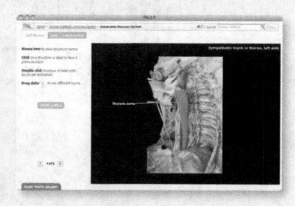

Need More Practice and Review?

Build your knowledge—and confidence!—in the Study Area of MasteringA&P® at www.masteringaandp.com with Pre-lab Quizzes, Post-lab Quizzes, Practice Anatomy Lab™ (PAL™) 3.0 virtual anatomy practice tool, PhysioEx™ 9.0 laboratory simulations, and A&P Flix™ with Quizzes.

PAL For this lab exercise, follow these navigation paths:
- PAL>Human Cadaver>Nervous System>Autonomic Nervous System
- PAL>Anatomical Models>Nervous System>Autonomic Nervous System

From Exercise 26 of *Laboratory Manual for Anatomy & Physiology featuring Martini Art*, Fifth Edition. Michael G. Wood.

ganglionic neuron (Figure 1). The axons of autonomic neurons are called *fibers*. **Preganglionic fibers** are axons that synapse with ganglionic neurons in the ganglion, whereas **ganglionic fibers** synapse with the effectors: smooth muscles, the heart, and glands.

The preganglionic neurons of both divisions release acetylcholine (ACh) into a ganglion, but the ganglionic neurons of the two divisions release different neurotransmitters to the target effector cells. During times of excitement, emotional stress, and emergencies, sympathetic ganglionic neurons release norepinephrine (NE) to effectors and cause a sympathetic **fight-or-flight response** that increases overall alertness. Heart rate, blood pressure, and respiratory rate all increase, sweat glands secrete, and digestive and urinary functions cease. Parasympathetic ganglionic neurons release ACh, which slows the body for normal, energy-conserving homeostasis. This parasympathetic **rest-and-digest response** decreases cardiovascular and respiratory activity and increases the rate at which food and wastes are processed and eliminated.

Make a Prediction

A 65-year-old male has outpatient surgery. While in the recovery room, he is told that he may go home once he urinates. Why is urination a good indicator that it is safe to allow the patient to go home?

The two major anatomical differences between the sympathetic and parasympathetic subdivisions of the ANS are the location of preganglionic exit points from the CNS and the location of autonomic ganglia in the PNS.

Figure 1 An Overview of ANS Pathways Sympathetic pathways consist of short preganglionic neurons that release acetylcholine (ACh) in sympathetic ganglia. They synapse with long ganglionic neurons that release norepinephrine (NE) at an effector. The sympathetic response is generalized as a fight-or-flight response. Parasympathetic pathways have long preganglionic neurons that exit the CNS either directly from the brain (shown) or by passing down the spinal cord to the sacral region (not shown). They release ACh in terminal and intramural ganglia located in or near the effector organ. Preganglionic parasympathetic neurons synapse with short ganglionic neurons that also release ACh. The general parasympathetic response is a rest-and-digest response.

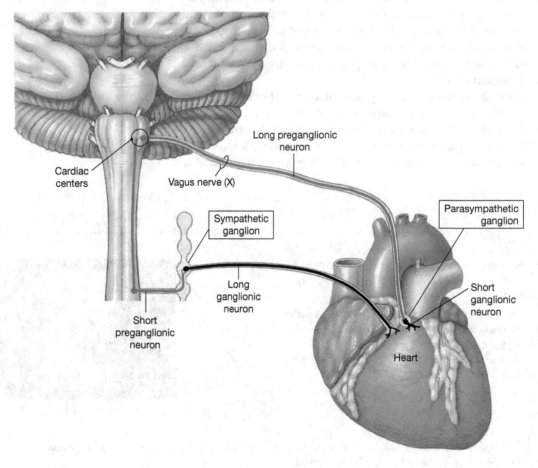

An easy way to remember the sympathetic fight-or-flight response is to consider how your organs must adjust their activities during an emergency situation, such as being chased by an animal. Sympathetic impulses increase your heart rate, blood pressure, and respiratory rate. Muscle tone increases in preparation for fighting off the animal or running for your life. As arterioles in skeletal muscles dilate, more blood flows into the muscles to support their high activity level. Sympathetic stimulation decreases the activity of your digestive tract. An emergency situation is not the time to work at digesting your lunch! With digestive actions slowed, the body shunts blood from the abdominal organs and delivers more blood to skeletal muscles. Once you are out of danger, sympathetic stimulation decreases and parasympathetic stimulation predominates to return your body to the routine "housekeeping" chores of digesting food, eliminating wastes, and conserving precious cell energy. ■

Location of Preganglionic Exit Points from CNS

Sympathetic preganglionic neurons exit the spinal cord at segments T_1 through L_2 and enter the thoracic and first two lumbar spinal nerves. Because of this nerve distribution, the sympathetic division is also called the **thoracolumbar** (tho-ra-kō-LUM-bar) **division.** In the parasympathetic division, the efferent neurons originating in the brain either exit the cranium in certain cranial nerves or descend the spinal cord and exit at the sacral level. The parasympathetic division is also called the **craniosacral** (krā-nē-ō-SĀ-krul) **division** (Figure 1).

Location of Autonomic Ganglia in PNS

All autonomic ganglia are in the PNS, but their proximity to the CNS provides another difference between the sympathetic and parasympathetic divisions. Sympathetic ganglia are located close to the spinal cord. This location results in short sympathetic preganglionic neurons and long sympathetic ganglionic neurons. Parasympathetic ganglia are located either near or within the visceral effectors. With the ganglia farther away from the CNS, parasympathetic preganglionic neurons are long and parasympathetic ganglionic neurons are short. In Figure 1, notice both the difference in the locations of the sympathetic and parasympathetic ganglia and the difference in the preganglionic and ganglionic lengths.

Lab Activity 1 The Sympathetic (Thoracolumbar) Division

The organization of the sympathetic division of the ANS is diagrammed in **Figure 2**. Preganglionic neurons originate in the pons and the medulla of the brain stem. These autonomic

Stress stimulates the body to increase sympathetic commands from the ANS. Appetite may decrease while blood pressure and general sensitivity to stimuli may increase. The individual may become irritable and have difficulty sleeping and coping with day-to-day responsibilities. Prolonged stress can lead to disease—coronary diseases, for example, are common in people with stressful occupations. ■

motor neurons descend in the spinal cord to the thoracic and lumbar segments, where their somae are located in the lateral gray horns. Preganglionic axons exit the spinal cord in ventral roots and pass into a spinal nerve which branches into a sympathetic chain ganglion. In the chain ganglion, the preganglionic neuron will either synapse with a ganglionic neuron or pass through the chain ganglion and synapse in a collateral ganglion or in the adrenal medulla.

In a typical sympathetic pathway, the short sympathetic preganglionic fibers release ACh at the synapse where ACh is excitatory to the ganglionic fiber. The long ganglionic axon then releases norepinephrine at its synapse with the effector. How the NE affects the effector depends on the type of NE receptors present in the effector's cell membrane. Generally, the sympathetic response is to prepare the body for increased activity or a crisis situation; this is the fight-or-flight response that occurs during exercise, excitement, and emergencies.

Figure 3 outlines the general distribution of the sympathetic pathways, showing the *sympathetic chain ganglia* positioned lateral to the lower portion of the spinal cord. For simplicity, the left side of the figure shows sympathetic nerves to structures of the skin, blood vessels, and adipose tissue; the right side of Figure 3 details sympathetic distribution to organs in the head and ventral body cavity. In real life, sympathetic distribution is the same on both sides of the spinal cord.

Three types of sympathetic ganglia occur in the body: sympathetic chain ganglia, collateral ganglia, and modified ganglia in the adrenal medulla. Preganglionic neurons extend from the thoracic and lumbar segments of the spinal cord and pass into sympathetic ganglia where they synapse with ganglionic neurons that exit the ganglia and innervate the effectors of the thoracic cavity, head, body wall, and limbs.

Sympathetic chain ganglia (Figure 3) are located lateral to the spinal cord and are also called **paravertebral ganglia.** All sympathetic preganglionic neurons pass through a sympathetic chain ganglion but only the ones that supply the head, body wall, and limbs will synapse in the chain with a ganglionic neuron. Neurons that supply the abdominopelvic cavity do not synapse in the chain ganglia; instead, they pass through the chain ganglia and synapse in collateral ganglia.

Collateral ganglia are located anterior to the vertebral column and contain ganglionic neurons that lead to organs in

Figure 2 Organization of the Sympathetic Division of the ANS Preganglionic neurons of the sympathetic division exit thoracic and lumbar segments of the spinal cord and enter sympathetic ganglia where they synapse with ganglionic neurons that supply the target organs with sympathetic control.

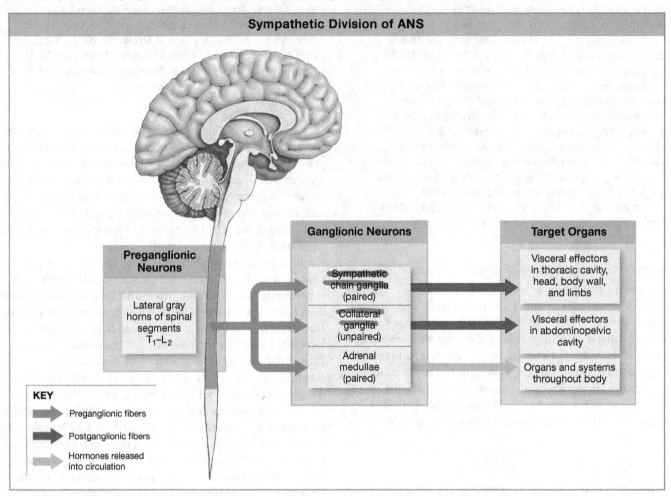

the abdominopelvic cavity. The preganglionic fibers associated with collateral ganglia pass through the sympathetic chain ganglia without synapsing and join to form a network called the **splanchnic** (SPLANK-nik) **nerves.** This network divides and sends branches into the collateral ganglia, where the preganglionic fibers synapse with ganglionic neurons. The ganglionic fibers then synapse with abdominopelvic effectors. The collateral ganglia are named after the adjacent blood vessels. The **celiac** (SĒ-lē-ak) **ganglion** supplies the liver, gallbladder, stomach, pancreas, and spleen. The **superior mesenteric** (mez-en-TER-ik) **ganglion** innervates the small intestine and parts of the large intestine. The **inferior mesenteric ganglion** controls most of the large intestine, the kidneys, the bladder, and the sex organs.

The third type of sympathetic ganglion is associated with the adrenal glands, also called *suprarenal glands,* which are positioned on top of the kidneys. Each adrenal gland has an outer cortex layer that produces hormones and an inner region called the **adrenal medulla.** It is this region that contains sympathetic ganglia and ganglionic neurons. During sympathetic stimulation, the ganglionic neurons in the medulla, like other sympathetic ganglionic neurons, release epinephrine into the bloodstream and contribute to the fight-or-flight response.

Sympathetic Pathways

Figure 4 shows the sympathetic pathways in more detail. The pathway utilizing the sympathetic chain ganglia passes through areas called the **white ramus** and the **gray ramus.** (Collectively, these two regions are known as the **rami communicantes.**) Once a preganglionic fiber enters a sympathetic chain ganglion via the white ramus, the fiber usually synapses with a ganglionic neuron, as shown in Figure 4a. The ganglionic fiber exits the sympathetic chain ganglion via either the gray ramus or an autonomic nerve. The gray ramus directs

Figure 3 Distribution of Sympathetic Innervation The distribution of sympathetic fibers is the same on both sides of the body. For clarity, the innervation of somatic structures is shown here on the left, and the innervation of visceral structures on the right.

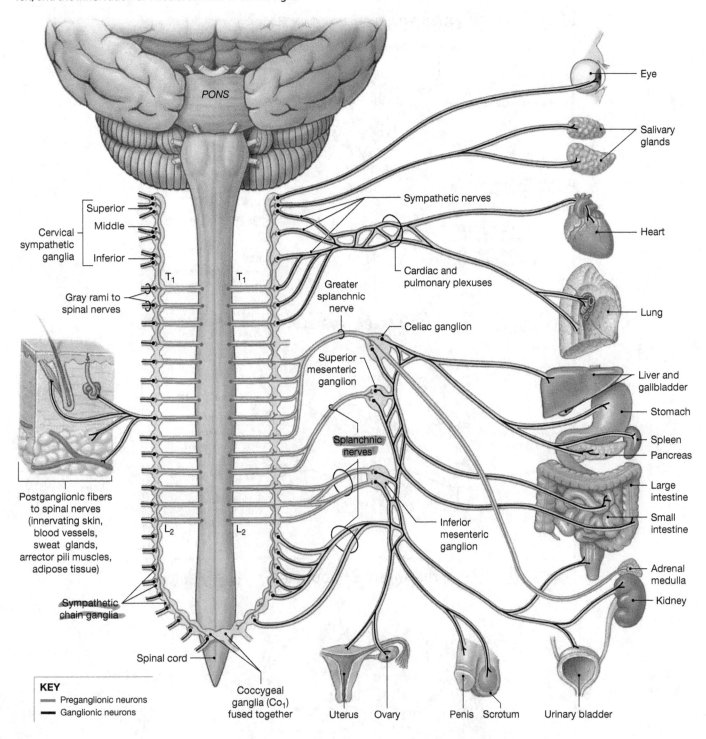

PONS

Cervical sympathetic ganglia
— Superior
— Middle
— Inferior

T_1

T_1

Gray rami to spinal nerves

Sympathetic nerves

Cardiac and pulmonary plexuses

Greater splanchnic nerve

Celiac ganglion

Superior mesenteric ganglion

Splanchnic nerves

Inferior mesenteric ganglion

Postganglionic fibers to spinal nerves (innervating skin, blood vessels, sweat glands, arrector pili muscles, adipose tissue)

L_2

L_2

Sympathetic chain ganglia

Spinal cord

Coccygeal ganglia (Co_1) fused together

Eye

Salivary glands

Heart

Lung

Liver and gallbladder

Stomach

Spleen

Pancreas

Large intestine

Small intestine

Adrenal medulla

Kidney

Uterus   Ovary   Penis Scrotum   Urinary bladder

KEY
— Preganglionic neurons
— Ganglionic neurons

Figure 4 Sympathetic Ganglia and Pathways Sympathetic ganglia are located in three regions: Sympathetic chain ganglia are lateral to the spinal cord; collateral ganglia supply the abdominal organs and are anterior to the spinal cord; and the adrenal medullae are the middle portions of the adrenal (suprarenal) glands. Sympathetic preganglionic neurons synapse in the medullae and ganglionic neurons release NE into the blood.

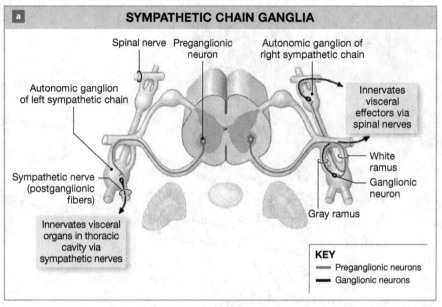

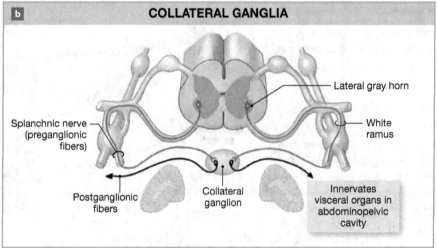

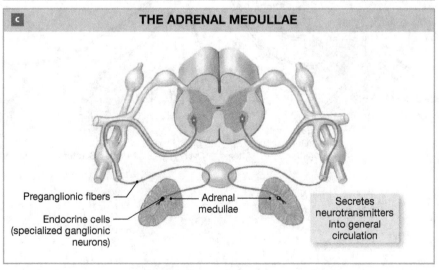

the ganglionic fiber into a spinal nerve leading to a general somatic structure, such as blood vessels supplying skeletal muscles. A ganglionic fiber in an autonomic nerve passes into the thoracic cavity to innervate the thoracic viscera.

Notice in Figure 4a that all the sympathetic chain ganglia on the same side of the spinal cord are interconnected. A single preganglionic neuron may enter one sympathetic chain ganglion and branch into many different chain ganglia, to synapse with up to 32 ganglionic neurons. This fanning out of preganglionic neurons within the sympathetic chain ganglia contributes to the widespread effect that sympathetic stimulation has on the body.

Figure 4b details the pathway involving collateral ganglia. Note how the preganglionic axons pass through the chain ganglia and enter the splanchnic nerve (described earlier) before entering the collateral ganglia. Sympathetic neurons supplying the adrenal gland do not synapse in a sympathetic chain ganglion or a collateral ganglion. Instead, the preganglionic fibers penetrate deep into the adrenal gland and synapse with ganglionic neurons in the adrenal medulla, as noted earlier.

QuickCheck Questions

1.1 Why is the sympathetic division of the ANS also called the thoracolumbar division?

1.2 What is the body's general response to sympathetic stimulation?

1.3 How do the heart, lungs, and digestive tract respond to sympathetic stimulation?

Study Tip Understanding Sympathetic Ganglia

Following is a brief summary of sympathetic ganglia:

- First, remember that all sympathetic ganglionic neurons enter chain ganglia.
- *Chain ganglia.* Sympathetic preganglionic neurons pass into chain ganglia, synapse with ganglionic neurons that exit the chain to innervate thoracic and integumentary organs.
- *Collateral ganglia.* Ganglionic neurons pass through chain ganglia and synapse with ganglionic neurons in collateral ganglia which supply organs in the abdomino-pelvic cavity.
- *Adrenal medullae.* Sympathetic ganglionic neurons pass through chain and collateral ganglia and enter the medulla of the adrenal glands where ganglionic neurons release adrenaline into the bloodstream. ▪

In the Lab 1

Materials

- ☐ Nervous system chart
- ☐ Spinal cord model

Procedures

1. Review the anatomy and sympathetic pathways presented in Figures 1 through 4. Complete the *Sketch to Learn* activity below.

 Sketch to Learn

Use the provided template and practice drawing sympathetic pathways.

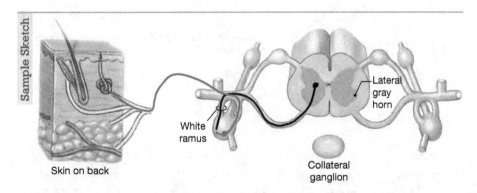

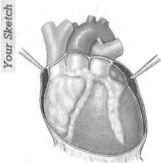

Step 1
- Draw a black line for the preganglionic neuron, which passes from the lateral gray horn to the sympathetic ganglion.

Step 2
- Draw a red line for the ganglionic neuron, which passes from the ganglion, to the gray ramus, and out the dorsal ramus to enter the skin.

Step 3
- On the right side of the template, draw a sympathetic pathway from the spinal cord to the heart, using black and red lines for the preganglionic and ganglionic neurons.

2. On the spinal cord model, locate the lateral gray horns, ventral roots, and the components of the rami communicantes.

3. On a chart of the nervous system, or in Figure 3, locate a sympathetic chain ganglion, a collateral ganglion, and the medulla of the adrenal gland.

4. On the nervous system chart, trace the following sympathetic pathways:

  a. Preganglionic fiber synapsing in a collateral ganglion

  b. Ganglionic fiber exiting a chain ganglion and passing into a spinal nerve

  c. Preganglionic fiber synapsing in the adrenal medulla ■

Lab Activity 2   The Parasympathetic (Craniosacral) Division

The organization of the parasympathetic division of the ANS is diagrammed in Figure 5. In this division, the preganglionic neurons leave the CNS either via cranial nerves III, VII, IX, and X, or via the sacral level of the spinal cord. Parasympathetic preganglionic neurons release acetylcholine, which is always excitatory to a ganglionic fiber. The parasympathetic ganglionic fibers also release ACh to their visceral effectors. How the ACh affects the effectors depends on the type of ACh receptors present in the cell membrane of the effector cells. Generally, the parasympathetic

Figure 5 Organization of the Parasympathetic Division of the ANS Preganglionic neurons of the parasympathetic division are in cranial nerves III, VII, IX, and X and in pelvic nerves in sacral spinal cord segments. Preganglionic neurons in these cranial and sacral nerves synapse in parasympathetic ganglia located near or within the effectors where they synapse with ganglionic neurons that supply the target organs with parasympathetic control.

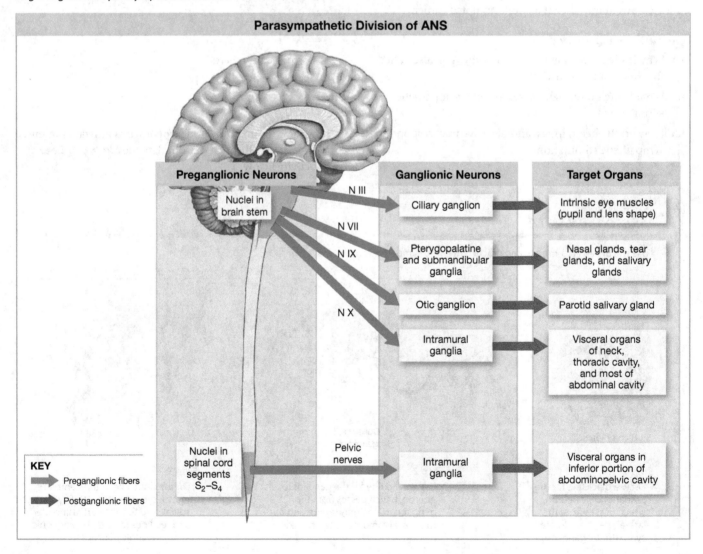

response is a rest-and-digest response that slows body functions and promotes digestion and waste elimination.

There are two main types of parasympathetic ganglia: terminal and intramural. **Terminal ganglia** are located near the eye and salivary glands; **intramural** (within walls) **ganglia** are embedded in the walls of effector organs. In the brain, parasympathetic preganglionic neurons branch into four cranial nerves: oculomotor, facial, glossopharyngeal, and vagus (Figure 6). For the first three of these nerves, there is a separate terminal ganglion for each one. The oculomotor nerve

Figure 6 Distribution of Parasympathetic Innervation Parasympathetic nerves are in cranial nerves III, VII, IX, and X and in sacral nerves of the sacral part of the spinal cord. For clarity, only the right side of the figure shows nerves but in real life each nerve is paired.

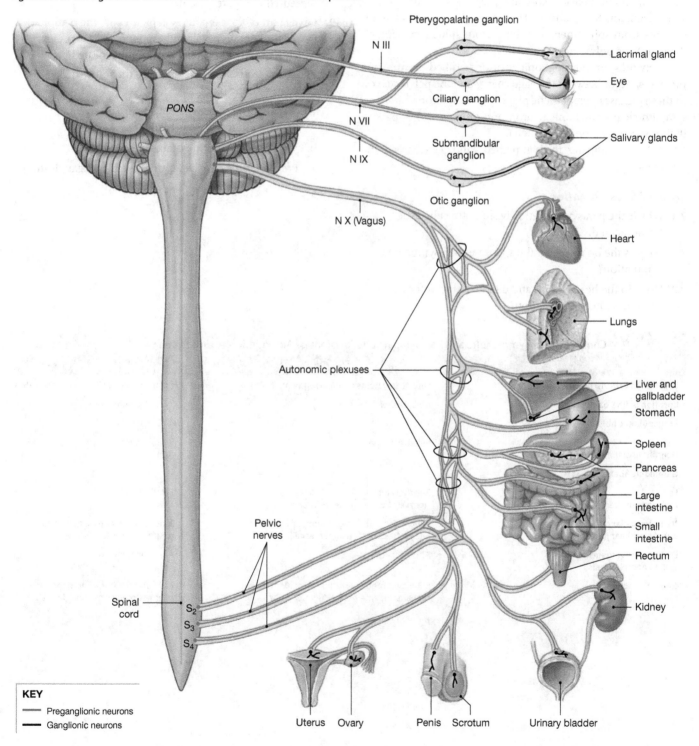

(N III) to the eyes enters the **ciliary ganglion,** the facial nerve (N VII) passes into the **pterygopalatine** (TER-i-gō-PAL-a-tin) and **submandibular ganglia,** and the glossopharyngeal nerve (N IX) includes the **otic ganglion.** Intramural ganglia receive preganglionic neurons in the vagus nerve (N X), which exits the brain, travels down the musculature of the neck, enters the ventral body cavity, and spreads into the intramural ganglia of the internal organs. The sacral portion of the parasympathetic division contains preganglionic neurons in sacral segments S_2, S_3, and S_4. The preganglionic fibers remain separate from spinal nerves and exit from spinal segments S_2 through S_4 as **pelvic nerves.**

Networks of preganglionic neurons, called **autonomic plexuses,** occur between the vagus nerve and the pelvic nerves. In these plexuses, sympathetic preganglionic neurons and parasympathetic preganglionic neurons intermingle as they pass to their respective autonomic ganglia.

Table 1 compares the sympathetic and parasympathetic divisions.

QuickCheck Questions

2.1 Why is the parasympathetic division also called the craniosacral division?

2.2 What is the body's general response to parasympathetic stimulation?

2.3 How do the heart, lungs, and digestive tract respond to parasympathetic stimulation?

Material

☐ Nervous system chart

Procedures

1. Review the anatomy and parasympathetic pathways presented in Figures 5 and 6.

2. On a chart of the nervous system, identify the oculomotor, facial, glossopharyngeal, and vagus cranial nerves. In which part of the brain are these nerves located?

3. On the nervous system chart, trace the following parasympathetic pathways:

   a. Preganglionic fiber entering a pelvic nerve and traveling to the urinary bladder

   b. Vagus nerve from the brain to the heart

   c. Preganglionic fiber synapsing in a ciliary ganglion ■

Table 1	Comparison of Sympathetic and Parasympathetic Divisions of Autonomic Nervous System	
Characteristic	**Sympathetic Division**	**Parasympathetic Division**
Location of CNS visceral motor neurons	Lateral gray horns of spinal segments T_1–L_2	Brain stem and spinal segments S_2–S_4
Location of PNS ganglia	Near vertebral column	Typically intramural
Preganglionic fibers		
Length Neurotransmitter released	Relatively short ACh	Relatively long ACh
Ganglionic fibers		
Length Neurotransmitter released	Relatively long Normally NE; sometimes ACh	Relatively short ACh
Neuromuscular or neuroglandular junction	Varicosities and enlarged terminal knobs that release transmitter near target cells	Junctions that release transmitter to special receptor surface
Degree of divergence from CNS to ganglion cells	Approximately 1:32	Approximately 1:6
General function(s)	Stimulates metabolism; increases alertness; prepares for emergency ("fight or flight")	Promotes relaxation, nutrient uptake, energy storage ("rest and digest")

Name _____

Date _____

Section _____

Autonomic Nervous System

A. Description

Write a brief description of each ANS structure listed.

1. preganglionic neuron

2. gray ramus

3. adrenal medulla

4. rami communicantes

5. thoracolumbar division of ANS

6. collateral ganglion

7. intramural ganglion

8. white ramus

9. ganglionic neuron

10. craniosacral division of ANS

B. Short-Answer Questions

1. Discuss the anatomy of the sympathetic chain ganglia. How do fibers enter and exit these ganglia?

2. Which cranial nerves are involved in the parasympathetic division of the ANS?

3. Compare the lengths of preganglionic and ganglionic neurons in the sympathetic and parasympathetic divisions of the ANS.

C. Drawing

1. **Draw It!** In Figure 7, draw the preganglionic and ganglionic neurons for a sympathetic pathway from the CNS to visceral effectors in the skin.

2. **Draw It!** In Figure 7, draw the preganglionic and ganglionic neurons for a sympathetic pathway from the CNS to the stomach.

Figure 7 Sympathetic Pathways

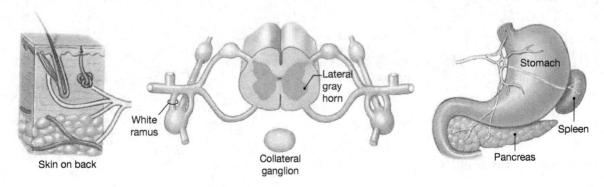

D. Analysis and Application

1. As a child, you might have been told to wait for up to an hour after eating before going swimming. Explain the rationale for this statement.

2. Compare the outflow of preganglionic neurons from the CNS in the sympathetic and parasympathetic divisions of the ANS.

E. Clinical Challenge

1. List four responses to sympathetic stimulation and four responses to parasympathetic stimulation.

2. Compare the effect that neurotransmitters from sympathetic and parasympathetic ganglionic fibers have on smooth muscle in the digestive tract, on cardiac muscle, and on arterioles in skeletal muscles.

Anatomy of the Heart
Wish List

Locate and identify structures of the heart using models or/and fixed specimens Remember that you will be required to be able to identify the structures marked with an * in the sheep heart. Also, make sure you compare the adult heart with the fetal heart. Illustrations of the fetal heart will be located at the end of the chapter on Systemic Circulation.

✓	Structure	Description
	Heart	
	myocardium	
	superior vena cava	
	inferior vena cava	
	right atrium	
	tricuspid valve	
	*right ventricle	
	*pulmonary (semilunar) valve	
	pulmonary trunk	
	pulmonary arteries	
	left atrium	
	pulmonary veins	
	*bicuspid (mitral) valve	
	*left ventricle	
	aortic (semilunar) valve	
	*aorta	
	aortic arch	
	descending aorta	
	pectinate muscles	
	trabeculae carnae	
	*papillary muscles	
	*chordae tendinae	
	*interventricular septum	
	interatrial septum	
	coronary artery	
	base	
	apex	

✓	Structure	Description
	Fetal heart	
	ductus venosus	
	ductus arteriosus	
	foramen ovale	

Anatomy of the Heart

Learning Outcomes

On completion of this exercise, you should be able to:

1. Describe the gross external and internal anatomy of the heart.

2. Identify and discuss the function of the valves of the heart.

3. Identify the major blood vessels of the heart.

4. Trace a drop of blood through the pulmonary circuit and the systemic circuit.

5. Identify the vessels of coronary circulation.

6. List the components of the conduction system of the heart.

7. Describe the anatomy of a sheep heart.

The cardiovascular system consists of blood; the heart, which pumps blood through the system; and all the blood vessels through which the blood flows. **Arteries** are the blood vessels that carry blood away from the heart, and **veins** are the blood vessels that return blood to the heart. In addition to arteries and veins, the cardiovascular system also contains small-diameter blood vessels called **capillaries.** It is across the walls of capillaries that gases, nutrients, and cellular waste products enter and exit the blood. The heart beats approximately 100,000 times daily to send blood flowing into thousands of miles of blood vessels, providing the body's cells with nutrients, regulating the amounts of substances and gases in the cells, and removing waste products from them. All organ systems of the body depend on the cardiovascular system. Damage to the heart often results in widespread disruption of homeostasis.

Lab Activities

1. Heart Wall

2. External and Internal Anatomy of the Heart

3. Coronary Circulation

4. Conducting System of the Heart

5. Sheep Heart Dissection

Clinical Applications

Mitral Valve Prolapse

Anastomoses and Infarctions

Need More Practice and Review?

Build your knowledge—and confidence!—in the Study Area of MasteringA&P® at www.masteringaandp.com with Pre-lab Quizzes, Post-lab Quizzes, Practice Anatomy Lab™ (PAL™) 3.0 virtual anatomy practice tool, PhysioEx™ 9.0 laboratory simulations, and A&P Flix™ with Quizzes.

PAL | practice anatomy lab™   For this lab exercise, follow these navigation paths:
- PAL>Human Cadaver>Cardiovascular System>Heart
- PAL>Anatomical Models>Cardiovascular System>Heart
- PAL>Histology>Cardiovascular System

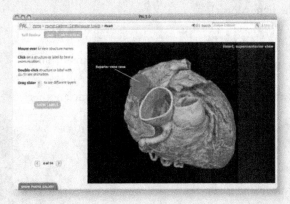

MasteringA&P®

Your laboratory studies in this exercise include the histology of cardiac muscle tissue, external and internal heart anatomy, and circulation of blood through the pulmonary and systemic circuits of the cardiovascular system. The dissection of a sheep heart will reinforce your observations of the human heart.

Lab Activity 1   Heart Wall

The heart is located in the **mediastinum** (mē-dē-as-TĪ-num) of the thoracic cavity (Figure 1). Blood vessels join the heart at the **base,** positioned medially in the mediastinum. Because the left side of the heart has more muscle mass than the right side, the **apex** at the inferior tip of the heart is more on the left side of the thoracic cavity. (Note from Figure 1a that the heart's base and apex are "upside down" relative to what we usually mean by those words. The base is anterior to the apex.) Within the mediastinum, the heart is surrounded by the **pericardial** (per-i-KAR-dē-al) **cavity** formed by the **pericardium,** the serous membrane of the heart. The pericardial cavity contains **serous fluid** to reduce friction during muscular contraction. The superficial **parietal pericardium** attaches to the heart in the mediastinum, and the deep **visceral pericardium,** or **epicardium,** covers the heart surface and is considered the outermost layer of the cardiac wall.

The heart wall is organized into three layers: epicardium, myocardium, and endocardium (Figure 2). The epicardium is the same structure as the visceral pericardium, as just noted. The myocardium constitutes most of the heart wall and is composed of **cardiac muscle cells,** also called **cardiocytes.** Each cardiac muscle cell is **uninucleated** (containing a single nucleus) and branched. Cardiac muscle cells interconnect at their branches via junctions called **intercalated** (in-TER-ka-lā-ted) **discs.** Deep to the myocardium is the **endocardium,** a thin layer that lines the chambers of the heart. The endocardium is composed of endothelial tissue resting on a layer of areolar connective tissue.

Make a Prediction

Why would the myocardium be thicker in the left ventricle than in the right ventricle?

QuickCheck Questions

1.1 List the three layers of the heart wall, from superficial to deep.

1.2 How are cardiac muscle cells connected to one another?

In the Lab   1

Materials

☐ Heart model and specimens
☐ Compound microscope
☐ Prepared slide of cardiac muscle

Procedures

1. Review the heart anatomy in Figures 1 and 2.
2. Identify the layers of the heart wall on the heart model and specimens.
3. With the microscope at low power, examine the microscopic structure of cardiac muscle, using Figure 2c for reference. Increase the magnification to high and locate several cardiac muscle cells. Note the single nucleus in each cell and where each cell branches into two arms. Intercalated discs are dark-stained lines where cardiac muscle cells connect together.
4. *Draw It!* Sketch several cardiac muscle cells and intercalated discs in the space provided. ■

Cardiac muscle cells

Lab Activity 2   External and Internal Anatomy of the Heart

The heart is divided into right and left sides, with each side having an upper and a lower chamber (Figure 3). The upper chambers are the **right atrium** (Ā-trē-um; chamber) and the **left atrium,** and the lower chambers are the **right ventricle** (VEN-tri-kl; little belly) and the **left ventricle.** The atria are receiving chambers and fill with blood returning to the heart in veins. Blood in the atria flows into the ventricles, the pumping chambers, which squeeze their walls together to pressurize the blood and eject it into two large arteries for distribution to the lungs and body tissues. Most of the blood in the atria flows into the ventricles because of pressure and gravity. Before the ventricles contract, the atria contract and "top off" the ventricles.

For a drop of blood to complete one circuit through the body, it must be pumped by the heart twice—through the **pulmonary circuit,** which directs deoxygenated blood to the lungs; and through the **systemic circuit,** which takes oxygenated blood to the rest of the body (Figure 3). Each circuit delivers blood to a series of arteries, then capillaries, and finally veins that drain into the opposite side of the heart.

Figure 1 **The Location of the Heart in the Thoracic Cavity** The heart is situated in the anterior part of the mediastinum, immediately posterior to the sternum.

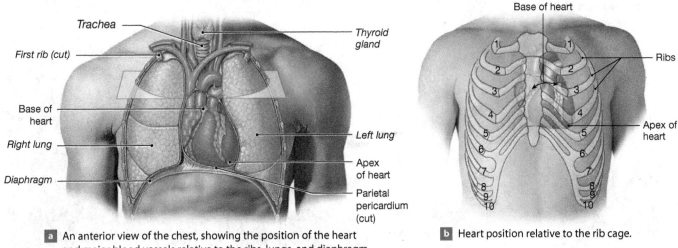

Trachea

Thyroid gland

First rib (cut)

Base of heart

Right lung

Diaphragm

Left lung

Apex of heart

Parietal pericardium (cut)

a An anterior view of the chest, showing the position of the heart and major blood vessels relative to the ribs, lungs, and diaphragm.

Base of heart

Ribs

Apex of heart

b Heart position relative to the rib cage.

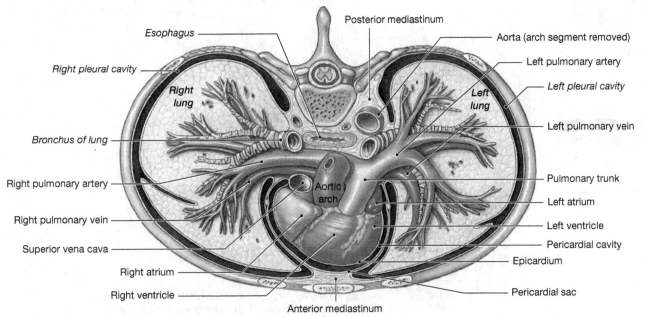

Esophagus

Right pleural cavity

Right lung

Bronchus of lung

Right pulmonary artery

Right pulmonary vein

Superior vena cava

Right atrium

Right ventricle

Posterior mediastinum

Aorta (arch segment removed)

Left pulmonary artery

Left pleural cavity

Left lung

Left pulmonary vein

Pulmonary trunk

Left atrium

Left ventricle

Pericardial cavity

Epicardium

Pericardial sac

Aortic arch

Anterior mediastinum

c A superior view of the organs in the mediastinum; portions of the lungs have been removed to reveal blood vessels and airways. The heart is situated in the anterior part of the mediastinum, immediately posterior to the sternum.

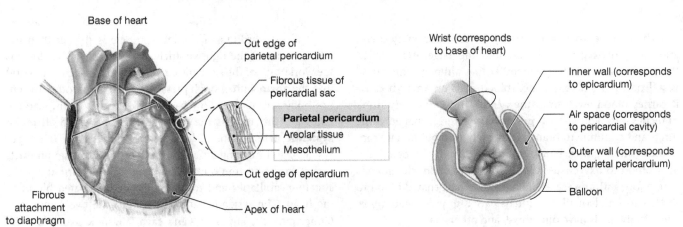

Base of heart

Cut edge of parietal pericardium

Fibrous tissue of pericardial sac

Parietal pericardium
Areolar tissue
Mesothelium

Cut edge of epicardium

Fibrous attachment to diaphragm

Apex of heart

Wrist (corresponds to base of heart)

Inner wall (corresponds to epicardium)

Air space (corresponds to pericardial cavity)

Outer wall (corresponds to parietal pericardium)

Balloon

d The relationship between the heart and the pericardial cavity; compare with the fist-and-balloon example.

333

Figure 2 The Heart Wall

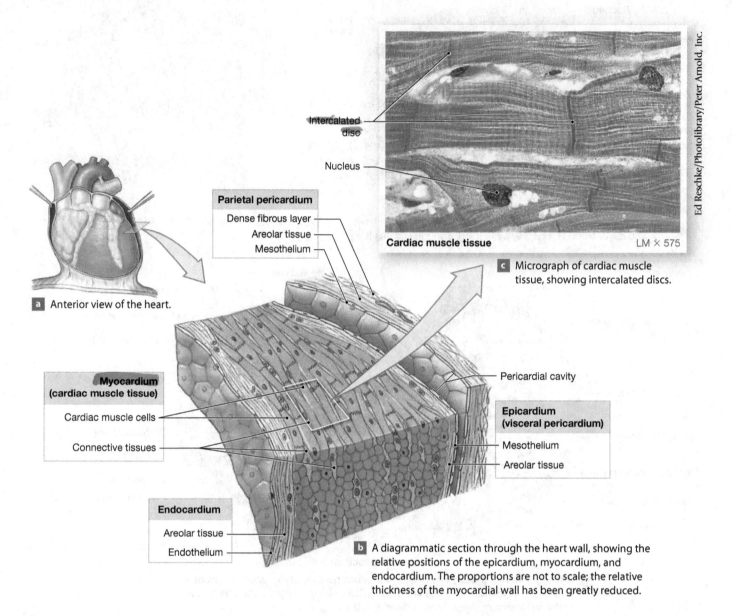

Intercalated disc

Nucleus

Cardiac muscle tissue

LM × 575

Ed Reschke/Photolibrary/Peter Arnold, Inc.

c Micrograph of cardiac muscle tissue, showing intercalated discs.

Parietal pericardium
Dense fibrous layer
Areolar tissue
Mesothelium

a Anterior view of the heart.

Myocardium (cardiac muscle tissue)
Cardiac muscle cells
Connective tissues

Pericardial cavity

Epicardium (visceral pericardium)
Mesothelium
Areolar tissue

Endocardium
Areolar tissue
Endothelium

b A diagrammatic section through the heart wall, showing the relative positions of the epicardium, myocardium, and endocardium. The proportions are not to scale; the relative thickness of the myocardial wall has been greatly reduced.

The right ventricle is the pump for the pulmonary circuit and ejects deoxygenated blood into the large artery called the **pulmonary trunk.** (Remember that although this blood vessel transports deoxygenated blood, it is an artery because it carries blood away from the heart.) The pulmonary trunk branches into right and left **pulmonary arteries** that enter the lungs and continue to branch ultimately into pulmonary capillaries, where gas exchange occurs to convert the deoxygenated blood to oxygenated blood. The pulmonary circuit ends where four **pulmonary veins** return the oxygenated blood to the left atrium. Not all individuals have four pulmonary veins; some individuals have only three, and others have five.

The myocardium of the left ventricle is thicker than the myocardium of the right ventricle. The thicker left ventricle is the workhorse of the systemic circuit; it ejects oxygenated blood into the **aorta** with enough pressure to deliver blood to the entire body and have it flow back to the heart to complete the pathway. The aorta is the main artery from which all major **systemic arteries** arise. The systemic arteries enter the organ systems, and exchange of gases, nutrients, and waste products occurs in the **systemic capillaries. Systemic veins** drain the systemic capillaries and transport the deoxygenated blood to the heart. The systemic veins merge into the two largest systemic veins: the **superior vena cava** (VĒ-na KĀ-vuh) and the

Figure 3 **Generalized View of the Pulmonary and Systemic Circuits** Blood flows through separate pulmonary and systemic circuits, driven by the pumping of the heart. Each circuit begins and ends at the heart and contains arteries, capillaries, and veins. Arrows indicate the direction of blood flow in each circuit.

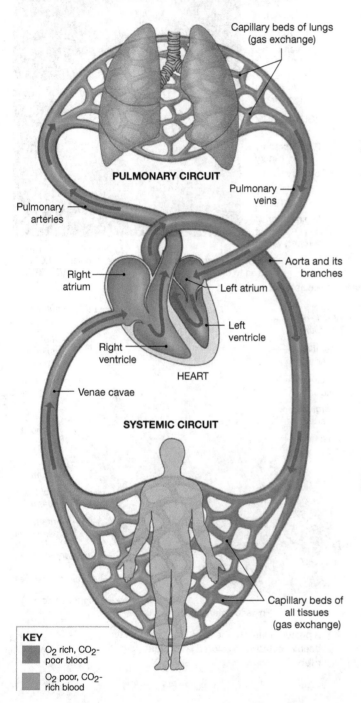

Capillary beds of lungs (gas exchange)

PULMONARY CIRCUIT

Pulmonary veins

Pulmonary arteries

Aorta and its branches

Right atrium

Left atrium

Left ventricle

Right ventricle

HEART

Venae cavae

SYSTEMIC CIRCUIT

Capillary beds of all tissues (gas exchange)

KEY
- O$_2$ rich, CO$_2$-poor blood
- O$_2$ poor, CO$_2$-rich blood

inferior vena cava, which empty the deoxygenated blood into the right atrium. The cycle of blood flow repeats as the deoxygenated blood enters the right ventricle and is pumped through the pulmonary circuit to the lungs to pick up oxygen for the next journey through the systemic circuit.

The external anatomy of the heart is detailed in **Figure 4.** The anterior surface of each atrium has an external flap called the **auricle** (AW-ri-kul; *auris,* ear), shown in Figure 4a. Adipose tissue and blood vessels occur along grooves in the heart wall. The **coronary sulcus** is a deep groove between the right atrium and right ventricle that extends to the posterior surface. The boundary between the right and left ventricles is marked anteriorly by the **anterior interventricular sulcus** and posteriorly by the **posterior interventricular sulcus.** Coronary blood vessels follow the sulci and branch to the myocardium. At the branch of the pulmonary trunk is the **ligamentum arteriosum,** a relic of a fetal vessel called the ductus arteriosus that joined the pulmonary trunk with the aorta.

Figure 5 details the internal anatomy of the heart. Note how much thicker the myocardium is in the left ventricle, as mentioned previously. The wall between the atria is called the **interatrial septum,** and the ventricles are separated by the **interventricular septum.** In the right atrium, a depression called the **fossa ovalis** is located on the interatrial septum. This is a remnant of fetal circulation, where the foramen ovale allowed blood to bypass the fetal pulmonary circuit. Lining the inside of the right atrium are muscular ridges, the **pectinate** (*pectin,* comb) **muscles.** Folds of muscle tissue called **trabeculae carneae** (tra-BEK-ū-lē KAR-nē-ē; *carneus,* fleshy) occur on the inner surface of each ventricle. The **moderator band** is a ribbon of muscle that passes electrical signals from the interventricular septum to muscles in the right ventricle.

To control and direct blood flow, the heart has two **atrioventricular (AV) valves** and two **semilunar valves.** The two pairs generally work in opposition: When the AV valves are open, the semilunar valves are either closed or preparing to close; when the semilunar valves are open, the AV valves are either closed or preparing to close. The two atrioventricular valves prevent blood from reentering the atria when the ventricles contract. The **right atrioventricular valve,** which joins the right atrium and right ventricle, has three flaps, or cusps, and is also called the **tricuspid** (trī-KUS-pid; *tri,* three; *cuspid,* flap) **valve.** The **left atrioventricular valve** between the left atrium and left ventricle has two cusps and is called either the **bicuspid valve** or the **mitral** (MĪ-tral) **valve.** The cusps of each AV valve have small cords, the **chordae tendineae** (KOR-dē TEN-di-nē-ē; *tendonlike cords*), which are attached to **papillary** (PAP-i-ler-ē) **muscles** on the floor of the ventricles. When the ventricles contract, the AV valves are held closed by the papillary muscles pulling on the chordae tendineae.

The two semilunar valves are the **aortic valve** and **pulmonary valve,** each located at the base of its artery. These valves prevent backflow of blood into the ventricles when the ventricles are relaxed. Each semilunar valve has three small cusps that, when the ventricles relax, fill with blood and close the base of the artery.

335

Figure 4 External Anatomy of the Heart

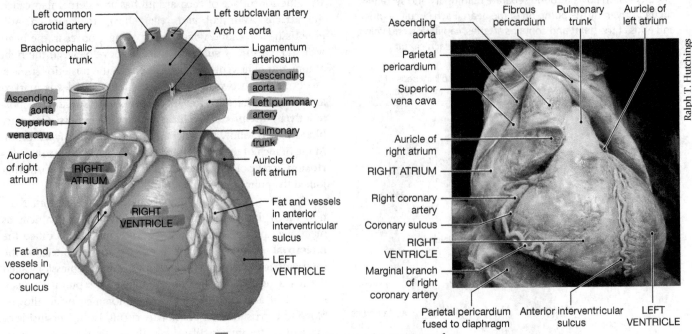

Left common carotid artery
Left subclavian artery
Arch of aorta
Brachiocephalic trunk
Ligamentum arteriosum
Descending aorta
Ascending aorta
Left pulmonary artery
Superior vena cava
Pulmonary trunk
Auricle of right atrium
RIGHT ATRIUM
Auricle of left atrium
RIGHT VENTRICLE
Fat and vessels in anterior interventricular sulcus
Fat and vessels in coronary sulcus
LEFT VENTRICLE

Fibrous pericardium
Pulmonary trunk
Auricle of left atrium
Ascending aorta
Parietal pericardium
Superior vena cava
Auricle of right atrium
RIGHT ATRIUM
Right coronary artery
Coronary sulcus
RIGHT VENTRICLE
Marginal branch of right coronary artery
Parietal pericardium fused to diaphragm
Anterior interventricular sulcus
LEFT VENTRICLE

Ralph T. Hutchings

a Major anatomical features on the anterior surface.

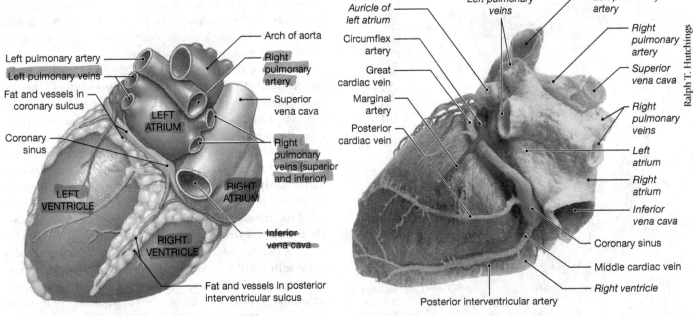

Left pulmonary artery
Left pulmonary veins
Fat and vessels in coronary sulcus
Coronary sinus
LEFT VENTRICLE
Arch of aorta
Right pulmonary artery
Superior vena cava
LEFT ATRIUM
Right pulmonary veins (superior and inferior)
RIGHT ATRIUM
RIGHT VENTRICLE
Inferior vena cava
Fat and vessels in posterior interventricular sulcus

b Major landmarks on the posterior surface. Coronary arteries (which supply the heart itself) are shown in red; coronary veins are shown in blue.

Auricle of left atrium
Left pulmonary veins
Left pulmonary artery
Circumflex artery
Right pulmonary artery
Great cardiac vein
Superior vena cava
Marginal artery
Right pulmonary veins
Posterior cardiac vein
Left atrium
Right atrium
Inferior vena cava
Coronary sinus
Middle cardiac vein
Right ventricle
Posterior interventricular artery

Ralph T. Hutchings

c A posterior view of the heart; the vessels have been injected with colored latex (liquid rubber).

336

Figure 5 **Internal Anatomy of the Heart**

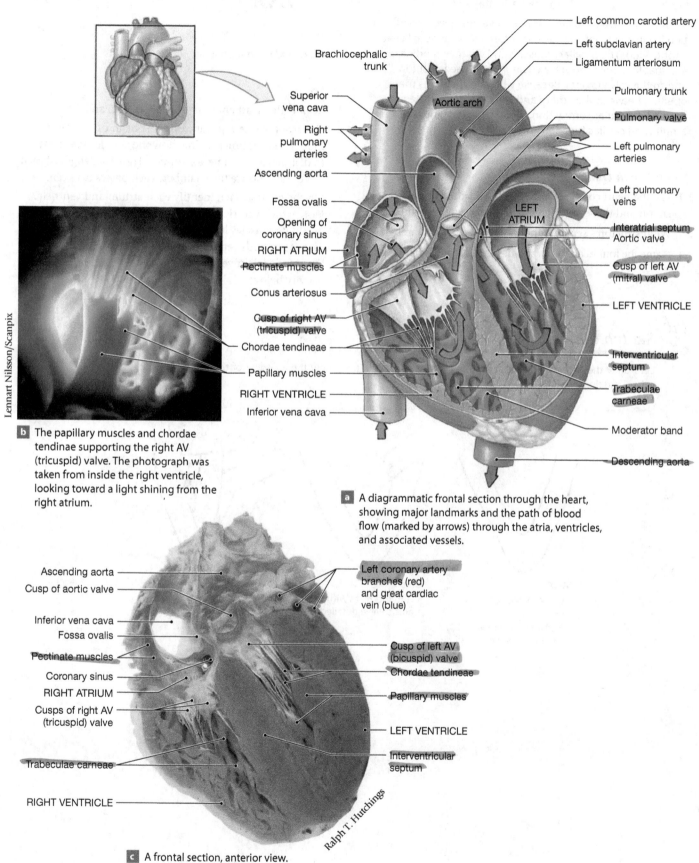

Left common carotid artery

Left subclavian artery

Ligamentum arteriosum

Brachiocephalic trunk

Pulmonary trunk

Aortic arch

Pulmonary valve

Superior vena cava

Left pulmonary arteries

Right pulmonary arteries

Left pulmonary veins

Ascending aorta

LEFT ATRIUM

Interatrial septum

Fossa ovalis

Aortic valve

Opening of coronary sinus

Cusp of left AV (mitral) valve

RIGHT ATRIUM

Pectinate muscles

LEFT VENTRICLE

Conus arteriosus

Cusp of right AV (tricuspid) valve

Interventricular septum

Chordae tendineae

Trabeculae carneae

Papillary muscles

RIGHT VENTRICLE

Moderator band

Inferior vena cava

Descending aorta

b The papillary muscles and chordae tendinae supporting the right AV (tricuspid) valve. The photograph was taken from inside the right ventricle, looking toward a light shining from the right atrium.

Lennart Nilsson/Scanpix

a A diagrammatic frontal section through the heart, showing major landmarks and the path of blood flow (marked by arrows) through the atria, ventricles, and associated vessels.

Ascending aorta

Cusp of aortic valve

Left coronary artery branches (red) and great cardiac vein (blue)

Inferior vena cava

Fossa ovalis

Cusp of left AV (bicuspid) valve

Pectinate muscles

Chordae tendineae

Coronary sinus

RIGHT ATRIUM

Papillary muscles

Cusps of right AV (tricuspid) valve

LEFT VENTRICLE

Trabeculae carneae

Interventricular septum

RIGHT VENTRICLE

Ralph T. Hutchings

c A frontal section, anterior view.

Clinical Application Mitral Valve Prolapse

A common valve problem is **mitral valve prolapse**, a condition in which the left AV valve reverses, like an umbrella in a strong wind. The papillary muscles and chordae tendineae are unable to hold the valve cusps in the closed position, and so the valve inverts. Because when this happens the opening between the atrium and ventricle is not sealed shut during ventricular contraction, blood backflows into the left atrium, and cardiac function is diminished. ■

QuickCheck Questions

2.1 List the heart chambers associated with the pulmonary circuit and those associated with the systemic circuit.

2.2 What structures separate the walls of the heart chambers?

2.3 Name the four heart valves and describe the function of each.

Materials

☐ Heart model and specimens

Procedures

1. Review the heart anatomy in Figures 3, 4, and 5.

2. Observe the external features of the heart on the heart model and specimens. Note how the auricles may be used to distinguish the anterior surface. Trace the length of each sulcus, and notice the chambers each passes between.

3. On the heart model, identify each atrium and ventricle. Note which ventricle has the thicker wall. Identify the pectinate muscles in the right atrium and the trabeculae carneae in both ventricles. Locate the moderator band in the inferior right ventricle. Complete the *Sketch to Learn* activity below.

Sketch to Learn

Let's draw the left ventricle, isolated from the rest of the heart, to show the anatomy of the ventricle, valves, and the aorta.

Sample Sketch

Step 1
- Draw a V shape for the ventricle.
- Add an outer line to complete the heart wall.

Step 2
- Add the aorta with the aortic valve detailed.

Step 3
- Sketch in the bicuspid valve and associated anatomy.
- Label your sketch.

Your Sketch

4. Identify the two AV valves, their cusps, and the two semilunar valves.

5. Identify the major arteries and veins at the base of the heart.

6. Starting at the superior vena cava, trace a drop of blood though the heart model, and distinguish between the pulmonary and systemic circuits. ■

Lab Activity 3 Coronary Circulation

To produce the pressure required for blood to reach all through the cardiovascular system, the heart can never completely rest. The branch of the systemic circuit known as the **coronary circulation** supplies the myocardium with the oxygen necessary for muscle contraction (Figure 6). The right and left **coronary arteries** of the coronary circulation are the first vessels to branch off the base of the ascending aorta and penetrate the myocardium to the outer heart wall. As the right coronary artery (RCA) passes along the coronary sulcus, many **atrial arteries** supply blood to the right atrium and one or more **marginal arteries** arise to supply the right ventricle. The **posterior interventricular branch** off the RCA supplies adjacent posterior regions of the ventricles.

The left coronary artery (LCA) branches to supply blood to the left atrium, left ventricle, and interventricular septum.

The LCA divides into a **circumflex artery** and an **anterior interventricular artery.** The anterior interventricular branch supplies the left ventricle. The circumflex branch follows the left side of the heart, turns inferior, and passes along the left ventricle as the **marginal artery.** The posterior branches of the RCA and LCA often unite in the posterior coronary sulcus.

The **cardiac veins** of the coronary circulation collect deoxygenated blood from the myocardium (Figure 6). The **great cardiac vein** follows along the anterior interventricular sulcus and curves around the left side of the heart to drain the myocardium supplied by the anterior interventricular branch. The **posterior cardiac vein** drains the myocardium supplied by the LCA posterior ventricular branch. The **small cardiac vein** drains the superior right area of the heart. The **middle cardiac vein** drains the myocardium supplied by the posterior interventricular branch of the RCA. The cardiac veins merge as a large **coronary sinus** situated in the posterior region of the coronary sulcus. The coronary sinus empties deoxygenated blood from the myocardium into the right atrium. As noted previously, the right atrium also receives deoxygenated blood from the venae cavae.

QuickCheck Questions

3.1 Where do the right and left coronary arteries arise?

3.2 Where do the cardiac veins drain?

Figure 6 Coronary Circulation Coronary arteries and cardiac veins supply and drain the myocardium of blood.

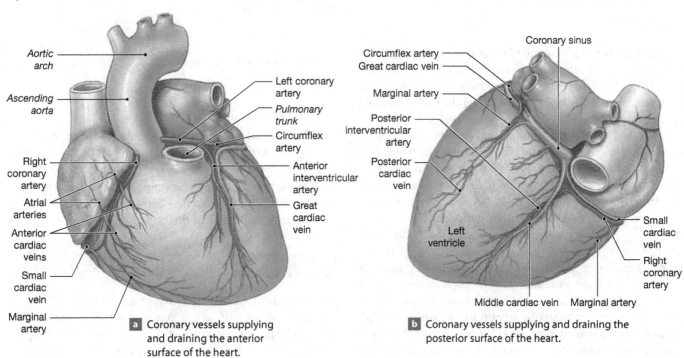

a Coronary vessels supplying and draining the anterior surface of the heart.

b Coronary vessels supplying and draining the posterior surface of the heart.

Anastomoses and Infarctions

The interventricular branches connect with one another, as do smaller arteries between the right coronary artery and the circumflex branch of the left coronary artery. These connections, called **anastomoses**, ensure that blood flow to the myocardium remains steady. In coronary artery disease, the arteries become narrower and narrower as fatty plaque is deposited on the interior walls of the vessels. As a result, blood flow is reduced. If enough plaque accumulates in critical areas, blood flow to that part of the heart becomes inadequate, and the heart muscle has an **infarction**, a heart attack. ■

In the Lab 3

Materials

☐ Heart model and specimens

Procedures

1. Review the blood vessels of the coronary circulation in Figure 6.
2. Follow the RCA and LCA on the heart model and identify their main branches.
3. Identify the cardiac veins and trace them into the coronary sinus. Identify where the coronary sinus drains. ■

Lab Activity 4   Conducting System of the Heart

Cardiac muscle tissue is unique in that it is *autorhythmic*, producing its own contraction and relaxation phases without stimulation from nerves. Nerves may increase or decrease the heart rate, but a living heart removed from the body continues to contract on its own.

Figure 7 details the **conducting system** of the heart. Special cells called **nodal cells** produce and conduct electrical currents to the myocardium, and it is these currents that coordinate the heart's contraction. The pacemaker of the heart is the **sinoatrial** (si-nō-Ā-trē-al) **node** (SA node), located where the superior vena cava empties into the upper right atrium. Nodal cells in the SA node self-excite faster than nodal cells in other areas of the heart and therefore set the pace for the heart's contraction. The **atrioventricular node** (AV node) is located on the lower medial floor of the right atrium. The SA node stimulates both the atria and the AV node, and the AV node then directs the impulse toward the ventricles through the **atrioventricular bundle,** also called the *bundle of His*. The atrioventricular bundle passes into the interventricular septum

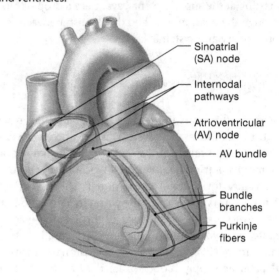

Figure 7 Conducting System of the Heart Components of the conducting system are specialized nodal cells that generate and distribute electrical signals, to coordinate the contraction of the atria and ventricles.

- Sinoatrial (SA) node
- Internodal pathways
- Atrioventricular (AV) node
- AV bundle
- Bundle branches
- Purkinje fibers

and branches into right and left **bundle branches.** The bundle branches divide into fine **Purkinje fibers,** which distribute the electrical impulses to the cardiocytes.

QuickCheck Questions

4.1 Where is the pacemaker of the heart located?

4.2 How is the AV node connected to the ventricles?

In the Lab 4

Materials

☐ Heart model and specimens

Procedures

1. Review the conducting system in Figure 7.
2. On the heart model, examine the sinus where the superior vena cava drains into the right atrium, and locate the SA node.
3. On the floor of the right atrium, locate the AV node. Trace the conducting path to the ventricles: AV bundle, bundle branches, and Purkinje fibers. ■

Lab Activity 5   Sheep Heart Dissection

The sheep heart, like all other mammalian hearts, is similar in structure and function to the human heart. One major difference is in where the great vessels join the heart. In four-legged animals, the inferior vena cava has a posterior connection to

Anatomy of the Heart

Safety Alert: Dissecting the Heart

You *must* practice the highest level of laboratory safety while handling and dissecting the heart. Keep the following guidelines in mind during the dissection.

1. Wear gloves and safety glasses to protect yourself from the fixatives used to preserve the specimen.
2. Do not dispose of the fixative from your specimen. You will later store the specimen in the fixative to keep the specimen moist and to keep it from decaying.
3. Be extremely careful when using a scalpel or other sharp instrument. Always direct cutting and scissor motion away from you to prevent an accident if the instrument slips on moist tissue.
4. Before cutting a given tissue, make sure it is free from underlying and/or adjacent tissues so that they will not be accidentally severed.
5. Never discard tissue in the sink or trash. Your instructor will inform you of the proper disposal procedure. ▲

the heart instead of the inferior connection found in humans. Dissecting a sheep heart will enhance your studies of models and charts of the human heart. Take your time while dissecting and follow the directions carefully.

QuickCheck Questions

5.1 What type of safety equipment should you wear as you dissect the sheep heart?

5.2 How should you dispose of the sheep heart and scrap tissue?

In the Lab 5

Materials

☐ Gloves
☐ Safety glasses
☐ Dissecting tools
☐ Dissecting pan
☐ Fresh or preserved sheep heart

Procedures

1. Put on gloves and safety glasses, and clear your work space before obtaining your dissection specimen.
2. Wash the sheep heart with cold water to flush out preservatives and blood clots. Minimize your skin and mucous membrane exposure to the preservatives.
3. Carefully follow the instructions in this section. Cut into the heart only as instructed.

External Anatomy

1. Figure 8 details the external anatomy of the sheep heart. Examine the surface of the heart to see if the pericardium is present. (Often this serous membrane has been removed from preserved specimens.) Carefully scrape the outer heart muscle with a scalpel to loosen the epicardium.
2. Locate the anterior surface by orienting the heart so that the auricles face you. Under the auricles are the right and left atria. Note the base of the heart above the atria, where the large blood vessels occur. Squeeze gently just above the apex to locate the right and left ventricles. Locate the anterior interventricular sulcus, the fat-laden groove between the ventricles. Carefully remove some of the adipose tissue with the scalpel to uncover coronary blood vessels. Identify two grooves—the coronary sulcus between the right atrium and ventricle and the posterior interventricular sulcus between the ventricles on the posterior surface.
3. Identify the aorta and then the pulmonary trunk anterior to the aorta. If on your specimen the pulmonary trunk was cut long, you may be able to identify the right and left pulmonary arteries branching off the trunk. The brachiocephalic artery is the first major branch of the aorta and is often intact in preserved material.

Figure 8 **External Anatomy of the Sheep Heart**

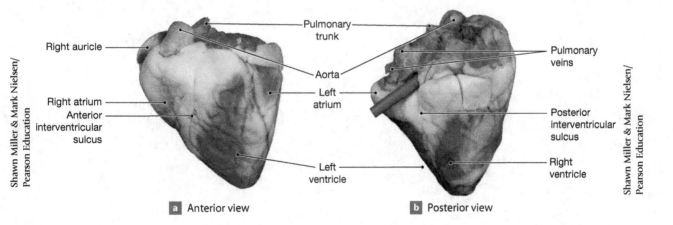

a Anterior view

b Posterior view

Shawn Miller & Mark Nielsen/Pearson Education

4. Follow along the inferior margin of the right auricle to the posterior surface. The prominent vessel at the termination of the auricle is the superior vena cava. At the base of this vessel is the inferior vena cava. Next, examine the posterior aspect of the left atrium and find the four pulmonary veins. You may need to carefully remove some of the adipose tissue around the superior region of the left atrium to locate these veins.

Internal Anatomy

1. Cut a frontal section passing through the aorta. Use Figure 9 as a reference to the internal anatomy.

2. Examine the two sides of the heart. Identify the right and left atria, right and left ventricles, and the interventricular septum. Compare the myocardium of the left ventricle with that of the right ventricle. Note the folds of trabeculae carneae along the inner ventricular walls. Examine the right atrium for the comblike pectinate muscles lining the inner wall.

3. Locate the tricuspid and bicuspid valves. Observe the papillary muscles with chordae tendineae attached.

4. Examine the wall of the left atrium for the openings of the four pulmonary veins.

5. At the entrance of the aorta, locate the small cusps of the aortic valve.

6. At the base of the pulmonary trunk, locate the pulmonary valve.

7. Locate the superior and inferior venae cavae, which drain into the right atrium.

8. Upon completion of the dissection, dispose of the sheep heart as directed by your instructor and wash your hands and dissecting instruments. ■

Figure 9 Internal Anatomy of the Sheep Heart The major anatomical features of the sheep heart as shown in a frontal section.

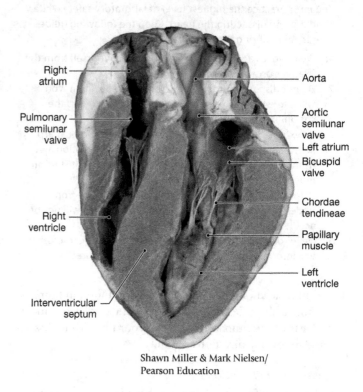

Shawn Miller & Mark Nielsen/
Pearson Education

Name _____

Date _____

Section _____

Anatomy of the Heart

A. Descriptions

Write a description of each heart structure.

1. tricuspid valve

2. superior vena cava

3. interventricular septum

4. left ventricle

5. pulmonary veins

6. semilunar valve

7. bicuspid valve

8. pulmonary trunk

9. circumflex artery

10. trabeculae carneae

11. coronary sinus

12. epicardium

B. Short-Answer Questions

1. List the layers of the heart wall.

2. Describe how the AV valves function.

3. List the order in which an electrical impulse spreads through the conducting system.

C. Labeling

1. Label the anatomy of the heart in Figure 10.

Figure 10 **Frontal Section Through the Heart**

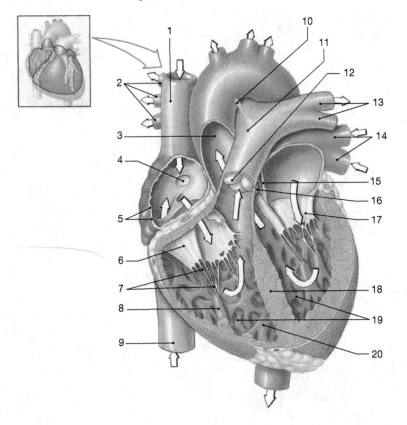

1. _____
2. _____
3. _____
4. _____
5. _____
6. _____
7. _____
8. _____
9. _____
10. _____
11. _____
12. _____
13. _____
14. _____
15. _____
16. _____
17. _____
18. _____
19. _____
20. _____

2. Label the major arteries and veins on the posterior of the heart in Figure 11.

Figure 11 Posterior Surface of the Heart

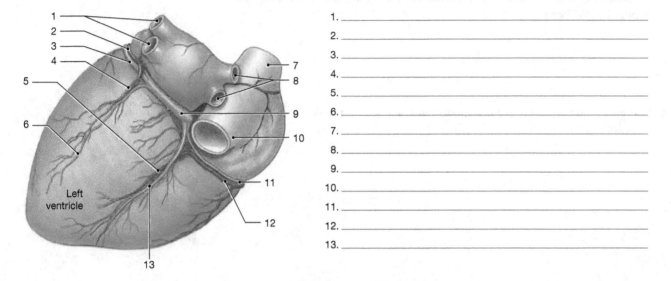

1. _____
2. _____
3. _____
4. _____
5. _____
6. _____
7. _____
8. _____
9. _____
10. _____
11. _____
12. _____
13. _____

D. Analysis and Application

1. Explain the difference between thickness of the myocardium in the right and left ventricles.

2. Does the pulmonary trunk transport oxygenated blood or deoxygenated blood? Why is it an artery rather than a vein?

3. Trace a drop of blood through the pulmonary and systemic circuits of the heart.

E. **Clinical Challenge**

1. Suppose a patient has a weakened bicuspid valve that does not close properly, a condition called mitral valve prolapse. How does this valve defect affect the flow of blood in the heart?

2. Coronary artery disease in the marginal arteries would affect which part of the myocardium?

Anatomy of the Systemic Circulation
Wish List

Locate and identify structures of the venous (v) and arterial (a) system using models.

	Structure	Description
	Veins (v) and Arteries (a)	-
	internal carotid a.	
	internal jugular v.	
	external carotid a	
	external jugular v.	
	brachiocephalic (a. & v.)	
	subclavian (a. & v.)	
	common carotid (right and left) a.	
	superior vena cava	
	thoracic aorta	
	inferior vena cava	
	abdominal aorta	

	Structure	Description
	celiac trunk	three branches
	hepatic a.	
	gastric a.	
	splenic a.	
	superior mesenteric a.	
	inferior mesenteric a.	
	renal (a. & v.)	

	Structure	Description
	Axillary (a. & v.)	
	Brachial (a. & v.)	
	Radial (a. & v.)	
	Ulnar (a. & v.)	
	(Superficial) palmar (a. & v.)	

	Structure	Description
	common iliac (a. & v.)	
	femoral (a. & v.)	

	Structure	Description
	Hepatic portal system	
	superior mesenteric v.	
	splenic v.	
	gastric v.	
	hepatic portal v.	

	Structure	Description
	Fetal Circulation	
	placenta prostatic	
	umbilical cord	
	umbilical a. and v.	

Anatomy of the Systemic Circulation

Learning Outcomes

On completion of this exercise, you should be able to:

1. Compare the histology of an artery, a capillary, and a vein.

2. Describe the difference in the blood vessels serving the right and left arms.

3. Describe the anatomy and importance of the circle of Willis.

4. Trace a drop of blood from the ascending aorta into each abdominal organ and into the lower limbs.

5. Trace a drop of blood returning to the heart from the foot.

6. Discuss the unique features of the fetal circulation.

Clinical Application

Arteriosclerosis

The body contains more than 60,000 miles of blood vessels to transport blood to the trillions of cells in the tissues. Arteries of the systemic circuit distribute oxygen and nutrient-rich blood to microscopic networks of thin-walled vessels called capillaries. At the capillaries, nutrients, gases, wastes, and cellular products diffuse either from blood to cells or from cells to blood. Veins drain deoxygenated blood from the systemic capillaries and direct it toward the heart, which then pumps it into the pulmonary circuit, to be carried to the lungs to pick up oxygen and release carbon dioxide.

In this exercise, you will study the major arteries and veins of the systemic circuit.

Need More Practice and Review?

Build your knowledge—and confidence!—in the Study Area of MasteringA&P® at www.masteringaandp.com with Pre-lab Quizzes, Post-lab Quizzes, Practice Anatomy Lab™ (PAL™) 3.0 virtual anatomy practice tool, PhysioEx™ 9.0 laboratory simulations, and A&P Flix™ with Quizzes.

PAL For this lab exercise, follow these navigation paths:
- PAL>Human Cadaver>Cardiovascular System>Blood Vessels
- PAL>Anatomical Models>Cardiovascular System>Veins
- PAL>Anatomical Models>Cardiovascular System>Arteries
- PAL>Histology> Cardiovascular System

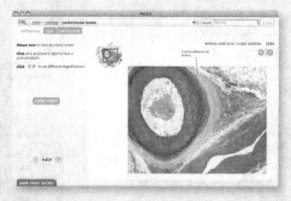

Lab Activity 1 Comparison of Arteries, Capillaries, and Veins

The walls of the body's blood vessels have three layers (Figure 1). The **tunica externa** is a layer of connective tissue that anchors the vessel to surrounding tissues. Collagen and elastic fibers give this layer strength and flexibility. The **tunica media** is a layer of smooth muscle tissue. In the tunica media of arteries are elastic fibers that allow the vessels to stretch and recoil in response to blood pressure changes. Veins have fewer elastic fibers; collagen fibers in the tunica media provide strength. Lining the inside of the vessels is the third layer, the **tunica intima,** a thin layer of simple squamous epithelium called **endothelium.** In arteries, the luminal surface of the endothelium has a thick, dark-staining **internal elastic membrane.**

Make a Prediction

Which vessels have greater pressure: arteries or veins, and which type of vessel has valves?

Because blood pressure is much higher in arteries than in veins and also because the pressure fluctuates more in arteries than in veins, the walls of arteries are thicker than those of veins. Notice how the artery cross section in the micrograph of Figure 1 is round and thick walled, whereas the adjacent vein is irregularly shaped and thin walled. In a slide preparation, the tunica intima of an artery may appear pleated because the vessel wall has recoiled due to a loss of pressure. In reality, the luminal surface is smooth and the vessel can expand and shrink to regulate blood flow.

A capillary consists of a single layer of endothelium that is continuous with the tunica intima of the artery and vein supplying and draining the capillary. Capillaries are so narrow that RBCs must line up in single file to squeeze through.

Veins have a thinner wall than arteries. The walls of a vein collapse if the vessel is emptied of blood. Blood pressure is low in veins; and to prevent backflow, the peripheral veins have valves that keep blood flowing in one direction, toward the heart.

QuickCheck Questions

1.1 Describe the three layers in the wall of an artery.

1.2 How do arterial walls differ from venous walls?

In the Lab 1

Materials

☐ Compound microscope

☐ Prepared slide of artery and vein

☐ Prepared slide of artery with plaque (atherosclerosis)

Procedures

1. Place the artery/vein slide on the microscope stage and locate the artery and vein at low magnification. Most slide preparations have one artery, an adjacent vein, and a nerve. The blood vessels are hollow and most likely have blood cells in the lumen. The nerve appears as a round, solid structure.

Figure 1 Comparison of the Structure of a Typical Artery and Vein Arteries have thicker walls and retain their shape compared to veins.

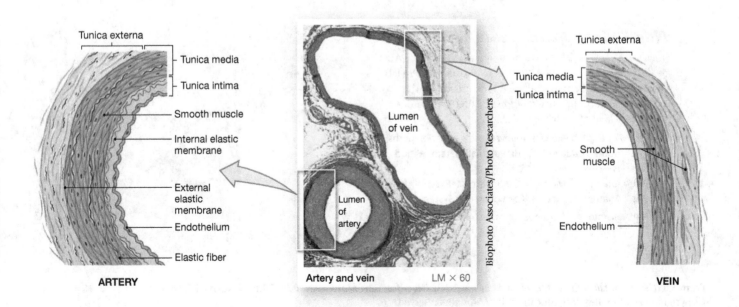

Tunica externa — Tunica media — Tunica intima — Smooth muscle — Internal elastic membrane — External elastic membrane — Endothelium — Elastic fiber

ARTERY

Lumen of vein — Lumen of artery

Biophoto Associates/Photo Researchers

Artery and vein LM × 60

Tunica externa — Tunica media — Tunica intima — Smooth muscle — Endothelium

VEIN

Clinical Application Arteriosclerosis

Arteriosclerosis (ar-tĕr-ē-o-skler-Ō-sis) is the thickening and hardening of an artery. In cases of **focal calcification,** calcium salts gradually accumulate and damage smooth muscle tissue in the tunica media of the vessel wall. **Atherosclerosis** (ath-ĕr-o-skler-Ō-sis) is the buildup of lipid deposits in the tunica media (**Figure 2**). The deposits, called atherosclerotic **plaque,** eventually damage the vessel's endothelium and obstruct blood flow. Plaque accumulation in coronary arteries greatly increases the risk of heart attack and stroke. During balloon angioplasty, a catheter with an inflatable tip is used to push the plaque against the vessel wall to restore blood flow. A stent is frequently inserted into the narrowed region of the vessel to keep the vessel open. To reduce the risk of arteriosclerosis, lower the consumption of dietary fats such as saturated fats, trans fats, and cholesterol found in red meat, dairy cream, and egg yolks. Monitoring blood pressure and cholestrol levels and controlling weight are important for good vascular health. ■

Figure 2 A Plaque Within an Artery

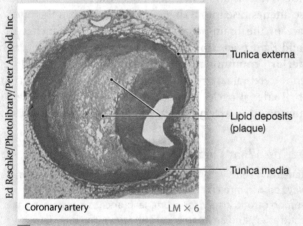

Coronary artery   LM × 6

a A cross-sectional view of a large plaque

- Tunica externa
- Lipid deposits (plaque)
- Tunica media

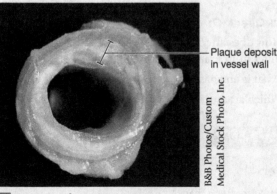

- Plaque deposit in vessel wall

b A section of a coronary artery narrowed by plaque formation

2. Increase the magnification to high and compare each arterial layer with its venous counterpart.

3. *Draw It!* Draw and label a cross section of an artery and a vein in the space provided. Include enough detail in your drawings to show the anatomical differences between the vessels.

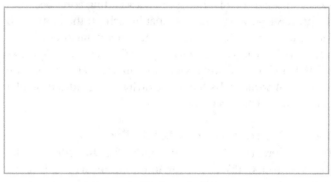

Artery cross section

Vein cross section

4. Examine the slide of an artery with atherosclerosis and note where the plaque has accumulated in the vessel. ■

Lab Activity 2 Arteries of the Head, Neck, and Upper Limb

Blood vessels are a continuous network of "pipes," and often there is little anatomical difference along the length of a given vessel as it passes from one region of the body to another. To facilitate identification and discussion, however, anatomists assign different names to a given vessel, depending on which part of the body the vessel is passing through. The subclavian artery becomes the axillary artery, for instance, and then the brachial artery. Each name is usually related to the name of a bone or organ adjacent to the vessel; therefore, because they often run parallel to each other, arteries and veins often have the same name.

The aorta receives oxygenated blood from the left ventricle of the heart and distributes the blood to the major arteries that

351

arise from the aorta and supply the head, limbs, and trunk. The initial portion of the aorta is curved like an inverted letter *U*, and the various regions have different names. The **ascending aorta** exits the base of the heart, curves upward and to the left to form the **aortic arch,** and then as the **descending aorta** descends behind the heart (Figure 3). At the point where it passes through the diaphragm, the descending aorta becomes the **abdominal aorta.** Arteries that branch off the aortic arch serve the head, neck, and upper limb. Intercostal arteries stem from the thoracic aorta and supply the thoracic wall. Branches off the abdominal aorta serve the abdominal organs. The abdominal aorta enters the pelvic cavity and divides to send a branch into each lower limb.

Three Branches of the Aortic Arch

The first branch of the aortic arch, the **brachiocephalic** (brā-kē-ō-se-FAL-ik) **trunk,** or **innominate artery,** is short and divides into the **right common carotid artery** and the **right subclavian artery** (Figure 4). The right common carotid artery supplies blood to the right side of the head and neck; the right subclavian artery supplies blood to the right upper limb. The second and third branches of the aortic arch are the **left common carotid artery,** which supplies the left side of the head and neck, and **left subclavian artery,** which supplies the left upper limb as well as the shoulder and head. Note that only the right common carotid artery and right subclavian artery are derived from the brachiocephalic trunk. The left common carotid artery and left subclavian artery arise directly from the peak of the aortic arch. A **vertebral artery** branches off each subclavian artery and supplies blood to the brain and spinal cord.

Subclavian Arteries Supply the Upper Limb

The subclavian arteries supply blood to the upper limbs. Each subclavian artery passes under the clavicle, crosses the armpit as the **axillary artery,** and continues into the arm as the **brachial artery** (Figure 4). (Blood pressure is usually taken at the brachial artery.) At the antecubitis (elbow), the brachial artery divides into the lateral **radial artery** and the medial **ulnar artery,** each named after the bone it follows. In the palm of the hand, these arteries are interconnected by the **superficial** and **deep palmar arches,** which send small **digital arteries** to the fingers. Except in the vicinity of the heart, where the right arterial pathway has a brachiocephalic trunk that is absent from the left pathway, the arrangement of the arteries supplying the left and right upper limbs is symmetrical.

Carotid Arteries Supply the Head

Each common carotid artery ascends deep in the neck and divides at the larynx into an **external carotid artery** and an **internal carotid artery** (Figure 5). The base of the internal carotid swells as the **carotid sinus** and contains baroreceptors to monitor blood pressure. The external carotid artery branches to supply blood to the neck and face. The pulse in the external carotid artery can be felt by placing your fingers lateral to your thyroid cartilage (Adam's apple). The external carotid artery branches into the **facial artery, maxillary artery,** and **superficial temporal artery** to serve the external structures of the head. The internal carotid artery ascends to the base of the brain and divides into three arteries: the **ophthalmic artery,** which supplies the eyes, and the **anterior cerebral artery** and **middle cerebral artery,** both of which supply the brain.

Cerebral Arterial Circle

Because of its high metabolic rate, the brain has a voracious appetite for oxygen and nutrients. A reduction in blood flow to the brain may result in permanent damage to the affected area. To ensure that the brain receives a continuous supply of blood, branches of the internal carotid arteries and other arteries interconnect, or **anastomose,** as the **cerebral arterial circle,** also called the **circle of Willis** (Figure 5). The right and left vertebral arteries ascend in the transverse foramina of the cervical vertebrae and enter the skull at the foramen magnum. These arteries fuse into a single **basilar artery** on the inferior surface of the brain stem. The basilar artery branches into left and right **posterior cerebral arteries** and left and right **posterior communicating arteries.** The right and left anterior cerebral arteries form the anterior portion of the cerebral arterial circle. Between these arteries is the **anterior communicating artery,** which completes the anastomosis.

> ### Study Tip What's in a Name?
> Arteries and veins with the term *common* as part of their name always branch into an external and an internal vessel. The common carotid artery, for example, branches into an external carotid artery and an internal carotid artery. The internal and external iliac veins join as the common iliac vein. ∎

QuickCheck Questions

2.1 How does arterial branching in the left side of the neck differ from branching in the right side?

2.2 What is an anastomosis?

2.3 Which arteries in the brain anastomose with one another?

In the Lab 2

Materials

- ☐ Vascular system chart
- ☐ Torso model
- ☐ Head model
- ☐ Upper limb model

Figure 3 **Overview of the Major Systemic Arteries**

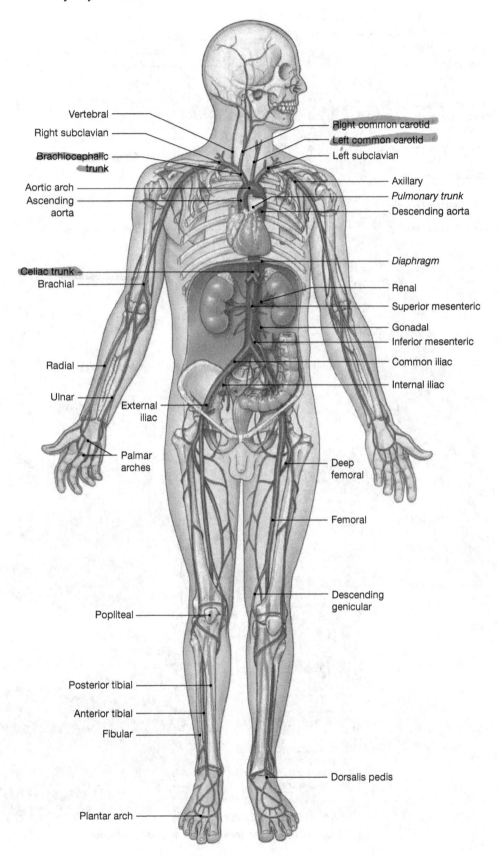

Vertebral
Right subclavian
Brachiocephalic trunk
Aortic arch
Ascending aorta
Celiac trunk
Brachial
Radial
Ulnar
External iliac
Palmar arches
Popliteal
Posterior tibial
Anterior tibial
Fibular
Plantar arch

Right common carotid
Left common carotid
Left subclavian
Axillary
Pulmonary trunk
Descending aorta
Diaphragm
Renal
Superior mesenteric
Gonadal
Inferior mesenteric
Common iliac
Internal iliac
Deep femoral
Femoral
Descending genicular
Dorsalis pedis

Figure 4 Arteries of the Chest and Upper Limb

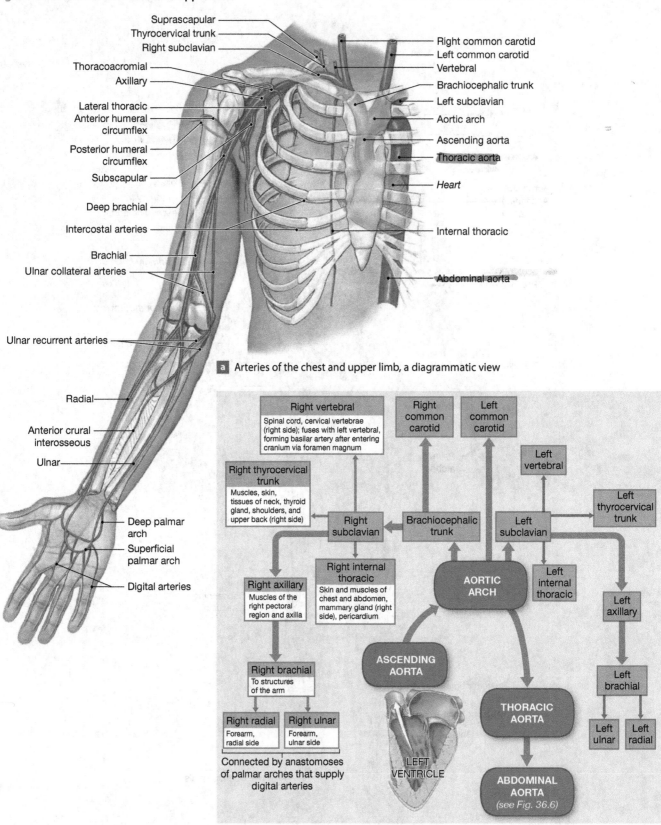

a Arteries of the chest and upper limb, a diagrammatic view

b A flowchart of the arteries of the chest and upper limb

Figure 5 Arteries of the Neck, Head, and Brain

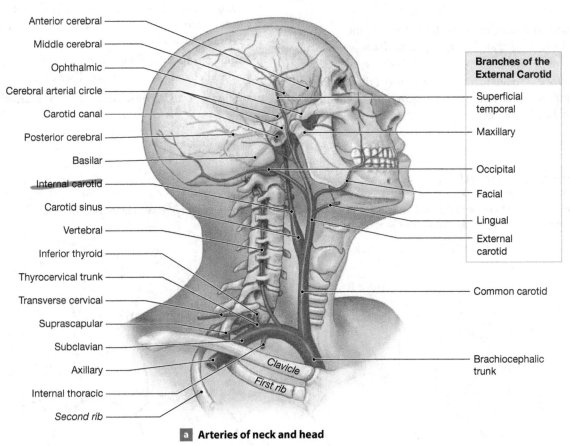

Anterior cerebral
Middle cerebral
Ophthalmic
Cerebral arterial circle
Carotid canal
Posterior cerebral
Basilar
Internal carotid
Carotid sinus
Vertebral
Inferior thyroid
Thyrocervical trunk
Transverse cervical
Suprascapular
Subclavian
Axillary
Internal thoracic
Second rib

Clavicle
First rib

Branches of the External Carotid

Superficial temporal
Maxillary
Occipital
Facial
Lingual
External carotid
Common carotid
Brachiocephalic trunk

a Arteries of neck and head

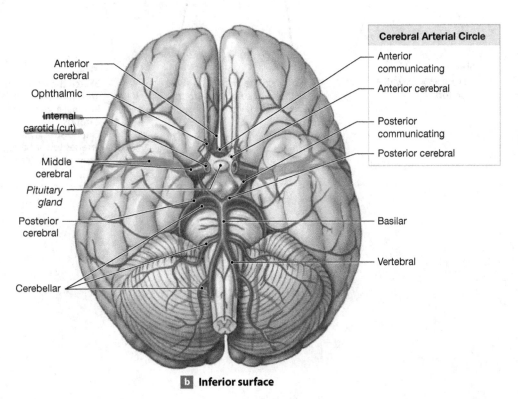

Anterior cerebral
Ophthalmic
Internal carotid (cut)
Middle cerebral
Pituitary gland
Posterior cerebral
Cerebellar

Cerebral Arterial Circle

Anterior communicating
Anterior cerebral
Posterior communicating
Posterior cerebral
Basilar
Vertebral

b Inferior surface

Procedures

1. Review the arteries in Figures 3, 4, and 5.

2. On the torso model, examine the aortic arch and identify the three branches arising from the superior margin of the arch.

3. On the torso model, identify the arteries of the shoulder and limb. Note the difference in origin of the right and left subclavian arteries.

4. On the head model, trace the arteries to the head and note the differences between the right and left common carotid arteries. Identify the arteries that converge at the cerebral arterial circle.

5. Using your index and middle fingers, locate the pulse in your radial and common carotid arteries.

For additional practice, complete the *Sketch to Learn* activity. ■

 Sketch to Learn!

An excellent way to remember blood vessels is to make simple "stick vessels." In this drawing we will show the arterial distribution branching from the aortic arch.

Sample Sketch

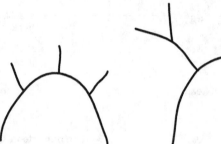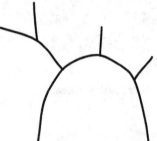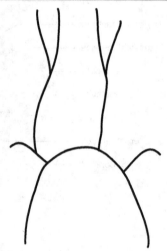

Step 1
• Draw an arch with 3 lines on top.

Step 2
• Branch the first line to show the right common carotid and subclavian arteries.

Step 3
• Sketch the left carotid and show branches of internal and external carotids.
• Extend subclavian arteries toward the "arms."
• Label your sketch.

Your Sketch

Lab Activity 3 Arteries of the Abdominopelvic Cavity and Lower Limb

The arteries stemming from the abdominal aorta are shown in Figure 3, as well as in Figures 6 and 7. An easy way to identify the branches of the abdominal aorta is to distinguish between paired arteries, which have right and left branches, and unpaired arteries. Also refer to the flowchart of arteries in Figure 6 for patterns and sequences of arteries as they arise from the abdominal aorta.

Celiac Trunk Has Three Branches

Three unpaired arteries arise from the abdominal aorta: celiac trunk, superior mesenteric artery, and inferior mesenteric artery. The short **celiac** (SĒ-lē-ak) **trunk** arises inferior to the diaphragm and splits into three arteries. The **common hepatic artery** divides to supply blood to the liver, gallbladder, and part of the stomach. The **left gastric artery** supplies the stomach. The **splenic artery** supplies the spleen, stomach, and pancreas.

Mesenteric Arteries Supply the Intestines

Inferior to the celiac trunk is the next unpaired artery, the **superior mesenteric** (mez-en-TER-ik) **artery.** This vessel supplies blood to the large intestine, parts of the small intestine, and other abdominal organs. The third unpaired artery, the **inferior mesenteric artery,** originates before the abdominal aorta divides to enter the pelvic cavity and lower limbs. This artery supplies parts of the large intestine and the rectum.

Four major sets of paired arteries arise off the abdominal aorta. The right and left **adrenal arteries** arise near the superior mesenteric artery and branch into the adrenal glands, located on top of the kidneys. The right and left **renal arteries,** which supply the kidneys, stem off the abdominal aorta just inferior to the adrenal arteries. The right and left

Figure 6 Arteries Supplying the Abdominopelvic Organs

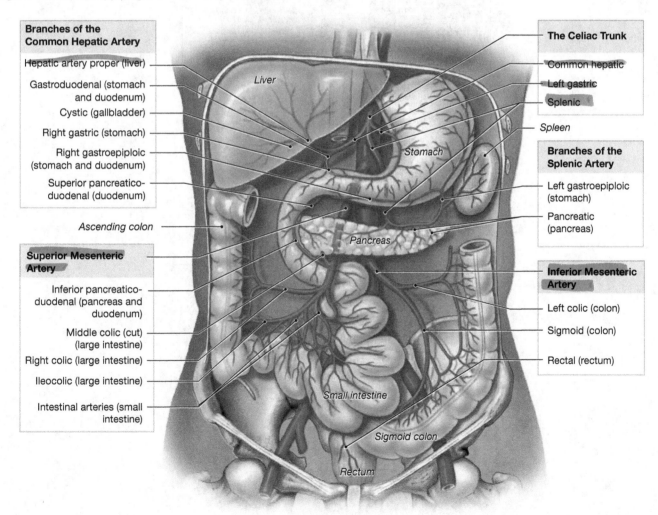

Figure 7 Flowchart of the Major Arteries of the Trunk

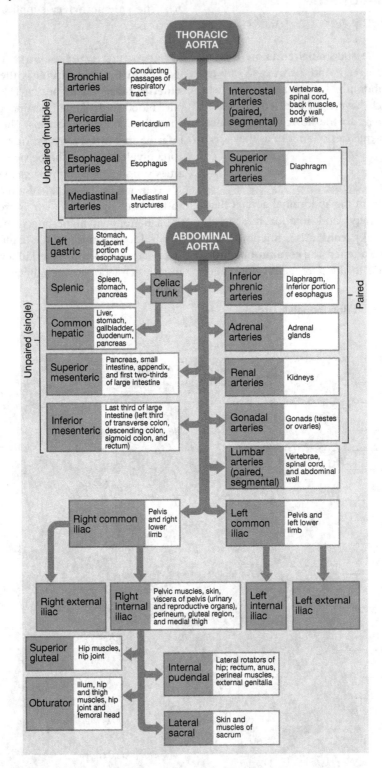

gonadal (gō-NAD-al) **arteries** arise near the inferior mesenteric artery and bring blood to the reproductive organs. The right and left **lumbar arteries** originate near the terminus of the abdominal aorta and service the lower body wall.

Iliac Arteries Branch to Supply the Pelvis and Lower Limb

At the level of the hips, the abdominal aorta divides into the right and left **common iliac** (IL-ē-ak) **arteries.** Each common iliac artery descends through the pelvic cavity and branches into an **external iliac artery,** which enters the lower limb, and an **internal iliac artery,** which supplies blood to the organs of the pelvic cavity. The external iliac artery pierces the abdominal wall and becomes the **femoral artery** of the thigh (Figure 8). A **deep femoral artery** arising off the femoral artery supplies deep thigh muscles. The femoral artery passes through the posterior knee as the **popliteal** (pop-LIT-ē-al) **artery** and divides into the **posterior tibial artery** and the **anterior tibial artery,** each supplying blood to the leg. The **fibular artery,** also called the *peroneal artery,* stems laterally off the posterior tibial artery. The arteries of the leg branch into the foot and anastomose at the **dorsal arch** and the **plantar arch.**

QuickCheck Questions

3.1 What are the three branches of the celiac trunk?

3.2 Which arteries supply the intestines?

3.3 What does the external iliac artery become in the lower limb?

In the Lab 3

Materials

- ☐ Vascular system chart
- ☐ Torso model
- ☐ Lower limb model

Procedures

1. Review the arteries in Figures 5 through 8.
2. On the torso model, locate the celiac trunk and its three branches. Identify the superior and inferior mesenteric arteries and the four sets of paired arteries stemming from the abdominal aorta.
3. On the torso model, observe how the abdominal aorta branches into the left and right common iliac arteries.
4. On the lower limb model, locate the major arteries supplying the lower limb.
5. On your body, trace the location of your abdominal aorta, common iliac artery, external iliac artery, femoral artery, popliteal artery, and posterior tibial artery. ■

Lab Activity 4 Veins of the Head, Neck, and Upper Limb

Once you have learned the major systemic arteries, identifying the systemic veins is easy because most arteries have a corresponding vein (Figure 9). Unlike arteries, many veins are superficial and easily seen under the skin. Systemic veins are usually painted blue on vascular and torso models to indicate that they transport deoxygenated blood. When identifying veins, work in the direction of blood flow, from the periphery toward the heart.

Jugular Veins Drain the Head

Blood in the brain drains into large veins called *sinuses* (Figure 10). Small-diameter veins deep inside the brain drain into progressively larger veins that empty into the **superior sagittal sinus** located in the falx cerebri separating the cerebral hemispheres. This large sinus drains into a **transverse sinus** on each side of the brain that, in turn, empties into a **sigmoid sinus.** The sigmoid sinus drains into the **internal jugular vein,** which exits the skull via the jugular foramen, descends the neck, and empties into the **brachiocephalic vein.** Superficial veins that drain the face and scalp empty into the **external jugular vein,** which descends the neck to join the **subclavian vein.** The **internal thoracic vein** joins the left brachiocephalic vein and drains the anterior thoracic wall. The right and left brachiocephalic veins merge at the **superior vena cava** and empty deoxygenated blood into the right atrium of the heart. The blood then enters the right ventricle, which contracts and pumps the blood to the lungs through the pulmonary circuit.

Study Tip Brachiocephalic Veins

One difference between the systemic arteries and the systemic veins is that the venous pathway has both a right and a left brachiocephalic vein, each formed by the merging of subclavian, vertebral, internal jugular, and external jugular veins. The arterial pathway has a single brachiocephalic trunk that branches into the right common carotid artery and right subclavian artery. On the left side of the body, the common carotid artery and subclavian artery originate directly off the aortic arch, as noted earlier. ■

Veins That Drain the Upper Limb

Figure 11 illustrates the venous drainage of the upper limb, chest, and abdomen. Figure 12 shows flowcharts of the venous circulation for the superior and inferior venae cavae. Small veins in the fingers drain into **digital veins** that

Figure 8 **Major Arteries of the Lower Limb**

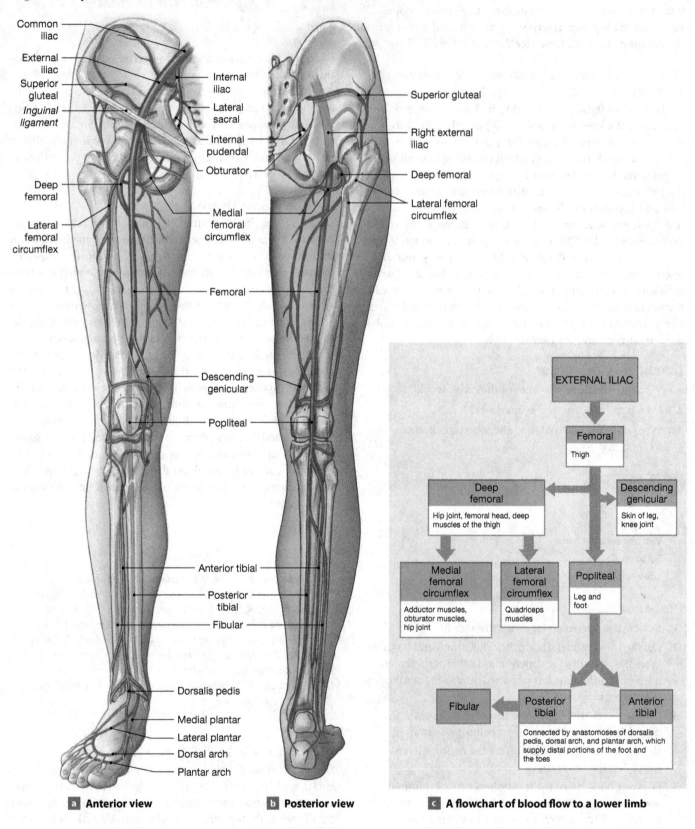

a **Anterior view**

b **Posterior view**

c **A flowchart of blood flow to a lower limb**

Figure 9 Overview of the Major Systemic Veins

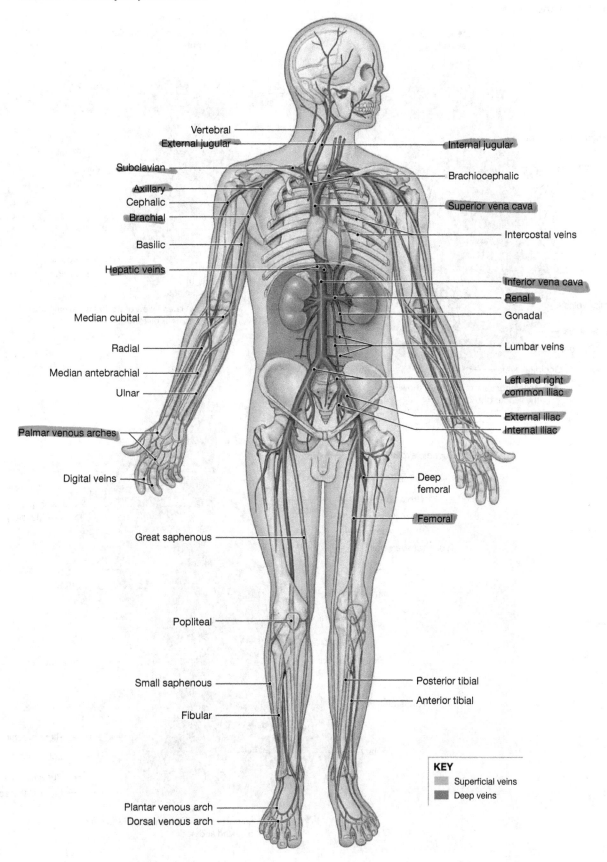

Vertebral
External jugular
Subclavian
Axillary
Cephalic
Brachial
Basilic
Hepatic veins
Median cubital
Radial
Median antebrachial
Ulnar
Palmar venous arches
Digital veins
Great saphenous
Popliteal
Small saphenous
Fibular
Plantar venous arch
Dorsal venous arch

Internal jugular
Brachiocephalic
Superior vena cava
Intercostal veins
Inferior vena cava
Renal
Gonadal
Lumbar veins
Left and right common iliac
External iliac
Internal iliac
Deep femoral
Femoral
Posterior tibial
Anterior tibial

KEY
Superficial veins
Deep veins

Figure 10 Major Veins of the Head, Neck, and Brain Veins draining the brain and the superficial and deep portions of the head and neck.

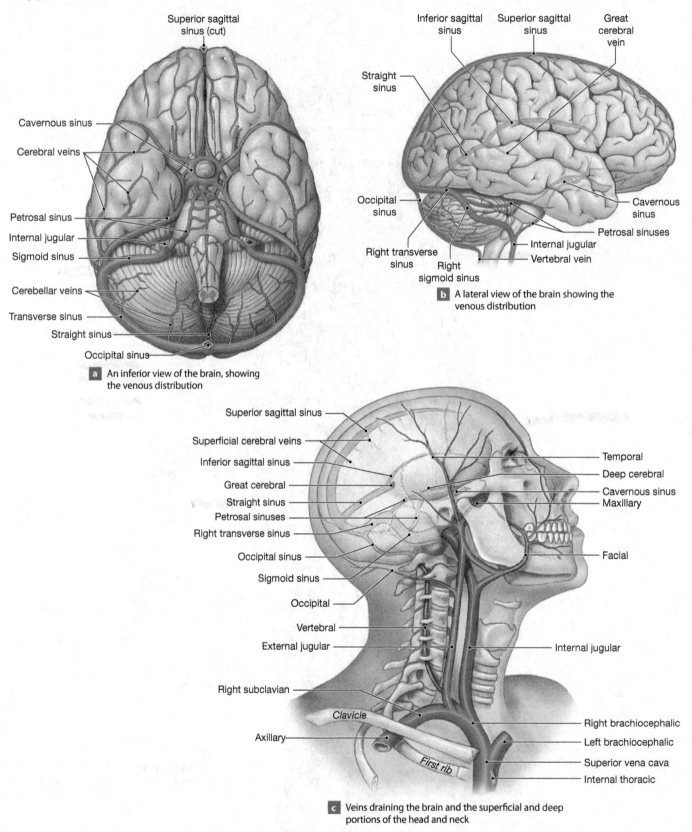

Superior sagittal sinus (cut)

Cavernous sinus

Cerebral veins

Petrosal sinus

Internal jugular

Sigmoid sinus

Cerebellar veins

Transverse sinus

Straight sinus

Occipital sinus

a An inferior view of the brain, showing the venous distribution

Inferior sagittal sinus

Superior sagittal sinus

Great cerebral vein

Straight sinus

Occipital sinus

Right transverse sinus

Right sigmoid sinus

Cavernous sinus

Petrosal sinuses

Internal jugular

Vertebral vein

b A lateral view of the brain showing the venous distribution

Superior sagittal sinus

Superficial cerebral veins

Inferior sagittal sinus

Great cerebral

Straight sinus

Petrosal sinuses

Right transverse sinus

Occipital sinus

Sigmoid sinus

Occipital

Vertebral

External jugular

Right subclavian

Clavicle

Axillary

First rib

Temporal

Deep cerebral

Cavernous sinus

Maxillary

Facial

Internal jugular

Right brachiocephalic

Left brachiocephalic

Superior vena cava

Internal thoracic

c Veins draining the brain and the superficial and deep portions of the head and neck

Figure 11 Veins of the Upper Limb, Chest, and Abdomen The head, neck, and upper limb drain into the superior vena cava; the abdominopelvic organs and lower limb drain into the inferior vena cava.

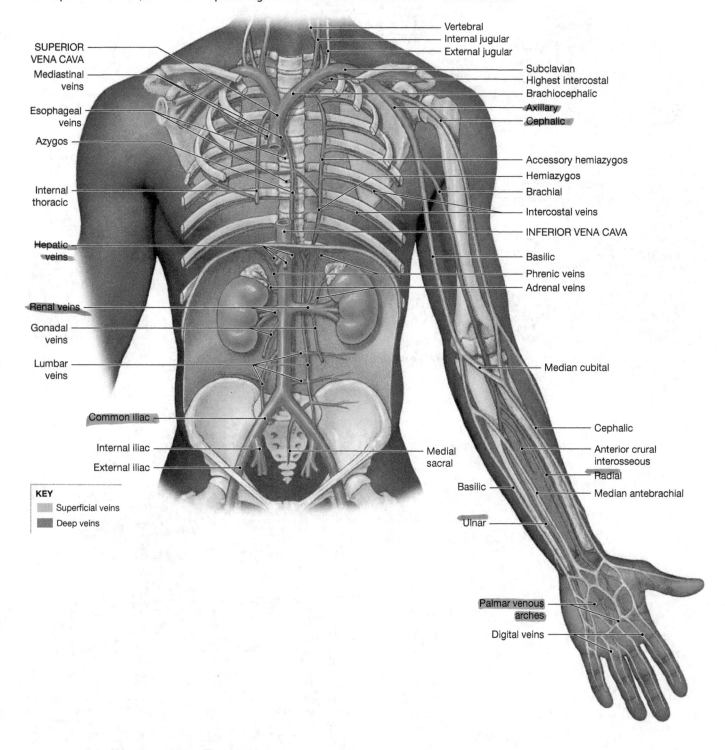

Figure 12 Flowchart of Circulation to the Two Venae Cavae

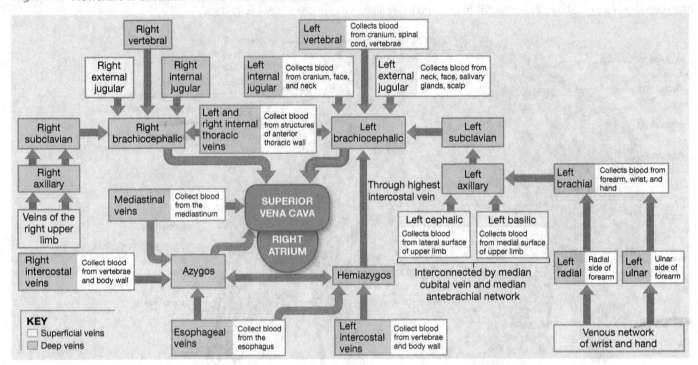

a Tributaries of the superior vena cava

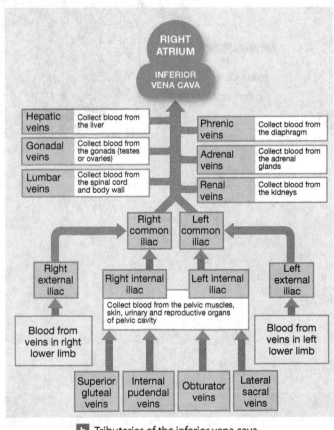

b Tributaries of the inferior vena cava

empty into a network of **palmar venous arches.** These vessels drain into the **cephalic vein,** which ascends along the lateral margin of the arm. The **median antebrachial vein** ascends to the elbow, is joined by the **median cubital vein** that crosses over from the cephalic vein, and becomes the **basilic vein.** The median cubital vein is often used to collect blood from an individual. Also in the forearm are the **radial** and **ulnar veins,** which fuse above the elbow into the **brachial vein.** The brachial and basilic veins meet at the armpit as the **axillary vein,** which joins the cephalic vein and becomes the subclavian vein. The subclavian vein plus veins from the neck and head drain into the brachiocephalic vein, which then empties into the superior vena cava, which empties into the right atrium. See Figure 12a for flowcharts of the venous circulation to the superior vena cava.

QuickCheck Questions

4.1 Which two veins combine to form the superior vena cava?

4.2 Where is the cephalic vein?

4.3 Where is the superior sagittal sinus?

In the Lab   4

Materials

☐ Vascular system chart
☐ Torso model
☐ Head model
☐ Upper limb model

Procedures

1. Review the head, neck, and upper limb veins in Figures 9 to 12.

2. On the head model, identify the superior sagittal sinus and other veins draining the head into the external and internal jugular veins.

3. Using the torso and upper limb models, start at one hand and name the veins draining the limb and shoulder. Notice how the right and left brachiocephalic veins join as the superior vena cava.

4. On your body, trace your cephalic vein, subclavian vein, brachiocephalic vein, and superior vena cava. ■

Lab Activity   5   Veins of the Abdominopelvic Cavity and Lower Limb

Veins that drain the lower limbs and abdominal organs empty into the **inferior vena cava,** the large vein that pierces the diaphragm and delivers deoxygenated blood to the right atrium

of the heart. Veins of the abdomen and lower limb are illustrated in Figures 13 and 14, as well as in Figures 9, 11, and 12.

Veins of the Abdomen

Six major veins from the abdominal organs drain blood into the inferior vena cava (Figure 11). The **lumbar veins** drain the muscles of the lower body wall and the spinal cord and empty into the inferior vena cava close to the common iliac veins. A pair of **gonadal veins** empty blood from the reproductive organs into the inferior vena cava above the lumbar veins. Pairs of **renal** and **adrenal veins** drain into the inferior vena cava next to their respective organs. Before entering the thoracic cavity to drain blood into the right atrium, the inferior vena cava collects blood from the **hepatic veins** draining the liver and the **phrenic veins** from the diaphragm. Figure 12b is a flowchart of the venous drainage into the inferior vena cava.

Hepatic Portal Vein

Veins leaving the digestive tract are diverted to the liver before continuing on to the heart. The **inferior** and **superior mesenteric veins** drain nutrient-rich blood from the digestive tract. These veins empty into the **hepatic portal vein** (Figure 13), which passes the blood through the liver, where blood sugar concentration is regulated. Phagocytic cells in the liver cleanse the blood of any microbes that may have entered it through the mucous membrane of the digestive system. Blood from the hepatic arteries and hepatic portal vein mixes in the liver and is returned to the inferior vena cava by the hepatic veins.

Veins of the Lower Limb

Figure 14 illustrates the venous drainage of the lower limb. Just like the hand, the foot contains digital veins, which in the foot drain into the **plantar venous arch** and the **dorsal venous arch,** which drain into the lateral **fibular vein** (also called *peroneal vein*) and the **anterior tibial vein,** located on the medial aspect of the anterior leg. These veins, along with the **posterior tibial vein,** merge and become the **popliteal vein** of the posterior knee. The **small saphenous** (sa-FĒ-nus) **vein,** which ascends from the ankle to the knee and drains blood from superficial veins, also empties into the popliteal vein. Superior to the knee, the popliteal vein becomes the **femoral vein,** which ascends along the femur to the inferior pelvic girdle, where it joins the **deep femoral vein** at the **external iliac vein.** The **great saphenous vein** ascends from the medial side of the ankle to the superior thigh and drains into the external iliac vein. In the pelvic cavity, the external iliac vein and the **internal iliac vein** fuse to form the **common iliac vein.** The right and left common iliac veins merge and drain into the inferior vena cava.

Figure 13 The Hepatic Portal System The hepatic portal vein receives blood from the superior and inferior mesenteric veins and passes the nutrient-rich blood into the liver for breakdown of toxins, removal of microbes, and regulation of blood sugar.

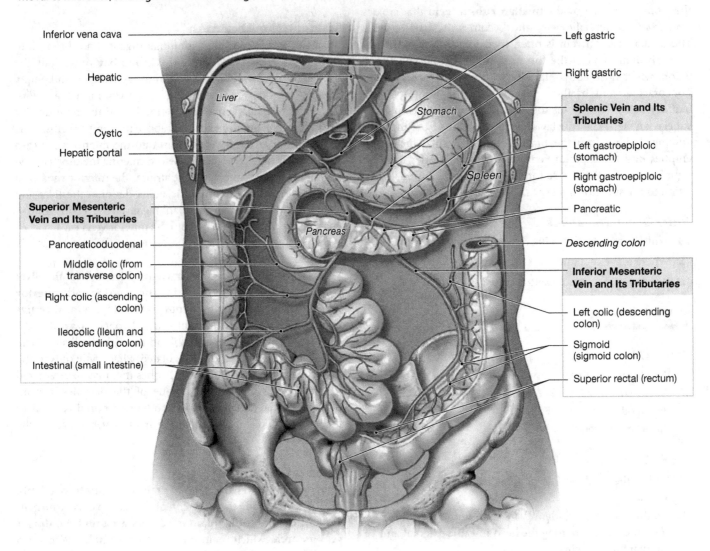

QuickCheck Questions

5.1 List the vessels that drain blood from the lower limb into the inferior vena cava.

5.2 Which veins drain into the hepatic portal vein?

In the Lab 5

Materials

☐ Vascular system chart
☐ Torso model
☐ Lower limb model

Procedures

1. Review the veins in Figures 11 through 14.

2. On the torso model, identify the veins draining the major abdominal organs. Locate where the superior and inferior mesenteric veins drain into the hepatic portal vein.

3. On the lower limb model, identify the veins that drain blood from the ankle to the inferior vena cava.

4. On your body, trace the location of the veins in your lower limb.

5. Although you have studied the arterial and venous divisions separately, they are anatomically connected to each other by capillaries. To reinforce this connectedness,

Figure 14 Veins of the Lower Limb

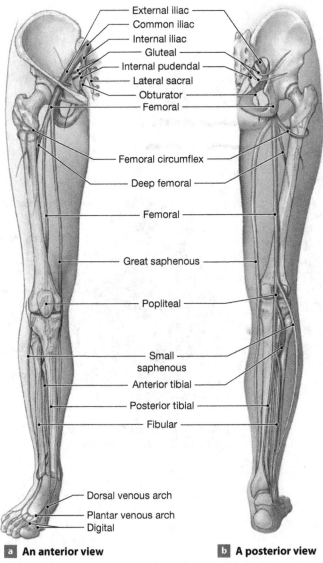

- External iliac
- Common iliac
- Internal iliac
- Gluteal
- Internal pudendal
- Lateral sacral
- Obturator
- Femoral
- Femoral circumflex
- Deep femoral
- Femoral
- Great saphenous
- Popliteal
- Small saphenous
- Anterior tibial
- Posterior tibial
- Fibular
- Dorsal venous arch
- Plantar venous arch
- Digital

a **An anterior view** **b** **A posterior view**

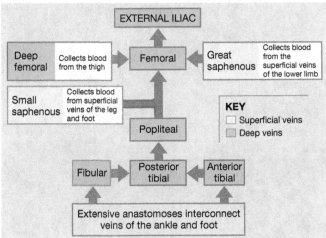

EXTERNAL ILIAC

| Deep femoral | Collects blood from the thigh |
| Femoral |
| Great saphenous | Collects blood from the superficial veins of the lower limb |

| Small saphenous | Collects blood from superficial veins of the leg and foot |

Popliteal

KEY
☐ Superficial veins
☐ Deep veins

| Fibular | Posterior tibial | Anterior tibial |

Extensive anastomoses interconnect veins of the ankle and foot

c **A flowchart of venous circulation from a lower limb**

practice identifying blood vessels while tracing the following systemic routes.

a. From the heart through the left upper limb and back to the heart

b. From the heart through the brain and back to the heart

c. From the heart through the liver and back to the heart

d. From the heart through the right lower limb and back to the heart ▪

Lab Activity 6 Fetal Circulation

A fetus receives oxygen from the mother through the **placenta,** a vascular organ that connects the fetus to the wall of the mother's uterus. During development, the fetal lungs are filled with amniotic fluid, and for efficiency some of the blood is shunted away from the fetal pulmonary circuit by several structures (**Figure 15**). The **foramen ovale** is a hole in the interatrial wall. Much of the blood entering the right atrium from the inferior vena cava passes through the foramen ovale to the left atrium and avoids the right ventricle and the pulmonary circuit. Some of the blood that enters the pulmonary trunk may bypass the lungs through a connection with the aorta, the **ductus arteriosus.** At birth, the foramen ovale closes and becomes a depression on the interatrial wall, the **fossa ovalis.** The ductus arteriosus closes and becomes the **ligamentum arteriosum.**

QuickCheck Questions

6.1 Where is the foramen ovale?

6.2 Which two structures are connected by the ductus arteriosus?

In the Lab 6

Material

☐ Heart model

Procedures

1. Review the fetal structures in Figure 15.

2. Identify the fossa ovalis on the heart model. What was this structure in the fetus?

3. At the point where the pulmonary trunk branches, find the ligamentum arteriosum. What was this structure in the fetus, and what purpose did it serve?

4. On the heart model, trace a drop of blood through the fetal structures of the heart, starting at the right atrium. ▪

Figure 15 Fetal Circulation

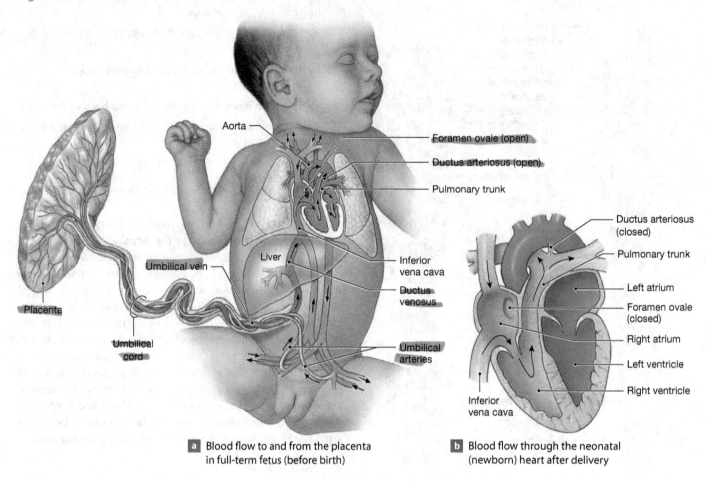

a Blood flow to and from the placenta in full-term fetus (before birth)

b Blood flow through the neonatal (newborn) heart after delivery

Name _____

Date _____

Section _____

Anatomy of the Systemic Circulation

A. Matching

Match each term in the left column with its correct description from the right column.

_____ 1. artery in armpit	**A.** subclavian
_____ 2. artery having three branches	**B.** superior mesenteric
_____ 3. vein used for taking blood samples	**C.** popliteal
_____ 4. artery on right side only	**D.** cephalic
_____ 5. long vein of leg	**E.** carotid
_____ 6. carries deoxygenated blood to liver	**F.** gonadal
_____ 7. artery to large intestine	**G.** valves
_____ 8. cerebral anastomosis	**H.** axillary
_____ 9. long vein of arm	**I.** great saphenous
_____ 10. vein in knee	**J.** median cubital
_____ 11. artery to reproductive organ	**K.** hepatic portal vein
_____ 12. major artery in neck	**L.** circle of Willis
_____ 13. vein under clavicle	**M.** celiac
_____ 14. found only in veins	**N.** brachiocephalic artery

B. Drawing

Draw It! Draw and label a simple line sketch of the arteries of the right upper limb starting at the aorta.

C. Labeling

1. Label the arteries in Figure 16.

Figure 16 Overview of the Major Systemic Arteries

1. _____

2. _____

3. _____

4. _____

5. _____

6. _____

7. _____

8. _____

9. _____

10. _____

11. _____

12. _____

13. _____

14. _____

15. _____

16. _____

17. _____

18. _____

19. _____

20. _____

21. _____

22. _____

23. _____

24. _____

25. _____

26. _____

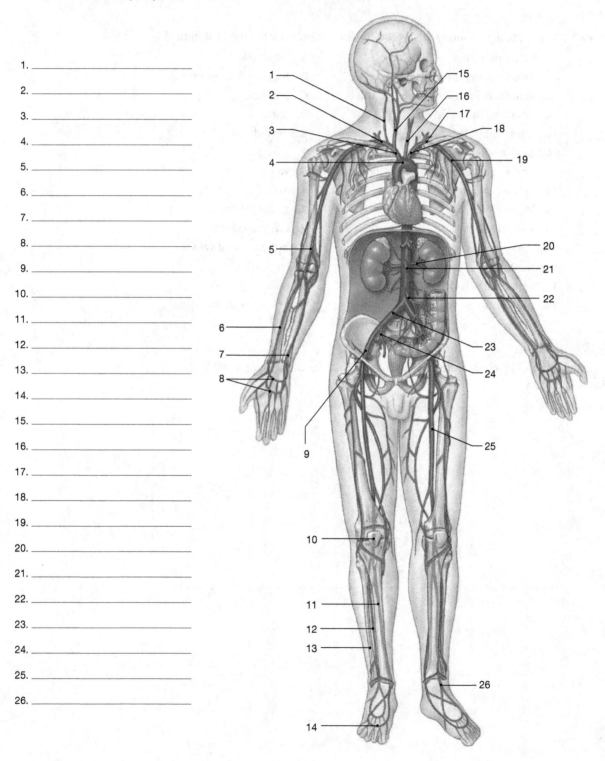

2. Label the veins in Figure 17.

Figure 17 **Overview of the Major Systemic Veins**

1. _____

2. _____

3. _____

4. _____

5. _____

6. _____

7. _____

8. _____

9. _____

10. _____

11. _____

12. _____

13. _____

14. _____

15. _____

16. _____

17. _____

18. _____

19. _____

20. _____

21. _____

22. _____

23. _____

24. _____

25. _____

26. _____

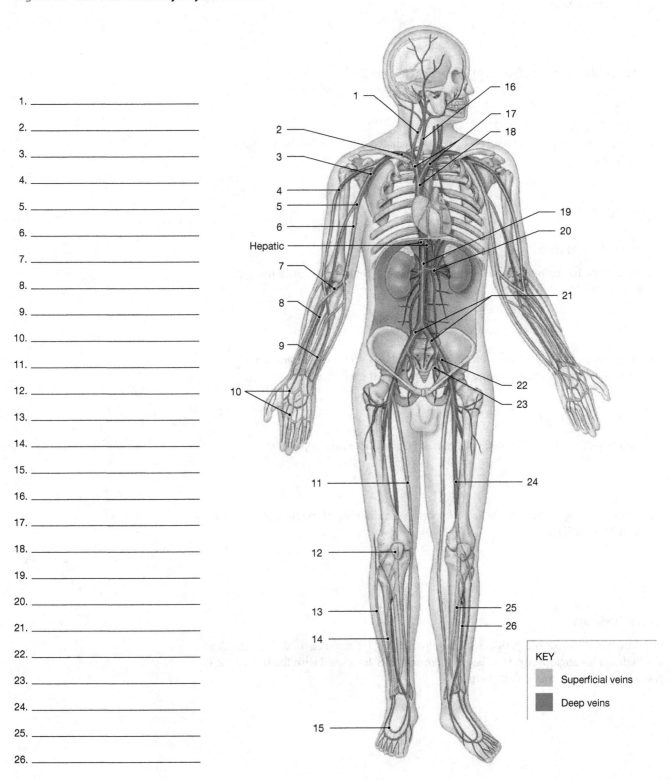

KEY

Superficial veins

Deep veins

D. Short-Answer Questions

1. List the vessels involved in supplying and draining blood from the small and large intestines.

2. What is the function of valves in the peripheral veins?

3. Describe the major vessels that return deoxygenated blood to the right atrium of the heart.

E. Analysis and Application

1. How does the cerebral arterial circle ensure that the brain has a constant supply of blood?

2. How is the anatomy of the arteries running from the aorta to the right arm different from that of the arteries running from the aorta to the left arm?

3. Which vessel is normally used to obtain a blood sample from a patient?

4. Explain the significance of the hepatic portal vein draining blood from the digestive tract into the liver.

F. Clinical Challenge

Mr. Brown is a 75-year-old patient with arteriosclerosis. He suffers a mild heart attack and is scheduled for angioplasty. How is his arteriosclerosis associated with the heart attack and will the balloon angioplasty help?

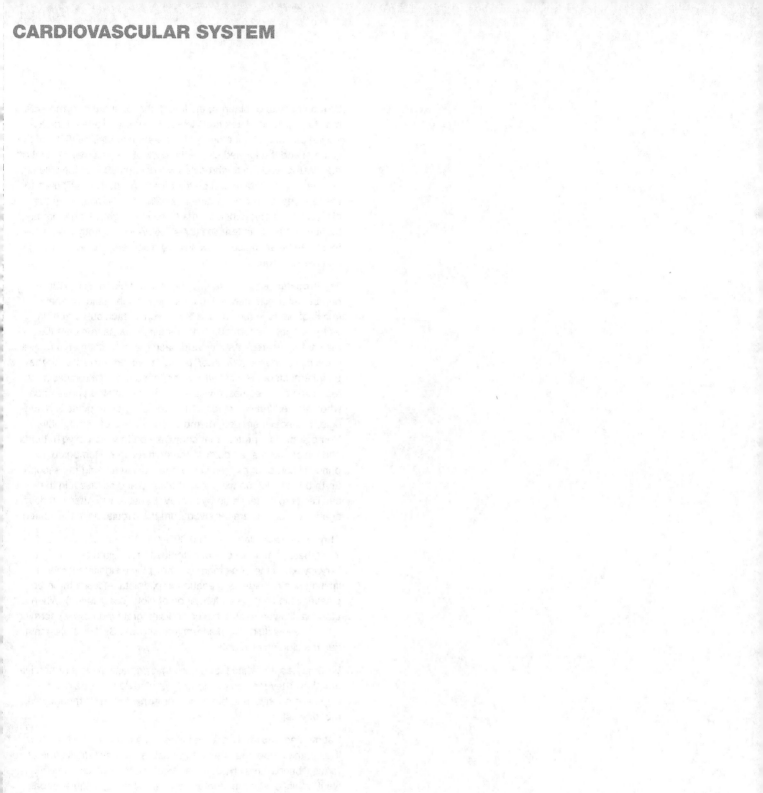

Blood consists of **plasma**, the liquid phase; and the **formed elements** (cells and platelets). Allowed to remain in a test tube following centrifugation, blood will separate into plasma (55% of the volume) and the formed elements (45% of the volume). Decant off the plasma, and the erythrocytes will occupy 99% of the volume, and the 1% leukocyte and platelet fraction ("buffy coat") rises to the top. The erythrocyte fraction is called the *hematocrit* in the clinical laboratory; generally, males have a slightly higher hematocrit (45–49% than females (37–47%). A significantly low hematocrit can be an indication of several disorders, including anemia and hemorrhage.

Erythrocytes (*erythro-*, red; *-cyte*, cell; red blood cells, RBCs) number approximately 4.5–6.2 million in each cubic millimeter (mm^3) of blood in men and 4–5.5 million in each cubic mm^3 in women. They are formed in the bone marrow as true cells (i.e., they are nucleated). As they approach maturity, each erythrocyte *loses its nucleus and most of its organelles* prior to entering the peripheral blood. Recently released immature erythrocytes may retain some ribosomes, giving a slightly reticulated appearance when stained (*reticulocytes*). The circulating erythrocyte is a non-rigid, biconcave-shaped, membrane-lined sac of hemoglobin. Hemoglobin is a protein that contains iron to which oxygen binds and which gives a red color to the erythrocytes. Hemoglobin is the principal carrier of oxygen in the body, plasma being the second. Erythrocytes pick up oxygen in the lungs and release it in the capillaries to be taken up by nearby tissues/cells. After 120 days, aged erythrocytes are removed from the circulation in the spleen.

Thrombocytes (platelets) (150,000–400,000/mL of blood; 2–5 μm in diameter) are small bits of cytoplasm from giant cells (*megakaryocytes*) of the bone marrow. They play a significant role in limiting hemorrhage: aggregation of platelets releases thromboplastin, which enhances formation of clots (*coagulation*). When blood is allowed to clot, the cells disintegrate (*hemolysis*), forming a thick yellow fluid called *serum* (not shown). Serum is plasma minus the clotting elements.

Leukocytes are white blood cells that primarily have a protective function. They may be **granular** (granulocytes include neutrophils, eosinophils, and basophils) or **nongranular** (lymphocytes, monocytes).

Segmented **neutrophils** arise in the bone marrow and live short lives in the blood and connective tissues (hours–4 days). Immature forms ("bands") may be seen in the blood during acute infections. Neutrophils destroy microorganisms and take up cellular debris.

Eosinophils exhibit colorful granules when properly stained. Eosinophils are phagocytic in immune reactions with allergens, and particularly against parasites.

Basophils contain dark-staining granules. Basophils are mediators of allergic reactions and parasitic infections.

Lymphocytes (20–45% of WBCs), which arise from bone marrow, roam lymphoid tissues as well as blood. Lymphocytes are associated with immunity.

Monocytes (2–8% of WBCs) arise in the bone marrow, mature in the blood, and then leave the circulation to enter the extracellular spaces as **macrophages**.

CARDIOVASCULAR SYSTEM
BLOOD & BLOOD ELEMENTS

CN: (1) Color the names and percentages of A and B and the contents of A and B of the tube at left. (2) Color the large arrow B pointing to the middle rectangular tube; color the name and percentage B[1], the border B of the middle tube and its primary contents, B[1]. Do not color the names and percentages at the top of the middle tube. (3) Color the name "Thrombocytes," C, and particles in the center of the page. (4) Leave the name "Leukocytes" below uncolored; color the six leukocytes below according to the color code: B blue, LB light blue, O orange, LO light orange, P purple, DP dark purple, LP light purple. Stipple the granules with the darkest color. (5) Color the five bands of leukocytes in the tube at upper right reflecting the relative distribution of these cells and their percentages in peripheral blood.

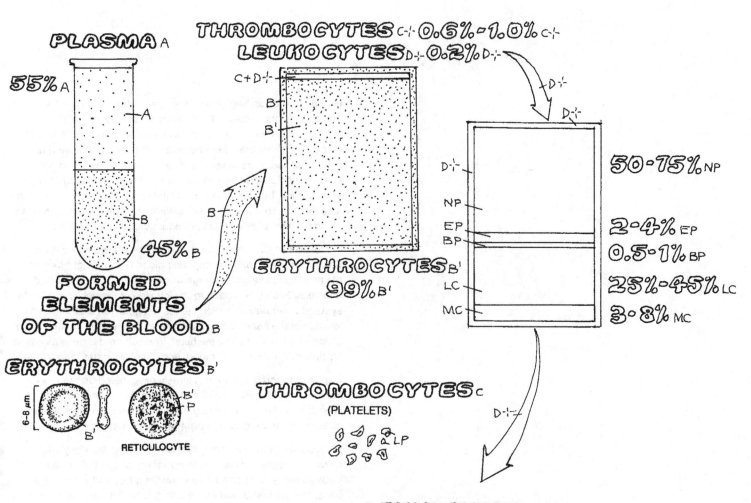

PLASMA A

55% A

THROMBOCYTES C∻ 0.6%~1.0% C∻
LEUKOCYTES D∻ 0.2% D∻

C+D∻
B
B¹

A

B

45% B

FORMED ELEMENTS OF THE BLOOD B

ERYTHROCYTES B'

6-8 µm

B'
B'
P

RETICULOCYTE

ERYTHROCYTES B'
99% B'

50-75% NP

2-4% EP
0.5-1% BP
25%-45% LC
3-8% MC

D∻
NP
EP
BP
B'
LC
MC

THROMBOCYTES C
(PLATELETS)

D∻
LP

D∻

LEUKOCYTES D∻
(WHITE BLOOD CELLS)

GRANULAR

NEUTROPHIL NP

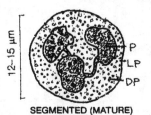

12-15 µm

Granules
Cytoplasm
Nucleus
P
LP
DP
LP
P
DP

SEGMENTED (MATURE)   BAND (IMMATURE)

EOSINOPHIL EP

O
LO
P

12-15 µm

BASOPHIL BP

LP
DP
P

NONGRANULAR

LYMPHOCYTE LC

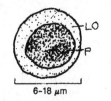

LO
P

6-18 µm

MONOCYTE MC

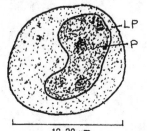

LP
P

12-20 µm

375

Blood circulation begins with the heart, which pumps blood into arteries and receives blood from veins. Regardless of the amount of oxygen (oxygenation) in that blood, arteries conduct blood away from the heart and veins conduct blood toward the heart. *Capillaries* are networks of extremely thin-walled vessels throughout the body tissues that permit the exchange of gases and nutrients between the vessel interior (vascular space) and the area external to the vessel (extracellular space). Capillaries receive blood from small arteries and conduct blood to small veins.

There are two circuits of blood flow: (1) the **pulmonary circulation** that conveys oxygen-depleted blood from the right side of the heart to the lungs for oxygenation/release of carbon dioxide and takes fresh blood back to the left side of the heart; and (2) the **systemic circulation**, which carries **oxygen-rich blood** from the left side of the heart to the body tissues and returns **oxygen-poor blood** to the right side of the heart. The color red is generally used for depicting oxygenated blood, and blue for oxygen-poor blood.

Capillary blood is mixed; it is largely oxygenated on the arterial side of the capillary bed, and is more deoxygenated on the venous side. This is a consequence of delivering oxygen to and picking up carbon dioxide from the tissues it supplies.

One *capillary network* generally exists between an artery and a vein. There are exceptions: the portal circulation of the liver involves two sets of capillaries between artery and vein (on this page, see the portal vein and the additional capillary network between the capillaries of the gastrointestinal tract and the heart). Other portal systems exist between the hypothalamus and the pituitary gland (the hypophyseal portal system); and within the kidney, between the glomerulus and the peritubular capillary plexus.

CARDIOVASCULAR SYSTEM
SCHEME OF BLOOD CIRCULATION

CN: (1) Color the upper central terms A-C first; use blue for A, purple for B, and red for C. Use colors for D and E that do not distract from A, B, and C. (1) Color the terms "Systemic Circulation," D, and "Pulmonary Circulation," E, the two figures, and the two capillaries, B, purple. (2) Color the brackets (D, E) of the circulatory scheme. Begin in the right atrium of the heart

(BEGIN HERE) and color the flow of oxygen-poor blood, A, into the lungs. The blood is oxygenated in the lungs, B to C. (3) The oxygenated blood, C, returns to the left side of the heart, and is pumped out into the systemic circulation to capillary networks throughout the body. Deoxygenated blood, A, is returned to the heart, to repeat the cycle.

OXYGEN-POOR BLOOD A
CAPILLARY BLOOD B
OXYGEN-RICH BLOOD C

SYSTEMIC CIRCULATION D

PULMONARY CIRCULATION E

SCHEME OF BLOOD CIRCULATION

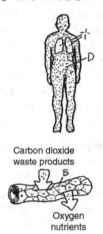

Carbon dioxide waste products

Oxygen nutrients

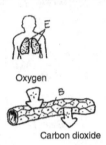

Oxygen

Carbon dioxide

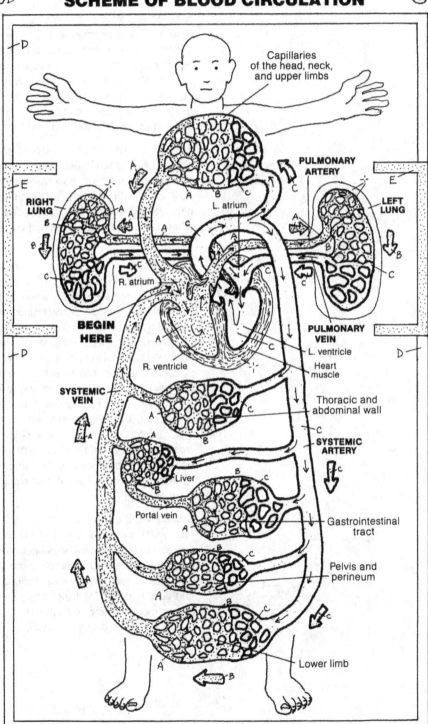

Capillaries of the head, neck, and upper limbs

PULMONARY ARTERY

RIGHT LUNG

LEFT LUNG

L. atrium

R. atrium

BEGIN HERE

PULMONARY VEIN

L. ventricle

Heart muscle

R. ventricle

SYSTEMIC VEIN

Thoracic and abdominal wall

SYSTEMIC ARTERY

Liver

Portal vein

Gastrointestinal tract

Pelvis and perineum

Lower limb

The *vascular system* is the name for the collection of **blood vessels** and lymph vessels of the body. Arteries take blood away from the heart (pump) and deliver it to capillary networks for distribution to cells and tissues. Veins bring the blood back to the heart from the capillary networks.

Arteries are characterized by smooth muscle and one or two elastic laminae in their walls. The layers of an arterial wall are generally distinctive except in the largest (endothelial-lined elastic tubes) and smallest (precapillaries). Small arteries (**arterioles**; resistance vessels) can cut off blood to a maze of capillaries when required. **Medium arteries** tend to be vessels of distribution, diverting flow as needed. **Large arteries** are the equivalent of elastic aqueducts, moving large volumes of blood out of the heart or aorta to distant parts (head, lower limbs, etc.). All arteries have a fibrous outer layer (**tunica externa** or adventitia). Within this tunic, much smaller nutrient blood vessels (*vasa vasorum*) and motor/sensor nerves (*nervi vasorum*) are found.

Arteries have the ability to respond to changing circumstances by vasodilating to increase flow and decrease blood pressure, by vasoconstricting to decrease flow and increase blood pressure, by diverting/redirecting blood flow, and literally shutting circulation down in a particular locale (e.g., capillary blanching when in shock, or suspension of bleeding in a traumatically amputated limb).

Veins generally lack significant layers of smooth muscle and elastic tissue in their walls. They function largely as conduits with considerable increased capacity when subjected to pressure loads. Large veins are especially capacious. **Venules** (small veins) are formed by the merging of capillaries and are of basically the same construction. Veins get progressively larger as they approach the heart. Veins, like rivers, have tributaries, not branches (except in portal circulations). Most medium veins of the neck and extremities have a series of small pockets, called *valves*, formed from the endothelial layer. These valves are paired and point in the direction of blood flow. They are particularly numerous in the lower limbs. Though offering no resistance to blood flow, a reversed blood flow closes the valves (and the lumen) of the vein. Venous flow in the lower limbs is enhanced by the contraction of skeletal muscles, whose contractile bulges give an antigravity boost to the movement of blood.

Capillaries, the smallest of the lot, are thin-walled, potentially porous endothelial tubes with some fibrous support. Lacking muscle and elastic tissues, capillaries are concerned with the release of nutrients, gases, and fluids to surrounding tissue, and the taking-up of carbon dioxide and other "unnecessary" gases and microparticulate matter. Capillaries can generally accommodate the passage of cells between endothelial cells. Specialized capillaries of this nature are called *sinusoids*.

CARDIOVASCULAR SYSTEM
BLOOD VESSELS

CN: Use red for A, purple for B, and blue for C (colors you used in the previous page) for the names and related types of blood vessels above.
(1) Begin with the name "Large Arteries" in the upper illustration, and color all the vessels and names.
(2) Color the names of the blood vessel types in the section titled "Vessel Structure," and their characteristic components. Use very light colors for D, F, and H. (3) Note that the vas and nervus vasorum in the fibrous tissue layer, H, of the lower arterial cross section are not to be colored. (4) In the two diagrams of the vein, C¹, at far right, note the closed venous valves in the lower vein, and the functioning valves in the upper vein. The blood between the two valves in the upper drawing is to be colored gray so as not to be confused with the vein structure.

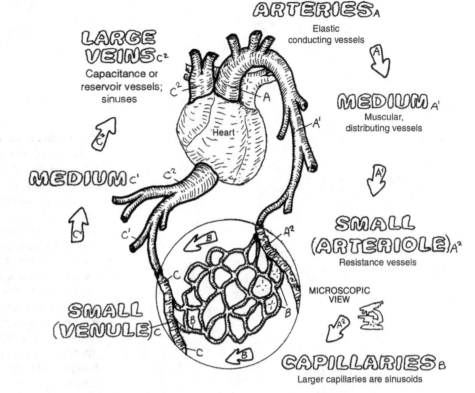

LARGE ARTERIES A
Elastic conducting vessels

MEDIUM A'
Muscular, distributing vessels

SMALL (ARTERIOLE) A²
Resistance vessels

MICROSCOPIC VIEW

CAPILLARIES B
Larger capillaries are sinusoids

LARGE VEINS C²
Capacitance or reservoir vessels; sinuses

MEDIUM C'

SMALL (VENULE) C

Heart

VESSEL STRUCTURE

TUNICA INTERNA
ENDOTHELIUM D
INTERNAL ELASTIC LAMINA E

TUNICA MEDIA
SMOOTH MUSCLE F
EXTERNAL ELASTIC LAMINA G

TUNICA EXTERNA
FIBROUS TISSUE H

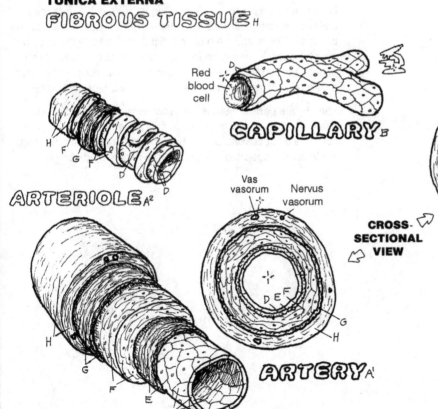

Red blood cell

CAPILLARY B

ARTERIOLE A²

Vas vasorum   Nervus vasorum

ARTERY A'

CROSS-SECTIONAL VIEW

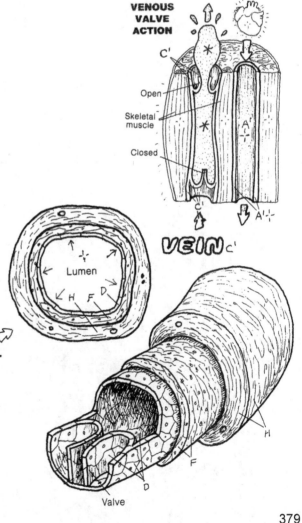

VENOUS VALVE ACTION

C'

Open

Skeletal muscle

Closed

A'

C'

Lumen

VEIN C'

Valve

379

The **mediastinum** (median partition) is a highly populated region in the thorax between and *excluding* the lungs. This is largely so because heart has many incoming and outgoing vessels that make up a significant fraction of the structure in the thorax. Learning the contents of the mediastinum by subdivision is a fairly standard academic drill because it is the best way to get a handle on the arrangement of key structures in a very crowded and busy area of the body. Note in the two upper illustrations the floor of the mediastinum, the thoracic *diaphragm*; the roof is fascial, surrounding structure entering/leaving the **superior mediastinum**; the lateral walls are parietal pleural membranes; the **posterior wall** is the anterior aspect of the thoracic vertebrae; the **anterior wall** is the sternum and costal cartilages. The mediastinum is divided into subdivisions (see sagittal view). Most (but not all) of the organs/vessels/nerves of significance in these subdivisions are listed at middle left and can be seen in the two views of the illustration page. The learning objective is to define the **subdivisions of the mediastinum** and cite the major contents in each.

The **heart wall** (lower part of the page) consists of an inner layer of simple squamous epithelium (**endocardium**) lining the cavities; it overlies a variably thick **myocardium** (cardiac muscle). External to the myocardium is a three-layered sac (**pericardium**). The innermost layer of this sac is the **visceral pericardium** (epicardium), clothing the heart. At the origin of the aortic arch, this layer turns (reflects) outward to become the **parietal pericardium** that surrounds the heart and encloses an empty **pericardial cavity**. Imagine a fist clutching the edges of a closed paper bag. Push the bag down and around the fist while it is still clutching the edges. Note that two layers of the paper bag, as well as the collapsed cavity of the bag, surround your fist—yet your fist is *not* inside the bag itself. The relationship of your fist that is outside the two layers of the bag is the relationship of the heart to the visceral and parietal pericardia. Except for serous fluid that allows friction-free movement of the heart in its sac, the pericardial cavity is empty.

The **fibrous pericardium** is the outer lining of the parietal pericardium. It is fibrous and fatty, and is strongly attached to the sternum, the great vessels, and the diaphragm. It keeps the twisting, contracting, squeezing heart within the middle mediastinum.

SUBDIVISIONS OF THE MEDIASTINUM

SUPERIOR ₐ
INFERIOR ⊹
   ANTERIOR ₈
   MIDDLE ᴄ
   POSTERIOR ᴅ

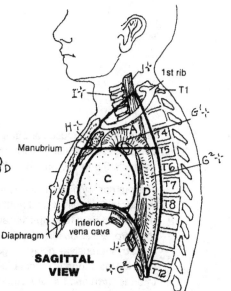

1st rib
T1
J⊹
I⊹
G'⊹
Manubrium
T4
T5
G²⊹
T6
T7
T8
B
C
D
Inferior vena cava
Diaphragm
J⊹
SAGITTAL VIEW
⊹ G²
T12

CN: Use your lightest colors for A-D; use blue for F and red for G. Begin with the "Subdivisions of the Mediastinum." (1) Color the names of the subdivisions and the four regions of the mediastinum at upper left. (2) Color the major structures within the mediastinum in the anterior view, and the related names at left. Do not color the lungs. The thymus, seen in the sagittal view, has been deleted in the anterior view to show the great vessels deep to it. (3) Color the walls of the heart and layers of pericardium, and their names, below. The pericardial cavity has been greatly exaggerated for coloring. It is normally only a potential space (contiguous membranes with a fluid interface).

STRUCTURES OF THE MEDIASTINUM

PERICARDIUM-LINED HEART ᴇ
GREAT VESSELS
   SUPERIOR VENA CAVA ꜰ
   PULMONARY TRUNK ꜰ'
   PULMONARY ARTERY ꜰ²
   PULMONARY VEIN ɢ
   AORTIC ARCH ɢ'
   THORACIC AORTA ɢ²⊹
THYMUS ʜ⊹
TRACHEA ɪ
ESOPHAGUS ᴊ
VAGUS NERVE ᴋ
PHRENIC NERVE ʟ

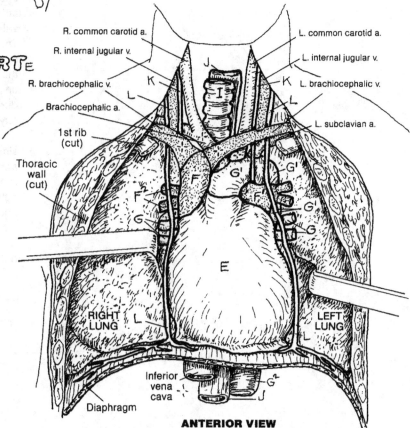

R. common carotid a.
R. internal jugular v.
R. brachiocephalic v.
Brachiocephalic a.
1st rib (cut)
Thoracic wall (cut)
L. common carotid a.
L. internal jugular v.
L. brachiocephalic v.
L. subclavian a.
J
I
K
K
L
L
F
G'
G'
F'
F'
G
G
G
E
RIGHT LUNG
L
LEFT LUNG
Inferior vena cava
G²
J
Diaphragm

ANTERIOR VIEW
(Lungs retracted to visualize deeper structures)

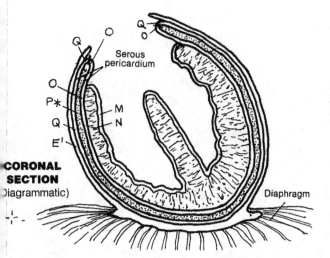

Q
O
O
Q
Serous pericardium
O
P✳
Q
M
N
E'
CORONAL SECTION
(Diagrammatic)
Diaphragm

WALLS OF THE HEART / PERICARDIUM

ENDOCARDIUM ᴍ
MYOCARDIUM ɴ
VISCERAL PERICARDIUM ᴏ
  PERICARDIAL CAVITY ᴘ✳
PARIETAL PERICARDIUM ꞯ
FIBROUS PERICARDIUM ᴇ'

The heart is the muscular pump of the blood vascular system. It contains four cavities (chambers): two on the right side (pulmonary heart) and two on the left (systemic heart).

The pulmonary heart includes the **right atrium** and **right ventricle**. The thin-walled right atrium receives poorly oxygenated blood from the **superior** and **inferior vena cavae** and from the coronary sinus (draining the cardiac vessels). The thin-walled **left atrium** receives richly oxygenated blood from **pulmonary veins**. Atrial blood is pumped at a pressure of about 5 mm Hg into the **right** and **left ventricles** simultaneously through the atrioventricular orifices, guarded by the three-cusp **tricuspid valve** on the right and the two-cusp **bicuspid valve** on the left. The cusps are like panels of a parachute, secured to the **papillary muscles** in the ventricles by **chordae tendineae** (tendons). These muscles contract with the ventricular muscles, tensing the cords and resisting cusp over-flap as ventricular blood bulges into them during ventricular contraction (*systole*). The right ventricle pumps oxygen-deficient blood to the lungs via the **pulmonary trunk** at a pressure of about 25 mm Hg (right ventricle), and the left ventricle simultaneously pumps oxygen-rich blood into the **ascending aorta** at a pressure of about 120 mm Hg. This pressure difference is reflected in the thicker walls of the left ventricle compared to the right. The pocket-like **pulmonary** and **aortic semilunar valves** guard the trunk and aorta, respectively. As blood falls back toward the ventricle from the trunk/aorta during the resting phase of the heartbeat (*diastole*), these pockets fill, closing off their respective orifices and preventing reflux into the ventricles.

CARDIOVASCULAR SYSTEM
CHAMBERS OF THE HEART

CN: Use blue for A–A⁴; dotted arrows represent venous blood flow in both illustrations. Use red for H–H⁴; clear arrows represent arterial blood flow in both illustrations. Use light colors for heart cavities B, C, I, and J. (1) Begin with arrows A⁴ in the left side of upper drawing above and below the right atrium, B; color A and A¹ In the list of names. Color the structures in the order of the list, A–H³. (2) Color the circulation chart below, beginning with the arrow A⁴ leading into the right atrium (numeral 1). Color the numerals, and their related arrows, in order from 1 to 4. Do not color the chambers or the vessels in the drawing at lower right.

SUPERIOR VENA CAVA A

INFERIOR VENA CAVA A'

 A⁴

RIGHT ATRIUM B

RIGHT VENTRICLE C

A-V TRICUSPID VALVE D

CHORDAE TENDINEAE E

PAPILLARY MUSCLE F

PULMONARY TRUNK A²

PULMONARY SEMILUNAR VALVE G

PULMONARY ARTERY A³

 H⁴

PULMONARY VEIN H

LEFT ATRIUM I

LEFT VENTRICLE J

A-V BICUSPID (MITRAL) VALVE D'

CHORDAE TENDINEAE E'

PAPILLARY MUSCLE F'

ASCENDING AORTA H'

AORTIC SEMILUNAR VALVE G'

AORTIC ARCH H²

THORACIC AORTA H³

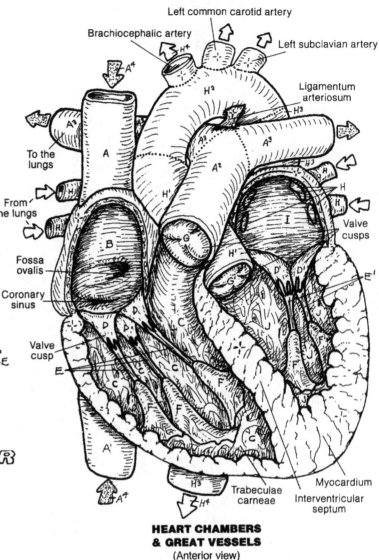

Left common carotid artery
Brachiocephalic artery
Left subclavian artery
Ligamentum arteriosum
To the lungs
From the lungs
Fossa ovalis
Coronary sinus
Valve cusp
Valve cusps
Myocardium
Trabeculae carneae
Interventricular septum

HEART CHAMBERS & GREAT VESSELS
(Anterior view)

OXYGENATED BLOOD ⇒ H⁴
DEOXYGENATED BLOOD ⇒ A⁴

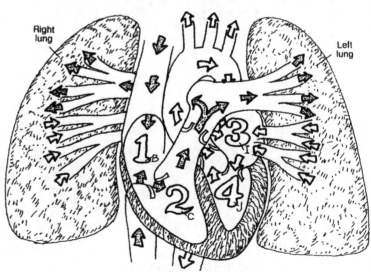

Right lung
Left lung

CIRCULATION THROUGH THE HEART
(Diagrammatic)

383

Cardiac muscle cells contract spontaneously. They do not require motor nerves to shorten. However, the intrinsic contraction rate of these cells is too slow and too unorganized for effective pumping of the heart. Happily, groups of more excitable but noncontractile cardiac cells take responsibility for initiating and conducting electrochemical impulses throughout the cardiac musculature. Such cells cause a coordinated, rhythmic sequence of cardiac muscle contractions that result in blood being moved through the cavities of the heart with appropriate volumes and pressures. These cells constitute the **cardiac conduction system**. Impulses generated at the **sinoatrial (SA) node** are distributed throughout the **atria** and to the **atrioventricular (AV) node** by way of nondiscrete **internodal pathways**. Impulses travel from the AV node, down the **AV bundle** and its **branches**, to the **Purkinje plexus** of cells embedded in the ventricular musculature.

The cardiac conduction system generates voltage changes around the heart. Some of these changes can be monitored, assessed, and measured by **electrocardiography (ECG; aka EKG)**. An ECG is essentially a voltmeter reading. It does not measure hemodynamic changes. Electrodes are placed on a number of body points on the skin. Recorded data (various waves of varying voltage over time) are displayed on an oscilloscope or a strip of moving paper. The shape and direction of wave deflections are dependent upon the spatial relationship of the electrodes (leads) on the body surface.

When the SA node fires, excitation/depolarization of the atrial musculature spreads out from the node. This is reflected in the ECG by an upward deflection of the resting (isoelectric) horizontal line (**P wave**). This deflection immediately precedes contraction of the atrial musculature and filling of the ventricles. The **P-Q interval** (**P-R interval** in the absence of a Q wave) reflects conduction of excitation from the atria to the Purkinje cell plexus in the ventricular myocardium. Prolongation of this interval beyond .20 seconds may reflect an AV conduction block. The **QRS complex** reflects depolarization of the ventricular myocardium. The term *complex* here refers to the combination of the three waves (Q, R, and S) immediately preceding ventricular contraction, wherein blood is forced into the pulmonary trunk and ascending aorta. The **S-T segment** reflects a continuing period of ventricular depolarization. Myocardial ischemia may induce a deflection of this normally horizontal segment. The **T wave** is an upward, prolonged deflection and reflects ventricular repolarization (recovery), during which the atria passively fill with blood from the vena cavae and pulmonary veins. The QT interval, corrected for heart rate (QTc), reflects ventricular depolarization and repolarization. Prolongation of this segment may suggest abnormal ventricular rhythms (arrhythmias). In a healthy heart at a low rate of beat, the P-Q, S-T, and **T-P segments** all are isoelectric (horizontal).

CARDIAC CONDUCTION SYSTEM & THE ECG

CN: Use blue for D and red for E. Use a very light color for B so that the patterns of dots identifying segments B–B³ of the ECG remain visible after coloring. The QRS complex and the S-T segment (ECG diagram) are colored similarly; they both reflect ventricular depolarization. (1) Begin at upper right and color the four large arrows identifying the atria, A², and ventricles, B³, as well as their names; do not color the atria and ventricles. Color the internodal and interatrial pathway arrows, A¹. (2) In the middle of the page, color the stages of blood flow through the heart and their related letters; they relate to voltage changes in the ECG below. (3) Color the ECG and related letters, starting at the left. (4) Color the horizontal bar below the time line.

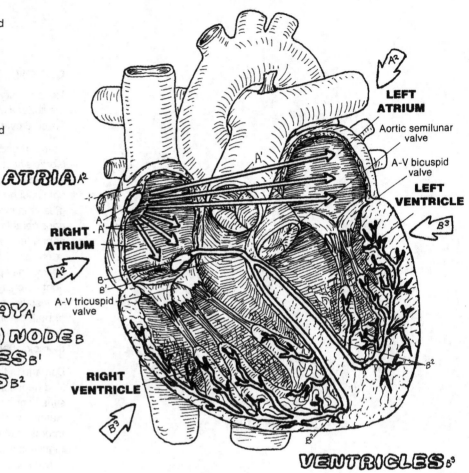

ATRIA A²

LEFT ATRIUM

Aortic semilunar valve

A-V bicuspid valve

LEFT VENTRICLE

RIGHT ATRIUM

A-V tricuspid valve

RIGHT VENTRICLE

VENTRICLES B³

CONDUCTION SYSTEM

SA (SINOATRIAL) NODE A
INTERNODAL PATHWAY A¹
AV (ATRIOVENTRICULAR) NODE B
AV BUNDLE/BRANCHES B¹
PURKINJE PLEXUS B²

BLOOD FLOW

OXYGEN-POOR D
OXYGEN-RICH E

P A³

L. atrium
L. ventricle
R. atrium
R. ventricle

QRS B³

T B³

ELECTROCARDIOGRAM (ECG)

P WAVE A³
P-Q (P-R) INTERVAL B-B²
QRS COMPLEX B³
S-T SEGMENT B³
T WAVE B³
T-P SEGMENT C

mV (Millivolt)

P A³

P-Q B-B²

R B³

S-T B³

T B³

T-P C

Q B³

S B³

TIME (sec.) 0   A³   .08 B-B¹ .12   B³   .20   B³ .24   B³   .40

← P-Q (R) INTERVAL → ← QT INTERVAL →

CORONARY ARTERIES

The coronary arteries form an upside-down crown (L. corona) on the surface of the heart. The arteries lie in grooves, or sulci, often covered over by the epicardium.

Both **left** and **right coronary arteries** arise from small openings (*aortic sinuses*) just above the two aortic semilunar valve cusps. Generally, the left coronary artery is somewhat larger than the right. During the cardiac cycle, the flow rate through the left is greater in most people than that through the right. There may be considerable variation in the anastomotic pattern of the left and right arterial branches. These branches terminate in multitudes of arterioles supplying the vast capillary network among the muscle fibers. The apparent multiple communications among the left and right coronary arteries notwithstanding, varying degrees of vascular insufficiency occur when there is significant obstruction of one or both coronary arteries. There is some extra-coronary arterial supply to the heart from epicardial vessels (branches of internal thoracic arteries) and aortic vasa vasorum.

Damage to the intimal layer of coronary arteries can occur with lipid deposition or inflammation. Platelet aggregation at these sites contributes to the formation of **plaque** (cell material, lipid, platelet, fibrin). Plaque builds up within the vessels, forming thrombi that occlude the vessels in progressively greater degrees. Significantly reduced blood flow to the myocardium (*ischemia*) can cause sharp pain (angina) to the chest, back, shoulder, and arm as well as permanent damage to the **myocardium (infarction)**, not to mention disability and death.

CARDIAC VEINS

The **cardiac veins** travel with the coronary arteries, but incompletely. Vast anastomoses of veins occur throughout the myocardium; most drain into the right atrium by way of the **coronary sinus**. The **anterior cardiac veins** conduct blood directly into the right atrium. Other small veins may drain directly into the right atrium as well. Some deep (arteriosinusoidal) veins drain directly into the atria and ventricles. Extracardiac venous drainage can also occur through the vasa vasorum of the vena cavae.

CARDIOVASCULAR SYSTEM
CORONARY ARTERIES & CARDIAC VEINS

RIGHT CORONARY ARTERYA
  MUSCULAR BRANCHA'
  MARGINAL BRANCHB
  POSTERIOR INTERVENTRICULAR
  (DESCENDING) BRANCHC

LEFT CORONARY ARTERYD
  ANTERIOR INTERVENTRICULAR
  (DESCENDING) BRANCHE
  MUSCULAR BRANCHE'
  CIRCUMFLEX BRANCHF

CN: Color only the arteries and veins on this page; do not color the heart. Use your brightest colors for A, D, and L. (1) When coloring the arteries, include the broken lines that represent vessels on the posterior surface of the heart. (2) Do the same with the veins. (3) Color the artery in front of the plaque in the circled view.

CORONARY ARTERIES

ARTERIOR VIEW

Left aortic sinus (Posterior)

Aorta

Pulmonary trunk

Pulmonary artery

Left atrium

Superior vena cava

Right aortic sinus (Anterior)

Right atrium

Right ventricle

Left ventricle

Plaque

MYOCARDIAL INFARCTION*'

CARDIAC VEINS

ANTERIOR VIEW

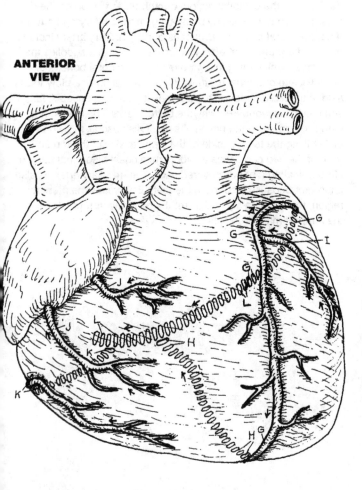

GREAT CARDIAC V.G
MIDDLE CARDIAC V.H
MARGINAL V.I
ANTERIOR CARDIAC V.J
SMALL CARDIAC V.K
CORONARY SINUSL

Arteries to the head and neck, principally the subclavian and the common carotid arteries, arise indirectly by way of the brachiocephalic trunk on the right side, and directly from the aortic arch on the left side. There are embryologic bases for this difference that can be visualized on the illustration page at lower right.

On the drawing at left, note the branches of the right subclavian artery (the branches of the left are not shown here, but see the anterior view). The branches of the left subclavian are essentially identical. The subclavian artery supplies the upper limb through the axillary artery.

The first branch of the subclavian artery is the internal thoracic artery, an important anastomotic artery between upper and lower limbs. Many vessels supplying the neck come from the thyrocervical and costocervical trunks. Particularly important is the inferior thyroid artery, to the thyroid gland, from the thyrocervical trunk.

Now follow the external carotid artery after the bifurcation of the common carotid. Note that its first branch is the superior thyroid artery supplying the critical larynx and thyroid gland. Follow out the arterial branches to the tongue (lingual), the facial muscles (facial), and the occipital region (occipital). At this point, the external carotid finishes by separating into maxillary and superficial temporal arteries. Branches of the maxillary artery include the middle meningeal artery, a critical vessel that supplies the dura mater while riding in a groove of the temporal bone. It is a potential site of arterial rupture with a hard fall on or a blow to the side of the head (epidural hematoma). If you are a baseball fan, you may have wondered why the batter wears a helmet with an extension covering the pitcher's side of his head. A thrown baseball striking the temple (side of the head level with the top and front of the ear) can cause a middle meningeal bleed that can be life-terminating if not discovered early. The maxillary artery is also important because it supplies the teeth, lower jaw, the pterygoid region, the nasal cavity and nose, the hard and soft palate, and the temporomandibular joint.

CARDIOVASCULAR SYSTEM
ARTERIES OF THE HEAD & NECK

CN: Use red for A and dark or bright colors for B and L. (1) Begin with the anterior view at lower right, coloring the names above it as well. (2) Color the lateral view at left, beginning with the brachiocephalic trunk, A. The broken lines at the side of the face represent vessels that run more deeply than the arteries with solid lines. (3) Color the arrows pointing to the four sites where the arterial pulse may be palpated.

BRACHIOCEPHALIC TRUNK A

RIGHT SUBCLAVIAN B
  INTERNAL THORACIC C
  VERTEBRAL D
  THYROCERVICAL TRUNK E
    INFERIOR THYROID F
    SUPRASCAPULAR G
    TRANSVERSE CERVICAL H
  COSTOCERVICAL TRUNK I
    DEEP CERVICAL J
    HIGHEST INTERCOSTAL K

RIGHT COMMON CAROTID L
  INTERNAL CAROTID M
    OPHTHALMIC N
  EXTERNAL CAROTID O
    SUPERIOR THYROID P
    LINGUAL Q
    FACIAL R
    OCCIPITAL S
    MAXILLARY T
      INFERIOR ALVEOLAR U
      SUPERIOR ALVEOLAR U'
      MIDDLE MENINGEAL V
    POSTERIOR AURICULAR W
    SUPERFICIAL TEMPORAL X
    TRANSVERSE FACIAL Y

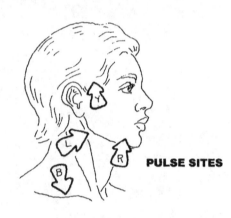

PULSE SITES

LEFT SUBCLAVIAN A. B'
LEFT COMMON CAROTID A. L'

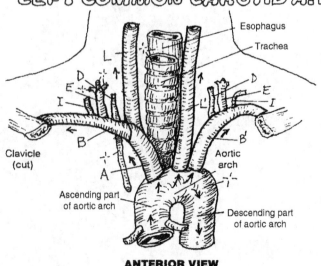

LATERAL VIEW
(Right side)

ANTERIOR VIEW

Two pairs of arteries provide the blood supply to the brain: the **internal carotid artery system** and the **vertebral artery system** (recall the previous page). The two internal carotid arteries ascend the neck to reach the *carotid canals* in the base of the skull to arrive in the middle cranial fossa just lateral to the optic chiasma. In the upper center illustration, note the cut ends of the internal carotid arteries (A). Each internal carotid artery ends by dividing into **anterior** and **middle cerebral arteries**. Just before that division, the internal carotid gives off the ophthalmic artery to the orbit via the superior orbital fissure (not shown).

The anterior cerebral arteries continue rostrally, close to one another where an **anterior communicating artery** connects them. The area of coverage for the anterior cerebral artery can be seen in all three views of arterial distribution. The **middle cerebral artery** heads laterally in the lateral fissure between the insula and the temporal lobe, giving off small, short lenticulo-striate arteries at right angles, directed to the basal ganglia. These "stroke arteries," as they are called, are common sources of intracerebral hemorrhage, often resulting in at least partial paralysis of the limb muscles on the side of the body opposite (contralateral to) the hemorrhage. Note the distribution of the anterior, middle, and posterior cerebral arteries on the surface of the cerebrum.

In the central illustration, note how vessels arising directly or indirectly from the vertebral arteries (F) supply the brain stem. The **anterior spinal arteries** arise from the paired **vertebral arteries**, as do the posterior inferior cerebellar arteries (PICAs). The vertebral arteries form the **basilar artery** at the pontine-medullary junction. On the anterior surface of the pons, the basilar artery sends branches to the cerebellum, the inner ear (labyrinthine arteries), and the pons, and terminates by splitting into two **posterior cerebral arteries** (the inferior part of the cerebral arterial circle).

The **posterior communicating artery** is the single direct connection of the vertebral system with the carotid system. There is, however, considerable variation in the components of the arterial circle as seen angiographically, including anomalies and severely narrowed vessels.

CARDIOVASCULAR SYSTEM
ARTERIES OF THE BRAIN

CN: (1) Color the vessels of the carotid system A–E. (2) Color the vessels of the vertebral system F–J, with contrasting colors. (3) Color the diagram at upper right. (4) Color the diagram of the arterial circle at left, beginning with A. (5) Color the vessels on the lateral and medial surface of the cerebral hemisphere.

INTERNAL CAROTID ᴀ   VERTEBRAL ꜰ
ANTERIOR CEREBRAL ʙ   BASILAR ɢ
    ANTERIOR COMMUNICATING ᴄ   CEREBELLAR (3) ʜ
MIDDLE CEREBRAL ᴅ   POSTERIOR CEREBRAL ɪ
POSTERIOR COMMUNICATING ᴇ   ANTERIOR SPINAL ᴊ

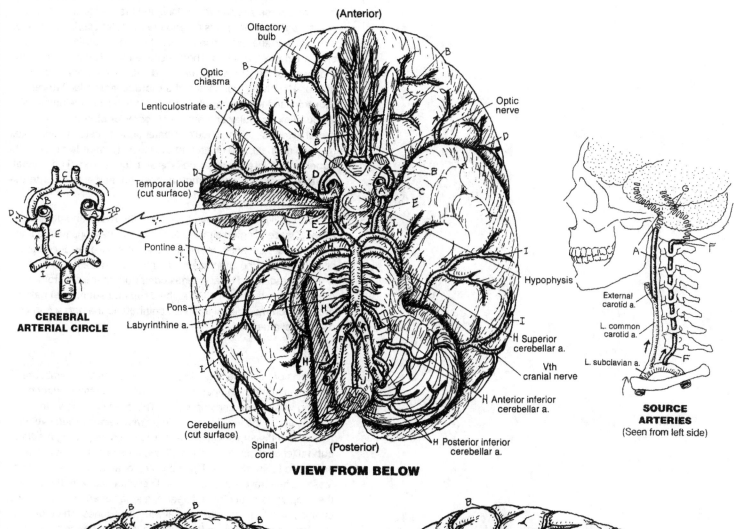

CEREBRAL
ARTERIAL CIRCLE

(Anterior)

Olfactory bulb

Optic chiasma

Lenticulostriate a.

Temporal lobe (cut surface)

Pontine a.

Pons

Labyrinthine a.

Cerebellum (cut surface)

Spinal cord

(Posterior)

VIEW FROM BELOW

Optic nerve

Hypophysis

H Superior cerebellar a.

Vth cranial nerve

H Anterior inferior cerebellar a.

H Posterior inferior cerebellar a.

External carotid a.

L. common carotid a.

L. subclavian a.

SOURCE ARTERIES
(Seen from left side)

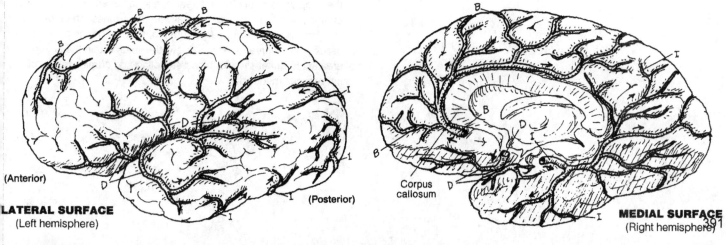

(Anterior)

LATERAL SURFACE
(Left hemisphere)

(Posterior)

Corpus callosum

MEDIAL SURFACE
(Right hemisphere)

391

ARTERIES

The principal artery to the free upper limb comes as an extension of the **brachiocephalic** and the **subclavian arteries** in the root of the limb deep to the clavicle: the **axillary artery**. On this page, looking at the arrangement of arteries, one can see a generally straight line of an artery (**brachial artery**) through the anterior-medial arm with a significant branch (**profunda** or **deep brachial artery**) descending the posterior arm and below the elbow. A complex of interconnecting vessels, constituting a pattern of collateral circulation, exists around the scapula (not shown) whereby branches of the subclavian, axillary, and brachial arteries form *circumscapular anastomoses* around the scapula, offering a route of blood flow to the forearm in the event the lower axillary and brachial arteries are blocked. There are anastomotic channels around the major joints: (1) the acromion and shoulder (*acromial rete* or network) involving branches of the **thoraco-acromial, lateral thoracic**, and **suprascapular arteries**; (2) neck of the humerus (**circumflex scapular** and **anterior/posterior circumflex humeral arteries**), (3) the shoulder (anterior and posterior circumflex humeral arteries), and (4) around the elbow (**profunda brachial, superior** and **inferior ulnar collateral arteries, radial** and **radial recurrent arteries**, and **common** [posterior and anterior] **interosseous arteries**).

The principal arteries of the forearm are the **radial** and **ulnar arteries.** Descending on either side of the interosseous membrane (ligament) are the anterior and posterior interosseous arteries (not shown, but see the interosseous membrane on the right). At the wrist, the radial and ulnar arteries contribute to the anastomoses of the wrist and hand, including the **deep** and **superficial palmar arches**. Common digital arteries contribute to the dorsal and palmar digital arteries.

VEINS

The veins of the upper limb, like the veins in the lower limb, are variable in number and pattern. There are two sets of interconnecting veins: deep and superficial. The deep set follows the arteries and is identically named (e.g., radial artery, **radial vein**). Not so with the superficial veins, e.g., **basilic, cephalic, median cubital** (*cubital*, referring to the elbow; for example, veins often employed for intravenous injections are located in the antecubital fossa). Often traveling in pairs (*venae comitantes*) with the arteries, the deep veins of the hand, forearm, and lower arm are not shown on this page; but know they travel with the arteries. The broken lines represent superficial (subcutaneous) veins on the posterior aspect of the forearm. At the elbow, the veins within the boxed area are frequent sites for blood sampling and administration of intravenous medication.

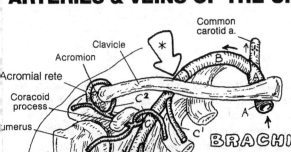

Common carotid a.

Clavicle

Acromion

Acromial rete

Coracoid process

Humerus

CN: (1) Color the arteries A-F² on the left in the direction of blood flow. (2) Color the pulse points gray. (3) Color the veins G¹-O on the right, starting at the bottom of the page.

Internal jugular v.

External jugular v.

ANTERIOR VIEW (Left limb)

◀ ARTERIES

BRACHIOCEPHALIC A

SUBCLAVIAN B

AXILLARY C

   SUPERIOR THORACIC C¹

   THORACO-ACROMIAL & BRANCHES C²

   LATERAL THORACIC C³

   SUBSCAPULAR C⁴

   ANTERIOR/POSTERIOR CIRCUMFLEX HUMERAL C⁵

BRACHIAL D

   PROFUNDA BRACHII & BRANCH D¹

   SUPERIOR ULNAR COLLATERAL D²

   INFERIOR ULNAR COLLATERAL D³

RADIAL E

   RADIAL RECURRENT E¹

ULNAR E²

   ANTERIOR ULNAR RECURRENT E³

   POSTERIOR ULNAR RECURRENT E⁴

   COMMON INTEROSSEOUS E⁵

SUPERFICIAL PALMAR ARCH F

COMMON PALMAR DIGITAL F¹

DEEP PALMAR ARCH F²

Middle collateral a.

Recurrent interosseous a.

Radius

Ulna

VEINS ▶

DORSAL DIGITAL G & NETWORK G¹

BASILIC H

MEDIAN V. OF FOREARM I

CEPHALIC J

MEDIAN CUBITAL K

BRACHIAL L

AXILLARY M

SUBCLAVIAN N

BRACHIOCEPHALIC O

PULSE POINTS *

ANTERIOR VIEW (Right limb)

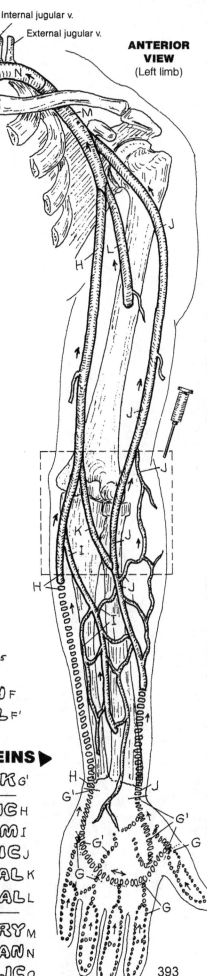

393

The **stem artery to the lower limb** begins in the lateral wall of the pelvis. Here the bilateral **common iliac arteries** taking off from the terminal abdominal aorta (right side shown here) give off the **internal iliac artery** supplying the pelvic wall and viscera. From this latter artery is derived some vessels of significance to the lower limb, including the **superior/inferior gluteal arteries** that exit the pelvis through the greater sciatic foramen above/below the piriformis muscle, respectively, to supply the glutei medius and minimus. The **obturator artery** and its fellow nerve pass through the obturator foramen; the artery primarily supplies the hip joint. Note the contribution of the inferior gluteal artery to the anastomoses around the hip joint.

The **external iliac artery** gives off a very important **inferior epigastric artery** just before reaching the inguinal ligament. This artery climbs up the deep surface of the anterior abdominal wall to the sheath of the rectus abdominis, where it connects with the superior epigastric artery. This is a major collateral route of flow to the lower limb in the event of occlusion of the abdominal aorta. The external iliac artery becomes the **femoral artery** upon passing under the inguinal ligament in company with the vein and nerve of the same name.

The femoral artery sends off the **profunda femoris artery** early in its course, then dives deep to the sartorius and pierces the medial muscular compartment (adductor canal) to gain access to the back of the knee and leg. Due in part to the considerable muscle mass in the posterior thigh, the profunda femoris artery is quite large, and its descending **perforating branches** are extensive. Note how the **medial** and **lateral circumflex arteries** contribute to the anastomoses about the femoral head/neck and the hip joint. The blood supply to the hip joint area can be compromised in several ways.

The **popliteal artery** is the distal continuation of the femoral artery at the top of the popliteal fossa. It is a relatively short artery, as it ends by dividing into **anterior** and **posterior tibial arteries**. The **genicular arteries** form a significant anastomotic pattern about the knee joint in company with the **circumflex fibular** and **anterior tibial recurrent arteries**. They can keep everything alive around the knee if there is an obstruction of the popliteal artery. The **anterior tibial artery** descends along the interosseous membrane, as does the **fibular artery** that supplies both lateral and posterior leg compartments. The **posterior tibial** and **fibular arteries** run deep to the gastrocnemius and soleus muscles. The anterior tibial artery exits the posterior leg compartment just below the knee, and descends on the interosseous membrane's anterior surface. In the event of occlusion of the posterior tibial artery, the fibular artery expands to pick up the load through multiple communicating vessels.

The primary artery to the dorsal foot is the **dorsalis pedis artery**, the pulse of which is palpable over the tarsal bones. The primary artery to the plantar region is the posterior tibial artery.

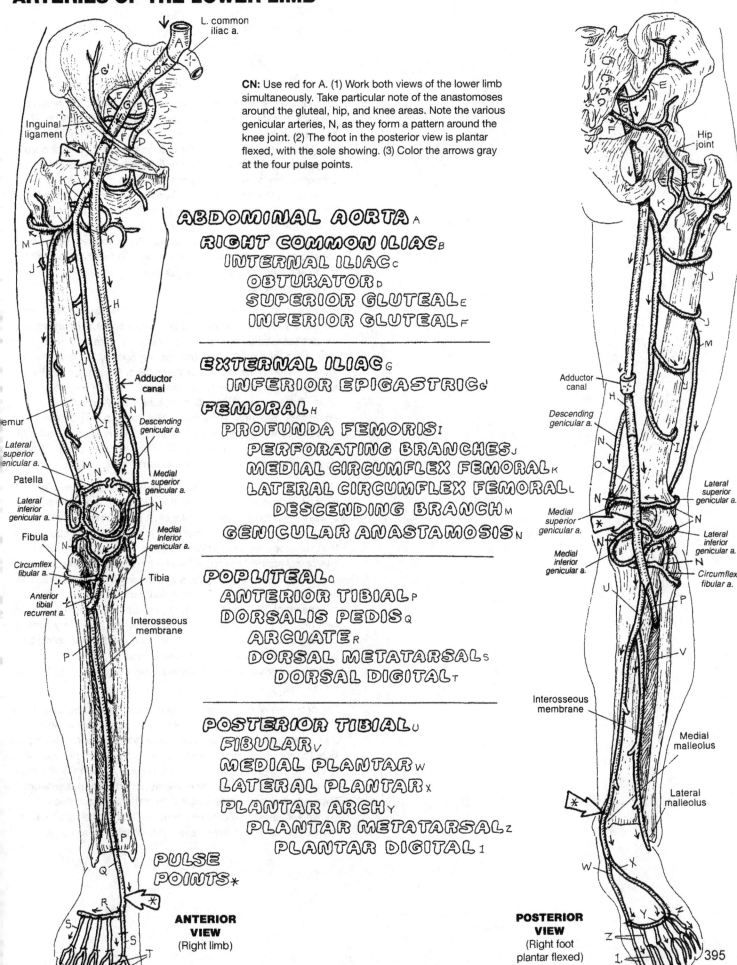

L. common iliac a.

CN: Use red for A. (1) Work both views of the lower limb simultaneously. Take particular note of the anastomoses around the gluteal, hip, and knee areas. Note the various genicular arteries, N, as they form a pattern around the knee joint. (2) The foot in the posterior view is plantar flexed, with the sole showing. (3) Color the arrows gray at the four pulse points.

Inguinal ligament

ABDOMINAL AORTA A
RIGHT COMMON ILIAC B
INTERNAL ILIAC C
OBTURATOR D
SUPERIOR GLUTEAL E
INFERIOR GLUTEAL F

EXTERNAL ILIAC G
INFERIOR EPIGASTRIC G'
FEMORAL H
PROFUNDA FEMORIS I
PERFORATING BRANCHES J
MEDIAL CIRCUMFLEX FEMORAL K
LATERAL CIRCUMFLEX FEMORAL L
DESCENDING BRANCH M
GENICULAR ANASTAMOSIS N

POPLITEAL O
ANTERIOR TIBIAL P
DORSALIS PEDIS Q
ARCUATE R
DORSAL METATARSAL S
DORSAL DIGITAL T

POSTERIOR TIBIAL U
FIBULAR V
MEDIAL PLANTAR W
LATERAL PLANTAR X
PLANTAR ARCH Y
PLANTAR METATARSAL Z
PLANTAR DIGITAL 1

Adductor canal

Femur

Lateral superior genicular a.

Patella

Lateral inferior genicular a.

Fibula

Circumflex fibular a.

Anterior tibial recurrent a.

Descending genicular a.

Medial superior genicular a.

Medial inferior genicular a.

Tibia

Interosseous membrane

PULSE POINTS *

ANTERIOR VIEW
(Right limb)

Hip joint

Adductor canal

Descending genicular a.

Medial superior genicular a.

Medial inferior genicular a.

Lateral superior genicular a.

Lateral inferior genicular a.

Circumflex fibular a.

Interosseous membrane

Medial malleolus

Lateral malleolus

POSTERIOR VIEW
(Right foot plantar flexed)

395

The aorta arises from the superior aspect of the left ventricle as the **ascending aorta;** the ascending part of the aortic arch. This large vessel is a classic "large artery" with a wall almost entirely composed of elastic tissue. It is characterized by a pair of **coronary arteries** that begin as two orifices in the first part of the ascending aorta. These open into two of the three cusps of the aortic valve. During systole, the blood is ejected from the left ventricle under high pressure, and the aortic valve cusps are pressed against the aortic wall. During diastole, the blood in the ascending aorta flows retrograde (backward), fills the cusps, and flows into the two coronary arteries. In this manner, the heart helps itself to the freshest blood in town! The aortic arch is at the level of the fourth thoracic vertebra.

From your right to your left, the branches of the **aortic arch** are the **brachiocephalic trunk**, the **left common carotid artery**, and the **left subclavian artery**. The descending thoracic aorta begins at the third rib (T5 vertebra), closely applied to the posterior thoracic wall on the left side of the midline. Small **bronchial** and **esophageal arterie**s come off the anterior wall of the thoracic aorta. The supreme (highest) intercostal artery, a branch of the **costocervical trunk**, supplies the first and second posterior intercostal spaces. The thoracic aorta gives off nine pairs of posterior intercostal arteries. Twelve ribs, eleven intercostal spaces. Where do the first two intercostal arteries come from?

Note the left **internal thoracic artery** (F) coming off the inferior surface of the subclavian artery. It lies in the anterior intercostal spaces deep to the costal cartilages. It gives off the anterior intercostal arteries (not shown) that meet in the intercostal spaces with the posterior intercostal arteries. Follow this artery to the sixth intercostal space; here it divides into the **musculophrenic** (ending on the diaphragm) and the **superior epigastric arteries**. The latter artery descends down the anterior abdominal wall deep to the sheath of the rectus abdominis. Its terminal branches connect with the terminal branches of the inferior epigastric artery coming up from the external iliac artery. *This is one of the most important anastomoses in the body*: by these connections, blood can get to the lower limbs even with a serious occlusion of the abdominal aorta.

The branches of the abdominal aorta are either visceral or parietal. The parietal branches are small, bilateral, segmental (**lumbar**) arteries supplying the body wall. These arteries are largely responsible for providing arterial blood to the spinal cord. The visceral branches may be paired (e.g., **gastric**, **renal**, **ovarian/testicular**) or not (e.g., **celiac**, **superior mesenteric**, **inferior mesenteric**). These parietal and visceral branches of the aorta are clearly shown and should be colored carefully. They will be presented in more detail with the relevant system of which they are a part.

CARDIOVASCULAR SYSTEM
AORTA, BRANCHES, & RELATED VESSELS

CN: Use red for A, A[1], and A[2]. (1) Color the aortic arch and its branches, A–E. Color the vessels supplying the anterior and posterior intercostal spaces 1–11, F–H. (2) Color the bronchial and esophageal arteries on the bronchi and esophagus. (3) Color the superior epigastric artery. (4) Color the branches of the abdominal aorta. The inferior vena cava (stippled) is shown for reference.

AORTIC ARCHₐ
CORONARYᵦ
BRACHIOCEPHALIC TRUNKc
LEFT COMMON CAROTIDᴅ
LEFT SUBCLAVIANᴇ
   INTERNAL THORACICꜰ
     MUSCULOPHRENICꜰ'
      SUPERIOR EPIGASTRICꜰ²
   COSTOCERVICAL TRUNKɢ
     HIGHEST INTERCOSTALₕ

THORACIC AORTAₐ'
BRONCHIALᵢ
ESOPHAGEALⱼ
POSTERIOR INTERCOSTAL (9)ₖ

ABDOMINAL AORTAₐ²
CELIAC TRUNKʟ
   LEFT GASTRICₘ
    SPLENICₙ
    COMMON HEPATICₒ
SUPERIOR MESENTERICₚ
RENALᵩ
TESTICULAR / OVARIANᵣ
LUMBARₛ
INFERIOR MESENTERICₜ
COMMON ILIACᵤ

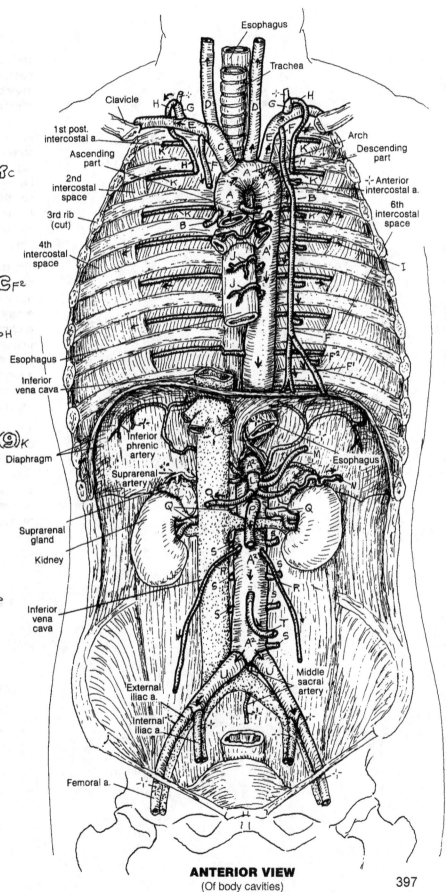

ANTERIOR VIEW
(Of body cavities)

397

The **celiac trunk**, the first single visceral artery off the abdominal aorta, comes off the abdominal **aorta** within the aortic hiatus of the thoracic diaphragm. It is a very short vessel that divides immediately into arteries to the liver, spleen, stomach, duodenum, and pancreas. Note the rich anastomotic pattern of arteries to the stomach. Both **left** and **right gastric arteries** cover the lesser curvature of the stomach, with branches of the left reaching and supplying the lower esophagus. The term -*epiploic* refers to the omentum, which is the fold of peritoneum between the stomach and the liver (lesser omentum), and between the stomach and the transverse colon (greater omentum). The **gastroepiploic arteries** supply the greater curvature of the stomach and run in the greater omentum.

The **superior mesenteric artery** supplies most of the small intestine, the head of the pancreas, the cecum, the ascending colon, and part of the transverse colon. It travels in the common mesentery that comes off the parietal peritoneum of the posterior abdominal wall. Anastomoses exist between the celiac and superior mesenteric arteries in the curve of the duodenum. The superior and inferior mesenteric arteries also interconnect via a marginal artery that runs along the length of the large intestine and is fed by both these arteries. The arteries to the ileum/jejunum (O, P) run in the common mesentery.

The **inferior mesenteric artery** supplies the transverse colon down to the rectum and anal canal. Its branches lie, for the most part, posterior to the peritoneum (*retroperitoneal*); the principal exception is the group of vessels to the sigmoid colon that run in the sigmoid mesocolon on the left. Note the anastomoses between branches of the **superior rectal artery** (from the inferior mesenteric artery) and those of the middle and inferior rectal arteries that come from the internal iliac artery, as does the internal pudendal artery.

ARTERIES TO GASTROINTESTINAL TRACT & RELATED ORGANS

CN: Color the aorta, A, red. Use the same colors for arteries labeled here B, J, K, L, and Q that were used for those arteries with different labels under the heading "Abdominal Aorta" on the preceding page. (1) Begin with the illustration at upper right for orientation. (2) Color the larger illustration in descending order.

AORTA A

CELIAC TRUNK B
HEPATIC: COMMON c /LEFT c' /RIGHT c²
RIGHT GASTRIC D
GASTRODUODENAL E
RIGHT GASTROEPIPLOIC F
LEFT GASTROEPIPLOIC G
PANCREATICO-DUODENAL (SUPERIOR) H
CYSTIC I
LEFT GASTRIC J
SPLENIC K

SUPERIOR MESENTERIC L
PANCREATICO-DUODENAL (INFERIOR) H'
MIDDLE COLIC M
RIGHT COLIC N
ILEO-COLIC O
BRANCHES TO SMALL INTESTINE P

INFERIOR MESENTERIC Q
LEFT COLIC R
SIGMOID BRANCHES S
SUPERIOR RECTAL T

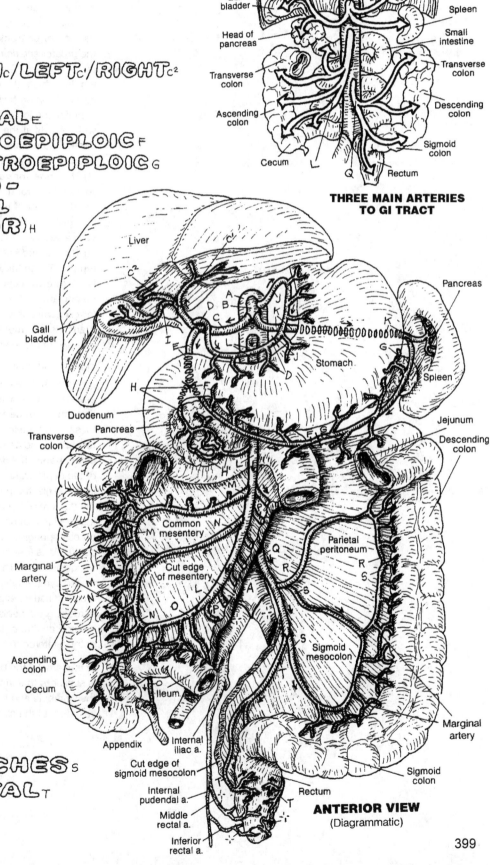

THREE MAIN ARTERIES TO GI TRACT

ANTERIOR VIEW
(Diagrammatic)

399

The **internal iliac artery** is the primary source of blood to the **pelvis** and **perineum**. Its branches are usually organized into posterior (parietal) and anterior (visceral) divisions/trunks. The vascular pattern is variable; the one shown is characteristic. From the **posterior trunk**, the **superior gluteal artery** passes through the *greater sciatic foramen above* the piriformis muscle to the upper buttock. The **inferior gluteal** and **internal pudendal arteries**, from the anterior trunk, depart the pelvis through the *lesser sciatic foramen below* the piriformis. The inferior gluteal artery supplies the lower buttock and maintains anastomotic channels with vessels at the hip joint. Proximal to the formation of the inferior gluteal and pudendal arteries, the **anterior trunk** of the internal iliac gives off four branches in both males and females. (1) The **superior vesical artery**, which arises from the proximal part of the **fetal umbilical artery**. When the umbilical cord is cut, the distal part of the artery atrophies, forming the medial umbilical ligament; the remaining umbilical artery becomes the superior vesical artery, supplying the upper bladder and ductus deferens. (2) The second branch is the **obturator artery** to the medial thigh region. (3) The third branch is the **uterine artery**; in the male, it is the **inferior vesical artery**. The **vaginal artery** comes off the uterine artery. The arteries to the prostate and seminal vesicles (not shown) come off the inferior vesical artery. (4) The fourth branch is the **middle rectal artery** that contributes to the significant set of rectal anastomoses around the rectum and anal canal.

The left and right **internal pudendal arteries** supply the external genital structures. The pudendal vessels (and nerve) leave the pelvic cavity by way of the lesser sciatic foramen, and descend through the **pudendal canal** in the lateral wall of the ischiorectal fossa along the inner surface of the inferior pubic ramus. The artery enters the deep perineal space. There the **artery to the bulb of the penis**, the **deep artery of the penis**, and the *dorsal artery of the penis* branch off to enter the posterior aspect of the bulb of the penis, the posterior aspect of the corpus cavernosum, and the dorsum of the penis, respectively. In the male, these arteries provide blood to the vascular spaces of erectile tissue of the corpus spongiosum and the larger corpus cavernosum, as well as the glans (dorsal artery). The corpus spongiosum terminates at the glans penis. The deep and dorsal arteries dilate in response to parasympathetic stimulation, increasing blood flow into the erectile tissues, expanding the erectile bodies, and erecting and hardening the penis. The erectile tissue of the glans is generally softer than that of the cavernous bodies, thus facilitating a softer entry in intercourse.

In the female, the branching pattern of the internal pudendal artery is similar to that in the male, with arterial branches to the bulb of the vestibule and the corpus cavernosum of the clitoris. The dorsal artery of the clitoris supplies the glans.

CN: Take note of the aorta in the two illustrations at right that is to be left uncolored. (1) Color the medial views of both pelves simultaneously. (2) Color both halves of the dissected perineum seen from below (inferior view). (3) The names listed under "Perineum" can be seen in one or more of the three views presented.

PELVIS

INTERNAL ILIAC A

POSTERIOR TRUNK A¹

ILIOLUMBAR B

SUPERIOR GLUTEAL C

LATERAL SACRAL D

ANTERIOR TRUNK A²

UMBILICAL (FETAL) E÷

SUPERIOR VESICAL /

A. TO VAS DEF. F

OBTURATOR G

UTERINE H

VAGINAL I

INFERIOR VESICAL J

MIDDLE RECTAL K

INFERIOR GLUTEAL L

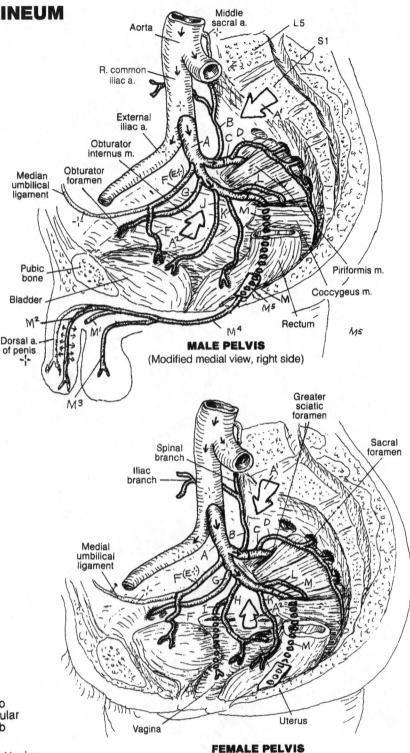

MALE PELVIS
(Modified medial view, right side)

FEMALE PELVIS
(Modified medial view, right side)

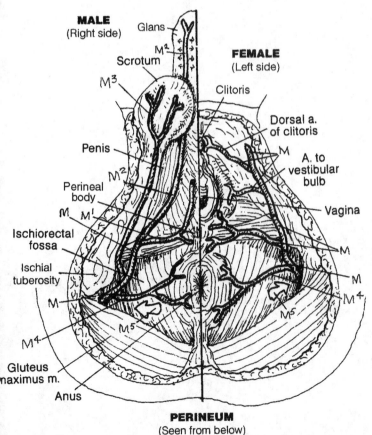

MALE
(Right side)

FEMALE
(Left side)

PERINEUM
(Seen from below)

PERINEUM

PUDENDAL M

A. TO THE BULB OF PENIS M¹

DEEP A. OF THE PENIS M²

POSTERIOR SCROTAL M³

INFERIOR RECTAL M⁴

PUDENDAL CANAL M⁵

401

402

CN: The arteries are shown bilaterally in the limbs only. Note that the figure is in the anatomical position, palms facing forward. (1) Using the preceding pages for reference as necessary, start with A and color in the order listed. You may wish to write each name with a graphite pencil to facilitate corrections (you may change your mind!), in which case, circle the letter or number at the beginning of the line with the appropriate color.
(See the end of this section for answers.)

A _____

ARTERIES OF THE UPPER LIMB
B _____
C _____
D _____
E _____
F _____
G _____
H _____
I _____
J _____

ARTERIES OF THE HEAD AND NECK
K _____
L _____
M _____

ARTERIES OF THE CHEST
A _____
A¹ _____
N _____
O _____
P _____
Q _____
R _____
S _____

ARTERIES OF THE ABDOMEN AND PELVIS
A² _____
T _____
U _____
V _____
W _____
X _____
Y _____
Z _____
1 _____
2 _____

ARTERIES OF THE LOWER LIMB
3 _____
4 _____
5 _____
6 _____
7 _____
8 _____
9 _____
10 _____
11 _____
12 _____
13 _____
14 _____

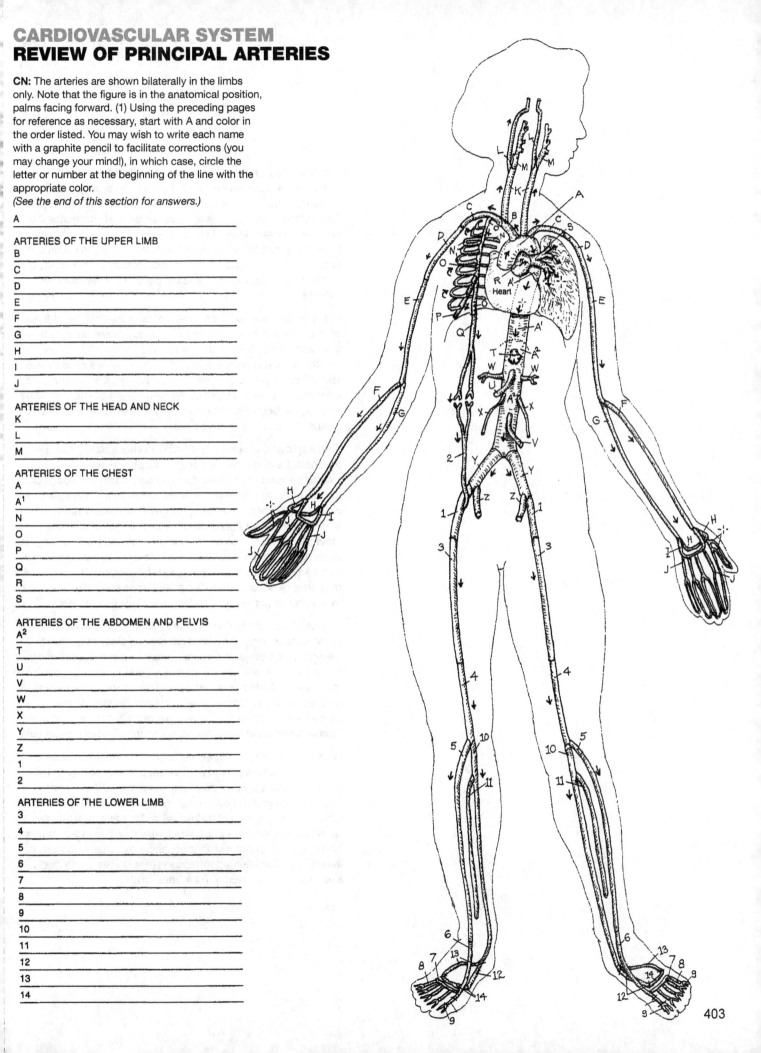

403

The brain lies in a bony cavity (cranium) with a bony "roof" (calvaria). Because the skull roof is composed of several bones, the term for the roof must be plural (-ia) rather than singular (-ium). The surface of that bony cavity is periosteal and constitutes the outer or periosteal layer of the dura mater. The inner (or meningeal) layer of the dura forms the dural sac that envelops the brain and spinal cord; it also splits off from the outer layer to form fibrous partitions that support and separate parts of the cerebrum and cerebellum.

Between the inner and outer layers of dura are endothelial-lined spaces called *dural venous sinuses*. Dural sinuses conduct blood from veins in the brain to the internal jugular veins, the facial veins, and the pterygoid plexuses of veins. These venous sinuses also take offerings from *diploic veins* between the tables of compact bone in skull bones, as well as the meningeal and *emissary veins* that pass through foramina of the skull to join veins and venous plexuses outside the cranium.

The deep cerebral veins, which collect venous blood from the thalamus, basal ganglia, and the diencephalon, merge into two *internal cerebral veins* under the splenium (posterior aspect) of the corpus callosum, and above the cerebellum to form the **great cerebral vein** *(of Galen)*. Here, the great vein drains into the anterior end of the **straight sinus**. The confluence of dural sinuses (**occipital**, *straight*, *transverse,* and **inferior** and **superior sagittal**) takes place near the occipital bone where the tent-shaped tentorium cerebelli merges with the midline falx cerebri. The confluence of venous blood drains into the paired **transverse sinuses** and on to the internal jugular vein via the paired **sigmoid sinuses**.

Venous blood from the anterior and middle cranial fossae and the facial veins flow into the paired **cavernous sinuses** by way of the ophthalmic veins. In the lateral walls of these sinuses can be found the oculomotor (third), trochlear (fourth), ophthalmic (V^1) and maxillary (V^2) (fifth) cranial nerves. Passing *through* the cavernous sinuses are the abducens (sixth) cranial nerve and the internal carotid artery. The cavernous sinuses drain into the **superior** and **inferior petrosal sinuses** that flow into the **internal jugular vein**.

On a practical note, the facial skin around the nose and cheeks often reveals little reddened mounds topped with pus (pustules). Squeezing these *pimples* (*blackheads, whiteheads*) with one's fingers or fingernails is dangerous and can lead to the uptake of infected debris by the ophthalmic veins. These veins deliver the debris to the cavernous sinus, which may then become obstructed. This may develop into a serious condition called *cavernous sinus thrombosis*, characterized by raccoon (black) eyes, periorbital swelling, and much worse. Think antiseptic!

CARDIOVASCULAR SYSTEM
VEINS OF THE HEAD & NECK

CN: Note the lists of tributaries; each indented *above* the vein with which they merge, and arranged in the direction of flow. This arrangement will hold for all pages concerning veins. Use lighter colors for the sinuses, A–K, represented in the lateral view by broken lines. (1) Begin above with the venous Sinuses of the Dura Mater. When coloring the falx and tentorium gray, color lightly over the vessels contained within: A, B, D, and E. Do not color the superior cerebral veins that join the superior sagittal sinus, A. The occipital sinus, K, is shown only in the lateral view below. (2) Color the veins of the head and neck at lower left.

SINUSES OF DURA MATER

SUPERIOR SAGITTAL SINUS A

INFERIOR SAGITTAL SINUS B
GREAT CEREBRAL V. C
STRAIGHT SINUS D

TRANSVERSE SINUS E
SIGMOID SINUS F

SUPERIOR OPHTHALMIC V. G
CAVERNOUS SINUS H
SUPERIOR PETROSAL SINUS I
INFERIOR PETROSAL SINUS J

OCCIPITAL SINUS K

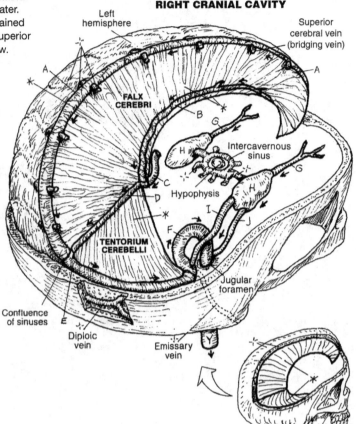

**INTERIOR VIEW
RIGHT CRANIAL CAVITY**

Left hemisphere

Superior cerebral vein (bridging vein)

FALX CEREBRI

Intercavernous sinus

Hypophysis

TENTORIUM CEREBELLI

Jugular foramen

Confluence of sinuses

Diploic vein

Emissary vein

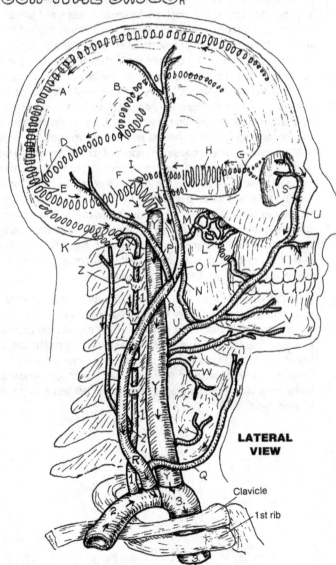

LATERAL VIEW

Clavicle

1st rib

VEINS OF HEAD & NECK

PTERYGOID PLEXUS L
MAXILLARY M
RETROMANDIBULAR N
SUPERFICIAL TEMPORAL O

POSTERIOR AURICULAR P
ANTERIOR JUGULAR Q
EXTERNAL JUGULAR R

ANGULAR S
DEEP FACIAL T
FACIAL U
LINGUAL V
SUPERIOR THYROID W
MIDDLE THYROID X
INTERNAL JUGULAR Y

DEEP CERVICAL Z
VERTEBRAL 1.
RIGHT SUBCLAVIAN 2.
RIGHT BRACHIOCEPHALIC 3.

405

The **superior vena cava** drains the head, neck, and upper limbs and flows directly into the right atrium of the heart. In addition, it drains the posterior intercostal and lumbar regions by way of a variable collection of veins called the **azygos system**. In conjunction with the veins of the vertebral canal (vertebral venous plexus), the azygos system (*azygos, accessory hemiazygos,* and *hemiazygos veins*) provides a secondary means of returning blood to the heart from the lower limbs and the posterior body wall in the event of obstruction of the **inferior vena cava**.

In general, arteries develop with a higher set of pressures than veins. As a consequence, veins (under lower pressure) are more numerous than arteries, more irregular in flow pattern, and their wall construction is thinner. Nowhere are these facts better seen than in the azygos system, for which there is no arterial corollary.

The **first posterior intercostal veins**, left and right, draining the first intercostal spaces, join directly with the brachiocephalic veins *on both sides*. The left and right second and third intercostal veins drain into a common vessel, the **superior intercostal vein**, but...surprise! The left superior intercostal joins the **left brachiocephalic vein**; the right superior intercostal joins the azygos vein. On the left, posterior intercostal veins 4–7 join up with the **accessory hemiazygos vein**, which turns to joins the azygos; lower on the left, posterior intercostal veins 8–12 join the **hemiazygos vein**, which crosses the vertebral column to join the azygos. On the right, the posterior intercostal veins flow segmentally into the azygos vein. The **azygos vein** originates at the inferior vena cava on the right; the hemiazygos vein arises from the **ascending lumbar vein** on the left. The azygos vein passes into the thorax through the aortic hiatus of the diaphragm. The azygos vein terminates on the posterior aspect of the superior vena cava at the level of the second costal cartilage. The anterior intercostal veins (not shown) drain into the internal thoracic veins (F), which join the subclavian vein bilaterally—the converse of the intercostal arteries with which you are already familiar. The inferior vena caval and azygos systems have no major tributaries draining the gastrointestinal tract, gall bladder, and pancreas. The liver, however, is drained by hepatic veins into the inferior vena cava, just below the diaphragm and the right atrium.

Note that the right testicular vein merges with the inferior vena cava on the right at an angle of about 20°, generating very little, if any, resistance to blood flow in the vein. On the left, the **testicular vein** joins the **renal vein** at a right angle (90°). The resistance to blood flow in the testicular vein created by the cross-current in the renal vein tends to push down the plexus of veins around the left testis, thus often (but not always) leaving the left testis a bit lower than the right.

CARDIOVASCULAR SYSTEM
CAVAL & AZYGOS SYSTEMS

CN: Use blue for the superior and inferior venae cavae, H and H[1]. Note that a large segment of the latter has been deleted to reveal the azygos vein, N. Use bright colors for the first posterior intercostal, D, and internal thoracic, F, veins, both of which drain into the brachiocephalic. Note that the majority of the posterior intercostal veins drain into the azygos vein, N, on the right, and the accessory hemiazygos, L, and hemiazygos veins, M, on the left.

SUPERIOR VENA CAVAL SYSTEM

SUPERIOR THYROID A
MIDDLE THYROID B
INTERNAL JUGULAR C
1ST POSTERIOR
          INTERCOSTAL D
INFERIOR THYROID E
INTERNAL THORACIC F
RIGHT BRACHIOCEPHALIC G
LEFT BRACHIOCEPHALIC G'
SUPERIOR VENA CAVA H

AZYGOS SYSTEM

POSTERIOR INTERCOSTAL D'
SUPERIOR INTERCOSTAL I
LUMBAR J
ASCENDING LUMBAR K
HEMIAZYGOS (ACCESSORY) L
HEMIAZYGOS M
AZYGOS N

INFERIOR VENA CAVAL SYSTEM

COMMON ILIAC O
TESTICULAR / OVARIAN P
RENAL Q
HEPATIC R
INFERIOR VENA CAVA H'

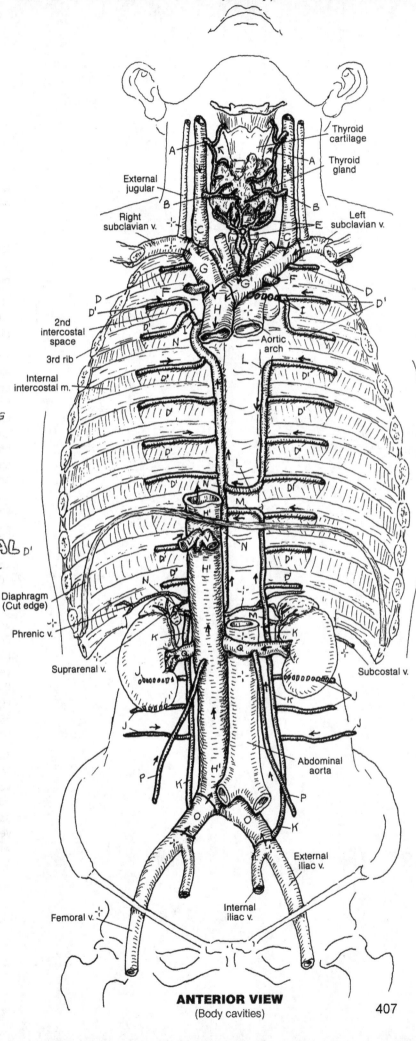

Thyroid cartilage
Thyroid gland
External jugular
Right subclavian v.
Left subclavian v.
2nd intercostal space
3rd rib
Internal intercostal m.
Aortic arch
Diaphragm (Cut edge)
Phrenic v.
Suprarenal v.
Subcostal v.
Abdominal aorta
External iliac v.
Internal iliac v.
Femoral v.

ANTERIOR VIEW
(Body cavities)

407

Deep veins travel in deep fascia with the arteries of the same name or destination. Like tributaries of rivers flowing into larger rivers, deep veins flow into larger veins. In the list of names of "Deep Veins," the larger vein is the last vein listed in each of the four groups of veins. Thus, A is a tributary of D that is a tributary of G that is a tributary of K that is a tributary of P. P takes the blood to the heart.

The **superficial veins** are drained by the **small saphenous vein**, a tributary of the **popliteal vein**, and the **great saphenous vein**, a tributary of the **femoral vein**.

The flow of blood in the deep veins of the lower limb is generally an uphill course. In concert with gravity, prolonged horizontal positioning of the legs (and other conditions) can result in slowed flow (*stasis*) in the deep veins, producing venous distention and inflammation (*phlebitis*). Formation of clots (*thrombi*) may follow (*deep vein thrombosis*) and inflammation as well (*thrombophlebitis*). In these conditions, thrombi may become detached and released into the venous circulation (*embolism*). The emboli continue up the venous pathway of ever-increasing size, easily pass into the right heart, and are pumped into the progressively *smaller* vessels of the lung, where they become stuck (*pulmonary embolism*).

Although deep veins generally travel with the arteries (*venae comitantes*), superficial veins do not. Instead, they travel with cutaneous nerves in the superficial fascia; many are easily visualized in the limbs. The blood in these long veins has to overcome gravity for a considerable distance, and their valves often come under weight-bearing stress. Happily, there exist a number of communicating vessels (*perforating veins*, or *perforators*, not shown) between superficial and deep veins that permit runoff into the deep veins. This significantly offsets the effect of incompetent valves that lead to pooling of blood and swelling in the lower superficial veins, with potential inflammation. In the chronic condition, the saphenous veins and their tributaries can become permanently deformed and dysfunctional (*varicosities*).

The blood *must* keep moving! Blood that is not moving will clot. To move the blood in leg veins along the lower limb to the inferior vena cava, it is helpful (even necessary) to routinely move the muscles of the foot and leg so that the venous blood gets some assistance in moving heartward. The muscles actually knead the veins and assist the movement of blood toward the heart. Imagine what exercise can do!

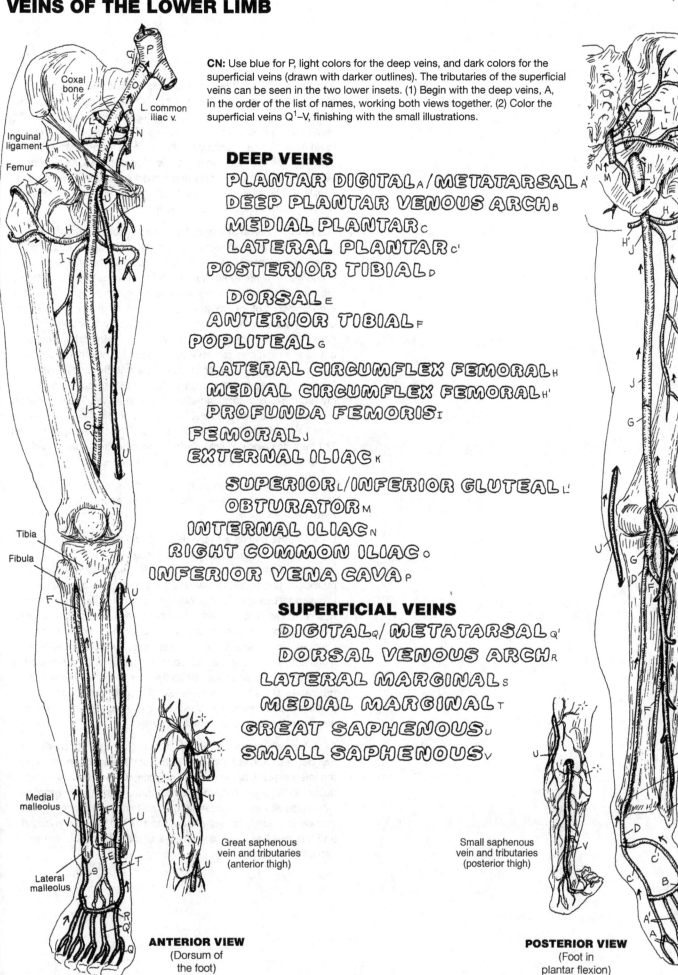

CN: Use blue for P, light colors for the deep veins, and dark colors for the superficial veins (drawn with darker outlines). The tributaries of the superficial veins can be seen in the two lower insets. (1) Begin with the deep veins, A, in the order of the list of names, working both views together. (2) Color the superficial veins Q^1–V, finishing with the small illustrations.

DEEP VEINS
PLANTAR DIGITAL A / METATARSAL A'
DEEP PLANTAR VENOUS ARCH B
MEDIAL PLANTAR C
LATERAL PLANTAR C'
POSTERIOR TIBIAL D

DORSAL E
ANTERIOR TIBIAL F
POPLITEAL G

LATERAL CIRCUMFLEX FEMORAL H
MEDIAL CIRCUMFLEX FEMORAL H'
PROFUNDA FEMORIS I
FEMORAL J
EXTERNAL ILIAC K

SUPERIOR L / INFERIOR GLUTEAL L'
OBTURATOR M
INTERNAL ILIAC N
RIGHT COMMON ILIAC O
INFERIOR VENA CAVA P

SUPERFICIAL VEINS
DIGITAL Q / METATARSAL Q'
DORSAL VENOUS ARCH R
LATERAL MARGINAL S
MEDIAL MARGINAL T
GREAT SAPHENOUS U
SMALL SAPHENOUS V

Coxal bone
L. common iliac v.
Inguinal ligament
Femur
Tibia
Fibula
Medial malleolus
Lateral malleolus
Medial malleolus
Lateral malleolus

Great saphenous vein and tributaries (anterior thigh)

Small saphenous vein and tributaries (posterior thigh)

ANTERIOR VIEW
(Dorsum of the foot)

POSTERIOR VIEW
(Foot in plantar flexion)

409

A *portal system* of veins is a system of vessels that transports blood from one capillary network to another without having gone through the heart between networks. It is the equivalent of loading crude oil into a length of oil-tank railroad cars, and taking the train to an oil refinery and unloading the crude oil for processing. In the human body, the liver is in the processing business. Its capillaries take in ingested nutrients and related molecules from the first capillary network in the intestines and process them in a second capillary network (sinusoids of the liver).

The **hepatic portal system** begins with the capillaries of the gastrointestinal tract, gallbladder, pancreas, and spleen. **Tributaries** of the hepatic portal vein drain these vessels. They are not branches; they are tributaries (like the tributaries of a river, merging with and flowing in the same direction as the river). Within the liver, *branches* of the portal vein (like those of an artery) discharge blood into capillaries (*sinusoids*) surrounded by liver cells. These cells remove digested (molecular) lipids, carbohydrates, amino acids, vitamins, and iron from the sinusoids. They then store them, alter their structure, and/or distribute them to the body tissues (and, in the case of unnecessary/undesirable molecules or degraded remains of toxic substances, the kidneys). The distribution process begins with the selective release of molecular substances from liver cells into the small tributaries of the three **hepatic veins**. The hepatic veins join the **inferior vena cava** immediately below the diaphragm, which is immediately below the right atrium.

The veins draining the viscera of the abdominal cavity generally follow the arteries supplying those viscera, and use the same name as the arteries.

Liver disease begins with the death of liver cells, followed by an inflammatory response with the laying-down of fibrous tissue around and among the dead cell debris. Liver cells cannot reproduce fast enough to avoid the ravages of fibrous tissue invasion following inflammation). As the amount of fibrous (scar) tissue increases, it invades the liver sinusoids and begins to block the blood flow through the involved part of the liver. As a consequence, over time, the **portal vein** and its tributaries enlarge significantly. This event is related to the lack of valves in the portal vein and its tributaries, as well as the inferior vena cava and its tributaries. Back flow of venous blood induces the formation of paths of lesser resistance. Venous blood must return to the right atrium of the heart, and it will find a way.

Such "ways" (routes; i.e., ★1, ★2) develop by way of **anastomoses** between and among veins of the portal system and veins of the inferior caval, superior caval, azygos, and vertebral venous systems. It's called **collateral circulation**. In time, with progression in the absence of treatment, these thin-walled anastomotic vessels (especially the esophageal and rectal) become enlarged and tortuous (*varices*), thin-walled, and subject to recurrent if not lethal hemorrhage.

HEPATIC PORTAL SYSTEM

CN: Use blue for I and a dark color for J. (1) Color the veins, A–J[1], and the related arrows. There are both *left* and *right* gastro-epiploic (D, D[1]) and *left* and *right* gastric (G, G[1]) veins. For the darkly outlined directional arrows adjacent to blood vessels, use the color of the adjacent blood vessel. (2) Color gray the term "Collateral Circulation & Site of Anastomosis", *[3], and the three large related colorable arrows, *[3], pointing out the connections between the portal circulation and the tributaries of the inferior vena cava, *[1], and the tributaries of the inferior vena cava, *[2].

HEPATIC PORTAL SYSTEM

SUPERIOR RECTAL A
INFERIOR MESENTERIC B
PANCREATIC C
LEFT GASTRO-
 EPIPLOIC D
SPLENIC E
RIGHT GASTRO-
 EPIPLOIC D'
SUPERIOR
 MESENTERIC F
RIGHT GASTRIC G
LEFT GASTRIC G'
CYSTIC H
PORTAL I
HEPATIC VEIN J
 & TRIBUTARIES J'
INFERIOR VENA CAVA *
TRIBUTARY *'
TRIBUTARY OF
 SUPERIOR
 VENA CAVA *²

COLLATERAL CIRCULATION
& SITE OF ANASTOMOSIS *³ ⇨

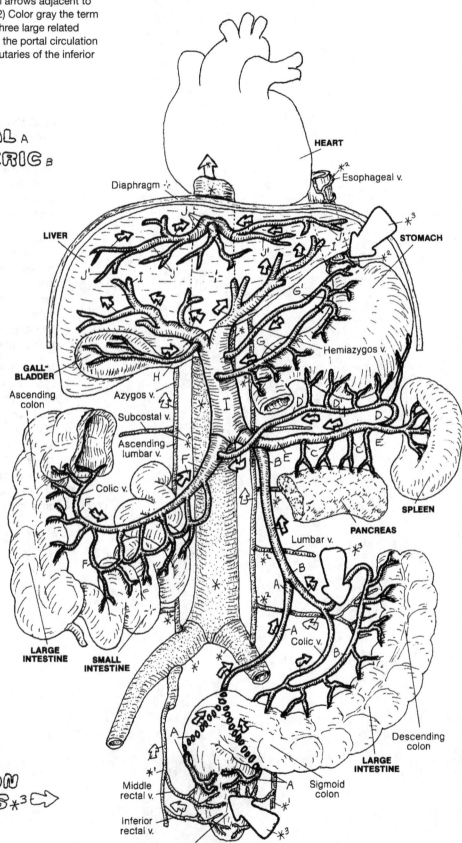

**PORTAL VEINS
& TRIBUTARIES**
(Anterior view, diagrammatic)

411

As all phlebotomists know, some veins are extremely variable in size and location. Why do they know this? Because they spend hours, over the length of a career, searching for a vessel in the antecubital fossa (front of elbow), for example, that is supposed to be there and, in this person, is not. There are folks who display a host of veins in front of the elbow for drawing blood, and others who don't seem have a single one within needle range!

Deep veins run with arteries of the same name (though the direction of flow is opposite). In the limbs, the veins are often paired (venae comitantes); the artery rarely so. Superficial veins generally have no companion arteries; they do tend to travel with cutaneous nerves. In review, it should be clear that arteries and portal veins have branches. All other veins have tributaries. Finally, it should be recognized that there are substantially more veins in the body than arteries.

Missing from this illustration are some of the anastomotic venous pathways between the upper chest and the lower limb, providing for venous return to the heart in the event the inferior vena cava is compromised in some way. The venous equivalents are veins of the same name, running in the same place (deep to the rectus abdominis), and terminating close to their arterial counterparts. There is also a collateral route between the lateral thoracic vein (from the axillary) and the superficial epigastric vein (a tributary of the great saphenous vein). These veins were not presented graphically.

CARDIOVASCULAR SYSTEM
REVIEW OF PRINCIPAL VEINS

CN: Superficial veins of the limbs are shown on the left and deep veins are shown on the right. Only a few are shown bilaterally. Palms are facing forward. (1) Using the preceding pages for reference as necessary, start with A (right hand) and color in the order listed. As you color each vein, write the name of the vein in graphite pencil (to make corrections easier), but circle the identifying numbers or letters in color. After completing the superficial veins in the limbs, color through the deep veins, starting at the hand/foot. (2) The deep veins travel with the arteries of the same name.
(See the end of this section for answers.)

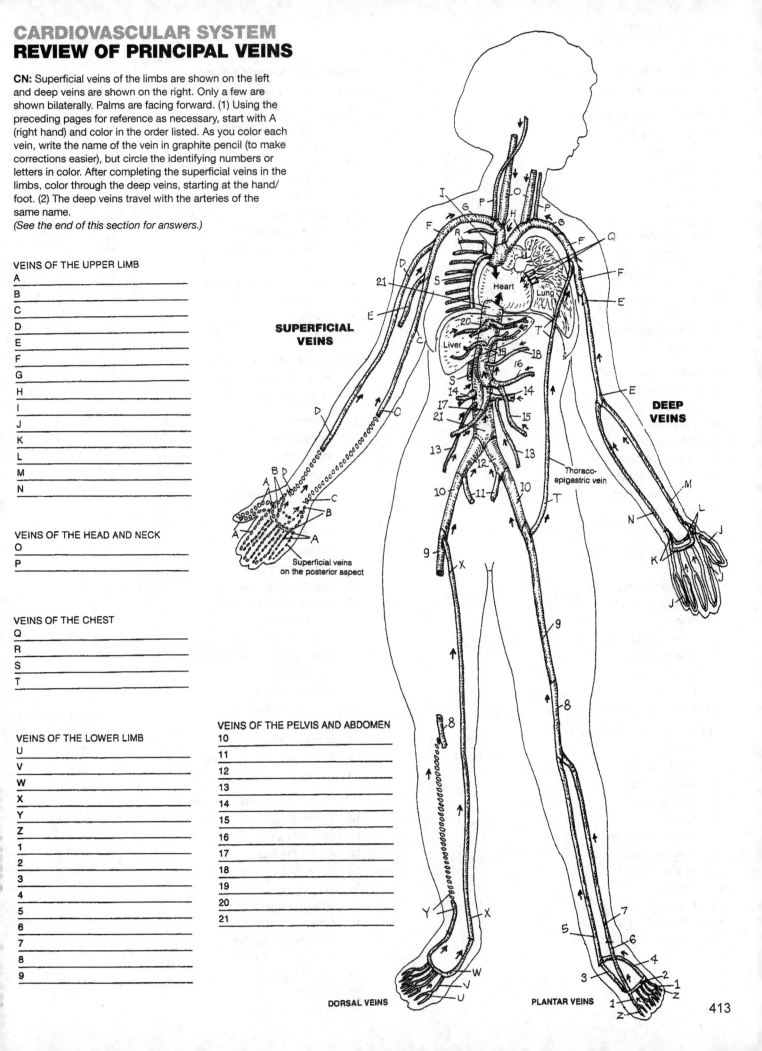

VEINS OF THE UPPER LIMB

A _____
B _____
C _____
D _____
E _____
F _____
G _____
H _____
I _____
J _____
K _____
L _____
M _____
N _____

VEINS OF THE HEAD AND NECK

O _____
P _____

VEINS OF THE CHEST

Q _____
R _____
S _____
T _____

VEINS OF THE LOWER LIMB

U _____
V _____
W _____
X _____
Y _____
Z _____
1 _____
2 _____
3 _____
4 _____
5 _____
6 _____
7 _____
8 _____
9 _____

VEINS OF THE PELVIS AND ABDOMEN

10 _____
11 _____
12 _____
13 _____
14 _____
15 _____
16 _____
17 _____
18 _____
19 _____
20 _____
21 _____

SUPERFICIAL VEINS

DEEP VEINS

Heart

Lung

Liver

Thoraco-epigastric vein

Superficial veins on the posterior aspect

DORSAL VEINS

PLANTAR VEINS

413

ANSWERS

Review of Principal Arteries

A   Aortic Arch

ARTERIES OF THE UPPER LIMB
B   Brachiocephalic
C   Subclavian
D   Axillary
E   Brachial
F   Radial
G   Ulnar
H   Deep palmar arch
I   Superficial palmar arch
J   Palmar digital

ARTERIES OF THE HEAD AND NECK
K   Common carotid
L   Internal carotid
M   External carotid

ARTERIES OF THE CHEST
A   Aortic arch
A^1 Thoracic aorta
N   Intercostal
O   Internal thoracic
P   Musculophrenic
Q   Superior epigastric
R   Pulmonary trunk
S   Pulmonary

ARTERIES OF THE ABDOMEN AND PELVIS
A^2 Abdominal aorta
T   Celiac
U   Superior mesenteric
V   Inferior mesenteric
W   Renal
X   Testicular/Ovarian
Y   Common iliac
Z   Internal iliac
1   External iliac
2   Inferior epigastric

ARTERIES OF THE LOWER LIMB
3   Femoral
4   Popliteal
5   Anterior tibial
6   Dorsalis pedis
7   Arcuate
8   Dorsal metatarsal
9   Dorsal digital
10   Posterior tibial
11   Fibular
12   Medial plantar
13   Lateral plantar
14   Plantar arch

Review of Principal Veins

VEINS OF THE UPPER LIMB
A   Dorsal digital
B   Dorsal digital network
C   Basilic
D   Cephalic
E   Brachial
F   Axillary
G   Subclavian
H   Brachiocephalic
I   Superior vena cava
J   Digital
K   Superficial palmar arch
L   Deep palmar arch
M   Radial
N   Ulnar

VEINS OF THE HEAD AND NECK
O   Internal jugular
P   External jugular

VEINS OF THE CHEST
Q   Pulmonary
R   Intercostal
S   Azygos
T   Thoracoepigastric

VEINS OF THE LOWER LIMB
U   Dorsal digital
V   Dorsal metatarsal
W   Dorsal venous arch
X   Great saphenous
Y   Lesser saphenous
Z   Plantar digital
1   Plantar metatarsal
2   Deep plantar venous arch
3   Medial plantar
4   Lateral plantar
5   Posterior tibial
6   Dorsal
7   Anterior tibial
8   Popliteal
9   Femoral

VEINS OF THE PELVIS AND ABDOMEN
10   External iliac
11   Internal iliac
12   Common iliac
13   Testicular/Ovarian
14   Renal
15   Inferior mesenteric
16   Splenic
17   Superior mesenteric
18   Gastric
19   Hepatic portal
20   Hepatic
21   Inferior vena cava

Anatomy of the Respiratory System
Wish List

Locate and identify structures listed below using the models as you work through this chapter's activities.

✓	Structure	Description
	external nares	_
	nasal vestibule	
	nasal cavity	
	nasal conchae	
	oral cavity	
	hard palate	
	soft palate	
	uvula	
	pharynx	
	nasopharynx	
	oropharynx	
	tonge	
	laryngopharynx	
	epiglottis	
	hyoid	
	larynx	
	vocal folds	
	cricoid cartilage	
	thyroid cartilage	
	trachea	
	tracheal (thoracic) rings (cartilage)	
	primary bronchi	
	lobar bronchi	
	lungs	
	right lung lobes (superior, middle, inferior)	
	left lung lobes (superior, inferior)	
	alveoli	
	diaphragm	

Anatomy of the Respiratory System

Learning Outcomes

On completion of this exercise, you should be able to:

1. Identify and describe the structures of the nasal cavity.

2. Distinguish among the three regions of the pharynx.

3. Identify and describe the cartilages and ligaments of the larynx.

4. Identify the gross and microscopic structure of the trachea.

5. Identify and describe the gross and microscopic structure of the lungs.

6. Classify the branches of the bronchial tree.

Lab Activities

1. Nose and Pharynx

2. Larynx

3. Trachea and Primary Bronchi

4. Lungs and Bronchial Tree

Clinical Application

Asthma

A ll cells require a constant supply of oxygen (O_2) for the oxidative reactions of mitochondrial ATP production. A major by-product of these reactions is carbon dioxide (CO_2). The respiratory system exchanges these two gases between the atmosphere and the blood. Specialized organs of the airway filter, warm, and moisten the inhaled air before it enters the lungs. Once the air is in the lungs, the O_2 gas in the air diffuses into the surrounding capillaries to oxygenate the blood. As the blood takes up this oxygen, CO_2 gas in the blood diffuses into the lungs and is exhaled. Pulmonary veins return the oxygenated blood to the heart, where it is pumped into arteries of the systemic circulation.

The respiratory system, shown in **Figure 1**, consists of the nose, nasal cavity, sinuses, pharynx, larynx, trachea, bronchi, and lungs. The **upper respiratory system** includes the nose, nasal cavity, sinuses, and pharynx. These structures filter, warm, and moisten air before it enters the **lower respiratory system,** which

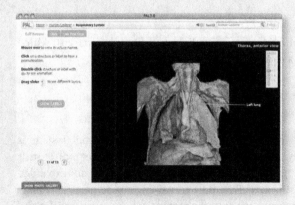

Need More Practice and Review?

Build your knowledge—and confidence!—in the Study Area of MasteringA&P® at www.masteringaandp.com with Pre-lab Quizzes, Post-lab Quizzes, Practice Anatomy Lab™ (PAL™) 3.0 virtual anatomy practice tool, PhysioEx™ 9.0 laboratory simulations, and A&P Flix™ with Quizzes.

PAL | For this lab exercise, follow these navigation paths:
- PAL>Human Cadaver>Respiratory System
- PAL>Anatomical Models>Respiratory System
- PAL>Histology>Respiratory System

MasteringA&P®

Figure 1 Structures of the Respiratory System Only the conducting portion of the respiratory system is shown; the smaller bronchioles and alveoli have been omitted.

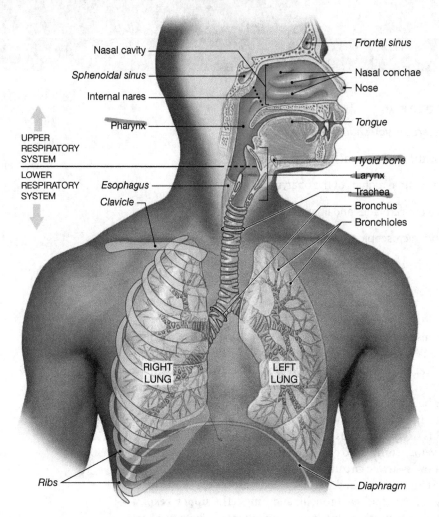

comprises the larynx, trachea, bronchi, and lungs. The larynx regulates the opening into the lower respiratory system and produces speech sounds. The trachea and bronchi maintain an open airway to the lungs where gas exchange occurs.

Make a Prediction

Predict which type of epithelial tissue lines the pharynx, which serves as a common passageway for food and air.

Lab Activity 1 Nose and Pharynx

The primary route for air entering the respiratory system is through two openings, the **external nares** (NA-rĕz), or nostrils (**Figure 2**). Just inside each external naris is an expanded **nasal vestibule** (VES-ti-būl) containing coarse hairs. The hairs help to prevent large airborne materials such as dirt particles and insects from entering the respiratory system. The external portion

of the nose is composed of **nasal cartilages** that form the bridge and tip of the nose.

The **nasal cavity** is the airway from the external nares to the superior part of the pharynx. The perpendicular plate of the ethmoid and the vomer create the **nasal septum,** which divides the nasal cavity into right and left sides. The **superior, middle,** and **inferior nasal conchae** are bony shelves that project from the lateral walls of the nasal cavity. The distal edge of each nasal concha curls inferiorly and forms a tube, or **meatus,** that causes inhaled air to swirl in the nasal cavity. This turbulence moves the air across the sticky pseudostratified ciliated columnar epithelium lining, where dust and debris are removed. The floor of the nasal cavity is the superior portion of the **hard palate,** formed by the maxillae, palatine bones, and muscular **soft palate.** Hanging off the posterior edge of the soft palate is the conical **uvula** (Ū-vū-luh). The **internal nares** are the two posterior openings of the nasal cavity that connect with the superior portion of the pharynx.

Figure 2 The Nose, Nasal Cavity, and Pharynx

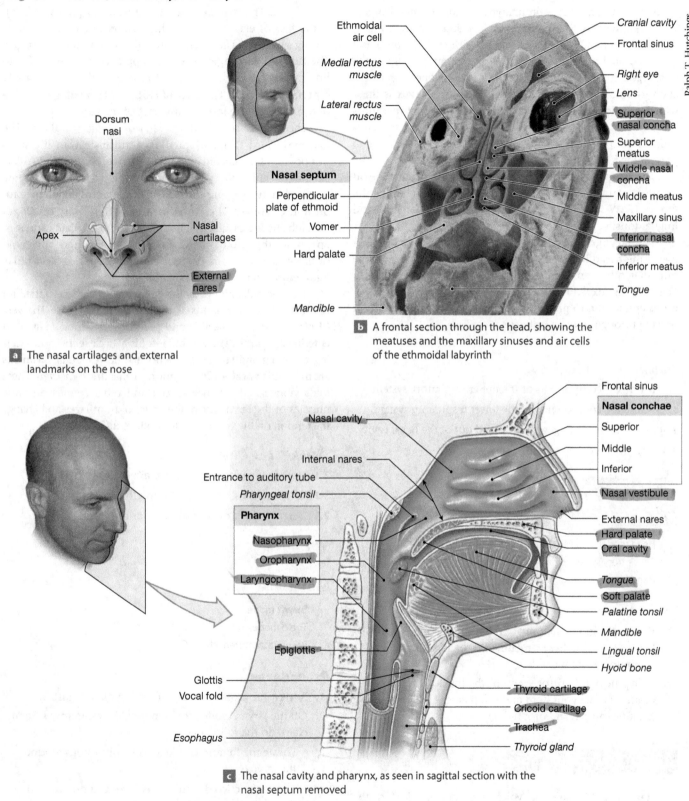

Ralph T. Hutchings

Dorsum nasi

Apex

Nasal cartilages

External nares

a The nasal cartilages and external landmarks on the nose

Ethmoidal air cell

Medial rectus muscle

Lateral rectus muscle

Nasal septum

Perpendicular plate of ethmoid

Vomer

Hard palate

Mandible

Cranial cavity

Frontal sinus

Right eye

Lens

Superior nasal concha

Superior meatus

Middle nasal concha

Middle meatus

Maxillary sinus

Inferior nasal concha

Inferior meatus

Tongue

b A frontal section through the head, showing the meatuses and the maxillary sinuses and air cells of the ethmoidal labyrinth

Nasal cavity

Internal nares

Entrance to auditory tube

Pharyngeal tonsil

Pharynx

Nasopharynx

Oropharynx

Laryngopharynx

Epiglottis

Glottis

Vocal fold

Esophagus

Frontal sinus

Nasal conchae

Superior

Middle

Inferior

Nasal vestibule

External nares

Hard palate

Oral cavity

Tongue

Soft palate

Palatine tonsil

Mandible

Lingual tonsil

Hyoid bone

Thyroid cartilage

Cricoid cartilage

Trachea

Thyroid gland

c The nasal cavity and pharynx, as seen in sagittal section with the nasal septum removed

The throat, or **pharynx** (FAR-inks), is divided into three regions: nasopharynx, oropharynx, and laryngopharynx. The **nasopharynx** (nā-zō-FAR-inks) is superior to the soft palate and serves as a passageway for airflow from the nasal cavity. Located on the posterior wall of the nasopharynx is the pharyngeal tonsil. On the lateral walls are the openings of the auditory (pharyngotympanic) tubes. The nasopharynx is lined with a pseudostratified ciliated columnar epithelium that functions to warm, moisten, and clean inhaled air. When a person is eating, food pushes past the uvula, and the soft palate raises to prevent the food from entering the nasopharynx.

The **oropharynx,** which extends inferiorly from the soft palate, is connected to the oral cavity at an opening called the **fauces** (FAW-sēz). The oropharynx contains the palatine and lingual tonsils.

The **laryngopharynx** (la-rin-gō-FAR-inks) is located between the hyoid bone and the entrance to the esophagus, the muscular tube connecting the oral cavity with the stomach. The oropharynx and laryngopharynx have a stratified squamous epithelium to protect from abrasion by swallowed food passing through to the esophagus.

QuickCheck Questions

1.1 Name the components of the upper respiratory system.

1.2 Name the components of the lower respiratory system.

1.3 Describe the passageways into and out of the nasal cavity.

1.4 List the three regions of the pharynx.

In the Lab 1

Materials

- ☐ Head model
- ☐ Respiratory system chart
- ☐ Hand mirror

Procedures

1. Review the gross anatomy of the nose and pharynx in Figure 2. Locate these structures on the head model and respiratory system chart.

2. Using the hand mirror, examine the inside of your mouth. Locate your hard and soft palates, uvula, fauces, palatine tonsils, and oropharynx. ■

Lab Activity 2 Larynx

The **larynx** (LAR-inks), or voice box, lies inferior to the laryngopharynx and anterior to cervical vertebrae C_4 through C_7. It consists of nine cartilages held together by **laryngeal ligaments.** The airway through the larynx is the **glottis** (Figure 2b).

Three large, unpaired cartilages form the body of the larynx (Figure 3). The first cartilage, the **epiglottis** (ep-i-GLOT-is), is the flap of elastic cartilage that lowers to cover the glottis during swallowing and helps direct the food to the esophagus. The **thyroid cartilage,** or Adam's apple, is composed of hyaline cartilage. It is visible under the skin on the anterior neck, especially in males. The **cricoid** (KRĪ-koyd) **cartilage** is a ring of hyaline cartilage forming the base of the larynx.

The larynx also has three pairs of smaller cartilages. The **arytenoid** (ar-i-TĒ-noyd) **cartilages** articulate with the superior border of the cricoid cartilage. **Corniculate** (kor-NIK-ū-lāt) **cartilages** articulate with the arytenoid cartilages and are involved in the opening and closing of the glottis and in the production of sound. The **cuneiform** (kū-NĒ-i-form) **cartilages** are club-shaped cartilages anterior to the corniculate cartilages. Spanning the glottis between the thyroid and arytenoid cartilages are two pairs of ligaments; the **superior vestibular ligaments** and the **inferior vocal ligaments**.

The vestibular and vocal ligaments are covered in epithelium that extend into the glottis as thick folds (Figure 4). The **vestibular folds** are inflexible and prevent foreign materials from entering the glottis. The vestibular folds also close the glottis during coughing and sneezing. Inferior to the vestibular ligaments are the elastic **vocal folds**, commonly called the *vocal cords*. These folds vibrate and produce speech and other sounds. Intrinsic muscles of the larynx move the arytenoid cartilages and change the tension on the vocal folds to produce different sounds.

QuickCheck Questions

2.1 How many pieces of cartilage are in the larynx?

2.2 What are the glottis and the epiglottis?

2.3 Describe the structures that produce speech.

In the Lab 2

Materials

- ☐ Larynx model
- ☐ Torso model
- ☐ Respiratory system chart

Procedures

1. Review the gross anatomy of the larynx in Figure 3.

2. On the larynx model, torso model, or respiratory system chart, do the following:

   - Locate the thyroid cartilage. Is it continuous around the larynx?

   - Locate the cricoid cartilage. Is it continuous around the larynx?

   - Study the position of the epiglottis. How does it act like a chute to direct food into the esophagus?

Figure 3 The Larynx

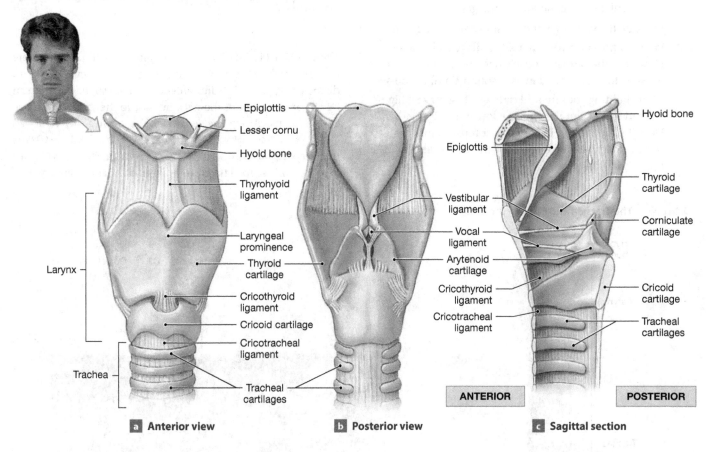

Epiglottis
Lesser cornu
Hyoid bone
Thyrohyoid ligament
Larynx
Laryngeal prominence
Thyroid cartilage
Cricothyroid ligament
Cricoid cartilage
Cricotracheal ligament
Trachea
Tracheal cartilages

a Anterior view

Vestibular ligament
Vocal ligament
Arytenoid cartilage
Cricothyroid ligament
Cricotracheal ligament

b Posterior view

Epiglottis
Hyoid bone
Thyroid cartilage
Corniculate cartilage
Cricoid cartilage
Tracheal cartilages

ANTERIOR   **POSTERIOR**

c Sagittal section

Figure 4 The Glottis

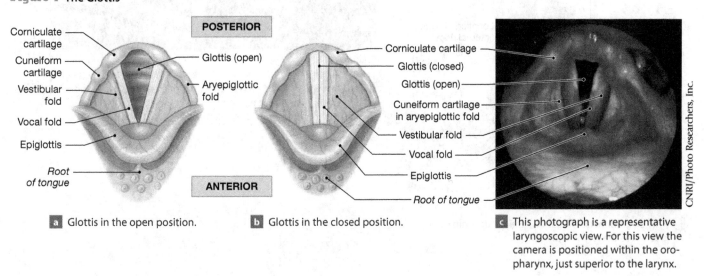

Corniculate cartilage
Cuneiform cartilage
Vestibular fold
Vocal fold
Epiglottis
Root of tongue

POSTERIOR

Glottis (open)
Aryepiglottic fold

ANTERIOR

a Glottis in the open position.

Corniculate cartilage
Glottis (closed)
Glottis (open)
Cuneiform cartilage in aryepiglottic fold
Vestibular fold
Vocal fold
Epiglottis
Root of tongue

b Glottis in the closed position.

c This photograph is a representative laryngoscopic view. For this view the camera is positioned within the oropharynx, just superior to the larynx.

CNRI/Photo Researchers, Inc.

421

- Open the larynx model, and identify the arytenoid, corniculate, and cuneiform cartilages.

  - Locate the vestibular and vocal ligaments and folds.

3. Put your finger on your thyroid cartilage and swallow. How does the cartilage move when you swallow? Is it possible to swallow and make a sound simultaneously?

4. While holding your thyroid cartilage, first make a high-pitched sound and then make a low-pitched sound. Describe the tension in your throat muscles for each sound, and relate the muscle tension to the tension in the vocal folds. ■

Lab Activity 3 Trachea and Primary Bronchi

The **trachea** (TRĀ-kē-uh), or windpipe, is a tubular structure approximately 11 cm (4.25 in.) long and 2.5 cm (1 in.) in diameter (Figure 5). It lies anterior to the esophagus and can be felt on the front of the neck inferior to the thyroid cartilage of the larynx. Along the length of the trachea are 15 to 20 C-shaped pieces of hyaline cartilage called **tracheal cartilages** that keep the airway open. The **trachealis muscle** holds the two tips of each C-shaped tracheal cartilage together posteriorly. This

Figure 5 **The Trachea and Primary Bronchi**

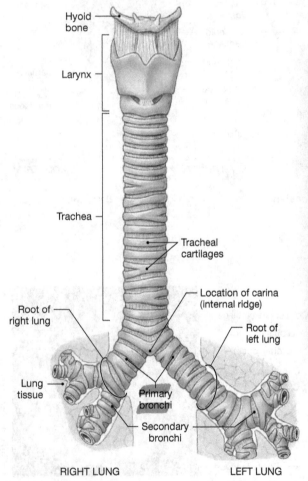

a This diagrammatic view shows the relationship of the trachea to the larynx and bronchi.

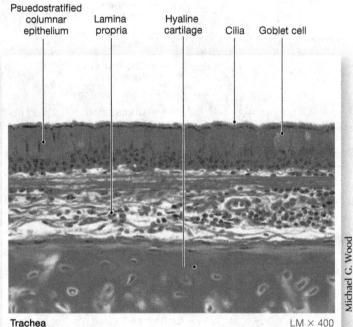

Trachea   LM × 400

b The lumen of the trachea is lined with a ciliated respiratory epithelium; the airway is kept open by hyaline cartilage formed into C-shaped rings called tracheal cartilages.

muscle allows the esophagus diameter to increase during swallowing so that the esophagus wall presses against the adjacent trachea wall and decreases the trachea diameter momentarily.

The trachea is lined with a pseudostratified ciliated columnar epithelium that is constantly sweeping the airway clean. Interspersed in the epithelium are goblet cells that secrete mucus to trap particles present in the inhaled air.

The trachea divides, at a ridge called the **carina,** into the left and right **primary bronchi** (BRONG-kī; singular *bronchus*). The right primary bronchus is wider and more vertical than the left primary bronchus. (For this reason, objects that are accidentally inhaled often enter the right primary bronchus.)

QuickCheck Questions

3.1 What is the lining epithelium of the trachea?

3.2 What is the connective tissue of a tracheal cartilage?

In the Lab 3

Materials

☐ Compound microscope
☐ Prepared slide of trachea
☐ Head model
☐ Torso model
☐ Lung model
☐ Respiratory system chart

Procedures

1. Review the gross anatomy of the trachea in Figure 5. Locate these structures on the head, torso, and lung models and the respiratory system chart. Palpate your trachea for the tracheal cartilages.

2. On the trachea slide, locate the structures labeled in Figure 5.

3. *Draw It!* Sketch a section of the trachea in the space provided.

Trachea section

4. Study the bronchial tree on the torso and/or lung models, and identify the right and left primary bronchi. ■.

Clinical Application Asthma

Asthma (AZ-ma) is a condition that occurs when the smooth muscle encircling the delicate bronchioles contracts and reduces the diameter of the airway. The airway is further compromised by increased mucus production and inflammation of the epithelial lining. The individual has difficulty breathing, especially during exhalation, as the narrowed passageways collapse under normal respiratory pressures. An asthma attack can be triggered by a number of factors, including allergies, chemical sensitivities, air pollution, stress, and emotion.

Daniela Andrea/iStockphoto.com

Bronchodilator drugs are used to relax the smooth muscle and open the airway; other drugs reduce inflammation of the mucosa. *Albuterol* is an important bronchodilator, usually administered as an inhalant sprayed from a nebulizer. ■

Lab Activity 4 Lungs and Bronchial Tree

Each lung sits inside a pleural cavity located between the two layers of the pleura (**Figure 6**). The parietal pleura lies against the thoracic wall and the visceral pleura adheres to the surface of the lung. The pleural cavity between these layers contains pleural fluid that reduces friction on the lungs during breathing.

The lungs are a pair of cone-shaped organs lying in the thoracic cavity (**Figure 7**). The **apex** is the conical top of each lung, and the broad inferior portion is the **base.** The anterior, lateral, and posterior surfaces of each lung face the thoracic cage, and the medial surface faces the mediastinum. The heart lies on a medial concavity of the left lung called the **cardiac notch.** Each lung has a slitlike **hilum** on the medial surface where the bronchi, blood vessels, lymphatic vessels, and nerves access the lung.

Each lung is divided into lobes, two in the left lung and three in the right lung. Both lungs have an **oblique fissure** forming the lobes, and the right lung also has a **horizontal fissure.** The oblique fissure of the left lung separates the lung into its **superior** and **inferior lobes.** The oblique fissure of

423

Figure 6 **The Relationship Between the Lungs and the Heart**   This transverse section was taken at the level of the cardia notch.

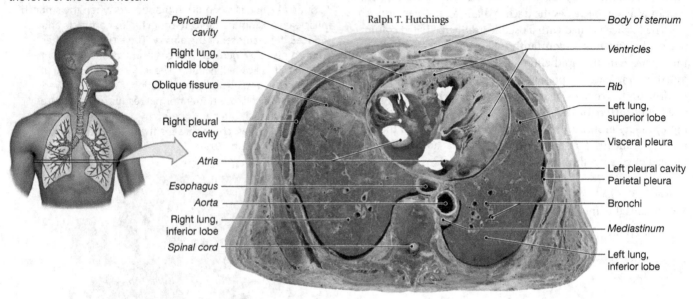

the right lung separates the **middle lobe** from the **inferior lobe,** and the horizontal fissure separates the middle lobe from the superior lobe.

The primary bronchi, called **extrapulmonary bronchi,** branch into increasingly smaller **intrapulmonary bronchi** to conduct air into the lungs (Figure 8). This branching pattern formed by the divisions of the bronchial structures is called the **bronchial tree.** At the superior terminus of the tree, the primary bronchi branch into as many **secondary bronchi** as there are lobes in each lung. The right lung has three lobes, and each lobe receives a secondary bronchus to supply it with air. The left lung has two lobes, and thus two secondary bronchi branch off the left primary bronchus. The secondary bronchi divide into **tertiary bronchi,** also called *segmental bronchi.* Smaller divisions called **bronchioles** branch into **terminal bronchioles.** The terminal bronchioles branch into **respiratory bronchioles,** which further divide into the narrowest passageways, the **alveolar ducts.**

As the bronchial tree branches from the primary bronchi to the respiratory bronchioles, cartilage is gradually replaced with smooth muscle tissue. The epithelial lining of the bronchial tree also changes from pseudostratified ciliated columnar at the superior end of the tree to simple squamous epithelium at the inferior end.

Inside a lobe, the region supplied by each tertiary bronchi is called a **bronchopulmonary segment** (Figure 9).

Subregions within each bronchopulmonary segment are called **lobules,** and each lobule is made up of numerous tiny air pockets called **alveoli** (al-VĒ-ō-lī; singular *alveolus*). Groups of alveoli clustered together are called **alveolar sacs.** Each lobule is served by a single terminal bronchiole. Inside a lobule, at the finest level of the bronchial tree, each alveolar duct serves a number of alveolar sacs.

The walls of the alveoli are constructed of simple squamous epithelium. Scattered throughout the simple squamous epithelium are **septal cells** that secrete an oily coating to prevent the alveoli from sticking together after exhalation. Also in the alveolar wall are macrophages that phagocytize debris. Pulmonary capillaries cover the exterior of the alveoli, and gas exchange occurs across the thin alveolar walls. Oxygen from inhaled air diffuses through the simple squamous epithelium of the alveolar wall, moves across the basal lamina membrane and the endothelium of the capillary, and enters the blood. The thickness of the combined alveolar wall and capillary wall is only about 0.5 mm, a size that permits rapid gas exchange between the alveoli and blood.

QuickCheck Questions

4.1 How many lobes does each lung have?

4.2 Which lung has the cardiac notch?

4.3 What is the bronchial tree?

Figure 7 Gross Anatomy of the Lungs

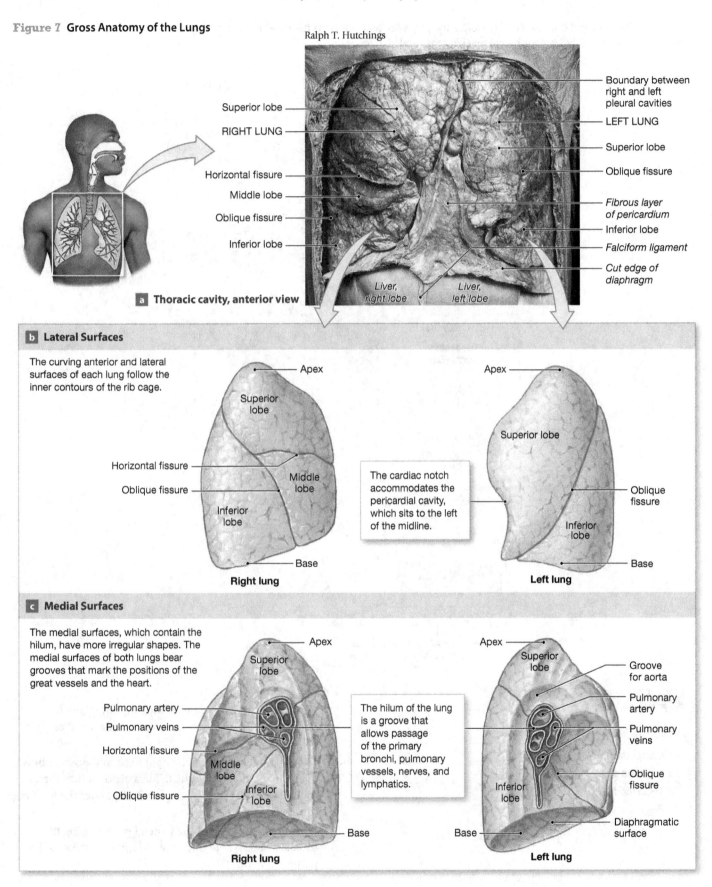

Ralph T. Hutchings

Superior lobe

RIGHT LUNG

Horizontal fissure

Middle lobe

Oblique fissure

Inferior lobe

Boundary between right and left pleural cavities

LEFT LUNG

Superior lobe

Oblique fissure

Fibrous layer of pericardium

Inferior lobe

Falciform ligament

Cut edge of diaphragm

Liver, right lobe

Liver, left lobe

a Thoracic cavity, anterior view

b Lateral Surfaces

The curving anterior and lateral surfaces of each lung follow the inner contours of the rib cage.

Apex

Superior lobe

Horizontal fissure

Oblique fissure

Middle lobe

Inferior lobe

Base

Right lung

Apex

Superior lobe

The cardiac notch accommodates the pericardial cavity, which sits to the left of the midline.

Oblique fissure

Inferior lobe

Base

Left lung

c Medial Surfaces

The medial surfaces, which contain the hilum, have more irregular shapes. The medial surfaces of both lungs bear grooves that mark the positions of the great vessels and the heart.

Apex

Superior lobe

Pulmonary artery

Pulmonary veins

Horizontal fissure

Middle lobe

Oblique fissure

Inferior lobe

Base

Right lung

The hilum of the lung is a groove that allows passage of the primary bronchi, pulmonary vessels, nerves, and lymphatics.

Apex

Superior lobe

Groove for aorta

Pulmonary artery

Pulmonary veins

Oblique fissure

Inferior lobe

Base

Diaphragmatic surface

Left lung

Figure 8 **Bronchi and Bronchioles** For clarity, the degree of branching has been reduced; an airway branches approximately 23 times before reaching the level of a lobule.

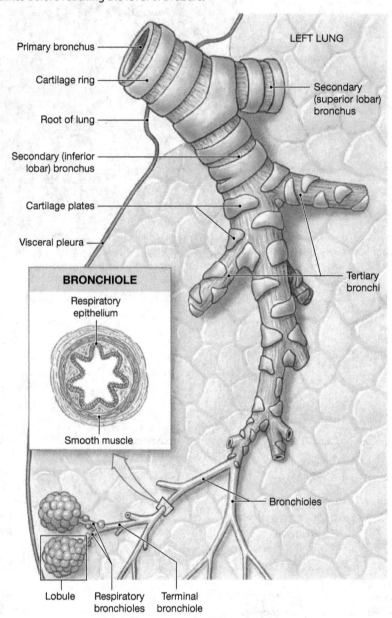

In the Lab 4

Materials

- ☐ Compound microscope
- ☐ Prepared slide of lung
- ☐ Torso model
- ☐ Respiratory system chart

Procedures

1. Review the gross anatomy of the lungs in Figure 6. Locate these structures on the torso models and on the respiratory system chart.

2. On the model, examine the right lung, and observe how the horizontal and oblique fissures divide it into three lobes. Note how the oblique fissure separates the left lung into two lobes.

3. Examine the model for the parietal pleura lining the thoracic wall. Where is the pleural cavity relative to the parietal pleura?

Figure 9 Lobules and Alveoli of the Lung

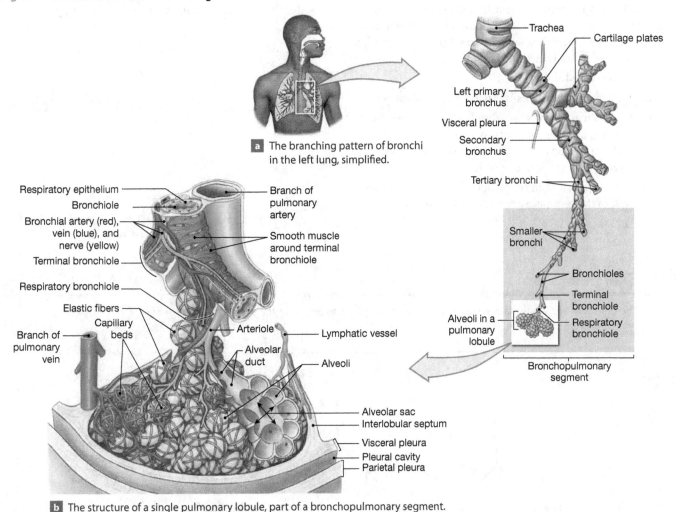

a The branching pattern of bronchi in the left lung, simplified.

Trachea

Cartilage plates

Left primary bronchus

Visceral pleura

Secondary bronchus

Tertiary bronchi

Smaller bronchi

Bronchioles

Terminal bronchiole

Alveoli in a pulmonary lobule

Respiratory bronchiole

Bronchopulmonary segment

Respiratory epithelium

Bronchiole

Bronchial artery (red), vein (blue), and nerve (yellow)

Terminal bronchiole

Respiratory bronchiole

Elastic fibers

Capillary beds

Branch of pulmonary vein

Branch of pulmonary artery

Smooth muscle around terminal bronchiole

Arteriole

Lymphatic vessel

Alveolar duct

Alveoli

Alveolar sac

Interlobular septum

Visceral pleura

Pleural cavity

Parietal pleura

b The structure of a single pulmonary lobule, part of a bronchopulmonary segment.

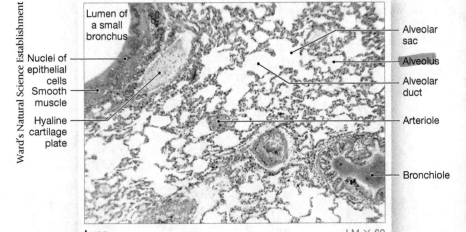

Lumen of a small bronchus

Nuclei of epithelial cells

Smooth muscle

Hyaline cartilage plate

Alveolar sac

Alveolus

Alveolar duct

Arteriole

Bronchiole

Lung   LM × 62

c This transverse section of lung shows a hyaline cartilage plate next to a small bronchus.

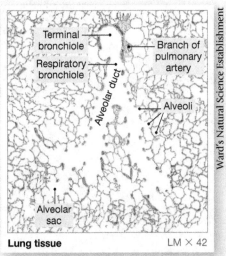

Terminal bronchiole

Respiratory bronchiole

Alveolar duct

Branch of pulmonary artery

Alveoli

Alveolar sac

Lung tissue   LM × 42

d This micrograph shows the distribution of a respiratory bronchiole that supplies a portion of a lobule.

4. Study the bronchial tree on the torso and/or lung models, and identify the primary bronchi, secondary bronchi, tertiary bronchi, bronchioles, terminal bronchioles, and respiratory bronchioles. For additional practice, complete the *Sketch to Learn* activity below.

5. On the prepared slide,

a. Identify the alveoli, using Figure 9d as a reference.

b. Locate an area where the alveoli appear to have been scooped out. This passageway is an alveolar duct. Follow the duct to its end, and observe the many alveolar sacs serviced by the duct.

c. At the opposite end of the duct, look for the thicker wall of the respiratory bronchiole and blood vessels.

6. *Draw It!* In the space provided, sketch the alveolar duct and several alveolar sacs, as seen in your prepared slide. ■

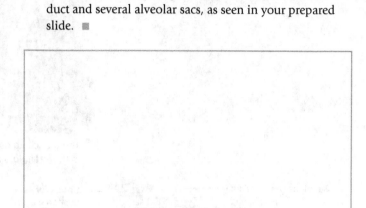

Alveolar ducts and sacs

 Sketch to Learn

The bronchial tree is easy to draw using simple branching lines to represent the various divisions of the bronchi and the bronchioles.

Sample Sketch

Step 1
• Draw lines for the trachea and primary bronchi.

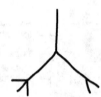

Step 2
• Add three secondary bronchi to the right primary bronchus and two secondaries on the left.

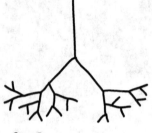

Step 3
• Draw branches off of each secondary bronchus.
• Add another set of branches for the bronchioles.
• Label your drawing

Your Sketch

Name _____

Date _____

Section _____

Anatomy of the Respiratory System

A. Matching

Match each structure in the left column with its correct description in the right column.

_____	**1.** C-shaped rings	**A.** voice box
_____	**2.** internal nares	**B.** elastic cartilage flap of larynx
_____	**3.** cricoid cartilage	**C.** serous membrane of lungs
_____	**4.** pleurae	**D.** left lung
_____	**5.** epiglottis	**E.** connects nasal cavity with throat
_____	**6.** larynx	**F.** tracheal cartilage
_____	**7.** vocal folds	**G.** vocal cords
_____	**8.** cardiac notch	**H.** protect vocal folds
_____	**9.** external nares	**I.** nostrils
_____	**10.** three lobes	**J.** base of larynx
_____	**11.** thyroid cartilage	**K.** right lung
_____	**12.** vestibular folds	**L.** Adam's apple

B. Short-Answer Questions

1. List the components of the upper and lower respiratory systems.

2. What are the functions of the superior, middle, and inferior conchae?

3. Where is the pharyngeal tonsil located?

4. Trace a breath of air from the external nares through the respiratory system to the alveolar sacs.

C. Labeling

Label the anatomy of the nose in Figure 10.

Figure 10 The Nose, Nasal Cavity, and Pharynx

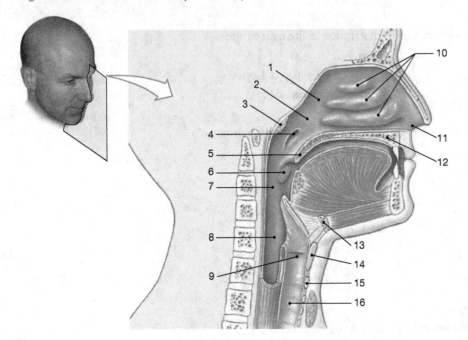

1. _____
2. _____
3. _____
4. _____
5. _____
6. _____
7. _____
8. _____
9. _____
10. _____
11. _____
12. _____
13. _____
14. _____
15. _____
16. _____

D. Analysis and Application

1. Where do goblet cells occur in the respiratory system, and what function do they serve?

2. What is the function of stratified squamous epithelium that lines the oropharynx and laryngopharynx?

E. Clinical Application

1. How does an asthma attack cause difficulty in breathing?

2. Emphysema from smoking and exposure to heavy pollution causes alveoli to expand and rupture. Describe how this would compromise respiratory function.

Anatomy of the Urinary System
Wish List

Locate and identify structures listed below using the models as you work through this chapter's activities.

✓	Structure	Description
	-	-
	Kidney	
	cortex	
	medulla	
	calyx (calices)	
	renal papilla	
	renal columns	
	renal artery	
	renal pyramids	
	renal pelvis	
	renal vein	
	nephron	
	renal corpuscle	
	afferent arteriole	
	glomerulus	
	glomerular (Bowman's) capsule	
	capsular space	
	efferent arteriole	
	proximal convoluted tubule	
	loop of Henle	
	distal convoluted tubule	
	collecting duct	

✓	Structure	Description
	ureter	

✓	Structure	Description
	urinary bladder	
	rugae	
	ureteral openings	

✓	Structure	Description
	urethra	female uretra has no separate divisions. Male has three divisions (see below)
	internal urethral sphincter	
	external urethral sphincter	

✓	Structure	Description
	male urethral divisions	
	prostatic urethra	
	membranous urethra	
	spongy urethra	

Anatomy of the Urinary System

Learning Outcomes

On completion of this exercise, you should be able to:

1. Identify and describe the basic anatomy of the urinary system.

2. Trace the blood flow through the kidney.

3. Explain the function of the kidney.

4. Identify the basic components of the nephron.

5. Describe the differences between the male and female urinary tracts.

The primary function of the urinary system is to control the composition, volume, and pressure of the blood. The system exerts this control by adjusting both the volume of the liquid portion of the blood (the *plasma*) and the concentration of solutes in the blood as they pass through the kidneys. Any excess water and solutes that accumulate in the blood and waste products are eliminated from the body via the urinary system. These eliminated products are collectively called *urine*. The urinary system, highlighted in Figure 1, comprises a pair of kidneys, a pair of ureters, a urinary bladder, and a urethra.

Lab Activity 1   Kidney

The kidneys lie on the posterior surface of the abdomen on either side of the vertebral column between vertebrae T_{12} and L_3. The right kidney is typically lower than the left kidney because of the position of the liver. The kidneys are *retroperitoneal*,

Need More Practice and Review?

Build your knowledge—and confidence!—in the Study Area of MasteringA&P® at www.masteringaandp.com with Pre-lab Quizzes, Post-lab Quizzes, Practice Anatomy Lab™ (PAL™) 3.0 virtual anatomy practice tool, PhysioEx™ 9.0 laboratory simulations, and A&P Flix with Quizzes.

PAL For this lab exercise, follow these navigation paths:
- PAL>Human Cadaver>Urinary System
- PAL>Anatomical Models>Urinary System
- PAL>Histology>Urinary System

MasteringA&P®

Figure 1 An Introduction of the Urinary System An anterior view of the urinary system, showing the positions of its components.

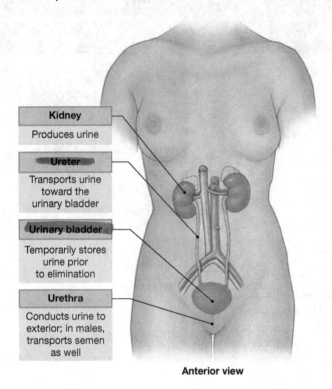

Kidney
Produces urine

Ureter
Transports urine toward the urinary bladder

Urinary bladder
Temporarily stores urine prior to elimination

Urethra
Conducts urine to exterior; in males, transports semen as well

Anterior view

meaning they are located outside of the peritoneal cavity, behind the parietal peritoneum. Each kidney is secured in the abdominal cavity by three layers of tissue: renal fascia, adipose capsule, and renal capsule. Superficially, the **renal fascia** anchors the kidney to the abdominal wall. The **perinephric fat capsule** is a mass of adipose tissue that envelopes the kidney, protects it from trauma, and helps to anchor it to the abdominal wall. Deep to the adipose capsule, on the surface of the kidney, the fibrous tissue of the **fibrous capsule** protects from trauma and infection.

A kidney is about 13 cm (5 in.) long and 2.5 cm (1 in.) thick. The medial aspect contains a **hilum** through which blood vessels, nerves, and other structures enter and exit the kidney (**Figure 2**). The hilus also leads to a cavity in the kidney called the **renal sinus.** The **cortex** is the outer, light red layer of the kidney, located just deep to the renal capsule. Deep to the cortex is a region called the **medulla,** which consists of triangular **renal pyramids** projecting toward the kidney center. Areas of the cortex extending between the renal pyramids are **renal columns.** A **renal lobe** is a renal pyramid and accompanying cortex, and the adjacent renal columns. At the apex of each renal pyramid is a **renal papilla** that empties urine into a small cuplike space called the **minor calyx** (KĀ-liks). Several minor calyces (KĀL-i-sēz) empty into a common space, the **major calyx.** These larger calyces merge to form the **renal pelvis.**

Figure 2 Structure of the Kidney

Ralph T. Hutchings

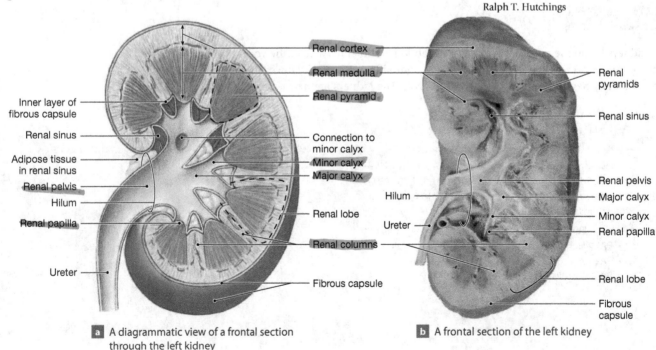

Inner layer of fibrous capsule

Renal sinus

Adipose tissue in renal sinus

Renal pelvis

Hilum

Renal papilla

Ureter

Renal cortex

Renal medulla

Renal pyramid

Connection to minor calyx

Minor calyx

Major calyx

Renal lobe

Renal columns

Fibrous capsule

a A diagrammatic view of a frontal section through the left kidney

Renal pyramids

Renal sinus

Renal pelvis

Major calyx

Minor calyx

Renal papilla

Renal lobe

Fibrous capsule

Hilum

Ureter

b A frontal section of the left kidney

1.1 What is the hilus?

1.2 Where are the renal pyramids located?

1.3 Where are the renal columns located?

In the Lab 1

Materials

☐ Kidney model
☐ Kidney chart

Procedures

1. Review the anatomy of the kidney in Figure 2.
2. Locate each structure shown in Figure 2 on the kidney model and/or chart. ■

Lab Activity 2 Nephron

Each kidney contains more than 1 million microscopic tubules called **nephrons** (NEF-ronz) that produce urine. As blood circulates through the blood vessels of the kidney, blood pressure forces materials such as water, excess ions, and waste products out of the blood and into the nephrons. This aqueous solution, called **filtrate,** circulates through the nephrons. As this circulation takes place, any substances in the filtrate still needed by the body move back into the blood. The remaining filtrate is excreted as urine.

Approximately 85% of the nephrons are **cortical nephrons,** which are found in the cortex and barely penetrate into the medulla (Figure 3). The remaining 15% are **juxtamedullary** (juks-ta-MED-ū-lar-ē) **nephrons,** located primarily at the junction of the cortex and the medulla and extending deep into the medulla before turning back toward the cortex. These longer nephrons produce a urine that is more concentrated than that produced by the cortical nephrons.

Each nephron, whether cortical or juxtamedullary, consists of two regions: a renal corpuscle and a renal tubule (Figure 3). The **renal corpuscle** is where blood is filtered. It consists of a **glomerular capsule,** also called **Bowman's capsule,** that houses a capillary called the **glomerulus** (glo-MER-ū-lus). As filtration occurs, materials are forced out of the blood that is in the glomerulus and into the **capsular space** in the glomerular capsule.

The renal corpuscle empties filtrate into the **renal tubule,** which consists of twisted and straight ducts of primarily cuboidal epithelium. The first segment of the renal tubule, coming right after the glomerular capsule, is a twisted segment called the **proximal convoluted tubule (PCT)** (Figure 3). The **nephron loop,** also called the **loop of Henle** (HEN-lē), is a straight portion that begins where the proximal convoluted tu-

bule turns toward the medulla. The nephron loop has both thick portions near the cortex and thin portions extending into the medulla. The **descending limb** is mostly a thin tubule that turns back toward the cortex as the **ascending limb.** The ascending limb leads to a second twisted segment, the **distal convoluted tubule (DCT).** The nephron ends where the distal convoluted tubule empties into a **connecting tubule,** which drains into a **collecting duct.** Adjacent nephrons join the same collecting duct that, in turn, joins other collecting ducts and collectively open into a common **papillary duct** that empties urine into a minor calyx. There are between 25 and 35 papillary ducts per renal pyramid.

At its superior end, the ascending limb of the nephron loop twists back toward the renal corpuscle and comes into contact with the blood vessel that supplies its glomerulus. This point of contact is called the **juxtaglomerular apparatus** (Figure 4). Here the cells of the renal tubule become tall and crowded together and form the **macula densa** (MAK-ū-la DEN-sa), which monitors NaCl concentrations in this area of the renal tubule.

The renal corpuscle is specialized for filtering blood, the physiological process that forces water, ions, nutrients, and wastes out of the blood and into the capsular space. The glomerular capsule has a superficial layer called the **parietal epithelium** *(capsular epithelium)* and a deep **visceral epithelium** *(glomerular epithelium),* the latter wrapping around the surface of the glomerulus. Between these two layers is the capsular space. The visceral epithelium consists of specialized cells called **podocytes** (PŌ-dō-sīts). These cells wrap extensions called **pedicels** around the endothelium of the glomerulus. Small gaps between the pedicels are pores called **filtration slits.** To be filtered out of the blood passing through the glomerulus, a substance must be small enough to pass through the capillary endothelium and its basement membrane and squeeze through the filtration slits to enter the capsular space. Any substance that can pass through these layers is removed from the blood as part of the filtrate. The filtrate therefore contains both essential materials and wastes.

QuickCheck Questions

2.1 What are the two main regions of a nephron?

2.2 What are the two kinds of nephrons?

In the Lab 2

Materials

☐ Kidney model
☐ Nephron model
☐ Compound microscope
☐ Prepared slide of kidney

Figure 3 Cortical and Juxtamedullary Nephrons

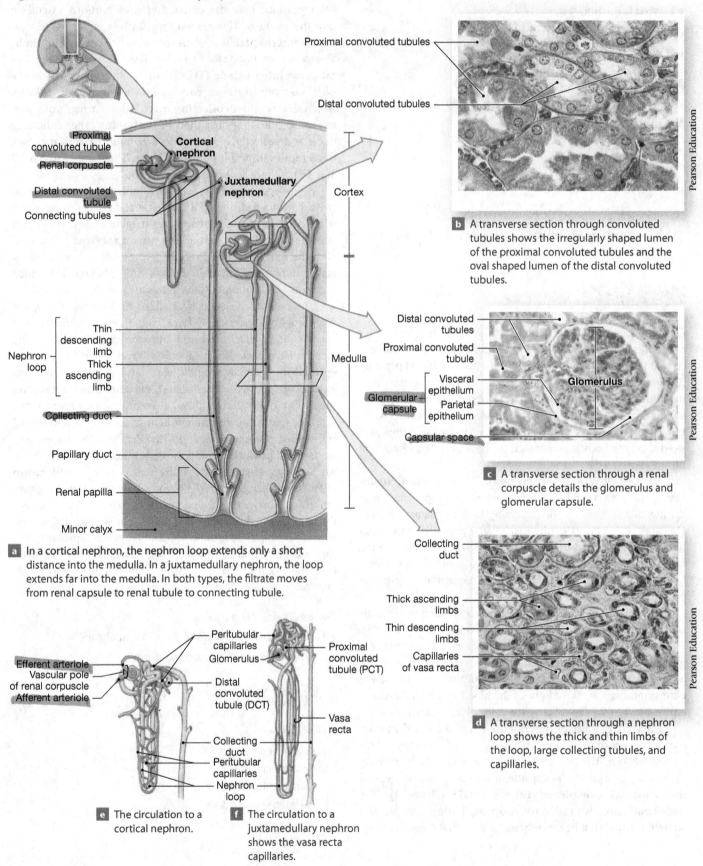

Proximal convoluted tubules

Distal convoluted tubules

Pearson Education

b A transverse section through convoluted tubules shows the irregularly shaped lumen of the proximal convoluted tubules and the oval shaped lumen of the distal convoluted tubules.

Proximal convoluted tubule

Renal corpuscle

Cortical nephron

Distal convoluted tubule

Connecting tubules

Juxtamedullary nephron

Cortex

Nephron loop {
Thin descending limb
Thick ascending limb
}

Medulla

Collecting duct

Papillary duct

Renal papilla

Minor calyx

a In a cortical nephron, the nephron loop extends only a short distance into the medulla. In a juxtamedullary nephron, the loop extends far into the medulla. In both types, the filtrate moves from renal capsule to renal tubule to connecting tubule.

Distal convoluted tubules

Proximal convoluted tubule

Glomerular capsule {
Visceral epithelium
Parietal epithelium
}

Glomerulus

Capsular space

Pearson Education

c A transverse section through a renal corpuscle details the glomerulus and glomerular capsule.

Collecting duct

Thick ascending limbs

Thin descending limbs

Capillaries of vasa recta

Pearson Education

d A transverse section through a nephron loop shows the thick and thin limbs of the loop, large collecting tubules, and capillaries.

Peritubular capillaries

Glomerulus

Efferent arteriole

Vascular pole of renal corpuscle

Afferent arteriole

Proximal convoluted tubule (PCT)

Distal convoluted tubule (DCT)

Vasa recta

Collecting duct

Peritubular capillaries

Nephron loop

e The circulation to a cortical nephron.

f The circulation to a juxtamedullary nephron shows the vasa recta capillaries.

Figure 4 The Renal Corpuscle This diagrammatic view shows the important structural features of a renal corpuscle.

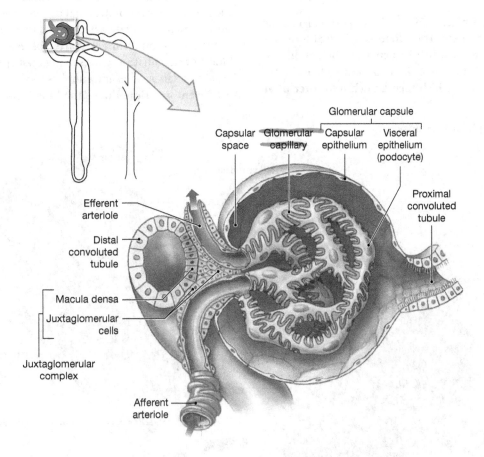

Procedures

1. Review the nephron anatomy in Figures 3 and 4.

2. Identify each structure of a kidney on the kidney model.

3. Identify each structure of a nephron on the nephron model.

4. Observe the kidney slide at low and medium magnifications and determine whether the renal capsule is present on the specimen. Increase the magnification to high and identify the renal cortex and, if present, the renal medulla. The medulla is usually not present on most kidney slides.

5. Examine several renal tubules, visible as ovals on the slide. Use the micrographs in Figure 3 as a guide. Cells of the PCT have microvilli facing the lumen of the tubule that make the lining appear fuzzy. The tubular cells of the DCT do not have microvilli and the lumen appears smoother as compared to the PCT.

6. Locate a renal corpuscle, which appears as a small knot in the cortex. Distinguish among the parietal and visceral epithelia of the glomerular capsule, the capsular space, and the glomerulus. The visceral epithelium is visible as the cells covering the glomerulus.

7. ***Draw It!*** Draw a section of the kidney slide in the space provided. Label the cortex, a renal corpuscle, and a renal tubule. ◼

Cross section of kidney

Lab Activity 3 — Blood Supply to the Kidney

Each minute, approximately 25% of the total blood volume travels through the kidneys. This blood is delivered to a kidney by the **renal artery,** which branches off the abdominal aorta. Once it enters the hilus, the renal artery divides into five **segmental arteries,** which then branch into **interlobar arteries,** which pass through the renal columns (**Figure 5**). The interlobar arteries divide into **arcuate** (AR-kū-āt) **arteries**, which cross the bases of the renal pyramids and enter the renal cortex as **cortical radiate arteries** *(interlobular arteries).*

In the nephron, an **afferent arteriole** branches off from one of the cortical radiate arteries serving the nephron, passes into the glomerular capsule, and supplies blood to the glomerulus. An **efferent arteriole** drains the blood from the glomerulus

Figure 5 Blood Supply to the Kidney

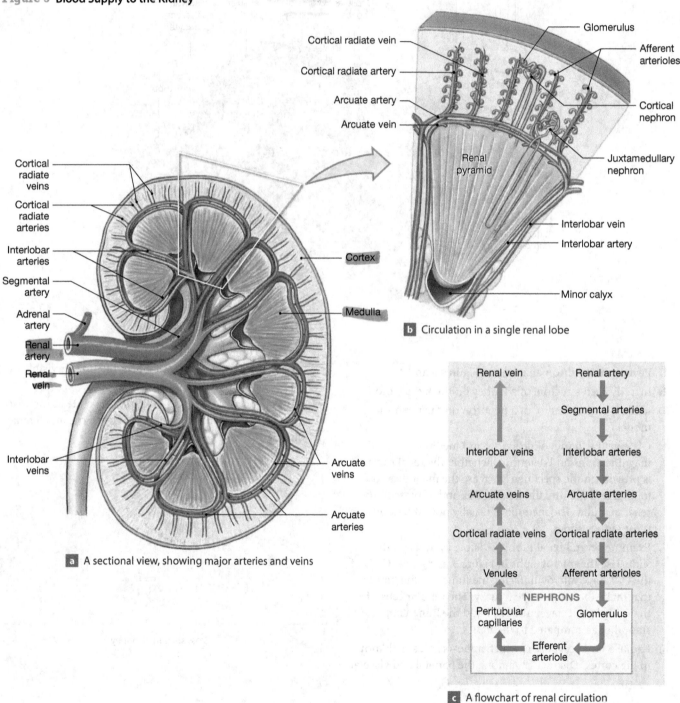

a A sectional view, showing major arteries and veins

b Circulation in a single renal lobe

c A flowchart of renal circulation

and branches into capillaries that surround the nephrons and reabsorb water, nutrients, and ions from the filtrate in the renal tubule. **Peritubular capillaries** in the cortex surround cortical nephrons and parts of juxtamedullary nephrons. The nephron loops of juxtamedullary nephrons have thin vessels collectively called the **vasa recta** (see Figure 3e, f). Both the peritubular capillaries and the vasa recta are involved in re-absorbing materials from the filtrate of the renal tubules back into the blood. Both networks drain into **cortical radiate veins,** which then drain into **arcuate veins** along the base of the renal pyramids. **Interlobar veins** pass through the renal columns and join the **renal vein,** which drains into the infe-rior vena cava. Although there are segmental arteries, there are no segmental veins.

QuickCheck Questions

3.1 Which vessel branches from the abdominal aorta to supply blood to the kidney?

3.2 Where are the interlobar and cortical radiate arteries located?

In the Lab 3

Materials

☐ Kidney model

☐ Nephron model

Procedures

1. Review the blood vessels depicted in Figure 5.
2. On the kidney and nephron models, identify the blood vessels that supply and drain the kidneys. Start with the renal artery and follow the blood supply to a renal corpuscle, the capillary beds, and the venous drainage toward the renal vein. For additional practice, complete the *Sketch to Learn* activity below. ■

 ## Sketch to Learn

This activity is helpful for reviewing gross anatomy of the kidney while highlighting the blood supply to this vital organ. First let's sketch the outline of a kidney, then we'll add internal features.

Sample Sketch

 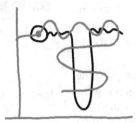 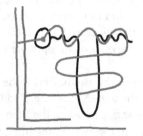

Step 1
- Draw a simple nephron as shown.
- In red, add a horizontal line for the arcuate artery and a vertical line for the cortical radiate artery.

Step 2
- Add the afferent arteriole entering the renal corpuscle and a glomerulus.
- Draw the efferent arteriole and the capillary beds that surround the nephron.

Step 3
- Use blue to draw the veins.
- Draw a vertical line for the cortical radiate (CR) vein.
- Connect the capillaries to this vein with a blue line.
- Make a horizontal line at the bottom of the CR vein for the arcuate vein.
- Label the vessels in your drawing.

Your Sketch

Lab Activity 4 Ureter, Urinary Bladder, and Urethra

Each kidney has a single **ureter** (ū-RĒ-ter), a muscular tube that transports urine from the renal pelvis to the **urinary bladder,** a hollow, muscular organ that stores urine temporarily (Figure 6). The two ureters conduct urine from kidney to bladder by means of gravity and peristalsis. Folds in the mucosa of the urinary bladder called **rugae** allow the bladder wall to expand and shrink as it fills with urine and then empties. The submucosa is deep to the mucosa. Deep to the submucosa, the muscular wall of the bladder is known as the **detrusor** (de-TROO-sor) **muscle.** In males (Figure 6a), the urinary bladder lies between the pubic symphysis and the rectum. In females (Figure 6b), the urinary bladder is posterior to the pubic symphysis, inferior to the uterus, and superior to the vagina.

A single duct, the **urethra** (ū-RĒ-thra), drains urine from the bladder out of the body (Figure 6). Around the opening to the urethra are two sphincter muscles that control the voiding of urine from the bladder, the **internal urethral sphincter** and the **external urethral sphincter.** In males, the urethra passes through the penis and opens at the distal tip of the penis. The **prostatic urethra** is the portion of the male urethra that passes through the prostate gland, located inferior to the bladder. The urethra in males transports urine and semen, each at the appropriate time. In females, the urethra is separate from the reproductive organs and opens anteriosuperior to the vaginal opening.

The point where the urethra exits the bladder plus the two points where the ureters enter the bladder on its posterior surface define a triangular area of the bladder wall called the **trigone** (TRĪ-gōn). In this region, the lumenal bladder wall is smooth rather than folded into rugae.

Make a Prediction

The urinary bladder expands and recoils as it fills and empties with urine. What type of lining epithelium does the urinary bladder have to facilitate this change in shape?

The ureter is lined with a mucosa consisting of a layer of **transitional epithelium** covering a **lamina propria** (Figure 7). The function of this mucus-producing covering is to protect the ureteral walls from the acidic urine. The ureters enter the bladder low on the posterior bladder surface.

Histological details of the bladder are shown in Figure 7b. Because the bladder is a passageway to the external environment,

Figure 6 Organs for Conducting and Storing Urine

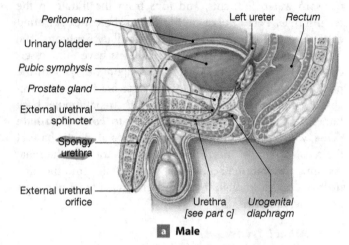

a Male

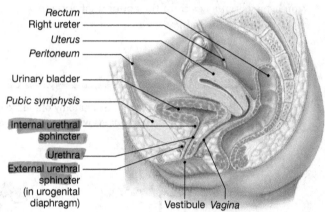

b Female

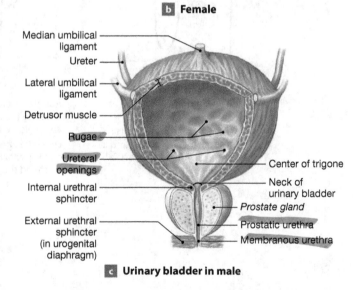

c Urinary bladder in male

Figure 7 **Histology of the Organs That Collect and Transport Urine**

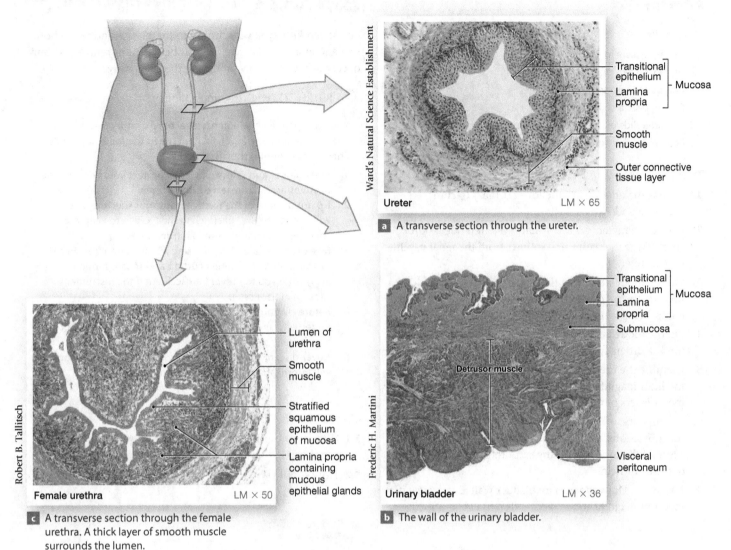

Ward's Natural Science Establishment

Transitional
epithelium
Lamina
propria
⎤ Mucosa

Smooth
muscle

Outer connective
tissue layer

Ureter   LM × 65

a A transverse section through the ureter.

Robert B. Tallitsch

Lumen of
urethra

Smooth
muscle

Stratified
squamous
epithelium
of mucosa

Lamina propria
containing
mucous
epithelial glands

Female urethra   LM × 50

c A transverse section through the female
urethra. A thick layer of smooth muscle
surrounds the lumen.

Frederic H. Martini

Transitional
epithelium
Lamina
propria
⎤ Mucosa

Submucosa

Detrusor muscle

Visceral
peritoneum

Urinary bladder   LM × 36

b The wall of the urinary bladder.

the mucosal lining facing the lumen is the superficial layer. This **mucosa** is made up of **transitional epithelium** overlying a **lamina propria.** The transitional epithelium consists of many different cell shapes to facilitate the stretching and recoiling of the bladder wall. Deep to the mucosa is the connective tissue of the **submucosa.** The detrusor muscle is deep to the submucosa.

Unlike the ureters and urinary bladder, the urethral mucosa is lined with stratified squamous epithelium rather than transitional epithelium. Deep to the epithelium is the lamina propria with mucous glands that secrete mucus to protect the urethral wall from the acidity of urine.

Clinical Application Floating Kidneys

Nephroptosis, or "floating kidneys," is the condition that results when the integrity of either the adipose capsule or the renal fascia is jeopardized, often because of excessive weight loss. There is less adipose tissue available to secure the kidneys around the renal fascia. This lack of support can result in the pinching or kinking of one or both ureters, preventing the normal flow of urine to the urinary bladder. ▪

QuickCheck Questions

4.1 Where do the ureters join the urinary bladder?

4.2 What is the trigone?

In the Lab 4

Materials

- ☐ Urinary system model
- ☐ Urinary system chart
- ☐ Compound microscope
- ☐ Prepared slide of the ureter
- ☐ Prepared slide of the urinary bladder
- ☐ Prepared slide of the urethra

Procedures

1. Review the anatomy of the lower urinary tract in Figures 6 and 7.

2. Locate the ureters on the urinary system model and/or chart. Trace the path urine follows from the renal papilla to the ureter.

3. On the model, examine the wall of the urinary bladder. Identify the trigone and the rugae. Which structures control emptying of the bladder?

4. On the model, examine the urethra. Note how the male urethra differs from the female urethra.

5. Examine the ureter slide with the microscope at low and medium magnifications. Refer to Figure 7 and identify the major layers of the ureteral wall.

6. Examine the urinary bladder slide at different magnifications. Observe transitional epithelium and rugae of the mucosa and the smooth muscle tissue of the detrusor muscle.

7. *Draw It!* Draw the urinary bladder wall as you view it at medium magnification.

Urinary bladder wall

8. Observe the urethral slide and note the lining epithelium in the mucosa and the mucous epithelia glands. ■

Lab Activity 5   Sheep Kidney Dissection

The sheep kidney is very similar to the human kidney in both size and anatomy. Dissection of a sheep kidney reinforces your observations of kidney models in the laboratory.

 Safety Alert: Dissecting a Kidney

You *must* practice the highest level of laboratory safety while handling and dissecting the kidney. Keep the following guidelines in mind during the dissection.

1. Wear gloves and safety glasses to protect yourself from the fixatives used to preserve the specimen.

2. Do not dispose of the fixative from your specimen. You will later store the specimen in the fixative to keep the specimen moist and to keep it from decaying.

3. Be extremely careful when using a scalpel or other sharp instrument. Always direct cutting and scissor motions away from you to prevent an accident if the instrument slips on moist tissue.

4. Before cutting a given tissue, make sure it is free from underlying and/or adjacent tissues so that they will not be accidentally severed.

5. Never discard tissue in the sink or trash. Your instructor will inform you of the proper disposal procedure. ▲

QuickCheck Questions

5.1 What type of safety equipment should you wear during the sheep kidney dissection?

5.2 How should you dispose of the sheep kidney and scrap tissue?

In the Lab 5

Materials

- ☐ Gloves
- ☐ Safety glasses
- ☐ Dissecting tools
- ☐ Dissecting pan
- ☐ Preserved sheep kidney

Procedures

1. Put on gloves and safety glasses, and clear your workspace before obtaining your dissection specimen.

2. Rinse the kidney with water to remove excess preservative. Minimize your skin and mucous membrane exposure to the preservatives.

3. Examine the external features of the kidney. Using Figure 8 as a guide, locate the hilus. Locate the renal capsule and gently lift it by teasing with a needle. Below this capsule is the light pink cortex.

4. With a scalpel, make a longitudinal cut to divide the kidney into anterior and posterior portions. A single long, smooth cut is less damaging to the internal anatomy than a sawing motion.

5. Distinguish between the cortex and the darker medulla, which is organized into many triangular renal pyramids. The base of each pyramid faces the cortex, and the tip narrows into a renal papilla.

6. The renal pelvis is the large, expanded end of the ureter. Extending from this area are the major calyces and then the smaller minor calyces into which the renal papillae project.

7. Upon completion of the dissection, dispose of the sheep kidney as directed by your instructor; then wash your hands and dissecting instruments. ■

Figure 8 Gross Anatomy of Sheep Kidney A frontal section of a sheep kidney that has been injected with latex dye to highlight arteries (red), veins (blue), and urinary passageways (yellow).

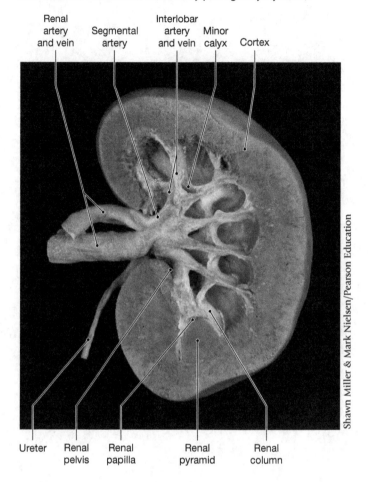

Renal artery and vein
Segmental artery
Interlobar artery and vein
Minor calyx
Cortex

Ureter
Renal pelvis
Renal papilla
Renal pyramid
Renal column

Shawn Miller & Mark Nielsen/Pearson Education

Name _____

Date _____

Section _____

Anatomy of the Urinary System

A. Definition

Define each term.

1. renal papilla

2. cortex

3. glomerular capsule

4. nephron loop

5. renal sinus

6. nephron

7. efferent arteriole

8. hilus

9. ureter

10. arcuate artery

11. renal capsule

12. renal column

B. Short-Answer Questions

1. Describe the components of the renal corpuscle.

2. What are two differences between cortical and juxtamedullary nephrons?

3. How does the urethra differ between males and females?

4. Where are the internal and external urethral sphincters located?

C. Labeling

Label the gross anatomy of the kidney in Figure 9.

Figure 9 Gross Anatomy of the Kidney

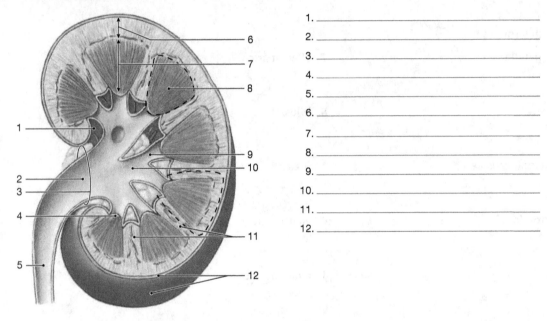

1. _____
2. _____
3. _____
4. _____
5. _____
6. _____
7. _____
8. _____
9. _____
10. _____
11. _____
12. _____

D. Analysis and Application

1. List the layers in the renal corpuscle through which filtrate must pass to enter the capsular space.

2. Trace a drop of blood from the abdominal aorta, through a kidney, and into the inferior vena cava.

3. Trace a drop of urine from a minor calyx to the urinary bladder.

E. Clinical Challenge

1. A patient has lost much weight while ill and now has difficulty urinating. Describe how a diagnosis of nephroptosis affects the urinary system.

2. Describe the effect of an enlarged prostate gland on the urinary function of a male.

Digestive System Wish List

Locate and identify the following digestive structures as you work through the chapter's activities.

✓	Structure	Description
	Digestive Tract	
	<u>Teeth</u>	
	incisor	
	canine (cuspid)	
	premolar (bicuspid)	
	molar (tricuspid)	

	oropharynx	
	tongue	
	esophagus	

	<u>Stomach</u>	
	greater curvature	
	lesser curvature	
	cardia (gastric region)	
	fundus	
	body	
	pylorus	
	rugae	
	pyloric sphincter	
	<u>muscle layers</u>	
	longitudinal	
	circular	
	oblique	

	<u>Small intestine</u>	
	duodenum	
	jejunum	
	ileum	
	ileocecal valve	

	Large intestine	
	cecum	
	ascending colon	
	transverse colon	
	descending colon	
	sigmoid colon	
	haustra	
	(veriform) appendix	

	rectum	
	anus	
	anal sphincter	

	Accesory Digestive Organs	
	salivary glands	
	parotid gland	
	submandibular gland	

	pancreas	
	pancreatic duct	

	liver	
	right lobe	
	left lobe	
	falciform ligament	
	round ligament	

	gallbladder	
	cystic duct	
	common bile duct	

	Support Tissue	
	greater omentum	
	mesentery	

Anatomy of the Digestive System

Learning Outcomes

On completion of this exercise, you should be able to:

1. Identify the major layers and tissues of the digestive tract.

2. Identify all digestive anatomy on laboratory models and charts.

3. Describe the histological structure of the various digestive organs.

4. Trace the secretion of bile from the liver to the duodenum.

5. List the organs of the digestive tract and the accessory organs that empty into them.

The five major processes of digestion are (1) ingestion of food into the mouth, (2) movement of food through the digestive tract, (3) mechanical and enzymatic digestion of food, (4) absorption of nutrients into the blood, and (5) formation and elimination of indigestible material and waste.

The **digestive tract** is a muscular tube extending from the mouth to the anus, a tube formed by the various hollow organs of the digestive system. Accessory organs outside the digestive tract plus the tract organs make up the **digestive system** (Figure 1). The accessory organs—salivary glands, teeth, liver, gallbladder, and pancreas—manufacture enzymes, hormones, and other compounds and secrete these substances onto the inner lining of the digestive tract. Food does not pass through the accessory organs.

The wet mucosal layer lining the mouth and the rest of the digestive tract is a mucous membrane. Glands drench the tissue surface with enzymes, mucus, hormones, pH buffers, and other compounds to orchestrate the step-by-step breakdown of food as it passes through the digestive tract.

Need More Practice and Review?

Build your knowledge—and confidence!—in the Study Area of MasteringA&P® at www.masteringaandp.com with Pre-lab Quizzes, Post-lab Quizzes, Practice Anatomy Lab™ (PAL™) 3.0 virtual anatomy practice tool, PhysioEx™ 9.0 laboratory simulations, and A&P Flix with Quizzes.

PAL For this lab exercise, follow these navigation paths:

- PAL>Human Cadaver>Digestive System
- PAL>Anatomical Models>Digestive System
- PAL>Histology>Digestive System

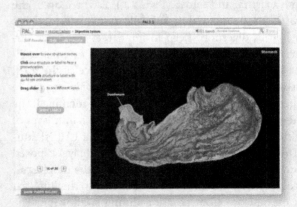

Figure 1 Components of the Digestive System

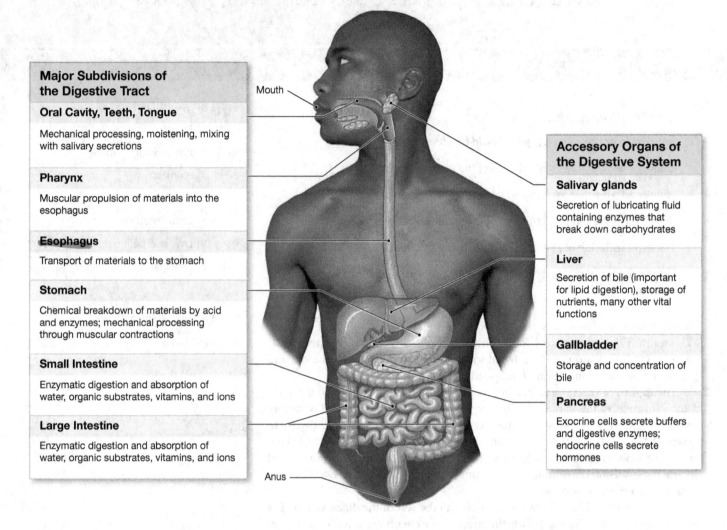

Major Subdivisions of the Digestive Tract

Oral Cavity, Teeth, Tongue

Mechanical processing, moistening, mixing with salivary secretions

Pharynx

Muscular propulsion of materials into the esophagus

Esophagus

Transport of materials to the stomach

Stomach

Chemical breakdown of materials by acid and enzymes; mechanical processing through muscular contractions

Small Intestine

Enzymatic digestion and absorption of water, organic substrates, vitamins, and ions

Large Intestine

Enzymatic digestion and absorption of water, organic substrates, vitamins, and ions

Mouth

Anus

Accessory Organs of the Digestive System

Salivary glands

Secretion of lubricating fluid containing enzymes that break down carbohydrates

Liver

Secretion of bile (important for lipid digestion), storage of nutrients, many other vital functions

Gallbladder

Storage and concentration of bile

Pancreas

Exocrine cells secrete buffers and digestive enzymes; endocrine cells secrete hormones

The histological organization of the digestive tract is similar throughout the length of the tract, and most of the tract consists of four major tissue layers: mucosa, submucosa, muscularis externa, and serosa (**Figure 2**). Each region of the digestive tract has anatomical specializations reflecting that region's role in digestion. Keep in mind that the inner surface where food is processed is considered the external environment and, therefore, is the superficial surface of the tract. The **mucosa** is the superficial layer exposed at the lumen of the tract. Three distinct layers in the mucosa can be identified: the **mucosal epithelium,** the **lamina propria,** and a thin layer of smooth muscle called the **muscularis** (mus-kū-LAR-is) **mucosae.** The mucosal epithelium is the superficial layer exposed to the lumen of the tract. From the mouth to the esophagus, the mucosal epithelium is stratified squamous epithelium that protects the mucosa from abrasion during swallowing. The mucosal epithelium in the stomach, small intestine, and large intestine is simple columnar epithelium, as food in these parts

of the tract is liquid and less abrasive. Deep to the mucosal epithelium is the lamina propria, a layer of connective tissue that attaches the epithelium and contains blood vessels, lymphatic vessels, and nerves. The muscularis mucosae is the deepest layer of the mucosa and in most organs has two layers, an inner circular layer that wraps around the tract and an outer longitudinal layer that extends along the length of the tract.

Deep to the mucosa is the **submucosa,** a loose connective-tissue layer containing blood vessels, lymphatic vessels, and nerves. Deep to the submucosa is a network of sensory and autonomic nerves, the **submucosal plexus,** that controls the tone of the muscularis mucosae.

Deep to the submucosal plexus is the **muscularis externa** layer, made up of two layers of smooth muscle tissue. Near the submucosa is a superficial circular muscle layer that wraps around the digestive tract; when this muscle contracts, the tract gets narrower. The deep layer is longitudinal muscle, with cells oriented parallel to the length of the tract. Contraction of

Figure 2 **Structure of the Digestive Tract** A diagrammatic view of a representative portion of the digestive tract. The features illustrated are typical of those of the small intestine.

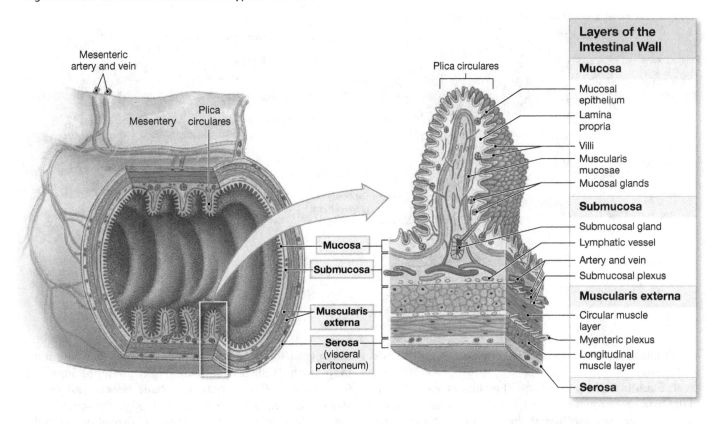

this muscle layer shortens the tract. The layers of the muscularis externa produce waves of contraction called **peristalsis** (per-i-STAL-sis), which move materials along the digestive tract. Between the circular and longitudinal muscle layers is the **myenteric** (mī-en-TER-ik) **plexus,** nerves that control the activity of the muscularis externa.

The deepest layer of the digestive tract is called the **adventitia** in the mouth, pharynx, esophagus, and inferior part of the large intestine and either the **serosa** or **visceral peritoneum** in the rest of the digestive tract. The adventitia is a network of collagen fibers, and the serosa is a serous membrane of loose connective tissue that attaches the digestive tract to the abdominal wall.

Lab Activity 1   Mouth

The mouth (**Figure 3**) is formally called either the **oral cavity** or the **buccal** (BUK-al) **cavity** and is defined by the space from the lips, or **labia,** posterior to the fauces. The cone-shaped uvula is suspended from the cavity roof just anterior to the fauces. The lateral walls of the cavity are composed of the **cheeks,** and the roof is the hard palate and the soft palate. The **vestibule** is the region

between the teeth and the interior surface of the mouth; thus, the vestibule is bounded by the teeth and the cheeks laterally and by the teeth and the upper and lower lips anteriorly. The floor of the mouth is muscular, mostly because of the muscles of the **tongue.** A fold of tissue, the **lingual frenulum** (FREN-ū-lum), anchors the tongue yet allows free movement for food processing and speech. Between the posterior base of the tongue and the roof of the mouth is the **palatoglossal** (pal-a-tō-GLOS-al) **arch.** At the fauces is the **palatopharyngeal arch.**

The mouth contains two structures that act as digestive-system accessory organs: the salivary glands and the teeth. Three pairs of major salivary glands, illustrated in **Figure 4,** produce the majority of the saliva, enzymes, and mucus of the oral cavity. The largest, the **parotid** (pa-ROT-id) **glands,** are anterior to each ear between the skin and the masseter muscle. The **parotid ducts** (*Stensen's ducts*) pierce the masseter and enter the oral cavity to secrete saliva at the upper second molar.

The **submandibular glands** are medial to the mandible and extend from the mandibular arch posterior to the ramus. The **submandibular ducts** (*Wharton's ducts*) pass through the lingual frenulum and open at the swelling on the central margin of this tissue. Submandibular secretions are thicker than that of the parotid glands because of the presence of **mucin,**

451

Figure 3 The Oral Cavity

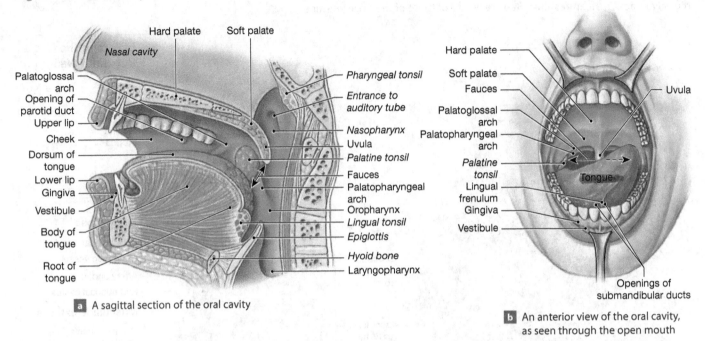

a A sagittal section of the oral cavity

b An anterior view of the oral cavity, as seen through the open mouth

a thick mucus that helps to keep food in a **bolus,** or ball, for swallowing.

The **sublingual** (sub-LING-gwal) **glands** are located deep to the base of the tongue. These glands secrete mucus-rich saliva into numerous **sublingual ducts** (*ducts of Rivinus*) that open along the base of the tongue.

Salivary glands predominately consist of two cell types; **serous cells** that produce a watery solution with enzymes and antibodies, and **mucous cells** that secrete the protein mucin for lubrication and sticking chewed food particles together for swallowing (Figure 4b). The cells have different responses to histological stains. The serous cells are *chromophilic* and pick up the dye and become dark-stained; the mucous cells are *chromophobic* and do not react with the stain so they appear much lighter than the chromophilic cells. The parotid glands are almost entirely serous cells and they secrete the bulk of the watery saliva. The submandibular gland consists of both serous and mucous cells and secretes saliva and mucin. Lingual glands are mostly mucous cells with few serous cells.

The teeth, as shown in **Figure 5,** are accessory digestive structures for chewing, or **mastication** (mas-ti-KA-shun). The **occlusal surface** is the superior area where food is ground, snipped, and torn by the tooth. Figure 5a details the anatomy of a typical adult tooth. The tooth is anchored in the alveolar bone of the jaw by a strong **periodontal ligament** that lines the embedded part of the tooth, the **root.** The **crown** is the portion of the tooth above the **gingiva** (JIN-ji-va), or gum. The crown and root meet at the **neck,** where the gingiva forms the **gingival sulcus,** a tight seal around the tooth.

Although a tooth has many distinct layers, only the inner **pulp cavity** is filled with living tissue, the **pulp.** Supplying the pulp are blood vessels, lymphatic vessels, and nerves, all of which enter the pulp cavity through the **apical foramen** at the inferior tip of the narrow U-shaped tunnel in the tooth root called the **root canal.** Surrounding the pulp cavity is **dentin** (DEN-tin), a hard, nonliving solid similar to bone matrix. Dentin makes up most of the structural mass of a tooth. In the root portion of the tooth, the dentin is covered by **cementum,** a material that provides attachment for the periodontal ligament. The crown is covered with **enamel,** the hardest substance produced by living organisms. Because of this hard enamel, which does not decompose, teeth are often used to identify accident victims and skeletal remains that have no other identifying features.

Humans have two sets of teeth during their lifetime. The first set, the **deciduous** (de-SID-ū-us; *decidua,* to shed) **dentition,** starts to appear at about the age of six months and is replaced by the **secondary dentition** (*permanent dentition*) starting at around the age of six years. The **deciduous teeth** (Figure 5d) are commonly called the *primary teeth, milk teeth,* or *baby teeth.* There are 20 of them, 5 in each jaw quadrant. (The mouth is divided into four quadrants: upper right, upper left, lower right, lower left.) Moving laterally from the midline of either jaw, the deciduous teeth are the **central incisor, lateral incisor, cuspid** (*canine*), **first molar,** and **second molar.** The secondary dentition consists of 32 adult teeth, each quadrant containing a central incisor, lateral incisor, cuspid, **first** and **second premolars** (*bicuspids*), and **first,**

Figure 4 Salivary Glands

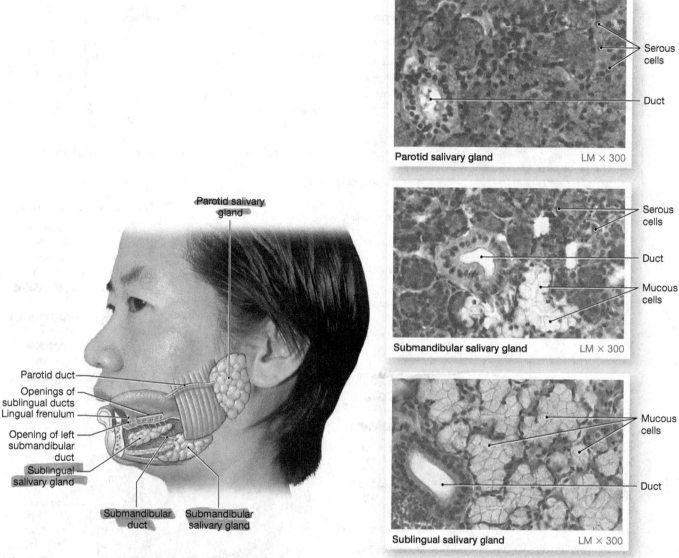

Robert B. Tallitsch

Parotid salivary gland — LM × 300

Serous cells

Duct

Submandibular salivary gland — LM × 300

Serous cells

Duct

Mucous cells

Sublingual salivary gland — LM × 300

Mucous cells

Duct

Parotid salivary gland

Parotid duct

Openings of sublingual ducts

Lingual frenulum

Opening of left submandibular duct

Sublingual salivary gland

Submandibular duct

Submandibular salivary gland

a Lateral view showing the relative positions of the salivary glands and ducts on the left side of the head. Much of the left half of the body and the left ramus of the mandible have been removed.

b Histological detail of the parotid, submandibular, and sublingual salivary glands. The parotid salivary gland produces saliva rich in enzymes. The gland is dominated by serous secretory cells. The submandibular salivary gland produces saliva containing enzymes and mucins, and it contains both serous and mucous secretory cells. The sublingual salivary gland produces saliva rich in mucins. This gland is dominated by mucous secretory cells.

second, and **third molars** (Figure 5c). The third molar is also called the *wisdom tooth.*

Each tooth is specialized for processing food. The incisors are used for snipping and biting off pieces of food. The cuspid is like a fang and is used to pierce and tear food. Premolars and molars are for grinding and processing food into smaller pieces for swallowing.

QuickCheck Questions

1.1 Which two mouth structures are digestive-system accessory organs?

1.2 Where is each salivary gland located?

1.3 Describe the main layers of a tooth.

Figure 5 Teeth

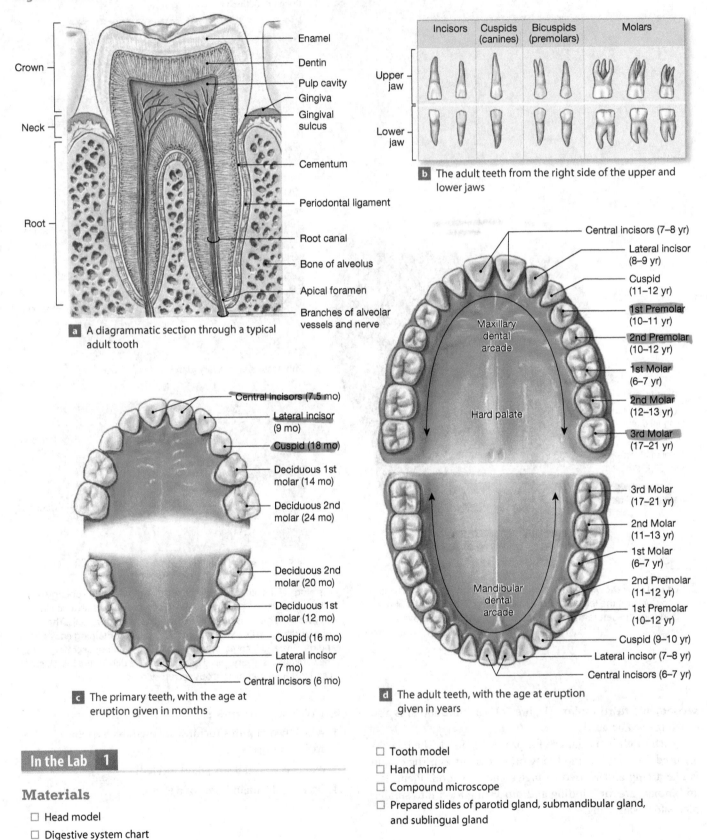

a A diagrammatic section through a typical adult tooth

Crown
Neck
Root

Enamel
Dentin
Pulp cavity
Gingiva
Gingival sulcus
Cementum
Periodontal ligament
Root canal
Bone of alveolus
Apical foramen
Branches of alveolar vessels and nerve

Incisors	Cuspids (canines)	Bicuspids (premolars)	Molars
Upper jaw			
Lower jaw			

b The adult teeth from the right side of the upper and lower jaws

c The primary teeth, with the age at eruption given in months

Central incisors (7.5 mo)
Lateral incisor (9 mo)
Cuspid (18 mo)
Deciduous 1st molar (14 mo)
Deciduous 2nd molar (24 mo)
Deciduous 2nd molar (20 mo)
Deciduous 1st molar (12 mo)
Cuspid (16 mo)
Lateral incisor (7 mo)
Central incisors (6 mo)

d The adult teeth, with the age at eruption given in years

Central incisors (7–8 yr)
Lateral incisor (8–9 yr)
Cuspid (11–12 yr)
1st Premolar (10–11 yr)
2nd Premolar (10–12 yr)
1st Molar (6–7 yr)
2nd Molar (12–13 yr)
3rd Molar (17–21 yr)
Maxillary dental arcade
Hard palate

3rd Molar (17–21 yr)
2nd Molar (11–13 yr)
1st Molar (6–7 yr)
2nd Premolar (11–12 yr)
1st Premolar (10–12 yr)
Cuspid (9–10 yr)
Lateral incisor (7–8 yr)
Central incisors (6–7 yr)
Mandibular dental arcade

In the Lab 1

Materials

☐ Head model
☐ Digestive system chart
☐ Tooth model
☐ Hand mirror
☐ Compound microscope
☐ Prepared slides of parotid gland, submandibular gland, and sublingual gland

Procedures

1. Review the mouth anatomy presented in Figure 3 and 4.

2. Identify the anatomy of the mouth on the head model and digestive system chart.

3. Use the hand mirror to locate your uvula, fauces, and palatoglossal arch. Lift your tongue and examine your submandibular duct.

4. Review the tooth anatomy in Figure 5.

5. Use the mirror to examine your teeth. Locate your incisors, cuspids, bicuspids, and molars. How many teeth do you have? Are you missing any because of extractions? Do you have any wisdom teeth?

6. Identify each salivary gland and duct on the head model and/or digestive system chart.

7. Examine the submandibular gland slide and distinguish between serous and mucous cells. Next view the parotid gland and note the abundance of serous cells. Observe the sublingual gland and locate the large clusters of mucous cells.

8. *Draw It!* Draw each salivary gland in the space provided. ◼

Submanbidular gland

Parotid gland

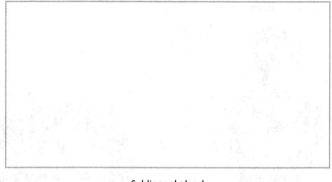

Sublingual gland

Lab Activity 2 Pharynx and Esophagus

The pharynx is a passageway for both nutrients and air, and is divided into three anatomical regions—nasopharynx, oropharynx, and laryngopharynx (see Figure 5). The nasopharynx is superior to the oropharynx, which is located directly posterior to the oral cavity. Muscles of the soft palate contract during swallowing and close the passageway to the nasopharynx to prevent food from entering the nasal cavity. When you swallow a bolus of food, it passes through the fauces into the oropharynx and then into the laryngopharynx. Toward the base of this area, the pharynx branches into the larynx of the respiratory system and the esophagus leading to the stomach. The epiglottis closes the larynx so that swallowed food enters only the esophagus and not the respiratory passageways. The lumen of the oropharynx and laryngopharynx is lined with stratified squamous epithelium to protect the walls from abrasion as swallowed food passes through this region of the digestive tract.

The food tube, or **esophagus,** connects the pharynx to the stomach. It is inferior to the pharynx and posterior to the trachea. The esophagus is approximately 25 cm (10 in.) long. It pierces the diaphragm at the **esophageal hiatus** (hī-Ā-tus) to connect with the stomach in the abdominal cavity. At the stomach, the esophagus terminates in a **lower esophageal sphincter,** a muscular valve that prevents stomach contents from backwashing into the esophagus. The four layers of the esophagus are shown in Figure 6, along with the three regions of the mucosa.

QuickCheck Questions

2.1 What are the three regions of the pharynx?

2.2 Which parts of the digestive tract does the esophagus connect?

2.3 Where is the esophageal hiatus?

Figure 6 Esophagus

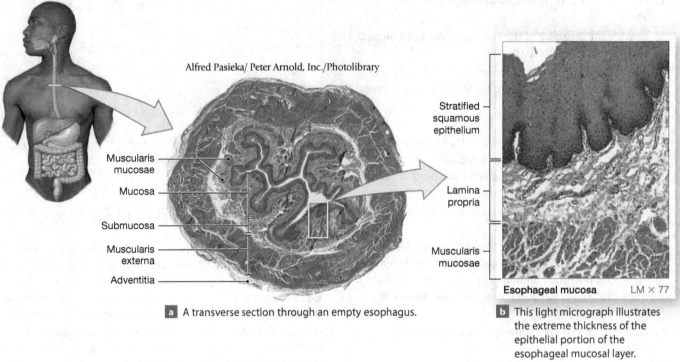

Alfred Pasieka/ Peter Arnold, Inc./Photolibrary

Muscularis mucosae

Mucosa

Submucosa

Muscularis externa

Adventitia

Stratified squamous epithelium

Lamina propria

Muscularis mucosae

Esophageal mucosa   LM × 77

Astrid and Hanns-Frieder Michler/SPL/ Photo Researchers, Inc.

a A transverse section through an empty esophagus.

b This light micrograph illustrates the extreme thickness of the epithelial portion of the esophageal mucosal layer.

Clinical Application   Acid Reflux

Acid reflux, also commonly called *heartburn,* occurs when stomach acid backflows into the esophagus and irritates the mucosal lining. The term *reflux* refers to a backflow, or regurgitation, of liquid—in this case, gastric juice, which is acidic. Some individuals have a weakened lower esophageal sphincter that allows the gastric juices to reflux during gastric mixing. Recent studies indicate that acid reflux is a major cause of esophageal and pharyngeal cancer. ■

In the Lab   2

Materials

☐ Head model
☐ Digestive system chart
☐ Torso model
☐ Hand mirror
☐ Compound microscope
☐ Prepared slide of esophagus

Procedures

1. Identify the anatomy of the pharynx and esophagus on the head model and digestive system chart.

2. Put your finger on your Adam's apple (thyroid cartilage of the larynx) and swallow. How does your larynx move, and what is the purpose of this movement?

3. Identify the anatomy of the esophagus on the torso model and digestive system chart.

4. Examine the esophagus slide at low magnification and observe the organization of the esophageal wall and identify the mucosa, submucosa, muscularis externa with its inner circular and outer longitudinal layers, and adventitia. Use Figure 6 for reference during your observations.

5. Increase the magnification and study the mucosa. Distinguish among the mucosal epithelium, which is stratified squamous epithelium, the lamina propria, and the muscularis mucosae. ■

Lab Activity 3   Stomach

The stomach is the J-shaped organ just inferior to the diaphragm (**Figure 7**). The four major regions of the stomach are the **cardia** (KAR-dē-uh), where the stomach connects with the esophagus; the **fundus** (FUN-dus), the superior rounded area; the **body,** the middle region; and the **pylorus** (pī-LOR-us), which joins the body at the **pyloric antrum** and moves into the **pyloric canal** at the distal end connected to the small intestine. The **pyloric sphincter** (also called the *pyloric valve*) controls movement of material from the stomach into the

Figure 7 Stomach

Ralph T. Hutchings

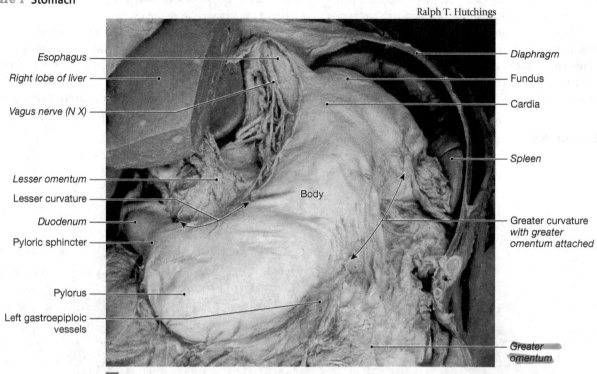

Esophagus

Right lobe of liver

Vagus nerve (N X)

Lesser omentum

Lesser curvature

Duodenum

Pyloric sphincter

Pylorus

Left gastroepiploic vessels

Diaphragm

Fundus

Cardia

Spleen

Body

Greater curvature with greater omentum attached

Greater omentum

a   The position and external appearance of the stomach, showing superficial landmarks

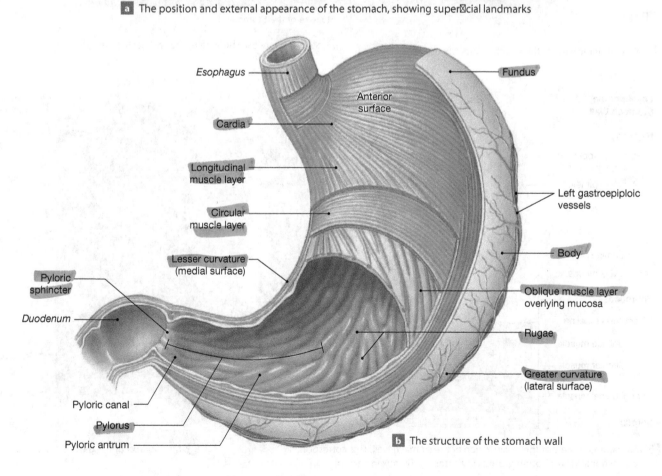

Esophagus

Cardia

Longitudinal muscle layer

Circular muscle layer

Lesser curvature (medial surface)

Pyloric sphincter

Duodenum

Pyloric canal

Pylorus

Pyloric antrum

Anterior surface

Fundus

Left gastroepiploic vessels

Body

Oblique muscle layer overlying mucosa

Rugae

Greater curvature (lateral surface)

b   The structure of the stomach wall

small intestine. The lateral, convex border of the stomach is the **greater curvature,** and the medial concave stomach margin is the **lesser curvature.** Extending from the greater curvature is the **greater omentum** (ō-MEN-tum), commonly referred to as the *fatty apron.* This fatty layer is part of the serosa of the stomach wall. Its functions are to protect the abdominal organs and to attach the stomach and part of the large intestine to the posterior abdominal wall. The **lesser omentum,** also part of the serosa, suspends the stomach from the liver.

Figure 8 shows the histology of the stomach wall. The mucosal epithelium is simple columnar epithelium with cells called **mucus neck cells.** The epithelium folds deep into the lamina propria as **gastric pits** that extend to the base of **gastric glands.** The glands consist of numerous **parietal cells,**

Figure 8 Stomach Wall

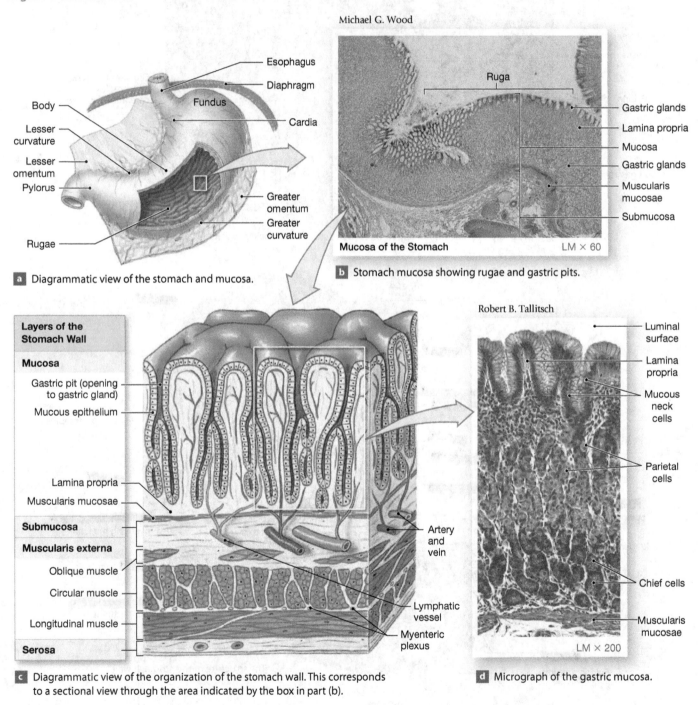

Michael G. Wood

a Diagrammatic view of the stomach and mucosa.

b Stomach mucosa showing rugae and gastric pits.

Mucosa of the Stomach   LM × 60

Robert B. Tallitsch

c Diagrammatic view of the organization of the stomach wall. This corresponds to a sectional view through the area indicated by the box in part (b).

d Micrograph of the gastric mucosa.

LM × 200

which secrete hydrochloric acid, and **chief cells,** which release an inactive protein-digesting enzyme called pepsinogen. The mucosa has **rugae** (ROO-gē), which are folds that enable the stomach to expand as it fills with food. Unlike what is found in other regions of the digestive tract, the muscularis externa of the stomach contains three layers of smooth muscle instead of two. The superficial layer (closest to the stomach lumen) is an **oblique layer,** surrounded by a **circular layer** and then a deep **longitudinal layer.** The three muscle layers contract and churn stomach contents, mixing gastric juice and liquefying the food into **chyme.** As mentioned previously, the serosa is expanded into the greater and lesser omenta.

QuickCheck Questions

3.1 What are the four major regions of the stomach?

3.2 How is the muscularis externa of the stomach unique?

3.3 Which structure of the stomach allows the organ to distend?

In the Lab   3

Materials

- ☐ Torso model
- ☐ Digestive system chart
- ☐ Preserved animal stomach (optional)
- ☐ Compound microscope
- ☐ Prepared slide of stomach

Procedures

1. Review the anatomy of the stomach in Figure 7.
2. Identify the gross anatomy of the stomach on the torso model and digestive system chart.
3. If specimens are available, examine the stomach of a cat or other animal. Locate the rugae, cardia, fundus, body, pylorus, greater and lesser omenta, lower esophageal sphincter, and pyloric sphincter.
4. Place the stomach slide on the microscope stage, focus at low magnification, and observe the rugae.
5. At medium magnification, identify the mucosa, submucosa, muscularis external, and serosa. Examine the muscularis externa and distinguish the three muscle layers.
6. Increase the magnification and, using Figure 8 as a guide, observe that the mucosal epithelium is simple columnar epithelium with mucous neck cells. Locate the numerous gastric pits, which appear as invaginations along the rugae. Within the pits, distinguish between parietal cells, which are more numerous in the upper areas, and chief cells, those that have nuclei at the basal region of the cells. ■

Lab Activity   4   Small Intestine

The small intestine (**Figure 9**) is approximately 6.4 m (21 ft) long and composed of three segments: duodenum, jejunum, and ileum. Sheets of serous membrane called the

Figure 9 Segments of the Small Intestine

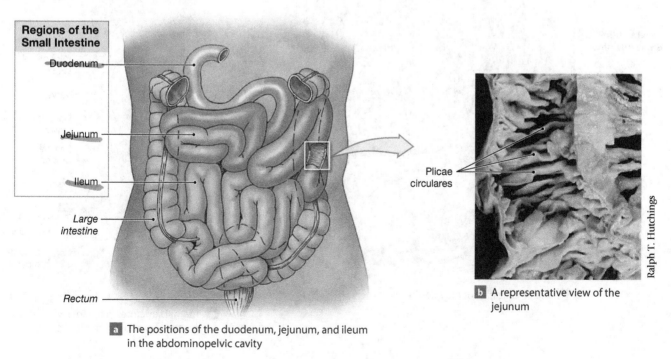

Regions of the Small Intestine

- Duodenum
- Jejunum
- Ileum
- Large intestine
- Rectum

Plicae circulares

Ralph T. Hutchings

b A representative view of the jejunum

a The positions of the duodenum, jejunum, and ileum in the abdominopelvic cavity

mesenteries (MEZ-en-ter-ēz) **proper** extend from the serosa to support and attach the small intestine to the posterior abdominal wall. The first 25 cm (10 in.) is the **duodenum** (doo-ō-DĒ-num) and is attached to the distal region of the pylorus. Digestive secretions from the liver, gallbladder, and pancreas flow into ducts that merge and empty into the duodenum. This anatomy is described further in the upcoming section on the liver. The **jejunum** (je-JOO-num) is

approximately 3.6 m (12 ft) long and is the site of most nutrient absorption. The last 2.6 m (8 ft) is the **ileum** (IL-ē-um), which terminates at the **ileocecal** (il-ē-ō-SĒ-kal) **valve** and empties into the large intestine.

The small intestine is the site of most digestive and absorptive activities and has specialized folds to increase the surface area for these functions (**Figure 10**; also see Figure 9). The submucosa and mucosa are creased together

Figure 10 Intestinal Wall

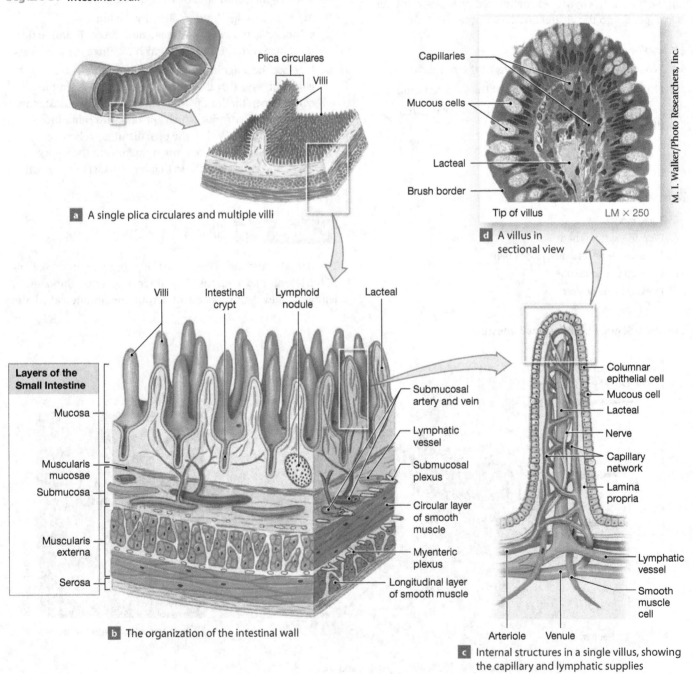

M. I. Walker/Photo Researchers, Inc.

a A single plica circulares and multiple villi

d A villus in sectional view

b The organization of the intestinal wall

c Internal structures in a single villus, showing the capillary and lymphatic supplies

into large folds called **plicae** (PLĪ-sē) **circulars** (sir-kū-LAR-ēs). Along the plicae circulares, the lamina propria is pleated into small, fingerlike **villi** lined with simple columnar epithelium. The epithelial cells have a **brush border** of minute cell-membrane extensions or folds called **microvilli.**

At the base of the villi the epithelium forms pockets of cells called **intestinal glands** *(crypts of Lieberkuhn)* that secrete intestinal juice rich in enzymes and pH buffers to neutralize

stomach acid. Interspersed among the columnar cells are oval mucus-producing goblet cells. In the middle of each villus is a **lacteal** (LAK-tē-ul), a lymphatic vessel that absorbs fatty acids and monoglycerides from lipid digestion.

Each segment of the small intestine has unique histological features that reflect the specialized functions of the segment (**Figure 11**). In the duodenal submucosa are scattered **submucosal** (Brunner's) **glands** that secrete an alkaline mucin to

Figure 11 Regional Specialization of the Small Intestine

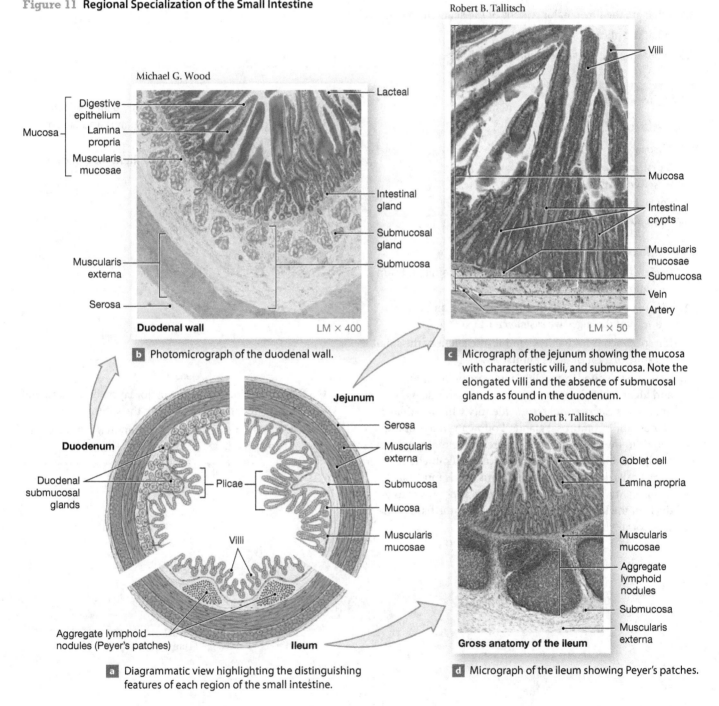

b Photomicrograph of the duodenal wall.

c Micrograph of the jejunum showing the mucosa with characteristic villi, and submucosa. Note the elongated villi and the absence of submucosal glands as found in the duodenum.

a Diagrammatic view highlighting the distinguishing features of each region of the small intestine.

d Micrograph of the ileum showing Peyer's patches.

protect the intestinal lining from the harsh acidic chyme arriving from the stomach. The jejunum has many intestinal crypts to manufacture enzymes for chemical digestion and elongated villi to increase surface area for nutrient absorption. The ileum has fewer plicae and the submucosa has **aggregate lymphoid nodules,** also called **Peyer's patches,** which are large lymphatic nodules that prevent bacteria from the colon entering the blood.

QuickCheck Questions

4.1 What are the three major regions of the small intestine?

4.2 What is a plica?

4.3 Where are the intestinal glands located?

In the Lab 4

Materials

- ☐ Torso model
- ☐ Digestive system chart
- ☐ Preserved animal intestines (optional)
- ☐ Compound microscope
- ☐ Prepared slides of duodenum, jejunum, and ileum

Procedures

1. Review the regions and organization of the small intestine in Figures 9 and 10.

2. Identify the anatomy of the small intestine on the torso model and the digestive system chart.

3. If a specimen is available, examine a segment of the small intestine of a cat or other animal.

4. Examine the duodenum slide at low magnification, and identify the features of the mucosa, submucosa, muscularis externa, and serosa. Identify villi, intestinal glands, and submucosal glands. Follow the ducts of the glands to the mucosal surface. Increase the magnification to high and identify the simple columnar epithelium, goblet cells, lamina propria, and muscularis mucosae, using Figure 11 as a guide. The lacteals appear as empty ducts in the lamina propria of the villi. At the base of the villi, locate the intestinal glands.

5. *Draw It!* Draw the duodenum at medium magnification in the space provided. For additional practice, complete the *Sketch to Learn* activity.

Duodenum

6. Observe the jejenum slide and identify features of the wall. Note the numerous intestinal glands and lack of submucosal glands.

7. *Draw It!* Draw the jejunum at medium magnification in the space provided.

Jejunum

8. On the ileum slide, locate the major layers of the wall and the aggregate lymphoid nodules in the submucosa.

9. *Draw It!* Sketch the ileum at medium magnification in the space provided. ■

Ileum

Sketch to Learn

Drawing the unique features of the duodenal wall is an excellent technique to reinforce your lab studies of the small intestine. Take your time drawing and labeling this sketch and you will have a great study guide to the small intestine!

Sample Sketch

Your Sketch

Step 1
- Draw two cones for villi.
- Add lines for the other layers of the intestinal wall.

Step 2
- Add a line over the villi and draw the cells of the digestive epithelium.
- Draw ovals in the epithelium for goblet cells.
- Add a space in each villus for a lacteal.

Step 3
- Add dots in the lamina propria and draw small ovals at base between villi for crypts.
- Add detail for muscularis mucosae and submucosal glands.

Lab Activity 5 Large Intestine

The large intestine is the site of electrolyte and water absorption and waste compaction. It is approximately 1.5 m (5 ft) long and divided into two regions: the **colon** (KŌ-lin), which makes up most of the intestine, and the **rectum** (Figure 12). The ileocecal valve regulates what enters the colon from the ileum. The first part of the colon, a pouchlike **cecum** (Sē-kum), is located in the right lumbar region. At the medial floor of the cecum is the wormlike **appendix.** Distal to the cecum, the **ascending colon** travels up the right side of the abdomen, bends left at the **right colic (hepatic) flexure,** and crosses the abdomen inferior to the stomach as the **transverse colon.** The **left colic (splenic) flexure** turns the colon inferiorly to become the **descending colon.**

The S-shaped **sigmoid** (SIG-moyd) **colon** passes through the pelvic cavity to join the **rectum,** which is the last 15 cm (6 in.) of the large intestine and the end of the digestive tract. The opening of the rectum, the **anus,** is controlled by an internal **anal sphincter** of smooth muscle and an **external anal sphincter** of skeletal muscle. Longitudinal folds called **anal columns** occur in the rectum where the digestive epithelium changes from simple columnar to stratified squamous.

In the colon, the longitudinal layer of the muscularis externa is modified into three bands of muscle collectively called the **taenia coli** (TĒ-neē-a KŌ-li). The muscle tone of the taenia coli constricts the colon wall into pouches called **haustra** (HAWS-truh, singular *haustrum*), which permit the colon wall to expand and stretch.

The wall of the colon lacks plicae and villi (Figure 13). It is thinner than the wall of the small intestine and contains more glands. The mucosal epithelium is simple columnar epithelium that folds into intestinal glands lined by goblet cells.

QuickCheck Questions

5.1 What are the major regions of the colon?

5.2 Where is the appendix located?

Figure 12 Large Intestine

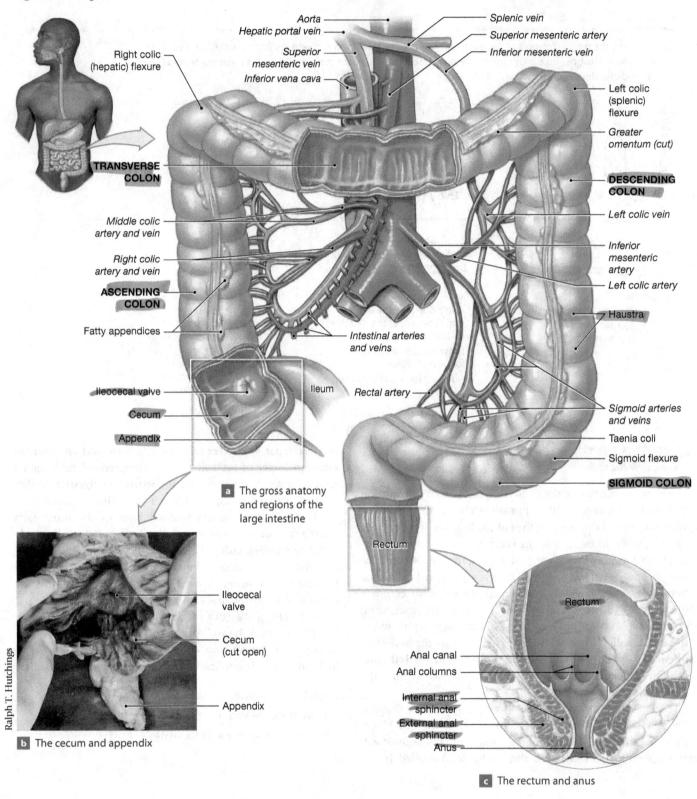

Aorta

Hepatic portal vein

Superior mesenteric vein

Inferior vena cava

Splenic vein

Superior mesenteric artery

Inferior mesenteric vein

Right colic (hepatic) flexure

Left colic (splenic) flexure

Greater omentum (cut)

TRANSVERSE COLON

DESCENDING COLON

Middle colic artery and vein

Left colic vein

Right colic artery and vein

Inferior mesenteric artery

ASCENDING COLON

Left colic artery

Fatty appendices

Haustra

Intestinal arteries and veins

Ileocecal valve

Ileum

Cecum

Rectal artery

Sigmoid arteries and veins

Appendix

Taenia coli

Sigmoid flexure

SIGMOID COLON

a The gross anatomy and regions of the large intestine

Rectum

Ileocecal valve

Cecum (cut open)

Appendix

Ralph T. Hutchings

b The cecum and appendix

Rectum

Anal canal

Anal columns

Internal anal sphincter

External anal sphincter

Anus

c The rectum and anus

Figure 13 Wall of the Colon

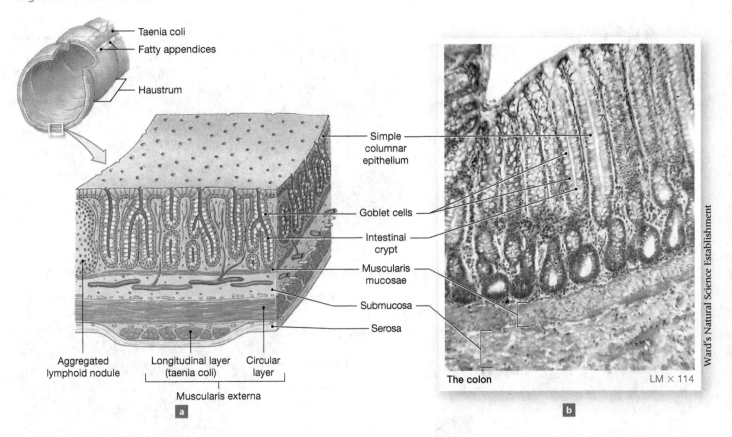

- Taenia coli
- Fatty appendices
- Haustrum

- Simple columnar epithelium
- Goblet cells
- Intestinal crypt
- Muscularis mucosae
- Submucosa
- Serosa

Aggregated lymphoid nodule | Longitudinal layer (taenia coli) | Circular layer

Muscularis externa

a

The colon — LM × 114

Ward's Natural Science Establishment

b

In the Lab 5

Materials

- ☐ Torso model
- ☐ Digestive system chart
- ☐ Preserved animal intestines (optional)
- ☐ Compound microscope
- ☐ Prepared slide of large intestine

Procedures

1. Review the anatomy of the large intestine in Figures 12 and 13.

2. Identify the gross anatomy of the large intestine on the torso model and the digestive system chart.

3. If a specimen is available, examine the colon of a cat or other animal. Locate each region of the colon, the left and right colic flexures, the taenia coli, and the haustra.

4. View the microscope slide of the large intestine and, referring to Figure 13, locate the intestinal glands. Distinguish between the simple columnar cells and goblet cells. ■

Lab Activity 6 Liver and Gallbladder

The liver is located in the right upper quadrant of the abdomen and is suspended from the inferior of the diaphragm by the **coronary ligament** (Figure 14). Historically the liver has been divided into four lobes visible in gross observation. Current medical and surgical classification of the liver is based on vascular supply to individual segments; however, the blood vessels are apparent only in dissection. For gross observations, we shall use the four-lobe description. The **right** and **left lobes** are separated by the **falciform ligament,** which attaches the lobes to the abdominal wall. Within the falciform ligament is the **round ligament,** where the fetal umbilical vein passed. The square **quadrate lobe** is located on the inferior surface of the right lobe, and the **caudate lobe** is posterior, near the site of the inferior vena cava.

Each lobe is organized into approximately 100,000 smaller lobules (Figure 15). In the lobules, cells called **hepatocytes** (he-PAT-ō-sīts) secrete **bile,** a watery substance that acts like dish soap and breaks down the fat in ingested food. The bile is released into small ducts called **bile canaliculi,** which empty into **bile ductules** (DUK-tūlz) surrounding

465

Figure 14 Anatomy of the Liver

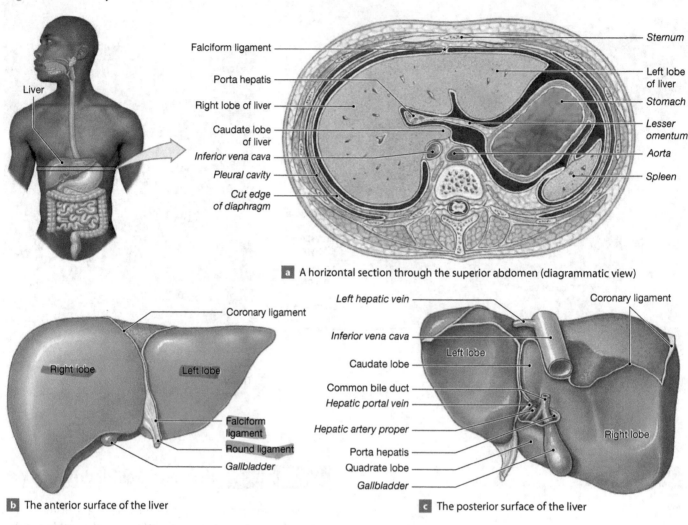

Falciform ligament

Porta hepatis

Right lobe of liver

Caudate lobe of liver

Inferior vena cava

Pleural cavity

Cut edge of diaphragm

Liver

Sternum

Left lobe of liver

Stomach

Lesser omentum

Aorta

Spleen

a A horizontal section through the superior abdomen (diagrammatic view)

Coronary ligament

Right lobe

Left lobe

Falciform ligament

Round ligament

Gallbladder

b The anterior surface of the liver

Left hepatic vein

Inferior vena cava

Caudate lobe

Common bile duct

Hepatic portal vein

Hepatic artery proper

Porta hepatis

Quadrate lobe

Gallbladder

Coronary ligament

Left lobe

Right lobe

c The posterior surface of the liver

Figure 15 Histology of the Liver

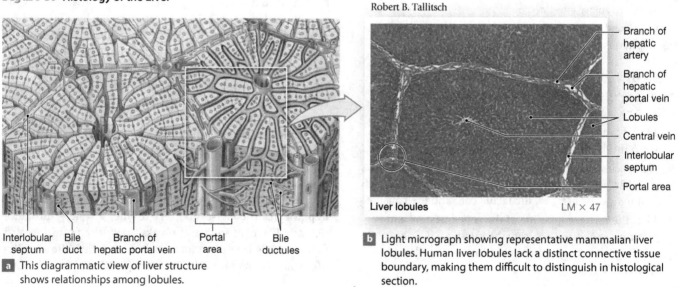

Robert B. Tallitsch

Interlobular septum

Bile duct

Branch of hepatic portal vein

Portal area

Bile ductules

a This diagrammatic view of liver structure shows relationships among lobules.

Branch of hepatic artery

Branch of hepatic portal vein

Lobules

Central vein

Interlobular septum

Portal area

Liver lobules   LM × 47

b Light micrograph showing representative mammalian liver lobules. Human liver lobules lack a distinct connective tissue boundary, making them difficult to distinguish in histological section.

each lobule. Progressively larger ducts drain bile into the **right** and **left hepatic ducts,** which then join a **common hepatic duct.** Blood flows through spaces called **sinusoids,** with each sinusoid receiving blood from a branch of either the hepatic artery or the hepatic portal vein. The sinusoids empty into a **central vein** in the middle of each lobule. Hepatocytes lining the sinusoids phagocytize wornout blood cells and reprocess the hemoglobin pigments for new blood cells.

The **gallbladder** is a small, muscular sac that stores and concentrates bile salts used in the digestion of lipids. It is located inferior to the right lobe of the liver (**Figure 16**). The wall of the gallbladder consists of three layers and does not include a muscularis mucosae or a submucosa., The mucosa is simple columnar epithelium that is folded and pinched into **mucosal crypts.** A **lamina propria** of connective tissue underlies the epithelium. The **muscularis externis** forms the outer wall and is organized into an inner (superficial to lumen) longitudinal and an outer (deep) circular layer.

The liver and gallbladder are connected with ducts to transport bile. The common hepatic duct from the liver meets the **cystic duct** of the gallbladder to form the **common bile duct.** This duct passes through the lesser omentum and continues on to a junction called the **duodenal ampulla** (am-PUL-luh). The ampulla projects into the lumen of the duodenum at the **duodenal papilla.** A band of muscle called the **hepatopancreatic sphincter** (*sphincter of Oddi*) regulates the flow of bile and other secretions into the duodenum.

QuickCheck Questions

6.1 What are the four visible lobes of the liver?

6.2 How does bile enter the small intestine?

Figure 16 Gallbladder and Bile Ducts

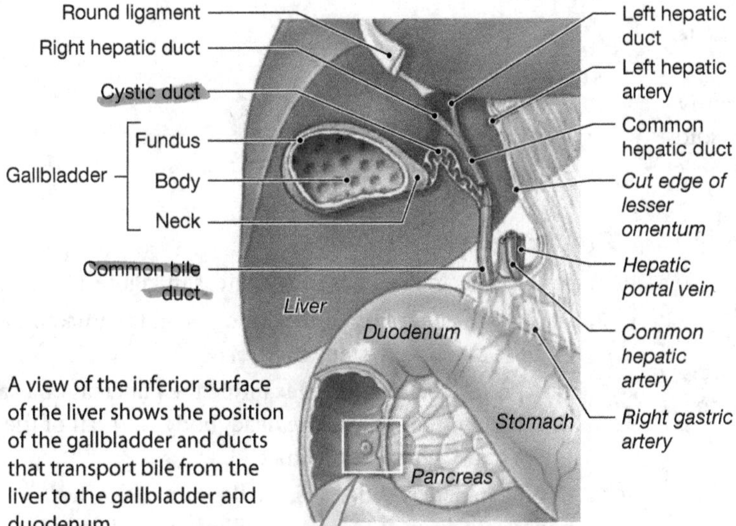

a A view of the inferior surface of the liver shows the position of the gallbladder and ducts that transport bile from the liver to the gallbladder and duodenum.

Robert B. Tallitsch

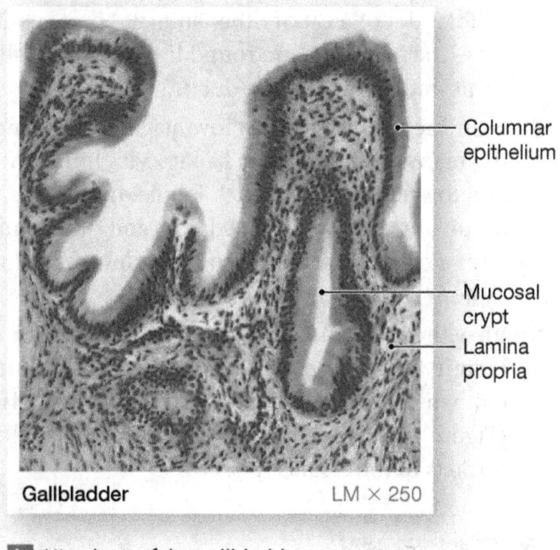

Gallbladder   LM × 250

b Histology of the gallbladder mucosa.

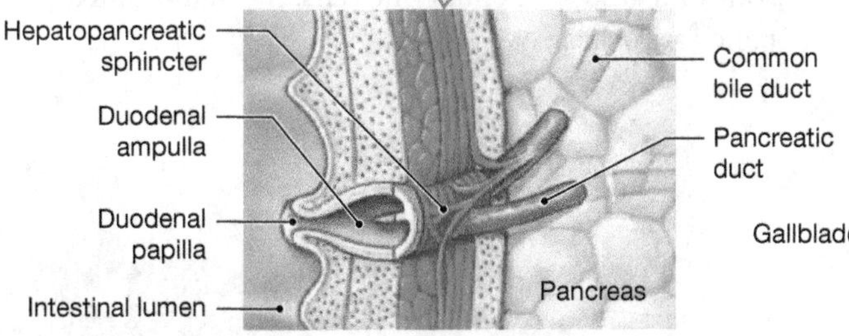

c A portion of the lesser omentum has been cut away to make it easier to see the relationships among the common bile duct, the hepatic duct, and the cystic duct.

Frederic H. Martini

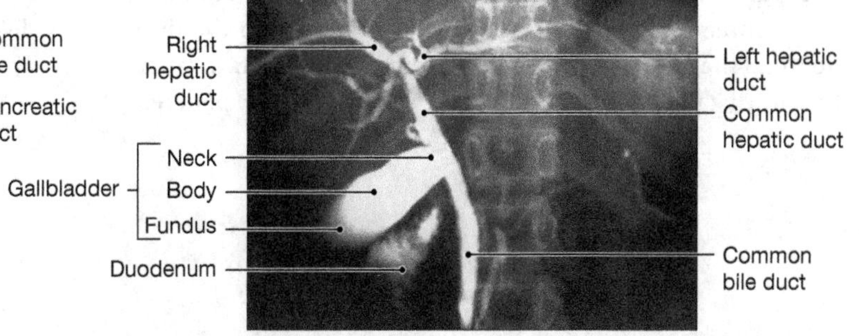

d A radiograph (cholangiogram, anterior-posterior view) of the gallbladder, biliary ducts, and pancreatic ducts.

In the Lab   6

Materials

- ☐ Torso model
- ☐ Digestive system chart
- ☐ Liver model
- ☐ Preserved animal liver and gallbladder (optional)
- ☐ Compound microscope
- ☐ Prepared slide of liver
- ☐ Prepared slide of gallbladder

Procedures

1. Review the anatomy of the liver in Figures 14 and 15.
2. Review the anatomy of the gallbladder in Figure 16.
3. Identify the gross anatomy of the liver and gallbladder on the torso model, liver model, and digestive system chart. Trace the ducts that transport bile from the liver and gallbladder into the small intestine.
4. If specimens are available, examine the liver and gallbladder of a cat or other animal. Locate each liver lobe, the falciform and round ligaments, and the hepatic, cystic, and common bile ducts.
5. Examine the liver slide at low magnification and identify the many lobules. Notice hepatocytes lining the sinusoids and the central vein of each lobule. In humans, the lobules are not well defined. Pigs and other animals have a connective tissue septum around each lobule; this septum can be seen in Figure 15b.
6. View the gallbladder slide at low magnification and identify the three components of the wall: columnar epithelium, lamina propria, and the muscularis externa (Figure 16). Observe how the epithelium is folded into pockets of mucosal crypts. ◼

Lab Activity 7   Pancreas

The **pancreas** is a gland located posterior to the stomach. It has three main regions: the **head** is adjacent to the duodenum, the **body** is the central region, and the **tail** tapers to the distal end of the gland (Figure 17). The pancreas is characterized as a *double gland,* which means it has both endocrine and exocrine functions. The endocrine cells occur in **pancreatic islets** and secrete hormones for sugar metabolism. Most of the glandular epithelium of the pancreas has an exocrine function. These exocrine cells, called **acini** (AS-i-nī) **cells,** secrete pancreatic juice into small ducts called **acini** located in the pancreatic glands. The acini drain into progressively larger ducts that merge as the **pancreatic duct** and, in some individuals, an **accessory pancreatic duct.** The pancreatic duct joins the common bile duct at the duodenal ampulla (see Figure 16).

QuickCheck Questions

7.1 What are the exocrine and endocrine functions of the pancreas?

7.2 Where does the pancreatic duct connect to the duodenum?

In the Lab   7

Materials

- ☐ Torso model
- ☐ Digestive system chart
- ☐ Preserved animal pancreas (optional)
- ☐ Compound microscope
- ☐ Prepared slide of pancreas

Procedures

1. Review the anatomy of the pancreas in Figure 17.
2. Identify the anatomy of the pancreas on the torso model and the digestive system chart.
3. If a specimen is available, examine the pancreas of a cat or other animal. Locate the head, body, and tail of the organ and the pancreatic duct.
4. On the pancreas slide, observe the numerous oval pancreatic ducts at low and medium magnifications. The exocrine cells are the dark-stained acini cells that surround groups of endocrine cells, the light-stained pancreatic islets. ◼

Figure 17 Pancreas

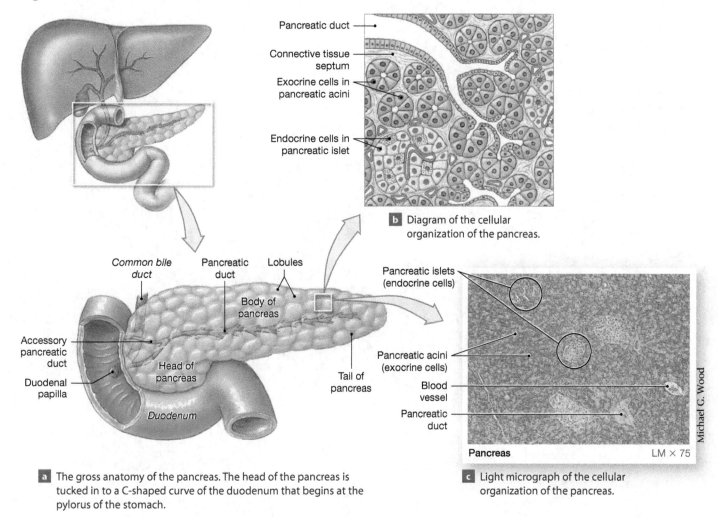

Pancreatic duct

Connective tissue septum

Exocrine cells in pancreatic acini

Endocrine cells in pancreatic islet

b Diagram of the cellular organization of the pancreas.

Common bile duct

Pancreatic duct

Lobules

Body of pancreas

Accessory pancreatic duct

Duodenal papilla

Head of pancreas

Tail of pancreas

Duodenum

Pancreatic islets (endocrine cells)

Pancreatic acini (exocrine cells)

Blood vessel

Pancreatic duct

Pancreas   LM × 75

Michael G. Wood

a The gross anatomy of the pancreas. The head of the pancreas is tucked in to a C-shaped curve of the duodenum that begins at the pylorus of the stomach.

c Light micrograph of the cellular organization of the pancreas.

Name _____

Date _____

Section _____

Anatomy of the Digestive System

A. Definition

Define or state an anatomical description for each of the following structures.

1. pyloric sphincter

2. greater omentum

3. incisor

4. haustra

5. muscularis mucosae

6. serosa

7. gingiva

8. enamel

9. rugae

10. plicae circulares

11. molar

12. common bile duct

B. Drawing

Draw It! Draw a transverse section of the stomach wall showing the four major layers and the unique regional specializations such as gastric pits.

C. Labeling

1. Label the structures of the digestive tract in Figure 18.

Figure 18 Small Intestine

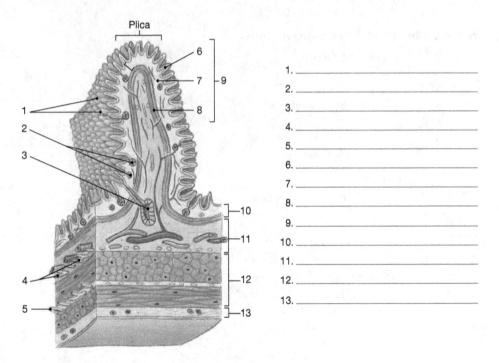

Plica

1. _____
2. _____
3. _____
4. _____
5. _____
6. _____
7. _____
8. _____
9. _____
10. _____
11. _____
12. _____
13. _____

2. Label the features of a typical tooth in Figure 19.

Figure 19 A Typical Tooth

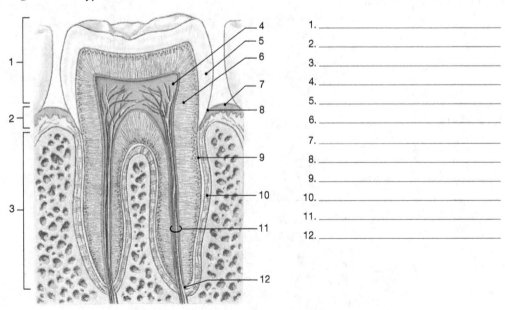

1. _____
2. _____
3. _____
4. _____
5. _____
6. _____
7. _____
8. _____
9. _____
10. _____
11. _____
12. _____

3. Label the anatomy of the liver in Figure 20.

Figure 20 **Liver**

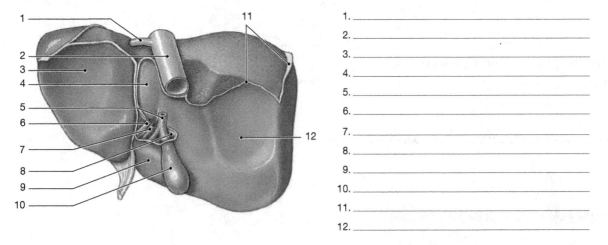

1. _____
2. _____
3. _____
4. _____
5. _____
6. _____
7. _____
8. _____
9. _____
10. _____
11. _____
12. _____

4. Label the structures of the stomach in Figure 21.

Figure 21 **Stomach**

1. _____
2. _____
3. _____
4. _____
5. _____
6. _____
7. _____
8. _____
9. _____
10. _____
11. _____
12. _____
13. _____
14. _____
15. _____
16. _____

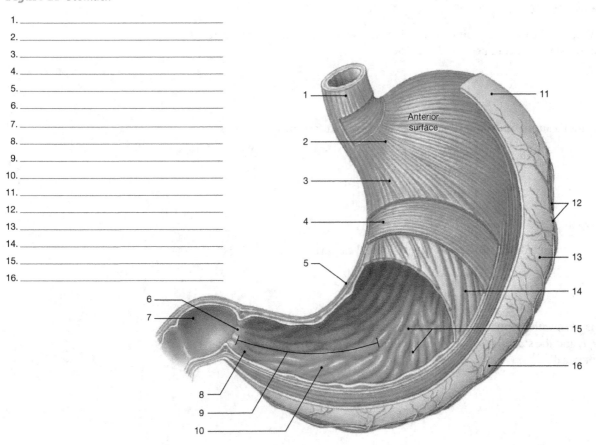

D. Short-Answer Questions

1. List the three major pairs of salivary glands and the type of saliva each gland secretes.

2. List the accessory organs of the digestive system.

3. How is the wall of the stomach different from the wall of the esophagus?

4. Describe the gross anatomy of the large intestine.

E. Analysis and Application

1. Trace a drop of bile from the point where it is produced to the point where it is released into the intestinal lumen.

2. List the modifications of the intestinal wall that increase surface area.

F. Clinical Challenge

1. How is chronic heartburn associated with esophageal cancer?

2. A baby is born with esophageal atresia, an incomplete connection between the esophagus and the stomach. What will most likely happen to the infant if this defect is not corrected?

Reproductive System Wish List

Locate and identify the following reproductive structures as you work through the chapter's activities.

✓	Structure	Description
	Female	
	ovary	
	uterine (fallopian) tube	
	fimbriae	
	infundibulum	
	ampulla	
	isthmus	
	uterus	
	perimetrium	
	myometrium	
	endometrium	
	uterine cavity	
	cervix	
	vagina	
	Male	
	scrotum	
	testes	
	seminiferous tubules	
	epididymis	
	ductus (vas) deferens	
	seminal vesicle	
	prostate gland	
	ejaculatory duct	
	bulbourethral gland	
	penis	
	Pregnant Uterus	
	uterus	
	placenta	
	umbilical cord	
	fetus	

Stages of Birth	
full term pregnancy	fetus in utero, cervix closed
dilation	fetus in utero, cervix opening
expulsion 1	fetus in utero, head emerging
expulsion 2	fetus in utero between pelvic bones. Head out of cervix
placental	placenta and umbilical cord still to be delivered

Anatomy of the Reproductive System

Learning Outcomes

On completion of this exercise, you should be able to:

1. Identify the male testes, ducts, and accessory glands.

2. Describe the composition of semen.

3. Identify the three regions of the male urethra.

4. Identify the structures of the penis.

5. Identify the female ovaries, ligaments, uterine tubes, and uterus.

6. Describe and recognize the three main layers of the uterine wall.

7. Identify the vagina and the features of the vulva.

8. Identify the structures of the mammary glands.

9. Compare the formation of gametes in males and females.

Lab Activities

1. Male: Testes, Epididymis, and Ductus Deferens

2. Male: Accessory Glands

3. Male: Penis

4. Male: Spermatogenesis

5. Female: Ovaries, Uterine Tubes, and Uterus

6. Female: Vagina and Vulva

7. Female: Mammary Glands

8. Female: Oogenesis

Clinical Applications

Vasectomy

Tubal Ligation

Whereas all the other systems of the body function to support the continued life of the organism, the reproductive system functions to ensure continuation of the species. The primary sex organs, or **gonads** (GŌ-nads), of the male and female are the **testes** (TES-tēz; singular *testis*) and **ovaries,** respectively. The testes produce the male sex cells, **spermatozoa** (sper-ma-tō-ZŌ-uh; singular **spermatozoon;** also called *sperm cell*), and the ovaries produce the female sex cells, **ova** (singular **ovum**). These reproductive cells, collectively called **gametes** (GAM-ĕts),

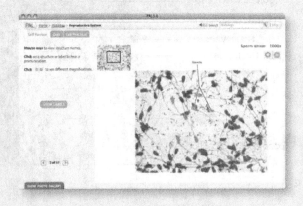

Need More Practice and Review?

Build your knowledge—and confidence!—in the Study Area of MasteringA&P® at www.masteringaandp.com with Pre-lab Quizzes, Post-lab Quizzes, Practice Anatomy Lab™ (PAL™) 3.0 virtual anatomy practice tool, PhysioEx™ 9.0 laboratory simulations, and A&P Flix with Quizzes.

PAL For this lab exercise, follow these navigation paths:
- PAL>Human Cadaver>Reproductive System
- PAL>Anatomical Models>Reproductive System
- PAL>Histology>Reproductive System

PhysioEx 9.0 For this lab exercise, go to this topic:
- PhysioEx Exercise 12: Serological Testing

From Exercise 45 of *Laboratory Manual for Anatomy & Physiology featuring Martini Art*, Fifth Edition. Michael G. Wood.
Copyright © 2013 by Pearson Education, Inc. All rights reserved.

are the parental cells that combine and become a new life. The gonads have important endocrine functions and secrete hormones that support maintenance of the male and female sex characteristics. The gametes are stored and transported in ducts, and several accessory glands in the reproductive system secrete products to protect and support the gametes.

Lab Activity 1 Male: Testes, Epididymis, and Ductus Deferens

In addition to the pair of testes, the male reproductive system consists of ducts, glands, and the penis (Figure 1). The testes are located outside the pelvic cavity, and the ducts transport the spermatozoa produced in the testes to inside the pelvic cavity, where glands add secretions to form a mixture

called **semen** (SĒ-men), the liquid that is ejaculated. The testes are located in the **scrotum** (SKRŌ-tum), a pouch of skin hanging from the pubis region. The pouch is divided into two compartments by the notch in the scrotum called the **raphe** (RĀ-fē) and by the **scrotal septum** (Figure 2). The **dartos** (DAR-tōs) **muscle** in the dermis also contributes to the septum separating the testes and is responsible for the wrinkling of the scrotum skin. Deep to the scrotal skin is the superficial scrotal fascia that encases the testes and the **spermatic cord** from which the testes are suspended. Other structures in the spermatic cord include blood and lymphatic vessels, nerves, and the **cremaster** (krĕ-MAS-ter) **muscle,** which encases the testes and raises or lowers them to maintain an optimum temperature for spermatozoa production.

Each testis is about 5 cm (2 in.) long and 2.5 cm (1 in.) in diameter. The scrotum and testes are lined with a serous

Figure 1 Male Reproductive System in Midsagittal View A sagittal section of the male reproductive organs.

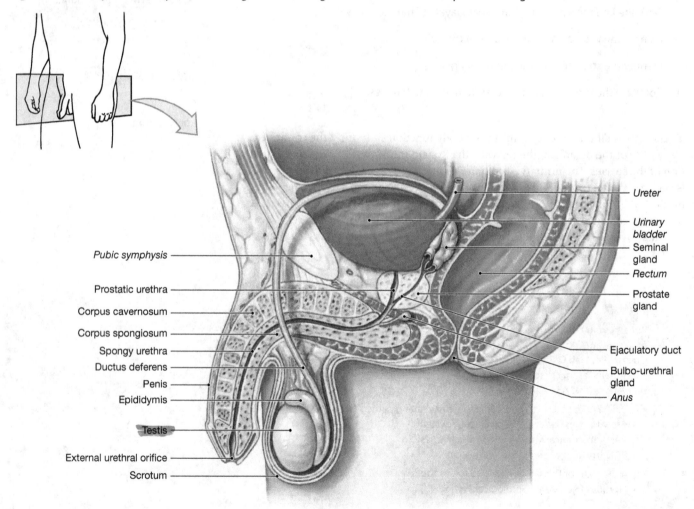

Pubic symphysis

Prostatic urethra

Corpus cavernosum

Corpus spongiosum

Spongy urethra

Ductus deferens

Penis

Epididymis

Testis

External urethral orifice

Scrotum

Ureter

Urinary bladder

Seminal gland

Rectum

Prostate gland

Ejaculatory duct

Bulbo-urethral gland

Anus

Figure 2 Male Reproductive System in Anterior View The frontal section of the scrotum to show the cremaster muscle and the spermatic cord.

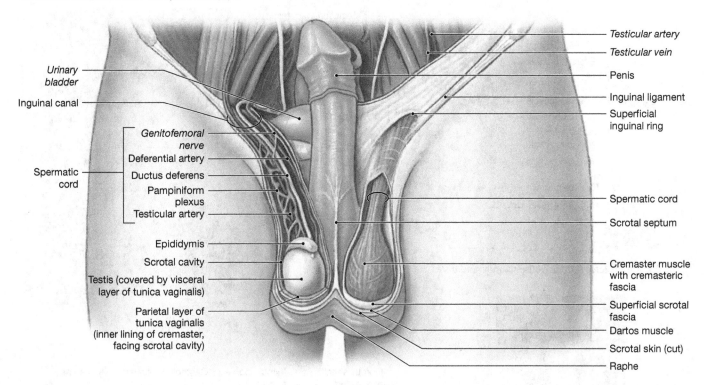

Urinary bladder

Inguinal canal

Spermatic cord

Genitofemoral nerve

Deferential artery

Ductus deferens

Pampiniform plexus

Testicular artery

Epididymis

Scrotal cavity

Testis (covered by visceral layer of tunica vaginalis)

Parietal layer of tunica vaginalis (inner lining of cremaster, facing scrotal cavity)

Testicular artery

Testicular vein

Penis

Inguinal ligament

Superficial inguinal ring

Spermatic cord

Scrotal septum

Cremaster muscle with cremasteric fascia

Superficial scrotal fascia

Dartos muscle

Scrotal skin (cut)

Raphe

membrane called the **tunica vaginalis** that allows for movement of the tests within the scrotum (**Figure 3**). Deep to the tunica vaginalis is the **tunica albuginea** (al-bū-JEN-ē-uh) that branches into septa that divide the testis into sections called **lobules** that contain highly coiled **seminiferous** (se-mi-NIF-e-rus) **tubules** where spermatozoa are produced. Between the seminiferous tubules are small clusters of cells called **interstitial cells** that secrete **testosterone,** the male sex hormone. Testosterone is responsible for the male sex drive and for development and maintenance of the male secondary sex characteristics, such as facial hair and increased muscle and bone development.

Spermatozoa are flagellated cells each with a **head** containing a nucleus with the male's genetic contribution to an offspring. The **acrosome** (ak-rō-SŌM) on the head contains enzymes to break down the outer layer of the egg so fertilization may occur. The **neck** of the spermatozoon contains centrioles; the **middle piece** has mitochondria to generate ATP that is required to whip the tail-like **flagellum** around to move the sperm.

After spermatozoa are produced in the seminiferous tubules, they pass through a series of tubules called the **rete testis** and enter the **epididymis** (ep-i-DID-i-mus), a highly coiled tubule

located on the posterior side of the testis (**Figure 4**). The wall of the epididymis consists mainly of smooth muscle tissue; the lumen is lined with pseudostratified columnar epithelium that has stereocilia to help transport the spermatozoa out of the epididymis during ejaculation. The spermatozoa mature in the epididymis and are stored until ejaculation out of the male reproductive system. Peristalsis of the smooth muscle of the epididymis and surface transport by the stereocilia propels the spermatozoa into the **ductus deferens** (DUK-tus DEF-e-renz), or *vas deferens*, the duct that empties into the urethra. The ductus deferens is 46 to 50 cm (18 to 20 in.) long and is lined with pseudostratified columnar epithelium. Peristaltic waves propel spermatozoa toward the urethra.

Within the scrotum, the ductus deferens ascends into the pelvic cavity as part of the spermatic cord. The ductus deferens passes through the **inguinal** (ING-gwi-nal) **canal** in the lower abdominal wall to enter the body cavity. This canal is a weak area and is frequently injured. An **inguinal hernia** occurs when portions of intestine protrude through the canal and slide into the scrotum. The ductus deferens continues around the posterior of the urinary bladder and widens into the **ampulla** (am-PŪL-uh) before joining the seminal vesicle at the ejaculatory duct.

Figure 3 Scrotum and Testes

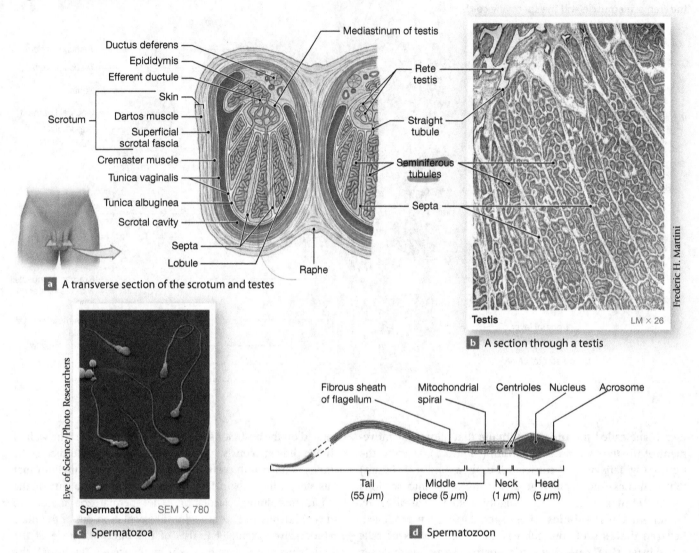

Ductus deferens
Epididymis
Efferent ductule
Skin
Scrotum — Dartos muscle
Superficial scrotal fascia
Cremaster muscle
Tunica vaginalis
Tunica albuginea
Scrotal cavity
Septa
Lobule

Mediastinum of testis
Rete testis
Straight tubule
Seminiferous tubules
Septa
Raphe

a A transverse section of the scrotum and testes

Testis LM × 26

Frederic H. Martini

b A section through a testis

Spermatozoa SEM × 780

Eye of Science/Photo Researchers

c Spermatozoa

Fibrous sheath of flagellum
Mitochondrial spiral
Centrioles Nucleus Acrosome

Tail (55 μm)
Middle piece (5 μm)
Neck (1 μm)
Head (5 μm)

d Spermatozoon

Clinical Application Vasectomy

A common method of birth control for men is a procedure called **vasectomy** (vaz-EK-tō-mē). Two small incisions are made in the scrotum, and a small segment of the ductus deferens on each side is removed. A vasectomized man still produces spermatozoa, but because the duct that transports them from the epididymis to the urethra is removed, the semen that is ejaculated contains no spermatozoa. As a result, no female ovum can be fertilized. Men who have had a vasectomy still produce testosterone and have a normal sex drive. They have orgasms, and the ejaculate is approximately the same volume as in men who have not been vasectomized. ■

QuickCheck Questions

1.1 Where are the testes located?

1.2 Where are spermatozoa stored?

1.3 Where does the ductus deferens enter the abdominal cavity?

In the Lab   1

Materials

- ☐ Male urogenital model and chart
- ☐ Compound microscope
- ☐ Prepared slide of testis
- ☐ Prepared slide of epididymis

Figure 4 The Epididymis

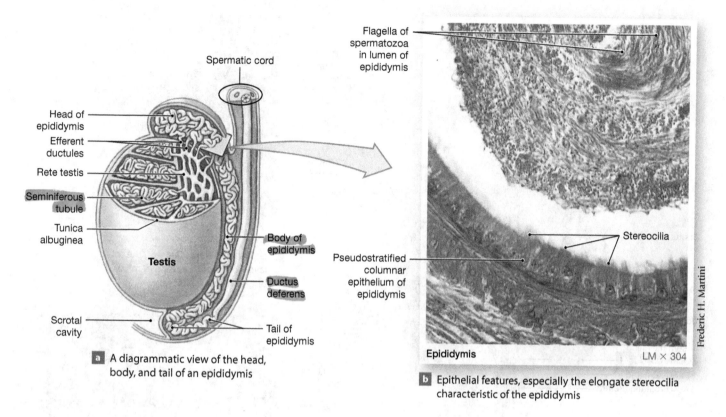

Spermatic cord

Head of epididymis

Efferent ductules

Rete testis

Seminiferous tubule

Tunica albuginea

Testis

Body of epididymis

Ductus deferens

Scrotal cavity

Tail of epididymis

a A diagrammatic view of the head, body, and tail of an epididymis

Flagella of spermatozoa in lumen of epididymis

Stereocilia

Pseudostratified columnar epithelium of epididymis

Epididymis LM × 304

Frederic H. Martini

b Epithelial features, especially the elongate stereocilia characteristic of the epididymis

Procedures

1. Review the male anatomy in Figures 1 and 2. Locate the scrotum, testes, epididymis, and ductus deferens on the urogenital model and chart.

2. Locate the spermatic cord, the cremaster muscle, and the inguinal canal on the model and chart.

3. Examine the testis slide at different magnifications and identify the rete testis, seminiferous tubules, and interstitial cells. At high magnification, look carefully in the lumen of the tubules for spermatozoa.

4. On the epididymis slide, examine the epithelium and observe the stereocilia extending into the lumen. Observe the layers of smooth muscle tissue of the wall. ■

Lab Activity 2   Male: Accessory Glands

Three accessory glands—seminal vesicles, prostate gland, and bulbo-urethral glands—produce fluids that nourish, protect, and support the spermatozoa (Figure 5). The spermatozoa and fluids from these glands mix together as semen. The average number of spermatozoa per milliliter of semen is between 50 million and 150 million, and the average volume of ejaculate is between 2 and 5 mL.

The **seminal** (SEM-i-nal) **vesicles** are a pair of glands posterior and lateral to the urinary bladder. Each gland is approximately 15 cm (6 in.) long and merges with the ductus deferens into an **ejaculatory duct.** The seminal vesicles contribute about 60% of the total volume of semen. They secrete a viscous, alkaline **seminal fluid** containing the sugar fructose. The alkaline nature of this liquid neutralizes the acidity of the male urethra and the female vagina. The fructose provides the energy needed by each spermatozoon for beating its flagellum tail to propel the cell on its way to an ovum. Seminal fluid also contains fibrinogen, which causes the semen to temporarily clot after ejaculation.

The **prostate** (PROS-tāt) **gland** is a single gland just inferior to the urinary bladder. The ejaculatory duct passes into the prostate gland and empties into the first segment of the urethra, the **prostatic urethra.** The prostate gland secretes a milky white, slightly acidic liquid that contains clotting enzymes to coagulate the semen. These secretions contribute about 20% to 30% of the semen volume.

The prostatic urethra exits the prostate gland and passes through the floor of the pelvis, the urogenital diaphragm, as the **membranous urethra.** A pair of **bulbo-urethral** (bul-bō-ū-RĒ-thral) **glands,** also called *Cowper's glands,* occur on either side of the membranous urethra and add an alkaline

Figure 5 Ductus Deferens and Accessory Glands

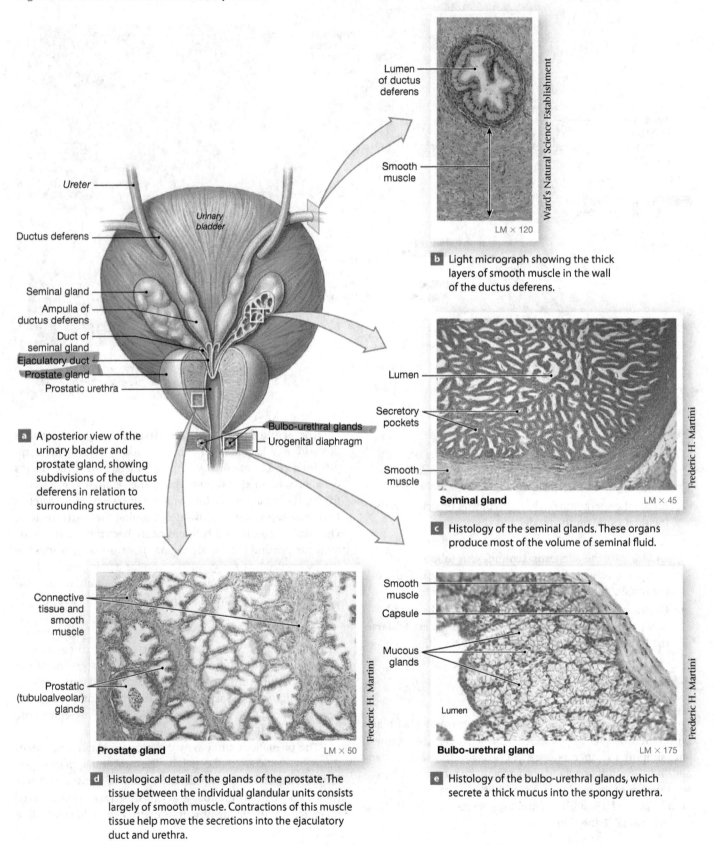

Ward's Natural Science Establishment

Lumen
of ductus
deferens

Smooth
muscle

LM × 120

b Light micrograph showing the thick
layers of smooth muscle in the wall
of the ductus deferens.

Ureter

Urinary
bladder

Ductus deferens

Seminal gland

Ampulla of
ductus deferens

Duct of
seminal gland

Ejaculatory duct

Prostate gland

Prostatic urethra

a A posterior view of the
urinary bladder and
prostate gland, showing
subdivisions of the ductus
deferens in relation to
surrounding structures.

Bulbo-urethral glands
Urogenital diaphragm

Lumen

Secretory
pockets

Smooth
muscle

Seminal gland   LM × 45

Frederic H. Martini

c Histology of the seminal glands. These organs
produce most of the volume of seminal fluid.

Connective
tissue and
smooth
muscle

Prostatic
(tubuloalveolar)
glands

Prostate gland   LM × 50

Frederic H. Martini

d Histological detail of the glands of the prostate. The
tissue between the individual glandular units consists
largely of smooth muscle. Contractions of this muscle
tissue help move the secretions into the ejaculatory
duct and urethra.

Smooth
muscle

Capsule

Mucous
glands

Lumen

Bulbo-urethral gland   LM × 175

Frederic H. Martini

e Histology of the bulbo-urethral glands, which
secrete a thick mucus into the spongy urethra.

mucus to the semen. Before ejaculation, the bulbo-urethral secretions neutralize the acidity of the urethra and lubricate the end of the penis for sexual intercourse. These glands contribute about 5% of the volume of semen.

QuickCheck Questions

2.1 What are the three accessory glands that contribute to the formation of semen?

2.2 Where is the membranous urethra located?

In the Lab 2

Materials

☐ Male urogenital model and chart

Procedures

1. Review the anatomy in Figure 5.

2. On the model and/or chart, trace each ductus deferens through the inguinal canal, behind the urinary bladder, to where each unites with a seminal vesicle. Identify the enlarged ampulla of the ductus deferens.

3. Identify the prostate gland, and note the ejaculatory duct that drains the ductus deferens and the seminal vesicle on each side of the body. Identify the prostatic urethra passing from the urinary bladder through the prostate gland.

4. Find the membranous urethra in the muscular pelvic floor. Identify the small bulbo-urethral glands on either side of the urethra. ■

Lab Activity 3   Male: Penis

The **penis,** detailed in Figure 6, is the male copulatory organ that delivers semen into the vagina of the female. The penis is cylindrical and has an enlarged, acorn-shaped head called the **glans.** Around the base of the glans is a margin called the **corona** (crown). On an uncircumcised penis, the glans is covered with a loose-fitting skin called the **prepuce** (PRĒ-pūs) or *foreskin*. **Circumcision** is surgical removal of the prepuce. The **spongy urethra** transports both semen and urine through the penis and ends at the **external urethral orifice** in the tip of the glans. The **root** of the penis anchors the penis to the pelvis. The **body** consists of three cylinders of erectile tissue: a pair of dorsal **corpora cavernosa** (KOR-po-ruh ka-ver-NŌ-suh), and a single ventral **corpus spongiosum** (spon-jē-Ō-sum). During sexual arousal, the three erectile tissues become engorged with blood and cause the penis to stiffen into an erection.

QuickCheck Questions

3.1 What is the enlarged structure at the tip of the penis?

3.2 Which structures fill with blood during erection?

3.3 What duct transports urine and semen in the penis?

In the Lab 3

Materials

☐ Male urogenital model and chart

Procedures

1. Review the anatomy of the penis in Figure 6.

2. Identify the glans, corona, body, and root of the penis on the model and/or chart.

3. On the model, identify the corpora cavernosa and the corpus spongiosum. ■

Lab Activity 4   Male: Spermatogenesis

Millions of spermatozoa are produced each day by the seminiferous tubules, in a process called **spermatogenesis** (sper-ma-tō-JEN-e-sis), shown in Figure 7. During this process, cells go through a series of cell divisions, called **meiosis** (mī-Ō-sis), that ultimately reduce the number of chromosomes in each cell to one-half the initial number. Cells containing this lower number of chromosomes are called **haploid** (HAP-loyd) cells. In females, a similar process (called *oogenesis* and discussed in Lab Activity 8) occurs in an ovary to produce a haploid ovum. When a haploid spermatozoon with its 23 chromosomes joins a haploid ovum with its 23 chromosomes, the resulting fertilized ovum has all 46 chromosomes and is **diploid** (DIP-loyd). From this first new diploid cell, called the **zygote,** an incomprehensible number of divisions ultimately shape a new human.

The term **somatic cells** refers to all the cells in the body except the cells that produce gametes. **Mitosis** (mī-TŌ-sis) is cell division in somatic cells, where one parent cell divides to produce two identical diploid daughter cells. Meiosis, as just noted, is cell division of cells in the testes and ovaries that produces haploid gametes. Meiosis occurs in two cycles, meiosis I and II, and in many ways is similar to mitosis. For simplicity, Figure 7 illustrates meiosis in a diploid cell containing 3 chromosome pairs (6 individual chromosomes) instead of the 23 pairs found in humans.

When a male reaches puberty, hormones stimulate the testes to begin spermatogenesis (Figure 8). Cells called **spermatogonia** (sper-ma-tō-GŌ-nē-uh) located in the outer wall of the seminiferous tubules divide by mitosis and produce, in addition to new (haploid) spermatogonia, some

Figure 6 The Penis

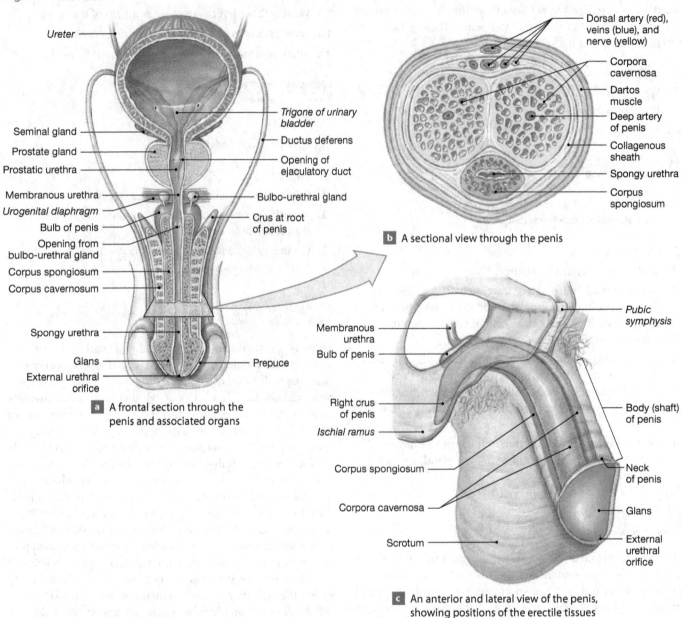

Ureter

Trigone of urinary bladder

Seminal gland

Prostate gland

Prostatic urethra

Membranous urethra
Urogenital diaphragm
Bulb of penis

Opening from bulbo-urethral gland

Corpus spongiosum

Corpus cavernosum

Spongy urethra

Glans

External urethral orifice

Ductus deferens

Opening of ejaculatory duct

Bulbo-urethral gland

Crus at root of penis

Prepuce

a A frontal section through the penis and associated organs

Dorsal artery (red), veins (blue), and nerve (yellow)

Corpora cavernosa

Dartos muscle

Deep artery of penis

Collagenous sheath

Spongy urethra

Corpus spongiosum

b A sectional view through the penis

Membranous urethra

Bulb of penis

Right crus of penis

Ischial ramus

Corpus spongiosum

Corpora cavernosa

Scrotum

Pubic symphysis

Body (shaft) of penis

Neck of penis

Glans

External urethral orifice

c An anterior and lateral view of the penis, showing positions of the erectile tissues

diploid **primary spermatocytes** (sper-MA-tō-sīts). A primary spermatocyte prepares for meiosis by duplicating its genetic material. After replication, each chromosome is double stranded and consists of two **chromatids.** Thus each original pair of chromosomes, which are called **homologous chromosomes,** now consists of four chromatids. The primary spermatocyte is now ready to proceed into meiosis.

Meiosis I begins as the nuclear membrane of the primary spermatocyte dissolves and the chromatids condense into chromosomes. The homologous chromosomes match into pairs in a process called **synapsis,** and the four

chromatids of the pair are collectively called a **tetrad.** Because each chromatid in a tetrad belongs to the same chromosome pair, genetic information may be exchanged between chromatids. This **crossing over,** or mixing, of the genes contained in the chromatids increases the genetic variation within the population.

Next the tetrads line up in the middle of the cell, and the critical step of reducing the chromosome number to haploid occurs. The tetrads separate, and the double-stranded chromosomes move to opposite sides of the cell. This separation step is called the **reduction division** of meiosis because haploid

Figure 7 Seminiferous Tubules and Meiosis

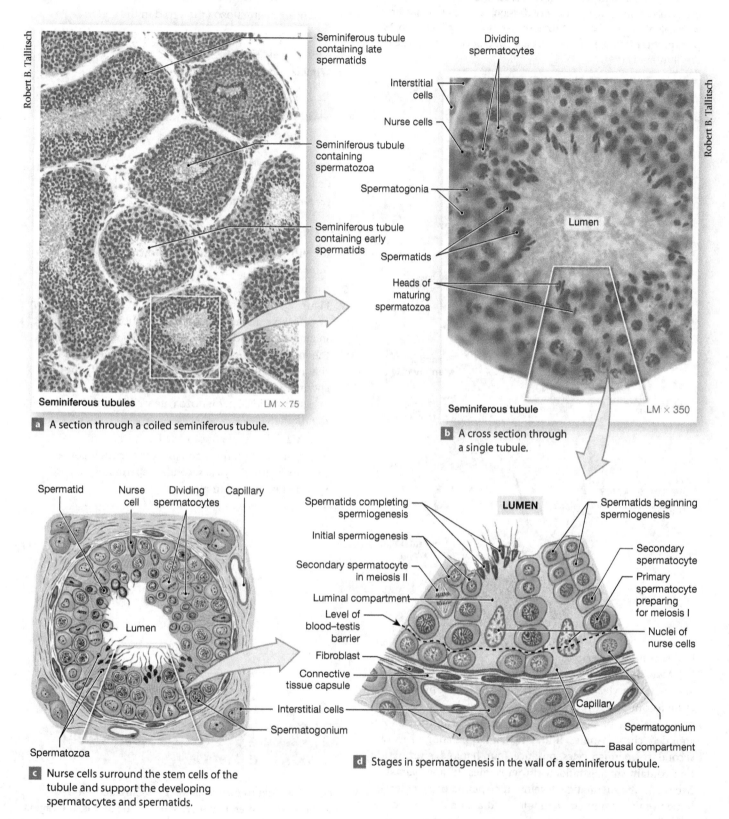

Robert B. Tallitsch

Seminiferous tubule containing late spermatids

Seminiferous tubule containing spermatozoa

Seminiferous tubule containing early spermatids

Seminiferous tubules LM × 75

a A section through a coiled seminiferous tubule.

Dividing spermatocytes

Interstitial cells

Nurse cells

Spermatogonia

Lumen

Spermatids

Heads of maturing spermatozoa

Robert B. Tallitsch

Seminiferous tubule LM × 350

b A cross section through a single tubule.

Spermatid   Nurse cell   Dividing spermatocytes   Capillary

Lumen

Spermatozoa

c Nurse cells surround the stem cells of the tubule and support the developing spermatocytes and spermatids.

Spermatids completing spermiogenesis

Initial spermiogenesis

Secondary spermatocyte in meiosis II

Luminal compartment

Level of blood–testis barrier

Fibroblast

Connective tissue capsule

Interstitial cells

Spermatogonium

LUMEN

Spermatids beginning spermiogenesis

Secondary spermatocyte

Primary spermatocyte preparing for meiosis I

Nuclei of nurse cells

Capillary

Spermatogonium

Basal compartment

d Stages in spermatogenesis in the wall of a seminiferous tubule.

Figure 8 Spermatogenesis Stem cells in the wall of the seminiferous tubule undergo meiosis, cell division that results in gametes with half of the number of chromosomes. Human cells contain 23 pairs of chromosomes in diploid stages, but for clarity only 3 pairs are illustrated here.

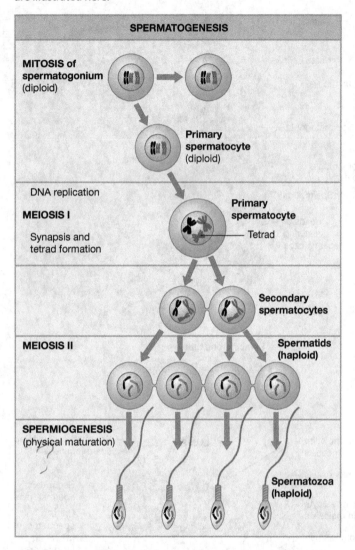

SPERMATOGENESIS

MITOSIS of spermatogonium (diploid)

Primary spermatocyte (diploid)

DNA replication

MEIOSIS I

Synapsis and tetrad formation

Primary spermatocyte

Tetrad

Secondary spermatocytes

MEIOSIS II

Spermatids (haploid)

SPERMIOGENESIS (physical maturation)

Spermatozoa (haploid)

cells are produced. Next the cell pinches apart into two haploid **secondary spermatocytes.**

Meiosis II is necessary because, although the secondary spermatocytes are haploid, they have double-stranded chromosomes that must be reduced to single-stranded chromosomes. The process is similar to mitosis, with the double-stranded chromosomes lining up and separating. The two secondary spermatocytes produce four haploid **spermatids** that contain single-stranded chromosomes. In approximately five weeks the spermatids develop into spermatozoa, enter the lumen of the seminiferous tubules, and are transported to the epididymis where they undergo several weeks of maturation into a mature, active spermatozoa.

QuickCheck Questions

4.1 Where are spermatozoa produced in the male?

4.2 What is the name of the cell that divides to produce a primary spermatocyte?

4.3 What is a tetrad?

In the Lab 4

Materials

☐ Meiosis models
☐ Compound microscope
☐ Prepared slide of testis

Procedures

1. Identify the different cell types shown on the meiosis models.

2. Examine the testis slide, using the micrographs in Figure 8 for reference. Scan the slide at low magnification and observe the many seminiferous tubules. Increase the magnification and locate the interstitial cells between the tubules. At high power, pick a seminiferous tubule that has distinct cells within the walls. Identify the spermatogonia, primary and secondary spermatocytes, and spermatids. Spermatozoa are visible in the lumen of the tubule.

3. *Draw It!* In the space provided, draw a section of a seminiferous tubule, and label the spermatogonia, primary spermatocytes, secondary spermatocytes, spermatids, and spermatozoa. ■

Seminiferous tubule

Lab Activity 5 Female: Ovaries, Uterine Tubes, and Uterus

The female reproductive system, highlighted in Figure 9, includes two ovaries, two uterine tubes, the uterus, the vagina, external genitalia, and two mammary glands. **Gynecology** is

Figure 9 Female Reproductive System in Sagittal Section A midsagittal section of the female pelvis showing the anatomical location of the reproductive organs.

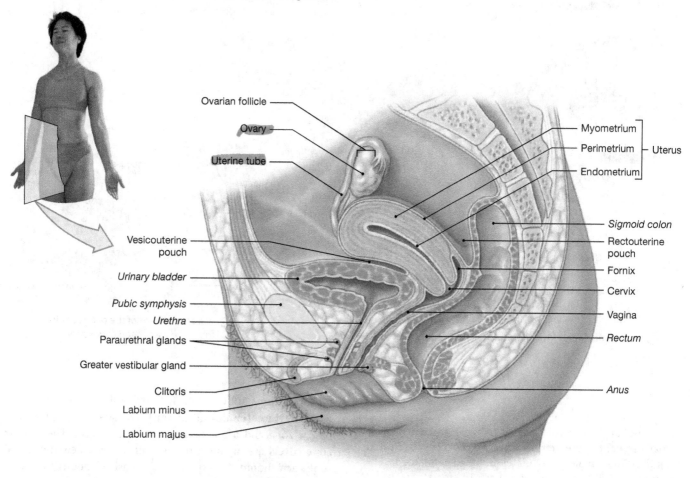

the branch of medicine that deals with the care and treatment of the female reproductive system.

The ovaries are paired structures approximately the size and shape of an almond and are located along the lateral walls of the pelvic cavity. A double-layered fold of peritoneum called the **mesovarium** (mes-ō-VAR-ē-um) holds the ovaries to the **broad ligament** of the uterus (Figure 10). The **suspensory ligaments** hold the ovaries to the wall of the pelvis, and the **ovarian ligaments** hold the ovaries to the uterus. The **round ligaments** extend laterally from the ovaries and provide posterior support.

Like around the testis, a layer of dense connective tissue called the **tunica albuginea** surrounds the ovary. The **stroma** or interior of the ovary has a central **medulla** and outer **cortex** where the ova are produced. The process of oogenesis, egg production, begins before birth, therefore, the cortex of a mature ovary is full of **egg nests** of immature eggs called **oocytes** (ō-ō-sīts) that can develop into **mature follicles** that can

ovulate ova for fertilization. (See Lab Activity 8 for the study of oogenesis.)

Upon ovulation, an ovum is released from ovary and transported to the uterus by one of two **uterine tubes,** commonly called *fallopian tubes* (Figure 11). At the tip of the uterine tubes are fingerlike projections called **fimbriae** (FIM-brē-ē). These projections sweep over the surface of the ovary to capture the released ovum and draw it into the expanded **infundibulum** region of the uterine tube. The lumen of the uterine tube is lined with **ciliated simple columnar epithelium** with an underlying bed of connective tissue called the **lamina propria** (Figure 11b). Deep to the lamina propria is smooth muscle. Once the ovum is inside the uterine tube, movements of the cilia and peristaltic waves of muscle contraction transport the ovum toward the uterus. The tube widens midway along its length in the **ampulla** and then narrows at the **isthmus** (IS-mus) to enter the uterus. Fertilization of the ovum usually occurs between the infundibulum and the ampulla of the uterine tube.

Figure 10 Ovaries and Their Relationships to the Uterine Tubes and Uterus

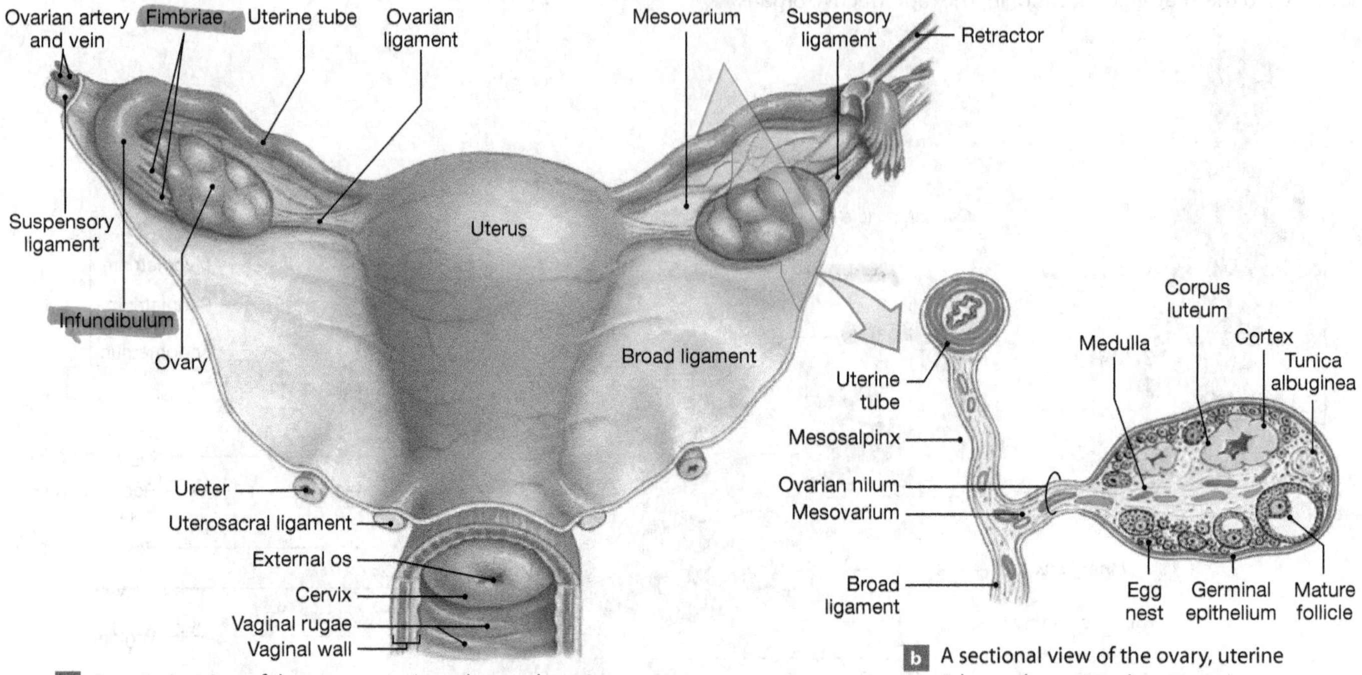

a A posterior view of the uterus, uterine tubes, and ovaries

b A sectional view of the ovary, uterine tube, and associated mesenteries

---

Clinical Application Tubal Ligation

Permanent birth control for females involves removing a small segment of the uterine tubes in a process called **tubal ligation.** The female still ovulates, but the spermatozoa cannot reach the ova to fertilize them. The female still has a monthly menstrual period. ■

The **uterus,** the pear-shaped muscular organ located between the urinary bladder and the rectum, is the site where a fertilized ovum is implanted and where the fetus develops during pregnancy. The uterus consists of three major regions: fundus, body, and cervix. The superior, dome-shaped portion of the uterus is the **fundus,** and the inferior, narrow portion is the **cervix** (SER-viks). The rest of the uterus is called the **body.** Within the uterus is a space called the **uterine cavity** that narrows at the cervix as the **cervical canal.**

The uterine wall consists of three main layers: perimetrium, myometrium, and endometrium. The **perimetrium** is the outer covering of the uterus. It is an extension of the visceral peritoneum and is therefore also called the *serosa*. The thick middle layer, the **myometrium** (mī-ō-MĒ-trē-um), is composed of three layers of smooth muscle and is responsible for the power-

ful contractions during labor. Exposed at the uterine cavity, the **endometrium** (en-dō-MĒ-trē-um), consists of two layers, a basilar zone and a functional zone (Figure 11c). The **basilar zone** covers the myometrium and produces a new functional zone each month. Superficial to the basilar zone is the **functional zone.** This layer is very glandular and is highly vascularized to support an implanted embryo. The functional zone is the endometrial layer that is shed each cycle during menstruation.

As a woman's monthly cycle progresses, the histology of the endometrium changes and the uterus prepares for the possibility of pregnancy (Figure 12). The cycle starts with bleeding, called **menses,** and is characterized by the breaking down of the functional zone. After menses, the functional zone is rebuilt during the **proliferative phase** and small uterine glands appear. Toward the end of the cycle, the **secretory phase** is distinguished by a thick endometrium with many elongated uterine glands. If pregnancy does not occur, the cycle repeats as menses occurs.

QuickCheck Questions

5.1 What structure transports an ovum from the ovary to the uterus?

5.2 What are the three layers of the uterine wall?

5.3 Which layer of the uterine wall is shed during menses?

Figure 11 Uterine Tubes and Uterus

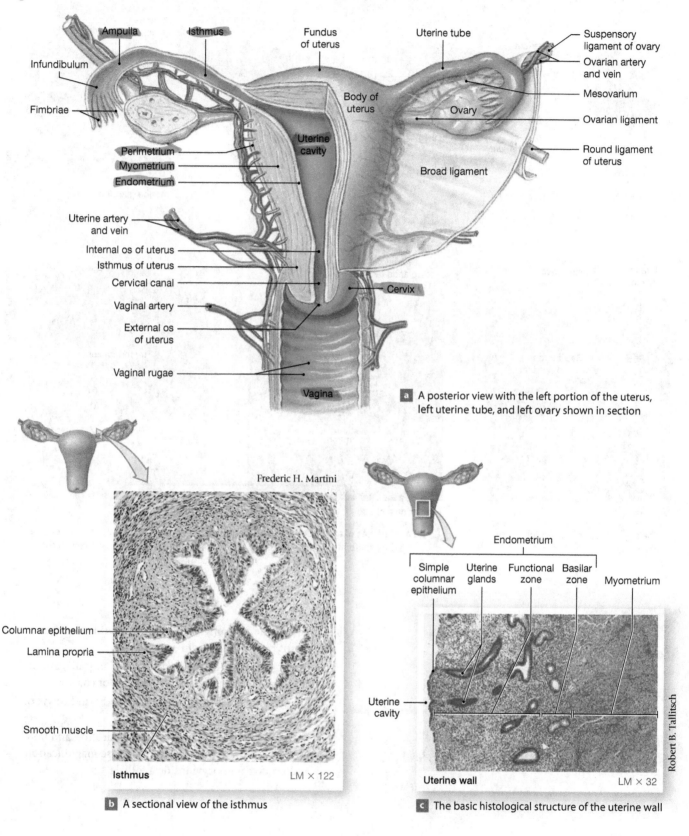

Ampulla

Isthmus

Fundus of uterus

Uterine tube

Suspensory ligament of ovary

Infundibulum

Ovarian artery and vein

Body of uterus

Mesovarium

Fimbriae

Ovary

Ovarian ligament

Perimetrium

Uterine cavity

Round ligament of uterus

Myometrium

Endometrium

Broad ligament

Uterine artery and vein

Internal os of uterus

Isthmus of uterus

Cervical canal

Cervix

Vaginal artery

External os of uterus

Vaginal rugae

Vagina

a A posterior view with the left portion of the uterus, left uterine tube, and left ovary shown in section

Frederic H. Martini

Columnar epithelium

Lamina propria

Smooth muscle

Isthmus

LM × 122

b A sectional view of the isthmus

Endometrium

Simple columnar epithelium

Uterine glands

Functional zone

Basilar zone

Myometrium

Uterine cavity

Uterine wall

LM × 32

Robert B. Tallitsch

c The basic histological structure of the uterine wall

489

Figure 12 Appearance of the Endometrium During the Uterine Cycle

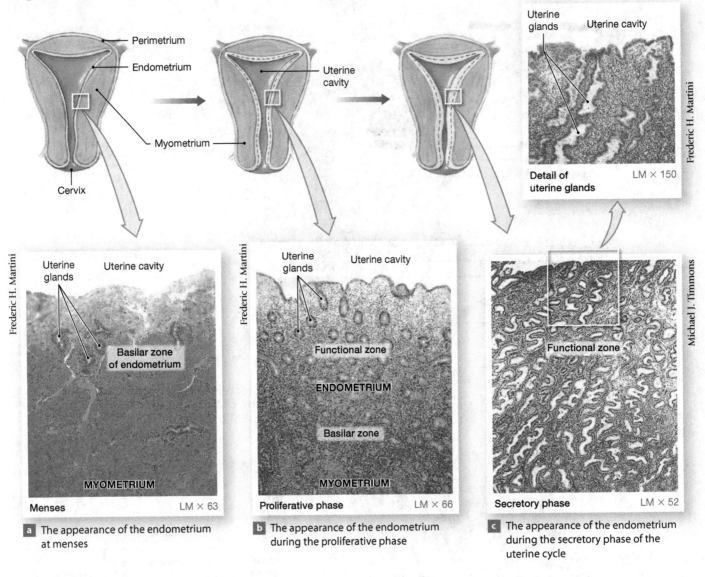

a The appearance of the endometrium at menses

b The appearance of the endometrium during the proliferative phase

c The appearance of the endometrium during the secretory phase of the uterine cycle

In the Lab 5

Materials

☐ Female reproductive system model and chart

☐ Compound microscope

☐ Prepared slide of ovary

☐ Prepared slide of uterine tube

☐ Prepared slide of uterus

☐ Prepared slides of endometrium series

Procedures

1. Review the anatomy of the ovaries, uterine tubes, and uterus presented in Figures 9, 10, and 11.

2. Identify the ovaries, uterine tubes, the ampulla, and the isthmus on the laboratory model and/or chart.

3. On the model, identify the fundus, body, and cervix of the uterus.

4. Examine the ovary slide at low magnification and note the cortex with many egg nests. Increase magnification and observe an oocyte inside a follicle.

5. **Draw It!** Draw some follicles in the space provided.

(blank drawing space)

Follicles of the ovary

6. Scan the uterine tube slide at low and medium magnifications. Observe the lining epithelium and smooth muscle tissue.

7. **Draw It!** Draw a section of the uterine tube in the space provided.

(blank drawing space)

Uterine tube

8. Observe the uterus slide and locate the perimetrium and the thick myometrium composed of smooth muscle tissue. Identify the endometrium.

9. **Draw It!** Draw a section of the uterine wall in the space provided.

(blank drawing space)

Uterine wall

10. Using Figure 12 for reference, examine the endometrium slide set and compare the functional zone and uterine glands during the menses, proliferative, and secretory phases. ■

Lab Activity 6 **Female: Vagina and Vulva**

The **vagina** is a muscular tube approximately 10 cm (4 in.) long (**Figure 13**). It is lined with stratified squamous epithelium and is the female copulatory organ, the pathway for menstrual flow, and the lower birth canal. The **fornix** is the pouch formed where the uterus protrudes into the vagina. The **vaginal orifice** is the external opening of the vagina. This opening may be partially or totally occluded by a thin fold of vascularized mucous membrane called the **hymen** (HĪ-men). On either side of the vaginal orifice are openings of the **greater vestibular glands,** glands that produce a mucous secretion that lubricates the vaginal entrance for sexual intercourse. These glands are similar to the bulbourethral glands of the male.

The **vulva** (VUL-vuh), which is the collective name for the female **external genitalia** (jen-i-TĀ-lē-uh), includes the following structures (**Figure 14**).

- The **mons pubis** is a pad of adipose over the pubic symphysis. The mons is covered with skin and pubic hair and serves as a cushion for the pubic symphysis.

- The **labia** (LĀ-bē-uh) **majora** are two fatty folds of skin extending from the mons pubis and continuing posteriorly. They are homologous to the scrotum of the male. They usually have pubic hair and contain many sudoriferous (sweat) and sebaceous (oil) glands.

- The **labia minora** (mi-NOR-uh) are two smaller parallel folds of skin containing many sebaceous glands. This pair of labia lacks hair.

- The **clitoris** (KLIT-ō-ris) is a small, cylindrical mass of erectile tissue analogous to the penis. Like the penis, the clitoris contains a small fold of covering skin called the prepuce. The exposed portion of the clitoris is called the **glans.**

- The **vestibule** is the area between the labia minora that contains the vaginal orifice, hymen, and external urethral orifice.

- **Paraurethral glands** (_Skene's glands_) surround the urethra.

- The **perineum** is the area between the legs from the clitoris to the anus. This area is of clinical significance because of the tremendous pressure exerted on it during childbirth. If the vagina is too narrow during childbirth, an **episiotomy** (e-pēz-ē-OT-uh-mē) is performed by making a small incision at the base of the vaginal opening toward the anus to expand the vaginal opening.

QuickCheck Questions

6.1 Where is the mons pubis located?

6.2 The vestibule is between what two sets of folds?

6.3 Which female organ has a glans?

Figure 13 **The Vagina**

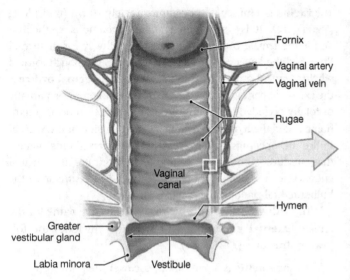

- Fornix
- Vaginal artery
- Vaginal vein
- Rugae
- Vaginal canal
- Hymen
- Greater vestibular gland
- Labia minora
- Vestibule

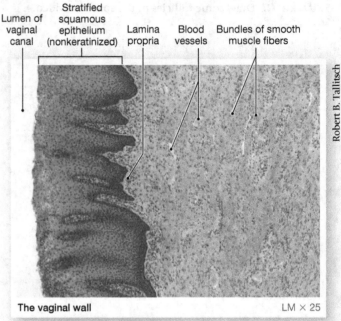

Lumen of vaginal canal · Stratified squamous epithelium (nonkeratinized) · Lamina propria · Blood vessels · Bundles of smooth muscle fibers

Robert B. Tallitsch

The vaginal wall — LM × 25

Figure 14 **Female External Genitalia** The external anatomy of the female is collectively called the vulva.

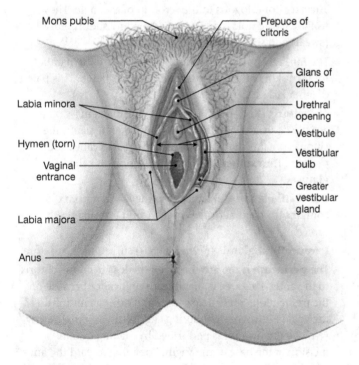

- Mons pubis
- Prepuce of clitoris
- Glans of clitoris
- Labia minora
- Urethral opening
- Vestibule
- Hymen (torn)
- Vestibular bulb
- Vaginal entrance
- Greater vestibular gland
- Labia majora
- Anus

In the Lab 6

Materials

☐ Female reproductive system model and chart
☐ Compound microscope
☐ Prepared slide of vagina

Procedures

1. Review the anatomy of the vulva in Figure 14.
2. Locate the vagina and vaginal orifice on the laboratory model and/or chart. Examine the fornix, which is the point where the cervix and vagina connect.
3. Observe the vagina slide and study the histology of the wall. Identify the stratified squamous epithelium, lamina propria, and smooth muscle.
4. ***Draw It!*** Draw and label the wall in the space provided.

Vaginal wall

5. Locate each component of the vulva. Note the positions of the clitoris, urethra, and vagina. ■

Figure 15 Mammary Glands

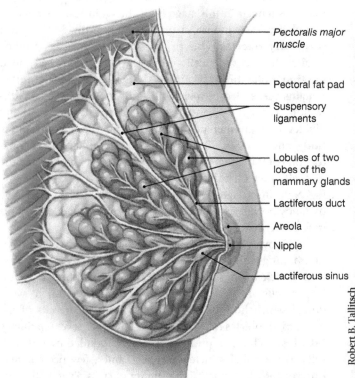

Pectoralis major muscle

Pectoral fat pad

Suspensory ligaments

Lobules of two lobes of the mammary glands

Lactiferous duct

Areola

Nipple

Lactiferous sinus

a The mammary glands of the left breast

Robert B. Tallitsch

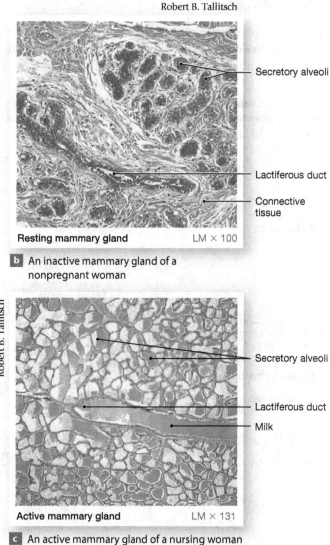

Secretory alveoli

Lactiferous duct

Connective tissue

Resting mammary gland LM × 100

b An inactive mammary gland of a nonpregnant woman

Robert B. Tallitsch

Secretory alveoli

Lactiferous duct

Milk

Active mammary gland LM × 131

c An active mammary gland of a nursing woman

Lab Activity 7 Mammary Glands

The **mammary glands** (Figure 15) are modified sweat glands that, in the process called **lactation** (lak-TĀ-shun), produce milk to nourish a newborn infant. At puberty, the release of estrogens stimulates an increase in the size of these glands. Fat deposition is the major contributor to the size of the breast, and size does not influence the amount of milk produced. Each gland consists of 15 to 20 lobes separated by fat and connective tissue. Each lobe contains smaller lobules that contain milk-secreting cells called **alveoli. Lactiferous** (lak-TIF-e-rus) **ducts** drain milk from the lobules toward the **lactiferous sinuses.** These sinuses empty the milk at the raised portion of the breast called the *nipple*. A circular pigmented area called the **areola** (a-RĒ-ō-luh) surrounds the nipple.

QuickCheck Questions

7.1 What are the milk-producing cells of the breast called?

7.2 What is the areola?

In the Lab 7

Materials

☐ Breast model
☐ Female reproductive system model and chart

Procedures

1. Review the anatomy of the breast presented in Figure 15.
2. On the model and chart, trace the pathway of milk from a lobule to the surface of the nipple. ◼

Lab Activity 8 Female: Oogenesis

Formation of the female gamete, the ovum (or *egg*), is called **oogenesis** (ō-ō-JEN-e-sis) and occurs in the ovaries (**Figure 16**). In a female fetus, meiosis I begins when cells

Figure 16 Oogenesis In oogenesis, a single primary oocyte produces an ovum and two nonfunctional polar bodies. Compare this diagram with Figure 3 which summarizes spermatogenesis.

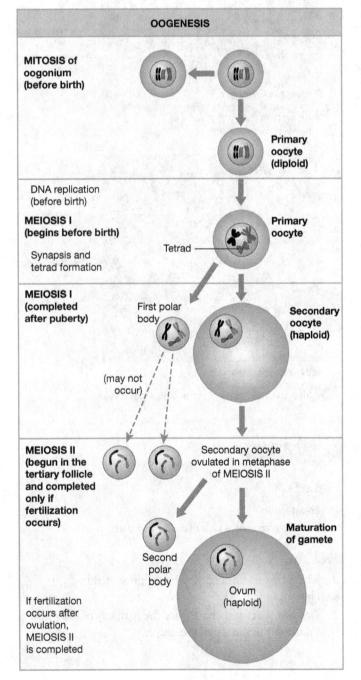

called **oogonia** (ō-ō-GŌ-nē-uh, singular *oogonium*) divide by mitosis and produce **primary oocytes** (ō-ō-sīts), which remain suspended in this stage until the child reaches puberty. At puberty, each month, a primary oocyte divides into two **secondary oocytes.** One of the secondary oocytes is much smaller than its sister cell and is a nonfunctional cell called the **first polar body** (Figure 8). The other secondary oocyte remains suspended in meiosis II until it is ovulated. If fertilization occurs, the secondary oocyte completes meiosis II and divides into another polar body, called the **second polar body,** and an ovum. The haploid ovum and haploid spermatozoon combine their haploid chromosomes and become the first cell of the offspring, the diploid zygote.

Note from Figure 16 that females produce only a single ovum by oogenesis, whereas in males, spermatogenesis results in four spermatozoa (Figure 8).

Each ovary contains 100,000 to 200,000 oocytes clustered in groupings called **egg nests.** Within the nests are **primordial follicles,** which are primary oocytes surrounded by follicular cells. **Figure 17** details the monthly ovarian cycle, during which hormones stimulate the follicular cells of the primordial follicles to proliferate and produce several **primary follicles,** each one a primary oocyte surrounded by follicular cells. These follicles increase in size, and a few become **secondary follicles** containing primary oocytes. Eventually, one secondary follicle develops into a **tertiary follicle,** also called a *mature Graafian* (GRAF-ē-an) *follicle.* By now the oocyte has completed meiosis I and is now a secondary oocyte starting meiosis II. The tertiary follicle fills with liquid and ruptures, casting out the secondary oocyte during ovulation. This follicle secretes **estrogen,** the hormone that stimulates rebuilding of the spongy lining of the uterus. After ovulation, the follicular cells of the tertiary follicle become the **corpus luteum** (LOO-tē-um) and secrete primarily the hormone **progesterone** (prō-JES-ter-ōn), which prepares the uterus for pregnancy. If the secondary oocyte is not fertilized, the corpus luteum degenerates into the **corpus albicans** (AL-bi-kanz), and most of the rebuilt lining of the uterus is shed as the menstrual flow.

QuickCheck Questions

8.1 Where are ova produced in the female?

8.2 Which structure ruptures during ovulation to release an ovum?

8.3 What are polar bodies?

Figure 17 The Ovarian Cycle Ovaries contain oocytes which become surrounded by follicle cells. Ovulation occurs when the tertiary follicle ruptures and releases the secondary oocyte from the ovary. The torn follicle develops into the corpus luteum and produces progesterone.

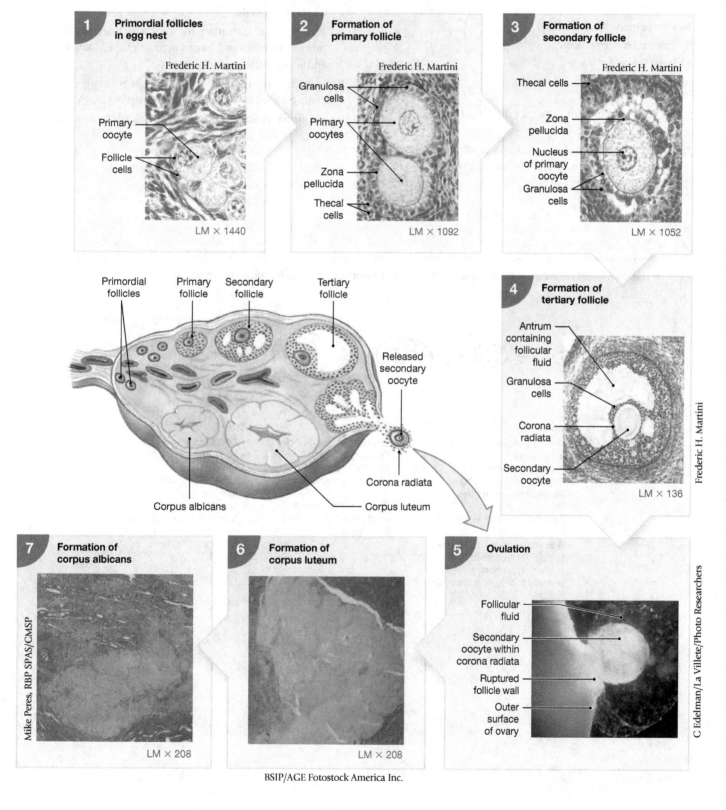

BSIP/AGE Fotostock America Inc.

495

In the Lab   8

Material

- ☐ Meiosis models
- ☐ Compound microscope
- ☐ Prepared slide of ovary

Procedures

1. Identify the different cell types shown on the meiosis models.

2. Using Figures 16 and 17 as references, scan the ovary slide at low magnification, and locate an egg nest along the periphery of the ovary.

3. Identify the primary follicles, which are larger than the primordial follicles in the nests. In the primary-follicle stage, the oocyte has increased in size and is surrounded by follicular cells.

4. Identify some secondary follicles, which are larger than primary follicles and have a separation between the outer and inner follicular cells.

5. Identify some tertiary follicles, which are easily distinguished by the large, liquid-filled space they contain.

For additional practice, complete the *Sketch to Learn* activity below. ■

 Sketch to Learn

In this drawing let's show the various stages of follicle development before and after ovulation of an oocyte.

Sample Sketch

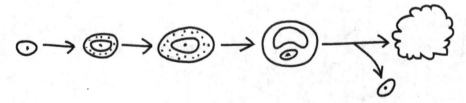

Step 1
- Draw a series of three ovals for oocytes.
- Add a circle close around the second oocyte and a larger circle around the third.
- Add dots in the outer circles for follicular cells.
- Add arrows between follicles.
- Label the three follicles in sequence; primordial follicle, primary follicle, and secondary follicle.

Step 2
Draw the Graafian follicle:
- Draw an oocyte.
- Draw a large circle around the oocyte with oocyte at bottom.
- Add an inner circle that wraps around the top of the oocyte.

Step 3
- Add a branched arrow.
- Show the oocyte out of follicle.
- Draw a large corpus luteum.
- Label the Graafian follicle in Step 2 and the corpus luteum and ovulated oocyte in Step 3.

Your Sketch

Name _____

Date _____

Section _____

Anatomy of the Reproductive System

A. Description

Write a description of each of the following structures.

1. epididymis

2. ductus deferens

3. bulbo-urethral gland

4. corpora cavernosa

5. prostatic urethra

6. seminiferous tubule

7. labia minora

8. myometrium

9. fundus

10. infundibulum

11. vulva

12. cervix

B. Labeling

1. Label the anatomy of the male in Figure 18.

Figure 18 **Male Reproductive System**

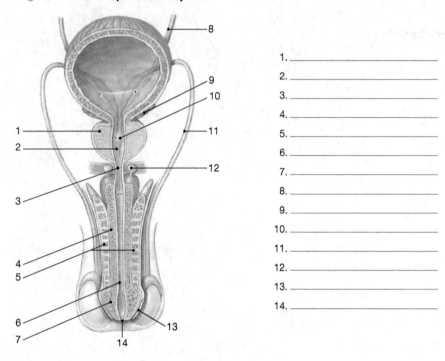

1. _____
2. _____
3. _____
4. _____
5. _____
6. _____
7. _____
8. _____
9. _____
10. _____
11. _____
12. _____
13. _____
14. _____

2. Label the anatomy of the vulva in Figure 19.

Figure 19 **The Vulva**

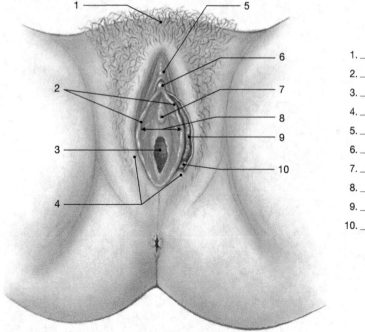

1. _____
2. _____
3. _____
4. _____
5. _____
6. _____
7. _____
8. _____
9. _____
10. _____

3. Label the anatomy of the female in Figure 20.

Figure 20 **Female Reproductive System**

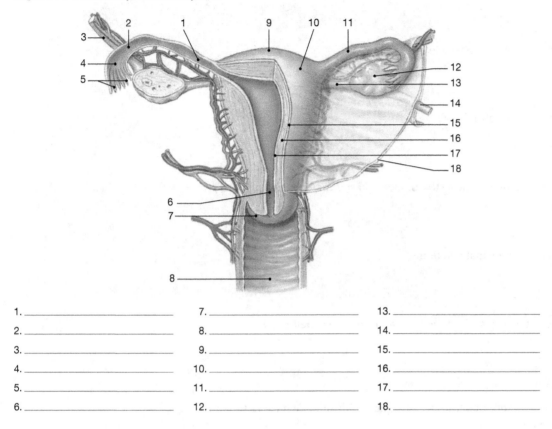

1. _____
2. _____
3. _____
4. _____
5. _____
6. _____

7. _____
8. _____
9. _____
10. _____
11. _____
12. _____

13. _____
14. _____
15. _____
16. _____
17. _____
18. _____

4. Label the anatomy of the seminiferous tubule in Figure 21.

Figure 21 **Seminiferous Tubule**

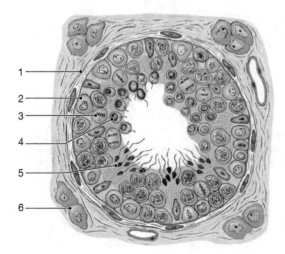

1. _____
2. _____
3. _____
4. _____
5. _____
6. _____

C. Short-Answer Questions

1. List the three layers of the uterus, from superficial to deep.

2. Describe the gross anatomy of the female breast.

3. List the components of the vulva.

4. How is temperature regulated in the testes for maximal spermatozoa production?

5. Name the three regions of the male urethra.

6. What are the three accessory glands of the male reproductive system?

D. Analysis and Application

1. Explain the division sequence that leads to four spermatids in male meiosis but only one ovum in female meiosis.

2. How are the clitoris and the penis similar to each other?

E. Clinical Challenge

1. How does a vasectomy or a tubal ligation sterilize an individual?

2. Do castration and vasectomy have the same effects on endocrine and reproductive functions?

Index

501